ONLY YESTERDAY

An Informal History of the 1920's

Frederick Lewis Allen

1931

CONTENTS

PREFACE

This book is an attempt to tell, and in some measure to interpret, the story of what in the future may be considered a distinct era in American history: the eleven years between the end of the war with Germany (November 11, 1918) and the stock-market panic which culminated on November 13, 1929, hastening and dramatizing the destruction of what had been known as Coolidge (and Hoover) Prosperity.

Obviously the writing of a history so soon after the event has involved breaking much new ground. Professor Preston William Slosson, in *The Great Crusade and After,* has carried his story almost to the end of this period, but the scheme of his book is quite different from that of mine; and although many other books have dealt with one aspect of the period or another, I have been somewhat surprised to find how many of the events of those years have never before been chronicled in full. For example, the story of the Harding scandals (in so far as it is now known) has never been written before except in fragments, and although the Big Bull Market has been analyzed and discussed a thousand times, it has never been fully presented in narrative form as the extraordinary economic and social phenomenon which it was.

Further research will undoubtedly disclose errors and deficiencies in the book, and the passage of time will reveal the shortsightedness of many of my judgments and interpretations. A contemporary history is bound to be anything but definitive. Yet half the enjoyment of writing it has lain in the effort to reduce to some sort of logical and coherent order a mass of material untouched by any previous historian; and I have wondered whether some readers might not be interested and perhaps amused to find events and circumstances which they remember well--which seem to have happened only yesterday--woven into a pattern which at least masquerades as history. One advantage the book will have over most histories: hardly anyone old enough to read it can fail to remember the entire period with which it deals.

As for my emphasis upon the changing state of the public mind and upon the sometimes trivial happenings with which it was preoccupied, this has been deliberate. It has seemed to me that one who writes at such close range, while recollection is still fresh, has a special opportunity to record the fads and fashions and follies of the time, the things which millions of people thought about and talked about and became excited about and which at once touched their daily lives: and that he may prudently leave to subsequent historians certain events and policies, particularly in the field of foreign affairs, the effect of which upon the life of the ordinary citizen was less immediate and may not be fully measurable for a long time. (I am indebted to Mr. Mark Sullivan for what he has done in the successive volumes of *Our Own Times* to develop this method of writing contemporary history.) Naturally I have attempted to bring together the innumerable threads of the story so as to reveal the fundamental trends in our national life and national thought during the nineteen-twenties.

In an effort to eliminate footnotes and at the same time to express my numerous obligations. I have added an appendix listing my principal sources.

F. L. A.

♦ I ♦
PRELUDE: MAY, 1919

If time were suddenly to turn back to the earliest days of the Postwar Decade, and you were to look about you, what would seem strange to you? since 1919 the circumstances of American life have been transformed--yes, but exactly how?

Let us refresh our memories by following a moderately well-to-do young couple of Cleveland or Boston or Seattle or Baltimore--it hardly matters which--through the routine of an ordinary day in May, 1919. (I select that particular date, six months after the Armistice of 1918, because by then the United States had largely succeeded in turning from the ways of war to those of peace, yet the profound alterations wrought by the Post-war Decade had hardly begun to take place.) There is no better way of suggesting what the passage of a few years has done to change you and me and the environment in which we live.

From the appearance of Mr. Smith as he comes to the breakfast table on this May morning in 1919, you would hardly know that you are not in the nineteen-thirties (though you might, perhaps, be struck by the narrowness of his trousers). The movement of men's fashions is glacial. It is different, however, with Mrs. Smith.

She comes to breakfast in a suit, the skirt of which--rather tight at the ankles--hangs just six inches from the ground. She has read in *Vogue* the alarming news that skirts may become even shorter, and that "not since the days of the Bourbons has the woman of fashion been visible so far above the ankle"; but six inches is still the orthodox clearance. She wears low shoes now, for spring has come; but all last winter she protected her ankles either with spats or with high laced "walking-boots," or with high patent-leather shoes with contrasting buckskin tops. Her stockings are black (or tan, perhaps, if she wears tan shoes); the idea of flesh-colored stockings would appall her. A few minutes ago Mrs. Smith was surrounding herself with an "envelope chemise" and a petticoat; and from the thick ruffles on her undergarments it was apparent that she was not disposed to make herself more boyish in form than ample nature intended.

Mrs. Smith may use powder, but she probably draws the line at paint. Although the use of cosmetics is no longer, in 1919, considered *prima facie* evidence of a scarlet career, and sophisticated young girls have already begun to apply them with some bravado, most well-brought-up women still frown upon rouge. The beauty-parlor industry is in its infancy; there are a dozen hair dressing parlors for every beauty parlor, and Mrs. Smith has never heard of such dark arts as that of face-lifting. When she puts on her hat to go shopping she will add a veil pinned neatly together behind her head. In the shops she will perhaps buy a bathing-suit for use in the summer; it will consist of an outer tunic of silk or cretonne over a tight knitted undergarment--worn, of course, with long stockings.

Her hair is long, and the idea of a woman ever frequenting a barber shop would never occur to her. If you have forgotten what the general public thought of short hair in those days, listen to the remark of the manager of the Palm Garden in New York when reporters asked him, one night in November, 1918, how he happened to rent his hall for a pro-Bolshevist meeting which had led to a riot. Explaining that a well-dressed woman had come in a fine automobile to make arrangements for the use of the auditorium, he added, "Had we noticed then, as we do now, that she had short hair, we would have refused to rent the hall." In Mrs. Smith's mind, as in that of the manager of the Palm Garden, short-haired women, like long-haired men, are associated with radicalism, if not with free love.

The breakfast to which Mr. and Mrs. Smith sit down may have been arranged with a view to the provision of a sufficient number of calories--they need only to go to Childs' to learn about calories--but in all probability neither of them has ever heard of a vitamin.

As Mr. Smith eats, he opens the morning paper. It is almost certainly not a tabloid, no matter how rudimentary Mr. Smith's journalistic tastes may be: for although Mr. Hearst has already experimented with small-sized picture papers, the first conspicuously successful tabloid is yet to be born. Not until June 26, 1919, will the New York *Daily News* reach the newsstands, beginning a career that will bring its daily circulation in one year to nearly a quarter of a million, in five years to over four-fifths of a million, and in ten years to the amazing total of over one million three hundred thousand.

Strung across the front page of Mr. Smith's paper are headlines telling of the progress of the American Navy seaplane, the

NC-4, on its flight across the Atlantic *via* the Azores. That flight is the most sensational news story of May, 1919. (Alcock and Brown have not yet crossed the ocean in a single hop; they will do it a few weeks hence, eight long years ahead of Lindbergh.) But there is other news, too: of the Peace Conference at Paris, where the Treaty is now in its later stages of preparation; of the successful oversubscription of the Victory Loan ("Sure, we'll finish the job!" the campaign posters have been shouting); of the arrival of another transport with soldiers from overseas; of the threat of a new strike; of a speech by Mayor Ole Hanson of Seattle denouncing that scourge of the times, the I. W. W.; of the prospects for the passage of the Suffrage Amendment, which it is predicted will enable women to take "a finer place in the national life"; and of Henry Ford's libel suit against the Chicago *Tribune*--in the course of which he will call Benedict Arnold a writer, and in reply to the question, "Have there been any revolutions in this country?" will answer, "Yes, in 1812."

If Mr. Smith attends closely to the sporting news, he may find obscure mention of a young pitcher and outfielder for the Boston Red Sox named Ruth. But he will hardly find the Babe's name in the headlines. (In April, 1919, Ruth made one home run; in May, two; but the season was much further advanced before sporting writers began to notice that he was running up a new record for swatting--twenty-nine home runs for the year; the season had closed before the New York Yankees, seeing gold in the hills, bought him for $125,000; and the summer of 1920 had arrived before a man died of excitement when he saw Ruth smash a ball into the bleachers, and it became clear that the mob had found a new idol. In 1919, the veteran Ty Cobb, not Ruth, led the American League in batting.)

The sporting pages inform Mr. Smith that Rickard has selected Toledo as the scene of a forthcoming encounter between the heavyweight champion, Jess Willard, and another future idol of the mob, Jack Dempsey. (They met, you may recall, on the Fourth of July, 1919, and sober citizens were horrified to read that 19,650 people were so depraved as to sit in a broiling sun to watch Dempsey knock out the six-foot-six-inch champion in the third round. How would the sober citizens have felt if they had known that eight years later a Dempsey-Tunney fight would bring in more than five times as much money in gate receipts as this battle of Toledo?) In the sporting pages there may be news of Bobby Jones, the seventeen-year-old Southern golf champion, or of William T. Tilden, Jr., who is winning tennis tournaments here and there, but neither of them is yet a national champion. And even if Jones were to win this year he would hardly become a great popular hero; for although golf is gaining every day in popularity, it has not yet become an inevitable part of the weekly ritual of the American business man. Mr. Smith very likely still scoffs at "grown men who spend their time knocking a little white ball along the ground"; it is quite certain that he has never heard of plus fours; and if he should happen to play golf he had better not show his knickerbockers in the city streets, or small boys will shout to him, "Hey, get some men's pants!"

Did I say that by May, 1919, the war was a thing of the past? There are still reminders of it in Mr. Smith's paper. Not only the news from the Peace Conference, not only the item about Sergeant Alvin York being on his way home; there is still that ugliest reminder of all, the daily casualty list.

Mr. and Mrs. Smith discuss a burning subject, the High Cost of Living. Mr. Smith is hoping for an increase in salary, but meanwhile the family income seems to be dwindling as prices rise. Everything is going up--food, rent, clothing, and taxes. These are the days when people remark that even the man without a dollar is fifty cents better off than he once was, and that if we coined seven-cent pieces for street-car fares, in another year we should have to discontinue them and begin to coin fourteen-cent pieces. Mrs. Smith, confronted with an appeal from Mr. Smith for economy, reminds him that milk has jumped since 1914 from nine to fifteen cents a quart, sirloin steak from twenty-seven to forty-two cents a pound, butter from thirty-two to sixty-one cents a pound, and fresh eggs from thirty-four to sixty-two cents a dozen. No wonder people on fixed salaries are suffering, and colleges are beginning to talk of applying the money-raising methods learned during the Liberty Loan campaigns to the increasing of college endowments. Rents are almost worse than food prices, for that matter; since the Armistice there has been an increasing shortage of houses and apartments, and the profiteering landlord has become an object of popular hate along with the profiteering middleman. Mr. Smith tells his wife that "these profiteers are about as bad as the I. W. W.'s." He could make no stronger statement.

Breakfast over, Mr. Smith gets into his automobile to drive to the office. The car is as likely to be a Lexington, a Maxwell, a Briscoe, or a Templar as to be a Dodge, Buick, Chevrolet, Cadillac, or Hudson, and it surely will not be a Chrysler; Mr. Chrysler has just been elected first vice-president of the General Motors Corporation. Whatever the make of the car, it stands higher than the cars of the nineteen-thirties;

the passengers look down upon their surroundings from an imposing altitude. The chances are nine to one that Mr. Smith's automobile is open (only 10.3 per cent of the cars manufactured in 1919 were closed). The vogue of the sedan is just beginning. Closed cars are still associated in the public mind with wealth; the hated profiteer of the newspaper cartoon rides in a limousine.

If Mr. Smith's car is one of the high, hideous, but efficient model T Fords of the day, let us watch him for a minute. He climbs in by the right-hand door (for there is no left-hand door by the front seat), reaches over to the wheel, and sets the spark and throttle levers in a position like that of the hands of a clock at ten minutes to three. Then, unless he has paid extra for a self-starter, he gets out to crank. Seizing the crank in his right hand carefully (for a friend of his once broke his arm cranking), he slips his left forefinger through a loop of wire that controls the choke. He pulls the loop of wire, he revolves the crank mightily, and as the engine at last roars, he leaps to the trembling running-board, leans in, and moves the spark and throttle to twenty-five minutes of two. Perhaps he reaches the throttle before the engine falters into silence, but if it is a cold morning perhaps he does not. In that case, back to the crank again and the loop of wire. Mr. Smith wishes Mrs. Smith would come out and sit in the driver's seat and pull that spark lever down before the engine has time to die.

Finally he is at the wheel with the engine roaring as it should. He releases the emergency hand-brake, shoves his left foot against the low-speed pedal, and as the car sweeps loudly out into the street, he releases his left foot, lets the car into high gear, and is off. Now his only care is for that long hill down the street; yesterday he burned his brake on it, and this morning he must remember to brake with the reverse pedal, or the low-speed pedal, or both, or all three in alternation. (Jam your foot down on any of the three pedals and you slow the car.)

Mr. Smith is on the open road--a good deal more open than it will be a decade hence. On his way to work he passes hardly a third as many cars as he will pass in 1929; there are less than seven million passenger cars registered in the United States in 1919, as against over twenty-three million cars only ten years later. He is unlikely to find many concrete roads in his vicinity, and the lack of them is reflected in the speed regulations. A few states like California and New York permit a rate of thirty miles an hour in 1919, but the average limit is twenty (as against thirty-five or forty in 1931). The Illinois rate of 1919 is characteristic of the day; it limits the driver to fifteen miles in residential parts of cities, ten miles in built-up sections, and six miles on curves. The idea of making a hundred-mile trip in two and a half hours--as will constantly be done in the nineteen-thirties by drivers who consider themselves conservative--would seem to Mr. Smith perilous, and with the roads of 1919 to drive on he would be right.

In the course of his day at the office, Mr. Smith discusses business conditions. It appears that things are looking up. There was a period of uncertainty and falling stock prices after the Armistice, as huge government contracts were canceled and plants which had been running overtime on war work began to throw off men by the thousand, but since then conditions have been better. Everybody is talking about the bright prospects for international trade and American shipping. The shipyards are running full tilt. There are too many strikes going on, to be sure; it seems as if the demands of labor for higher and higher wages would never be satisfied, although Mr. Smith admits that in a way you can't blame the men, with prices still mounting week by week. But there is so much business activity that the men being turned out of army camps to look for jobs are being absorbed better than Mr. Smith ever thought they would be. It was back in the winter and early spring that there was so much talk about the ex-servicemen walking the streets without work; it was then that *Life* ran a cartoon which represented Uncle Sam saying to a soldier, "Nothing is too good for you, my boy! What would you like?" and the soldier answering, "A job." Now the boys seem to be sifting slowly but surely into the ranks of the employed, and the only clouds on the business horizon are strikes and Bolshevism and the dangerous wave of speculation in the stock market.

"Bull Market Taxes Nerves of Brokers," cry the headlines in the financial pages, and they speak of "Long Hours for Clerks." Is there a familiar ring to those phrases? Does it seem natural to you, remembering as you do the Big Bull Market of 1928 and 1929, that the decision to keep the Stock Exchange closed over the 31st of May, 1919, should elicit such newspaper comments as this: "The highly specialized machine which handles the purchase and sales of stocks and bonds in the New York market is fairly well exhausted and needs a rest"? Then listen; in May, 1919, it was a long series of *million-and-a-half-share* days which was causing financiers to worry and the Federal Reserve Board to consider issuing a warning against speculation. During that year a new record of six two-million-share days was set up, and on only 145 days did the trading amount to over a million shares. What would Mr. Smith and his associates think if they were to be told that within eleven years there would occur a sixteen-million-share day; and that they would see the time when three-million-share days would be referred to as "virtual stagnation" or as "listless trading by professionals only, with the general public refusing to become interested"? The price of a seat on the New York Stock Exchange in 1919 ranged between $60,000 and a new high record of $110,000; it would be hard for Mr. Smith to believe that before the end of the decade seats on the Exchange would fetch a half million.

In those days of May, 1919, the record of daily Stock Exchange transactions occupied hardly a newspaper column. The Curb Market record referred to trading on a real curb--to that extraordinary outdoor market in Broad Street, New York, where boys with telephone receivers clamped to their heads hung out of windows high above the street and grimaced and wigwagged through the din to traders clustered on the pavement below. And if there was anything Mrs. Smith was certain not to have on her mind as she went shopping, it was the price of stocks. Yet the "unprecedented bull market" of 1919 brought fat profits to those who participated in it. Between February 15th and May 14th, Baldwin Locomotive rose from 72 to 93, General Motors from 130 to 191, United States Steel from 90 to 104 $^1/_2$, and International Mercantile Marine common (to which traders were attracted on account of the apparently boundless possibilities of shipping) from 23 to 47 $^5/_8$.

When Mr. Smith goes out to luncheon, he has to proceed to his club in a roundabout way, for a regiment of soldiers just returned from Europe is on parade and the central thoroughfares of the city are blocked with crowds. It is a great season for parades, this spring of 1919. As the transports from Brest swing up New York Harbor, the men packed solid on the decks are greeted by Major Hylan's Committee of Welcome, represented sometimes by the Mayor's spruce young secretary, Grover Whalen, who in later years is to reduce welcoming to a science and raise it to an art. New York City has built in honor of the homecoming troops a huge plaster arch in Fifth Avenue at Madison Square, toward the design of which forty artists are said to have contributed. ("But the result," comments the New York *Tribune,* sadly, "suggests four hundred rather than forty. It holds everything that was ever on an arch anywhere, the lay mind suspects, not forgetting the horses on top of a certain justly celebrated Brandenburg Gate.") Farther up the Avenue, before the Public Library, there is a shrine of pylons and palms called the Court of the Heroic Dead, of whose decorative effect the *Tribune* says, curtly, "Add perils of death." A few blocks to the north an arch of jewels is suspended above the Avenue "like a net of precious stones, between two white pillars surmounted by stars"; on this arch colored searchlights play at night with superb effect. The Avenue is hung with flags from end to end; and as the Twenty-seventh Division parades under the arches the air is white with confetti and ticker tape, and the sidewalks are jammed with cheering crowds. Nor is New York alone in its enthusiasm for the returning soldiers; every other city has its victory parade, with the city elders on the reviewing stand and flags waving and the bayonets of the troops glistening in the spring sunlight and the bands playing "The Long, Long Trail." Not yet disillusioned, the nation welcomes its heroes--and the heroes only wish the fuss were all over and they could get into civilian clothes and sleep late in the mornings and do what they please, and try to forget.

Mr. and Mrs. Smith have been invited to a tea dance at one of the local hotels, and Mr. Smith hurries from his office to the scene of revelry. If the hotel is up to the latest wrinkles, it has a jazz-band instead of the traditional orchestra for dancing, but not yet does a saxophone player stand out in the foreground and contort from his instrument that piercing music, "endlessly sorrowful yet endlessly unsentimental, with no past, no memory, no future, no hope," which William Bolitho called the *Zeitgeist* of the Post-war Age. The jazz-band plays "I'm Always Chasing Rainbows," the tune which Harry Carroll wrote in wartime after Harrison Fisher persuaded him that Chopin's "Fantasie Impromptu" had the makings of a good ragtime tune. It plays, too, "Smiles" and "Dardanella" and "Hindustan" and "Japanese Sandman" and "I Love You Sunday," and that other song which is to give the Post-war Decade one of its most persistent and wearisome slang phrases, "I'll Say She Does." There are a good many military uniforms among the fox-trotting dancers. There is one French officer in blue; the days are not past when a foreign uniform adds the zest of war-time romance to any party. In the more dimly lighted palm-room there may be a juvenile petting party or two going on, but of this Mr. and Mrs. Smith are doubtless oblivious. F. Scott Fitzgerald has yet to confront a horrified republic with the Problem of the Younger Generation.

After a few dances, Mr. Smith wanders out to the bar (if this is not a dry state). He finds there a group of men downing Bronxes and Scotch highballs, and discussing with dismay the approach of prohibition. On the 1st of July the so-called Wartime Prohibition Law is to take effect (designed as a war measure, but not signed by the

President until after the Armistice), and already the ratification of the Eighteenth Amendment has made it certain that prohibition is to be permanent. Even now, distilling and brewing are forbidden. Liquor is therefore expensive, as the frequenters of midnight cabarets are learning to their cost. Yet here is the bar, still quite legally doing business. Of course there is not a woman within eyeshot of it; drinking by women is unusual in 1919, and drinking at a bar is an exclusively masculine prerogative. Although Mr. and Mrs. Smith's hosts may perhaps serve cocktails before dinner this evening, Mr. and Mrs. Smith have never heard of cocktail parties as a substitute for tea parties.

As Mr. Smith stands with his foot on the brass rail, he listens to the comments on the coming of prohibition. There is some indignant talk about it, but even here the indignation is by no means unanimous. One man, as he tosses off his Bronx, says that he'll miss his liquor for a time, he supposes, but he thinks "his boys will be better off for living in a world where there is no alcohol"; and two or three others agree with him. Prohibition has an overwhelming majority behind it throughout the United States; the Spartan fervor of war-time has not yet cooled. Nor is there anything ironical in the expressed assumption of these men that when the Eighteenth Amendment goes into effect, alcohol will be banished from the land. They look forward vaguely to an endless era of actual drought.

At the dinner party to which Mr. and Mrs. Smith go that evening, some of the younger women may be bold enough to smoke, but they probably puff their cigarettes self-consciously, even defiantly. (The national consumption of cigarettes in 1919, excluding the very large sizes, is less than half of what it will be by 1930.)

After dinner the company may possibly go to the movies to see Charlie Chaplin in "Shoulder Arms" or Douglas Fairbanks in "The Knickerbocker Buckaroo" or Mary Pickford in "Daddy Long Legs," or Theda Bara, or Pearl White, or Griffith's much touted and much wept-at "Broken Blossoms." Or they may play auction bridge (not contract, of course). Mah Jong, which a few years hence will be almost obligatory, is still over the horizon. They may discuss such best sellers of the day as *The Four Horsemen of the Apocalypse,* Tarkington's *The Magnificent Ambersons.* Conrad's *Arrow of Gold,* Brand Whitlock's *Belgium,* and Wells's *The Undying Fire.* (The *Outline of History* is still unwritten.) They may go to the theater: the New York successes of May, 1919, include "Friendly Enemies," "Three Faces East," and "The Better Ole," which have been running ever since war-time and are still going strong, and also "Listen, Lester," Gillette in "Dear Brutus,"

Frances Starr in "Tiger! Tiger!" and--to satisfy a growing taste for bedroom farce--such tidbits as "Up in Mabel's Room." The Theater Guild is about to launch its first drama, Ervine's "John Ferguson." The members of the senior class at Princeton have just voted "Lightnin'" their favorite play (after "Macbeth" and "Hamlet," for which they cast the votes expected of educated men), and their favorite actresses, in order of preference, are Norma Talmadge, Elsie Ferguson, Marguerite Clark, Constance Talmadge, and Madge Kennedy.

One thing the Smiths certainly will not do this evening. They will not listen to the radio.

For there is no such thing as radio broadcasting. Here and there a mechanically inclined boy has a wireless set, with which, if he knows the Morse code, he may listen to messages from ships at sea and from land stations equipped with sending apparatus. The radiophone has been so far developed that men flying in an airplane over Manhattan have talked with other men in an office-building below. But the broadcasting of speeches and music--well, it was tried years ago by DeForest, and "nothing came of it." Not until the spring of 1920 will Frank Conrad of the Westinghouse Company of East Pittsburgh, who has been sending out phonograph music and baseball scores from the barn which he has rigged up as a spare-time research station, find that so many amateur wireless operators are listening to them that a Pittsburgh newspaper has had the bright idea of advertising radio equipment "which may be used by those who listen to Dr. Conrad's programs." And not until this advertisement appears will the Westinghouse officials decide to open the first broadcasting station in history in order to stimulate the sale of their supplies.

One more word about Mr. and Mrs. Smith and we may dismiss them for the night. Not only have they never heard of radio broadcasting; they have never heard of Coué, the Dayton Trial, cross-word puzzles, bathing-beauty contests, John J. Raskob, racketeers, Teapot Dome, Coral Gables, the *American Mercury,* Sacco and Vanzetti, companionate marriage, brokers' loan statistics, Michael Arlen, the Wall Street explosion, confession magazines, the Hall-Mills case, radio stock, speakeasies, Al Capone, automatic traffic lights, or Charles A. Lindbergh.

The Post-war Decade lies before them.

◆ II ◆
BACK TO NORMALCY

§ 1

Early on the morning of November 11, 1918, President Woodrow Wilson wrote in pencil, on an ordinary sheet of White House stationery, a message to the American people:

My Fellow Countrymen: The armistice was signed this morning. Everything for which America fought has been accomplished. It will now be our fortunate duty to assist by example, by sober, friendly counsel, and by material aid in the establishment of just democracy throughout the world.

Never was a document more Wilsonian. In those three sentences spoke the Puritan schoolmaster, cool in a time of great emotions, calmly setting the lesson for the day: the moral idealist, intent on a peace of reconciliation rather than a peace of hate; and the dogmatic prophet of democracy, who could not dream that the sort of institutions in which he had believed all his life were not inevitably the best for all nations everywhere. Yet the spirit of the message suggests, at the same time, that of another war President. It was such a document as Lincoln might have written.

But if the man in the White House was thinking of Abraham Lincoln as he wrote those sentences--and no doubt he was--there was something which perhaps he overlooked. Counsels of idealism sometimes fail in the relaxation that comes with peace. Lincoln had not lived to see what happens to a policy of "sober, friendly counsel" in a post-war decade; he had been taken off in the moment of triumph.

Woodrow Wilson was not to be so fortunate.

§ 2

What a day that 11th of November was! It was not quite three o'clock in the morning when the State Department gave out to the dozing newspapermen the news that the Armistice had really been signed. Four days before, a false report of the end of hostilities had thrown the whole United States into a delirium of joy. People had poured out of offices and shops and paraded the streets singing and shouting, ringing bells, blowing tin horns, smashing one another's hats, cheering soldiers in uniform, draping themselves in American flags, gathering in closely packed crowds before the newspaper bulletin boards, making a wild and hilarious holiday; in New York, Fifth Avenue had been closed to traffic and packed solid with surging men and women, while down from the windows of the city fluttered 155 tons of ticker tape and torn paper. It did not seem possible that such an outburst could be repeated. But it was.

By half-past four on the morning of the 11th, sirens, whistles, and bells were rousing the sleepers in a score of American cities, and newsboys were shouting up and down the dark streets. At first people were slow to credit the report; they had been fooled once and were not to be fooled again. Along an avenue in Washington, under the windows of the houses of government officials, a boy announced with painstaking articulation, "THE WAR IS OVAH! OFFICIAL GOVERNMENT ANNOUNCEMENT CONFIRMS THE NEWS!" He did not mumble as newsboys ordinarily do; he knew that this was a time to convince the skeptical by being intelligible and specific. The words brought incredible relief. A new era of peace and of hope was beginning--had already begun.

So the tidings spread throughout the country. In city after city mid-morning found offices half deserted, signs tacked up on shop doors reading "Closed for the Kaiser's Funeral," people marching up and down the streets again as they had four days previously, pretty girls kissing every soldier they saw, automobiles slowly creeping through the crowds and intentionally backfiring to add to the noise of horns and rattles and every other sort of din-making device. Eight hundred Barnard College girls snake-danced on Morningside Heights in New York; and in Times Square, early in the morning, a girl mounted the platform of "Liberty Hall," a building set up for war-campaign purposes, and sang the "Doxology" before hushed crowds.

Yet as if to mock the Wilsonian statement about "sober, friendly counsel," there were contrasting celebrations in which the mood was not that of pious thanksgiving, but of triumphant hate. Crowds burned the Kaiser in effigy. In New York, a dummy of the Kaiser was washed down Wall Street with a firehose; men carried a coffin made of soapboxes up and down Fifth Avenue, shouting that the Kaiser was within it, "resting in pieces"; and on Broadway at Seventieth Street a boy drew pictures of the Kaiser over and over again on the sidewalk, to give the crowds the delight of trampling on them.

So the new era of peace began.

But a million men--to paraphrase Bryan--cannot spring from arms overnight. There were still over three and a half million Americans in the military service, over two million of them in Europe. Uniforms were everywhere. Even after the tumult and shouting of November 11th had died, the Expeditionary Forces were still in the trenches, making ready for the long, cautious march into Germany; civilians were still saving sugar and eating strange dark breads and saving coal; it was not until ten days had passed that the "lightless" edict of the Fuel Administration was withdrawn, and Broadway and a dozen lesser white ways in other cities blazed once more; the railroads were still operated by the government, and one bought one's tickets at United States Railroad Administration Consolidated Ticket Offices; the influenza epidemic, which had taken more American lives than had the Germans, and had caused thousands of men and women to go about fearfully with white cloth masks over their faces, was only just abating; the newspapers were packed with reports from the armies in Europe, news of the revolution in Germany, of Mr. Wilson's peace preparations, of the United War Work Campaign, to the exclusion of almost everything else; and day after day, week after week, month after month, the casualty lists went on, and from Maine to Oregon men and women searched them in daily apprehension.

November would normally have brought the climax of the football season, but now scratch college teams, made up mostly of boys who had been wearing the uniform of the Students' Army Training Corps, played benefit games "to put the War Work Fund over the top"; and further to strengthen the will to give, Charlie Brickley of Harvard drop-kicked a football across Wall Street into the arms of Jack Gates of Yale on the balcony of the Stock Exchange. Not only the news columns of the papers, but the advertisements also, showed the domination of wartime emotions. Next to an editorial on "The Right to Hate the Huns," or a letter suggesting that the appropriate punishment for the Kaiser would be to deport him from country to country, always as an "undesirable alien," the reader would find a huge United War Work Fund advertisement, urging him to GIVE--GIVE--GIVE! On another page, under the title of PREPARING AMERICA TO REBUILD THE WORLD, he would find a patriotic blast beginning, "Now that liberty has triumphed, now that the forces of Right have begun their reconstruction of humanity's morals, the world faces a material task of equal magnitude," and not until he had waded through several more sentences of sonorous rhetoric would he discover that this "material task" was to be accomplished through the use of Blank's Steel Windows.

And even as the process of demobilization got definitely under way, as the soldiers began to troop home from the camps, as censorship was done away with and lights were permitted to burn brightly again and women began to buy sugar with an easy conscience; even as this glorious peace began to seem a reality and not a dream, the nation went on thinking with the mind of people at war. They had learned during the preceding nineteen months to strike down the thing they hated--not to argue or hesitate, but to strike. Germany had been struck down, but it seemed that there was another danger on the horizon. Bolshevism was spreading from Russia through Europe; Bolshevism might spread to the United States. They struck at it--or at what they thought was it. A week after the Armistice, Mayor Hylan of New York forbade the display of the red flag in the streets and ordered the police to "disperse all unlawful assemblages." A few nights later, while the Socialists were holding a mass meeting in Madison Square Garden, five hundred soldiers and sailors gathered from the surrounding streets and tried to storm the doors. It took twenty-two mounted policemen to break up the milling mob and restore order. The next evening there was another riot before the doors of the Palm Garden, farther up town, where a meeting of sympathy for Revolutionary Russia was being held under the auspices of the Women's International League. Again soldiers and sailors were the chief offenders. They packed Fifty-eighth Street for a block, shouting and trying to break their way into the Palm Garden, and in the *mêlée* six persons were badly beaten up. One of the victims was a conservative stockbroker. He was walking up Lexington Avenue with a lady, and seeing the yelling crowd, he asked someone what all the excitement was about. A sailor called out, "Hey, fellows, here's another of the Bolsheviks," and in a moment a score of men had leaped upon him, ripped off his tie, and nearly knocked him unconscious. These demonstrations were to prove the first of a long series of post-war anti-Red riots.

The nation at war had formed the habit of summary action, and it was not soon unlearned. The circumstances and available methods had changed, that was all. Employers who had watched with resentment the rising scale of wages paid to labor, under the encouragement of a government that wanted no disaffection in the ranks of the workers, now felt that their chance had come. The Germans were beaten; the next thing to do was to teach labor a lesson. Labor agitators were a bunch of Bolsheviks, anyhow, and it was about time that a man had a chance to make a decent profit in his business. Meanwhile labor, facing a steadily mounting cost of living, and realizing that it was no longer unpatriotic to strike for higher wages, decided to teach the silk-stockinged profiteering employer a lesson in his turn. The result was a bitter series of strikes and lockouts.

There was a summary action with regard to liquor, too. During the war alcohol had been an obvious menace to the fighting efficiency of the nation. The country, already largely dry by state law and local option, had decided to banish the saloon once and for all. War-time psychology was dominant; no halfway measure would serve. The War-time Prohibition Act was already on the books and due to take effect July 1, 1919. But this was not enough. The Eighteenth Amendment, which would make prohibition permanent and (so it was thought) effective, had been passed by Congress late in 1917, and many of the states had ratified it before the war ended. With the convening of the state legislatures in January, 1919, the movement for ratification went ahead with amazing speed. The New York *Tribune* said that it was "as if a sailing-ship on a windless ocean were sweeping ahead, propelled by some invisible force." "Prohibition seems to be the fashion, just as drinking once was," exclaimed the *Times* editorially. By January 16th--within nine weeks of the Armistice--the necessary thirty-six States had ratified the Amendment. Even New York State fell in line a few days later. Whisky and the "liquor ring" were struck at as venomously as were the Reds. There were some misgivings, to be sure; there were those who pointed out that three million men in uniform might not like the new dispensation; but the country was not in the mood to think twice. Prohibition went through on the tide of the war spirit of "no compromise."

Yet though the headlong temper of war-time persisted after the Armistice, in one respect the coming of peace brought about a profound change. During the war the nation had gone about its tasks in a mood of exaltation. Top sergeants might remark that the only good Hun was a dead one and that this stuff about making the world safe for democracy was all bunk; four-minute speakers might shout that the Kaiser ought to be boiled in oil; the fact remained that millions of Americans were convinced that they were fighting in a holy cause, for the rights of oppressed nations, for the end of all war forever, for all that the schoolmaster in Washington so eloquently preached. The singing of the "Doxology" by the girl in Times Square represented their true feeling as truly as the burning of the Kaiser in effigy. The moment the Armistice was signed, however, a subtle change began.

Now those who had never liked Wilson, who thought that he had stayed out of the war too long, that milk and water ran in his veins instead of blood, that he should never have been forgiven for his treatment of Roosevelt and Wood, that he was a dangerous radical at heart and a menace to the capitalistic system, that he should never have appealed to the country for the election of a Democratic Congress, or that his idea of going to Paris himself to the Peace Conference was a sign of egomania--these people began to speak out freely. There were others who were tired of applauding the French, or who had ideas of their own about the English and the English attitude toward Ireland, or who were sick of hearing about "our noble Allies" in general, or who thought that we had really gone into the war to save our own skins and that the Wilsonian talk about making the world safe for democracy was dangerous and hypocritical nonsense. They, too, began to speak out freely. Now one could say with impunity, "We've licked the Germans and we're going to lick these damned Bolsheviki, and it's about time we got after Wilson and his crew of pacifists." The tension of the war was relaxing, the bubble of idealism was pricked. As the first weeks of peace slipped away, it began to appear doubtful whether the United States was quite as ready as Woodrow Wilson had thought "to assist in the establishment of just democracy throughout the world."

§ 3

But the mind of Mr. Wilson, too, had been molded by the war. Since April, 1917, his will had been irresistible. In the United States open opposition to his leadership had been virtually stifled: it was unpatriotic to differ with the President. His message and speeches had set the tone of popular thought about American war aims and the terms of eventual peace. In Europe his eloquence had proved so effective that statesmen had followed his lead perforce and allowed the Armistice to be made upon his terms. All over the world there were millions upon millions of men and women to whom his words were as those of a Messiah. Now that he envisioned a new world order based upon a League of Nations, it seemed inevitable to him that he himself should go to Paris, exert this vast and beneficent power, and make the vision a reality. The splendid dream took full possession of him. Critics like Senator Lodge and even associates like Secretary Lansing might object that he ought to leave the negotiations to subordinates, or that peace should be made with Germany first, and discussion of the League postponed, in order to bring an unsettled world back to equilibrium without delay; but had he not silenced critics during the war and could he not silence them again? On the 4th of December-- less than a month after the Armistice--the President sailed from New York on the *George Washington.* As the crowds along the waterfront shouted their tribute and the vessels in the harbor tooted their whistles and the guns roared in a presidential salute, Woodrow Wilson, standing on the bridge of the *George Washington,* eastward bound, must have felt that destiny was on his side.

The events of the next few weeks only confirmed him in this feeling. He toured France and England and Italy in incredible triumph. Never had such crowds greeted a foreigner on British soil. His progress through the streets of London could be likened only to a Coronation procession. In Italy the streets were black with people come to do him honor. "No one has ever had such cheers," wrote William Bolitho; "I, who heard them in the streets of Paris, can never forget them in my life. I saw Foch pass, Clemenceau pass, Lloyd George, generals, returning troops, banners, but Wilson heard from his carriage something different, inhuman--or superhuman." Seeing those overwhelming crowds and hearing their shouts of acclaim, how could Woodrow Wilson doubt that he was still invincible? If, when the Conference met, he could only speak so that they might hear, no diplomatists of the old order could withstand him. Destiny was taking him, and the whole world with him, toward a future bright with promise.

But, as it happened, destiny had other plans. In Europe, as well as in America, idealism was on the ebb. Lloyd George, that unfailing barometer of public opinion, was campaigning for reëlection on a "Hang the Kaiser" platform; and shout as the crowds might for Wilson and justice, they voted for Lloyd George and vengeance. Now that the Germans were beaten, a score of jealous European politicians were wondering what they could get out of the settlement at Paris for their own national ends and their own personal glory. They wanted to bring home the spoils of war. They heard the mob applaud Wilson, but they knew that mobs are fickle and would applaud annexations and punitive reparations with equal fervor. They went to Paris determined to make a peace which would give them plunder to take home.

And meanwhile in the Senate Chamber at Washington opposition to Wilson's League and Wilson's Fourteen Points increased in volume. As early as December 21, 1918, Henry Cabot Lodge, intellectual leader of the Republicans in the Senate, announced that the Senate had equal power with the President in treaty-making and should make its wishes known in advance of the negotiations. He said that there would be quite enough to do at Paris without raising the issue of the League. And he set forth his idea of the sort of peace which ought to be made--an idea radically different from President Wilson's. Lodge and a group of his associates wanted Germany to be disarmed, saddled with a terrific bill for reparations, and if possible dismembered. They were ready to give to the Allies large concessions in territory. And above all, they wanted nothing to be included in the peace settlement which would commit the United States to future intervention in European affairs. They prepared to examine carefully any plan for a League of Nations which might come out of the Conference and to resist it if it involved "entangling alliances." Thus to opposition from the diplomats of Europe was added opposition of another sort from the Senate and public opinion at home. Wilson was between two fires. He might not realize how they threatened him, but they were spreading.

The tide of events, had Wilson but known it, was turning against him. Human nature, the world over, was beginning to show a new side, as it has shown it at the end of every war in history. The compulsion for unity was gone, and division was taking its place. The compulsion for idealism was gone, and realism was in the ascendant.

Nor did destiny work only through the diplomats of the Old World and the senatorial patriots of the New. It worked also through the peculiar limitations in the mind and character of Woodrow Wilson himself. The very singleness of purpose, the very uncompromising quality of mind that had made him a great prophet, forced him to take upon his own shoulders at Paris an impossible burden of responsible negotiation. It prevented him from properly acquainting his colleagues with what he himself was doing at the sessions of the Council of Ten or the Council of Four, and from getting the full benefit of their suggestions and objections. It prevented him from taking the American correspondents at Paris into his confidence and thus gaining valuable support at home. It made him play a lone hand. Again, his intelligence was visual rather than oral. As Ray Stannard Baker has well put it, Wilson was "accustomed to getting his information, not from people, but out of books, documents, letters--the written word," and consequently "underestimated the value of . . . human contacts." At written negotiations he was a past master, but in the oral give and take about a small conference table he was at a disadvantage. When Clemenceau and Lloyd George and Orlando got him into the Council of Four behind closed doors, where they could play the game of treaty-making like a four-handed card game, they had already half defeated him. A superman might have gone to Paris and come home completely victorious, but Woodrow Wilson could not have been what he was and have carried the day.

This is no place to tell the long and bitter story of the President's fight for his ideals at Paris. Suffice it to say that he fought stubbornly and resourcefully, and succeeded to a creditable extent in moderating the terms of the Treaty. The European diplomats wanted to leave the discussion of the League until after the territorial and military settlements had been made, but he forced them to put the League first. Sitting as chairman of the commission appointed to draw up the League Covenant, he brought out a preliminary draft which met, as he supposed, the principal objections to it made by men at home like Taft and Root and Lodge. In Paris he confronted a practically unanimous sentiment for annexation of huge slices of German territory and of all the German colonies; even the British dominions, through their premiers, came out boldly for annexation and supported one another in their colonial claims; yet he succeeded in getting the Conference to accept the mandate principle. He forced Clemenceau to modify his demands for German territory, though he had to threaten to leave Paris to get his way. He forced Italy to accept less land than she wanted, though he had to venture a public appeal to the conscience of the world to do it. Again and again it was he, and he only, who prevented territories from being parceled out among the victors without regard to the desires of their inhabitants. To read the day-to-day story of the Conference is to realize that the settlement would have been far more threatening to the future peace of the world had Woodrow Wilson not struggled as he did to bring about an agreement fair to all. Yet the result, after all, was a compromise. The Treaty followed in too many respects the provisions of the iniquitous secret treaties of war-time; and the League Covenant which Wilson had managed to imbed securely in it was too rigid and too full of possible military obligations to suit an American people tired of war and ready to get out of Europe once and for all.

The President must have been fully aware of the ugly imperfections in the Treaty of Versailles as he sailed back to America with it at the end of June, 1919, more than six months after his departure for France. He must have realized that, despite all his efforts, the men who had sat about the council table at Paris had been more swayed by fear and hate and greed and narrow nationalism than by the noble motives of which he had been the mouthpiece. No rational man with his eyes and ears open could have failed to sense the disillusionment which was slowly settling down upon the world, or the validity of many of the objections to the Treaty which were daily being made in the Senate at Washington. Yet what could Wilson do?

Could he come home to the Senate and the American people and say, in effect: "This Treaty is a pretty bad one in some respects. I shouldn't have accepted the Shantung clause or the Italian border clause or the failure to set a fixed German indemnity or the grabbing of a lot of German territory by France and others unless I had had to, but under the circumstances this is about the best we could do and I think the League will make up for the rest"? He could not; he had committed himself to each and every clause; he had signed the Treaty, and must defend it. Could he admit that the negotiators at Paris had failed to act in the unselfish spirit which he had proclaimed in advance that they would show? To do this would be to admit his own failure and kill his own prestige. Having proclaimed before the Conference that the settlement would be righteous and having insisted during the Conference that it was righteous, how could he admit afterward that it had not been righteous? The drift of events had caught him in a predicament from which there seemed to be but one outlet of escape. He must go home and vow that the Conference had been a love-feast, that every vital decision had been based on the Fourteen Points, that Clemenceau and Orlando and Lloyd George and the rest had been animated by an overpowering love for humanity, and that the salvation of the world depended on the complete acceptance of the Treaty as the charter of a new and idyllic world order.

That is what he did; and because the things he said about the Treaty were not true, and he must have known--sometimes, at least-- that they were not, the story of Woodrow Wilson from this point on is sheer tragedy. He fell into the pit which is dug for every idealist. Having failed to embody his ideal in fact, he distorted the fact. He pictured the world, to himself and to others, not as it was, but as he wished it to be. The optimist became a sentimentalist. The story of the Conference which he told to the American people when he returned home was a very beautiful romance of good men and true laboring without thought of selfish advantage for the welfare of humanity. He said that if the United States did not come to the aid of mankind by endorsing all that had been done at Paris, the heart of the world would be broken. But the only heart which was broken was his own.

§ 4

Henry Cabot Lodge was a gentleman, a scholar, and an elegant and persuasive figure in the United States Senate. As he strolled down the aisle of the Senate Chamber--slender, graceful, gray-haired, gray-bearded, the embodiment of all that was patrician--he caught and held the eye as might William Gillette on a crowded stage. He need not raise his voice, he need only turn for a moment and listen to a sentence or two of some colleague's florid speech and then walk indifferently on, to convince a visitor in the gallery that the speech was unworthy of attention. It was about Lodge that the opposition to Wilson gathered.

He believed in Americanism. He believed that the essence of American foreign policy should be to keep the country clear of foreign entanglements unless our honor was involved, to be ready to fight and fight hard the moment it became involved, and, when the fight was over, to disentangle ourselves once more, stand aloof, and mind our own business. (Our honor, as Lodge saw it, was involved if our prerogatives were threatened; to Woodrow Wilson, on the other hand, national honor was a moral matter: only by shameful conduct could a nation lose it.) As chairman of the Foreign Relations Committee, Lodge conceived it to be his duty to see that the United States was not drawn into any international agreement which would endanger this time-honored policy. He did not believe that the nations of the world could be trusted to spend the rest of their years behaving like so many Boy Scouts; he knew that, to be effective, a treaty must be serviceable in eras of bad feeling as well as good; and he saw in the present one many an invitation to trouble.

Senator Lodge was also a politician. Knowing that his Massachusetts constituents numbered among them hundreds of thousands of Irish, he asked the overworked peace delegates at Paris to give a hearing to Messrs. Frank P. Walsh, Edward F. Dunn, and Michael J. Ryan, the so-called American Commission for Irish Independence, though it was difficult for anyone but an Irishman to say what Irish independence had to do with the Treaty. Remembering, too, the size of the Italian vote, Lodge was willing to embarrass President Wilson, in the midst of the Italian crisis at the Conference, by saying in a speech to the Italians of Boston that Italy ought to have Fiume and control the Adriatic. Finally, Lodge had no love for Woodrow Wilson. So strongly did he feel that Wilson's assumption of the right to speak for American opinion was unwarranted and iniquitous, that when Henry White, the only Republican on the American Peace Commission, sailed for Europe, Lodge put into White's hands a secret memorandum containing his own extremely un-Wilsonian idea of what peace terms the American people would stand for, and suggested that White show it in strict confidence to Balfour, Clemenceau, and Nitti, adding, "This knowledge may in certain circumstances be very important to them in strengthening their position." No honorable man could have made such a suggestion unless he believed the defeat of the President's program to be essential to the country's welfare.

United with Lodge in skepticism about the Treaty, if in nothing else, was a curious combination of men and of influences. There were hard-shelled tories like Brandegee; there were Western idealists like Borah, who distrusted any association with foreign diplomats as the blond country boy of the old-fashioned melodrama distrusted association with the slick city man; there were chronic dissenters like La Follette and Jim Reed; there were Republicans who were not sorry to put the Democratic President into a hole, and particularly a President who had appealed in war-time for the election of a Democratic Congress; there were Senators anxious to show that nobody could make a treaty without the advice as well as the consent of the Senate, and get away with it; and there were not a few who, in addition to their other reasons for opposition, shared Lodge's personal distaste for Wilsonian rhetoric. Outside the Senate there was opposition of still other varieties. The Irish were easily inflamed against a League of Nations that gave "six seats to England." The Italians were ready to denounce a man who had refused to let Italy have Fiume. Many Germans, no matter how loyal to the United States they may have been during the war, had little enthusiasm for the hamstringing of the German Republic and the denial to Germany of a seat in the League. There were some people who thought that America had got too little out of the settlement. And there were a vast number who saw in the League Covenant, and especially in Article X, obligations with which they were not willing to have the nation saddled.

Aside from all these groups, furthermore, there was another factor to be reckoned with: the growing apathy of millions of Americans toward anything which reminded them of the war. They were fast becoming sick and tired of the whole European mess. They wanted to be done with it. They didn't want to be told of new sacrifices to be made--they had made plenty. Gone was the lift of the day when a girl singing the "Doxology" in Times Square could express their feelings about victory. This was all over now, the Willard-Dempsey fight and the arrival of the British dirigible R-34 at Long Island were much more interesting.

On the 10th of July, 1919, the President, back in Washington again, laid the Treaty of Versailles before the Senate, denying that the compromises which had been accepted as inevitable by the American negotiators "cut to the heart of any principle." In his words as he addressed the Senate was all the eloquence which only a few months ago had swayed the world. "The stage is set, the destiny disclosed. It has come about by no plan of our conceiving, but by the hand of God who led us into the way. We cannot turn back. We can only go forward, with lifted eyes and freshened spirit, to follow the vision. It was of this that we dreamed at our birth. America shall in truth show the way. The light streams upon the path ahead and nowhere else."

Fine words--but they brought no overwhelming appeal from the country for immediate ratification. The country was tired of going forward with lifted eyes, and Woodrow Wilson's prose style, now all too familiar, could no longer freshen its spirit. The Treaty--a document as long as a novel--was referred to Lodge's Committee on Foreign Relations, which settled down to study it at leisure. A month later Lodge rose in the Senate to express his preference for national independence and security, to insist that Articles X and XI of the League Covenant gave "other powers" the right "to call out American troops and American ships to any part of the world," and to reply to Wilson: "We would not have our politics distracted and embittered by the dissensions of other lands. We would not have our country's vigor exhausted, or her moral force abated, by everlasting meddling and muddling in every quarrel, great and small, which afflicts the world." And within a fortnight Lodge's committee began voting--although by a narrow margin in each case--to amend the Treaty; to give Shantung to China, to relieve the United States of membership in international commissions, to give the United States the same vote as Great Britain in the League, and to shut off the representatives of the British dominions from voting on questions affecting the British Empire. It began to look as if the process of making amendments and reservations might go on indefinitely. Woodrow Wilson decided to play his last desperate card. He would go to the people. He would win them to his cause, making a speaking trip through the West.

His doctors advised against it, for physically the President was almost at the end of his rope. Never robust, for months he had been under a terrific strain. Again and again during the Peace Conference, Ray Stannard Baker would find him, after a long day of nerve-wracking sessions, looking "utterly beaten, worn out, his face quite haggard and one side of it twitching painfully." At one time he had broken down--had been taken with a sudden attack of influenza, with violent paroxysms of coughing and a fever of 103°--only to be up again and at his labors within a few days. Now, in September, his nerves frayed by continued overwork and by the thought of possible failure of all he had given his heart and strength for, he was like a man obsessed. He could think of nothing but the Treaty and the League. He cared for nothing but to bring them through to victory. And so, despite all that those about him could say, he left Washington on September 3rd to undergo the even greater strain of a speaking trip--the preparation and delivery of one or even two speeches a day in huge sweltering auditoriums (and without amplifiers to ease the strain on his voice); the automobile processions through city after city (during which he had to stand up in his car and continuously wave his hat to the crowds); the swarms of reporters, the hand-shaking, the glare of publicity, and the restless sleep of one who travels night in and night out on a swaying train.

Again and again on that long trip of his, Woodrow Wilson painted the picture of the Treaty and the League that lived in his own mind, a picture which bore fainter and fainter resemblance to the reality. He spoke of the "generous, high-minded, statesman-like coöperation" which had been manifest at the Paris Conference; he said that "the hearts of men like Clemenceau and Lloyd George and Orlando beat with the people of the world," and that the heart of humanity beat in the document which they had produced. He represented America, and indeed every other country, as thrilling to a new ideal. "The whole world is now in a state where you can fancy that there are hot tears upon every cheek, and those hot tears are tears of sorrow. They are also tears of hope." He warned his audiences that if the Treaty were not ratified, disorder would shake the foundations of the world, and he envisioned "this great nation marching at the fore of a great procession" to "those heights upon which there rests nothing but the pure light of the justice of God." Every one of those forty speeches was different from every other, and each was perfectly ordered, beautifully phrased, and thrilling with passion. As an intellectual feat the delivery of them was remarkable. Yet each pictured a dream world and a dream Treaty, and instinctively the country knew it. (Perhaps, indeed, there were moments of terrible sanity when, as the President lay sleepless in his private car, he himself knew how far from the truth he had departed.) The expected surge of public opinion toward Wilson's cause failed to materialize. The Senate went right on discussing reservations. On September 24th, the first test vote went against the President 43 to 40.

On the night of the next day Wilson came to the end of his strength. For some time he had had indigestion and had slept little. After his long speech at Pueblo on the evening of September 25th he could not sleep at all. The train was stopped and Mr. and Mrs. Wilson took a walk together on a country road. When he returned to the train he was feverish and "as he slept under a narcotic, his mouth drooled. His body testified in many ways to an impending crash." The next morning when he tried to get up he could hardly stand. The train hurried on toward Washington and all future speaking engagements were canceled. Back to the White House the sick man went. A few days later a cerebral thrombosis partially paralyzed his left side. Another act of the tragedy had come to an end. He had given all he had to the cause, and it had not been enough.

§ 5

There followed one of the most extraordinary periods in the whole history of the Presidency. For weeks Woodrow Wilson lay seriously ill, sometimes unable even to sign documents awaiting his signature. He could not sit up in a chair for over a month, or venture out for a ride in the White House automobile for five months. During all the rest of his term--which lasted until March 4, 1921, seventeen months after his breakdown--he remained in feeble and precarious health, a sick man lying in bed or sitting in an invalid's chair, his left side and left leg and left arm partially paralyzed. Within the White House he was immured as if in a hospital. He saw almost nobody, transacted only the most imperative business of his office. The only way of communicating with him was by letter, and as during most of this time all letters must pass through the hands of Mrs. Wilson or Admiral Grayson or others in the circle of attendants upon the invalid, and few were answered, there was often no way of knowing who was responsible for a failure to answer them or to act in accordance with the suggestions embodied in them. Sometimes, in fact, it was suspected that it was Mrs. Wilson who was responsible for many a White House decision--that the country was in effect being governed by a regency.

With the President virtually unable to function, the whole executive machine came almost to a stop. It could, to be sure, continue its routine tasks; and an aggressive member of the Cabinet like Attorney-General Palmer could go blithely ahead rounding up radicals and deporting them and getting out injunctions against strikers as if he had the full wisdom and power of the Presidency behind him; but most matters of policy waited upon the White House, and after a while it became clear that guidance from that quarter could hardly be expected. There were vital problems clamoring for the attention of the Executive: the high cost of living, the subsequent breakdown of business prosperity and increase of unemployment; the intense bitterness between capital and labor, culminating in the great steel and coal strikes; the reorganization of the government departments on a peace basis; the settlement of innumerable questions of foreign policy unconnected with the Treaty or the League. Yet upon most of these problems the sick man had no leadership to offer. Meanwhile his influence with Congress and the country, far from being increased by his martyrdom for the League, dwindled to almost nothing.

The effect of this strange state of affairs upon official Washington was well described a year or two later by Edward G. Lowry in *Washington Close-ups:*

"For a long time the social-political atmosphere of Washington had been one of bleak and chill austerity suffused and envenomed by hatred of a sick chief magistrate that seemed to poison and blight every human relationship. The White House was isolated. It had no relation with the Capitol or the local resident and official community. Its great iron gates were closed and chained and locked. Policemen guarded its approaches. It was in a void apart. . . . It all made for bleakness and bitterness and a general sense of frustration and unhappiness."

Mr. Wilson's mind remained clear. When the report went about that he was unable "to discharge the powers and duties" of his office and should, therefore, under the provisions of the Constitution, be supplanted by the Vice-President (and reports of this sort were frequent in those days) Senators Fall and Hitchcock visited him in behalf of the Senate to determine his mental condition. They found him keenly alive to the humor of their embarrassing mission; he laughed and joked with them and showed a complete grasp of the subjects under discussion. Nevertheless, something had gone out of him. His messages were lifeless, his mind was sterile of new ideas. He could not meet new situations in a new way: reading his public documents, one felt that his brain was still turning over old ideas, rearranging old phrases, that he was still living in that dream world which he had built about himself during the days of his fight for the League.

He had always been a lonely man; and now, as if pursued by some evil demon, he broke with one after another of those who still tried to serve him. For long years Colonel House had been his chief adviser as well as his affectionate friend. During the latter days of the Peace Conference a certain coolness had been noticed in Wilson's attitude toward House. This very conciliatory man had been perhaps a little too conciliatory in his negotiations during the President's absence from Paris: rightly or wrongly, the President felt that House had unwittingly played into the hands of the wily Clemenceau. Nevertheless, House hoped, on his return from Paris, to be able to effect a rapprochement between his broken chief and the defiant Senators. House wrote to suggest that Wilson accept certain reservations to the Treaty. There was no answer to the letter. House wrote again. No answer. There was never any explanation. The friendship and the political relationship, long so valuable to the President and so influential in the direction of policy, were both at an end--that was all one could say.

Robert Lansing had been at odds with the President over many things before and during the Peace Conference; yet he remained as Secretary of State and believed himself to be on good terms with his chief. During Wilson's illness, deciding that something must be done to enable the government to transact business, he called meetings of the Cabinet, which were held in the Cabinet Room at the White House offices. He was peremptorily dismissed. Last of all to go was the faithful Joe Tumulty, who had been Wilson's secretary through fair weather and foul, in the Governor's office at Trenton and for eight years at Washington. Although the break with Tumulty happened after Wilson left the White House, it deserves mention here because it so resembles the others and reveals what poison was working in the sick man's mind. In April, 1922, there was to be held in New York a Democratic dinner. Before the dinner Tumulty visited Wilson and got what he supposed to be an oral message to the effect that Wilson would "support any man [for the Presidency] who will stand for the salvation of America, and the salvation of America is justice to all classes." It seemed an innocuous message, and after ten years of association with Wilson, Tumulty had reason to suppose that he knew when Wilson might be quoted and when he might not. But as it happened, Governor Cox spoke at the Democratic dinner, and the message, when Tumulty gave it, was interpreted as an endorsement of Cox; whereupon Wilson wrote a curt letter to the *New York Times* denying that he had authorized anybody to give a message from him. Tumulty at once wrote to Wilson to explain that he had acted in good faith and to apologize like a true friend for having caused the President embarrassment. His letter was "courteously answered by Mrs. Wilson" (to use Tumulty's own subsequent words), but Wilson himself said not a word more. Again Tumulty wrote loyally, saying that he would always regard Mr. Wilson with affection and would be "always around the corner when you need me." There was no answer.

On the issue of the Treaty and the League Woodrow Wilson remained adamant to the end. Call it unswerving loyalty to principle or call it stubbornness, as you will--he would consent to no reservations except (when it was too late) some innocuous "interpretive" ones, framed by Senator Hitchcock, which went down to defeat. While the President lay critically ill, the Senate went right on proposing reservation after reservation, and on November 19, 1919, it defeated the Treaty. Only a small majority of the Senators were at that time irreconcilable opponents of the pact; but they were enough to carry the day. By combining forces with Wilson's Democratic supporters who favored the passage of the Treaty without change, they secured a majority against the long list of reservations proposed by Lodge's committee. Then by combining forces with Lodge and the other reservationists, they defeated the Treaty minus the reservations. It was an ironical result, but it stood. A few months later the issue was raised again, and once more the Treaty went down to defeat. Finally a resolution for a separate peace with Germany was passed by both Houses--and vetoed by Wilson as "an action which would place an ineffaceable stain upon the gallantry and honor of the United States." (A similar peace resolution was ultimately signed by President Harding.) President Wilson's last hope was that the election of 1920 would serve as a "great and solemn referendum" in which the masses of the people--those masses who, he had always claimed, were on his side--would rise to vindicate him and the country. They rose--and swamped the pro-League candidate by a plurality of seven million.

It is not pleasant to imagine the thoughts of the sick man in the White House as defeat after defeat overwhelmed his cause and mocked the great sacrifice he had made for it. How soon the realization came upon him that everything was lost we do not know. After his breakdown, as he lay ill in the White House, did he still hope? It seems likely. All news from the outside world was filtered to him through those about him. With his life hanging in the balance, it would have been quite natural--if not inevitable--for them to wish to protect him from shock, to tell him that all was going well on the Hill, that the tide had swung back again, that this token and that showed that the American people would not fail him. On such a theory one might explain the break with Colonel House. Possibly any suggestion for compromise with the Lodge forces seemed to the President simply a craven proposal for putting up the white flag in the moment of victory. But whether or not this theory is justified, sooner or later the knowledge must have come, as vote after vote turned against the Treaty, and must have turned the taste of life to bitterness. Wilson's icy repudiation of faithful Joe Tumulty was the act of a man who has lost his faith in humankind.

§ 6

Back in the early spring of 1919, while Wilson was still at Paris, Samuel G. Blythe, an experienced observer of the political scene, had written in the *Saturday Evening Post* of the temper of the leaders of the Republican Party as they faced the issues of peace:

"You cannot teach an Old Guard new tricks. . . . The Old Guard surrenders but it never dies. Right at this minute, the ancient and archaic Republicans who think they control the destinies of the Republican Party--think they do!--are operating after the manner and style of 1896. The war hasn't made a dent in them. . . . The only way they look is backward."

The analysis was sound; but the Republican bosses, however open to criticism they may have been as statesmen, were at least good politicians. They had their ears where a good politician's should be--to the ground--and what they heard there was a rumble of discontent with Wilson and all that he represented. They determined that at the election of 1920 they would choose as the Republican standard-bearer somebody who would present, both to themselves and to the country, a complete contrast with the idealist whom they detested. As the year rolled round and the date for the Republican Convention approached, they surveyed the field. The leading candidate was General Leonard Wood, a blunt soldier, an inheritor of Theodore Roosevelt's creed of fearing God and keeping your powder dry; he made a fairly good contrast with Wilson, but he promised to be almost as unmanageable. Then there was Governor Lowden of Illinois--but he, too, did not quite fulfill the ideal. Herbert Hoover, the reliever of Belgium and war-time Food Administrator, was conducting a highly amateur campaign for the nomination; the politicians dismissed him with a sour laugh. Why, this man Hoover hadn't known whether he was a Republican or Democrat until the campaign began! Hiram Johnson was in the field, but he also might prove stiff-necked, although it was to his advantage that he was a Senator. The bosses' inspired choice was none of these men: it was Warren Gamaliel Harding, a commonplace and unpretentious Senator from Ohio.

Consider how perfectly Harding met the requirements. Wilson was a visionary who liked to identify himself with "forward-looking men"; Harding, as Mr. Lowry put it, was as old-fashioned as those wooden Indians which used to stand in front of cigar stores, "a flower of the period before safety razors." Harding believed that statesmanship had come to its apogee in the days of McKinley and

Foraker. Wilson was cold; Harding was an affable small-town man, at ease with "folks"; an ideal companion, as one of his friends expressed it, "to play poker with all Saturday night." Wilson had always been difficult of access; Harding was accessible to the last degree. Wilson favored labor, distrusted businessmen as a class, and talked of "industrial democracy"; Harding looked back with longing eyes to the good old days when the government didn't bother businessmen with unnecessary regulations, but provided them with fat tariffs and instructed the Department of Justice not to have them on its mind. Wilson was at logger-heads with Congress, and particularly with the Senate; Harding was not only a Senator, but a highly amenable Senator. Wilson had been adept at making enemies; Harding hadn't an enemy in the world. He was genuinely genial. "He had no knobs, he was the same size and smoothness all the way round," wrote Charles Willis Thompson. Wilson thought in terms of the whole world; Harding was for America first. And finally, whereas Wilson wanted America to exert itself nobly, Harding wanted to give it a rest. At Boston, a few weeks before the Convention, he had correctly expressed the growing desire of the people of the country and at the same time had unwittingly added a new word to the language, when he said, "America's present need is not heroics but healing; not nostrums but normalcy; not revolution but restoration; . . . not surgery but serenity." Here was a man whom a country wearied of moral obligations and the hope of the world could take to its heart.

It is credibly reported that the decision in favor of Harding was made by the Republican bosses as early as February, 1920, four months before the Convention. But it was not until four ballots had been taken at the Convention itself--with Wood leading, Lowden second, and Harding fifth--and the wilted delegates had dispersed for the night, that the leaders finally concluded to put Harding over. Harding's political manager, an Ohio boss named Harry M. Daugherty, had predicted that the Convention would be deadlocked and that the nomination would be decided upon by twelve or thirteen men "at two o'clock in the morning, in a smoke-filled room." He was precisely right. The room was Colonel George Harvey's, in the Hotel Blackstone. Boies Penrose, lying mortally ill in Philadelphia, had given his instructions by private wire to John T. Adams. The word was passed round, and the next afternoon Harding was nominated.

The Democrats, relieved that Wilson's illness had disqualified him, duly nominated another equally undistinguished Ohio politician, Governor James M. Cox. This nominee had to swallow the League of

Nations and did. He swung manfully around the circle, shouting himself hoarse, pointing with pride. But he hadn't a chance in the world. Senator Harding remained in his average small town and conducted a McKinley-esque front-porch campaign; he pitched horseshoes behind the house with his Republican advisers like an average small-town man and wore a McKinley carnation; he said just enough in behalf of "an association of nations" to permit inveterate Republicans who favored the League to vote for him without twinges of conscience, and just enough against Wilson's League to convince the majority that with him in the White House they would not be called upon to march to the aid of suffering Czechoslovakia; and the men and women of the United States woke up on the morning of November 3rd to find that they had swept him into the Presidency by a margin of sixteen million to nine million. Governor Cox, the sacrificial victim, faded rapidly into the mists of obscurity.

The United States had rendered its considered judgment on "our fortunate duty to assist by example, by sober, friendly counsel, and by material aid in the establishment of just democracy throughout the world." It had preferred normalcy.

§ 7

Woodrow Wilson lived on in Washington--in a large and comfortable house on S Street--for over three years after this final crushing defeat. Those who came to call upon him toward the end found a man prematurely old, huddled in a big chair by the fireplace in a sunny south room. He sat with his hands in his lap, his head a little on one side. His face and body were heavier than they had been in his days of power; his hair, now quite gray, was brushed back over an almost bald head. As he talked he did not move his head--only his eyes followed his visitor, and his right arm swung back and forth and occasionally struck the arm of the chair for emphasis as he made his points. The old-time urbanity was in his manner as he said, "You must excuse my not rising; I'm really quite lame." But as he talked of the foreign policy of the United States and of his enemies, his tone was full of hatred. This was no time to sprinkle rose-water round, he said; it was a time for fighting--there must be a party fight, "not in a partisan spirit, but on party lines." Still he clung to the last shred of hope that his party might follow the gleam. Of the men who had made the fulfillment of his great project impossible he spoke in unsparing terms.

"I've got to get well, and then I'm going out to get a few scalps." So he nursed his grievance; an old man, helpless and bitter.

On Armistice Day, five years after the triumphant close of the war, he stood on the steps of his house--supported so that he should not fall--and spoke to a crowd that had gathered to do him honor. "I am not," said he, "one of those that have the least anxiety about the triumph of the principles I have stood for. I have seen fools resist Providence before and I have seen their destruction, as will come upon these again--utter destruction and contempt. That we shall prevail is as sure as that God reigns."

Three months later he was dead.

♦ III ♦
THE BIG RED SCARE

§ 1

If the American people turned a deaf ear to Woodrow Wilson's plea for the League of Nations during the early years of the Post-war Decade, it was not simply because they were too weary of foreign entanglements and noble efforts to heed him. They were listening to something else. They were listening to ugly rumors of a huge radical conspiracy against the government and institutions of the United States. They had their ears cocked for the detonation of bombs and the tramp of Bolshevist armies. They seriously thought--or at least millions of them did, millions of otherwise reasonable citizens--that a Red revolution might begin in the United States the next month or next week, and they were less concerned with making the world safe for democracy than with making America safe for themselves.

Those were the days when column after column of the front pages of the newspapers shouted the news of strikes and anti-Bolshevist riots; when radicals shot down Armistice Day paraders in the streets of Centralia, Washington, and in revenge the patriotic citizenry took out of the jail a member of the I. W. W.--a white American, be it noted--and lynched him by tying a rope around his neck and throwing him off a bridge; when properly elected members of the Assembly of New York State were expelled (and their constituents thereby disfranchised) simply because they had been elected as members of the venerable Socialist Party; when a jury in Indiana took two minutes to acquit a man for shooting and killing an alien because he had shouted, "To hell with the United States"; and when the Vice-President of the nation cited as a dangerous manifestation of radicalism in the women's colleges the fact that the girl debaters of Radcliffe had upheld the affirmative in an intercollegiate debate on the subject: "Resolved, that the recognition of labor unions by employers is essential to successful collective bargaining." It was an era of lawless and disorderly defense of law and order, of unconstitutional defense of the Constitution, of suspicion and civil conflict--in a very literal sense, a reign of terror.

For this national panic there was a degree of justification. During the war the labor movement had been steadily gaining in momentum and prestige. There had been hundreds of strikes, induced chiefly by the rising prices of everything that the laboring-man needed in order to live, but also by his new consciousness of his power. The government, in order to keep up production and maintain industrial peace, had encouraged collective bargaining, elevated Samuel Gompers to one of the seats of the mighty in the war councils at Washington, and given the workers some reason to hope that with the coming of peace new benefits would be showered upon them. Peace came, and hope was deferred. Prices still rose, employers resisted wage increases with a new solidarity and continued to insist on long hours of work, Woodrow Wilson went off to Europe in quest of universal peace and forgot all about the laboring-men; and in anger and despair, they took up the only weapon ready to their hand--the strike. All over the country they struck. There were strikes in the building trades, among the longshoremen, the stockyard workers, the shipyard men, the subway men, the shoe-workers, the carpenters, the telephone operators, and so on *ad infinitum,* until by November, 1919, the total number of men and women on strike in the industrial states was estimated by Alvin Johnson to be at least a million, with enough more in the non-industrial states, or voluntarily abstaining from work though not engaged in recognized strikes, to bring the grand total to something like two million.

Nor were all of these men striking merely for recognition of their unions or for increases in pay or shorter hours--the traditional causes. Some of them were demanding a new industrial order, the displacement of capitalistic control of industry (or at least of their own industry) by government control: in short, something approaching a social régime. The hitherto conservative railroad workers came out for the Plumb Plan, by which the government would continue to direct the railroads and labor would have a voice in the management. When in September, 1919, the United Mine Workers voted to strike, they boldly advocated the nationalization of the mines; and a delegate who began his speech before the crowded convention with the words, "Nationalization is impossible," was drowned out by boos and jeers and cries of "Coal operator! Throw him out!" In the Northwest the I. W. W. was fighting to get the whip hand over capital through One Big Union. In North Dakota and the adjoining grain states, two hundred thousand farmers joined Townley's Non-Partisan League, described by its enemies--with some truth--as an agrarian soviet. (Townley's candidate for governor of Minnesota in 1916, by the way, had been a Swedish-American named Charles A. Lindbergh, who would have been amazed to hear that his family was destined to be allied by marriage to that of a Morgan partner.) There was an unmistakable trend toward socialistic ideas both in the ranks of labor and among liberal intellectuals. The Socialist party, watching the success of the Russian Revolution, was flirting with the idea of violent mass-action. And there was, too, a rag-tag-and-bobtail collection of communists and anarchists, many of them former Socialists, nearly all of them foreign-born, most of them Russian, who talked of going still further, who took their gospel direct from Moscow and, presumably with the aid of Russian funds, preached it aggressively among the slum and factory-town population.

This latter group of communists and anarchists constituted a very narrow minority of the radical movement--absurdly narrow when we consider all the to-do that was made about them. Late in 1919 Professor Gordon S. Watkins of the University of Illinois, writing in the *Atlantic Monthly,* set the membership of the Socialist party at 39,000, of the Communist Labor party at from 10,000 to 30,000, and of the Communist party at from 30,000 to 60,000. In other words, according to this estimate, the Communists could muster at the most hardly more than one-tenth of one per cent of the adult population of the country; and the three parties together--the majority of whose members were probably content to work for their ends by lawful means--brought the proportion to hardly more than two-tenths of one per cent, a rather slender nucleus, it would seem, for a revolutionary mass movement.

But the American businessman was in no mood to consider whether it was a slender nucleus or not. He, too, had come out of the war with his fighting blood up, ready to lick the next thing that stood in his way. He wanted to get back to business and enjoy his profits. Labor stood in his way and threatened his profits. He had come out of the war with a militant patriotism; and mingling his idealistic with his selfish motives, after the manner of all men at all times, he developed a fervent belief that 100-per-cent Americanism and the Welfare of God's Own Country and Loyalty to the Teachings of the Founding

Fathers implied the right of the businessman to kick the union organizer out of his workshop. He had come to distrust anything and everything that was foreign, and this radicalism he saw as the spawn of long-haired Slavs and unwashed East-Side Jews. And, finally, he had been nourished during the war years upon stories of spies and plotters and international intrigue. He had been convinced that German sympathizers signaled to one another with lights from mountain-tops and put ground glass into surgical dressings, and he had formed the habit of expecting tennis courts to conceal gun-emplacements. His credulity had thus been stretched until he was quite ready to believe that a struggle of American laboring-men for better wages was the beginning of an armed rebellion directed by Lenin and Trotsky, and that behind every innocent professor who taught that there were arguments for as well as against socialism there was a bearded rascal from eastern Europe with a money bag in one hand and a smoking bomb in the other.

§ 2

The events of 1919 did much to feed this fear. On the 28th of April--while Wilson was negotiating the Peace Treaty at Paris, and homecoming troops were parading under Victory Arches--an infernal machine "big enough to blow out the entire side of the County-City Building" was found in Mayor Ole Hanson's mail at Seattle. Mayor Hanson had been stumping the country to arouse it to the Red Menace. The following afternoon a colored servant opened a package addressed to Senator Thomas R. Hardwick at his home in Atlanta, Georgia, and a bomb in the package blew off her hands. Senator Hardwick, as chairman of the Immigration Committee of the Senate, had proposed restricting immigration as a means of keeping out Bolshevism.

At two o'clock the next morning Charles Caplan, a clerk in the parcel post division of the New York Post Office, was on his way home to Harlem when he read in a newspaper about the Hardwick bomb. The package was described in this news story as being about six inches long and three inches wide; as being done up in brown paper and, like the Hanson bomb, marked with the (false, of course) return address of Gimbel Brothers in New York. There was something familiar to Mr. Caplan about this description. He thought he remembered having seen some packages like that. He racked his brain, and suddenly it all came back to him. He hurried back to the Post Office--and found, neatly laid away on a shelf where he had put them because of insufficient postage, sixteen little brown-paper packages with the Gimbel return address on them. They were addressed to Attorney-General Palmer, Postmaster-General Burleson, Judge Landis of Chicago, Justice Holmes of the Supreme Court, Secretary of Labor Wilson, Commissioner of Immigration Caminetti, J. P. Morgan, John D. Rockefeller, and a number of other government officials and capitalists. The packages were examined by the police in a neighboring firehouse, and found to contain bombs. Others had started on their way through the mails; the total number ultimately accounted for reached thirty-six. (None of the other packages were carelessly opened, it is hardly necessary to say; for the next few days people in high station were very circumspect about undoing brown-paper packages.) The list of intended recipients was strong evidence that the bombs had been sent by an alien radical.

Hardly more than a month later there was a series of bomb explosions, the most successful of which damaged the front of Attorney-General Palmer's house in Washington. It came in the evening; Mr. Palmer had just left the library on the ground floor and turned out the lights and gone up to bed when there was a bang as of something hitting the front door, followed by the crash of the explosion. The limbs of a man blown to pieces were found outside, and close by, according to the newspaper reports, lay a copy of *Plain Words,* a radical publication.

The American public read the big headlines about these outrages and savagely resolved to get back at "these radicals."

How some of them did so may be illustrated by two incidents out of dozens which took place during those days. Both of them occurred on May Day of 1919--just after Mr. Caplan had found the brown-paper packages on the Post Office shelf. On the afternoon of May Day the owners and staff of the *New York Call,* a Socialist paper, were holding a reception to celebrate the opening of their new office. There were hundreds of men, women, and children gathered in the building for innocent palaver. A mob of soldiers and sailors stormed in and demanded that the "Bolshevist" posters be torn down. When the demand was refused, they destroyed the literature on the tables, smashed up the offices, drove the crowd out into the street, and clubbed them so vigorously--standing in a semicircle outside the front door and belaboring them as they emerged--that seven members of the *Call* staff went to the hospital.

In Cleveland, on the same day, there was a Socialist parade headed by a red flag. An army lieutenant demanded that the flag be lowered, and thereupon with a group of soldiers leaped into the ranks of the procession and precipitated a free-for-all fight. The police came and charged into the *mêlée*--and from that moment a series of riots began which spread through the city. Scores of people were injured, one man was killed, and the Socialist headquarters were utterly demolished by a gang that defended American institutions by throwing typewriters and office furniture out into the street.

The summer of 1919 passed. The Senate debated the Peace Treaty. The House passed the Volstead Act. The Suffrage Amendment passed Congress and went to the States. The R-34 made the first transatlantic dirigible flight from England to Mineola, Long Island, and returned safely. People laughed over *The Young Visiters* and wondered whether Daisy Ashford was really James M. Barrie. The newspapers denounced sugar-hoarders and food profiteers as the cost of living kept on climbing. The first funeral by airplane was held. Ministers lamented the increasing laxity of morals among the young. But still the fear and hatred of Bolshevism gripped the American mind as new strikes broke out and labor became more aggressive and revolution spread like a scourge through Europe. And then, in September, came the Boston police strike, and the fear was redoubled.

§ 3

The Boston police had a grievance: their pay was based on a minimum of $1,100, out of which uniforms had to be bought, and $1,100 would buy mighty little at 1919 prices. They succumbed to the epidemic of unionism, formed a union, and affiliated with the American Federation of Labor. Police Commissioner Curtis, a stiff-necked martinet, had forbidden them to affiliate with any outside organization, and he straightway brought charges against nineteen officers and members of the union for having violated his orders, found them guilty, and suspended them. The Irish blood of the police was heated, and they threatened to strike. A committee appointed by the mayor to adjust the dispute proposed a compromise, but to Mr. Curtis this looked like surrender. He refused to budge. Thereupon, on September 9, 1919, a large proportion of the police walked out at the time of the evening roll call.

With the city left defenseless, hoodlums proceeded to enjoy themselves. That night they smashed windows and looted stores. Mayor Peters called for State troops. The next day the Governor called out the State Guard, and a volunteer police force began to try to cope with the situation. The Guardsmen and volunteer police--ex-servicemen, Harvard students, cotton brokers from the Back Bay--were inexperienced, and the hoodlums knew it. Guardsmen were goaded into firing on a mob in South Boston and killed two people. For days there was intermittent violence, especially when Guardsmen upheld the majesty of the law by breaking up crap games in that garden of sober Puritanism, Boston Common. The casualty list grew, and the country looked on with dismay as the Central Labor Union, representing the organized trade unionists of the city, debated holding a general strike on behalf of the policemen. Perhaps, people thought, the dreaded revolution was beginning here and now.

But presently it began to appear that public opinion in Boston, as everywhere else, was overwhelmingly against the police and that theirs was a lost cause. The Central Labor Union prudently decided not to call a general strike. Mr. Curtis discharged the nineteen men whom he had previously suspended and began to recruit a new force.

Realizing that the game was nearly up, old Samuel Gompers, down in Washington, tried to intervene. He wired to the Governor of Massachusetts that the action of the Police Commissioner was unwarranted and autocratic.

The Governor of Massachusetts was an inconspicuous, sour-faced man with a reputation for saying as little as possible and never jeopardizing his political position by being betrayed into a false move. He made the right move now. He replied to Gompers that there was "no right to strike against the public safety by anybody, anywhere, any time"--and overnight he became a national hero. If there had been any doubt that the strike was collapsing, it vanished when the press of the whole country applauded Calvin Coolidge. For many a week to come, amateur policemen, pressed into emergency service, would come home at night to the water side of Beacon Street to complain that directing traffic was even more arduous than a whole day of golf at the Country Club; it took time to recruit a new force. But recruited it was, and Boston breathed again.

Organized labor, however, was in striking mood. A few days later, several hundred thousand steel-workers walked out of the mills--after Judge Gary had shown as stiff a neck as Commissioner Curtis and had refused to deal with their union representatives.

Now there was little radicalism among the steel strikers. Their strike was a protest against low wages and long hours. A considerable proportion of them worked a twelve-hour day, and they had a potentially strong case. But the steel magnates had learned something from the Boston Police Strike. The public was jumpy and would condemn any cause on which the Bolshevist label could be pinned. The steel magnates found little difficulty in pinning a Bolshevist label on the strikers. William Z. Foster, the most energetic and intelligent of the strike organizers, had been a syndicalist (and later, although even Judge Gary didn't know it then, was to become a Communist). Copies of a syndicalist pamphlet by Foster appeared in newspaper offices and were seized upon avidly to show what a revolutionary fellow he was. Foster was trying to substitute unions organized by industries for the ineffective craft unions, which were at the mercy of a huge concern like the Steel Corporation; therefore, according to the newspapers, Foster was a "borer from within" and the strike was part of a radical conspiracy. The public was sufficiently frightened to prove more interested in defeating borers from within than in mitigating the lot of obscure Slavs who spent twelve hours a day in the steel mills.

The great steel strike had been in progress only a few weeks when a great coal strike impended. In this case nobody needed to point out to the public the Red specter lurking behind the striking miners. The miners had already succeeded in pinning the Bolshevist label on themselves by their enthusiastic vote for nationalization; and to the undiscriminating newspaper reader, public control of the mining industry was all of a piece with communism, anarchism, bomb-throwing, and general Red ruin. Here was a new threat to the Republic. Something must be done. The Government must act.

It acted. A. Mitchell Palmer, Attorney-General of the United States, who enjoyed being called the "Fighting Quaker," saw his shining opportunity and came to the rescue of the Constitution.

§ 4

There is a certain grim humor in the fact that what Mr. Palmer did during the next three months was done by him as the chief legal officer of an Administration which had come into power to bring about the New Freedom. Woodrow Wilson was ill in the White House, out of touch with affairs, and dreaming only of his lamented League: that is the only explanation.

On the day before the coal strike was due to begin, the Attorney-General secured from a Federal Judge in Indianapolis an order enjoining the leaders of the strike from doing anything whatever to further it. He did this under the provisions of a food-and-fuel-control Act which forbade restriction of coal production during the war. In actual fact the war was not only over, it had been over for nearly a year: but legally it was not over--the Peace Treaty still languished in the Senate. This food-and-fuel-control law, in further actual fact, had been passed by the Senate after Senator Husting had explicitly declared that he was "authorized by the Secretary of Labor, Mr. Wilson, to say that the Administration does not construe this bill as prohibiting strikes and peaceful picketing and will not so construe it." But Mr. Palmer either had never heard of this assurance or cared nothing about it or decided that unforeseen conditions had arisen. He got his injunction, and the coal strike was doomed, although the next day something like four hundred thousand coal miners, now leaderless by decree of the Federal Government, walked out of the mines.

The public knew nothing of the broken pledge, of course; it would have been a bold newspaper proprietor who would have published Senator Husting's statement, even had he known about it. It took genuine courage for a paper even to say, as did the *New York World* at that time, that there was "no Bolshevist menace in the United States and no I. W. W. menace that an ordinarily capable police force is not competent to deal with." The press applauded the injunction as it had applauded Calvin Coolidge. The Fighting Quaker took heart. His next move was to direct a series of raids in which Communist leaders were rounded up for deportation to Russia, *via* Finland, on the ship *Buford,* jocosely known as the "Soviet Ark." Again there was enthusiasm--and apparently there was little concern over the right of the Administration to tear from their families men who had as yet committed no crime. Mr. Palmer decided to give the American public more of the same; and thereupon he carried through a new series of raids which set a new record in American history for executive transgression of individual constitutional rights.

Under the drastic war-time Sedition Act, the Secretary of Labor had the power to deport aliens who were anarchists, or believed in or advocated the overthrow of the government by violence, or were affiliated with any organization that so believed or advocated. Mr. Palmer now decided to "cooperate" with the Secretary of Labor by rounding up the alien membership of the Communist party for wholesale deportation. His under-cover agents had already worked their way into the organization; one of them, indeed, was said to have become a leader in his district (which raised the philosophical question whether government agents in such positions would have imperiled their jobs by counseling moderation among the comrades).

In scores of cities all over the United States, when the Communists were simultaneously meeting at their various headquarters on New Year's Day of 1920, Mr. Palmer's agents and police and voluntary aides fell upon them--fell upon everybody, in fact, who was in the hall, regardless of whether he was a Communist or not (how could one tell?)--and bundled them off to jail, with or without warrant. Every conceivable bit of evidence--literature, membership lists, books, papers, pictures on the wall, everything--was seized, with or without a search warrant. On this and succeeding nights other Communists and suspected Communists were seized in their homes. Over six thousand men were arrested in all, and thrust summarily behind the bars for days or weeks--often without any chance to learn what was the explicit charge against them. At least one American citizen, not a Communist, was jailed for days through some mistake--probably a confusion of names--and barely escaped deportation. In Detroit, over a hundred men were herded into a bullpen measuring twenty-four by thirty feet and kept there for a week under conditions which the mayor of the city called intolerable. In Hartford, while the suspects were in jail the authorities took the further precaution of arresting and incarcerating all visitors who came to see them, a friendly call being regarded as *prima facie* evidence of affiliation with the Communist party.

Ultimately a considerable proportion of the prisoners were released for want of sufficient evidence that they were Communists. Ultimately, too, it was divulged that in the whole country-wide raid upon these dangerous men--supposedly armed to the teeth--exactly three pistols were found, and no explosives at all. But at the time the newspapers were full of reports from Mr. Palmer's office that new evidence of a gigantic plot against the safety of the country had been unearthed; and although the steel strike was failing, the coal strike was failing, and any danger of a socialistic régime, to say nothing of a revolution, was daily fading, nevertheless to the great mass of the American people the Bolshevist bogey became more terrifying than ever.

Mr. Palmer was in full cry. In public statements he was reminding the twenty million owners of Liberty bonds and the nine million farm-owners and the eleven million owners of savings accounts that the Reds proposed to take away all they had. He was distributing boiler-plate propaganda to the press, containing pictures of horrid-looking Bolsheviks with bristling beards, and asking if such as these should rule over America. Politicians were quoting the suggestion of Guy Empey that the proper implements for dealing with the Reds could be "found in any hardware store," or proclaiming, "My motto for the Reds is S. O. S.--ship or shoot. I believe we should place them all on a ship of stone, with sails of lead, and that their first stopping-place should be hell." College graduates were calling for the dismissal of professors suspected of radicalism; schoolteachers were being made to sign oaths of allegiance; businessmen with unorthodox political or economic ideas were learning to hold their tongues if they wanted to hold their jobs. Hysteria had reached its height.

§ 5

Nor did it quickly subside. For the professional super-patriot (and assorted special propagandists disguised as super-patriots) had only begun to fight. Innumerable patriotic societies had sprung up, each with its executive secretary, and executive secretaries must live, and therefore must conjure up new and ever greater menaces. Innumerable other gentlemen now discovered that they could defeat whatever they wanted to defeat by tarring it conspicuously with the Bolshevist brush. Big-navy men, believers in compulsory military service, drys, anti-cigarette campaigners, anti-evolution Fundamentalists, defenders of the moral order, book censors, Jew-haters, Negro-haters, landlords, manufacturers, utility executives, upholders of every sort of cause, good, bad, and indifferent, all wrapped themselves in Old Glory and the mantle of the Founding Fathers and allied their opponents with Lenin. The open shop, for example, became the "American plan." For years a pestilence of speakers and writers continued to afflict the country with tales of "sinister and subversive agitators." Elderly ladies in gilt chairs in ornate drawing-rooms heard from executive secretaries that the agents of the government had unearthed new radical conspiracies too fiendish to be divulged before the proper time. Their husbands were told at luncheon clubs that the colleges were honeycombed with Bolshevism. A cloud of suspicion hung in the air, and intolerance became an American virtue.

William J. Burns put the number of resident Communists at 422,000, and S. Stanwood Menken of the National Security League made it 600,000--figures at least ten times as large as those of Professor Watkins. Dwight Braman, president of the Allied Patriotic Societies, told Governor Smith of New York that the Reds were holding 10,000 meetings in the country every week and that 350 radical newspapers had been established in the preceding six months.

But not only the Communists were dangerous; they had, it seemed, well-disguised or unwitting allies in more respectable circles. The Russian Famine Fund Committee, according to Ralph Easley of the National Civic Federation, included sixty pronounced Bolshevist sympathizers. Frederick J. Libby of the National Council for the Reduction of Armaments was said by one of the loudest of the super-patriots to be a Communist educated in Russia who visited Russia for instructions (although as a matter of fact the pacifist churchman had never been in Russia, had no affiliations with Russia, and had on his board only American citizens). *The Nation, The New Republic,* and *The Freeman* were classed as "revolutionary" by the executive secretary of the American Defense Society. Even *The Survey* was denounced by the writers of the Lusk Report as having "the endorsement of revolutionary groups." Ralph Easley pointed with alarm to the National League of Women Voters, the Federal Council of Churches, and the Foreign Policy Association. There was hardly a liberal civic organization in the land at which these protectors of the nation did not bid the citizenry to shudder. Even the National Information Bureau, which investigated charities and was headed by no less a pillar of New York respectability than Robert W. DeForest, fell under suspicion. Mr. DeForest, it was claimed, must be too busy to pay attention to what was going on; for along with him were people like Rabbi Wise and Norman Thomas and Oswald Villard and Jane Addams and Scott Nearing and Paul U. Kellogg, many of whom were tainted by radical associations.

There was danger lurking in the theater and the movies. The Moscow Art Theater, the Chauve Souris, and Fyodor Chaliapin were viewed by Mr. Braman of the Allied Patriotic Societies as propagandizing agencies of the Soviets; and according to Mr. Whitney of the American Defense Society, not only Norma Talmadge but--yes--Charlie Chaplin and Will Rogers were mentioned in "Communist files."

Books, too, must be carefully scanned for the all-pervasive evil. Miss Hermine Schwed, speaking for the Better America Federation, a band of California patriots, disapproved of *Main Street* because it "created a distaste for the conventional good life of the American," and called John Dewey and James Harvey Robinson "most dangerous to young people." And as for the schools and colleges, here the danger was more insidious and far-reaching still. According to Mr.

Whitney, Professors Felix Frankfurter and Zacharia Chafee *(sic)* of Harvard and Frederick Wells Williams and Max Solomon Mandell of Yale were "too wise not to know that their words, publicly uttered and even used in classrooms, are, to put it conservatively, decidedly encouraging to the Communists." The schools must be firmly taken in hand: textbooks must be combed for slights to heroes of American history, none but conservative speakers must be allowed within the precincts of school or college, and courses teaching reverence for the Constitution must be universal and compulsory.

The effect of these admonitions was oppressive. The fear of the radicals was accompanied and followed by a fear of being thought radical. If you wanted to get on in business, to be received in the best circles of Gopher Prairie or Middletown, you must appear to conform. Any deviation from the opinions of Judge Gary and Mr. Palmer was viewed askance. A liberal journalist, visiting a formerly outspoken Hoosier in his office, was not permitted to talk politics until his frightened host had closed and locked the door and closed the window (which gave on an airshaft perhaps fifty feet wide, with offices on the other side where there might be ears to hear the words of heresy). Said a former resident of a Middle Western city, returning to it after a long absence: "These people are all afraid of something. What is it?" The authors of *Middletown* quoted a lonely political dissenter forced into conformity by the iron pressure of public opinion as saying, bitterly, "I just run away from it all to my books." He dared not utter his economic opinions openly; to deviate ever so little from those of the Legion and the Rotary Club would be to brand himself as a Bolshevist.

"America," wrote Katharine Fullerton Gerould in *Harper's Magazine* as late as 1922, "is no longer a free country, in the old sense; and liberty is, increasingly, a mere rhetorical figure. . . . No thinking citizen, I venture to say, can express in freedom more than a part of his honest convictions. I do not of course refer to convictions that are frankly criminal. I do mean that everywhere, on every hand, free speech is choked off in one direction or another. The only way in which an American citizen who is really interested in all the social and political problems of his country can preserve any freedom of expression, is to choose the mob that is most sympathetic to him, and abide under the shadow of that mob."

Sentiments such as these were expressed so frequently and so vehemently in later years that it is astonishing to recall that in 1922 it required some temerity to put them in print. When Mrs. Gerould's article was published, hundreds of letters poured into the *Harper's* office and into her house--letters denouncing her in scurrilous terms as subversive and a Bolshevist, letters rejoicing that at last someone had stood up and told the truth. To such a point had the country been carried by the shoutings of the super-patriots.

§ 6

The intolerance of those days took many forms. Almost inevitably it took the form of an ugly flare-up of feeling against the Negro, the Jew, and the Roman Catholic. The emotions of group loyalty and of hatred, expanded during war-time and then suddenly denied their intended expression, found a perverted release in the persecution not only of supposed radicals, but also of other elements which to the dominant American group--the white Protestants--seemed alien or "un-American."

Negroes had migrated during the war by the hundreds of thousands into the industrial North, drawn thither by high wages and by the openings in mill and factory occasioned by the draft. Wherever their numbers increased they had no choice but to move into districts previously reserved for the whites, there to jostle with the whites in street cars and public places, and in a hundred other ways to upset the delicate equilibrium of racial adjustment. In the South as well as in the North the Negroes had felt the stirrings of a new sense of independence; had they not been called to the colors just as the whites had been, and had they not been fighting for democracy and oppressed minorities? When peace came, and they found they were to be put in their place once more, some of them showed their resentment; and in the uneasy atmosphere of the day this was enough to kindle the violent racial passions which smoulder under the surface of human nature. Bolshevism was bad enough, thought the whites, but if the niggers ever got beyond control . . .

One sultry afternoon in the summer of 1919 a seventeen-year-old colored boy was swimming in Lake Michigan by a Chicago bathing-beach. Part of the shore had been set aside by mutual understanding for the use of the whites, another part for the Negroes. The boy took hold of a railroad tie floating in the water and drifted across the invisible line. Stones were thrown at him; a white boy started to swim toward him. The colored boy let go of the railroad tie, swam a few strokes, and sank. He was drowned. Whether he had been hit by any of the stones was uncertain, but the Negroes on the shore accused the whites of stoning him to death, and a fight began. This small incident struck the match that set off a bonfire of race hatred. The Negro population of Chicago had doubled in a decade, the blacks had crowded into white neighborhoods, and nerves were raw. The disorder spread to other parts of the city--and the final result was that for nearly a week Chicago was virtually in a state of civil war; there were mobbings of Negroes, beatings, stabbings, gang raids through the Negro district, shootings by Negroes in defense, and wanton destruction of houses and property; when order was finally restored it was found that fifteen whites and twenty-three Negroes had been killed, five hundred and thirty-seven people had been injured, and a thousand had been left homeless and destitute.

Less than a year later there was another riot of major proportions in Tulsa. Wherever the colored population had spread, there was a new tension in the relations between the races. It was not alleviated by the gospel of white supremacy preached by speakers and writers such as Lothrop Stoddard, whose *Rising Tide of Color* proclaimed that the dark-skinned races constituted a worse threat to Western civilization than the Germans or the Bolsheviks.

The Jews, too, fell under the suspicion of a majority bent upon an undiluted Americanism. Here was a group of inevitably divided loyalty, many of whose members were undeniably prominent among the Bolsheviki in Russia and among the radical immigrants in America. Henry Ford discovered the menace of the "International Jew," and his *Dearborn Independent* accused the unhappy race of plotting the subjugation of the whole world and (for good measure) of being the source of almost every American affliction, including high rents, the shortage of farm labor, jazz, gambling, drunkenness, loose morals, and even short skirts. The Ford attack, absurd as it was, was merely an exaggerated manifestation of a widespread anti-Semitism. Prejudice became as pervasive as the air. Landlords grew less disposed to rent to Jewish tenants, and schools to admit Jewish boys and girls; there was a public scandal at Annapolis over the hazing of a Jewish boy; Harvard College seriously debated limiting the number of Jewish students; and all over the country Jews felt that a barrier had fallen between them and the Gentiles. Nor did the Roman Catholics escape censure in the regions in which they were in a minority. Did not the members of this Church take their orders from a foreign pope, and did not the pope claim temporal power, and did not Catholics insist upon teaching their children in their own way rather than in the American public schools, and was not all this un-American and treasonable?

It was in such an atmosphere that the Ku Klux Klan blossomed into power.

The Klan had been founded as far back as 1915 by a Georgian named Colonel William Joseph Simmons, but its first five years had been lean. When 1920 arrived, Colonel Simmons had only a few hundred members in his amiable patriotic and fraternal order, which drew its inspiration from the Ku Klux Klan of Reconstruction days and stood for white supremacy and sentimental Southern idealism in general. But in 1920 Simmons put the task of organizing the Order into the hands of one Edward Y. Clarke of the Southern Publicity Association. Clarke's gifts of salesmanship, hitherto expended on such blameless causes as the Roosevelt Memorial Association and the Near East Relief, were prodigious. The time was ripe for the Klan, and he knew it. Not only could it be represented to potential members as the defender of the white against the black, of Gentile against Jew, and of Protestant against Catholic, and thus trade on all the newly inflamed fears of the credulous small-towner, but its white robe and hood, its flaming cross, its secrecy, and the preposterous vocabulary of its ritual could be made the vehicle for all that infantile love of hocus-pocus and mummery, that lust for secret adventure, which survives in the adult whose lot is cast in drab places. Here was a chance to dress up the village bigot and let him be a Knight of the Invisible Empire. The formula was perfect. And there was another inviting fact to be borne in mind. Well organized, such an Order could be made a paying proposition.

The salesmen of memberships were given the entrancing title of Kleagles; the country was divided into Realms headed by King Kleagles, and the Realms into Domains headed by Grand Goblins; Clarke himself, as chief organizer, became Imperial Kleagle, and the art of nomenclature reached its fantastic pinnacle in the title bestowed upon Colonel Simmons: he became the Imperial Wizard. A membership cost ten dollars; and as four of this went into the pocket of the Kleagle who made the sale, it was soon apparent that a diligent Kleagle need not fear the wolf at the door. Kleagling became one of the profitable industries of the decade. The King Kleagle of the Realm and Grand Goblin of the Domain took a small rake-off from the remaining six dollars of the membership fee, and the balance poured into the Imperial Treasury at Atlanta.

An inconvenient congressional investigation in 1921--brought about largely by sundry reports of tarrings and featherings and floggings, and by the disclosure of many of the Klan's secrets by the

New York World--led ultimately to the banishment of Imperial Kleagle Clarke, and Colonel Simmons was succeeded as Imperial Wizard by a Texas dentist named Hiram Wesley Evans, who referred to himself, perhaps with some justice, as "the most average man in America"; but a humming sales organization had been built up and the Klan continued to grow. It grew, in fact, with such inordinate rapidity that early in 1924 its membership had reached--according to the careful estimates of Stanley Frost--the staggering figure of nearly four and a half million. It came to wield great political power, dominating for a time the seven states of Oregon, Oklahoma, Texas, Arkansas, Indiana, Ohio, and California. Its chief strongholds were the New South, the Middle West, and the Pacific coast, but it had invaded almost every part of the country and had even reached the gates of that stronghold of Jewry, Catholicism, and sophistication, New York City. So far had Clarke's genius and the hospitable temper of the times carried it.

The objects of the Order as stated in its Constitution were "to unite white male persons, native-born Gentile citizens of the United States of America, who owe no allegiance of any nature to any foreign government, nation, institution, sect, ruler, person, or people; whose morals are good, whose reputations and vocations are exemplary . . . to cultivate and promote patriotism toward our Civil Government; to practice an honorable Klanishness toward each other; to exemplify a practical benevolence; to shield the sanctity of the home and the chastity of womanhood; to maintain forever white supremacy, to reach and faithfully inculcate a high spiritual philosophy through an exalted ritualism, and by a practical devotion to conserve, protect, and maintain the distinctive institutions, rights, privileges, principles, traditions and ideals of a pure Americanism."

Thus the theory. In practice the "pure Americanism" varied with the locality. At first, in the South, white supremacy was the Klan's chief objective, but as time went on and the organization grew and spread, opposition to the Jew and above all to the Catholic proved the best talking point for Kleagles in most localities. Nor did the methods of the local Klan organizations usually suggest the possession of a "high spiritual philosophy." These local organizations were largely autonomous and beyond control from Atlanta. They were drawn, as a rule, mostly from the less educated and less disciplined elements of the white Protestant community. ("You think the influential men belong here?" commented an outspoken observer in an Indiana city. "Then look at their shoes when they march in parade. The sheet doesn't cover the shoes.") Though Imperial Wizard Evans inveighed against lawlessness, the members of the local Klans were not always content with voting against allowing children to attend parochial schools, or voting against Catholic candidates for office, or burning fiery crosses on the hilltop back of the town to show the niggers that the whites meant business. The secrecy of the Klan was an invitation to more direct action.

If a white girl reported that a colored man had made improper advances to her--even if the charge were unsupported and based on nothing more than a neurotic imagination--a white-sheeted band might spirit the Negro off to the woods and "teach him a lesson" with tar and feathers or with the whip. If a white man stood up for a Negro in a race quarrel, he might be kidnapped and beaten up. If a colored woman refused to sell her land at an arbitrary price which she considered too low, and a Klansman wanted the land, she might receive the K. K. K. ultimatum--sell or be thrown out. Klan members would boycott Jewish merchants, refuse to hire Catholic boys, refuse to rent their houses to Catholics. A hideous tragedy in Louisiana, where five men were kidnapped and later found bound with wire and drowned in a lake, was laid to Klansmen. R. A. Patton, writing in *Current History,* reported a grim series of brutalities from Alabama: "A lad whipped with branches until his back was ribboned flesh; a Negress beaten and left helpless to contract pneumonia from exposure and die; a white girl, divorcée, beaten into unconsciousness in her own home; a naturalized foreigner flogged until his back was a pulp because he married an American woman; a Negro lashed until he sold his land to a white man for a fraction of its value."

Even where there were no such outrages, there was at least the threat of them. The white-robed army paraded, the burning cross glowed across the valley, people whispered to one another in the darkness and wondered "who they were after this time," and fear and suspicion ran from house to house. Furthermore, criminals and gangs of hoodlums quickly learned to take advantage of the Klan's existence: if they wanted to burn someone's barn or raid the slums beyond the railroad tracks, they could do it with impunity now: would not the Klan be held responsible? Anyone could chalk the letters K. K. K. on a fence and be sure that the sheriff would move warily. Thus, as in the case of the Red hysteria, a movement conceived in fear perpetuated fear and brought with it all manner of cruelties and crimes.

Slowly, as the years passed and the war-time emotions ebbed, the power of the Klan waned, until in many districts it was dead and in others it had become merely a political faction dominated by

57

spoilsmen: but not until it had become a thing of terror to millions of men and women.

§ 7

After the Palmer raids at the beginning of 1920 the hunt for radicals went on. In April the five Socialist members of the New York State Assembly were expelled on the ground that (as the report of the Judiciary Committee put it) they were members of "a disloyal organization composed exclusively of perpetual traitors." When Young Theodore Roosevelt spoke against the motion to expel, he was solemnly rebuked by Speaker Sweet, who mounted the rostrum and read aloud passages from the writings of T. R. senior, in order that the Americanism of the father might be painfully contrasted with the un-Americanism of the son. When Assemblyman Cuvillier, in the midst of a speech, spied two of the Socialist members actually occupying the seats to which they had been elected, he cried: "These two men who sit there with a smile and a smirk on their faces are just as much representatives of the Russian Soviet Government as if they were Lenin and Trotsky themselves. They are little Lenins, little Trotskys in our midst." The little Lenins and Trotskys were thrown out by an overwhelming vote, and the *New York Times* announced the next day that "It was an American vote altogether, a patriotic and conservative vote. An immense majority of the American people will approve and sanction the Assembly's action." That statement, coming from the discreet *Times,* is a measure of the temper of the day.

Nevertheless, the tide was almost ready to turn. Charles Evans Hughes protested against the Assembly's action, thereby almost causing apoplexy among some of his sedate fellow-members of the Union League Club, who wondered if such a good Republican could be becoming a parlor pink. May Day of 1920 arrived in due course, and although Mr. Palmer dutifully informed the world in advance that May Day had been selected by the radicals as the date for a general strike and for assassinations, nothing happened. The police, fully mobilized, waited for a revolutionary onslaught that never arrived. The political conventions rolled round, and although Calvin Coolidge was swept into the Republican nomination for Vice-President on his record as the man who broke the Boston police strike, it was noteworthy that the Democratic Convention did not sweep the Fighting Quaker into anything at all, and that there was a certain unseemly levity among his opponents, who insisted upon referring to him as the quaking fighter, the faking fighter, and the quaking quitter. It began to look as if the country were beginning to regain its sense of humor.

Strikes and riots and legislative enactments and judicial rulings against radicals continued, but with the coming of the summer of 1920 there were at least other things to compete for the attention of the country. There was the presidential campaign; the affable Mr. Harding was mouthing orotund generalizations from his front porch, and the desperate Mr. Cox was steaming about the country, trying to pull Woodrow Wilson's chestnuts out of the fire. There was the ticklish business situation: people had been revolting against high prices for months, and overall parades had been held, and the Rev. George M. Elsbree of Philadelphia had preached a sermon in overalls, and there had been an overall wedding in New York (parson, bride, and groom all photographed for the rotogravure section in overalls), and the department stores had been driven to reduce prices, and now it was apparent that business was riding for a fall, strikes or no strikes, radicals or no radicals.

There was the hue and cry over the discovery of the bogus get-rich-quick schemes of Charles Ponzi of Boston. There was Woman Suffrage, now at last a fact, with ratification of the Amendment by the States completed on August 18th. Finally, there was Prohibition, also at last a fact, and an absorbing topic at dinner tables. In those days people sat with bated breath to hear how So-and-so had made very good gin right in his own cellar, and just what formula would fulfill the higher destiny of raisins, and how bootleggers brought liquor down from Canada. It was all new and exciting. That the Big Red Scare was already perceptibly abating by the end of the summer of 1920 was shown by the fact that the nation managed to keep its head surprisingly well when a real disaster, probably attributable to an anarchist gang, took place on the 16th of September.

If there was one geographical spot in the United States that could justly be called the financial center of the country, it was the junction of Broad and Wall Streets in New York. Here, on the north side of Wall Street, stood the Sub-Treasury Building, and next to it the United States Assay Office; opposite them, on the southeast corner, an ostentatiously unostentatious three-story limestone building housed the firm of J. P. Morgan & Company, the most powerful nexus of capitalism in the world; on the southwest corner yawned the excavation where the New York Stock Exchange was presently to build its annex, and next to this, on Broad Street, rose the Corinthian pillars of the Exchange itself. Government finance, private finance, the passage of private control of industry from capitalistic hand to hand: here stood their respective citadels cheek by jowl, as if to symbolize the union into one system of the government and the money power and the direction of business--that system which the radicals so bitterly decried.

Almost at this precise spot, a moment before noon on September 16th, just as the clerks of the neighborhood were getting ready to go out for luncheon, there was a sudden blinding flash of bluish-white light and a terrific crashing roar, followed by the clatter of falling glass from innumerable windows and by the screams of men and women. A huge bomb had gone off in the street in front of the Assay Office and directly opposite the House of Morgan--gone off with such appalling violence that it killed thirty people outright and injured hundreds, wrecked the interior of the Morgan offices, smashed windows for blocks around, and drove an iron slug through the window of the Bankers' Club on the thirty-fourth floor of the Equitable Building.

A great mushroom-shaped cloud of yellowish-green smoke rose slowly into the upper air between the skyscrapers. Below it, the air was filled with dust pouring out of the Morgan windows and the windows of other buildings--dust from shrapnel-bitten plaster walls. And below that, the street ran red with the blood of the dead and dying. Those who by blind chance had escaped the hail of steel picked themselves up and ran in terror as glass and fragments of stone showered down from the buildings above; then there was a surge of people back to the horror again, a vast crowd milling about and trying to help the victims and not knowing what to do first and bumping into one another and shouting; then fire engines and ambulances clanged to the scene and police and hospital orderlies fought their way through the mob and brought it at last to order.

In the House of Morgan, one man had been killed, the chief clerk; dozens were hurt, seventeen had to be taken to hospitals. But only one partner had been cut in the hand by flying glass; the rest were in conference on the other side of the building or out of town. Mr. Morgan was abroad. The victims of the explosion were not the financial powers of the country, but bank clerks, brokers' men, Wall Street runners, stenographers.

In the Stock Exchange, hardly two hundred feet away, trading had been proceeding at what in those days was considered "good volume"--at the rate of half a million shares or so for the day. Prices had been rising. Reading was being bid up $2\frac{1}{8}$ points to $93\frac{3}{4}$,

Baldwin Locomotive was going strong at 110 $^3/_4$, there was heavy trading in Middle States Oil, Steel was doing well at 89 $^3/_8$. The crash came, the building shook, and the big windows smashed down in a shower of glass; those on the Broad Street side had their heavy silk curtains drawn, or dozens of men would have been injured. For a moment the brokers, not knowing what had happened, scampered for anything that looked like shelter. Those in the middle of the floor, where an instant before the largest crowd of traders had been gathered around the Reading post, made for the edges of the room lest the dome should fall. But William H. Remick, president of the Exchange, who had been standing with the "money crowd" at the side of the room, kept his head. Remarking to a friend, "I guess it's about time to ring the gong," he mounted the rostrum, rang the gong, and thereby immediately ended trading for the day. (The next day prices continued to rise as if nothing had happened.)

Out in the middle of Wall Street lay the carcass of a horse blown to pieces by the force of the explosion, and here and there were assembled bits of steel and wood and canvas which, with the horse's shoes and the harness, enabled the police to decide that a TNT bomb had gone off in a horse-drawn wagon, presumably left unattended as its driver escaped from the scene. For days and months and years detectives and Federal agents followed up every possible clue. Every wagon in the city, to say nothing of powder wagons, was traced. The slugs which had imbedded themselves in the surrounding buildings were examined and found to be window sash-weights cut in two--but this, despite endless further investigation, led to nothing more than the conclusion that the explosion was a premeditated crime. The horse's shoes were identified and a man was found who had put them on the horse a few days before; he described the driver as a Sicilian, but the clue led no further. Bits of steel and tin found in the neighborhood were studied, manufacturers consulted, records of sale run through. One fragment of iron proved to be the knob of a safe, and the safe was identified; a detective followed the history of the safe from its manufacture through various hands until it went to France with the Army during the war and returned to Hoboken--but there its trail was lost. Every eye-witness's story was tested and analyzed. Reports of warnings of disaster received by businessmen were run down but yielded nothing of real value. Suspected radicals were rounded up without result. One bit of evidence remained, but how important it was one could not be sure. At almost the exact minute of the explosion, a letter-carrier was said to have found in a post-box two or three blocks from the scene--a box which had been emptied only half an hour before--five sheets of paper on which was crudely printed, with varying misspellings,

Rememer
We will not tolerate
any longer
Free the politiCal
prisoniers or it will be
sure death to all oF you
American   Anarchists
    Fighters

A prominent coal operator who was sitting in the Morgan offices when the explosion took place promptly declared that there was no question in his mind that it was the work of Bolshevists. After years of fruitless investigation, there was still a question in the minds of those who tried to solve the mystery. But in the loose sense in which the coal operator used the term, he was probably right.

The country followed the early stages of the investigation with absorbed interest. Yet no marked increase in anti-Bolshevist riots took place. If the explosion had occurred a few months earlier, it might have had indirect consequences as ugly as the damage which it did directly. But by this time the American people were coming to their senses sufficiently to realize that no such insane and frightful plot could ever command the support of more than a handful of fanatics.

♦ IV ♦
AMERICA CONVALESCENT

§ 1

The Big Red Scare was slowly--very slowly--dying.

What killed it?

The realization, for one thing, that there had never been any sufficient cause for such a panic as had convulsed the country. The localization of Communism in Europe, for another thing: when Germany and other European nations failed to be engulfed by the Bolshevist tide, the idea of its sweeping irresistibly across the Atlantic became a little less plausible. It was a fact, too, that radicalism was noticeably ebbing in the United States. The Fighting Quaker's inquisitorial methods, whatever one may think of them, had at least had the practical effect of scaring many Reds into a pale pinkness. By 1921 the A. F. of L. leaders were leaning over backward in their effort to appear as conservative as Judge Gary, college professors were canceling their subscriptions to liberal magazines on the ground that they could not afford to let such literature be seen on their tables, and the social reformers of a year or two before were tiring of what seemed a thankless and hopeless fight. There was also, perhaps, a perceptible loss of enthusiasm for governmental action against the Reds on the part of the growing company of the wets, who were acquiring a belated concern for personal liberty and a new distrust of federal snoopers. Yet there was another cause more important, perhaps, than any of these. The temper of the aftermath of war was at last giving way to the temper of peace. Like an overworked businessman beginning his vacation, the country had had to go through a period of restlessness and irritability, but was finally learning how to relax and amuse itself once more.

A sense of disillusionment remained; like the suddenly liberated vacationist, the country felt that it ought to be enjoying itself more than it was, and that life was futile and nothing mattered much. But in the meantime it might as well play--follow the crowd, take up the new toys that were amusing the crowd, go in for the new fads, savor the amusing scandals and trivialities of life. By 1921 the new toys and fads and scandals were forthcoming, and the country seized upon them feverishly.

§ 2

First of all was the radio, which was destined ultimately to alter the daily habits of Americans as profoundly as anything that the decade produced.

The first broadcasting station had been opened in East Pittsburgh on November 2, 1920--a date which school children may some day have to learn--to carry the Harding-Cox election returns. This was station KDKA, operated by the Westinghouse Company. For a time, however, this new revolution in communication and public entertainment made slow headway. Auditors were few. Amateur wireless operators objected to the stream of music--mostly from phonograph records--which issued from the Westinghouse station and interfered with their important business. When a real orchestra was substituted for the records, the resonance of the room in which the players sat spoiled the effect. The orchestra was placed out-of-doors, in a tent on the roof--and the tent blew away. The tent was thereupon pitched in a big room indoors, and not until then was it discovered that the cloth hangings which subsequently became standard in broadcasting studios would adequately muffle the sound.

Experiment proceeded, however; other radio stations were opened, market reports were thrown on the air, Dr. Van Etten of Pittsburgh permitted the services at Calvary Church to be broadcasted, the University of Wisconsin gave radio concerts, and politicians spouted into the strange instruments and wondered if anybody was really listening. Yet when Dempsey fought Carpentier in July, 1921, and three men at the ringside told the story of the slaughter into telephone transmitters to be relayed by air to eighty points throughout the country, their enterprise was reported in an obscure corner of the *New York Times* as an achievement in "wireless telephony"; and when the Unknown Soldier was buried at Arlington Cemetery the following November, crowds packed into Madison Square Garden in New York and the Auditorium in San Francisco to hear the speeches issue from huge amplifiers, and few in those crowds had any idea that soon they could hear all the orations they wanted without stirring from the easy-chair in the living-room. The great awakening had not yet come.

That winter, however--the winter of 1921-22--it came with a rush. Soon everybody was talking, not about wireless telephony, but about radio. A San Francisco paper described the discovery that millions were making: "There is radio music in the air, every night, everywhere. Anybody can hear it at home on a receiving set, which any boy can put up in an hour." In February President Harding had an outfit installed in his study, and the Dixmoor Golf Club announced that it would install a "telephone" to enable golfers to hear church services. In April, passengers on a Lackawanna train heard a radio concert, and Lieutenant Maynard broke all records for modernizing Christianity by broadcasting an Easter sermon from an airplane. Newspapers brought out radio sections and thousands of hitherto utterly unmechanical people puzzled over articles about regenerative circuits, sodion tubes, Grimes reflex circuits, crystal detectors, and neutrodynes. In the Ziegfeld "Follies of 1922" the popularity of "My Rambler Rose" was rivaled by that of a song about a man who hoped his love might hear him as she was "listening on the radio." And every other man you met on the street buttonholed you to tell you how he had sat up until two o'clock the night before, with earphones clamped to his head, and had actually *heard Havana!* How could one bother about the Red Menace if one was facing such momentous questions as how to construct a loop aërial?

In the *Readers' Guide to Periodical Literature* for the years 1919-21, in which were listed all the magazine articles appearing during those years, there were two columns of references to articles on Radicals and Radicalism and less than a quarter of a column of references to articles on Radio. In the *Readers' Guide* for 1922-24, by contrast, the section on Radicals and Radicalism shrank to half a column and the section on Radio swelled to nineteen columns. In that change there is an index to something more than periodical literature.

§ 3

Sport, too, had become an American obsession. When Jack Kearns persuaded Tex Rickard to bring together Dempsey and the worn-out but engaging Georges Carpentier at Boyle's Thirty Acres in Jersey City in 1921, the public responded as they had never before responded in the history of the country. Nearly seventy-five thousand people paid over a million and a half dollars--over three times as much as the Dempsey-Willard fight had brought in--to see the debonair Frenchman flattened in the fourth round, and the metropolitan papers, not content with a few columns in the sporting section, devoted page after page the next day to every conceivable detail of the fight. It was the first of the huge million-dollar bouts of the decade. Babe Ruth raised his home-run record to fifty-nine, and the 1921 World Series broke records for gate receipts and attendance. Sport-hungry crowds who had never dreamed of taking a college-entrance examination swarmed to college football games, watched Captain Malcolm Aldrich of Yale and George Owen of Harvard, and devoured hundreds of columns of dopesters' gossip about Penn State and Pittsburgh and Iowa and the "praying Colonels" of Centre College. Racing had taken on a new lease of life with the unparalleled success of Man o' War in 1920. Tennis clubs were multiplying, and businessmen were discovering by the hundreds of thousands that a par-four hole was the best place to be in conference. There were food-fads, too, as well as sport-fads: such was the sudden and overwhelming craze for Eskimo Pie that in three months the price of cocoa beans on the New York market rose 50 per cent.

Another new American institution caught the public eye during the summer of 1921--the bathing beauty. In early July a Costume and Beauty Show was held at Washington's bathing beach on the Potomac, and the prize-winners were so little touched by the influence of Mack Sennett and his moving-picture bathers that they wore tunic bathing-suits, hats over their long curls, and long stockings--all but one, who daringly rolled her stockings below her knees. In early September Atlantic City held its first Beauty Pageant--a similar show, but with a difference. "For the time being, the censor ban on bare knees and skintight bathing suits was suspended," wrote an astonished reporter, "and thousands of spectators gasped as they applauded the girls." Miss Washington was declared the most beautiful girl of the cities of America, the one-piece suit became overnight the orthodox wear for bathing beauties (though taffetas and sateens remained good enough for genuine seagoing bathers for a season or two to come), promoters of seashore resorts began to plan new contests, and the rotogravure and tabloid editors faced a future bright with promise.

The tabloids, indeed, were booming--and not without effect. There was more than coincidence in the fact that as they rose, radicalism fell. They presented American life not as a political and economic struggle, but as a three-ring circus of sport, crime, and sex, and in varying degrees the other papers followed their lead under the pressure of competition. Workmen forgot to be class-conscious as they gloated over pictures of Miss Scranton on the Boardwalk and followed the Stillman case and the Arbuckle case and studied the racing dope about Morvich.

Readers with perceptibly higher brows, too, had their diversions from the affairs of the day. Though their heads still reeled from *The Education of Henry Adams,* they were wading manfully through paleontology as revealed in the *Outline of History* (and getting bogged, most of them. somewhere near the section on Genghis Khan). They were asking one another whether America was truly as ugly as Sinclair Lewis made it in *Main Street* and Tahiti truly as enchanting as Frederick O'Brien made it in *White Shadows of the South Seas;* they were learning about hot love in hot places from *The Sheik,* and lapping up Mrs. Asquith's gossip of the British ruling classes, and having a good old-fashioned cry over *If Winter Comes.*

Further diversions were on the way, too. If there had been any doubt, after the radio craze struck the country, that the American people were learning to enjoy such diversions with headlong unanimity, the events of 1922 and 1923 dispelled it. On the 16th of September, 1922, the murder of the decade took place: The Reverend Edward Wheeler Hall and Mrs. James Mills, the choir leader in his church, were found shot to death on an abandoned farm near New Brunswick, New Jersey. The Hall-Mills case had all the elements needed to satisfy an exacting public taste for the sensational. It was better than the Elwell case of June, 1920. It was grisly, it was dramatic (the bodies being laid side by side as if to emphasize an unhallowed union), it involved wealth and respectability, it had just the right amount of sex interest--and in addition it took place close to the great metropolitan nerve-center of the American press. It was an illiterate American who did not shortly become acquainted with DeRussey's Lane, the crab-apple tree, the pig woman and her mule, the precise mental condition of Willie Stevens, and the gossip of the choir members.

§ 4

By this time, too, a new game was beginning its conquest of the country. In the first year or two after the war, Joseph P. Babcock,

Soochow representative of the Standard Oil Company, had become interested in the Chinese game of Mah Jong and had codified and simplified the rules for the use of Americans. Two brothers named White had introduced it to the English-speaking clubs of Shanghai, where it became popular. It was brought to the United States, and won such immediate favor that W. A. Hammond, a San Francisco lumber merchant, was encouraged to import sets on an ambitious scale. By September, 1922, he had already imported fifty thousand dollars' worth. A big campaign of advertising, with free lessons and exhibitions, pushed the game, and within the next year the Mah Jong craze had become so universal that Chinese makers of sets could no longer keep up with the demand and American manufacture was in full swing. By 1923, people who were beginning to take their radio sets for granted now simply left them turned on while they "broke the wall" and called "pung" or "chow" and wielded the Ming box and talked learnedly of bamboos, flowers, seasons, South Wind, and Red Dragon. The wealthy bought five-hundred-dollar sets; dozens of manufacturers leaped into the business; a Mah Jong League of America was formed; there was fierce debate as to what rules to play by, what system of scoring to use, and what constituted a "limit hand"; and the correct dinner party wound up with every one setting up ivory and bamboo tiles on green baize tables.

Even before Mah Jong reached its climax, however, Emil Coué had arrived in America, preceded by an efficient ballyhoo; in the early months of 1923 the little dried-up Frenchman from Nancy was suddenly the most-talked-of person in the country. Coué Institutes were established, and audiences who thronged to hear the master speak were hushed into awesome quiet as he repeated, himself, the formula which was already on everybody's lips: "Day by day in every way I am getting better and better." A few weeks later there was a new national thrill as the news of the finding of the tomb of King Tut-Ankh-Amen, cabled all the way from Egypt, overshadowed the news of the Radical trials and Ku Klux Klan scandals, and dress manufacturers began to plan for a season of Egyptian styles. Finally, the country presently found still a new obsession--in the form of a song: a phrase picked up from an Italian fruit-vender and used some time before this as a "gag-line" by Tad Dorgan, the cartoonist, was worked into verse, put to music which drew liberally from the "Hallelujah Chorus" and "I Dreamt That I Dwelt in Marble Halls" and "Aunt Dinah's Quilting Party," was tried out in a Long Island roadhouse, and then was brought to New York, where it quickly superseded "Mr. Gallagher and Mr.

Shean" in popular acclaim. Before long "Yes, We Have No Bananas" had penetrated to the remotest farmhouse in the remotest county.

Though the super-patriots still raged and federal agents still pursued the nimble Communists and an avowed Socialist was still regarded with as much enthusiasm as a leper, and the Ku Klux Klan still grew, the Big Red Scare was dying. There were too many other things to think about.

Perhaps, though, there was still another reason for the passing of the Red Menace. Another Menace was endangering the land--and one which could not possibly be attributed to the machinations of Moscow. The younger generation was on the rampage, as we shall presently see.

§ 5

Only one dispute, during the rest of the Post-war Decade, drew the old line of 1919 and 1920 between liberal and conservative throughout the nation.

At the height of the Big Red Scare--in April, 1920--there had taken place at South Braintree, Massachusetts, a crime so unimportant that it was not even mentioned in the *New York Times* of the following day--or, for that matter, of the whole following year. It was the sort of crime which was taking place constantly all over the country. A paymaster and his guard, carrying two boxes containing the pay-roll of a shoe factory, were killed by two men with pistols, who thereupon leaped into an automobile which drew up at the curb, and drove away across the railroad tracks. Two weeks later a couple of Italian radicals were arrested as the murderers, and a year later--at about the time when the Washington bathing beauties were straightening their long stockings to be photographed and David Sarnoff was supervising the reporting of the Dempsey-Carpentier fight by "wireless telephone"-- the Italians were tried before Judge Webster Thayer and a jury and found guilty. The trial attracted a little attention, but not much. A few months later, however, people from Maine to California began to ask what this Sacco-Vanzetti case was all about. For a very remarkable thing had happened.

Three men in a bleak Boston office--a Spanish carpenter, a Jewish youth from New York, and an Italian newspaperman--had been writing industriously about the two Italians to the radicals and the radical press of France and Italy and Spain and other countries in Europe and Central and South America. The result: A bomb exploded in Ambassador Herrick's house in Paris. Twenty people were killed by another bomb in a Paris Sacco-Vanzetti demonstration. Crowds menaced the American Embassy in Rome. There was an attempt to bomb the home of the Consul-General at Lisbon. There was a general strike and an attempt to boycott American goods at Montevideo. The case was discussed in the radical press of Algiers, Porto Rico, and Mexico. Under the circumstances it could not very well help becoming a *cause célèbre* in the United States.

But bombings and boycotts, though they attracted attention to the case, could never have aroused widespread public sympathy for Sacco and Vanzetti. What aroused it, as the case dragged on year after year and one appeal after another was denied, was the demeanor of the men themselves. Vanzetti in particular was clearly a remarkable man-- an intellectual of noble character, a philosophical anarchist of a type which it seemed impossible to associate with a pay-roll murder. New evidence made the guilt of the men seem still more doubtful. When, in 1927--seven long years after the murder--Judge Thayer stubbornly denied the last appeal and pronounced the sentence of death, public opinion forced Governor Fuller of Massachusetts to review the case and consider pardoning Sacco and Vanzetti. The Governor named as an advisory committee to make a further study of the case, President Lowell of Harvard, President Stratton of the Massachusetts Institute of Technology, and Judge Robert Grant--all men respected by the community. A few weeks later the committee reported: they believed Sacco and Vanzetti to be guilty. There was no pardon. On the night of August 22, 1927, these two men who had gathered about their cause the hopes and fears of millions throughout the world were sent to the electric chair.

Whether they were actually guilty or not will probably never be definitely determined--though no one can read their speeches to the court and their letters without doubting if justice was done. The record of the case was of vast length and full of technicalities, it was discussed *ex-parte* by vehement propagandists on both sides, and the division of public opinion on the case was largely a division between those who thought radicals ought to be strung up on general principles and those who thought that the test of a country's civilization lay in the scrupulousness with which it protected the rights of minorities. The passions of the early days of the decade were revived as pickets marched before the Boston State House, calling on the Governor to release Sacco and Vanzetti, and the Boston police--whose strike not eight years before had put Calvin Coolidge in the White House which he now occupied--arrested the pickets and bore them off to the lock-up.

The bull market was now in full swing, the labor movement was enfeebled, prosperity had given radicalism what seemed to be its *coup de grâce*--but still the predicament of these two simple Italians had the power briefly to recall the days of Mitchell Palmer's Red raids and to arouse fears and hatreds long since quieted. People who had almost forgotten whether they were conservatives or liberals found themselves in bitter argument once more, and friendships were disrupted over the identification of Sacco's cap or the value of Captain Proctor's testimony about the fatal bullet. But only briefly. The headlines screamed that Sacco and Vanzetti had been executed, and men read them with a shiver, and wondered, perhaps, if this thing which had been done with such awful finality were the just desserts of crime or a hideous mistake--and glanced at another column to find where Lindbergh was flying today, and whipped open the paper to the financial page. . . . What was General Motors doing?

♦ V ♦
THE REVOLUTION IN MANNERS AND MORALS

§ 1

A first-class revolt against the accepted American order was certainly taking place during those early years of the Post-war Decade, but it was one with which Nikolai Lenin had nothing whatever to do. The shock troops of the rebellion were not alien agitators, but the sons and daughters of well-to-do American families, who knew little about Bolshevism and cared distinctly less, and their defiance was expressed not in obscure radical publications or in soap-box speeches, but right across the family breakfast table into the horrified ears of conservative fathers and mothers. Men and women were still shivering at the Red Menace when they awoke to the no less alarming Problem of the Younger Generation, and realized that if the constitution were not in danger, the moral code of the country certainly was.

This code, as it currently concerned young people, might have been roughly summarized as follows: Women were the guardians of morality; they were made of finer stuff than men and were expected to act accordingly. Young girls must look forward in innocence (tempered perhaps with a modicum of physiological instruction) to a romantic love match which would lead them to the altar and to living-happily-ever-after, and until the "right man" came along they must allow no male to kiss them. It was expected that some men would succumb to the temptations of sex, but only with a special class of outlawed women; girls of respectable families were supposed to have no such temptations. Boys and girls were permitted large freedom to work and play together, with decreasing and well-nigh nominal chaperonage, but only because the code worked so well on the whole that a sort of honor system was supplanting supervision by their elders; it was taken for granted that if they had been well brought up they would never take advantage of this freedom. And although the attitude toward smoking and drinking by girls differed widely in different strata of society and different parts of the country, majority opinion held that it was morally wrong for them to smoke and could hardly imagine them showing the effects of alcohol.

The war had not long been over when cries of alarm from parents, teachers, and moral preceptors began to rend the air. For the boys and girls just growing out of adolescence were making mincemeat of this code.

The dresses that the girls--and for that matter most of the older women--were wearing seemed alarming enough. In July, 1920, a fashion-writer reported in the *New York Times* that "the American woman . . . has lifted her skirts far beyond any modest limitation," which was another way of saying that the hem was now all of nine inches above the ground. It was freely predicted that skirts would come down again in the winter of 1920-21, but instead they climbed a few scandalous inches farther. The flappers wore thin dresses, short-sleeved and occasionally (in the evening) sleeveless; some of the wilder young things rolled their stockings below their knees, revealing to the shocked eyes of virtue a fleeting glance of shin-bones and knee-cap; and many of them were visibly using cosmetics. "The intoxication of rouge," earnestly explained Dorothy Speare in *Dancers in the Dark,* "is an insidious vintage known to more girls than mere man can ever believe." Useless for frantic parents to insist that no lady did such things; the answer was that the daughters of ladies were doing it, and even retouching their masterpieces in public. Some of them, furthermore, were abandoning their corsets. "The men won't dance with you if you wear a corset," they were quoted as saying.

The current mode in dancing created still more consternation. Not the romantic violin but the barbaric saxophone now dominated the orchestra, and to its passionate crooning and wailing the fox-trotters moved in what the editor of the Hobart College *Herald* disgustedly called a "syncopated embrace." No longer did even an inch of space separate them; they danced as if glued together, body to body, cheek to cheek. Cried the *Catholic Telegraph* of Cincinnati in righteous indignation, "The music is sensuous, the embracing of partners--the female only half dressed--is absolutely indecent; and the motions--they are such as may not be described, with any respect for propriety, in a family newspaper. Suffice it to say that there are certain houses appropriate for such dances; but those houses have been closed by law."

Supposedly "nice" girls were smoking cigarettes--openly and defiantly, if often rather awkwardly and self-consciously. They were drinking--somewhat less openly but often all too efficaciously. There were stories of daughters of the most exemplary parents getting drunk--"blotto," as their companions cheerfully put it--on the contents of the hip-flasks of the new prohibition régime, and going out joyriding with men at four in the morning. And worst of all, even at well-regulated dances they were said to retire where the eye of the most sharp-sighted chaperon could not follow, and in darkened rooms or in parked cars to engage in the unspeakable practice of petting and necking.

It was not until F. Scott Fitzgerald, who had hardly graduated from Princeton and ought to know what his generation was doing, brought out *This Side of Paradise* in April, 1920, that fathers and mothers realized fully what was afoot and how long it had been going on. Apparently the "petting party" had been current as early as 1916, and was now widely established as an indoor sport. "None of the Victorian mothers--and most of the mothers were Victorian--had any idea how casually their daughters were accustomed to be kissed," wrote Mr. Fitzgerald. ". . . Amory saw girls doing things that even in his memory would have been impossible: eating three-o'clock, after-dance suppers in impossible cafés, talking of every side of life with an air half of earnestness, half of mockery, yet with a furtive excitement that Amory considered stood for a real moral let-down. But he never realized how widespread it was until he saw the cities between New York and Chicago as one vast juvenile intrigue." The book caused a shudder to run down the national spine; did not Mr. Fitzgerald represent one of his well-nurtured heroines as brazenly confessing, "I've kissed dozens of men. I suppose I'll kiss dozens more"; and another heroine as saying to a young man *(to a young man!)*, "Oh, just one person in fifty has any glimmer of what sex is. I'm hipped on Freud and all that, but it's rotten that every bit of real love in the world is ninety-nine per cent passion and one little *soupçon* of jealousy?"

It was incredible. It was abominable. What did it all mean? Was every decent standard being thrown over? Mothers read the scarlet words and wondered if they themselves "had any idea how often their daughters were accustomed to be kissed." . . . But no, this must be an exaggerated account of the misconduct of some especially depraved group. Nice girls couldn't behave like that and talk openly about passion. But in due course other books appeared to substantiate the findings of Mr. Fitzgerald: *Dancers in the Dark, The Plastic Age, Flaming Youth.* Magazine articles and newspapers reiterated the scandal. To be sure, there were plenty of communities where nice girls did not, in actual fact, "behave like that"; and even in the more sophisticated urban centers there were plenty of girls who did not. Nevertheless, there was enough fire beneath the smoke of these sensational revelations to make the Problem of the Younger Generation a topic of anxious discussion from coast to coast.

The forces of morality rallied to the attack. Dr. Francis E. Clark, the founder and president of the Christian Endeavor Society, declared that the modern "indecent dance" was "an offense against womanly purity, the very fountainhead of our family and civil life." The new style of dancing was denounced in religious journals as "impure, polluting, corrupting, debasing, destroying spirituality, increasing carnality," and the mothers and sisters and church members of the land were called upon to admonish and instruct and raise the spiritual tone of these dreadful young people. President Murphy of the University of Florida cried out with true Southern warmth, "The low-cut gowns, the rolled hose and short skirts are born of the Devil and his angels, and are carrying the present and future generations to chaos and destruction." A group of Episcopal church-women in New York, speaking with the authority of wealth and social position (for they included Mrs. J. Pierpont Morgan, Mrs. Borden Harriman, Mrs. Henry Phipps, Mrs. James Roosevelt, and Mrs. E. H. Harriman), proposed an organization to discourage fashions involving an "excess of nudity" and "improper ways of dancing." The Y. W. C. A. conducted a national campaign against immodest dress among high-school girls, supplying newspapers with printed matter carrying headlines such as "Working Girls Responsive to Modesty Appeal" and "High Heels Losing Ground Even in France." In Philadelphia a Dress Reform Committee of prominent citizens sent a questionnaire to over a thousand clergymen to ask them what would be their idea of a proper dress, and although the gentlemen of the cloth showed a distressing variety of opinion, the committee proceeded to design a "moral gown" which was endorsed by ministers of fifteen denominations. The distinguishing characteristics of this moral gown were that it was very loose-fitting, that the sleeves reached just below the elbows, and that the hem came within seven and a half inches of the floor.

Not content with example and reproof, legislators in several states introduced bills to reform feminine dress once and for all. The *New York American* reported in 1921 that a bill was pending in Utah providing fine and imprisonment for those who wore on the streets "skirts higher than three inches above the ankle." A bill was laid before the Virginia legislature which would forbid any woman from wearing shirtwaists or evening gowns which displayed "more than three inches of her throat." In Ohio the proposed limit of décolletage was two inches; the bill introduced in the Ohio legislature aimed also to prevent the sale of any "garment which unduly displays or accentuates the lines of the female figure," and to prohibit any "female over fourteen years of age" from wearing "a skirt which does not reach to that part of the foot known as the instep."

Meanwhile innumerable families were torn with dissension over cigarettes and gin and all-night automobile rides. Fathers and mothers lay awake asking themselves whether their children were not utterly lost; sons and daughters evaded questions, lied miserably and unhappily, or flared up to reply rudely that at least they were not dirty-minded hypocrites, that they saw no harm in what they were doing and proposed to go right on doing it. From those liberal clergymen and teachers who prided themselves on keeping step with all that was new came a chorus of reassurance: these young people were at least franker and more honest than their elders had been; having experimented for themselves, would they not soon find out which standards were outworn and which represented the accumulated moral wisdom of the race? Hearing such hopeful words, many good people took heart again. Perhaps this flare-up of youthful passion was a flash in the pan, after all. Perhaps in another year or two the boys and girls would come to their senses and everything would be all right again.

They were wrong, however. For the revolt of the younger generation was only the beginning of a revolution in manners and morals that was already beginning to affect men and women of every age in every part of the country.

§ 2

A number of forces were working together and interacting upon one another to make this revolution inevitable.

First of all was the state of mind brought about by the war and its conclusion. A whole generation had been infected by the eat-drink-and-be-merry-for-tomorrow-we-die spirit which accompanied the departure of the soldiers to the training camps and the fighting front. There had been an epidemic not only of abrupt war marriages, but of less conventional liaisons. In France, two million men had found themselves very close to filth and annihilation and very far from the American moral code and its defenders; prostitution had followed the flag and willing mademoiselles from Armentières had been plentiful; American girls sent over as nurses and war workers had come under the influence of continental manners and standards without being subject to the rigid protections thrown about their continental sisters of the respectable classes; and there had been a very widespread and very natural breakdown of traditional restraints and reticences and taboos. It was impossible for this generation to return unchanged when the ordeal was over. Some of them had acquired under the pressure of war-time conditions a new code which seemed to them quite defensible; millions of them had been provided with an emotional stimulant from which it was not easy to taper off. Their torn nerves craved the anodynes of speed, excitement, and passion. They found themselves expected to settle down into the humdrum routine of American life as if nothing had happened, to accept the moral dicta of elders who seemed to them still to be living in a Pollyanna land of rosy ideals which the war had killed for them. They couldn't do it, and they very disrespectfully said so.

"The older generation had certainly pretty well ruined this world before passing it on to us," wrote one of them (John F. Carter in the *Atlantic Monthly,* September, 1920), expressing accurately the sentiments of innumerable contemporaries. "They give us this thing, knocked to pieces, leaky, red-hot, threatening to blow up; and then they are surprised that we don't accept it with the same attitude of pretty, decorous enthusiasm with which they received it, way back in the 'eighties."

The middle generation was not so immediately affected by the war neurosis. They had had time enough, before 1917, to build up habits of conformity not easily broken down. But they, too, as the let-down of 1919 followed the war, found themselves restless and discontented, in a mood to question everything that had once seemed to them true and worthy and of good report. They too had spent themselves and wanted a good time. They saw their juniors exploring the approaches to the forbidden land of sex, and presently they began to play with the idea of doing a little experimenting of their own. The same disillusion which had defeated Woodrow Wilson and had caused strikes and riots and the Big Red Scare furnished a culture in which the germs of the new freedom could grow and multiply.

The revolution was accelerated also by the growing independence of the American woman. She won the suffrage in 1920. She seemed, it is true, to be very little interested in it once she had it; she voted, but mostly as the unregenerate men about her did, despite the efforts of women's clubs and the League of Women Voters to awaken her to womanhood's civic opportunity; feminine candidates for office were few, and some of them--such as Governor Ma Ferguson of Texas--scarcely seemed to represent the starry-eyed spiritual influence which, it had been promised, would presently ennoble public life. Few of the younger women could rouse themselves to even a passing interest in politics: to them it was a sordid and futile business, without flavor and without hope. Nevertheless, the winning of the suffrage had its effect. It consolidated woman's position as man's equal.

Even more marked was the effect of woman's growing independence of the drudgeries of housekeeping. Smaller houses were being built, and they were easier to look after. Families were moving into apartments, and these made even less claim upon the housekeeper's time and energy. Women were learning how to make lighter work of the preparation of meals. Sales of canned foods were growing, the number of delicatessen stores had increased three times as fast as the population during the decade 1910-20, the output of bakeries increased by 60 per cent during the decade 1914-24. Much of what had once been housework was now either moving out of the home entirely or being simplified by machinery. The use of commercial laundries, for instance, increased by 57 per cent between 1914 and 1924. Electric washing-machines and electric irons were coming to the aid of those who still did their washing at home; the manager of the local electric power company at "Middletown," a typical small American city, estimated in 1924 that nearly 90 per cent of the homes in the city already had electric irons. The housewife was learning to telephone her shopping orders, to get her clothes ready-made and spare herself the rigors of dress-making, to buy a vacuum cleaner and emulate the lovely carefree girls in the magazine advertisements who banished dust with such delicate fingers. Women were slowly becoming emancipated from routine to "live their own lives."

And what were these "own lives" of theirs to be like? Well, for one thing, they could take jobs. Up to this time girls of the middle classes who had wanted to "do something" had been largely restricted to school-teaching, social-service work, nursing, stenography, and clerical work in business houses. But now they poured out of the schools and colleges into all manner of new occupations. They besieged the offices of publishers and advertisers; they went into tea-room management until there threatened to be more purveyors than consumers of chicken patties and cinnamon toast; they sold antiques, sold real estate, opened smart little shops, and finally invaded the department stores. In 1920 the department store was in the mind of the average college girl a rather bourgeois institution which employed "poor shop girls"; by the end of the decade college girls were standing in line for openings in the misses' sports-wear department and even selling behind the counter in the hope that some day fortune might smile upon them and make them buyers or stylists. Small-town girls who once would have been contented to stay in Sauk Center all their days were now borrowing from father to go to New York or Chicago to seek their fortunes--in Best's or Macy's or Marshall Field's. Married women who were encumbered with children and could not seek jobs consoled themselves with the thought that home-making and child-rearing were really "professions," after all. No topic was so furiously discussed at luncheon tables from one end of the country to the other as the question whether the married woman should take a job, and whether the mother had a right to. And as for the unmarried woman, she no longer had to explain why she worked in a shop or an office; it was idleness, nowadays, that had to be defended.

With the job--or at least the sense that the job was a possibility--came a feeling of comparative economic independence. With the feeling of economic independence came a slackening of husbandly and parental authority. Maiden aunts and unmarried daughters were leaving the shelter of the family roof to install themselves in kitchenette apartments of their own. For city-dwellers the home was steadily becoming less of a shrine, more of a dormitory--a place of casual shelter where one stopped overnight on the way from the restaurant and the movie theater to the office. Yet even the job did not provide the American woman with that complete satisfaction which the management of a mechanized home no longer furnished. She still had energies and emotions to burn; she was ready for the revolution.

Like all revolutions, this one was stimulated by foreign propaganda. It came, however, not from Moscow, but from Vienna. Sigmund Freud had published his first book on psychoanalysis at the end of the nineteenth century, and he and Jung had lectured to American psychologists as early as 1909, but it was not until after the war that the Freudian gospel began to circulate to a marked extent among the American lay public. The one great intellectual force which had not suffered disrepute as a result of the war was science; the more-or-less educated public was now absorbing a quantity of popularized information about biology and anthropology which gave a general impression that men and women were merely animals of a rather intricate variety, and that moral codes had no universal validity and were often based on curious superstitions. A fertile ground was ready for the seeds of Freudianism, and presently one began to hear even from the lips of flappers that "science taught" new and disturbing things about sex. Sex, it appeared, was the central and pervasive force which moved mankind. Almost every human motive was attributable to it: if you were patriotic or liked the violin, you were in the grip of sex--in a sublimated form. The first requirement of mental health was to have an uninhibited sex life. If you would be well and happy, you must obey your libido. Such was the Freudian gospel as it imbedded itself in the American mind after being filtered through the successive minds of interpreters and popularizers and guileless readers and people who had heard guileless readers talk about it. New words and phrases began to be bandied about the cocktail-tray and the Mah Jong table-- inferiority complex, sadism, masochism, Œdipus complex. Intellectual ladies went to Europe to be analyzed; analysts plied their new trade in American cities, conscientiously transferring the affections of their fair patients to themselves; and clergymen who preached about the virtue of self-control were reminded by outspoken critics that self-control was out-of-date and really dangerous.

The principal remaining forces which accelerated the revolution in manners and morals were all 100 per cent American. They were prohibition, the automobile, the confession and sex magazines, and the movies.

When the Eighteenth Amendment was ratified, prohibition seemed, as we have already noted, to have an almost united country behind it. Evasion of the law began immediately, however, and strenuous and sincere opposition to it--especially in the large cities of the North and East--quickly gathered force. The results were the bootlegger, the speakeasy, and a spirit of deliberate revolt which in many communities made drinking "the thing to do." From these facts in turn flowed further results: the increased popularity of distilled as against fermented liquors, the use of the hip-flask, the cocktail party, and the general transformation of drinking from a masculine prerogative to one shared by both sexes together. The old-time saloon had been overwhelmingly masculine; the speakeasy usually catered to both men and women. As Elmer Davis put it, "The old days when father spent his evenings at Cassidy's bar with the rest of the boys are gone, and probably gone forever; Cassidy may still be in business at the old stand and father may still go down there of evenings, but since prohibition mother goes down with him." Under the new régime not only the drinks were mixed, but the company as well.

Meanwhile a new sort of freedom was being made possible by the enormous increase in the use of the automobile, and particularly of the closed car. (In 1919 hardly more than 10 per cent of the cars produced in the United States were closed; by 1924 the percentage had jumped to 43, by 1927 it had reached 82.8.) The automobile offered an almost universally available means of escaping temporarily from the supervision of parents and chaperons, or from the influence of neighborhood opinion. Boys and girls now thought nothing, as the Lynds pointed out in *Middletown,* of jumping into a car and driving off at a moment's notice--without asking anybody's permission--to a dance in another town twenty miles away, where they were strangers and enjoyed a freedom impossible among their neighbors. The closed car, moreover, was in effect a room protected from the weather which could be occupied at any time of the day or night and could be moved at will into a darkened byway or a country lane. The Lynds quoted the judge of the juvenile court in "Middletown" as declaring that the automobile had become a "house of prostitution on wheels," and cited the fact that of thirty girls brought before his court in a year on charges of sex crimes, for whom the place where the offense had occurred was recorded, nineteen were listed as having committed it in an automobile.

Finally, as the revolution began, its influence fertilized a bumper crop of sex magazines, confession magazines, and lurid motion pictures, and these in turn had their effect on a class of readers and movie-goers who had never heard and never would hear of Freud and the libido. The publishers of the sex adventure magazines, offering stories with such titles as "What I Told My Daughter the Night Before Her Marriage," "Indolent Kisses," and "Watch Your Step-ins," learned to a nicety the gentle art of arousing the reader without arousing the censor. The publishers of the confession magazines, while always instructing their authors to provide a moral ending and to utter pious sentiments, concentrated on the description of what they euphemistically called "missteps." Most of their fiction was faked to order by hack writers who could write one day "The Confessions of a Chorus Girl" and the next day recount, again in the first person, the temptations which made it easy for the taxidriver to go wrong. Both classes of magazines became astonishingly numerous and successful. Bernarr Macfadden's *True-Story,* launched as late as 1919, had over 300,000 readers by 1923; 848,000 by 1924; over a million and a half by 1925; and almost two million by 1926--a record of rapid growth probably unparalleled in magazine publishing.

Crowding the news stands along with the sex and confession magazines were motion-picture magazines which depicted "seven movie kisses" with such captions as "Do you recognize your little friend, Mae Busch? She's had lots of kisses, but she never seems to grow *blasé.* At least you'll agree that she's giving a good imitation of a person enjoying this one." The movies themselves, drawing millions to their doors every day and every night, played incessantly upon the same lucrative theme. The producers of one picture advertised "brilliant men, beautiful jazz babies, champagne baths, midnight revels, petting parties in the purple dawn, all ending in one terrific smashing climax that makes you gasp"; the venders of another promised "neckers, petters, white kisses, red kisses, pleasure-mad daughters, sensation-craving mothers, . . . the truth--bold, naked, sensational." Seldom did the films offer as much as these advertisements promised, but there was enough in some of them to cause a sixteen-year-old girl (quoted by Alice Miller Mitchell) to testify, "Those pictures with hot love-making in them, they make girls and boys sitting together want to get up and walk out, go off somewhere, you know. Once I walked out with a boy before the picture was even over. We took a ride. But my friend, she all the time had to get up and go out with her boyfriend."

A storm of criticism from church organizations led the motion-picture producers, early in the decade, to install Will H. Hays, President Harding's Postmaster-General, as their arbiter of morals and of taste, and Mr. Hays promised that all would be well. "This industry must have," said he before the Los Angeles Chamber of Commerce, "toward that sacred thing, the mind of a child, toward that clean virgin thing, that unmarked slate, the same responsibility, the same care about the impressions made upon it, that the best clergyman or the most inspired teacher of youth would have." The result of Mr. Hays's labors in behalf of the unmarked slate was to make the moral ending as obligatory as in the confession magazines, to smear over sexy pictures with pious platitudes, and to blacklist for motion-picture production many a fine novel and play which, because of its very honesty, might be construed as seriously or intelligently questioning the traditional sex ethics of the small town. Mr. Hays, being something of a genius, managed to keep the churchmen at bay. Whenever the threats of censorship began to become ominous he would promulgate a new series of moral commandments for the producers to follow. Yet of the practical effects of his supervision it is perhaps enough to say that the quotations given above all date from the period of his dictatorship. Giving lip-service to the old code, the movies diligently and with consummate vulgarity publicized the new.

Each of these diverse influences--the post-war disillusion, the new status of women, the Freudian gospel, the automobile, prohibition, the sex and confession magazines, and the movies--had its part in bringing about the revolution. Each of them, as an influence, was played upon by all the others; none of them could alone have changed to any great degree the folkways of America; together their force was irresistible.

§ 3

The most conspicuous sign of what was taking place was the immense change in women's dress and appearance.

In Professor Paul H. Nystrom's *Economics of Fashion,* the trend of skirt-length during the Post-war Decade is ingeniously shown by the sort of graph with which business analysts delight to compute the ebb and flow of car-loadings or of stock averages. The basis of this graph is a series of measurements of fashion-plates in the *Delineator;* the statistician painstakingly measured the relation, from month to month, of the height of the skirt hem above the ground to the total height of the figure, and plotted his curve accordingly. This very unusual graph shows that in 1919 the average distance of the hem above the ground was about 10 per cent of the woman's height--or to put it in another way, about six or seven inches. In 1920 it curved upward from 10 to about 20 per cent. During the next three years it gradually dipped to 10 per cent again, reaching its low point in 1923. In 1924, however, it rose once more to between 15 and 20 per cent, in 1925 to more than 20 per cent; and the curve continued steadily upward until by 1927 it had passed the 25 per cent mark--in other words, until the skirt had reached the knee. There it remained until late in 1929.

This graph, as Professor Nystrom explains, does not accurately indicate what really happened, for it represents for any given year or month, not the average length of skirts actually worn, but the length of the skirt which the arbiters of fashion, not uninfluenced by the manufacturers of dress goods, expected and wanted women to wear. In actual fact, the dip between 1921 and 1924 was very slight. Paris dressmakers predicted the return of longer skirts, the American stylists and manufacturers followed their lead, the stores bought the longer skirts and tried to sell them, but women kept on buying the shortest skirts they could find. During the fall of 1923 and the spring of 1924, manufacturers were deluged with complaints from retailers that skirts would have to be shorter. Shorter they finally were, and still shorter. The knee-length dress proved to be exactly what women wanted. The unlucky manufacturers made valiant efforts to change the fashion. Despite all they could do, however, the knee-length skirt remained standard until the decade was approaching its end.

With the short skirt went an extraordinary change in the weight and material and amount of women's clothing. The boyishly slender figure became the aim of every woman's ambition, and the corset was so far abandoned that even in so short a period as the three years from 1924 to 1927 the combined sales of corsets and brassières in the department stores of the Cleveland Federal Reserve District fell off 11 per cent. Silk or rayon stockings and underwear supplanted cotton, to the distress of cotton manufacturers and the delight of rayon manufacturers; the production of rayon in American plants, which in 1920 had been only eight million pounds, had by 1925 reached fifty-three million pounds. The flesh-colored stocking became as standard as the short skirt. Petticoats almost vanished from the American scene; in fact, the tendency of women to drop off one layer of clothing after another became so pronounced that in 1928 the *Journal of Commerce* estimated that in 15 years the amount of material required for a woman's complete costume (exclusive of her stockings) had declined from 19 $\frac{1}{4}$ yards to 7 yards. All she could now be induced to wear, it seemed, was an overblouse (2 yards), a skirt (2 $\frac{1}{4}$ yards), vest or shirt ($\frac{3}{4}$), knickers (2), and stockings--and all of them were made of silk or rayon! This latter statement, it is true, was a slight exaggeration; but a survey published in 1926 by the National Retail Dry Goods Association, on the basis of data from department stores all over the country, showed that only 33 per cent of the women's underwear sold was made of cotton, whereas 36 per cent was made of rayon, and 31 per cent of silk. No longer were silk stockings the mark of the rich; as the wife of a workingman with a total family income of $1,638 a year told the authors of *Middletown,* "No girl can wear cotton stockings to high school. Even in winter my children wear silk stockings with lisle or imitations underneath."

Not content with the freedom of short and skimpy clothes, women sought, too, the freedom of short hair. During the early years of the decade the bobbed head--which in 1918, as you may recall, had been regarded by the proprietor of the Palm Garden in New York as a sign of radicalism--became increasingly frequent among young girls, chiefly on the ground of convenience. In May, 1922, the *American Hairdresser* predicted that the bob, which persisted in being popular, "will probably last through the summer, anyway." It not only did this, it so increased in popularity that by 1924 the same journal was forced to feature bobbed styles and give its subscribers instructions in the new art, and was reporting the progress of a lively battle between the professional hairdressers and the barbers for the cream of this booming business. The ladies' hairdressers very naturally objected to women going to barbers' shops; the barbers, on the other hand, were trying to force legislation in various states which would forbid the "hairdressing profession" to cut hair unless they were licensed as barbers. Said the *Hairdresser,* putting the matter on the loftiest basis, "The effort to bring women to barber shops for haircutting is against the best interests of the public, the free and easy atmosphere often prevailing in barber shops being unsuitable to the high standard of American womanhood." But all that American womanhood appeared to insist upon was the best possible shingle. In the latter years of the decade bobbed hair became almost universal among girls in their twenties, very common among women in their thirties and forties, and by no means rare among women of sixty; and for a brief period the hair was not only bobbed, but in most cases cropped close to the head like a man's. Women universally adopted the small cloche hat which fitted tightly on the bobbed head, and the manufacturer of milliner's materials joined the hair-net manufacturer, the hair-pin manufacturer, and the cotton goods and woolen goods and corset manufacturers, among the ranks of depressed industries.

For another industry, however, the decade brought new and enormous profits. The manufacturers of cosmetics and the proprietors of beauty shops had less than nothing to complain of. The vogue of rouge and lipstick, which in 1920 had so alarmed the parents of the younger generation, spread swiftly to the remotest village. Women who in 1920 would have thought the use of paint immoral were soon applying it regularly as a matter of course and making no effort to disguise the fact; beauty shops had sprung up on every street to give "facials," to apply pomade and astringents, to make war against the wrinkles and sagging chins of age, to pluck and trim and color the eyebrows, and otherwise to enhance and restore the bloom of youth; and a strange new form of surgery, "face-lifting," took its place among the applied sciences of the day. Back in 1917, according to Frances

Fisher Dubuc, only two persons in the beauty culture business had paid an income tax; by 1927 there were 18,000 firms and individuals in this field listed as income-tax payers. The "beautician" had arrived.

As for the total amount of money spent by American women on cosmetics and beauty culture by the end of the decade, we may probably accept as conservative the prodigious figure of three-quarters of a billion dollars set by Professor Paul H. Nystrom in 1930; other estimates, indeed, ran as high as two billion. Mrs. Christine Frederick tabulated in 1929 some other equally staggering figures: for every adult woman in the country there were being sold annually over a pound of face powder and no less than eight rouge compacts; there were 2,500 brands of perfume on the market and 1,500 face creams; and if all the lipsticks sold in a year in the United States were placed end to end, they would reach from New York to Reno--which to some would seem an altogether logical destination.

Perhaps the readiest way of measuring the change in the public attitude toward cosmetics is to compare the advertisements in a conservative periodical at the beginning of the decade with those at its end. Although the June, 1919, issue of the *Ladies' Home Journal* contained four advertisements which listed rouge among other products, only one of them commented on its inclusion, and this referred to its rouge as one that was "imperceptible if properly applied." In those days the woman who used rouge--at least in the circles in which the *Journal* was read--wished to disguise the fact. (Advertisements of talc, in 1919, commonly displayed a mother leaning affectionately over a bouncing baby.) In the June, 1929, issue, exactly ten years later, the *Journal* permitted a lipstick to be advertised with the comment, "It's comforting to know that the alluring note of scarlet will stay with you for hours." (Incidentally, the examination of those two magazines offers another contrast: in 1919 the Listerine advertisement said simply, "The prompt application of Listerine may prevent a minor accident from becoming a major infection," whereas in 1929 it began a tragic rhapsody with the words, "Spring! for everyone but her . . .").

These changes in fashion--the short skirt, the boyish form, the straight, long-waisted dresses, the frank use of paint--were signs of a real change in the American feminine ideal (as well, perhaps, as in men's idea of what was the feminine ideal). Women were bent on freedom--freedom to work and to play without the trammels that had bound them heretofore to lives of comparative inactivity. But what they sought was not the freedom from man and his desires which had put the suffragists of an earlier day into hard straw hats and mannish suits and low-heeled shoes. The woman of the nineteen-twenties wanted to be able to allure man even on the golf links and in the office; the little flapper who shingled her hair and wore a manageable little hat and put on knickerbockers for the weekends would not be parted from her silk stockings and her high-heeled shoes. Nor was the post-war feminine ideal one of fruitful maturity or ripened wisdom or practiced grace. On the contrary: the quest of slenderness, the flattening of the breasts, the vogue of short skirts (even when short skirts still suggested the appearance of a little girl), the juvenile effect of the long waist--all were signs that, consciously or unconsciously, the women of this decade worshiped not merely youth, but unripened youth. They wanted to be--or thought men wanted them to be--men's casual and light-hearted companions; not broad-hipped mothers of the race, but irresponsible playmates. Youth was their pattern, but not youthful innocence: the adolescent whom they imitated was a hard-boiled adolescent, who thought not in terms of romantic love, but in terms of sex, and who made herself desirable not by that sly art which conceals art, but frankly and openly. In effect, the woman of the Post-war Decade said to man, "You are tired and disillusioned, you do not want the cares of a family or the companionship of mature wisdom, you want exciting play, you want the thrills of sex without their fruition, and I will give them to you." And to herself she added, "But I will be free."

§ 4

One indication of the revolution in manners which her headlong pursuit of freedom brought about was her rapid acceptance of the cigarette. Within a very few years millions of American women of all ages followed the lead of the flappers of 1920 and took up smoking. Custom still generally frowned upon their doing it on the street or in the office, and in the evangelical hinterlands the old taboo died hard; but in restaurants, at dinner parties and dances, in theater lobbies, and in a hundred other places they made the air blue. Here again the trend in advertising measured the trend in public opinion. At the beginning of the decade advertisers realized that it would have been suicidal to portray a woman smoking; within a few years, however, they ventured pictures of pretty girls imploring men to blow some of the smoke their way; and by the end of the decade billboards boldly displayed a smart-looking woman cigarette in hand, and in some of the magazines, despite floods of protests from rural readers, tobacco manufacturers were announcing that "now women may enjoy a companionable smoke with their husbands and brothers." In the ten years between 1918 and 1928 the total production of cigarettes in the United States *more than doubled.* Part of this increase was doubtless due to the death of the one-time masculine prejudice against the cigarette as unmanly, for it was accompanied by somewhat of a decrease in the production of cigars and smoking tobacco, as well as-- mercifully--of chewing tobacco. Part of it was attributable to the fact that the convenience of the cigarette made the masculine smoker consume more tobacco than in the days when he preferred a cigar or a pipe. But the increase could never have been so large had it not been for the women who now strewed the dinner table with their ashes, snatched a puff between the acts, invaded the masculine sanctity of the club car, and forced department stores to place ornamental ash-trays between the chairs in their women's shoe departments. A formidable barrier between the sexes had broken down. The custom of separating them after formal dinners, for example, still lingered, but as an empty rite. Hosts who laid in a stock of cigars for their male guests often found them untouched; the men in the dining-room were smoking the very same brands of cigarettes that the ladies consumed in the living- room.

Of far greater social significance, however, was the fact that men and women were drinking together. Among well-to-do people the serving of cocktails before dinner became almost socially obligatory. Mixed parties swarmed up to the curtained grills of speakeasies and uttered the mystic password, and girls along with men stood at the speakeasy bar with one foot on the old brass rail. The late afternoon cocktail party became a new American institution. When dances were held in hotels, the curious and rather unsavory custom grew up of hiring hotel rooms where reliable drinks could be served in suitable privacy; guests of both sexes lounged on the beds and tossed off mixtures of high potency. As houses and apartments became smaller, the country club became the social center of the small city, the suburb, and the summer resort; and to its pretentious clubhouse, every Saturday night, drove men and women (after a round of cocktails at somebody's house) for the weekly dinner dance. Bottles of White Rock and of ginger ale decked the tables, out of capacious masculine hip pockets came flasks of gin (once the despised and rejected of bartenders, now the most popular of all liquors), and women who a few years before would have gasped at the thought that they would ever be "under the influence of alcohol" found themselves matching the men drink for drink and enjoying the uproarious release. The next day gossip would report that the reason Mrs. So-and-so disappeared from the party at eleven was because she had had too many cocktails and had been led to the dressing-room to be sick, or that somebody would have to meet the club's levy for breakage, or that Mrs. Such-and-such really oughtn't to drink so much because three cocktails made her throw bread about the table. A passing scandal would be created by a dance at which substantial married men amused themselves by tripping up waiters, or young people bent on petting parties drove right out on the golf-links and made wheel-tracks on the eighteenth green.

Such incidents were of course exceptional and in many communities they never occurred. It was altogether probable, though the professional wets denied it, that prohibition succeeded in reducing the total amount of drinking in the country as a whole and in reducing it decidedly among the workingmen of the industrial districts. The majority of experienced college administrators agreed--rather to the annoyance of some of their undergraduates--that there was less drinking among men students than there had been before prohibition and that drinking among girl students, at least while they were in residence, hardly offered a formidable problem. Yet the fact remained that among the prosperous classes which set the standards of national social behavior, alcohol flowed more freely than ever before and lubricated an unprecedented informality--to say the least--of manners.

It lubricated, too, a new outspokenness between men and women. Thanks to the spread of scientific skepticism and especially to Sigmund Freud, the dogmas of the conservative moralists were losing force and the dogma that salvation lay in facing the facts of sex was gaining. An upheaval in values was taking place. Modesty, reticence, and chivalry were going out of style; women no longer wanted to be "ladylike" or could appeal to their daughters to be "wholesome"; it was too widely suspected that the old-fashioned lady had been a sham and that the "wholesome" girl was merely inhibiting a nasty mind and would come to no good end. "Victorian" and "Puritan" were becoming terms of opprobrium: up-to-date people thought of Victorians as old ladies with bustles and inhibitions, and of Puritans as blue-nosed, ranting spoilsports. It was better to be modern--everybody wanted to be modern--and sophisticated, and smart, to smash the conventions and to be devastatingly frank. And with a cocktail glass in one's hand it was easy at least to be frank.

"Listen with a detached ear to a modern conversation," wrote Mary Agnes Hamilton in 1927, "and you will be struck, first, by the restriction of the vocabulary, and second, by the high proportion in that vocabulary of words such as, in the older jargon, 'no lady could use.'" With the taste for strong liquors went a taste for strong language. To one's lovely dinner partner, the inevitable antithesis for "grand" and "swell" had become "lousy." An unexpected "damn" or "hell" uttered on the New York stage was no longer a signal for the sudden sharp laughter of shocked surprise; such words were becoming the commonplace of everyday talk. The barroom anecdote of the decade before now went the rounds of aristocratic bridge tables. Every one wanted to be unshockable; it was delightful to be considered a little shocking; and so the competition in boldness of talk went on until for a time, as Mrs. Hamilton put it, a conversation in polite circles was like a room decorated entirely in scarlet--the result was over-emphasis, stridency, and eventual boredom.

Along with the new frankness in conversation went a new frankness in books and the theater. Consider, for example, the themes of a handful of the best plays produced in New York during the decade: *What Price Glory?* which represented the amorous marines interlarding their talk with epithets new to the stage; *The Road to Rome,* the prime comic touch of which was the desire of a Roman matron to be despoiled by the Carthaginians; *Strange Interlude,* in which a wife who found there was insanity in her husband's family but wanted to give him a child decided to have the child by an attractive young doctor, instead of by her husband, and forthwith fell in love with the doctor; *Strictly Dishonorable,* in which a charming young girl walked blithely and open-eyed into an affair of a night with an opera-singer; and *The Captive,* which revealed to thousands of innocents the fact that the world contained such a phenomenon as homosexuality. None of these plays could have been tolerated even in New York before the Post-war Decade; all of them in the nineteen-twenties were not merely popular, but genuinely admired by intelligent audiences. The effect of some of them upon these audiences is suggested by the story of the sedate old lady who, after two acts of *What Price Glory?* reprimanded her grandson with a "God damn it, Johnny, sit down!"

The same thing was true of the novels of the decade; one after another, from *Jurgen* and *Dark Laughter* through the tales of Michael Arlen to *An American Tragedy* and *The Sun Also Rises* and *The Well of Loneliness* and *Point Counter Point,* they dealt with sex with an openness or a cynicism or an unmoral objectivity new to the English-speaking world. Bitterly the defenders of the Puritan code tried to stem the tide, but it was too strong for them. They banned *Jurgen*--and made a best seller of it and a public reputation for its author. They dragged Mary Ware Dennett into court for distributing a pamphlet for children which explained some of the mysteries of sex--only to have her upheld by a liberal judge and endorsed by intelligent public opinion. In Boston, where they were backed by an alliance between stubborn Puritanism and Roman Catholicism, they banned books wholesale, forbade the stage presentation of *Strange Interlude,* and secured the conviction of a bookseller for selling *Lady Chatterley's Lover*--only to find that the intellectuals of the whole country were laughing at them and that ultimately they were forced to allow the publication of books which they would have moved to ban ten years before. Despite all that they could do, the taste of the country demanded a new sort of reading matter.

Early in the decade a distinguished essayist wrote an article in which she contended that the physical processes of childbirth were humiliating to many women. She showed it to the editor of one of the best magazines, and he and she agreed that it should not be printed: too many readers would be repelled by the subject matter and horrified by the thesis. Only a few years later, in 1927, the editor recalled this manuscript and asked if he might see it again. He saw it--and wondered why it had ever been disqualified. Already such frankness seemed quite natural and permissible. The article was duly published, and caused only the mildest of sensations.

If in 1918 the editors of a reputable magazine had accepted a story in which one gangster said to another, "For Christ's sake, Joe, give her the gas. Some lousy bastard has killed Eddie," they would have whipped out the blue pencil and changed the passage to something like "For the love of Mike, Joe, give her the gas. Some dirty skunk has killed Eddie." In 1929 that sentence appeared in a story accepted by a magazine of the most unblemished standing, and was printed without alteration. A few readers objected, but not many. Times had changed. Even in the great popular periodicals with huge circulations and a considerable following in the strongholds of rural Methodism the change in standards was apparent. Said a short-story writer in the late nineteen-twenties, "I used to write for magazines like the *Saturday Evening Post* and the *Pictorial Review* when I had a nice innocuous tale to tell and wanted the money, and for magazines like *Harper's* and *Scribner's* when I wanted to write something searching and honest. Now I find I can sell the honest story to the big popular magazines too."

§ 5

With the change in manners went an inevitable change in morals. Boys and girls were becoming sophisticated about sex at an earlier age; it was symptomatic that when the authors of *Middletown* asked 241 boys and 315 girls of high-school age to mark as true or false, according to their opinion, the extreme statement, "Nine out of every ten boys and girls of high-school age have petting parties," almost precisely half of them marked it as true. How much actual intercourse there was among such young people it is of course impossible to say; but the lurid stories told by Judge Lindsay--of girls who carried contraceptives in their vanity cases, and of "Caroline," who told the judge that fifty-eight girls of her acquaintance had had one or more sex experiences without a single pregnancy resulting-- were matched by the gossip current in many a town. Whether prostitution increased or decreased during the decade is likewise uncertain; but certain it is that the prostitute was faced for the first time with an amateur competition of formidable proportions.

As for the amount of outright infidelity among married couples, one is again without reliable data, the private relations of men and women being happily beyond the reach of the statistician. The divorce rate, however, continued its steady increase; for every 100 marriages there were 8.8 divorces in 1910, 13.4 divorces in 1920, and 16.5 divorces in 1928--almost one divorce for every six marriages. There was a corresponding decline in the amount of disgrace accompanying divorce. In the urban communities men and women who had been divorced were now socially accepted without question; indeed, there was often about the divorced person just enough of an air of unconventionality, just enough of a touch of scarlet, to be considered rather dashing and desirable. Many young women probably felt as did the New York girl who said, toward the end of the decade, that she was thinking of marrying Henry, although she didn't care very much for him, because even if they didn't get along she could get a divorce and "it would be much more exciting to be a divorcée than to be an old maid."

The petting party, which in the first years of the decade had been limited to youngsters in their teens and twenties, soon made its appearance among older men and women: when the gin-flask was passed about the hotel bedroom during a dance, or the musicians stilled their saxophones during the Saturday-night party at the country club, men of affairs and women with half-grown children had their little taste of raw sex. One began to hear of young girls, intelligent and well born, who had spent week-ends with men before marriage and had told their prospective husbands everything and had been not merely forgiven, but told that there was nothing to forgive; a little "experience," these men felt, was all to the good for any girl. Millions of people were moving toward acceptance of what a *bon-vivant* of earlier days had said was his idea of the proper state of morality--"A single standard, and that a low one."

It would be easy, of course, to match every one of these cases with contrasting cases of men and women who still thought and behaved at the end of the decade exactly as the president of the Epworth League would have wished. Two women who conducted newspaper columns of advice in affairs of the heart testified that the sort of problem which was worrying young America, to judge from their bulging correspondence, was not whether to tell the boyfriend about the illegitimate child, but whether it was proper to invite the boyfriend up on the porch if he hadn't yet come across with an invitation to the movies, or whether the cake at a pie social should be cut with a knife. In the hinterlands there was still plenty of old-fashioned sentimental thinking about sex, of the sort which expressed itself in the slogan of a federated women's club: "Men are God's trees, women are His flowers." There were frantic efforts to stay the tide of moral change by law, the most picturesque of these efforts being the ordinance actually passed in Norphelt, Arkansas, in 1925, which contained the following provisions:

"Section 1. Hereafter it shall be unlawful for any man and woman, male or female, to be guilty of committing the act of sexual intercourse between themselves at any place within the corporate limits of said town.

"Section 3. Section One of this ordinance shall not apply to married persons as between themselves, and their husband and wife, unless of a grossly improper and lascivious nature."

Nevertheless, there was an unmistakable and rapid trend away from the old American code toward a philosophy of sex relations and of marriage wholly new to the country: toward a feeling that the virtues of chastity and fidelity had been rated too highly, that there was something to be said for what Mrs. Bertrand Russell defined as "the right, equally shared by men and women, to free participation in sex experience," that it was not necessary for girls to deny themselves this right before marriage or even for husbands and wives to do so after marriage. It was in acknowledgment of the spread of this feeling that Judge Lindsay proposed, in 1927, to establish "companionate marriage" on a legal basis. He wanted to legalize birth control (which, although still outlawed, was by this time generally practiced or believed in by married couples in all but the most ignorant classes) and to permit legal marriage to be terminated at any time in divorce by mutual consent, provided there were no children. His suggestion created great consternation and was widely and vigorously denounced; but the mere fact that it was seriously debated showed how the code of an earlier day had been shaken. The revolution in morals was in full swing.

§ 6

A time of revolution, however, is an uneasy time to live in. It is easier to tear down a code than to put a new one in its place, and meanwhile there is bound to be more or less wear and tear and general unpleasantness. People who have been brought up to think that it is sinful for women to smoke or drink, and scandalous for sex to be discussed across the luncheon table, and unthinkable for a young girl to countenance strictly dishonorable attentions from a man, cannot all at once forget the admonitions of their childhood. It takes longer to hard-boil a man or a woman than an egg. Some of the apostles of the new freedom appeared to imagine that habits of thought could be changed overnight, and that if you only dragged the secrets of sex out into the daylight and let everyone do just as he pleased at the moment, society would at once enter upon a state of barbaric innocence like that of the remotest South Sea Islanders. But it couldn't be done. When you drag the secrets of sex out into the daylight, the first thing that the sons and daughters of Mr. and Mrs. Grundy do is to fall all over themselves in the effort to have a good look, and for a time they can think of nothing else. If you let every one do just as he pleases, he is as likely as not to begin by making a nuisance of himself. He may even shortly discover that making a nuisance of himself is not, after all, the recipe for lasting happiness. So it happened when the old codes were broken down in the Postwar Decade.

One of the most striking results of the revolution was a widely pervasive obsession with sex. To listen to the conversation of some of the sons and daughters of Mr. and Mrs. Grundy was to be reminded of the girl whose father said that she would talk about anything; in fact, she hardly ever talked about anything else. The public attitude toward any number of problems of the day revealed this obsession: to give a single example, the fashionable argument against women's colleges at this period had nothing to do with the curriculum or with the intellectual future of the woman graduate, but pointed out that living with girls for four years was likely to distort a woman's sex life. The public taste in reading matter revealed it: to say nothing of the sex magazines and the tabloids and the acres of newspaper space devoted to juicy scandals like that of Daddy Browning and his Peaches, it was significant that almost every one of the novelists who were ranked most highly by the postwar intellectuals was at outs with the censors, and that the Pulitzer Prize juries had a hard time meeting the requirement that the prize-winning novel should "present the wholesome atmosphere of American life and the highest standard of American manners and manhood," and finally had to alter the terms of the award, substituting "whole" for "wholesome" and omitting reference to "highest standards." There were few distinguished novels being written which one could identify with a "wholesome atmosphere" without making what the Senate would call interpretive reservations. Readers who considered themselves "modern-minded" did not want them: they wanted the philosophical promiscuity of Aldous Huxley's men and women, the perfumed indiscretions of Michael Arlen's degenerates, Ernest Hemingway's unflinching account of the fleeting amours of the drunken Brett Ashley, Anita Loos's comedy of two kept women and their gentlemen friends, Radclyffe Hall's study of homosexuality. Young men and women who a few years before would have been championing radical economic or political doctrines were championing the new morality and talking about it everywhere and thinking of it incessantly. Sex was in the limelight, and the Grundy children could not turn their eyes away.

Another result of the revolution was that manners became not merely different, but--for a few years--unmannerly. It was no mere coincidence that during this decade hostesses--even at small parties-- found that their guests couldn't be bothered to speak to them on arrival or departure, that "gatecrashing" at dances became an accepted practice; that thousands of men and women made a point of not getting to dinners within half an hour of the appointed time lest they seem insufficiently *blasé;* that house parties of flappers and their wide-trousered swains left burning cigarettes on the mahogany tables, scattered ashes light-heartedly on the rugs, took the porch cushions out in the boats and left them there to be rained on, without apology; or that men and women who had had--as the old phrase went-- "advantages" and considered themselves highly civilized, absorbed a few cocktails and straightway turned a dinner party into a boisterous rout, forgetting that a general roughhouse was not precisely the sign of a return to the Greek idea of the good life. The old bars were down, no new ones had been built, and meanwhile the pigs were in the pasture. Someday, perhaps, the ten years which followed the war may aptly be known as the Decade of Bad Manners.

Nor was it easy to throw overboard the moral code and substitute another without confusion and distress. It was one thing to proclaim that married couples should be free to find sex adventure wherever they pleased and that marriage was something independent of such casual sport; it was quite another thing for a man or woman in whom the ideal of romantic marriage had been ingrained since early childhood to tolerate infidelities when they actually took place. Judge Lindsay told the story of a woman who had made up her mind that her husband might love whom he pleased; she would be modern and think none the less of him for it. But whenever she laid eyes on her rival she was physically sick. Her mind, she discovered, was hard-boiled only on the surface. That woman had many a counterpart during the revolution in morals; behind the grim statistics of divorce there was many a case of husband and wife experimenting with the new freedom and suddenly finding that there was dynamite in it which wrecked that mutual confidence and esteem without which marriage--even for the sake of their children--could not be endured.

The new code had been born in disillusionment, and beneath all the bravado of its exponents and the talk about entering upon a new era the disillusionment persisted. If the decade was ill-mannered, it was also unhappy. With the old order of things had gone a set of values which had given richness and meaning to life, and substitute values were not easily found. If morality was dethroned, what was to take its place? Honor, said some of the prophets of the new day: "It doesn't matter much what you do so long as you're honest about it." A brave ideal--yet it did not wholly satisfy; it was too vague, too austere, too difficult to apply. If romantic love was dethroned, what was to take its place? Sex? But as Joseph Wood Krutch explained, "If love has come to be less often a sin, it has also come to be less often a supreme privilege." And as Walter Lippmann, in *A Preface to Morals,* added after quoting Mr. Krutch, "If you start with the belief that love is the pleasure of a moment, is it really surprising that it yields only a momentary pleasure?" The end of the pursuit of sex alone was emptiness and futility--the emptiness and futility to which Lady Brett Ashley and her friends in *The Sun Also Rises* were so tragically doomed.

There were not, to be sure, many Brett Ashleys in the United States during the Post-war Decade. Yet there were millions to whom in some degree came for a time the same disillusionment and with it the same unhappiness. They could not endure a life without values, and the only values they had been trained to understand were being undermined. Everything seemed meaningless and unimportant. Well, at least one could toss off a few drinks and get a kick out of physical passion and forget that the world was crumbling. . . . And so the saxophones wailed and the gin-flask went its rounds and the dancers made their treadmill circuit with half-closed eyes, and the outside world, so merciless and so insane, was shut away for a restless night. . . .

It takes time to build up a new code. Not until the decade was approaching its end did there appear signs that the revolutionists were once more learning to be at home in their world, to rid themselves of their obsession with sex, to adjust themselves emotionally to the change in conventions and standards, to live the freer and franker life of this new era gracefully, and to discover among the ruins of the old dispensation a new set of enduring satisfactions.

♦ VI ♦
HARDING AND THE SCANDALS

§ 1

Having been personal attorney for Warren G. Harding before he was Senator from Ohio and while he was Senator, and thereafter until his death.

--And for Mrs. Harding for a period of several years, and before her husband was elected President and after his death,

--And having been attorney for the Midland National Bank of Washington Court House, O., and for my brother, M. S. Daugherty,

--And having been Attorney-General of the United States during the time that President Harding served as President,

--And also for a time after President Harding's death under President Coolidge,

--And with all of those named, as attorney, personal friend, and Attorney-General, my relations were of the most confidential character as well as professional,

--I refuse to testify and answer questions put to me, because:

The answer I might give or make and the testimony I might give might tend to incriminate me.

--Harry M. Daugherty's written reply when called upon by Judge Thacher for information for the Federal Grand Jury in New York March 31, 1926 (punctuation revised).

On the morning of March 4, 1921--a brilliant morning with a frosty air and a wind which whipped the flags of Washington--Woodrow Wilson, broken and bent and ill, limped from the White House door to a waiting automobile, rode down Pennsylvania Avenue to the Capitol with the stalwart President-elect at his side, and returned to the bitter seclusion of his private house in S Street. Warren Gamaliel Harding was sworn in as President of the United States. The reign of normalcy had begun.

March 4, 1921: what do those cold figures mean to you? Let us turn back for a moment to that day and look about us.

The war had been over for more than two years, although, as the Treaty of Versailles had been thrown out by the Senate and Woodrow Wilson had refused to compromise with the gentlemen at the other end of the Avenue, a technical state of war still existed between Germany and the United States. Business, having boomed until the middle of 1920, was collapsing into the depths of depression and dragging down with it the price-level which had caused so much uproar about the High Cost of Living. The Big Red Scare was gradually ebbing, although the super-patriots still raged and Sacco and Vanzetti had not yet come to trial before Judge Thayer. The Ku Klux Klan was acquiring its first few hundred thousand members. The Eighteenth Amendment was entering upon its second year, and rum-runners and bootleggers were beginning to acquire confidence. The sins of the flappers were disturbing the nation; it was at about this time that Philadelphia produced the "moral gown" and the *Literary Digest* featured a symposium entitled, "Is the Younger Generation in Peril?" The first radio broadcasting station in the country was hardly four months old and the radio craze was not yet. Skirts had climbed halfway to the knee and seemed likely to go down again, a crime commission had just been investigating Chicago's crime wave, Judge Landis had become the czar of baseball, Dempsey and Carpentier had signed to meet the following summer at Boyle's Thirty Acres, and *Main Street* and *The Outline of History* were becoming best sellers.

The nation was spiritually tired. Wearied by the excitements of the war and the nervous tension of the Big Red Scare, they hoped for quiet and healing. Sick of Wilson and his talk of America's duty to humanity, callous to political idealism, they hoped for a chance to pursue their private affairs without governmental interference and to forget about public affairs. There might be no such word in the dictionary as normalcy, but normalcy was what they wanted.

Every new administration at Washington begins in an atmosphere of expectant good will, but in this case the airs which lapped the capital were particularly bland. The smile of the new President was as warming as a spring thaw after a winter of discontent. For four long years the gates of the White House had been locked and guarded with sentries. Harding's first official act was to throw them open, to permit a horde of sight-seers to roam the grounds and flatten their noses against the executive window-panes and photograph one another under the great north portico; to permit flivvers and trucks to detour from Pennsylvania Avenue up the driveway and chortle right past the presidential front door. The act seemed to symbolize the return of the government to the people. Wilson had been denounced as an autocrat, had proudly kept his own counsel; Harding modestly said he would rely on the "best minds" to advise him, and took his oath of office upon the verse from Micah which asks, "What doth the Lord require of thee but to do justly, and to love mercy, and to walk humbly with thy God?" Wilson had seemed to be everlastingly prying into the affairs of business and had distrusted most business men; Harding meant to give them as free a hand as possible "to resume their normal onward way." And finally, whereas Wilson had been an austere academic theorist, Harding was "just folks": he radiated an unaffected good nature, met reporters and White House visitors with a warm handclasp and a genial word, and touched the sentimental heart of America by establishing in the White House a dog named Laddie Boy. "The Washington atmosphere of today is like that of Old Home Week or a college class reunion," wrote Edward G. Lowry shortly after Harding took office. "The change is amazing. The populace is on a broad grin." An era of good will seemed to be beginning.

Warren Harding had two great assets, and these were already apparent. First, he looked as a President of the United States should. He was superbly handsome. His face and carriage had a Washingtonian nobility and dignity, his eyes were benign; he photographed well and the pictures of him in the rotogravure sections won him affection and respect. And he was the friendliest man who ever had entered the White House. He seemed to like everybody, he wanted to do favors for everybody, he wanted to make everybody happy. His affability was not merely the forced affability of the cold-blooded politician; it was transparently and touchingly genuine. "Neighbor," he had said to Herbert Hoover at their first meeting, during the war, "I want to be helpful." He meant it; and now that he was President, he wanted to be helpful to neighbors from Marion and neighbors from campaign headquarters and to the whole neighborly American public.

His liabilities were not at first so apparent, yet they were disastrously real. Beyond the limited scope of his political experience he was "almost unbelievably ill-informed," as William Allen White put it. His mind was vague and fuzzy. Its quality was revealed in the clogged style of his public addresses, in his choice of turgid and maladroit language ("noninvolvement" in European affairs, "adhesion" to a treaty), and in his frequent attacks of suffix trouble ("normalcy" for normality, "betrothment" for betrothal). It was revealed even more clearly in his helplessness when confronted by questions of policy to which mere good nature could not find the answer. White tells of Harding's coming into the office of one of his secretaries after a day of listening to his advisers wrangling over a tax problem, and crying out: "John, I can't make a damn thing out of this tax problem. I listen to one side and they seem right, and then--God!--I talk to the other side and they seem just as right, and here I am where I started. I know somewhere there is a book that will give me the truth, but, hell, I couldn't read the book. I know somewhere there is an economist who knows the truth, but I don't know where to find him and haven't the sense to know him and trust him when I find him. God! What a job!" His inability to discover for himself the essential facts of a problem and to think it through made him utterly dependent upon subordinates and friends whose mental processes were sharper than his own.

If he had been discriminating in the choice of his friends and advisers, all might have been well. But discrimination had been left out of his equipment. He appointed Charles Evans Hughes and Herbert Hoover and Andrew Mellon to Cabinet positions out of a vague sense that they would provide his administration with the necessary amount of statesmanship, but he was as ready to follow the lead of Daugherty or Fall or Forbes. He had little notion of technical fitness for technical jobs. Offices were plums to him, and he handed them out like a benevolent Santa Claus--beginning with the boys from Marion. He made his brother-in-law Superintendent of Prisons; he not only kept the insignificant Doctor Sawyer, of Sawyer's Sanitarium at Marion, as his personal physician, but bestowed upon him what a White House announcement called a "brigadier-generalcy" (suffix trouble again) and deputed him to study the possible coordination of the health agencies of the government; and for Comptroller of the Currency he selected D. R. Crissinger, a Marion lawyer whose executive banking experience was limited to a few months as president of the National City Bank and Trust Company--of Marion.

Nor did Harding appear to be able to distinguish between honesty and rascality. He had been trained in the sordid school of practical Ohio politics. He had served for years as the majestic Doric false front behind which Ohio lobbyists and fixers and purchasers of privilege had discussed their "business propositions" and put over their "little deals"--and they, too, followed him to Washington, along with the boys from Marion. Some of them he put into positions of power, others he saw assuming positions of power; knowing them intimately, he must have known--if he was capable of a minute's clear and unprejudiced thought--how they would inevitably use those positions; but he was too fond of his old cronies, too anxious to have them share his good fortune, and too muddle-minded to face the issue until it was too late. He liked to slip away from the White House to the house in H Street where the Ohio gang and their intimates reveled and liquor flowed freely without undue regard for prohibition, and a man could take his pleasure at the poker table and forget the cares of state; and the easiest course to take was not to inquire too closely into what the boys were doing, to hope that if they were grafting a little on the side they'd be reasonable about it and not do anything to let old Warren down.

And why did he choose such company? The truth was that under his imposing exterior he was just a common small-town man, an "average sensual man," the sort of man who likes nothing better in the world than to be with the old bunch when they gather at Joe's place for an all-Saturday-night session, with waistcoats unbuttoned and cigars between their teeth and an ample supply of bottles and cracked ice at hand. His private life was one of cheap sex episodes; as one reads the confessions of his mistress, who claims that as President he was supporting an illegitimate baby born hardly a year before his election, one is struck by the shabbiness of the whole affair: the clandestine meetings in disreputable hotels, in the Senate Office Building (where Nan Britton believed their child to have been conceived), and even in a coat-closet in the executive offices of the White House itself. (Doubts have been cast upon the truth of the story told in *The President's Daughter,* but is it easy to imagine anyone making up out of whole cloth a supposedly autobiographical story compounded of such ignoble adventures?) Even making due allowance for the refraction of Harding's personality through that of Nan Britton, one sees with deadly clarity the essential ordinariness of the man, the commonness of his "Gee, dearie" and "Say, you darling," his being swindled out of a hundred dollars by card sharpers on a train ride, his naïve assurance to Nan, when detectives broke in upon them in a Broadway hotel, that they could not be arrested because it was illegal to detain a Senator while "en route to Washington to serve the people." Warren Harding's ambitious wife had tailored and groomed him into outward respectability and made a man of substance of him; yet even now, after he had reached the White House, the rowdies of the Ohio gang were fundamentally his sort. He had risen above them, he could mingle urbanely with their superiors, but it was in the smoke-filled rooms of the house in H Street that he was really most at home.

Harding had no sooner arrived at the White House than a swarm of practical politicians of the McKinley-Foraker vintage reappeared in Washington. Blowsy gentlemen with cigars stuck in their cheeks and rolls of very useful hundred-dollar bills in their pockets began to infest the Washington hotels. The word ran about that you could do business with the government now--if you only fixed things up with the right man. The oil men licked their chops; had they not lobbied powerfully at the Chicago convention for the nomination of just such a man as Harding, who did not take this conservation nonsense too seriously, and would not Harding's Secretary of the Interior, Albert B. Fall, let them develop the national resources on friendly and not too stringent terms? The Ohio gang chuckled over the feast awaiting them: the chances for graft at Columbus had been a piker's chance compared with those which the mastery of the federal government would offer him. Warren Harding wanted to be helpful. Well, he would have a chance to be.

§ 2

The public at large, however, knew little and cared less about what was happening behind the scenes. Their eyes--when they bothered to look at all--were upon the well-lighted stage where the Harding Administration was playing a drama of discreet and seemly statesmanship.

Peace with Germany, so long deferred, was made by a resolution signed by the President on July 2, 1921. The Government of the United States was put upon a unified budget basis for the first time in history by the passage of the Budget Act of 1921, and Charles G. Dawes, becoming Director of the Budget, entranced the newspaper-reading public with his picturesque language, his underslung pipe, and his broom-waving histrionics when he harangued the bureau chiefs on behalf of business efficiency. Immigration was restricted, being put upon a quota basis, to the satisfaction of labor and the relief of those who felt that the amount of melting being done in the melting-pot was disappointingly small. Congress raised the tariff, as all good Republican Congresses should. Secretary Mellon pleased the financial powers of the country by arguing for the lowering of the high surtaxes upon large incomes; and although an obstreperous Farm Bloc joined with the Democrats to keep the maximum surtax at 50 per cent, Wall Street at least felt that the Administration's heart was in the right place. Every foe of union labor was sure of this when Attorney-General Daugherty confronted the striking railway shopmen with an injunction worthy of Mitchell Palmer himself. In January, 1923, an agreement for the funding of the British war debt to the United States was made in Washington; it was shortly ratified by the Senate. The outstanding achievement of the Harding Administration, however, was undoubtedly the Washington Conference for the Limitation of Armaments--or, as the newspapers insisted upon calling it, the "Arms Parley."

Since the war the major powers of the world had begun once more their race for supremacy in armament. England, the United States, and Japan were all building ships for dear life. The rivalry between them was rendered acute by the growing tension in the Pacific. During the war Japan had seized her golden opportunity for the expansion of her commercial empire: her rivals being very much occupied elsewhere, she had begun to regard China as her special sphere of interest and to treat it as a sort of protectorate where her commerce would have prior rights to that of other nations. Her hand was strengthened by an alliance with England. When Charles Evans Hughes became Secretary of State and began to stand up for American rights in the Orient, applying once more the traditional American policy of the Open Door, it was soon apparent that the situation was ticklish. Japan wanted her own way; the Americans opposed it: and there lay the Philippines, apparently right under Japan's thumb if trouble should break out! All three powers. Britain, Japan, and the United States, would be the gainers by an amicable agreement about the points under dispute in the Pacific, by the substitution of a three-cornered agreement for the Japanese-British alliance, and by an arrangement for the limitation of fleets. Senator Borah proposed an international conference. Harding and Hughes took up his suggestion, the conference was called, and on November 12, 1921--the day following the solemn burial of America's Unknown Soldier at Arlington Cemetery--the delegates assembled in Washington.

President Harding opened the first session with a cordial if profuse speech of welcome, and true to his policy of leaving difficult problems to be solved by the "best minds," left Secretary Hughes and his associates to do the actual negotiating. In this case his hands-off policy worked well. Hughes not only had a brilliant mind, he had a definite program and a masterly grasp of the complicated issues at stake. President Harding had hardly walked out of Memorial Continental Hall when the Secretary of State, installed as chairman of the conference, began what seemed at first only the perfunctory address of greeting--and then, to the amazement of the delegates assembled about the long conference tables, came out with a definite and detailed program: a ten-year naval holiday, during which no capital ships should be built; the abandonment of all capital-shipbuilding plans, either actual or projected; the scrapping, by the three nations, of almost two million tons of ships built or building; and the limitation of replacement according to a 5-5-3 ratio (the American and British navies to be kept at parity and the Japanese at three-fifths of the size of each).

"With the acceptance of this plan," concluded Secretary Hughes amid a breathless silence, "the burden of meeting the demands of competition in naval armament will be lifted. Enormous sums will be released to aid the progress of civilization. At the same time the proper demands of national defense will be adequately met and the nations will have ample opportunity during the naval holiday of ten years to consider their future course. Preparation for offensive naval war will stop now."

The effect of this direct and specific proposal was prodigious. At the proposal of a naval holiday William Jennings Bryan, sitting among the newspapermen, expressed his enthusiasm with a yell of delight. At the conclusion of Hughes's speech the delegates broke into prolonged applause. It was echoed by the country and by the press of the world. People's imaginations were so stirred by the boldness and effectiveness of the Hughes plan that the success of the conference became almost inevitable.

After three months of negotiation the delegates of Japan, Great Britain, and the United States had agreed upon a treaty which followed the general lines of the Hughes program; had joined with the French in an agreement to respect one another's insular possessions in the Pacific, and to settle all disagreements by conciliatory negotiations; had prepared the way for the withdrawal of Japan from Shantung and Siberia; and had agreed to respect the principle of the Open Door in China. The treaties were duly ratified by the Senate. The immediate causes of friction in the Pacific were removed; and although cynics might point out that competition in cruisers and submarines was little abated and that battleships were almost obsolete anyhow, the Naval Treaty at least lessened the burden of competition, as Secretary

Hughes had predicted, and in addition set a precedent of profound importance. The armaments which a nation built were now definitely recognized as being a matter of international concern, subject to international agreement.

Outwardly, then, things seemed to be going well for Warren Harding. He was personally popular; his friendly attitude toward business satisfied the conservative temper of the country; his Secretary of the Treasury was being referred to, wherever two or three bankers or industrialists gathered together, as the "greatest since Alexander Hamilton"; his Secretary of Commerce, Herbert Hoover, was aiding trade as efficiently as he had aided the Belgians; and even discouraged idealists had to admit that the Washington Conference had been no mean achievement. Though there were rumors of graft and waste and mismanagement in some departments of the Government, and the director of the Veterans' Bureau had had to leave his office in disgrace, and there was noisy criticism in Congress of certain leases of oil lands to Messrs. Doheny and Sinclair, these things attracted only a mild public interest. When Harding left in the early summer of 1923 for a visit to Alaska, few people realized that anything was radically wrong with his administration. When, on his way home, he fell ill with what appeared to be ptomaine poisoning, and on his arrival at San Francisco his illness went into pneumonia, the country watched the daily headlines with affectionate concern. And when, just as the danger appeared to have been averted, he died suddenly--on August 2, 1923-- of what his physicians took to be a stroke of apoplexy, the whole nation was plunged into deep and genuine grief.

The President's body was placed upon a special train, which proceeded across the country at the best possible speed to Washington. All along the route, thousands upon thousands of men, women, and children were gathered to see it slip by. Cowboys on the Western hills dismounted and stood uncovered as the train passed. In the cities the throngs of mourners were so dense that the engineer had to reduce his speed and the train fell hours behind schedule. "It is believed," wrote a reporter for the *New York Times,* "to be the most remarkable demonstration in American history of affection, respect, and reverence for the dead." When Warren Harding's body, after lying in state at Washington, was taken to Marion for burial, his successor proclaimed a day of public mourning, business houses were closed, memorial services were held from one end of the country to the other, flags hung at half mast, and buildings were draped in black.

The innumerable speeches made that day expressed no merely perfunctory sentiments; everywhere people felt that a great-hearted man, bowed down with his labors in their behalf, had died a martyr to the service of his country. The dead President was called "a majestic figure who stood out like a rock of consistency"; it was said that "his vision was always on the spiritual"; and Bishop Manning of New York, speaking at a memorial service in the Cathedral of St. John the Divine, seemed to be giving the fallen hero no more than his due when he cried, "If I could write one sentence upon his monument it would be this, 'He taught us the power of brotherliness.' It is the greatest lesson that any man can teach us. It is the spirit of the Christian religion. In the spirit of brotherliness and kindness we can solve all the problems that confront us. . . . May God ever give to our country leaders as faithful, as wise, as noble in spirit, as the one whom we now mourn."

But as it happens, there are some problems--at least for a President of the United States--that the spirit of brotherliness and kindness will not alone solve. The problem, for example, of what to do when those to whom you have been all too brotherly have enmeshed your administration in graft, and you know that the scandal cannot long be concealed, and you feel your whole life-work toppling into disgrace. That was the problem which had killed Warren Harding.

A rumor that the President committed suicide by taking poison later gained wide currency through the publication of Samuel Hopkins Adams's *Revelry,* a novel largely based on the facts of the Harding Administration. Gaston B. Means, a Department of Justice detective and a member of the gang which revolved about Daugherty, implied only too clearly in *The Strange Death of President Harding* that the President was poisoned by his wife, with the connivance of Doctor Sawyer. The motive, according to Means, was a double one: Mrs. Harding had found out about Nan Britton and the illegitimate daughter and was consumed with a bitter and almost insane jealousy; and she had learned enough about the machinations of Harding's friends and the power that they had over him to feel that only death could save him from obloquy. Both the suicide theory and the Means story are very plausible. The ptomaine poisoning came, it was said, from eating crab meat on the presidential boat on the return from Alaska, but the list of supplies in the steward's pantry contained no crab meat and no one else in the presidential party was taken ill; furthermore, the fatal "stroke of apoplexy" occurred when the President was recovering from pneumonia, Mrs. Harding was apparently alone with him at the time, and the verdict of the physicians, not being based upon an autopsy, was hardly more than an expression of opinion. Yet it is not necessary to accept any such melodramatic version of the tragedy to acknowledge that Harding died a victim of the predicament in which he was caught. He knew too much of what had been going on in his administration to be able to face the future. On the Alaskan trip, he was clearly in a state of tragic fear; according to William Allen White, "he kept asking Secretary Hoover and the more trusted reporters who surrounded him what a President should do whose friends had betrayed him." Whatever killed him--poison or heart failure--did so the more easily because he had lost the will to live.

Of all this, of course, the country as a whole guessed nothing at the time. Their friend and President was dead, they mourned his death, and they applauded the plans of the Harding Memorial Association to raise a great monument in his honor. It was only afterward that the truth came out, piece by piece.

§ 3

The martyred President had not been long in his grave when the peculiar circumstances under which the Naval Oil Reserves at Teapot Dome and Elk Hills had been leased began to be unearthed by the Senate Committee on Public Lands, and there was little by little disclosed what was perhaps the gravest and most far-reaching scandal of the Harding Administration. The facts of the case, as they were ultimately established, were, briefly, as follows:

Since 1909, three tracts of oil-bearing government land had been legally set aside for the future hypothetical needs of the United States navy--as a sort of insurance policy against a possible shortage of oil in time of emergency. They were Naval Reserve No. 1, at Elk Hills, California; No. 2, at Buena Vista, California; and No. 3, at Teapot Dome, Wyoming. As time went on, it became apparent that the oil under these lands might be in danger of being drawn off by neighboring wells, the flow of oil under the earth being such that if you drill a well you are likely to bring up not only the oil from under your own land, but also that from under your neighbor's land. As to the extent of this danger to these particular properties there was wide disagreement; but when gushers were actually opened up right on the threshold of the Elk Hills Reserve, Congress took action. In 1920 it gave the Secretary of the Navy almost unlimited power to meet as he saw fit the problem of conserving the Reserves. Clearly there were at least two possible courses of action open to him. He might arrange to have offset wells drilled along the edge of the Reserves to neutralize the drainage, or he might lease the Reserves to private operators on condition that they store an equitable amount of the oil--or of fuel oil-- for the future requirements of the national defense. Secretary Daniels preferred to have offset wells drilled.

But when Albert B. Fall became Secretary of the Interior under President Harding, he decided otherwise. During 1921--on the eve of the Conference for the Limitation of Armaments--certain high officers in the navy were sufficiently nervous about possible trouble with Japan to declare that the navy must at once have fuel oil storage depots built and filled and ready for use at Pearl Harbor and other strategic points. This idea suited Mr. Fall perfectly. He had come into office as the ally of certain big oil interests, and being a politician without illusions, he saw a chance to do them a favor. He would lease the Reserves in their entirety to private operators, and meet the needs of the navy by using the royalty oil which these operators paid the Government for the purpose of buying fuel oil tanks and filling them with fuel oil. To be sure, the Secretary of the Navy alone had power to lease the Reserves, and Fall was not the Secretary of the Navy; but that was not an insuperable difficulty.

Less than three months after President Harding took office, he signed an Executive Order transferring the Reserves from the custody of the Secretary of the Navy to that of the Secretary of the Interior. On April 7, 1922, Fall secretly and without competitive bidding leased Reserve No. 3, the Teapot Dome Reserve, to Harry F. Sinclair's Mammoth Oil Company. On December 11, 1922, he secretly and without competitive bidding leased Reserve No. 1, the Elk Hills Reserve, to Edward F. Doheny's Pan-American Company. It has been argued that these leases were fair to the Government and that no undue profits would have accrued to the lessees if the contracts had been allowed to stand. It has been argued that the necessity for keeping secret what were thought of as military arrangements was sufficient excuse for the absence of competitive bidding and the complete absence of publicity. But it was later discovered that Fall had received from Sinclair some $260,000 in Liberty bonds, and that Fall had been "lent" by Doheny--without interest and without security--$100,000 in cash.

After a long series of Senate investigations, governmental lawsuits, and criminal trials which dragged out through the rest of the decade, the Doheny lease was voided by the Supreme Court as "illegal and fraudulent," the Sinclair lease was also voided, and Secretary Fall was found guilty of accepting a bribe from Doheny and sentenced to a year in prison. Secretary of the Navy Denby--who had amiably approved the transfer of the Reserves from his charge to that of Fall-- was driven from office by public criticism. Paradoxically, both Doheny and Sinclair were acquitted. But Sinclair had to serve a double term in prison in 1929: first, for contempt of the Senate in refusing to answer questions put to him by the Committee on Public Lands, and second, for contempt of court in having the jury at his first trial shadowed by Burns detectives. (One of the jurors declared that a man had approached him with the suggestion that if he voted right he would have an automobile "as long as this block.")

Such are the bare facts of the oil lease transactions. But they are only a part of the story. For after the Senate Committee's first important disclosures, early in 1924, and President Coolidge's appointment of the useful Mr. Owen Roberts and the ornamental Ex-Senator Atlee Pomerene as a bi-partisan team of Government prosecutors to take whatever legal action might be called for on behalf of the Government, Messrs. Roberts and Pomerene discovered that certain bonds transferred by Sinclair to Fall had come from the exchequer of a hitherto unheard-of concern called the Continental Trading Company, Ltd., of Canada. And the history of the Continental Trading Company, Ltd., as it was gradually dragged to light, was not only highly sensational but highly illuminating as a case-study in current American business ethics. This is what had happened:

On the 17th of November, 1921--a few months before the Fall-Sinclair contract was made--a little group of men gathered in a room at the Hotel Vanderbilt in New York for a business session. They included Colonel E. A. Humphreys, the owner of the rich Mexia oil field; Harry M. Blackmer of the Midwest Oil Company; James E. O'Neil of the Prairie Oil Company; Colonel Robert W. Stewart, chairman of the board of the Standard Oil Company of Indiana; and Harry F. Sinclair, head of the Sinclair Consolidated Oil Company. At that meeting Colonel Humphreys agreed to sell 33,333,333 barrels of oil from his oil field at $1.50 a barrel. But he discovered that he was not, as he had supposed, to sell this oil directly to the companies represented by the other men present. He was asked to sell it to a concern of which he had never heard, a concern which had only just been incorporated--the Continental Trading Company, Ltd. The contract of sale was guaranteed on behalf of the mysterious Continental Company by Sinclair and O'Neil. And the Continental straightway resold the oil to Sinclair's and O'Neil's companies, not at

$1.50 a barrel, *but at $1.75 a barrel*--thereby diverting to the coffers of the Continental a nice profit of twenty-five cents a barrel which might otherwise have gone to the other companies whose executives were gathered together. A profit, it might be added, which in the course of time should amount to over eight million dollars.

As a matter of fact, it never amounted to as much as that. For after a year or more the Senate became unduly inquisitive and it was thought best to wind up the affairs of the Continental Trading Company, Ltd., and destroy its records. But before this was done, the profit of that little deal pulled off at the Hotel Vanderbilt had piled up to more than three millions.

With these millions, as they rolled in, President Osler, the distinguished Canadian attorney who headed the Continental, purchased Liberty bonds. And the bulk of these bonds (after taking out a 2-per-cent share for himself) he turned over, in packages, to four of the gentlemen who had sat in on the conference at the Vanderbilt, as follows:

To Harry M. Blackmer, approximately $763,000.
To James E. O'Neil, approximately $800,000.
To Colonel Robert W. Stewart, approximately $759,000.
To Harry F. Sinclair, approximately $757,000.

And did these gentlemen at once report to their directors and stockholders the receipt of the bonds and put them into the corporate treasuries? They did not.

Blackmer, according to the subsequent (very subsequent) testimony of his counsel, put his share in a safety deposit box at the Equitable Trust Company in New York, where in 1928 it still remained.

O'Neil turned over his share to his company, but not until May, 1925.

Stewart handed his share to an employee of the Standard Oil Company of Indiana to be held in trust for the company in the vaults of the company, but never told any other associates of this except one member of the company's legal staff, and never disclosed to his directors what he had done until 1928, when he finally turned over the bonds to them. The trust agreement was written in pencil.

Sinclair, according to his own testimony, did not take the directors or officers of his company into his confidence until 1928, and kept his share of the bonds in a vault in his home. He did not keep all of them there very long, however, or the brave history of the Continental Trading Company, Ltd., might never have come to light.

A goodly portion of them (as we have already seen) he turned over to Fall. Another goodly portion, amounting to $185,000, he "loaned" (in addition to an outright gift of $75,000), to the Republican National Committee, later getting back $100,000 of it. The "loan" was made to Will H. Hays, who had been chairman of the Republican National Committee during the Harding-Cox campaign of 1920, had later been appointed Postmaster-General by President Harding, and had finally resigned to become supervisor of morals for the motion-picture industry. Mr. Hays was czar of the movies by the time Sinclair handed him the bonds, but being a conscientious man, he was trying to get the 1920 Republican campaign debt paid off. To this end he attempted to use the Sinclair "loan" in a very interesting way. He and his lieutenants approached a number of wealthy men, potential donors to the cause, and told them that if they would contribute to meet the deficit they might have Sinclair bonds to the amount of their contributions. How long they might keep the bonds was not made clear--at least in Hays's testimony before the Senate Committee on Public Lands. This method of concealing an enormous Sinclair contribution was euphemistically called, by the moral supervisor of the movies, "using the bonds in efforts to raise money for the deficit."

§ 4

So much for our little lesson in governmental practice and in the fiduciary duties of business executives in behalf of their stockholders. Now let us turn to the lighter side of the oil scandals. Lighter, that is, for those who were in no way implicated. There is a certain grim humor in the twistings and turnings of unwilling witnesses under the implacable cross-examination of Senator Walsh of Montana, without whose resourceful work the truth might never have been run to earth. Some of the scenes in the slowly-unfolding drama of the investigations, some of the sojourns of interested parties on foreign shores, some of the odd tricks of memory revealed, are not without an element of entertainment. Let us go back over the record of that long investigation and study a few of them, item by item.

Item One. Who Loaned Fall the Money?

In the autumn of 1923--not long after Harding's lamented death--Senator Walsh's committee learned of a recent sudden rise to affluence on the part of Secretary Fall. For some time previously Fall had been in financial straits; he had not even paid his local taxes for several years. But now all was changed. Mr. Fall had even purchased additional land near his New Mexican ranch, and in this purchase had used a considerable number of hundred-dollar bills. The Walsh committee at once became bloodhounds on the scent: hundred-dollar bills are as exciting to investigators as refusals to testify or refusals to waive immunity. From whom had Fall been receiving money? Fall wrote the committee a long letter, denying absolutely that he had ever received a dollar from Mr. Doheny or Mr. Sinclair, and in tones of outraged innocence explained that he had received a loan of $100,000 from Edward B. McLean of Washington, a millionaire newspaper-owner whose ample hospitality Harding and his associates had often enjoyed.

Mr. McLean was in Palm Beach and unable to come to Washington to testify about this loan. The committee might perhaps have been expected to let the matter go at that. But they did not. Mr. McLean was wanted--and it began to appear that he was extremely unwilling to be examined. He and his friends engaged in a voluminous correspondence by coded telegrams with his aides in Washington, discussing the progress of affairs in messages such as

Haxpw sent over buy bonka and householder bonka sultry tkvouep prozoics sepic bepelt goal hocusing this pouted proponent

Finally Senator Walsh all too obligingly journeyed to Palm Beach to take McLean's testimony there. Yes, McLean had made a loan to Fall. But he had made it in the form of three checks. Secretary Fall had shortly returned the checks; they had not even passed through the banks, and there was no record whatever of the transaction.

Clearly this brief and unusual financial transaction threw little light on the prosperity of the Ex-Secretary of the Interior or his use of cash in large denominations. Another explanation was necessary. Whereupon--on January 24, 1924--the lessee of Naval Reserve No. 1, Edward L. Doheny, took the stand. He, too, had loaned $100,000 to Fall. The money had been carried from New York to Washington in a satchel. But the loan had nothing to do with any lease of oil-bearing land. It was a bona fide loan made to accommodate an old friend. The elderly oil magnate drew a touching picture of his long years of comradeship with Fall. Was $100,000 a rather large sum to be loaned this way in cash? Why, no, it was "just a bagatelle" to him. It was not at all unusual for him "to make a remittance that way." Was there a note given for the loan? Yes; Doheny would search for it. Later he produced it--or rather, a fragment of it. The signature was missing. Fearing that he might die and that Fall might be unduly pressed for payment by cold-blooded executors, Doheny had torn the note in half and given the part with the signature to Mrs. Doheny--and she had mislaid it. The explanation was perfect--though some years later the Supreme Court seemed to regard it with skepticism.

Item Two. Six or Eight Cows

Just before the generous Doheny took the stand, the newspapers had been treated to a first-class front-page story. Archie Roosevelt, son of the great T. R. and brother of the lesser T. R. (who was Harding's Assistant Secretary of Navy), had come before the Walsh Committee as a volunteer witness. Archie Roosevelt was an officer in one of the Sinclair companies, and he had something to get off his mind. His brother had urged him to tell all. He (Archie) had been told by one G. D. Wahlberg, confidential secretary to Sinclair, that Sinclair had paid $68,000 to the manager of Fall's ranch, a circumstance which, in view of the relentless way in which Senator Walsh was running down evidence, apparently had caused Wahlberg some uneasiness. Furthermore, Sinclair had sailed for Europe--not only had sailed, but had done so very quietly, without letting his name appear on the passenger list. The committee called Wahlberg. This gentleman was even more uneasy at the committee table than he had been in talking to Archie Roosevelt, but he had a charming explanation for what he was said to have said. Roosevelt must have misunderstood him. He had said nothing about $68,000. What he must have said was that Sinclair had sent "six or eight cows" to Fall's ranch. (Which was true, after a manner of speaking: Sinclair had indeed made a present of live stock to Fall; not precisely "six or eight cows," but a horse, six hogs, a bull, and six heifers.) You see how the misunderstanding arose? You see how much "sixty-eight thous" sounds like "six or eight cows"?

The Committee on Public Lands did not seem to see. They lifted a collective eyebrow. So a little later Wahlberg tried again. This time his explanation was even more delightful. He had been consulting his memory, and had decided that what he must actually have said when he sounded as if he were talking about $68,000 going to the manager of the Fall ranch, or the Fall farm, was that $68,000 was going to the manager of the "horse farm"--by which he had meant the trainer at Sinclair's celebrated Rancocas Stables. This $68,000 represented the salary of Hildreth, the trainer, together with his share of the winnings of Zev and other Sinclair horses.

"Horse farm"--there seemed to be something less than idiomatic about the phrase. The collective eyebrow was not lowered.

Item Three. The Silences of Colonel Stewart--and Others

The Senate committee was hot on the trail--or rather on two trails. But then and thereafter the various gentlemen who could give it the greatest assistance in following these trails to the end revealed a strange reluctance to talk and a strange condition of memory when they did talk. Secretary Fall was declared by his physicians to be a "very sick man" who ought not to be pressed to testify. When he finally did testify, he refused to answer questions which might "tend to incriminate" him. Sinclair, as Archie Roosevelt had told the committee, had gone to Europe; after he returned, he too refused to answer questions; it was this refusal which led to his conviction for contempt. After his acquittal on the graver charge of conspiracy to defraud the government he at last spoke out; he admitted that he had turned over the bonds to Fall, but insisted that they were given in payment for a one-third interest in Fall's ranching and cattle business.

Blackmer had gone to Europe and could not be induced to return. O'Neil had gone to Europe and could not be induced to return. Osler of the Continental Trading Company was somewhere at the ends of the earth. And as for Colonel Stewart, only the insistence of John D. Rockefeller, Jr., induced him to come from Cuba to face the committee. When he did face it, early in 1928, he testified as follows: "I did not personally receive any of these bonds. I did not make one dollar out of the transaction." Less than two months later, after Sinclair's acquittal had somewhat reduced the tension, he admitted that over three-quarters of a million dollars' worth of these bonds had been delivered to him, and that he had not told the directors of his company about them for several years.

Item Four. The Testimony of Mr. Hays

In 1924 Will H. Hays, preceptor of motion-picture morality, was called before the Senate committee. He was asked how much money Sinclair had contributed to the Republican Party. Seventy-five thousand dollars, he said.

In 1928, after the history of the Continental bonds had become somewhat clearer, Mr. Hays was asked to face the committee again. He told them the full story of Sinclair's "loan" of $185,000 in addition to his gift. Why had he not told this before? He had not been "asked about any bonds."

Item Five. The Reticence of Mr. Mellon

A few days after Mr. Hays gave his second and improved version of the Sinclair contributions, the cashier of Charles Pratt & Company was called before the committee to testify about $50,000 worth of Sinclair-Continental Liberty bonds which had been left by Hays with the late John T. Pratt, to be held against a contribution of the same amount--after the ingenious Hays plan--by Mr. Pratt to the Republican Committee. The cashier produced a card on which Mr. Pratt had noted the disposal of the bonds and the payment of his contribution. And in the corner of this card was a minute notation in pencil, as follows:

$50,000

Andy Weeks

DuPont

Butler

Senator Walsh examined the card.

Senator Walsh: I can make out "Weeks," and I can make out "DuPont," and I can make out "Butler," but what is this other name? It looks like Andy.

The Cashier (using a magnifying glass): It's Weeks, DuPont, Butler, and the other name must be Candy. . . . Yes, it might be Andy.

Senator Nye: And who is Andy?

The Cashier: I have no idea who Andy can be. I can think of no one known as Andy.

There was a roar from the crowd in the room. Everybody knew who Andy must be. Senator Walsh dispatched a note to Andrew W. Mellon, Secretary of the Treasury, to ask him if he could explain the notation. This Mr. Mellon obligingly did without delay.

Late in 1923, Mr. Mellon explained--at just about the time when the Teapot Dome investigation was getting under way--Hays had sent him some bonds. "When Mr. Hays called shortly thereafter, he told me that he had received the bonds from Mr. Sinclair and suggested that I hold the bonds and contribute an equal amount to the fund. This I declined to do."

The Secretary had acted with strict integrity. He had sent the bonds back, and instead of following Hays's suggestion he had made an outright contribution of $50,000. He added that he had "had no knowledge of what has developed since, that is, of the Teapot Dome lease matter."

It is perhaps worth noting, however, that this testimony was given in 1928. For more than three years not only the Senate committee, but Messrs. Roberts and Pomerene, the public attorneys appointed by President Coolidge to prosecute the government suits, had been trying to discover just what had become of the Continental bonds, and during all that time the Secretary of the Treasury was aware that in 1923 he had been offered Liberty bonds which came from Sinclair. He said nothing until that little card turned up with Andy (or possibly Candy) penciled on it. A small matter, perhaps; but surely it revealed the Secretary as a paragon of reticence when his testimony might cast discredit on the money-raising methods of his party.

Thus comes to an end--as of this writing, at least--the remarkable story of Teapot Dome and Elk Hills and the Continental Trading Company, Ltd. The Executive Order transferring the leases, which may be said to have begun it all, was promulgated in June, 1921, when Harding was new in office, and the Stillman divorce trial was impending, and Dempsey was preparing to meet Carpentier, and young Charles Lindbergh had not yet taken his first ride in an airplane. By the time Sinclair and Stewart had told their stories and Hays had revised himself and Secretary Mellon had overcome his reticence, Lindbergh had flown to Europe and Herbert Hoover was corralling delegates for the Republican nomination; by the time Harry Sinclair emerged from his unwelcome term of service as apothecary in the Washington jail, the bull market had come down in ruin and the Post-war Decade was dying. Secretary Fall's term as guardian of the national resources for the Harding Administration had been brief, but the aftermath had been as long and harrowing as it was instructive.

Oh yes--there is one more thing to add. The oil: what became of the oil that started it all, the oil that the patriots of the Navy Department had been so anxious to have immediately available in case of trouble in the Pacific? There had been a good deal of excitement about bonds and hundred-thousand-dollar loans, but everybody seemed to have forgotten about that oil. Production in the properties leased to Sinclair and Doheny was stopped; but you may recall that the danger of drainage into neighboring wells had been much discussed in 1921. The neighboring wells went right on producing, and it is said that part of the oil from them--including, in all probability, some drawn from within the Reserves--was sold to the Japanese Government!

§ 5

The oil cases were the aristocrats among the scandals of the Harding Administration, but there were other scandals juicier and more reeking. Let us hold our noses for a moment and examine a few of them briefly.

There was, for example, the almost incredible extravagance and corruption of the Veterans' Bureau under Charles R. Forbes, a buccaneer of fortune (and one-time deserter from the army) whom Harding had fallen in with on a visit to Hawaii. Harding was so taken with Forbes that in 1921 he put him in charge of the Government's work for those disabled war heroes in whose behalf every public man considered it his duty to shed an appreciative tear. Forbes held office for less than two years, and during that time it was estimated that over two hundred million dollars went astray in graft and flagrant waste on the part of his Bureau. Forbes went on a notorious junket through the country, supposedly selecting hospital sites which in reality had already been chosen. His Bureau let contracts for veterans' hospitals almost without regard for price; for instance, a contract for a hospital at Northampton was let to a firm which asked some thirty thousand dollars more than the lowest bidder. It was charged that Forbes had an arrangement with the builders of some hospitals whereby he was to pocket a third of the profits. Preposterous purchases of hospital supplies were made: the Veterans' Bureau bought $70,000 worth of floor wax and floor cleaner, for instance--enough, it was said, to last a hundred years--and for the cleaner it paid 98 cents a gallon, although expert testimony later brought out the fact that it was worth less than 4 cents a gallon exclusive of the water which it contained. Quantities of surplus goods were sold with the same easy disregard for price: 84,000 brand-new sheets which had cost $1.37 each were sold at 26 or 27 cents apiece, although at that very moment the Bureau was purchasing 25,000 new ones at $1.03 apiece. "At one time," reported Bruce

Bliven, "sheets just bought were actually going in at one end of the warehouse [at Perryville, Maryland] as the ones just sold were going out the other, and some of them by mistake went straight in and out again." More than 75,000 towels which had cost 19 cents each were sold for 3 cents each. These few facts are enough to show with what generous abandon Forbes spent the money appropriated to care for the defenders of the Republic. Forbes went to Leavenworth in 1926 for fraud.

There was rampant graft in the office of the Alien Property Custodian as well. Gaston B. Means has charged that attorneys who came to Washington to file claims for the return of properties taken over from Germans during the war were advised to consult a Boston lawyer named Thurston, that Thurston would charge them a big fee for his services, the claim would be allowed, and the fee would be split with those in authority. Be that as it may, the evidence brought out in the American Metal Company case was sufficient to indicate the sort of transaction which was permitted to take place.

The American Metal Company was an internationally-owned concern 49 per cent of whose stock had been taken over by the Alien Property Custodian during the war on the ground that it belonged to Germans. This stock had been sold for $6,000,000. In 1921 a certain Richard Merton appeared at the Custodian's office with the claim that this 49 per cent had not been German, but Swiss, and that the Swiss owners, whom he represented, should be reimbursed. The claim was allowed after Merton had paid $441,000 in Liberty bonds to John T. King, Republican National Committeeman from Connecticut, for "services" which consisted of introducing him to Colonel T. W. Miller, the Custodian, and to Jess Smith, Attorney-General Daugherty's man Friday. It was brought out at Miller's trial that at least $200,000 of this $441,000 was paid over to Jess Smith "for expediting the claim through his acquaintance in Washington"; that Mal S. Daugherty, brother of the Attorney-General, sold at least $40,000 worth of Merton Liberty bonds and shortly thereafter deposited $49,165 to his brother's account; and that Colonel Miller also got a share of the money. Miller was convicted in 1927 of conspiracy to defraud the Government of his unbiased services and was sentenced to eighteen months in prison. Daugherty was also brought to trial, but got off. After two juries had been unable to agree as to his guilt or innocence, the indictment against him was dismissed--but not before it had been brought out that in 1925 this former chief legal officer of the Government had gone to his brother's bank at Washington Court House, Ohio, and had taken out and burned the ledger sheets covering his own account there, and his brother's account, and another account known as "Jesse Smith Extra."

It was during the grand jury investigation which preceded the American Metal Company case that Harding's Attorney-General wrote the remarkable statement which appears at the head of this chapter. During his trial Daugherty failed to take the stand in his own defense, and his attorney, Max Steuer, later explained this failure in another equally remarkable statement:

"It was not anything connected with this case which impelled him to refrain from so doing. . . . He feared . . . that Mr. Buckner would cross-examine him about matters political that would not involve Mr. Daugherty, concerning which he knew and as to which he would never make disclosure. . . . If the jury knew the real reason for destroying the ledger sheets they would commend rather than condemn Mr. Daugherty, but he insisted on silence."

Could there be more deliberate implication that Harding's Attorney-General could not tell the truth for fear of blackening the reputation of his dead chief? Call Daugherty's silence, if you wish, the silence of loyalty, or call those statements an effort to hide behind the dead President; in either case the Harding Administration appears in a strange light.

Charges still more damaging were boldly made by Gaston B. Means in 1930. He stated that as a henchman of the Ohio gang he used to engage two adjoining rooms at a New York hotel for the collection of prohibition graft from bootleggers who were willing to pay for federal protection; that he would place a big goldfish-bowl in one of the rooms, on a table which he could see by peeping through the door from the next room that each bootlegger would come at his appointed hour and minute and leave in the bowl huge amounts of cash in thousand-dollar or five-hundred-dollar bills; that as soon as the bootlegger left, Means would enter, count the money, and check off the contribution; and that in this way he collected a total of fully seven million dollars which he turned over to Jess Smith, the collector-in-chief for the Ohio Gang, who shared an apartment in Washington with Attorney-General Daugherty.

Means further asserted that the swag from this and other forms of graft was kept hidden--many thousand dollars at a time--in a metal box buried in the back yard of the house which he occupied at 903 Sixteenth Street in Washington; he described this house and yard as being protected with a high wire fence and fitted out with a code signal system and other secret devices such as would delight a gang of small boys playing pirate.

Jess Smith committed suicide--at least that was the official verdict--in 1923 in the apartment which he shared with Harry Daugherty. Means claimed that just before this tragedy took place, the gang had discovered that Smith--like the careful shopkeeper he had been before he was brought to Washington by Daugherty to occupy a desk in the Department of Justice--had kept a record of all the cash which had passed through his hands, and that Smith, terrified at the thought of his guilt and his secret knowledge, had been playing with the idea of turning state's witness against the gang. According to Means, the gang thereupon decided that Smith must be disposed of. Although Smith was afraid of firearms, he was persuaded to purchase a revolver on one of his trips to Ohio. And the "suicide" which followed--so Means plainly indicated, as many others had already suspected--was no suicide at all.

Finally, Means drew attention to the astonishing mortality among those who had been in on the secrets of the gang. Not only had Smith dropped out of the picture, but also John T. King (who had received the Merton bonds), C. F. Hately (a Department of Justice agent), C. F. Cramer (attorney for the Veterans' Bureau), Thurston (the Boston lawyer who represented many clients before the Alien Property Custodian), T. B. Felder (attorney for the Harding group), President Harding, Mrs. Harding, and General Sawyer. They had all died--most of them suddenly--within a few years of the end of the Harding Administration.

No matter how much or how little credence one may give to these latter charges and their implications, the proved evidence is enough to warrant the statement that the Harding Administration was responsible in its short two years and five months for more concentrated robbery and rascality than any other in the whole history of the Federal Government.

§ 6

And how did the American people take these disclosures? Did they rise in wrath to punish the offenders?

When the oil scandals were first spread across the front pages of the newspapers, early in 1924, there was a wave of excitement sufficient to force the resignations of Denby and Daugherty and to bring about the appointment by the new President, Calvin Coolidge, of special Government counsel to deal with the oil cases. But the harshest condemnation on the part of the press and the public was reserved, not for those who had defrauded the government, but for those who insisted on bringing the facts to light. Senator Walsh, who led the investigation of the oil scandals, and Senator Wheeler, who investigated the Department of Justice, were called by the *New York Tribune* "the Montana scandalmongers." The *New York Evening Post* called them "mud-gunners." The *New York Times,* despite its Democratic leanings, called them "assassins of character." In these and other newspapers throughout the country one read of the "Democratic lynching-bee" and "poison-tongued partisanship, pure malice, and twittering hysteria," and the inquiries were called "in plain words, contemptible and disgusting."

Newspaper-readers echoed these amiable sentiments. Substantial businessmen solemnly informed one another that mistakes might have been made but that it was unpatriotic to condemn them and thus to "cast discredit on the Government," and that those who insisted on probing them to the bottom were "nothing better than Bolsheviki." One of the leading super-patriots of the land, Fred R. Marvin of the Key Men of America, said the whole oil scandal was the result of "a gigantic international conspiracy . . . of the internationalists, or shall we call them socialists and communists?" A commuter riding daily to New York from his suburb at this period observed that on the seven-o'clock train there was some indignation at the scandals, but that on the eight-o'clock train there was only indignation at their exposure and that on the nine-o'clock train they were not even mentioned. When, a few months later, John W. Davis, campaigning for the Presidency on the Democratic ticket, made political capital of the Harding scandals, the opinion of the majority seemed to be that what he said was in bad taste, and Davis was snowed under at the polls. The fact was that any relentless investigation of the scandals threatened to disturb, if only slightly, the *status quo,* and disturbance of the *status quo* was the last thing that the dominant business class or the country at large wanted.

They had voted for normalcy and they still believed in it. The most that they required of the United States Government was that it should keep its hands off business (except to give it a lift now and then through the imposition of favorable tariffs and otherwise) and be otherwise unobtrusive. They did not look for bold and far-seeing statesmanship at Washington; their idea of statesmanship on the part of the President was that he should let things alone, give industry and trade a chance to garner fat profits, and not "rock the boat." They realized that their selection of Harding had been something of a false start toward the realization of this modest ideal. Harding had been a little too hail-fellow-well-met, and his amiability had led him into associations which brought about unfortunate publicity, and unfortunate publicity had a tendency to rock the boat. But the basic principle remained sound: all the country needed now was a President who combined with unobtrusiveness and friendliness toward business an unimpeachable integrity and an indisposition to have his leg pulled; and this sort of President they now had. The inscrutable workings of Providence had placed in the office left vacant by Harding the precise embodiment of this revised presidential ideal. Calvin Coolidge was unobtrusive to the last degree; he would never try to steer the ship of state into unknown waters; and at the same time he was sufficiently honest and circumspect to prevent any unseemly revelry from taking place on the decks. Everything was, therefore, as it should be. Why weaken public confidence in Harding's party, and thus in Harding's successor, by going into the unfortunate episodes of the past? The best thing to do was to let bygones be bygones.

As the years went by and the scandals which came to light grew in number and in scope, it began to appear that the "mistakes" of 1921-23 had been larger than the friends of normalcy had supposed when they vented their spleen upon Senator Walsh. But the testimony, coming out intermittently as it did, was confusing and hard to piece together; plain citizens could not keep clear in their minds such complicated facts as those relating to the Continental bonds or the Daugherty bank-accounts; and the steady passage of time made the later investigations seem like a washing of very ancient dirty linen. Business was good, the Coolidge variety of normalcy was working to the satisfaction of the country. Coolidge was honest; why dwell unnecessarily on the past? Resentment at the scandals and resentment at the scandal-mongers both gave way to a profound and untroubled apathy. When the full story of the Continental Trading Company deal became known, John D. Rockefeller, Jr., as a large stockholder in the

Standard Oil of Indiana, waged war against Colonel Stewart and managed to put him out of the chairmanship of the company; but the business world as a whole seemed to find nothing wrong in Colonel Stewart's performance. The voice of John the Baptist was a voice crying in the wilderness.

Yet the reputation of the martyred President sank slowly and quietly lower. For years the great tomb at Marion, Ohio, that noble monument to which a sorrowing nation had so freely subscribed, remained undedicated. Clearly a monument to a President of the United States could hardly be dedicated by anybody but a President of the United States; Harding's successors, however, seemed to find it inconvenient to come to Marion for the ceremony. Late in 1930, over seven years after Harding's death, the Harding Memorial Association met to consider what should be done in this embarrassing situation. That dauntless friend of the late President, Harry M. Daugherty, who had once refrained from testifying because he knew things "as to which he would never make disclosure," made a florid speech in which he declared that the American people had never been swayed "by the lip of libel or the tongue of falsehood." He proposed that the dedication be indefinitely postponed. The resolution was duly passed. Later, however, it was decided by those in high position that the matter could not very well be left in this unsatisfactory position, and that good Republicans had better swallow their medicine and be done with it. President Hoover and ex-President Coolidge accepted invitations to take part in the dedication of the tomb in June, 1931, and the dedication accordingly took place at last. But a certain restraint was manifest in the proceedings. It was not so easy in 1931 as it had been in 1923 to compose panegyrics upon the public virtues of that good-natured man who had "taught us the power of brotherliness."

♦ VII ♦
COOLIDGE PROSPERITY

§ 1

Business was booming when Warren Harding died, and in a primitive Vermont farmhouse, by the light of an old-fashioned kerosene lamp, Colonel John Coolidge administered to his son Calvin the oath of office as President of the United States. The hopeless depression of 1921 had given way to the hopeful improvement of 1922 and the rushing revival of 1923.

The prices of common stocks, to be sure, suggested no unreasonable optimism. On August 2, 1923, the day of Harding's death, United States Steel (paying a five-dollar dividend) stood at 87, Atchison (paying six dollars) at 95, New York Central (paying seven) at 97, and American Telephone and Telegraph (paying nine) at 122; and the total turnover for the day on the New York Stock Exchange amounted to only a little over 600,000 shares. The Big Bull Market was still far in the future. Nevertheless the tide of prosperity was in full flood.

Pick up one of those graphs with which statisticians measure the economic ups and downs of the Post-war Decade. You will find that the line of business activity rises to a jagged peak in 1920, drops precipitously into a deep valley in late 1920 and 1921, climbs uncertainly upward through 1922 to another peak at the middle of 1923, dips somewhat in 1924 (but not nearly so far as in 1921), rises again in 1925 and 1926, dips momentarily but slightly toward the end of 1927, and then zigzags up to a perfect Everest of prosperity in 1929--only to plunge down at last into the bottomless abyss of 1930 and 1931.

Hold the graph at arm's-length and glance at it again, and you will see that the clefts of 1924 and 1927 are mere indentations in a lofty and irregular plateau which reaches from early 1923 to late 1929. That plateau represents nearly seven years of unparalleled plenty; nearly seven years during which men and women might be disillusioned about politics and religion and love, but believed that at the end of the rainbow there was at least a pot of negotiable legal tender consisting of the profits of American industry and American salesmanship; nearly seven years during which the businessman was, as Stuart Chase put it, "the dictator of our destinies," ousting "the statesman, the priest, the philosopher, as the creator of standards of ethics and behavior" and becoming "the final authority on the conduct of American society." For nearly seven years the prosperity bandwagon rolled down Main Street.

Not everyone could manage to climb aboard this wagon. Mighty few farmers could get so much as a fingerhold upon it. Some dairymen clung there, to be sure, and fruit-growers and truck-gardeners. For prodigious changes were taking place in the national diet as the result of the public's discovery of the useful vitamin, the propaganda for a more varied menu, and the invention of better methods of shipping perishable foods. Between 1919 and 1926 the national production of milk and milk products increased by one-third and that of ice-cream alone took a 45-percent jump. Between 1919 and 1928, as families learned that there were vitamins in celery, spinach, and carrots, and became accustomed to serving fresh vegetables the year round (along with fresh fruits), the acreage of nineteen commercial truck vegetable crops nearly doubled. But the growers of staple crops such as wheat and corn and cotton were in a bad way. Their foreign markets had dwindled under competition from other countries. Women were wearing less and less cotton. Few agricultural raw materials were used in the new economy of automobiles and radios and electricity. And the more efficient the poor farmer became, the more machines he bought to increase his output and thus keep the wolf from the door, the more surely he and his fellows were faced by the specter of overproduction. The index number of all farm prices, which had coasted from 205 in 1920 to 116 in 1921--"perhaps the most terrible toboggan slide in all American agricultural history," to quote Stuart Chase again--regained only a fraction of the ground it had lost: in 1927 it stood at 131. Loudly the poor farmers complained, desperately they and their Norrises and Brookharts and Shipsteads and La Follettes campaigned for federal aid, and by the hundreds of thousands they left the farm for the cities.

There were other industries unrepresented in the triumphal march of progress. Coal-mining suffered, and textile-manufacturing, and shipbuilding, and shoe and leather manufacturing. Whole regions of the country felt the effects of depression in one or more of these industries. The South was held back by cotton, the agricultural Northwest by the dismal condition of the wheat growers, New England by the paralysis of the textile and shoe industries. Nevertheless, the prosperity bandwagon did not lack for occupants, and their good fortune outweighed and outshouted the ill fortune of those who lamented by the roadside.

§ 2

In a position of honor rode the automobile manufacturer. His hour of destiny had struck. By this time paved roads and repair shops and filling stations had become so plentiful that the motorist might sally forth for the day without fear of being stuck in a mudhole or stranded without benefit of gasoline or crippled by a dead spark plug. Automobiles were now made with such precision, for that matter, that the motorist need hardly know a spark plug by sight; thousands of automobile owners had never even lifted the hood to see what the engine looked like. Now that closed cars were in quantity production, furthermore, the motorist had no need of Spartan blood, even in January. And the stylish new models were a delight to the eye. At the beginning of the decade most cars had been somber in color, but with the invention of pyroxylin finishes they broke out (in 1925 and 1926) into a whole rainbow of colors, from Florentine cream to Versailles violet. Bodies were swung lower, expert designers sought new harmonies of line, balloon tires came in, and at last even Henry Ford capitulated to style and beauty.

If any sign had been needed of the central place which the automobile had come to occupy in the mind and heart of the average American, it was furnished when the Model A Ford was brought out in December, 1927. Since the previous spring, when Henry Ford had shut down his gigantic plant, scrapped his Model T and the thousands of machines which brought it into being, and announced that he was going to put a new car on the market, the country had been in a state of suspense. Obviously he would have to make drastic changes. Model T had been losing to Chevrolet its leadership in the enormous low-priced-car market, for the time had come when people were no longer content with ugliness and a maximum speed of forty or forty-five miles an hour; no longer content, either, to roar slowly uphill with a weary left foot jammed against the low-speed pedal while robin's-egg blue Chevrolets swept past in second. Yet equally obviously Henry

Ford was the mechanical genius of the age. What miracle would he accomplish?

Rumor after rumor broke into the front pages of the newspapers. So intense was the interest that even the fact that an automobile dealer in Brooklyn had "learned something of the new car through a telegram from his brother Henry" was headline stuff. When the editor of the Brighton, Michigan, *Weekly Argus* actually snapped a photograph of a new Ford out for a trial spin, newspaper-readers pounced on the picture and avidly discussed its every line. The great day arrived when this newest product of the inventive genius of the age was to be shown to the public. The Ford Motor Company was running in 2,000 daily newspapers a five-day series of full-page advertisements at a total cost of $1,300,000; and everyone who could read was reading them. On December 2, 1927, when Model A was unveiled, one million people--so the *Herald-Tribune* figured--tried to get into the Ford headquarters in New York to catch a glimpse of it; as Charles Merz later reported in his life of Ford, "one hundred thousand people flocked into the showrooms of the Ford Company in Detroit; mounted police were called out to patrol the crowds in Cleveland; in Kansas City so great a mob stormed Convention Hall that platforms had to be built to lift the new car high enough for everyone to see it." So it went from one end of the United States to the other. Thousands of orders piled up on the Ford books for Niagara Blue roadsters and Arabian Sand phaetons. For weeks and months, every new Ford that appeared on the streets drew a crowd. To the motor-minded American people the first showing of a new kind of automobile was no matter of merely casual or commercial interest. It was one of the great events of the year 1927; not so thrilling as Lindbergh's flight, but rivaling the execution of Sacco and Vanzetti, the Hall-Mills murder trial, the Mississippi flood, and the Dempsey-Tunney fight at Chicago in its capacity to arouse public excitement.

In 1919 there had been 6,771,000 passenger cars in service in the United States; by 1929 there were no less than 23,121,000. There you have possibly the most potent statistic of Coolidge Prosperity. As a footnote to it I suggest the following: even as early as the end of 1923 there were two cars for every three families in "Middletown," a typical American city. The Lynds and their investigators interviewed 123 working-class families of "Middletown" and found that 60 of them had cars. Of these 60, 26 lived in such shabby-looking houses that the investigators thought to ask whether they had bathtubs, and discovered that as many as 21 of the 26 had none. The automobile came even before the tub!

And as it came, it changed the face of America. Villages which had once prospered because they were "on the railroad" languished with economic anæmia; villages on Route 61 bloomed with garages, filling stations, hot-dog stands, chicken-dinner restaurants, tearooms, tourists' rests, camping sites, and affluence. The interurban trolley perished, or survived only as a pathetic anachronism. Railroad after railroad gave up its branch lines, or saw its revenues slowly dwindling under the competition of mammoth interurban busses and trucks snorting along six-lane concrete highways. The whole country was covered with a network of passenger bus-lines. In thousands of towns, at the beginning of the decade a single traffic officer at the junction of Main Street and Central Street had been sufficient for the control of traffic. By the end of the decade, what a difference!--red and green lights, blinkers, oneway streets, boulevard stops, stringent and yet more stringent parking ordinances--and still a shining flow of traffic that backed up for blocks along Main Street every Saturday and Sunday afternoon. Slowly but surely the age of steam was yielding to the gasoline age.

§ 3

The radio manufacturer occupied a less important seat than the automobile manufacturer on the prosperity bandwagon, but he had the distinction of being the youngest rider. You will remember that there was no such thing as radio broadcasting to the public until the autumn of 1920, but that by the spring of 1922 radio had become a craze--as much talked about as Mah Jong was to be the following year or cross-word puzzles the year after. In 1922 the sales of radio sets, parts, and accessories amounted to $60,000,000. People wondered what would happen when the edge wore off the novelty of hearing a jazz orchestra in Schenectady or in Davenport, Iowa, play "Mr. Gallagher and Mr. Shean." What actually did happen is suggested by the cold figures of total annual radio sales for the next few years:

1922-- $60,000,000 (as we have just seen)
1923--$136,000,000
1924--$358,000,000
1925--$430,000,000
1926--$506,000,000

1927--$425,600,000
1928--$650,550,000
1929--$842,548,000 (an increase over the 1922 figures of 1,400 per cent!)

Don't hurry past those figures. Study them a moment, remembering that whenever there is a dip in the curve of national prosperity there is likely to be a dip in the sales of almost every popular commodity. There was a dip in national prosperity in 1927, for instance; do you see what it did to radio sales? But there was also a dip in 1924, a worse one in fact. Yet radio sales made in that year the largest proportional increase in the whole period. Why? Well, for one thing, that was the year in which the embattled Democrats met at Madison Square Garden in New York to pick a standard-bearer, and the deadlock between the hosts of McAdoo and the hosts of Al Smith lasted day after day after day, and millions of Americans heard through loud-speakers the lusty cry of, "Alabama, twenty-four votes for Underwoo--ood!" and discovered that a political convention could be a grand show to listen to and that a seat by the radio was as good as a ticket to the Garden. Better, in fact; for at any moment you could turn a knob and get "Barney Google" or "It Ain't Gonna Rain No More" by way of respite. At the age of three and a half years, radio broadcasting had attained its majority.

Behind those figures of radio sales lies a whole chapter of the life of the Post-war Decade: radio penetrating every third home in the country; giant broadcasting stations with nationwide hook-ups; tenement-house roofs covered with forests of antennæ; Roxy and his Gang, the Happiness Boys, the A & P Gypsies, and Rudy Vallee crooning from antique Florentine cabinet sets; Graham McNamee's voice, which had become more familiar to the American public than that of any other citizen of the land, shouting across your living room and mine: "*And* he did it! Yes, sir, he did it! It's a touchdown! Boy, I want to tell you this is one of the finest games . . ."; the Government belatedly asserting itself in 1927 to allocate wavelengths among competing radio stations; advertisers paying huge sums for the privilege of introducing Beethoven with a few well-chosen words about yeast or toothpaste; and Michael Meehan personally conducting the common stock of the Radio Corporation of America from a 1928 low of 85 $^1/_4$ to a 1929 high of 549.

There were other riders on the prosperity band-wagon. Rayon, cigarettes, refrigerators, telephones, chemical preparations (especially cosmetics), and electrical devices of various sorts all were in growing demand. While the independent storekeeper struggled to hold his own, the amount of retail business done in chain stores and department stores jumped by leaps and bounds. For every $100 worth of business done in 1919, by 1927 the five-and-ten-cent chains were doing $260 worth, the cigar chains $153 worth, the drug chains $224 worth, and the grocery chains $387 worth. Mrs. Smith no longer patronized her "naborhood" store; she climbed into her two-thousand-dollar car to drive to the red-fronted chain grocery and save twenty-seven cents on her daily purchases. The movies prospered, sending their celluloid reels all over the world and making Charlie Chaplin, Douglas Fairbanks, Gloria Swanson, Rudolph Valentino, and Clara Bow familiar figures to the Eskimo, the Malay, and the heathen Chinee; while at home the attendance at the motion-picture houses of "Middletown" during a single month (December, 1923) amounted to four and a half times the entire population of the city. Men, women, and children, rich and poor, the Middletowners went to the movies at an average rate of better than once a week!

Was this Coolidge Prosperity real? The farmers did not think so. Perhaps the textile manufacturers did not think so. But the figures of corporation profits and wages and incomes left little room for doubt. Consider, for example, two significant facts at opposite ends of the scale of wealth. Between 1922 and 1927, the purchasing power of American wages increased at the rate of more than two per cent annually. And during the three years between 1924 and 1927 alone there was a leap from 75 to 283 in the number of Americans who paid taxes on incomes of more than a million dollars a year.

§ 4

Why did it happen? What made the United States so prosperous?

Some of the reasons were obvious enough. The war had impoverished Europe and hardly damaged the United States at all; when peace came the Americans found themselves the economic masters of the world. Their young country, with enormous resources in materials and in human energy and with a wide domestic market, was ready to take advantage of this situation. It had developed mass production to a new point of mechanical and managerial efficiency. The Ford gospel of high wages, low prices, and standardized manufacture on a basis of the most minute division of machine-tending labor was working smoothly not only at Highland Park, but in thousands of other factories. Executives, remembering with a shudder the piled-up inventories of 1921, had learned the lesson of cautious hand-to-mouth buying; and they were surrounded with more expert technical consultants, research men, personnel managers, statisticians, and business forecasters than had ever before invaded that cave of the winds, the conference room. Their confidence was strengthened by their almost superstitious belief that the Republican Administration was their invincible ally. And they were all of them aided by the boom in the automobile industry. The phenomenal activity of this one part of the body economic--which was responsible, directly or indirectly, for the employment of nearly four million men--pumped new life into all the rest.

Prosperity was assisted, too, by two new stimulants to purchasing, each of which mortgaged the future but kept the factories roaring while it was being injected. The first was the increase in installment buying. People were getting to consider it old-fashioned to limit their purchases to the amount of their cash balance; the thing to do was to "exercise their credit." By the latter part of the decade, economists figured that 15 per cent of all retail sales were on an installment basis, and that there were some six billions of "easy payment" paper outstanding. The other stimulant was stock-market speculation. When stocks were skyrocketing in 1928 and 1929 it is probable that hundreds of thousands of people were buying goods with money which represented, essentially, a gamble on the business profits of the nineteen-thirties. It was fun while it lasted. If these were the principal causes of Coolidge Prosperity, the salesman and the advertising man were at least its agents and evangels. Business had learned as never before the immense importance to it of the ultimate consumer. Unless he could be persuaded to buy and buy lavishly, the whole stream of six-cylinder cars, super-heterodynes, cigarettes, rouge compacts, and electric ice-boxes would be dammed at its outlet. The salesman and the advertising man held the key to this outlet. As competition increased their methods became more strenuous. No longer was it considered enough to recommend one's goods in modest and explicit terms and to place them on the counter in the hope that the ultimate consumer would make up his mind to purchase. The advertiser must plan elaborate national campaigns, consult with psychologists, and employ all the eloquence of poets to cajole, exhort, or intimidate the consumer into buying--to "break down consumer resistance." Not only was each individual concern struggling to get a larger share of the business in its own field, but whole industries shouted against one another in the public's ear. The embattled candy manufacturers took full-page space in the newspapers to reply to the American Tobacco Company's slogan of "Reach for a Lucky instead of a sweet." Trade journals were quoted by the *Reader's Digest* as reporting the efforts of the furniture manufacturers to make the people "furniture conscious" and of the clothing manufacturers to make them "tuxedo conscious." The salesman must have the ardor of a zealot, must force his way into people's houses by hook or by crook, must let nothing stand between him and the consummation of his sale. As executives put it, "You can't be an order-taker any longer--you've got to be a *salesman.*" The public, generally speaking, could be relied upon to regard with complacence the most flagrant assaults upon its credulity by the advertiser and the most outrageous invasions of its privacy by the salesman; for the public was in a mood to forgive every sin committed in the holy name of business.

Never before had such pressure been exerted upon salesmen to get results. Many concerns took up the quota system, setting as the objective for each sales representative a figure 20 or 25 per cent beyond that of the previous year, and putting it up to him to reach this figure or lose his employer's favor and perhaps his job. All sorts of sales contests and other ingenious devices were used to stimulate the force. Among the schemes suggested by the Dartnell Company of Chicago, which had more than ten thousand American business organizations subscribing to its service, was that of buying various novelties and sending them to the salesman at weekly intervals: one week a miniature feather duster with a tag urging him to "dust his territory," another week an imitation cannon cracker with the injunction to "make a big noise," and so on. The American Slicing Machine Company offered a turkey at Christmas to every one of its salesmen who beat his quota for the year. "We asked each man," explained the sales manager afterward, "to appoint a child in his family as a mascot, realizing that every one of them would work his head off to make some youngster happy at Christmas. The way these youngsters took hold of the plan was amusing, and at times the intensity of their interest was almost pathetic." The sales manager of another concern reported cheerfully that "one of his stunts" was "to twit one man at the good work of another until he is almost sore enough to be ready to fight." And according to Jesse Rainsford Sprague, still another company invented--and boasted of--a method of goading its salesmen which for sheer inhumanity probably set a record for the whole era of Coolidge Prosperity. It gave a banquet at which the man with the best score was served with oysters, roast turkey, and a most elaborate ice; the man with the second best score had the same dinner but without the oysters; and so on down to the man with the worst score, before whom was laid a small plate of boiled beans and a couple of crackers.

If the salesman was sometimes under pressure such as this, it is not surprising that the consumer felt the pressure, too. Let two extreme instances (both cited by Jesse Rainsford Sprague) suffice to suggest the trend in business methods. A wholesale drug concern offered to the trade a small table with a railing round its top for the display of "specials"; it was to be set up directly in the path of customers, "whose attention," according to *Printer's Ink,* "will be attracted to the articles when they fall over it, bump into it, kick their shins upon it, or otherwise come in contact with it." And *Selling News* awarded one of its cash prizes for "sales ideas" to a vender of electric cleaners who told the following story of commercial prowess. One day he looked up from the street and saw a lady shaking a rug out of a second-story window. "The door leading to her upstairs rooms was open. I went right in and up those stairs without knocking, greeting the lady with the remark: 'Well, I am here right on time. What room do you wish me to start in?' She was very much surprised, assuring me that I had the wrong number. But during my very courteous apologies I had managed to get my cleaner connected and in action. The result was that I walked out minus the cleaner, plus her contract and check for a substantial down payment." The readers of *Selling News* were apparently not expected to be less than enthusiastic at the prospect of a man invading a woman's apartment and setting up a cleaner in it without permission and under false pretenses. For if you could get away with such exploits, it helped business, and good business helped prosperity, and prosperity was good for the country.

§ 5

The advertisers met the competition of the new era with better design, persuasively realistic photographs, and sheer volume: the amount of advertising done in 1927, according to Francis H. Sisson, came to over a billion and a half dollars. They met it with a new frankness, introducing to staid magazine readers the advantages of Odo-ro-no and Kotex. And they met it, furthermore, with a subtle change in technique. The copywriter was learning to pay less attention to the special qualities and advantages of his product, and more to the study of what the mass of unregenerate mankind wanted--to be young and desirable, to be rich, to keep up with the Joneses, to be envied. The winning method was to associate his product with one or more of these ends, logically or illogically, truthfully or cynically; to draw a lesson from the dramatic case of some imaginary man or woman whose fate was altered by the use of X's soap, to show that in the most fashionable circles people were choosing the right cigarette in blindfold tests, or to suggest by means of glowing testimonials--often bought and paid for--that the advertised product was used by women of fashion, movie stars, and non-stop flyers. One queen of the films was said to have journeyed from California all the way to New York to spend a single exhausting day being photographed for testimonial purposes in dozens of costumes and using dozens of commercial articles, many of which she had presumably never laid eyes on before--and all because the appearance of these testimonials would help advertise her newest picture. Of what value were sober facts from the laboratory: did not a tooth-powder manufacturer try to meet the hokum of emotional toothpaste advertising by citing medical authorities, and was not his counter-campaign as a breath in a gale? At the beginning of the decade advertising had been considered a business; in the early days of Coolidge Prosperity its fulsome prophets were calling it a profession; but by the end of the decade many of its practitioners, observing the overwhelming victory of methods taken over from tabloid journalism, were beginning to refer to it--among themselves-- as a racket.

A wise man of the nineteen-twenties might have said that he cared not who made the laws of the country if he only might write its national advertising. For here were the sagas of the age, romances and tragedies depicting characters who became more familiar to the populace than those in any novel. The man who distinctly remembered Mr. Addison Sims of Seattle. . . . The four out of five who, failing to use Forhan's, succumbed to pyorrhea, each of them with a white mask mercifully concealing his unhappy mouth. . . . The pathetic figure of the man, once a golf champion, "now only a wistful onlooker" creeping about after the star players, his shattered health due to tooth neglect. . . . The poor fellow sunk in the corner of a taxicab, whose wife upbraided him with not having said a word all evening (when he might so easily have shone with the aid of the *Elbert Hubbard Scrap Book*). . . . The man whose conversation so dazzled the company that the envious dinner-coated bystanders could only breathe in amazement, "I think he's quoting from Shelley." . . . The woman who would undoubtedly do something about B. O. if people only said to her what they really thought. . . . The man whose friends laughed when the waiter spoke to him in French. . . . The girl who thought filet mignon was a kind of fish. . . . The poor couple who faced one another in humiliation after their guests were gone, the wife still holding the door knob and struggling against her tears, the husband biting his nails with shame (When Your Guests Are Gone--Are You Sorry You Ever Invited Them? . . . Be Free From All Embarrassment! Let the Famous *Book of Etiquette* Tell You Exactly What to Do, Say, Write, or Wear on Every Occasion). . . . The girl who merely carried the daisy chain, yet she had athlete's foot. . . . These men and women of the advertising pages, suffering or triumphant, became a part of the folklore of the day.

Sometimes their feats were astonishing. Consider, for example, the man who had purchased Nelson Doubleday's *Pocket University,* and found himself, one evening, in a group in which some one mentioned Ali Baba:

"Ali Baba? I sat forward in my chair. I could tell them all about this romantic, picturesque figure of fiction.

"I don't know how it happened, but they gathered all around me. And I told them of golden ships that sailed the seven seas, of a famous man and his donkey who wandered unknown ways, of the brute-man from whom we are all descended. I told them things they never knew of Cleopatra, of the eccentric Diogenes, of Romulus and the founding of Rome. I told them of the unfortunate death of Sir Raleigh *(sic),* of the tragic end of poor Anne Boleyn. . . .

"'You must have traveled all over the world to know so many marvelous things.'"

Skeptics might smile, thanking themselves that they were not of the company on that interminable evening; but the advertisement stuck in their minds. And to others, less sophisticated, it doubtless opened shining vistas of delight. They, too, could hold the dinner party spellbound if only they filled out the coupon. . . .

By far the most famous of these dramatic advertisements of the Postwar Decade was the long series in which the awful results of halitosis were set forth through the depiction of a gallery of unfortunates whose closest friends would not tell them. "Often a bridesmaid but never a bride. . . . Edna's case was really a pathetic one." . . . "Why did she leave him that way?" . . . *That's* why you're a failure," . . . and then that devilishly ingenious display which capitalized on the fears aroused by earlier tragedies in the series: the picture of a girl looking at a Listerine advertisement and saying to herself, "This *can't* apply to me!" Useless for the American Medical Association to insist that Listerine was "not a true deodorant," that it simply covered one smell with another. Just as useless as for the Life Extension Institute to find "one out of twenty with pyorrhea, rather than Mr. Forhan's famous four-out-of-five" (to quote Stuart Chase once more). Halitosis had the power of dramatic advertising behind it, and Listerine swept to greater and greater profits on a tide of public trepidation.

§ 6

As year followed year of prosperity, the new diffusion of wealth brought marked results. There had been a great boom in higher education immediately after the war, and the boom continued, although at a somewhat slackened pace, until college trustees were beside themselves wondering how to find room for the swarming applicants. There was an epidemic of outlines of knowledge and books of etiquette for those who had got rich quick and wanted to get cultured quick and become socially at ease. Wells's *Outline of History,* the best-selling non-fiction book of 1921 and 1922, was followed by Van Loon's *Story of Mankind,* J. Arthur Thomson's *Outline of Science* (both of them best sellers in 1922), the Doubleday mail-order *Book of Etiquette* and Emily Post's *Book of Etiquette* (which led the non-fiction list in 1923), *Why We Behave Like Human Beings* (a big success of 1926), and *The Story of Philosophy,* which ran away from all other books in the non-fiction list of 1927.

There was a rush of innocents abroad. According to the figures of the Department of Commerce, over 437,000 people left the United States by ship for foreign parts in the year 1928 alone, to say nothing of 14,000 odd who entered Canada and Mexico by rail, and over three million cars which crossed into Canada for a day or more. The innocents spent freely: the money that they left abroad, in fact (amounting in 1928 to some $650,000,000), solved for a time a difficult problem in international finance: how the United States could continue to receive interest on her foreign debts and foreign investments without permitting foreign goods to pass the high tariff barrier in large quantities.

The United States became the banker and financial arbitrator for the world. When the financial relations between Germany and the Allies needed to be straightened out, it was General Charles G. Dawes and Owen D. Young who headed the necessary international commission's--not only because their judgment was considered wise, and impartial as between the countries of Europe, but because the United States was in a position to call the tune. Americans were called in to reorganize the finances of one country after another. American investments abroad increased by leaps and bounds. The squat limestone building at the corner of Broad and Wall Streets, still wearing the scars of the shrapnel which had struck it during the 1920 explosion, had become the undisputed financial center of the world. Only occasionally did the United States have to intervene by force of arms in other countries. The Marines ruled Haiti and restored order in Nicaragua; but in general the country extended its empire not by military conquest or political dictation, but by financial penetration.

At home, one of the most conspicuous results of prosperity was the conquest of the whole country by urban tastes and urban dress and the urban way of living. The rube disappeared. Girls in the villages of New Hampshire and Wyoming wore the same brief skirts and used the same lipsticks as their sisters in New York. The proletariat--or what the radicals of the Big Red Scare days had called the proletariat--gradually lost its class consciousness; the American Federation of Labor dwindled in membership and influence; the time had come when workingmen owned second-hand Buicks and applauded Jimmy Walker, not objecting in the least, it seemed, to his exquisite clothes, his valet, and his frequent visits to the millionaire-haunted sands of Palm Beach. It was no accident that men like Mellon and Hoover and Morrow found their wealth an asset rather than a liability in public office, or that there was a widespread popular movement to make Henry Ford President in 1924. The possession of millions was a sign of success, and success was worshipped the country over.

§ 7

Business itself was regarded with a new veneration. Once it had been considered less dignified and distinguished than the learned professions, but now people thought they praised a clergyman highly when they called him a good businessman. College alumni, gathered at their annual banquets, fervently applauded the banker trustees who spoke of education as one of the greatest American industries and compared the president and the dean to business executives. The colleges themselves organized business courses and cheerfully granted credit to candidates for degrees in the arts and sciences for their work in advertising copy-writing, marketing methods, elementary stenography, and drug-store practice. Even Columbia University drew men and women into its home-study courses by a system of follow-up letters worthy of a manufacturer of refrigerators, and sent out salesmen to ring the door bells of those who expressed a flicker of interest; even the great University of Chicago made use of what André Siegfried has called "the mysticism of success" by heading an advertisement of its correspondence courses with the admonition to "DEVELOP POWER AT HOME, to investigate, persevere, achieve." . . . The Harvard Business School established annual advertising awards, conferring academic *éclat* upon well-phrased sales arguments for commercial products. It was not easy for the churches to resist the tide of business enthusiasm. The Swedish Immanuel Congregational Church in New York, according to an item in the *American Mercury,* recognized the superiority of the business to the spiritual appeal by offering to all who contributed one hundred dollars to its building fund "an engraved certificate of investment in preferred capital stock in the Kingdom of God." And a church billboard in uptown New York struck the same persuasive note: "Come to Church. Christian Worship Increases Your Efficiency. Christian F. Reisner, Pastor."

In every American city and town, service clubs gathered the flower of the middle-class citizenry together for weekly luncheons noisy with good fellowship. They were growing fast, these service clubs. Rotary, the most famous of them, had been founded in 1905; by 1930 it had 150,000 members and boasted--as a sign of its international influence--as many as 3,000 clubs in 44 countries. The number of Kiwanis Clubs rose from 205 in 1920 to 1,800 in 1929; the Lions Clubs, of which the first was not formed until 1917, multiplied until at the end of the decade there were 1,200 of them. Nor did these clubs content themselves with singing songs and conducting social-

139

service campaigns; they expressed the national faith in what one of their founders called "the redemptive and regenerative influence of business." The speakers before them pictured the businessman as a builder, a doer of great things, yes, and a dreamer whose imagination was ever seeking out new ways of serving humanity. It was a popular note, for in hundreds of directors' rooms, around hundreds of conference tables, the American businessmen of the era of Coolidge Prosperity were seeing themselves as men of vision with eyes steadfastly fixed on the long future. At the end of the decade, a cartoon in the *New Yorker* represented an executive as saying to his heavy-jowled colleagues at one of these meetings: "We have ideas. Possibly we tilt at windmills--just seven Don Juans tilting at windmills." It was a perfect bit of satire on business sentimentality. The service club specialized in this sort of mysticism: was not a speaker before the Rotarians of Waterloo, Iowa, quoted by the *American Mercury* as declaring that "Rotary is a manifestation of the divine"?

Indeed, the association of business with religion was one of the most significant phenomena of the day. When the National Association of Credit Men held their annual convention at New York, there were provided for the three thousand delegates a special devotional service at the Cathedral of St. John the Divine and five sessions of prayer conducted by Protestant clergymen, a Roman Catholic priest, and a Jewish rabbi; and the credit men were uplifted by a sermon by Dr. S. Parkes Cadman on "Religion in Business." Likewise the Associated Advertising Clubs, meeting in Philadelphia, listened to a keynote address by Doctor Cadman on "Imagination and Advertising," and at the meeting of the Church Advertising Department the subjects discussed included "Spiritual Principles in Advertising" and "Advertising the Kingdom through Press-Radio Service." The fact that each night of the session a cabaret entertainment was furnished to the earnest delegates from 11:30 to 2 and that part of the Atlantic City Beauty Pageant was presented was merely a sign that even men of high faith must have their fun.

So frequent was the use of the Bible to point the lessons of business and of business to point the lessons of the Bible that it was sometimes difficult to determine which was supposed to gain the most from the association. Fred F. French, a New York builder and real-estate man, told his salesmen, "There is no such thing as a reason why not," and continued: "One evidence of the soundness of this theory may be found in the command laid down in Matthew vii:7 by the Greatest Human-nature Expert that ever lived, 'Knock and it shall be opened unto you.'" He continued by quoting "the greatest command of them all--'Love Thy Neighbor as Thyself'"--and then stated that by following such high principles the Fred F. French salesmen had "immeasurably strengthened their own characters and power, so that during this year they will serve our stockholders at a lower commission rate, and yet each one will earn more money for himself than in nineteen hundred twenty-five." In this case Scripture was apparently taken as setting a standard for business to meet--to its own pecuniary profit. Yet in other cases it was not so certain that business was not the standard, and Scripture complimented by being lifted to the business level.

Witness, for example, the pamphlet on *Moses, Persuader of Men* issued by the Metropolitan Casualty Insurance Company (with an introduction by the indefatigable Doctor Cadman), which declared that "Moses was one of the greatest salesmen and real-estate promoters that ever lived," that he was a "Dominant, Fearless, and Successful Personality in one of the most magnificent selling campaigns that history ever placed upon its pages." And witness, finally, the extraordinary message preached by Bruce Barton in *The Man Nobody Knows,* which so touched the American heart that for two successive years--1925 and 1926--it was the best-selling non-fiction book in the United States. Barton sold Christianity to the public by showing its resemblance to business. Jesus, this book taught, was not only "the most popular dinner guest in Jerusalem" and "an outdoor man," but a great executive. "He picked up twelve men from the bottom ranks of business and forged them into an organization that conquered the world. . . . Nowhere is there such a startling example of executive success as the way in which that organization was brought together." His parables were "the most powerful advertisements of all time. . . . He would be a national advertiser today." In fact, Jesus was "the founder of modern business." Why, you ask? Because he was the author of the ideal of service.

The Gospel According to Bruce Barton met a popular demand. Under the beneficent influence of Coolidge Prosperity, business had become almost the national religion of America. Millions of people wanted to be reassured that this religion was altogether right and proper, and that in the rules for making big money lay all the law and the prophets.

Was it strange that during the very years when the Barton Gospel was circulating most vigorously, selling and advertising campaigns were becoming more cynical and the American business world was refusing to exercise itself over the Teapot Dome disclosures and the sordid history of the Continental Trading Company? Perhaps; but it must be remembered that in all religions there is likely to be a gap between faith and works. The businessman's halo did not always fit, but he wore it proudly.

§ 8

So the prosperity band-wagon rolled along with throttle wide open and siren blaring. But what of the man on the driver's seat, the man whose name this era bore?

He did not have a jutting chin, a Powerful Personality, or an irresistible flow of selling talk. If you had come from Timbuctoo and found him among a crowd of Chamber of Commerce boosters, he would have been the last man you would have picked as their patron saint. He had never been in business. His canonization by the hosts of quantity production and high-pressure salesmanship was a sublime paradox--and yet it was largely justified. Almost the most remarkable thing about Coolidge Prosperity was Calvin Coolidge.

He was a meager-looking man, a Vermonter with a hatchet face, sandy hair, tight lips, and the expression, as William Allen White remarked, of one "looking down his nose to locate that evil smell which seemed forever to affront him." He was pale and diffident. In private he could be garrulous, but in public he was as silent as a cake of ice. When his firmness in the Boston police strike captured the attention of the country and brought him to Washington as Vice-President, not even the affable warmth of the Harding Administration could thaw him. The Vice-President has to go to many a formal dinner; Coolidge went--and said nothing. The hostesses of Washington were dismayed and puzzled. "Over the Alps lay Italy, they thought, but none of them had won the summit and so they couldn't be sure that the view was worth the climb," wrote Edward G. Lowry. Coolidge became President, and still the frost continued.

Nor did this silence cloak a wide-ranging mind. Coolidge knew his American history, but neither he nor his intellect had ever ventured far abroad. Go through his addresses and his smug *Autobiography,* and the most original thing you will find in them is his uncompromising unoriginality. Calvin Coolidge still believed in the old American copybook maxims when almost everybody else had half forgotten them or was beginning to doubt them. "The success which is made in any walk of life is measured almost exactly by the amount of hard work that is put into it. . . . There is only one form of political strategy in which I have any confidence, and that is to try to do the right thing and sometimes be able to succeed. . . . If society lacks learning and virtue it will perish. . . . The nation with the greatest moral power will win. . . ." This philosophy of hard work and frugal living and piety crowned with success might have been brought down from some Vermont attic where *McGuffy's Reader* gathered dust. But it was so old that it looked new; it was so exactly what uncounted Americans had been taught at their mother's knee that it touched what remained of the pioneer spirit in their hearts; and Coolidge set it forth with refreshing brevity. So completely did it win over the country that if the President had declared that a straight line is the shortest distance between two points, one wonders if editorial pages would not have paid tribute to his concise wisdom.

He was not a bold leader, nor did he care to be. He followed no gleam, stormed no redoubt. Considering the fact that he was in the White House for five years and seven months, his presidential record was surprisingly negative. But it was just the sort of record that he preferred.

In its foreign policy, his Administration made little effort to persuade the American people that they were not happily isolated from the outside world. Bankers might engage in determining the amount of German reparations, unofficial observers might sit in on European negotiations, but the Government, remembering the decline and fall of Woodrow Wilson, shrewdly maintained an air of magnificent unconcern. Coolidge proposed, as had Harding before him, that the United States should join the World Court, but so gently that when the Senate eventually ratified the proposal with reservations which the other member nations were unable to accept, and the President went out of office without having achieved his end, nobody felt that his prestige suffered much thereby. A second naval conference was held at Geneva in 1927, but ended in failure. A Nicaraguan revolution was settled--after considerable turmoil and humiliation--with the aid of the Marines and of Henry L. Stimson's plan for a new election under American supervision. An even more bitter dispute with Mexico over the legal status of oil lands owned by American interests was finally moderated through the wisdom and tact of Coolidge's Amherst classmate and ambassador, Dwight W. Morrow. But the most conspicuous achievement of the Coolidge Administration in foreign affairs was the leading part it took in securing the Kellogg-Briand Treaty renouncing war as an instrument of national policy--a fine gesture which every nation was delighted to make but which had very little noticeable influence on the actualities of international relations. Aside from the belated solution of the Nicaraguan and Mexican difficulties and the championship of this somewhat innocuous treaty, the policy of the Coolidge Administration was to collect the money due it (even at the expense of considerable ill-feeling), to keep a watchful eye on the expansion of the American financial empire, and otherwise to let well enough alone.

Coolidge's record in domestic affairs was even less exciting. He was nothing if not cautious. When the Harding scandals came to light, he did what was necessary to set in motion an official prosecution, he adroitly jockeyed the notorious Daugherty out of the Cabinet, and from that moment on he exhibited an unruffled and altogether convincing calm. When there was a strike in the anthracite coal mines he did not leap into the breach; he let Governor Gifford Pinchot of Pennsylvania do it. On the one burning political issue of the day, that of prohibition, he managed to express no opinion except that the laws should be enforced. There was dynamite in prohibition; Calvin Coolidge remained at a safe distance and looked the other way.

He maintained the *status quo* for the benefit of business. Twice he vetoed farm relief legislation--to the immense satisfaction of the industrial and banking community which constituted his strongest support--on the ground that the McNary-Haugen bills were economically unsound. He vetoed the soldier bonus, too, on the ground of its expense, though in this case his veto was overruled. His proudest boast was that he cut down the cost of running the Government by systematic cheeseparing, reduced the public debt, and brought about four reductions in federal taxes, aiding not only those with small incomes but even more conspicuously those with large. Meanwhile his Secretary of Commerce, Herbert Hoover, ingeniously helped business to help itself; on the various governmental commissions, critics of contemporary commercial practices were replaced, as far as possible, by those who would look upon business with a lenient eye; and the serene quiet which lay about the White House was broken only by occasional flattering pronouncements upon business and assurances that prosperity was securely founded.

An uninspired and unheroic policy, you suggest? But it was sincere: Calvin Coolidge honestly believed that by asserting himself as little as possible and by lifting the tax burdens of the rich he was benefiting the whole country--as perhaps he was. And it was perfectly in keeping with the uninspired and unheroic political temper of the times. For the lusty businessmen who in these fat years had become the arbiters of national opinion did not envisage the Government as an agency for making over the country into something a little nearer to their hearts' desire, as a champion of human rights or a redresser of wrongs. The prosperity band-wagon was bringing them rapidly toward their hearts' desire, and politics might block the traffic. They did not want a man of action in the Presidency; they wanted as little government as possible, at as low cost as possible, and this dour New Englander who drove the prosperity band-wagon with so slack a rein embodied their idea of supreme statesmanship.

Statesmanship of a sort Calvin Coolidge certainly represented. Prosperity has its undeniable advantages, and a President who is astute enough to know how to encourage it without getting himself into hot water may possibly be forgiven such complacency as appears in his *Autobiography*. There is perhaps a cool word to be said, too, for the prudence which deliberately accepts the inevitable, which does not even try to be bolder or more magnanimous than circumstances will safely permit. The great god Business was supreme in the land, and Calvin Coolidge was fortunate enough to become almost a demi-god by doing discreet obeisance before the altar.

♦ VIII ♦
THE BALLYHOO YEARS

§ 1

All nations, in all eras of history, are swept from time to time by waves of contagious excitement over fads or fashions or dramatic public issues. But the size and frequency of these waves is highly variable, as is the nature of the events which set them in motion. One of the striking characteristics of the era of Coolidge Prosperity was the unparalleled rapidity and unanimity with which millions of men and women turned their attention, their talk, and their emotional interest upon a series of tremendous trifles--a heavyweight boxing-match, a murder trial, a new automobile model, a transatlantic flight.

Most of the *causes célèbres* which thus stirred the country from end to end were quite unimportant from the traditional point of view of the historian. The future destinies of few people were affected in the slightest by the testimony of the "pig woman" at the Hall-Mills trial or the attempt to rescue Floyd Collins from his Kentucky cave. Yet the fact that such things could engage the hopes and fears of unprecedented numbers of people was anything but unimportant. No account of the Coolidge years would be adequate which did not review that strange procession of events which a nation tired of "important issues" swarmed to watch, or which did not take account of that remarkable chain of circumstances which produced as the hero of the age, not a great public servant, not a reformer, not a warrior, but a stunt flyer who crossed the ocean to win a money prize.

By the time Calvin Coolidge reached the White House, the tension of the earlier years of the Post-war Decade had been largely relaxed. Though Woodrow Wilson still clung feebly to life in the sunny house in S Street, the League issue was dead and only handfuls of irreconcilable idealists imagined it to have a chance of resuscitation. The radicals were discouraged, the labor movement had lost energy and prestige since the days of the Big Red Scare, and under the beneficent influence of easy riches--or at least of easy Fords and

Chevrolets--individualistic capitalism had settled itself securely in the saddle. The Ku Klux Klan numbered its millions, yet already it was beginning to lose that naïve ardor which had lighted its fires on a thousand hilltops; it was becoming less of a crusade and more of a political racket. Genuine public issues, about which the masses of the population could be induced to feel intensely, were few and far between. There was prohibition, to be sure; anybody could get excited about prohibition; but because the division of opinion on liquor cut across party lines, every national politician, almost without exception, did his best to thrust this issue into the background. In the agricultural Northwest and Middle West there was a violent outcry for farm relief, but it could command only a scattered and half-hearted interest throughout the rest of a nation which was becoming progressively urbanized. Public spirit was at low ebb; over the World Court, the oil scandals, the Nicaraguan situation, the American people as a whole refused to bother themselves. They gave their energies to triumphant business, and for the rest they were in holiday mood. "Happy," they might have said, "is the nation which has no history--and a lot of good shows to watch." They were ready for any good show that came along.

It was now possible in the United States for more people to enjoy the same good show at the same time than in any other land on earth or at any previous time in history. Mass production was not confined to automobiles; there was mass production in news and ideas as well. For the system of easy nation-wide communication which had long since made the literate and prosperous American people a nation of faddists was rapidly becoming more widely extended, more centralized, and more effective than ever before.

To begin with, there were fewer newspapers, with larger circulations, and they were standardized to an unprecedented degree by the increasing use of press-association material and syndicated features. Between 1914 and 1926, as Silas Bent has pointed out, the number of daily papers in the country dropped from 2,580 to 2,001, the number of Sunday papers dropped from 571 to 541, and the aggregate circulation per issue rose from somewhat over 28,000,000 to 36,000,000. The city of Cleveland, which a quarter of a century before had had three morning papers, now had but one; Detroit, Minneapolis, and St. Louis had lost all but one apiece; Chicago, during a period in which it had doubled in population, had seen the number of its morning dailies drop from seven to two. Newspapers all over the country were being gathered into chains under more or less centralized direction: by 1927 the success of the Hearst and Scripps-Howard systems and the hope of cutting down overhead costs had led to the formation of no less than 55 chains controlling 230 daily papers with a combined circulation of over 13,000,000.

No longer did the local editor rely as before upon local writers and cartoonists to fill out his pages and give them a local flavor; the central office of the chain, or newspaper syndicates in New York, could provide him with editorials, health talks, comic strips, sob-sister columns, household hints, sports gossip, and Sunday features prepared for a national audience and guaranteed to tickle the mass mind. Andy Gump and Dorothy Dix had their millions of admirers from Maine to Oregon, and the words hammered out by a reporter at Jack Dempsey's training-camp were devoured with one accord by real-estate men in Florida and riveters in Seattle.

Meanwhile, the number of national magazines with huge circulations had increased, the volume of national advertising had increased, a horde of publicity agents had learned the knack of associating their cause or product with whatever happened to be in the public mind at the moment, and finally there was the new and vastly important phenomenon of radio broadcasting, which on occasion could link together a multitude of firesides to hear the story of a World Series game or a Lindbergh welcome. The national mind had become as never before an instrument upon which a few men could play. And these men were learning, as Mr. Bent has also shown, to play upon it in a new way--to concentrate upon *one tune at a time.*

Not that they put their heads together and deliberately decided to do this. Circumstances and self-interest made it the almost inevitable thing for them to do. They discovered--the successful tabloids were daily teaching them--that the public tended to become excited about one thing at a time. Newspaper owners and editors found that whenever a Dayton trial or a *Vestris* disaster took place, they sold more papers if they gave it all they had--their star reporters, their front-page display, and the bulk of their space. They took full advantage of this discovery: according to Mr. Bent's compilations, the insignificant Gray-Snyder murder trial got a bigger "play" in the press than the sinking of the *Titanic;* Lindbergh's flight, than the Armistice and the overthrow of the German Empire. Syndicate managers and writers, advertisers, press agents, radio broadcasters, all were aware that mention of the leading event of the day, whatever it might be, was the key to public interest. The result was that when something happened which promised to appeal to the popular mind, one had it hurled at one in huge headlines, waded through page after page of syndicated discussion of it, heard about it on the radio, was reminded of it again and again in the outpourings of publicity-seeking orators and preachers, saw pictures of it in the Sunday papers and in the movies, and (unless one was a perverse individualist) enjoyed the sensation of vibrating to the same chord which thrilled a vast populace.

The country had bread, but it wanted circuses--and now it could go to them a hundred million strong.

§ 2

Mah Jong was still popular during the winter of 1923-24--the winter when Calvin Coolidge was becoming accustomed to the White House, and the Bok Peace Prize was awarded, and the oil scandals broke, and Woodrow Wilson died, and General Dawes went overseas to preside over the reparations conference, and *So Big* outsold all other novels, and people were tiring of "Yes, We Have No Bananas," and to the delight of every rotogravure editor the lid of the stone sarcophagus of King Tutankhamen's tomb was raised at Luxor. Mah Jong was popular, but it had lost its novelty.

It was during that winter--on January 2, 1924, to be precise-- that a young man in New York called on his aunt. The aunt had a relative who was addicted to the cross-word puzzles which appeared every Sunday in the magazine supplement of the *New York World,* and asked the young man whether there was by any chance a book of these puzzles; it might make a nice present for her relative. The young man, on due inquiry, found that there was no such thing as a book of them, although cross-word puzzles dated back at least to 1913 and had been published in the *World* for years. But as it happened, he himself (his name was Richard Simon) was at that very moment launching a book-publishing business with his friend Schuster--and with one girl as their entire staff. Simon had a bright idea, which he communicated to Schuster the next day: *they* would bring out a cross-word-puzzle book. The two young men asked Prosper Buranelli, F. Gregory Hartswick, and Margaret Petherbridge, the puzzle editors of the *World,* to prepare it; and despite a certain coolness on the part of the book-sellers, who told them that the public "wasn't interested in puzzle books," they brought it out in mid-April. Their promotion campaign was ingenious and proved to be prophetic, for from the very beginning they advertised their book by drawing the following parallel:

1921--Coué
1922--Mah Jong
1923--Bananas
1924--THE CROSS-WORD-PUZZLE BOOK

Within a month this odd-looking volume with a pencil attached to it had become a best seller. By the following winter its sales had mounted into the hundreds of thousands, other publishers were falling over themselves to get out books which would reap an advantage from the craze, it was a dull newspaper which did not have its daily puzzle, sales of dictionaries were bounding, there was a new demand for that ancient and honorable handmaid of the professional writer, Roget's *Thesaurus,* a man had been sent to jail in New York for refusing to leave a restaurant after four hours of trying to solve a puzzle, and Mrs. Mary Zaba of Chicago was reported to be a "cross-word widow," her husband apparently being so busy with puzzles that he had no time to support her. The newspapers carried the news that a Pittsburgh pastor had put the text of his sermon into a puzzle. The Baltimore and Ohio Railroad placed dictionaries in all the trains on its main line. A traveler between New York and Boston reported that 60 per cent of the passengers were trying to fill up the squares in their puzzles, and that in the dining-car five waiters were trying to think of a five-letter word which meant "serving to inspire fear." Anybody you met on the street could tell you the name of the Egyptian sun-god or provide you with the two-letter word which meant a printer's measure.

The cross-word puzzle craze gradually died down in 1925. It was followed by a minor epidemic of question-and-answer books; there was a time when ladies and gentlemen with vague memories faced frequent humiliation after dinner because they were unable to identify John Huss or tell what an ohm was. Not until after contract bridge was introduced in the United States in 1926 did they breathe easily. Despite the decline of the cross-word puzzle, however, it remained throughout the rest of the decade a daily feature in most newspapers; and Simon and Schuster, bringing out their sixteenth series in 1930, figured their total sales since early 1924 at nearly three-quarters of a million copies, and the grand total, including British and Canadian sales, at over two million.

§ 3

This craze, like the Mah Jong craze which preceded it, was a fresh indication of the susceptibility of the American people to fads, but it was not in any real sense a creature of the new ballyhoo newspaper technique. The newspapers did not pick it up until it was well on its way. The greatest demonstrations of the power of the press to excite the millions over trifles were yet to come.

There was, of course, plenty to interest the casual newspaper reader in 1924 and early 1925, when everybody was doing puzzles. There was the presidential campaign, though this proved somewhat of an anticlimax after the sizzling Democratic Convention at Madison Square Garden, that long-drawn-out battle between the forces of William G. McAdoo and Al Smith which ended in a half-hearted stampede to John W. Davis; so much emotional energy had been expended by the Westerners in hating the Tammany Catholic and by the Tammanyites in singing "The Sidewalks of New York," that the Democratic party never really collected itself, and the unimpassioned Calvin, with his quiet insistence upon economy and tax reduction and his knack for making himself appear the personal embodiment of prosperity, was carried into office by a vast majority. There was also the trial of Leopold and Loeb for the murder of Bobby Franks in Chicago. There was the visit of the Prince of Wales to Long Island, during which he danced much, played polo, went motor-boating, and was detected in the act of reading *The Life and Letters of Walter Hines Page.* (It was in 1924, by the way, that those other importations from Britain, the voluminous gray flannel trousers known as Oxford bags, first hung about the heels of the up-and-coming young male.) There was a noteworthy alliance between a representative of the nobility of France and a representative of the nobility of Hollywood: Gloria Swanson married the Marquis de la Falaise de la Coudray. There was a superb eclipse of the sun, providentially arranged for the delectation of the Eastern seaboard cities. There was Paavo Nurmi: watch in hand, his heels thudding on the board track, Nurmi outran the chesty taxi-driver, Joie Ray, and later performed the incredible feat of covering two miles in less than nine minutes. There was the hullabaloo over bringing the serum to Nome to end a diphtheria epidemic, which for a few days made national heroes of Leonard Seppalla, Gunnar Kasson, and the dog Balto. And there was Floyd Collins imprisoned in his cave.

It was the tragedy of Floyd Collins, perhaps, which gave the clearest indication up to that time of the unanimity with which the American people could become excited over a quite unimportant event if only it were dramatic enough.

Floyd Collins was an obscure young Kentuckian who had been exploring an underground passage five miles from Mammoth Cave, with no more heroic purpose than that of finding something which might attract lucrative tourists. Some 125 feet from daylight he was caught by a cave-in which pinned his foot under a huge rock. So narrow and steep was the passage that those who tried to dig him out had to hitch along on their stomachs in cold slime and water and pass back from hand to hand the earth and rocks that they pried loose with hammers and blow-torches. Only a few people might have heard of Collins's predicament if W. B. Miller of the *Louisville Courier-Journal* had not been slight of stature, daring, and an able reporter. Miller wormed his way down the slippery, tortuous passageway to interview Collins, became engrossed in the efforts to rescue the man, described them in vivid dispatches--and to his amazement found that the entire country was turning to watch the struggle. Collinses plight contained those elements of dramatic suspense and individual conflict with fate which make a great news story, and every city editor, day after day, planted it on page one. When Miller arrived at Sand Cave he had found only three men at the entrance, warming themselves at a fire and wondering, without excitement, how soon their friend would extricate himself. A fortnight later there was a city of a hundred or more tents there and the milling crowds had to be restrained by barbed-wire barriers and state troops with drawn bayonets; and on February 17, 1925, even the *New York Times* gave a three-column page-one headline to the news of the dénouement:

FIND FLOYD COLLINS DEAD IN CAVE TRAP ON 18TH DAY; LIFELESS AT LEAST 24 HOURS; FOOT MUST BE AMPUTATED TO GET BODY OUT

Within a month, as Charles Merz later reminded the readers of the *New Republic,* there was a cave-in in a North Carolina mine in which 71 men were caught and 53 actually lost. It attracted no great notice. It was "just a mine disaster." Yet for more than two weeks the plight of a single commonplace prospector for tourists riveted the attention of the nation on Sand Cave, Kentucky. It was an exciting show to watch, and the dispensers of news were learning to turn their spotlights on one show at a time.

Even the Collins thriller, however, was as nothing beside the spectacle which was offered a few months later when John Thomas Scopes was tried at Dayton, Tennessee, for teaching the doctrine of evolution in the Central High School.

The Scopes case had genuine significance. It dramatized one of the most momentous struggles of the age--the conflict between religion and science. Yet even this trial, so diligently and noisily was it ballyhooed, took on some of the aspects of a circus.

§ 4

If religion lost ground during the Post-war Decade, the best available church statistics gave no sign of the fact. They showed, to be sure, a very slow growth in the number of churches in use; but this was explained partly by the tendency toward consolidation of existing churches and partly by the trend of population toward the cities--a trend which drew the church-going public into fewer churches with larger congregations. The number of church *members,* on the other hand, grew just about as fast as the population, and church wealth and expenditures grew more rapidly still. On actual attendance at services there were no reliable figures, although it was widely believed that an increasing proportion of the nominally faithful were finding other things to do on Sunday morning. Statistically, the churches apparently just about maintained their position in American life.

Yet it is difficult to escape the conclusion that they maintained it chiefly by the force of momentum--and to some extent, perhaps, by diligent attention to the things which are Cæsar's: by adopting, here and there, the acceptable gospel according to Bruce Barton; by strenuous membership and money-raising campaigns (such as Bishop Manning's high-pressure drive in New York for a "house of prayer for all people," which proved to be a house of prayer under strictly Episcopal auspices); and by the somewhat secular lure of church theatricals, open forums, basket-ball and swimming pools, and muscular good fellowship for the young. Something spiritual had gone out of the churches--a sense of certainty that theirs was the way to salvation. Religion was furiously discussed; there had never been so many books on religious topics in circulation, and the leading divines wrote constantly for the popular magazines; yet all this discussion was itself a sign that for millions of people religion had become a debatable subject instead of being accepted without question among the traditions of the community.

If church attendance declined, it was perhaps because, as Walter Lippmann put it, people were not so certain that they were going to meet God when they went to church. If the minister's prestige declined, it was in many cases because he had lost his one-time conviction that he had a definite and authoritative mission. The Reverend Charles Stelzle, a shrewd observer of religious conditions, spoke bluntly in an article in the *World's Work:* the church, he said, was declining largely because "those who are identified with it do not actually believe in it." Mr. Stelzle told of asking groups of Protestant ministers what there was in their church programs which would prompt them, if they were outsiders, to say, "That is great; that is worth lining up for," and of receiving in no case an immediate answer which satisfied even the answerer himself. In the congregations, and especially among the younger men and women, there was an undeniable weakening of loyalty to the church and an undeniable vagueness as to what it had to offer them--witness, for example, the tone of the discussions which accompanied the abandonment of compulsory chapel in a number of colleges.

This loss of spiritual dynamic was variously ascribed to the general let-down in moral energy which followed the strain of the war; to prosperity, which encouraged the comfortable belief that it profited a man very considerably if he gained a Cadillac car and a laudatory article in the *American Magazine;* to the growing popularity of Sunday golf and automobiling; and to disapproval in some quarters of the political lobbying of church organizations, and disgust at the connivance of many ministers in the bigotry of the Klan. More important than any of these causes, however, was the effect upon the churches of scientific doctrines and scientific methods of thought.

The prestige of science was colossal. The man in the street and the woman in the kitchen, confronted on every hand with new machines and devices which they owed to the laboratory, were ready to believe that science could accomplish almost anything; and they were being deluged with scientific information and theory. The newspapers were giving columns of space to inform (or misinform) them of the latest discoveries: a new dictum from Albert Einstein was now front-page stuff even though practically nobody could understand it. Outlines of knowledge poured from the presses to tell people about the planetesimal hypothesis and the constitution of the atom, to describe for them in unwarranted detail the daily life of the cave-man, and to acquaint them with electrons, endocrines, hormones, vitamins, reflexes, and psychoses. On the lower intellectual levels, millions of people were discovering for the first time that there was such a thing as the venerable theory of evolution. Those who had assimilated this doctrine without disaster at an early age were absorbing from Wells, Thomson, East, Wiggam, Dorsey, and innumerable other popularizers and interpreters of science a collection of ideas newer and more disquieting: that we are residents of an insignificant satellite of a very average star obscurely placed in one of who-knows-how-many galaxies scattered through space; that our behavior depends largely upon chromosomes and ductless glands; that the Hottentot obeys impulses similar to those which activate the pastor of the First Baptist Church, and is probably already better adapted to his Hottentot environment than he would be if he followed the Baptist code, that sex is the most important thing in life, that inhibitions are not to be tolerated, that sin is an out-of-date term, that most untoward behavior is the result of complexes acquired at an early age, and that men and women are mere bundles of behavior-patterns, anyhow. If some of the scientific and pseudoscientific principles which lodged themselves in the popular mind contradicted one another, that did not seem to matter: the popular mind appeared equally ready to believe with East and Wiggam in the power of heredity and with Watson in the power of environment.

Of all the sciences it was the youngest and least scientific which most captivated the general public and had the most disintegrating effect upon religious faith. Psychology was king. Freud, Adler, Jung, and Watson had their tens of thousands of votaries; intelligence-testers invaded the schools in quest of I.Q.s; psychiatrists were installed in business houses to hire and fire employees and determine advertising policies; and one had only to read the newspapers to be told with complete assurance that psychology held the key to the problems of waywardness, divorce, and crime.

The word science had become a shibboleth. To preface a statement with "Science teaches us" was enough to silence argument. If a sales manager wanted to put over a promotion scheme or a clergyman to recommend a charity, they both hastened to say that it was scientific.

The effect of the prestige of science upon churchmen was well summed up by Dr. Harry Emerson Fosdick at the end of the decade:

"The men of faith might claim for their positions ancient tradition, practical usefulness, and spiritual desirability, but one query could prick all such bubbles: Is it scientific? That question has searched religion for contraband goods, stripped it of old superstitions, forced it to change its categories of thought and methods of work, and in general has so cowed and scared religion that many modern-minded believers . . . instinctively throw up their hands at the mere whisper of it. . . . When a prominent scientist comes out strongly for religion, all the churches thank Heaven and take courage as though it were the highest possible compliment to God to have Eddington believe in Him. Science has become the arbiter of this generation's thought, until to call even a prophet and a seer scientific is to cap the climax of praise."

So powerful was the invasion of scientific ideas and of the scientific habit of reliance upon proved acts that the Protestant churches--which numbered in their membership five out of every eight adult church members in the United States--were broken into two warring camps. Those who believed in the letter of the Bible and refused to accept any teaching, even of science, which seemed to conflict with it, began in 1921 to call themselves Fundamentalists. The Modernists (or Liberals), on the other hand, tried to reconcile their beliefs with scientific thought: to throw overboard what was out of date, to retain what was essential and intellectually respectable, and generally to mediate between Christianity and the skeptical spirit of the age.

The position of the Fundamentalists seemed almost hopeless. The tide of all rational thought in a rational age seemed to be running against them. But they were numerous, and at least there was no doubt about where they stood. Particularly in the South they controlled the big Protestant denominations. And they fought strenuously. They forced the liberal Doctor Fosdick out of the pulpit of a Presbyterian church and back into his own Baptist fold, and even caused him to be tried for heresy (though there was no churchman in America more influential than he). They introduced into the legislatures of nearly half the states of the Union bills designed to forbid the teaching of the doctrine of evolution; in Texas, Louisiana, Arkansas, and South Carolina they pushed such bills through one house of the legislature only to fail in the other; and in Tennessee, Oklahoma, and Mississippi they actually succeeded in writing their anachronistic wishes into law.

The Modernists had the *Zeitgeist* on their side, but they were not united. Their interpretations of God--as the first cause, as absolute energy, as idealized reality, as a righteous will working in creation, as the ideal and goal toward which all that is highest and best is moving-- were confusingly various and ambiguous. Some of these

156

interpretations offered little to satisfy the worshiper: one New England clergyman said that when he thought of God he thought of "a sort of oblong blur." And the Modernists threw overboard so many doctrines in which the bulk of American Protestants had grown up believing (such as the Virgin birth, the resurrection of the body, and the Atonement) that they seemed to many to have no religious cargo left except a nebulous faith, a general benevolence, and a disposition to assure everyone that he was really just as religious as they. Gone for them, as Walter Lippmann said, was "that deep, compulsive, organic faith in an external fact which is the essence of religion for all but that very small minority who can live within themselves in mystical communion or by the power of their understanding." The Modernists, furthermore, had not only Fundamentalism to battle with, but another adversary, the skeptic nourished on outlines of science; and the sermons of more than one Modernist leader gave the impression that Modernism, trying to meet the skeptic's arguments without resorting to the argument from authority, was being forced against its will to whittle down its creed to almost nothing at all.

All through the decade the three-sided conflict reverberated. It reached its climax in the Scopes case in the summer of 1925.

The Tennessee legislature, dominated by Fundamentalists, passed a bill providing that "it shall be unlawful for any teacher in any of the universities, normals and all other public schools of the State, which are supported in whole or in part by the public school funds of the State, to teach any theory that denies the story of the Divine creation of man as taught in the Bible, and to teach instead that man has descended from a lower order of animals."

This law had no sooner been placed upon the books than a little group of men in the sleepy town of Dayton, Tennessee, decided to put it to the test. George Rappelyea, a mining engineer, was drinking lemon phosphates in Robinson's drug store with John Thomas Scopes, a likeable young man of twenty-four who taught biology at the Central High School, and two or three others. Rappelyea proposed that Scopes should allow himself to be caught red-handed in the act of teaching the theory of evolution to an innocent child, and Scopes--half serious, half in joke--agreed. Their motives were apparently mixed; it was characteristic of the times that (according to so friendly a narrator of the incident as Arthur Garfield Hays) Rappelyea declared that their action would put Dayton on the map. At all events, the illegal deed was shortly perpetrated and Scopes was arrested. William Jennings Bryan forthwith volunteered his services to the prosecution; Rappelyea wired the Civil Liberties Union in New York and secured for Scopes the legal assistance of Clarence Darrow, Dudley Field Malone, and Arthur Garfield Hays; the trial was set for July, 1925, and Dayton suddenly discovered that it was to be put on the map with a vengeance.

There was something to be said for the right of the people to decide what should be taught in their tax-supported schools, even if what they decided upon was ridiculous. But the issue of the Scopes case, as the great mass of newspaper readers saw it, was nothing so abstruse as the rights of taxpayers versus academic freedom. In the eyes of the public, the trial was a battle between Fundamentalism on the one hand and twentieth-century skepticism (assisted by Modernism) on the other. The champions of both causes were headliners. Bryan had been three times a candidate for the Presidency, had been Secretary of State, and was a famous orator; he was the perfect embodiment of old-fashioned American idealism--friendly, naïve, provincial. Darrow, a radical, a friend of the underdog, an agnostic, had recently jumped into the limelight of publicity through his defense of Leopold and Loeb. Even Tex Rickard could hardly have staged a more promising contest than a battle between these two men over such an emotional issue.

It was a strange trial. Into the quiet town of Dayton flocked gaunt Tennessee farmers and their families in mule-drawn wagons and ramshackle Fords; quiet, godly people in overalls and gingham and black, ready to defend their faith against the "foreigners," yet curious to know what this new-fangled evolutionary theory might be. Revivalists of every sort flocked there, too, held their meetings on the outskirts of the town under the light of flares, and tacked up signs on the trees about the courthouse--"Read Your Bible Daily for One Week," and "Be Sure Your Sins Will Find You Out," and at the very courthouse gate:

THE KINGDOM OF GOD
The sweetheart love of Jesus Christ and Paradise Street is at hand. Do you want to be a sweet angel? Forty days of prayer. Itemize your sins and iniquities for eternal life. If you come clean, God will talk back to you in voice.

Yet the atmosphere of Dayton was not simply that of rural piety. Hot-dog venders and lemonade venders set up their stalls along the streets as if it were circus day. Booksellers hawked volumes on biology. Over a hundred newspapermen poured into the town. The

Western Union installed twenty-two telegraph operators in a room off a grocery store. In the courtroom itself, as the trial impended, reporters and cameramen crowded alongside grim-faced Tennessee countrymen; there was a buzz of talk, a shuffle of feet, a ticking of telegraph instruments, an air of suspense like that of a first-night performance at the theater. Judge, defendant, and counsel were stripped to their shirt sleeves--Bryan in a pongee shirt turned in at the neck. Darrow with lavender suspenders, Judge Raulston with galluses of a more sober judicial hue--yet fashion was not wholly absent: the news was flashed over the wires to the whole country that the judge's daughters, as they entered the courtroom with him, wore rolled stockings like any metropolitan flapper's. Court was opened with a pious prayer--and motion-picture operators climbed upon tables and chairs to photograph the leading participants in the trial from every possible angle. The evidence ranged all the way from the admission of fourteen-year-old Howard Morgan that Scopes had told him about evolution and that it hadn't hurt him any, to the estimate of a zoologist that life had begun something like six hundred million years ago (an assertion which caused gasps and titters of disbelief from the rustics in the audience). And meanwhile two million words were being telegraphed out of Dayton, the trial was being broadcast by the *Chicago Tribune's* station WGN, the Dreamland Circus at Coney Island offered "Zip" to the Scopes defense as a "missing link," cable companies were reporting enormous increases in transatlantic cable tolls, and news agencies in London were being besieged with requests for more copy from Switzerland, Italy, Germany, Russia, China, and Japan. Ballyhoo had come to Dayton.

It was a bitter trial. Attorney-General Stewart of Tennessee cried out against the insidious doctrine which was "undermining the faith of Tennessee's children and robbing them of their chance of eternal life." Bryan charged Darrow with having only one purpose, "to slur at the Bible." Darrow spoke of Bryan's "fool religion." Yet again and again the scene verged on farce. The climax--both of bitterness and of farce--came on the afternoon of July 20th, when on the spur of the moment Hays asked that the defense be permitted to put Bryan on the stand as an expert on the Bible, and Bryan consented.

So great was the crowd that afternoon that the judge had decided to move the court outdoors, to a platform built against the courthouse under the maple trees. Benches were set out before it. The reporters sat on the benches, on the ground, anywhere, and scribbled their stories. On the outskirts of the seated crowd a throng stood in the hot sunlight which streamed down through the trees. And on the platform sat the shirt-sleeved Clarence Darrow, a Bible on his knee, and put the Fundamentalist champion through one of the strangest examinations which ever took place in a court of law.

He asked Bryan about Jonah and the whale, Joshua and the the sun, where Cain got his wife, the date of the Flood, the significance of the Tower of Babel. Bryan affirmed his belief that the world was created in 4004 B.C. and the Flood occurred in or about 2348 B.C.; that Eve was literally made out of Adam's rib; that the Tower of Babel was responsible for the diversity of languages in the world; and that a "big fish" had swallowed Jonah. When Darrow asked him if he had ever discovered where Cain got his wife, Bryan answered: "No, sir; I leave the agnostics to hunt for her." When Darrow inquired, "Do you say you do not believe that there were any civilizations on this earth that reach back beyond five thousand years?" Bryan stoutly replied, "I am not satisfied by any evidence I have seen." Tempers were getting frazzled by the strain and the heat; once Darrow declared that his purpose in examining Bryan was "to show up Fundamentalism . . . to prevent bigots and ignoramuses from controlling the educational system of the United States," and Bryan jumped up, his face purple, and shook his fist at Darrow, crying, "To protect the word of God against the greatest atheist and agnostic in the United States!"

It was a savage encounter, and a tragic one for the ex-Secretary of State. He was defending what he held most dear. He was making--though he did not know it--his last appearance before the great American public which had once done him honor (he died scarcely a week later). And he was being covered with humiliation. The sort of religious faith which he represented could not take the witness stand and face reason as a prosecutor.

On the morning of July 21st Judge Raulston mercifully refused to let the ordeal of Bryan continue and expunged the testimony of the previous afternoon. Scopes's lawyers had been unable to get any of their scientific evidence before the jury, and now they saw that their only chance of making the sort of defense they had planned for lay in giving up the case and bringing it before the Tennessee Supreme Court on appeal. Scopes was promptly found guilty and fined one hundred dollars. The State Supreme Court later upheld the anti-evolution law but freed Scopes on a technicality, thus preventing further appeal.

Theoretically, Fundamentalism had won, for the law stood. Yet really Fundamentalism had lost. Legislators might go on passing anti-evolution laws, and in the hinterlands the pious might still keep their religion locked in a science-proof compartment of their minds; but civilized opinion everywhere had regarded the Dayton trial with amazement and amusement, and the slow drift away from Fundamentalist certainty continued.

The reporters, the movie men, the syndicate writers, the telegraph operators shook the dust of Dayton from their feet. This monkey trial had been a good show for the front pages, but maybe it was a little too highbrow in its implications. What next? . . . How about a good clean fight without any biology in it?

§ 5

The year 1925 drew slowly toward its close. The *Shenandoah*--a great navy dirigible--was wrecked, and for a few days the country supped on horror. The Florida real-estate boom reached its dizziest height. And then the football season revealed what the ballyhoo technique could do for a football star. Nobody needed a course in biology to appreciate Red Grange.

The Post-war Decade was a great sporting era. More men were playing golf than ever before--playing it in baggy plus-fours, with tassels at the knee and checked stockings. There were five thousand golf-courses in the United States, there were said to be two million players, and it was estimated that half a billion dollars was spent annually on the game. The ability to play it had become a part of the almost essential equipment of the aspiring business executive. The country club had become the focus of social life in hundreds of communities. But it was an even greater era for watching sports than for taking part in them. Promoters, chambers of commerce, newspaper-owners, sports writers, press agents, radio broadcasters, all found profit in exploiting the public's mania for sporting shows and its willingness to be persuaded that the great athletes of the day were supermen. Never before had such a blinding light of publicity been turned upon the gridiron, the diamond, and the prize ring.

Men who had never learned until the nineteen-twenties the difference between a brassie and a niblick grabbed their five-star editions to read about Bobby Jones's exploits with his redoubtable putter, Calamity Jane. There was big money in being a successful golf professional: Walter Hagen's income for several years ranged between forty and eighty thousand dollars, and for a time he received thirty thousand a year and a house for lending the prestige of his presence and his name to a Florida real-estate development. World Series baseball crowds broke all records. So intense was the excitement over football that stadia seating fifty and sixty and seventy thousand people were filled to the last seat when the big teams met, while scores of thousands more sat in warm living-rooms to hear the play-by-play story over the radio and to be told by Graham McNamee that it certainly was cold on the upper rim of the amphitheater. The Yale Athletic Association was said to have taken in over a million dollars in ticket money in a single season. Teams which represented supposed institutions of learning went barnstorming for weeks at a time, imbibing what academic instruction they might on the sleeping-car between the Yankee Stadium and Chicago or between Texas and the Tournament of Roses at Pasadena. More Americans could identify Knute Rockne as the Notre Dame coach than could tell who was the presiding officer of the United States Senate. The fame of star football players, to be sure, was ephemeral compared with that of Jones in golf, or of Ruth in baseball, or of Tilden in tennis. Aldrich, Owen, Bo McMillin, Ernie Nevers, Grange, the Four Horsemen, Benny Friedman, Caldwell, Cagle, and Albie Booth all reigned briefly. But the case of Red Grange may illustrate to what heights a hero of the stadium could rise in the consulship of Calvin Coolidge, when pockets were full and the art of ballyhoo was young and vigorous.

"Harold E. Grange--the middle name is Edward--was born in Forksville, Sullivan County, Pennsylvania, on June 13, 1903," announced a publicity item sent out to the press to put the University of Illinois on the map by glorifying its greatest product. "His father, Lyle N. Grange, in his youth had been the king of lumberjacks in the Pennsylvania mountains, being renowned for his strength, skill, and daring. His mother, a sweet and lovely girl, died when 'Red' was five years old, and it was this which determined his father to move from Pennsylvania to Wheaton, Illinois. . . . The father, who never married again, is deputy sheriff at Wheaton."

But the publicity item (which continues in this rhapsodic tone for many a paragraph) is perhaps too leisurely. Suffice it to say that Red Grange--the "Wheaton iceman," as they called him--played football exceedingly well for the University of Illinois, so well that at the end of the season of 1925 (his senior year) he decided not to bother any further with education at the moment, but to reap the harvest of his fame. Let a series of items summarizing the telegraphic press dispatches tell the story:

Nov. 2--Grange is carried two miles by students.

Nov. 3--His football jersey will be framed at Illinois.

Nov. 11--Admirers circulate petition nominating him for Congress despite his being under age. Is silent on $40,000 offer from New York Giants for three games.

Nov. 17--Is offered $120,000 a year by real-estate firm.

Nov. 21--Plays last game with Illinois, turns professional.

Nov. 22--Signs with Chicago Bears.

Nov. 26--Plays first professional game with Bears and collects $12,000.

Dec. 6--Collects $30,000 in first New York game.

Dec. 7--Signs $300,000 movie contract with Arrow Picture Corporation; may earn $100,000 by June.

Dec. 8--Is presented to President Coolidge.

The public is Fickle, however. Within a few months Gertrude Ederle and the first mother to swim the English Channel were being welcomed in New York with thunderous applause. Dempsey and Tunney were preparing for their Philadelphia fight, and the spotlight had left Red Grange. Five years later he was reported to be working in a night club in Hollywood, while that other hero of the backfield, Caldwell of Yale, was running a lunchroom in New Haven. *Sic transit.*

The public mania for vicarious participation in sport reached its climax in the two Dempsey-Tunney fights, the first at Philadelphia in September, 1926, the second at Chicago a year later. Prize-fighting, once outlawed, had become so respectable in American eyes that gentlefolk crowded into the ringside seats and a clergyman on Long Island had to postpone a meeting of his vestrymen so that they might listen in on one of the big bouts. The newspapers covered acres of paper for weeks beforehand with gossip and prognostications from the training-camps; public interest was whipped up by such devices as signed articles--widely syndicated--in which the contestants berated each other (both sets of articles, in one case, being written by the same "ghost"), and even a paper so traditionally conservative in its treatment of sports as the *New York Times* announced the result of a major bout with three streamer headlines running all the way across its front page. One hundred and thirty thousand people watched Tunney outbox a weary Dempsey at Philadelphia and paid nearly two million dollars for the privilege; one hundred and forty-five thousand people watched the return match at Chicago and the receipts reached the incredible sum of $2,600,000. Compare that sum with the trifling $452,000 taken in when Dempsey gained his title from Willard in 1919 and you have a measure of what had happened in a few years. So enormous was the amphitheater at Chicago that two-thirds of the people in the outermost seats did not know who had won when the fight was over. Nor was the audience limited to the throng in Chicago, for millions more--forty million, the radio people claimed--heard the breathless story of it, blow by blow, over the radio. During the seventh round--when Tunney fell and the referee, by delaying the beginning of his count until Dempsey had reached his corner, gave Tunney some thirteen seconds to recover--five Americans dropped dead of heart failure at their radios. Five other deaths were attributed to the excitement of hearing the radio story of the fight.

Equally remarkable was the aftermath of these two mighty contests. Dempsey had been a mauler at the beginning of the decade; he was an ex-mauler at its end. Not so Tunney. From the pinnacle of his fame he stepped neatly off on to those upper levels of literary and fashionable society in which heavyweight champions, haloed by publicity, were newly welcome. Having received $1,742,282 in three years for his prowess in the ring, Tunney lectured on Shakespeare before Professor Phelps's class at Yale, went for a walking trip in Europe with Thornton Wilder (author of the best-selling novel of the year, *The Bridge of San Luis Rey*), married a young gentlewoman of Greenwich, Connecticut, and after an extensive stay abroad returned to the United States with his bride, giving out on his arrival a prepared statement which, if not quite Shakespearian or Wilderesque in its style, at least gave evidence of effort:

It is hard to realize as our ship passes through the Narrows that fifteen months have elapsed since the *Mauretania* was carrying me in the other direction. During those fifteen months Mrs. Tunney and I have visited many countries and have met some very interesting people. We thoroughly enjoyed our travels, but find the greatest joy of all in again being home with our people and friends.

The echo of a rumor at home that I am contemplating returning to the boxing game to defend the heavyweight championship reached me in Italy. This is in no sense true, for I have permanently ended my public career. My great work now is to live quietly and simply, for this manner of living brings me most happiness.

The sports writers were decidedly cool toward Tunney's post-boxing career. But he was simply exercising the ancient democratic prerogative of rising higher than his source. Ballyhoo had exalted him to the skies, and he took advantage of it to leave the dubious atmosphere of the pugilistic world and seek more salubrious airs.

§ 6

As 1925 gave way to 1926, the searchlight of public attention had shifted from Red Grange to the marriage of Irving Berlin and Ellin Mackay, showing that the curiosity of millions is no respecter of personal privacy; to the gallant rescue of the men of the steamship *Antinoë* in mid-ocean by Captain Fried of the *President Roosevelt;* to the exclusion from the United States of Vera, Countess Cathcart, on the uncomplimentary ground of moral turpitude; to Byrd's daring flight over the North Pole; and, as the summer of 1926 arrived, to the disappearance from a bathing beach of Aimee Semple McPherson, evangelist of a Four-Square Gospel made in California--a disappearance that was to prove the first of a series of opera-bouffe episodes which for years attracted wide-eyed tourists in droves to Mrs. McPherson's Angelus Temple.

The summer passed--the summer when the English Channel was full of swimmers, the brown jacket of *The Private Life of Helen of Troy* ornamented thousands of cottage tables, girls in knee-length skirts and horizontally striped sweaters were learning to dance the Charleston, and the Philadelphia Sesquicentennial was sinking deeper and deeper into the red despite the aid of the Dempsey-Tunney fight. Toward the season's end there was a striking demonstration of what astute press-agentry could do to make a national sensation. A young man named Rudolph Alfonzo Raffaele Pierre Filibert Guglielmi di Valentina d'Antonguolla died in New York at the age of thirty-one. The love-making of Rudolph Valentino (as he had understandably preferred to call himself) had quickened the pulses of innumerable motion-picture addicts; with his sideburns and his passionate air, "the sheik" had set the standard for masculine sex appeal. But his lying in state in an undertaker's establishment on Broadway would hardly have attracted a crowd which stretched through eleven blocks if his manager had not arranged the scenes of grief with uncanny skill, and if Harry C. Klemfuss, the undertaker's press agent, had not provided the newspapers with everything they could desire--such as photographs, distributed in advance, of the chamber where the actor's body would lie, and posed photographs of the funeral cortège. (One of these latter pictures, according to Silas Bent, was on the streets in one newspaper before the funeral procession started.) With such practical assistance, the press gave itself to the affair so whole-heartedly that mobs rioted about the undertaker's and scores of people were injured. Sweet are the uses of publicity: Valentino had been heavily in debt when he died, but his posthumous films, according to his manager's subsequent testimony, turned the debt into a $600,000 balance to the credit of his estate. High-minded citizens regretted that the death of Charles William Eliot, which occurred at about the same time, occasioned no such spectacular lamentations. But the president emeritus of Harvard had had no professional talent to put over his funeral in a big way.

Tunney beat Dempsey, a hurricane contributed the *coup-de-grâce* to the Florida boom, Queen Marie of Rumania sniffed the profits of ballyhoo from afar and made a royal visit to the United States; and then for months on end in the winter of 1926-27 the American people waded deep in scandal and crime.

It was four long years since the Reverend Edward W. Hall and Mrs. Eleanor R. Mills had been found murdered near the crab-apple tree by DeRussey's Lane outside New Brunswick, New Jersey. In 1922 the grand jury had found no indictment. But in 1926 a tabloid newspaper in search of more circulation dug up what purported to be important new evidence and got the case reopened. Mrs. Hall was arrested--at such an unholy hour of the night that the reporters and photographers of this tabloid got a scoop--and she and her two brothers, Henry and Willie Stevens, were brought to trial, thus providing thrills for the readers not only of the tabloid in question, but of every other newspaper in the United States.

The most sensational scene in this most sensational trial of the decade took place when Jane Gibson, the "pig woman," who was supposed to be dying, was brought from her hospital to the courtroom on a stretcher and placed on a bed facing the jury. Mrs. Gibson told a weird story. She had been pestered by corn-robbers, it seemed, and on the night of the murder, hearing the rattle of a wagon that she thought might contain the robbers, she saddled Jenny, her mule, and followed the wagon down DeRussey's Lane, "peeking and peeking and peeking." She saw a car in the Lane, with two people in it whom she identified as Mrs. Hall and Willie Stevens. She tethered Jenny to a cedar tree, heard the sound of a quarrel and a voice saying, "Explain these letters"; she saw Henry and Willie Stevens in the gleam of a flashlight, she heard shots, and then she fled in terror all the way

166

home--only to find that she had left a moccasin behind. Despite her fear, she went all the way back to get that moccasin, and heard what she thought was the screeching of an owl, but found it was a woman crying--"a big white-haired woman doing something with her hand, crying something." She said this woman was Mrs. Hall. All this testimony the "pig woman" gave from her bed in a wailing voice, while trained nurses stood beside her and took her pulse; then, crying out to the defendants, "I have told the truth! So help me God! And you know I've told the truth!" she was borne from the room.

The testimony of the "pig woman" did not gain in force from what was brought out about her previous checkered career; it would have made even less impression upon the jury had they known that their "dying witness," whose appearance in the courtroom had been so ingeniously staged, was destined to live four years more. Mrs. Hall and her brothers came magnificently through their ordeal, slow-witted Willie Stevens in particular delighting millions of murder-trial fans by the way in which he stoutly resisted the efforts of Senator Simpson to bullyrag him into confusion. The new evidence dug up by the tabloid-- consisting chiefly of a calling-card which was supposed to have Willie Steven's fingerprint on it--did not impress the jury.

But though the prosecution's case thus collapsed, the reputation of the Stevens family had been butchered to make a Roman holiday of the first magnitude for newspaper readers. Five million words were written and sent from Somerville, New Jersey, during the first eleven days of the trial. Twice as many newspapermen were there as at Dayton. The reporters included Mary Roberts Rinehart, the novelist, Billy Sunday, the revivalist, and James Mills, the husband of the murdered choir-singer; and the man who had claimed the mantle of Bryan as the leader of Fundamentalism, the Reverend John Roach Straton, wrote a daily editorial moralizing about the case. Over wires jacked into the largest telegraph switchboard in the world traveled the tidings of lust and crime to every corner of the United States, and the public lapped them up and cried for more.

So insistently did they cry that when, a few short months later, an art editor named Albert Snyder was killed with a sash-weight by his wife and her lover, a corset salesman named Judd Gray, once more the forces of ballyhoo got into action. In this case there was no mystery, nor was the victim highly placed; the only excuses for putting the Snyder-Gray trial on the front page were that it involved a sex triangle and that the Snyders were ordinary people living in an ordinary New York suburb--the sort of people with whom the ordinary reader could easily identify himself. Yet so great was the demand for vicarious horrors that once more the great Western Union switchboard was brought into action, an even more imposing galaxy of special writers interpreted the sordid drama (including David Wark Griffith, Peggy Joyce, and Will Durant, as well as Mrs. Rinehart, Billy Sunday, and Doctor Straton), and once more the American people tasted blood.

In the interval between the Hall-Mills case and the Snyder-Gray case, they had had a chance to roll an even riper scandal on their tongues. Frances Heenan Browning, known to the multitude as "Peaches," brought suit for separation from Edward W. Browning, a New York real-estate man who had a penchant for giving to very young girls the delights of a Cinderella. Supposedly sober and reputable newspapers recited the unedifying details of "Daddy" Browning's adventures; and when the *New York Graphic*, a tabloid, printed a "composograph" of Browning in pajamas shouting "Woof! Woof! Don't be a goof!" to his half-clad wife because--according to the caption--she "refused to parade nude," even the *Daily News,* which in the past had shown no distaste for scandal, expressed its fear that if such things went on the public would be "drenched in obscenity."

A great many people felt as the *Daily News* did, and regarded with dismay the depths to which the public taste seemed to have fallen. Surely a change must come, they thought. This carnival of commercialized degradation could not continue.

The change came--suddenly.

§ 7

The owner of the Brevoort and Lafayette Hotels in New York, Raymond Orteig, had offered--way back in 1919--a prize of $25,000 for the first non-stop flight between New York and Paris. Only a few days after the conclusion of the Snyder-Gray trial, three planes were waiting for favorable weather conditions to hop off from Roosevelt Field, just outside New York, in quest of this prize: the *Columbia,* which was to be piloted by Clarence Chamberlin and Lloyd Bertaud; the *America,* with Lieutenant-Commander Byrd of North Pole fame in command; and the *Spirit of St. Louis,* which had abruptly arrived from the Pacific coast with a lone young man named Charles A. Lindbergh at the controls. There was no telling which of the three planes would get off first, but clearly the public favorite was the young man from the West. He was modest, he seemed to know his business, there was something particularly daring about his idea of making the perilous journey alone, and he was as attractive-looking a youngster as ever had faced a camera man. The reporters--to his annoyance--called him "Lucky Lindy" and the "Flying Fool." The spotlight of publicity was upon him. Not yet, however, was he a god.

On the evening of May 19, 1927, Lindbergh decided that although it was drizzling on Long Island, the weather reports gave a chance of fair skies for his trip and he had better get ready. He spent the small hours of the next morning in sleepless preparations, went to Curtiss Field, received further weather news, had his plane trundled to Roosevelt Field and fueled, and a little before eight o'clock--on the morning of May 20th--climbed in and took off for Paris.

Then something very like a miracle took place.

No sooner had the word been flashed along the wires that Lindbergh had started than the whole population of the country became united in the exaltation of a common emotion. Young and old, rich and poor, farmer and stockbroker, Fundamentalist and skeptic, highbrow and lowbrow, all with one accord fastened their hopes upon the young man in the *Spirit of St. Louis*. To give a single instance of the intensity of their mood: at the Yankee Stadium in New York, where the Maloney-Sharkey fight was held on the evening of the 20th, forty thousand hard-boiled boxing fans rose as one man and stood with bared heads in impressive silence when the announcer asked them to pray for Lindbergh. The next day came the successive reports of Lindbergh's success--he had reached the Irish coast, he was crossing over England, he was over the Channel, he had landed at Le Bourget to be enthusiastically mobbed by a vast crowd of Frenchmen--and the American people went almost mad with joy and relief. And when the reports of Lindbergh's first few days in Paris showed that he was behaving with charming modesty and courtesy, millions of his countrymen took him to their hearts as they had taken no other human being in living memory.

Every record for mass excitement and mass enthusiasm in the age of ballyhoo was smashed during the next few weeks. Nothing seemed to matter, either to the newspapers or to the people who read them, but Lindbergh and his story. On the day the flight was completed the *Washington Star* sold 16,000 extra copies, the *St. Louis Post-Dispatch* 40,000, the *New York Evening World* 114,000. The huge headlines which described Lindbergh's triumphal progress from day to day in newspapers from Maine to Oregon showed how thorough was public agreement with the somewhat extravagant dictum of the *Evening World* that Lindbergh had performed "the greatest feat of a solitary man in the records of the human race." Upon his return to the United States, a single Sunday issue of a single paper contained one hundred columns of text and pictures devoted to him. Nobody appeared to question the fitness of President Coolidge's action in sending a cruiser of the United States navy to bring this young private citizen and his plane back from France. He was greeted in Washington at a vast open-air gathering at which the President made--according to Charles Merz--"the longest and most impressive address since his annual message to Congress." The Western Union having provided form messages for telegrams of congratulations to Lindbergh on his arrival, 55,000 of them were sent to him--and were loaded on a truck and trundled after him in the parade through Washington. One telegram, from Minneapolis, was signed with 17,500 names and made up a scroll 520 feet long, under which ten messenger boys staggered. After the public welcome in New York, the Street Cleaning Department gathered up 1,800 tons of paper which had been torn up and thrown out of windows of office buildings to make a snowstorm of greeting--1,800 tons as against a mere 155 tons swept up after the premature Armistice celebration of November 7, 1918!

Lindbergh was commissioned Colonel, and received the Distinguished Flying Cross, the Congressional Medal of Honor, and so many foreign decorations and honorary memberships that to repeat the list would be a weary task. He was offered two and a half million dollars for a tour of the world by air, and $700,000 to appear in the films; his signature was sold for $1,600; a Texas town was named for him, a thirteen-hundred-foot Lindbergh tower was proposed for the city of Chicago, "the largest dinner ever tendered to an individual in modern history" was consumed in his honor, and a staggering number of streets, schools, restaurants, and corporations sought to share the glory of his name.

Nor was there any noticeable group of dissenters from all this hullabaloo. Whatever else people might disagree about, they joined in praise of him.

To appreciate how extraordinary was this universal outpouring of admiration and love--for the word love is hardly too strong--one must remind oneself of two or three facts.

Lindbergh's flight was not the first crossing of the Atlantic by air. Alcock and Brown had flown direct from Newfoundland to Ireland in 1919. That same year the N-C 4, with five men aboard, had crossed by way of the Azores, and the British dirigible R-34 had flown from Scotland to Long Island with 31 men aboard, and then had turned about and made a return flight to England. The German dirigible ZR-3 (later known as the *Los Angeles)* had flown from Friedrichshafen to Lakehurst, New Jersey, in 1924 with 32 people aboard. Two Round-the-World American army planes had crossed the North Atlantic by way of Iceland, Greenland, and Newfoundland in 1924. The novelty of Lindbergh's flight lay only in the fact that he went all the way from New York to Paris instead of jumping off from Newfoundland, that he reached his precise objective, and that he went alone.

Furthermore, there was little practical advantage in such an exploit. It brought about a boom in aviation, to be sure, but a not altogether healthy one, and it led many a flyer to hop off blindly for foreign shores in emulation of Lindbergh and be drowned. Looking back on the event after a lapse of years, and stripping it of its emotional connotations, one sees it simply as a daring stunt flight--the longest up to that time--by a man who did not claim to be anything but a stunt flyer. Why, then, this idolization of Lindbergh?

The explanation is simple. A disillusioned nation fed on cheap heroics and scandal and crime was revolting against the low estimate of human nature which it had allowed itself to entertain. For years the American people had been spiritually starved. They had seen their early ideals and illusions and hopes one by one worn away by the corrosive influence of events and ideas--by the disappointing aftermath of the war, by scientific doctrines and psychological theories which undermined their religion and ridiculed their sentimental notions, by the spectacle of graft in politics and crime on the city streets, and finally by their recent newspaper diet of smut and murder. Romance, chivalry and self-dedication had been debunked; the heroes of history had been shown to have feet of clay, and the saints of history had been revealed as people with queer complexes. There was the god of business to worship--but a suspicion lingered that he was made of brass. Ballyhoo had given the public contemporary heroes to bow down before--but these contemporary heroes, with their fat profits from moving-picture contracts and ghost-written syndicated articles, were not wholly convincing. Something that people needed, if they were to live at peace with themselves and with the world, was missing from their lives. And all at once Lindbergh provided it. Romance, chivalry, self-dedication--here they were, embodied in a modern Galahad for a generation which had foresworn Galahads. Lindbergh did not accept the moving-picture offers that came his way, he did not sell testimonials, did not boast, did not get himself involved in scandal, conducted himself with unerring taste--and was handsome and brave withal. The machinery of ballyhoo was ready and waiting to lift him up where every eye could see him. Is it any wonder that the public's reception of him took on the aspects of a vast religious revival?

Lindbergh did not go back on his admirers. He undertook a series of exhibition flights and good-will flights--successfully and with quiet dignity. He married a daughter of the ambassador to Mexico, and in so doing delighted the country by turning the tables on ballyhoo itself--by slipping away with his bride on a motor-boat and remaining hidden for days despite the efforts of hundreds of newspapermen to spy upon his honeymoon. Wherever he went, crowds fought for a chance to be near him, medals were pinned upon him, tributes were showered upon him, his coming and going was news. He packed away a good-sized fortune earned chiefly as consultant for aviation companies, but few people grudged him that. Incredibly, he kept his head and his instinct for fine conduct.

And he remained a national idol.

Even three and four years after his flight, the roads about his New Jersey farm were blocked on week-ends with the cars of admirers who wanted to catch a glimpse of him, and it was said that he could not even send his shirts to a laundry because they did not come back-- they were too valuable as souvenirs. His picture hung in hundreds of schoolrooms and in thousands of houses. No living American--no dead American, one might almost say, save perhaps Abraham Lincoln-- commanded such unswerving fealty. You might criticize Coolidge or Hoover or Ford or Edison or Bobby Jones or any other headline hero; but if you decried anything that Lindbergh did, you knew that you had wounded your auditors. For Lindbergh was a god.

Pretty good, one reflects, for a stunt flyer. But also, one must add, pretty good for the American people. They had shown that they had better taste in heroes than anyone would have dared to predict during the years which immediately preceded the 20th of May, 1927.

§ 8

After Lindbergh's flight the profits of heroism were so apparent that a horde of seekers after cash and glory appeared, not all of whom seemed to realize that one of the things which had endeared Lindbergh to his admirers had been his indifference both to easy money and to applause. The formula was simple. You got an airplane, some financial backing, and a press agent, and made the first non-stop flight from one place to another place (there were still plenty of places that nobody had flown between). You arranged in advance to sell your personal story to a syndicate if you were successful. If necessary you could get a good deal of your equipment without paying for it, on condition that the purveyors of your oil or your flying suit or your five-foot shelf might say how useful you had found it. Having landed at your destination--and on the front pages--you promptly sold your book, your testimonials, your appearance in vaudeville, your appearance in the movies, or whatever else there was demand for. If you did not know how to pilot a plane you could still be a passenger; a woman passenger, in fact, had better news value than a male pilot. And if flying seemed a little hazardous for your personal taste, you could get useful publicity by giving a prize for other people to fly after.

When Chamberlin followed Lindbergh across the Atlantic, Charles A. Levine, the owner of the plane, was an extremely interested passenger. He got an official welcome at New York. Everybody was getting official welcomes at New York. Grover Whalen, the well-dressed Police Commissioner, was taking incessant advantage of what Alva Johnston called the great discovery that anybody riding up Broadway at noon with a motorcycle escort would find thousands of people gathered there in honor of luncheon. British open golf champions, Channel swimmers, and the Italian soccer team were greeted by Mr. Whalen as deferentially as the Persian Minister of Finance and the Mayor of Leipzig, and it was always fun for the citizenry to have an excuse to throw ticker tape and fragments of the Bronx telephone directory out the window.

Byrd and his men hopped off from Roosevelt Field a few weeks after Chamberlin and Levine, and came down in the sea--but so close to the French coast that they waded ashore. Brock and Schlee not only crossed the Atlantic, but continued on in a series of flights till they reached Japan. And then a good-looking dentist's assistant from Lakeland. Florida, named Ruth Elder, who had been taking flying lessons from George Haldeman, got a citrus-grower and a real-estate man to back her, and Haldeman to pilot her, and set out to become the first woman transatlantic airplane rider. She dropped into the sea much too far out to wade ashore, as it happened; but what matter? She and Haldeman were picked up providentially by a tanker; her manager did good business for her; and she got her welcome--though the City of New York spent only $333.90 on greeting her, as compared with more than $1,000 for Levine, $12,000 for the President of the Irish Free State, $26,000 for Byrd, and $71,000 for Lindbergh.

After Ruth Elder there were so many flights, successful or disastrous, that one could hardly keep track of them. They were always front-page news, but they were less exciting than the unveiling of the new Ford (in December, 1927) and the sinking of the steamship *Vestris,* which (late in 1928) was so hysterically reported that one might have imagined it to be the greatest marine disaster in history. There were no more Lindberghs.

The procession of sporting heroes continued. Bobby Jones went on from triumph to triumph, until no one could doubt that he was the greatest golfer of all time. Babe Ruth remained the home-run king. Cagle and Booth gave the football writers a chance to be the romantic fellows they longed to be. Tilden was slipping, but could still beat almost anybody but a Frenchman. Prize-fighting, however, languished, and there were signs that the public taste in sporting exhibitions was becoming a little jaded. The efforts to find something novel enough to arouse the masters of ballyhoo became almost pathological: Marathon dancers clung to one another by the hour and day and week, shuffling about the floor in an agony of weariness, and the unhappy participants in C. C. Pyle's "Bunion Derby" ran across the continent with results painful both to their feet and to Mr. Pyle's fortunes as a promoter. Thousands stood and gaped while Alvin Shipwreck Kelly sat on a flagpole. There was still money in breaking records, even if your achievement was that of perching on a flagpole in Baltimore for 23 days and 7 hours, having your food and drink hoisted to you in a bucket, and hiring a man to shout at you if you showed signs of dozing for more than twenty minutes at a time. But nobody seemed to be persuaded that there was anything epic about Mr. Kelly. Flagpole sitting and Marathon dancing were just freak shows to watch in an idle moment.

Perhaps the bloom of youth was departing from ballyhoo: the technique was becoming a little too obvious. Perhaps Lindbergh had spoiled the public for lesser heroes. Perhaps the grim execution of Sacco and Vanzetti in 1927 and the presidential campaign of 1928 reminded a well-fed people that there were such things as public issues, after all. But perhaps, too, there was some significance in the fact that in March, 1928, only a few months after the new Ford appeared and less than a year after Lindbergh's flight, the Big Bull Market went into its sensational phase. A ten-point gain in Radio common in a single day promised more immediate benefits than all the non-stop flyers and heavyweight champions in the world.

♦ IX ♦
THE REVOLT OF THE HIGHBROWS

§ 1

"Here was a new generation . . . grown up to find all Gods dead, all wars fought, all faiths in man shaken."
--F. Scott Fitzgerald's *This Side of Paradise.*

By the end of the war with Germany, social compulsion had become a national habit. The typical American of the old stock had never had more than a half-hearted enthusiasm for the rights of the minority; bred in a pioneer tradition, he had been accustomed to set his community in order by the first means that came to hand--a sumptuary law, a vigilance committee, or if necessary a shotgun. Declarations of Independence and Bills of Rights were all very well in the history books, but when he was running things himself he had usually been open to the suggestion that liberty was another name for license and that the Bill of Rights was the last resort of scoundrels. During the war he had discovered how easy it was to legislate and propagandize and intimidate his neighbors into what seemed to him acceptable conduct, and after peace was declared he went on using the same sort of methods to see that they continued to conform.

From Liberty-loan campaigns--with a quota for everybody and often a threat for those who were slow to contribute--he turned to community-chest drives and college-endowment-fund drives and church-membership drives and town-boosting drives and a multitude of other public campaigns: committees and subcommittees were organized, press agents distributed their canned releases, orators bellowed, and the man who kept a tight grip on his pocketbook felt the uncomfortable pressure of mass opinion. From the coercion of alien enemies and supposed pro-Germans it was a short step, as we have seen, to the coercion of racial minorities and supposed Bolsheviks. From war-time censorship it was a short step to peace-time censorship of newspapers and books and public speech. And from legislating sobriety in war-time it was a short step to imbedding prohibition permanently in the Constitution and trying to write the moral code of the majority into the statute-books. Business, to be sure, was freed of most of the shackles which had bound it in 1917 and 1918, for the average American now identified his own interests with those of business. But outside of business he thought he knew how people ought to behave, and he would stand for no nonsense.

After the early days of the Big Red Scare, the American middle-class majority met with little resistance in its stern measures against radicalism and its insistence upon *laissez faire* for business. While labor was being cowed by the police or lured into compliance by stock ownership and the hope of riches, the educated liberals who a few years before had been ready to die at the barricades for minimum-wage laws and equal suffrage and the right to collective bargaining were sinking into hopeless discouragement. Politics, they were deciding, was a vulgar mess; the morons always outnumbered the enlightened, the tobacco-spitting district leaders held the morons in a firm grip, and the right to vote was a joke. Welfare work was equally futile: it was stuffy, sentimental, and presumptuous. The bright young college graduate who in 1915 would have risked disinheritance to march in a Socialist parade yawned at Socialism in 1925, called it old stuff, and cared not at all whether the employees of the Steel Corporation were underpaid or overpaid. Fashions had changed: now the young insurgent enraged his father by arguing against monogamy and God.

When, however, the middle-class majority turned from persecuting political radicals to regulating personal conduct, they met with bitter opposition not only from the bright young college graduate but from the whole of a newly class-conscious group. The intellectuals of the country--the "civilized minority," as the *American Mercury* liked to call them--rose in loud and bitter revolt.

They were never an organized group, these embattled highbrows. They differed vehemently among themselves, and even if they had agreed, the idea of organizing would have been repugnant to them as individualists. They were widely dispersed; New York was their chief rallying-point, but groups of them were to be found in all the other urban centers. They consisted mostly of artists and writers, professional people, the intellectually restless element in the college towns, and such members of the college-educated business class as could digest more complicated literature than was to be found in the *Saturday Evening Post* and *McCall's Magazine;* and they were followed by an ill-assorted mob of faddists who were ready to take up with the latest idea. They may be roughly and inclusively defined as the men and women who had heard of James Joyce, Proust, Cézanne, Jung, Bertrand Russell, John Dewey, Petronius, Eugene O'Neill, and Eddington; who looked down on the movies but revered Charlie Chaplin as a great artist, could talk about relativity even if they could not understand it, knew a few of the leading complexes by name, collected Early American furniture, had ideas about progressive education, and doubted the divinity of Henry Ford and Calvin Coolidge. Few in numbers though they were, they were highly vocal, and their influence not merely dominated American literature but filtered down to affect by slow degrees the thought of the entire country.

These intellectuals felt the full disenchantment of the Peace of Versailles while the returning heroes of Armageddon were still parading past the reviewing-stands. The dreary story of a brutal war and a sordid settlement was spread before their resentful eyes in books like Sir Philip Gibb's *Now It Can Be Told,* John Dos Passos's *Three Soldiers,* E. E. Cummings's *The Enormous Room,* and John Maynard Keynes's *Economic Consequences of the Peace.* They were early converts to the devastating new psychology; the more youthful of them, in fact, were petting according to Freud while their less tutored contemporaries were petting simply because they liked it and could get away with it. Many of the intellectuals had felt the loss of certainty which resulted from new scientific knowledge long before the word Fundamentalism had even been coined or the Einstein theory had reached the research laboratories. Their revolt against the frock-coated respectability and decorous formality of American literature had been under way for several years; Theodore Dreiser, Willa Cather, Carl Sandburg, Edgar Lee Masters, Robert Frost, Vachel Lindsay, Amy Lowell, and the Imagists and exponents of free verse had been breaking new ground since before the war. When twenty of the intellectuals collaborated in the writing of *Civilization in the United States* (published in 1922 under the editorship of Harold Stearns) they summed up the opinion of thousands of their class in their agreement that "the most amusing and pathetic fact in the social life of America today is its emotional and æsthetic starvation." But the revolt of the highbrows against this emotional and æsthetic starvation, and against "the mania for petty regulation" to which it led, would hardly have gathered imposing force as soon as it did had Sinclair Lewis not brought out *Main Street* in October, 1920, and *Babbitt* some two years later.

The effect of these two books was overwhelming. In two volumes of merciless literary photography and searing satire, Lewis revealed the ugliness of the American small town, the cultural poverty of its life, the tyranny of its mass prejudices, and the blatant vulgarity and insularity of the booster. There were other things which he failed to reveal--such as the friendly sentiment and easy generosity of the Gopher Prairies and Zeniths of America--but his books were all the more widely devoured for their very one-sidedness. By the end of 1922 the sale of *Main Street* had reached 390,000 copies. The intellectuals had only to read Lewis's books to realize that the qualities in American life which they most despised and feared were precisely the ones which he put under the microscope for cold-blooded examination. It was George F. Babbitt who was the arch enemy of the enlightened, and it was the Main Street state of mind which stood in the way of American civilization.

After *Babbitt,* a flood of books reflected the dissatisfaction of the highbrows with the rule of America by the businessman and their growing disillusionment. The keynoter of this revolt, its chief tomtom beater, was H. L. Mencken.

§ 2

For several years Mencken, a Baltimorean trained in newspaper work on the *Baltimore Sun,* had been editing the *Smart Set* in company with George Jean Nathan. The *Smart Set* did not prosper; its name and its somewhat dubious previous reputation were against it. When it was languishing Alfred A. Knopf, the book-publisher, engaged Mencken and Nathan to conduct a new monthly magazine addressed to the intellectual left wing, and the first issue of the *American Mercury* appeared at the close of 1923. This--if you are uncertain about dates--was a few weeks before Woodrow Wilson's death; it was at the moment when Senator Walsh was trying to find out who had bestowed money upon Secretary Fall, when Richard Simon was about to hatch the *Cross-Word Puzzle Book* idea, and the Bok Peace Prize was about to be awarded to Charles H. Levermore.

The green cover of the *Mercury* and its format were as sedate as the marble-trimmed façade of Mencken's house in Baltimore, but its contents were explosive. It carried over from the *Smart Set* as regular features Mencken's literary notes, Nathan's theatrical criticisms, a series of editorial jottings which had been called Répétition Generale and now became Clinical Notes, and a museum of American absurdities known as Americana. Every month Mencken occupied several pages with a polemic against the lowbrow majority and its works. The magazine lustily championed writers such as Dreiser, Cabell, Sherwood Anderson, Willa Cather, and Sinclair Lewis, who defied the polite traditions represented by the American Academy of Arts and Letters; it poured critical acid upon sentimentality and evasion and academic pomposity in books and in life; it lambasted Babbitts, Rotarians, Methodists, and reformers, ridiculed both the religion of Coolidge Prosperity and what Mencken called the "bilge of idealism," and looked upon the American scene in general with raucous and profane laughter.

The *Mercury* made an immediate hit. It was new, startling, and delightfully destructive. It crystallized the misgivings of thousands. Soon its green cover was clasped under the arms of the young iconoclasts of a score of college campuses. Staid small-town executives, happening upon it, were shocked and bewildered; this man Mencken, they decided, must be a debauched and shameless monster if not a latter-day emissary of the devil. When Mencken visited Dayton to report the Scopes trial and called the Daytonians yokels, hillbillies, and peasants, the Reverend A. C. Stribling replied that Mencken was a "cheap blatherskite of a pen-pusher"; and to such retorts there was a large section of outraged public opinion ready to cry Amen. After a few years so much abuse had been heaped upon the editor of the *Mercury* that it was possible to publish for the delectation of his admirers a *Schimpflexicon*--a book made up entirely of highly uncomplimentary references to him. Meanwhile the circulation of his magazine climbed to more than 77,000 by 1927; and in that same year Walter Lippmann called him, without exaggeration, "the most powerful personal influence on this whole generation of educated people."

To many readers it seemed as if Mencken were against everything. This was not true, but certainly rebellion was the breath of his life. He was "against all theologians, professors, editorial-writers, right thinkers, and reformers" (to quote his own words). He was "against patriotism because it demands the acceptance of propositions that are obviously imbecile--*e.g.,* that an American Presbyterian is the equal of Anatole France, Brahms, or Ludendorff." He did not believe that "civilized life was possible under a democracy." He spoke of socialists and anarchists as fools. He was against prohibition, censorship, and all other interferences with personal liberty. He scoffed at morality and Christian marriage. There was an apparent inconsistency in this formidable collection of prejudices: how, some of his critics asked, could one expect an aristocracy of intellect, such as he preferred, to permit such liberties as he insisted upon, unless it happened to be made up entirely of Menckens--a rather unlikely premise? Inconsistencies, however, bothered Mencken not at all, and at first bothered few of his followers. For it was not easy to be coolly analytical in the face of such a prose style as he commanded.

He brought to his offensive against the lowbrows an unparalleled vocabulary of invective. He pelted his enemies with words and phrases like mountebank, charlatan, swindler, numskull, swine, witch-burner, *homo boobiens,* and imbecile; he said of sentimentalists that they squirted rosewater about, of Bryan that "he was born with a roaring voice and it had a trick of inflaming half-wits," of books which he disliked that they were garbage; he referred to the guileless farmers of Tennessee as "gaping primates" and "the anthropoid rabble." On occasion--as in his scholarly book on *The American Language*--Mencken could write measured and precise English, but when his blood was up, his weapons were gross exaggeration and gross metaphors. The moment he appeared the air was full of flying brick-bats; and to read him for the first time gave one, if not blind rage, the sort of intense visceral delight which comes from heaving baseballs at crockery in an amusement park.

The years when Mencken's wholesale idol-smashing first attracted wide attention, be it remembered, were the very years when the prosperity chorus was in full voice, Bruce Barton was revising Christian doctrine for the glorification of the higher salesmanship, the Fundamentalists were on the rampage against evolution, and the Methodist Board of Temperance, Prohibition, and Public Morals was trying to mold the country into sober conformity. Up to this time the intellectuals had been generally on the defensive. But now, with Mencken's noisy tub-thumping to give them assurance, they changed their tone. Other magazines joined, though less stridently, in the cry of dissent: *Harper's* put on an orange cover in 1925 and doubled its circulation by examining American life with a new critical boldness, *The Forum* debated subjects which Main Street considered undebatable, the *Atlantic* published the strictures of James Truslow Adams, and by the end of the decade even *Scribner's* was banned from the newsstands of Boston for printing a Hemingway serial. Books reflecting the intellectual minority's views of the United States and of life gushed from the presses. Slowly the volume of protest grew, until by 1926 or 1927 anybody who uttered a good word for Rotary or Bryan in any house upon whose walls hung a reproduction of Picasso or Marie Laurencin, or upon whose shelves stood *The Sun Also Rises* or *Notes on Democracy,* was likely to be set down as an incurable moron.

§ 3

What was the credo of the intellectuals during these years of revolt? Not many of them accepted all the propositions in the following rough summary; yet it suggests, perhaps, the general drift of their collective opinion:

1. They believed in a greater degree of sex freedom than had been permitted by the strict American code; and as for discussion of sex, not only did they believe it should be free, but some of them appeared to believe it should be continuous. They formed the spearhead of the revolution in manners and morals which has been described in Chapter Five. From the early days of the decade, when they thrilled at the lackadaisical petting of F. Scott Fitzgerald's young thinkers and at the boldness of Edna St. Vincent Millay's announcement that her candle burned at both ends and could not last the night, to the latter days when they were all agog over the literature of homosexuality and went by the thousand to take Eugene O'Neill's five-hour lesson in psychopathology, *Strange Interlude,* they read about sex, talked about sex, thought about sex, and defied anybody to say No.

2. In particular, they defied the enforcement of propriety by legislation and detested all the influences to which they attributed it. They hated the Methodist lobby, John S. Sumner, and all other defenders of censorship; they pictured the Puritan, even of Colonial days, as a blue-nosed, cracked-voiced hypocrite; and they looked at Victorianism as half indecent and half funny. The literary reputations of Thackeray, Tennyson, Longfellow, and the Boston *literati* of the last century sank in their estimation to new lows for all time. Convinced that the era of short skirts and literary dalliance had brought a new enlightenment, the younger intellectuals laughed at the "Gay Nineties" as depicted in *Life* and joined Thomas Beer in condescending scrutiny of the voluminous dresses and fictional

indirections of the Mauve Decade. Some of them, in fact, seemed to be persuaded that all periods prior to the coming of modernity had been ridiculous--with the exception of Greek civilization, Italy at the time of Casanova, France at the time of the great courtesans, and eighteenth-century England.

3. Most of them were passionate anti-prohibitionists, and this fact, together with their dislike of censorship and their skepticism about political and social regeneration, made them dubious about all reform movements and distrustful of all reformers. They emphatically did not believe that they were their brothers' keepers; anybody who did not regard tolerance as one of the supreme virtues was to them intolerable. If one heard at a single dinner party of advanced thinkers that there were "too many laws" and that people ought to be let alone, one heard it at a hundred. In 1915 the word reformer had been generally a complimentary term; in 1925 it had become--among the intellectuals, at least--a term of contempt.

4. They were mostly, though not all, religious skeptics. If there was less shouting agnosticism and atheism in the nineteen-twenties than in the eighteen-nineties it was chiefly because disbelief was no longer considered sensational and because the irreligious intellectuals, feeling no evangelical urge to make over others in their own image, were content quietly to stay away from church. It is doubtful if any college undergraduate of the 'nineties or of any other previous period in the United States could have said "No intelligent person believes in God any more" as blandly as undergraduates said it during the discussions of compulsory college chapel which raged during the 'twenties. Never before had so many books addressed to the thinking public assumed at the outset that their readers had rejected the old theology.

5. They were united in a scorn of the great bourgeois majority which they held responsible for prohibition, censorship, Fundamentalism, and other repressions. They emulated Mencken in their disgust at Babbitts, Rotarians, the Ku Klux Klan, Service-with-a-Smile, boosters, and super-salesmen. Those of them who lived in the urban centers prided themselves on their superiority to the denizens of the benighted outlying cities and towns where Babbittry flourished; witness, for example, the motto of the *New Yorker* when it was first established in the middle of the decade: "Not for the old lady from Dubuque." Particularly did they despise the mobs of prosperous American tourists which surged through Europe; one could hardly occupy a steamer chair next to anybody who had Aldous Huxley's

latest novel on his lap without being told of a delightful little restaurant somewhere in France which was quite "unspoiled by Americans."

6. They took a particular pleasure in overturning the idols of the majority; hence the vogue among them of the practice for which W. E. Woodward, in a novel published in 1923, invented the word "debunking." Lytton Strachey's *Queen Victoria,* which had been a best seller in the United States in 1922, was followed by a deluge of debunking biographies. Rupert Hughes removed a few coats of whitewash from George Washington and nearly caused a riot when he declared in a speech that "Washington was a great card-player, a distiller of whisky, and a champion curser, and he danced for three hours without stopping with the wife of his principal general." Other American worthies were portrayed in all their erring humanity, and the notorious rascals of history were rediscovered as picturesque and glamorous fellows; until for a time it was almost taken for granted that a biographer, if he were to be successful, must turn conventional white into black and *vice versa.*

7. They feared the effect upon themselves and upon American culture of mass production and the machine, and saw themselves as fighting at the last ditch for the right to be themselves in a civilization which was being leveled into monotony by Fordismus and the chain-store mind. Their hatred of regimentation gave impetus to the progressive school movement and nourished such innovations in higher education as Antioch, Rollins, Meiklejohn's Experimental College at Wisconsin, and the honors plan at Swarthmore and elsewhere. It gave equal impetus to the little-theater movement, which made remarkable headway from coast to coast, especially in the schools. The heroes of current novels were depicted as being stifled in the air of the home town, and as fleeing for their cultural lives either to Manhattan or, better yet, to Montparnasse or the Riviera. In any café in Paris one might find an American expatriate thanking his stars that he was free from standardization at last, oblivious of the fact that there was no more standardized institution even in the land of automobiles and radio than the French sidewalk café. The intellectuals lapped up the criticisms of American culture offered them by foreign lecturers imported in record-breaking numbers, and felt no resentment when the best magazines flaunted before their eyes, month after month, titles like "Our American Stupidity" and "Childish Americans." They quite expected to be told that America was sinking into barbarism and was an altogether impossible place for a civilized person to live in--as

when James Truslow Adams lamented in the *Atlantic Monthly,* "I am wondering, as a personal but practical question, just how and where a man of moderate means who prefers simple living, simple pleasures, and the things of the mind is going to be able to live any longer in his native country."

Few of the American intellectuals of the nineteen-twenties, let it be repeated, subscribed to all the propositions in this credo; but he or she who accepted none of them was suspect among the enlightened. He was not truly civilized, he was not modern. The prosperity bandwagon rolled on, but by the wayside stood the highbrows with voices upraised in derision and dismay.

§ 4

Mencken enjoyed his battle enormously, cynic though he was. He went on to meet the armed men, and said among the trumpets, Haha. Everything might be wrong with American civilization, but at least it made a lovely target for his blunderbuss. "If you find so much that is unworthy of reverence in the United States, then why do you live here?" he asked himself in the Fifth Series of his *Prejudices,* only to answer, "Why do men go to zoos?" Nobody had such a good time in the American zoo as Mencken; he even got a good laugh out of the Tennessee anthropoids.

Not so, however, with most of his *confrères* in the camp of the intellectuals. The word disillusionment has been frequently employed in this history, for in a sense disillusionment (except about business and the physical luxuries and improvements which business would bring) was the keynote of the nineteen-twenties. With the majority of Americans its workings were perhaps unconscious; they felt a queer disappointment after the war, they felt that life was not giving them all they had hoped it would, they knew that some of the values which had once meant much to them were melting away, but they remained cheerful and full of gusto, quite unaware of the change which was taking place beneath the surface of their own minds. Most of the intellectuals, however, in America as elsewhere, knew all too well that they were disillusioned. Few of them, unfortunately, had grown up with as low expectations for humanity as Mencken. You cannot fully enjoy a zoo if you have been led to think of it as the home of an enlightened citizenry.

The intellectuals believed in a greater degree of sex freedom-- and many of them found it disappointing when they got it, either in person or vicariously through books and plays. They were discovering that the transmutation of love into what Krutch called a "carefully catalogued psychosis" had robbed the loveliest passages of life of their poetry and their meaning. "Emotions," as Krutch said, "cannot be dignified unless they are first respected," and love was becoming too easy and too biological to be an object of respect. Elmer Davis referred in one of his essays to the heroine of a post-war novel who "indulged in 259 amours, if I remember correctly, without getting the emotional wallop out of any of them, or out of all of them together, that the lady of Victorian literature would have derived from a single competently conducted seduction." This busy heroine had many a literary counterpart and doubtless some in real life; and if one thing became clear to them, it was that romance cannot be put into quantity production, that the moment love becomes casual, it becomes commonplace as well. Even their less promiscuous contemporaries felt something of the sense of futility which came when romantic love was marked down.

As enemies of standardization and repression, the intellectuals believed in freedom--but freedom for what? Uncomfortable as it was to be harassed by prohibition agents and dictated to by chambers of commerce, it was hardly less comfortable in the long run to have their freedom and not know what to do with it. In all the nineteen-twenties there was no more dismal sight than that described by Richmond Barrett in an article in *Harper's* entitled "Babes in the Bois"--the sight of young Americans dashing to Paris to be free to do what Buffalo or Iowa City would not permit, and after being excessively rude to everybody they met and tasting a few short and tasteless love-affairs and soaking themselves in gin, finally passing out undecoratively under a table in the Café du Dôme. Mr. Barrett, to be sure, was portraying merely the lunatic fringe of the younger generation of intellectuals; but who during the nineteen-twenties did not recognize the type characterized in the title of one of Scott Fitzgerald's books as "All the Sad Young Men"? Wrote Walter Lippmann, "What most distinguishes the generation who have approached maturity since the débâcle of idealism at the end of the war is not their rebellion against the religion and the moral code of their parents, but their disillusionment with their own rebellion. It is common for young men and women to rebel, but that they should rebel sadly and without faith in their rebellion, and that they should distrust the new freedom no less than the old certainties--that is something of a novelty." It may be added that there were older and wiser heads than these who, in quite different ways, felt the unanswerability of the question, After freedom, what next?

They believed also, these intellectuals, in scientific truth and the scientific method--and science not only took their God away from them entirely, or reduced Him to a principle of order in the universe or a figment of the mind conjured up to meet a psychological need, but also reduced man, as Krutch pointed out in *The Modern Temper,* to a creature for whose ideas of right and wrong there was no transcendental authority. No longer was it possible to say with any positiveness, This is right, or, This is wrong; an act which was considered right in Wisconsin might be (according to the ethnologists) considered wrong in Borneo, and even in Wisconsin its merits seemed to be a matter of highly fallible human opinion. The certainty had departed from life. And what was worse still, it had departed from science itself. In earlier days those who denied the divine order had still been able to rely on a secure order of nature, but now even this was wabbling. Einstein and the quantum theory introduced new uncertainties and new doubts. Nothing, then, was sure; the purpose of life was undiscoverable, the ends of life were less discoverable still; in all this fog there was no solid thing on which a man could lay hold and say, This is real; this will abide.

§ 5

Yet in all this uncertainty there was new promise for the intellectual life of the country. With the collapse of fixed values went a collapse of the old water-tight critical standards in the arts, opening the way for fresh and independent work to win recognition. Better still, the idea was gaining ground that this fresh and independent work might as well be genuinely native, that the time had come when the most powerful nation in the world might rid itself of its cultural subjection to Europe.

It was still hard to persuade the *cognoscenti* that first-class painting or music might come out of America. Rejecting scornfully the pretty confections of the Academicians, art collectors went in so wholeheartedly for the work of the French moderns and their imitators that the United States became almost--from the artistic point of view-- a French colony. American orchestras remained under the domination of foreign conductors, played foreign compositions almost exclusively, and gave scant opportunity to the native composer. Even in art and music, however, there were signs of change. Artists were beginning to open their eyes to the pictorial possibilities of the skyscraper and the machine, and collectors waited only for George Bellows to die to bid up his rugged oils and lithographs of the American prize-ring. Music-lovers recognized at last the glory of the Negro spirituals, dabbled with the idea that George Gershwin might bridge the gap between popular jazz and vital music, permitted singers with such un-European names as Marion Talley and Lawrence Tibbett to become stars at the Metropolitan, and listened approvingly to an American opera (without, to be sure, an American subject) composed by Deems Taylor.

In architecture there was a somewhat more eager welcome for the indigenous product. Though the usual American country house was still a Georgian manor-house or a French farmhouse or a Spanish villa fitted out with bathrooms and a two-car garage, but trying to recapture, even in Lake Forest, what the real-estate agents called "Old World charm"; though the American bank was still a classical temple and there were still architects who tried to force the life of a modern American university into a medieval Gothic frame; nevertheless there was an increasing agreement with Lewis Mumford that new materials and new uses for them called for new treatment without benefit of the Beaux Arts. The *Chicago Tribune's* competition early in the decade, and particularly the startling design by Saarinen which won second prize, suggested new possibilities for the skyscraper--possibilities at which Louis Sullivan and Frank Lloyd Wright and Cass Gilbert's Woolworth Building had already hinted. The skyscraper was peculiarly American--why not solve this problem of steel construction in a novel and American way? Gradually an American architecture began to evolve. Goodhue's Public Library in Los Angeles, his Nebraska State Capitol, Arthur Loomis Harmon's Shelton Hotel in New York, the Barclay-Vesey Telephone Building (by McKenzie, Voorhees & Gmelin and Ralph Thomas Loamas), and other fine achievements at least paved the way for something which might be the logical and beautiful expression of an American need.

Finally, in literature the foreign yoke was almost completely thrown off. Even if the intellectuals bought more foreign books than ever before and migrated by the thousands to Montparnasse and Antibes, they expected to write and to appreciate American literature. Their writing and their appreciation were both stimulated by Mencken's strenuous praise of uncompromisingly native work, by the establishment of good critical journals (such as the *Saturday Review of Literature*), and by researches into the American background which disclosed such native literary material as the Paul Bunyan legends and the cowboy ballads and such potential material as the desperadoes of the frontier and the show-boats of the rivers. There was a new ferment working, and at last there was an audience quite unconvinced that American literature must be forever inferior or imitative. Certainly a decade which produced Sinclair Lewis's *Arrowsmith*, Dreiser's *An American Tragedy*, Hemingway's *A Farewell to Arms*, Willa Cather's novels, Benet's *John Brown's Body*, some of the plays of Eugene O'Neill, and such short stories as Ring Lardner's "Golden Honeymoon"--to make invidious mention of only a few performances--could lay claim to something better than mere promise for the future.

§ 6

Gradually the offensive against Babbittry spent itself, if only because the novelty of rebellion wore off. The circulation of the *Mercury* (and with it, perhaps, the influence of its editor) reached its peak in 1927 and thereafter slowly declined. The *New Yorker* forgot the old lady from Dubuque and developed a casual and altogether charming humor with malice toward none; the other magazines consumed by the urban intelligentsia tired somewhat of viewing the American scene with alarm. Sex fiction began to seem a little less adventurous and the debunking fad ran its course. And similarly there began to be signs, here and there, that the mental depression of the intellectuals might have seen its worst days.

In 1929--the very year which produced Krutch's *The Modern Temper,* a dismally complete statement of the philosophical disillusionment of the times--Walter Lippmann tried to lay the foundations for a new system of belief and of ethics which might satisfy even the disillusioned. The success of *A Preface to Morals* suggested that many people were tired of tobogganing into mental chaos. That same year there was a great hue and cry among the highbrows over humanism. The humanist fad was not without its comic aspect, since very few of those who diligently talked about it were clear as to which of three or four varieties of humanism they had in mind, and such cloistered beings as Paul Elmer More and Irving Babbitt were hardly the leaders to rally a popular movement of any dimensions; but it gave further evidence of a disposition among the doubters to dig in and face confusion along a new line of defense. There was also a widespread effort to find in the scientific philosophizing of Whitehead and Eddington and Jeans some basis for a belief that life might be worth living, after all. Perhaps the values which had been swept away during the post-war years had departed never to return, but at least there was a groping for new ones to take their place.

If there was, it came none too soon. For to many men and women the new day so sonorously heralded by the optimists and propagandists of war-time had turned into night before it ever arrived, and in the uncertain blackness they did not know which way to turn. They could revolt against stupidity and mediocrity, they could derive a meager pleasure from regarding themselves with pity as members of a lost generation, but they could not find peace.

◆ X ◆
ALCOHOL AND AL CAPONE

§ 1

If in the year 1919--when the Peace Treaty still hung in the balance, and Woodrow Wilson was chanting the praises of the League, and the Bolshevist bogey stalked across the land, and fathers and mothers were only beginning to worry about the younger generation-- you had informed the average American citizen that prohibition was destined to furnish the most violently explosive public issue of the nineteen-twenties, he would probably have told you that you were crazy. If you had been able to sketch for him a picture of conditions as they were actually to be--rum-ships rolling in the sea outside the twelve-mile limit and transferring their cargoes of whisky by night to fast cabin cruisers, beer-running trucks being hijacked on the interurban boulevards by bandits with Thompson sub-machine guns, illicit stills turning out alcohol by the carload, the fashionable dinner party beginning with contraband cocktails as a matter of course, ladies and gentlemen undergoing scrutiny from behind the curtained grill of the speakeasy, and Alphonse Capone, multi-millionaire master of the Chicago bootleggers, driving through the streets in an armor-plated car with bullet-proof windows--the innocent citizen's jaw would have dropped. The Eighteenth Amendment had been ratified, to go into effect on January 16, 1920; and the Eighteenth Amendment, he had been assured and he firmly believed, had settled the prohibition issue. You might like it or not, but the country was going dry.

Nothing in recent American history is more extraordinary, as one looks back from the nineteen-thirties, than the ease with which-- after generations of uphill fighting by the drys--prohibition was finally written upon the statute-books. The country accepted it not only willingly, but almost absent-mindedly. When the Eighteenth

ALLEN

Amendment came before the Senate in 1917, it was passed by a one-sided vote after only thirteen hours of debate, part of which was conducted under the ten-minute rule. When the House of Representatives accepted it a few months later, the debate upon the Amendment as a whole occupied only a single day. The state legislatures ratified it in short order; by January, 1919, some two months after the Armistice, the necessary three-quarters of the states had fallen into line and the Amendment was a part of the Constitution. (All the rest of the states but two subsequently added their ratifications--only Connecticut and Rhode Island remained outside the pale.) The Volstead Act for the enforcement of the Amendment, drafted after a pattern laid down by the Anti-Saloon League, slipped through with even greater ease and dispatch. Woodrow Wilson momentarily surprised the country by vetoing it, but it was promptly repassed over his veto. There were scattered protests--a mass-meeting in New York, a parade in Baltimore, a resolution passed by the American Federation of Labor demanding modification in order that the workman might not be deprived of his beer, a noisy demonstration before the Capitol in Washington--but so half-hearted and ineffective were the forces of the opposition and so completely did the country as a whole take for granted the inevitability of a dry régime, that few of the arguments in the press or about the dinner table raised the question whether the law would or would not prove enforceable; the burning question was what a really dry country would be like, what effect enforced national sobriety would have upon industry, the social order, and the next generation.

How did it happen? Why this overwhelming, this almost casual acceptance of a measure of such huge importance?

As Charles Merz has clearly shown in his excellent history of the first ten years of the prohibition experiment, the forces behind the Amendment were closely organized; the forces opposed to the Amendment were hardly organized at all. Until the United States entered the war, the prospect of national prohibition had seemed remote, and it is always hard to mobilize an unimaginative public against a vague threat. Furthermore, the wet leadership was discredited; for it was furnished by the dispensers of liquor, whose reputation had been unsavory and who had obstinately refused to clean house even in the face of a growing agitation for temperance.

The entrance of the United States into the war gave the dry leaders their great opportunity. The war diverted the attention of those who might have objected to the bone-dry program: with the very

191

existence of the nation at stake, the future status of alcohol seemed a trifling matter. The war accustomed the country to drastic legislation conferring new and wide powers upon the Federal Government. It necessitated the saving of food and thus commended prohibition to the patriotic as a grain-saving measure. It turned public opinion against everything German--and many of the big brewers and distillers were of German origin. The war also brought with it a mood of Spartan idealism of which the Eighteenth Amendment was a natural expression. Everything was sacrificed to efficiency, production, and health. If a sober soldier was a good soldier and a sober factory hand was a productive factory hand, the argument for prohibition was for the moment unanswerable. Meanwhile the American people were seeing Utopian visions; if it seemed possible to them that the war should end all wars and that victory should bring a new and shining world order, how much easier to imagine that America might enter an endless era of efficient sobriety! And finally, the war made them impatient for immediate results. In 1917 and 1918, whatever was worth doing at all was worth doing at once, regardless of red tape, counter-arguments, comfort, or convenience. The combination of these various forces was irresistible. Fervently and with headlong haste the nation took the shortcut to a dry Utopia.

Almost nobody, even after the war had ended, seemed to have any idea that the Amendment would be really difficult to enforce. Certainly the first Prohibition Commissioner, John F. Kramer, displayed no doubts. "This law," he declared in a burst of somewhat Scriptural rhetoric, "will be obeyed in cities, large and small, and in villages, and where it is not obeyed it will be enforced. . . . The law says that liquor to be used as a beverage must not be manufactured. We shall see that it is not manufactured. Nor sold, nor given away, nor hauled in anything on the surface of the earth or under the earth or in the air." The Anti-Saloon League estimated that an appropriation by Congress of five million dollars a year would be ample to secure compliance with the law (including, presumably, the prevention of liquor-hauling "under the earth"). Congress voted not much more than that, heaved a long sigh of relief at having finally disposed of an inconvenient and vexatious issue, and turned to other matters of more pressing importance. The morning of January 16, 1920, arrived and the era of promised aridity began. Only gradually did the dry leaders, or Congress, or the public at large begin to perceive that the problem with which they had so light-heartedly grappled was a problem of gigantic proportions.

§ 2

Obviously the surest method of enforcement was to shut off the supply of liquor at its source. But consider what this meant.

The coast lines and land borders of the United States offered an 18,700-mile invitation to smugglers. Thousands of druggists were permitted to sell alcohol on doctors' prescriptions, and this sale could not be controlled without close and constant inspection. Near-beer was still within the law, and the only way to manufacture near-beer was to brew real beer and then remove the alcohol from it--and it was excessively easy to fail to remove it from the entire product. The manufacture of industrial alcohol opened up inviting opportunities for diversion which could be prevented only by watchful and intelligent inspection--and after the alcohol left the plant where it was produced, there was no possible way of following it down the line from purchaser to purchaser and making sure that the ingredients which had been thoughtfully added at the behest of the Government to make it undrinkable were not extracted by ingenious chemists. Illicit distilling could be undertaken almost anywhere, even in the householder's own cellar; a commercial still could be set up for five hundred dollars which would produce fifty or a hundred highly remunerative gallons a day, and a one-gallon portable still could be bought for only six or seven dollars.

To meet all these potential threats against the Volstead Act, the Government appropriations provided a force of prohibition agents which in 1920 numbered only 1,520 men and as late as 1930 numbered only 2,836; even with the sometimes unenthusiastic aid of the Coast Guard and the Customs Service and the Immigration Service, the force was meager. Mr. Merz puts it graphically: if the whole army of agents in 1920 had been mustered along the coasts and borders--paying no attention for the moment to medicinal alcohol, breweries, industrial alcohol, or illicit stills--there would have been one man to patrol every twelve miles of beach, harbor, headland, forest, and river-front. The agents' salaries in 1920 mostly ranged between $1,200 and $2,000; by 1930 they had been munificently raised to range between $2,300 and $2,800. Anybody who believed that men employable at thirty-five or forty or fifty dollars a week would surely have the expert technical knowledge and the diligence to supervise successfully the complicated chemical operations of industrial-alcohol plants or to outwit the craftiest devices of smugglers and bootleggers, and that they would surely have the force of character to resist corruption by men whose pockets were bulging with money, would be ready to believe also in Santa Claus, perpetual motion, and pixies.

Yet even this body of prohibition agents, small and underpaid as it was in view of the size and complexity of its task and the terrific pressure of temptation, might conceivably have choked off the supply of alcohol if it had had the concerted backing of public opinion. But public opinion was changing. The war was over; by 1920 normalcy was on the way. The dry cause confronted the same emotional let-down which defeated Woodrow Wilson and hastened the Revolution in Manners and Morals. Spartan idealism was collapsing. People were tired of girding up their loins to serve noble causes. They were tired of making the United States a land fit for heroes to live in. They wanted to relax and be themselves. The change of feeling toward prohibition was bewilderingly rapid. Within a few short months it was apparent that the Volstead Act was being smashed right and left and that the formerly inconsiderable body of wet opinion was growing to sizable proportions. The law was on the statute-books, the Prohibition Bureau was busily plying its broom against the tide of alcohol, and the corner saloon had become a memory; but the liquorless millennium had nevertheless been indefinitely postponed.

§ 3

The events of the next few years present one of those paradoxes which fascinate the observer of democratic government. Obviously there were large sections of the country in which prohibition was not prohibiting. A rational observer would have supposed that the obvious way out of this situation would be either to double or treble or quadruple the enforcement squad or to change the law. But nothing of the sort was done. The dry leaders, being unwilling to admit that the task of mopping up the United States was bigger than they had expected, did not storm the Capitol to recommend huge increases in the appropriations for enforcement; it was easier to denounce the opponents of the law as Bolshevists and destroyers of civilization and to hope that the tide of opinion would turn again. Congress was equally unwilling to face the music; there was a comfortable dry majority in both Houses, but it was one thing to be a dry and quite another to insist on enforcement at whatever cost and whatever inconvenience to some of one's influential constituents. The Executive was as wary of the prohibition issue as of a large stick of dynamite; the contribution of Presidents Harding and Coolidge to the problem--aside from negotiating treaties which increased the three-mile limit to twelve miles, and trying to improve the efficiency of enforcement without calling for too much money from Congress--consisted chiefly of uttering resounding platitudes on the virtues of law observance. The state governments were supposed to help the Prohibition Bureau, but by 1927 their financial contribution to the cause was about one-eighth of the sum they spent enforcing their own fish and game laws. Some legislatures withdrew their aid entirely, and even the driest states were inclined to let Uncle Sam bear the brunt of the Volstead job. Local governments were supposed to war against the speakeasy, but did it with scant relish except where local opinion was insistent. Nor could the wets, for their part, agree upon any practical program. It seemed almost hopeless to try to repeal or modify the Amendment, and for the time being they contented themselves chiefly with loud and indignant lamentation. The law was not working as it had been intended to, but nobody seemed willing or able to do anything positive about it one way or the other.

Rum-ships plied from Bimini or Belize or St. Pierre, entering American ports under innocent disguises or transferring their cargoes to fast motor-boats which could land in any protected cove. Launches sped across the river at Detroit with good Canadian whisky aboard. Freighters brought in cases of contraband gin mixed among cases of other perfectly legal and properly labeled commodities. Liquor was hidden in freight-cars crossing the Canadian border; whole carfuls of whisky were sometimes smuggled in by judicious manipulation of seals. These diverse forms of smuggling were conducted with such success that in 1925 General Lincoln C. Andrews, Assistant Secretary of the Treasury in charge of enforcement, hazarded the statement that his agents succeeded in intercepting only about 5 per cent of the liquor smuggled into the country; and the value of the liquor which filtered in during the single year 1924 was estimated by the Department of Commerce at $40,000,000! Beer leaked profusely from the breweries; alley breweries unknown to the dry agents flourished and coined money. The amount of industrial alcohol illegally diverted was variously estimated in the middle years of the decade at from thirteen to fifteen million gallons a year; and even in 1930, after the Government had improved its technique of dealing with this particular source of supply (by careful control of the permit system and

195

otherwise), the Director of Prohibition admitted that the annual diversion still amounted to nine million gallons, and other estimates ran as high as fifteen million. (Bear in mind that one gallon of diverted alcohol, watered down and flavored, was enough to furnish three gallons of bogus liquor, bottled with lovely Scotch labels and described by the bootlegger at the leading citizen's door as "just off the boat.")

As for illicit distilling, as time went on this proved the most copious of all sources of supply. At the end of the decade it furnished, on the testimony of Doctor Doran of the prohibition staff, perhaps seven or eight times as much alcohol as even the process of diversion. If anything was needed to suggest how ubiquitous was the illicit still in America, the figures for the production of corn sugar provided it. Between 1919 and 1929 the output of this commodity increased *sixfold,* despite the fact that, as the Wickersham Report put it, the legitimate uses of corn sugar "are few and not easy to ascertain." Undoubtedly corn whisky was chiefly responsible for the vast increase.

This overwhelming flood of outlaw liquor introduced into the American scene a series of picturesque if unedifying phenomena: hip flasks uptilted above faces both masculine and feminine at the big football games; the speakeasy, equipped with a regular old-fashioned bar, serving cocktails made of gin turned out, perhaps, by a gang of Sicilian alky-cookers (seventy-five cents for patrons, free to the police); well-born damsels with one foot on the brass rail, tossing off Martinis; the keg of grape juice simmering hopefully in the young couple's bedroom closet, subject to periodical inspection by a young man sent from a "service station"; the business executive departing for the trade convention with two bottles of gin in his bag; the sales manager serving lavish drinks to the visiting buyer as in former days he had handed out lavish boxes of cigars; the hotel bellhop running to Room 417 with another order of ginger ale and cracked ice, provided by the management on the ironical understanding that they were "not to be mixed with spirituous liquors"; federal attorneys padlocking nightclubs and speakeasies, only to find them opening shortly at another address under a different name; Izzy Einstein and Moe Smith, prohibition agents extraordinary, putting on a series of comic-opera disguises to effect miraculous captures of bootleggers; General Smedley Butler of the Marines advancing in military formation upon the rum-sellers of Philadelphia, and retiring in disorder after a few strenuous months with the admission that politics made it impossible to dry up the city; the Government putting wood alcohol and other poisons into industrial alcohol to prevent its diversion, and the wets thereupon charging the Government with murder; Government agents, infuriated by their failure to prevent liquor-running by polite methods, finally shooting to kill--and sometimes picking off an innocent by-stander; the good ship *I'm Alone,* of Canadian registry, being pursued by a revenue boat for two and a half days and sunk at a distance of 215 miles from the American coast, to the official dismay of the Canadian Government; the federal courts jammed with prohibition cases, jurymen in wet districts refusing to pronounce bootleggers guilty, and the coin of corruption sifting through the hands of all manner of public servants.

Whatever the contribution of the prohibition régime to temperance, at least it produced intemperate propaganda and counter-propaganda. Almost any dry could tell you that prohibition was the basis of American prosperity, as attested by the mounting volume of savings-banks deposits and by what some big manufacturer had said about the men returning to work on Monday morning with clear eyes and steady hands. Or that prohibition had reduced the deaths from alcoholism, emptied the jails, and diverted the workman's dollar to the purchase of automobiles, radios, and homes. Almost any wet could tell you that prohibition had nothing to do with prosperity but had caused the crime wave, the increase of immorality and of the divorce rate, and a disrespect for all law which imperiled the very foundations of free government. The wets said the drys fostered Bolshevism by their fanatical zeal for laws which were inevitably flouted; the drys said the wets fostered Bolshevism by their cynical lawbreaking. Even in matters of supposed fact you could find, if you only read and listened, any sort of ammunition that you wanted. One never saw drunkards on the streets any more; one saw more drunkards than ever. Drinking in the colleges was hardly a problem now; drinking in the colleges was at its worst. There was a still in every other home in the mining districts of Pennsylvania; drinking in the mining districts of Pennsylvania was a thing of the past. Cases of poverty as a result of drunkenness were only a fraction of what they used to be; the menace of drink in the slums was three times as great as in pre-Volstead days. Bishop A and Doctor B and Governor C were much encouraged by the situation; Bishop X and Doctor Y and Governor Z were appalled by it. And so the battle raged, endlessly and loudly, back and forth.

The mass of statistics dragged to light by professional drys and professional wets and hurled at the public need not detain us here.

Many of them were grossly unreliable, and the use of most of them would have furnished an instructor in logic with perfect specimens of the *post hoc* fallacy. It is perhaps enough to point out a single anomaly--that with the Eighteenth Amendment and the Volstead Act in force, there should actually have been constant and vociferous argument throughout the nineteen-twenties over the question whether there was more drinking or less in the United States than before the war. Presumably there was a good deal less except among the prosperous; but the fact that it was not transparently obvious that there was less, showed how signal was the failure of the law to accomplish what almost everyone in 1919 had supposed it would accomplish.

§ 4

By 1928 the argument over prohibition had reached such intensity that it could no longer be kept out of presidential politics. Governor Smith of New York was accepted as the Democratic nominee despite his unterrified wetness, and campaigned lustily for two modifications: first, an amendment to the Volstead law giving a "scientific definition of the alcoholic content of an intoxicating beverage" (a rather large order for science), each state being allowed to fix its own standard if this did not exceed the standard fixed by Congress; and second, "an amendment in the Eighteenth Amendment which would give to each individual state itself, only after approval by a referendum popular vote of its people, the right wholly within its borders to import, manufacture, or cause to be manufactured and sell alcoholic beverages, the sale to be made only by the state itself and not for consumption in any public place." The Republican candidate, in reply, stepped somewhat definitely off the fence on the dry side. Herbert Hoover's dry declaration, to be sure, left much unsaid; he called prohibition "a great social and economic experiment, noble in motive and far-reaching in purpose," but he did not claim nobility for its results. The omission, however, was hardly noticed by an electorate which regarded endorsement of motives as virtually equivalent to endorsement of performance. Hoover was considered a dry.

The Republican candidate was elected in a landslide, and the drys took cheer. Despite the somewhat equivocal results of various state referenda and straw ballots, they had always claimed that they had a substantial majority in the country as well as in Congress; now they were sure of it. Still the result of the election left room for haunting doubts. Who could tell whether the happy warrior from the

East Side had been defeated because he was a wet, or because he was a Roman Catholic, or because he was considered a threat to the indefinite continuance of the delights of Coolidge Prosperity, or because he was a Democrat?

But Herbert Hoover had done more than endorse the motives of the prohibitionists. He had promised a study of the enforcement problem by a governmental commission. Two and a half months after his arrival at the White House, the commission, consisting of eleven members under the chairmanship of George W. Wickersham of New York, was appointed and immersed itself in its prodigious task.

By the time the Wickersham Commission emerged from the sea of fact and theory and contention in which it had been delving, and handed its report to the President, the Post-war Decade was dead and done with. Not until January, 1931, nineteen months after his appointment, did Mr. Wickersham lay the bulky findings of the eleven investigators upon the presidential desk. Yet the report calls for mention here, if only because it represented the findings of a group of intelligent and presumably impartial people with regard to one of the critical problems of the nineteen-twenties.

It was a paradoxical document. In the first place, the complete text revealed very clearly the sorry inability of the enforcement staff to dry up the country. In the second place, each of the eleven commissioners submitted a personal report giving his individual views, and only five of the eleven--a minority--favored further trial for the prohibition experiment without substantial change; four of them favored modification of the Amendment, and two were for outright repeal. But the commission *as a whole* cast its vote for further trial, contenting itself with suggesting a method of modification if time proved that the experiment was a failure. The confusing effect of the report was neatly satirized in Flaccus's summary of it in F. P. A.'s column in the *New York World:*

Prohibition is an awful flop.
> We like it.
It can't stop what it's meant to stop.
> We like it.
It's left a trail of graft and slime,
It's filled our land with vice and crime,
It don't prohibit worth a dime,
>> Nevertheless we're for it.

Yet if the Wickersham report was confusing, this was highly appropriate; for so also was the situation with which it dealt. Although it seemed reasonably clear to an impartial observer that the country had chosen the wrong road in 1917-20, legislating with a sublime disregard for elementary chemistry--which might have taught it how easily alcohol may be manufactured--and for elementary psychology-- which might have suggested that common human impulses are not easily suppressed by fiat--it was nevertheless very far from clear how the country could best extricate itself from the morass into which it had so blithely plunged. How could people who had become gin- drinkers be expected to content themselves with light wines and beers, as some of the modificationists suggested? How could any less drastic system of governmental regulation or governmental sale of liquor operate without continued transgression and corruption, now that a large element had learned how to live with impunity on the fruits of lawbreaking? To what sinister occupations might not the bootlegging gentry turn if outright repeal took their accustomed means of livelihood away from them? How could any new national policy toward alcohol be successfully put into effect when there was still violent disagreement, even among those who wanted the law changed, as to whether alcohol should be regarded as a curse, as a blessing to be used in moderation, or as a matter of personal rather than public concern? Even if a clear majority of the American people were able to decide to their own satisfaction what was the best way out of the morass, what chance was there of putting through their program when thirteen dry states could block any change in the Amendment? No problem which had ever faced the United States had seemed more nearly insoluble.

§ 5

In 1920, when prohibition was very young, Johnny Torrio of Chicago had an inspiration. Torrio was a formidable figure in the Chicago underworld. He had discovered that there was big money in the newly outlawed liquor business. He was fired with the hope of getting control of the dispensation of booze to the whole city of Chicago. At the moment there was a great deal too much competition; but possibly a well-disciplined gang of men handy with their fists and their guns could take care of that, by intimidating rival bootleggers and persuading speakeasy proprietors that life might not be wholly comfortable for them unless they bought Torrio liquor. What Torrio needed was a lieutenant who could mobilize and lead his shock troops.

Being a graduate of the notorious Five Points gang in New York and a disciple of such genial fellows as Lefty Louie and Gyp the Blood (he himself had been questioned about the murder of Herman Rosenthal in the famous Becker case in 1912), he naturally turned to his *alma mater* for his man. He picked for the job a bullet-headed twenty-three-year-old Neapolitan roughneck of the Five Points gang, and offered him a generous income and half the profits of the bootleg trade if he would come to Chicago and take care of the competition. The young hoodlum came, established himself at Torrio's gambling-place, the Four Deuces, opened by way of plausible stage setting an innocent-looking office which contained among its properties a family Bible, and had a set of business cards printed:

ALPHONSE CAPONE

Second Hand Furniture Dealer   2220 South Wabash Avenue

Torrio had guessed right--in fact, he had guessed right three times. The profits of bootlegging in Chicago proved to be prodigious, allowing an ample margin for the mollification of the forces of the law. The competition proved to be exacting: every now and then Torrio would discover that his rivals had approached a speakeasy proprietor with the suggestion that he buy their beer instead of the Torrio-Capone brand, and on receipt of an unfavorable answer had beaten the proprietor senseless and smashed up his place of business. But Al Capone had been an excellent choice as leader of the Torrio offensives; Capone was learning how to deal with such emergencies.

Within three years it was said that the boy from the Five Points had seven hundred men at his disposal, many of them adept in the use of the sawed-off shotgun and the Thompson sub-machine gun. As the profits from beer and "alky-cooking" (illicit distilling) rolled in, young Capone acquired more finesse--particularly finesse in the management of politics and politicians. By the middle of the decade he had gained complete control of the suburb of Cicero, had installed his own mayor in office, had posted his agents in the wide-open gambling-resorts and in each of the 161 bars, and had established his personal headquarters in the Hawthorne Hotel. He was taking in millions now. Torrio was fading into the background; Capone was becoming the Big Shot. But his conquest of power did not come without bloodshed. As the rival gangs--the O'Banions, the Gennas, the Aiellos--disputed his growing domination, Chicago was afflicted with such an epidemic of killings as no civilized modern city had ever before seen, and a new technique of wholesale murder was developed.

One of the standard methods of disposing of a rival in this warfare of the gangs was to pursue his car with a stolen automobile full of men armed with sawed-off shotguns and sub-machine guns; to draw up beside it, forcing it to the curb, open fire upon it--and then disappear into the traffic, later abandoning the stolen car at a safe distance. Another favorite method was to take the victim "for a ride": in other words, to lure him into a supposedly friendly car, shoot him at leisure, drive to some distant and deserted part of the city, and quietly throw his body overboard. Still another was to lease an apartment or a room overlooking his front door, station a couple of hired assassins at the window, and as the victim emerged from the house some sunny afternoon, to spray him with a few dozen machine-gun bullets from behind drawn curtains. But there were also more ingenious and refined methods of slaughter.

Take, for example, the killing of Dion O'Banion, leader of the gang which for a time most seriously menaced Capone's reign in Chicago. The preparation of this particular murder was reminiscent of the kiss of Judas. O'Banion was a bootlegger and a gangster by night, but a florist by day: a strange and complex character, a connoisseur of orchids and of manslaughter. One morning a sedan drew up outside his flower shop and three men got out, leaving the fourth at the wheel. The three men had apparently taken good care to win O'Banion's trust, for although he always carried three guns, now for the moment he was off his guard as he advanced among the flowers to meet his visitors. The middle man of the three cordially shook hands with O'Banion--*and then held on* while his two companions put six bullets into the gangster-florist. The three conspirators walked out, climbed into the sedan, and departed. They were never brought to justice, and it is not recorded that any of them hung themselves to trees in remorse. O'Banion had a first-class funeral, gangster style: a ten-thousand-dollar casket, twenty-six truck-loads of flowers, and among them a basket of flowers which bore the touching inscription, "From Al."

In 1926 the O'Banions, still unrepentant despite the loss of their leader, introduced another novelty in gang warfare. In broad daylight, while the streets of Cicero were alive with traffic, they raked Al Capone's headquarters with machine-gun fire from eight touring cars. The cars proceeded down the crowded street outside the Hawthorne Hotel in solemn line, the first one firing blank cartridges to disperse the innocent citizenry and to draw the Capone forces to the doors and windows, while from the succeeding cars, which followed a block behind, flowed a steady rattle of bullets, spraying the hotel and the adjoining buildings up and down. One gunman even got out of his car, knelt carefully upon the sidewalk at the door of the Hawthorne, and played one hundred bullets into the lobby--back and forth, as one might play the hose upon one's garden. The casualties were miraculously light, and Scarface Al himself remained in safety, flat on the floor of the Hotel Hawthorne restaurant; nevertheless, the bombardment quite naturally attracted public attention. Even in a day when bullion was transported in armored cars, the transformation of a suburban street into a shooting-gallery seemed a little unorthodox.

The war continued, one gangster after another crumpling under a rain of bullets; not until St. Valentine's Day of 1929 did it reach its climax in a massacre which outdid all that had preceded it in ingenuity and brutality. At half-past ten on the morning of February 14, 1929, seven of the O'Banions were sitting in the garage which went by the name of the S. M. C. Cartage Company, on North Clark Street, waiting for a promised consignment of hijacked liquor. A Cadillac touring-car slid to the curb, and three men dressed as policemen got out, followed by two others in civilian dress. The three supposed policemen entered the garage alone, disarmed the seven O'Banions, and told them to stand in a row against the wall. The victims readily submitted; they were used to police raids and thought nothing of them; they would get off easily enough, they expected. But thereupon the two men in civilian clothes emerged from the corridor and calmly mowed down all seven O'Banions with sub-machine gun fire as they stood with hands upraised against the wall. The little drama was completed when the three supposed policemen solemnly marched the two plain-clothes killers across the sidewalk to the waiting car, and all five got in and drove off--having given to those in the wintry street a perfect tableau of an arrest satisfactorily made by the forces of the law!

These killings--together with that of "Jake" Lingle, who led a double life as reporter for the *Chicago Tribune* and as associate of gangsters, and who was shot to death in a crowded subway leading to the Illinois Central suburban railway station in 1930--were perhaps the most spectacular of the decade in Chicago. But there were over five hundred gang murders in all. Few of the murderers were apprehended; careful planning, money, influence, the intimidation of witnesses, and the refusal of any gangster to testify against any other, no matter how treacherous the murder, met that danger. The city of Chicago was giving the whole country, and indeed the whole world, an astonishing object lesson in violent and unpunished crime. How and why could such a thing happen?

To say that prohibition--or, if you prefer, the refusal of the public to abide by prohibition--caused the rise of the gangs to lawless power would be altogether too easy an explanation. There were other causes: the automobile, which made escape easy, as the officers of robbed banks had discovered; the adaptation to peace-time use of a new arsenal of handy and deadly weapons; the murderous traditions of the Mafia, imported by Sicilian gangsters; the inclination of a wet community to wink at the by-products of a trade which provided them with beer and gin; the sheer size and unwieldiness of the modern metropolitan community, which prevented the focusing of public opinion upon any depredation which did not immediately concern the average individual citizen; and, of course, the easy-going political apathy of the times. But the immediate occasion of the rise of gangs was undoubtedly prohibition--or, to be more precise, beer-running. (Beer rather than whisky on account of its bulk; to carry on a profitable trade in beer one must transport it in trucks, and trucks are so difficult to disguise that the traffic must be protected by bribery of the prohibition staff and the police and by gunfire against bandits.) There was vast profit in the manufacture, transportation, and sale of beer. In 1927, according to Fred D. Pasley, Al Capone's biographer, federal agents estimated that the Capone gang controlled the sources of a revenue from booze of something like sixty million dollars a year, and much of this--perhaps most of it--came from beer. Fill a man's pockets with money, give him a chance at a huge profit, put him into an illegal business and thus deny him recourse to the law if he is attacked, and you have made it easy for him to bribe and shoot. There have always been gangs and gangsters in American life and doubtless always will be; there has always been corruption of city officials and doubtless always will be; yet it is ironically true, none the less, that the outburst of corruption and crime in Chicago in the nineteen-twenties was immediately occasioned by the attempt to banish the temptations of liquor from the American home.

The young thug from the Five Points, New York, had traveled fast and far since 1920. By the end of the decade he had become as widely renowned as Charles Evans Hughes or Gene Tunney. He had become an American portent. Not only did he largely control the sale of liquor to Chicago's ten thousand speakeasies; he controlled the sources of supply, it was said, as far as Canada and the Florida coast. He had amassed, and concealed, a fortune the extent of which nobody knew; it was said by federal agents to amount to twenty million. He was arrested and imprisoned once in Philadelphia for carrying a gun, but otherwise he seemed above the law. He rode about Chicago in an armored car, a traveling fortress, with another car to patrol the way ahead and a third car full of his armed henchmen following behind; he went to the theater attended by a body-guard of eighteen young men in dinner coats, with guns doubtless slung under their left armpits in approved gangster fashion; when his sister was married, thousands milled about the church in the snow, and he presented the bride with a nine-foot wedding cake and a special honeymoon car; he had a fine estate at Miami where he sometimes entertained seventy-five guests at a time; and high politicians--and even, it has been said, judges--took orders from him over the telephone from his headquarters in a downtown Chicago hotel. And still he was only thirty-two years old. What was Napoleon doing at thirty-two?

Meanwhile gang rule and gang violence were quickly penetrating other American cities. Toledo had felt them, and Detroit, and New York, and many another. Chicago was not alone. Chicago had merely led the way.

§ 6

By the middle of the decade it was apparent that the gangs were expanding their enterprises. In Mr. Pasley's analysis of the gross income of the Capone crew in 1927, as estimated by federal agents, the item of $60,000,000 from beer and liquor, including alky-cooking, and the items of $25,000,000 from gambling-establishments and dog-tracks, and of $10,000,000 from vice, dance-halls, roadhouses, and other resorts, were followed by this entry: Rackets, $10,000,000. The bootlegging underworld was venturing into fresh fields and pastures new.

The word "racket," in the general sense of an occupation which produces easy money, is of venerable age: it was employed over fifty years ago in Tammany circles in New York. But it was not widely used in its present meaning until the middle nineteen-twenties, and the derived term "racketeering" did not enter the American vocabulary until the year when Sacco and Vanzetti were executed and Lindbergh flew the Atlantic and Calvin Coolidge did not choose to run--the year 1927. The name was a product of the Post-war Decade; and so was the activity to which it was attached.

Like the murderous activities of the bootlegging gangs, racketeering grew out of a complex of causes. One of these was violent labor unionism. Since the days of the Molly Maguires, organized labor had now and again fought for its rights with brass knuckles and bombs. During the Big Red Scare the labor unions had lost the backing of public opinion, and Coolidge Prosperity was making things still more difficult for them by persuading thousands of their members that a union card was not the only ticket to good fortune. More than one fighting labor leader thereupon turned once more to dynamite in the effort to maintain his job and his power. Gone was the ardent radicalism of 1919, the hope of a new industrial order; the labor leader now found himself simply a man who hoped to get his when others were getting theirs, a man tempted to smash the scab's face or to blow the roof off the anti-union factory to show that he meant business and could deliver the goods. In many cases he turned for aid to the hired thug, the killer; he protected himself from the law by bribery or at least by political influence; he connived with businessmen who were ready to play his game for their own protection or for profit. These unholy alliances were now the more easily achieved because the illicit liquor trade was making the underworld rich and confident and quick on the trigger and was accustoming many politicians and businessmen to large-scale graft and conspiracy. Gangsters and other crafty fellows learned of the labor leader's tricks and went out to organize rackets on their own account. Thus by 1927 the city which had nourished Al Capone was nourishing also a remarkable assortment of these curious enterprises.

Some of them were labor unions perverted to criminal ends; some were merely conspiracies for extortion masquerading as labor unions; others were conspiracies masquerading as trade associations, or were combinations of these different forms. But the basic principle was fairly uniform: the racket was a scheme for collecting cash from businessmen to protect them from damage, and it prospered because the victim soon learned that if he did not pay, his shop would be bombed, or his trucks wrecked, or he himself might be shot in cold blood--and never a chance to appeal to the authorities for aid, because the authorities were frightened or fixed.

There was the cleaners' and dyers' racket, which collected heavy dues from the proprietors of retail cleaning shops and from master cleaners, and for a time so completely controlled the industry in Chicago that it could raise the price which the ordinary citizen paid for having his suit cleaned from $1.25 to $1.75. A cleaner and dyer who defied this racket might have his place of business bombed, or his delivery truck drenched with gasoline and set on fire, or he might be disciplined in a more devilish way: explosive chemicals might be sewn into the seams of trousers sent to him to be cleaned. There was the garage racket, product of the master mind of David Ablin, alias "Cockeye" Mulligan: if a garage owner chose not to join in the Mid-West Garage Association, as this enterprise was formally entitled, his garage would be bombed, or his mechanics would be slugged, or thugs would enter at night and smash windshields or lay about among the sedans with sledge-hammers, or tires would be flattened by the expert use of an ice-pick. There was the window-washing racket; when Max Wilner, who had been a window-washing contractor in Cleveland, moved to Chicago and tried to do business there, and was told that he could not unless he bought out some contractor already established, and refused to do so, he was not merely slugged or cajoled with explosives--he was shot dead. The list of rackets and of crimes could be extended for pages; in 1929, according to the State Attorney's office, there were ninety-one rackets in Chicago, seventy-five of them in active operation, and the Employers' Association figured the total cost to the citizenry at $136,000,000 a year.

As the favorite weapon of the bootlegging gangster was the machine gun, so the favorite weapon of the racketeer was the bomb. He could hire a bomber to do an ordinary routine job with a black-powder bomb for $100, but a risky job with a dynamite bomb might cost him all of $1,000. In the course of a little over fifteen months-- from October 11, 1927, to January 15, 1929--no less than 157 bombs were set or exploded in the Chicago district, and according to Gordon L. Hostetter and Thomas Quinn Beesley, who made a careful compilation of these outrages in *It's a Racket,* there was no evidence that the perpetrators of *any of them* were brought to book.

A merry industry, and reasonably safe, it seemed--for the racketeers. Indeed, before the end of the decade racketeering had made such strides in Chicago that businessmen were turning in desperation to Al Capone for protection; Capone's henchmen were quietly attending union meetings to make sure that all proceeded according to the Big Shot's desires, and it was said that there were few more powerful figures in the councils of organized labor than the lord of the bootleggers had come to be. Racketeering, like gang warfare, had invaded other American cities, too. New York had laughed at Chicago's lawlessness, had it? New York was acquiring a handsome crop of rackets of its own--a laundry racket, a slot-machine racket, a fish racket, a flour racket, an artichoke racket, and others too numerous to mention. In every large urban community the racketeer was now at least a potential menace. In the course of a few short years he had become a national institution.

§ 7

The prohibition problem, the gangster problem, the racket problem: as the Post-war Decade bowed itself out, all of them remained unsolved, to challenge the statesmanship of the nineteen-thirties. Still the rum-running launch slipped across the river, the alky-cooker's hidden apparatus poured forth alcohol, *entrepreneurs* of the contraband liquor industry put one another "on the spot," "typewriters" rattled in the Chicago streets, automobiles laden with roses followed the gangster to his grave, professional sluggers swung on non-union workmen, bull-necked gentlemen with shifty eyes called on the tradesman to suggest that he do business with them or they could not be responsible for what might happen, bombs reduced little shops to splintered wreckage; and tabloid-readers, poring over the stories of gangster killings, found in them adventure and splendor and romance.

♦ XI ♦
HOME, SWEET FLORIDA

§ 1

... "GO TO FLORIDA--
"WHERE ENTERPRISE IS ENTHRONED--
"Where you sit and watch at twilight the fronds of the graceful palm, latticed against the fading gold of the sun-kissed sky--
"Where sun, moon and stars, at eventide, stage a welcome constituting the glorious galaxy of the firmament--
"Where the whispering breeze springs fresh from the lap of Caribbean and woos with elusive cadence like unto a mother's lullaby--

"Where the silver cycle is heaven's lavalier, and the full orbit [*sic*] its glorious pendant."

This outburst of unbuttoned rhetoric was written in the autumn of 1925, when the Scopes trial was receding into memory, Santa Barbara was steadying itself from the shock of earthquake, Red Grange was plunging to fame, the cornerstone of Bishop Manning's house of prayer for all people was about to be laid, Brigadier-General Smedley Butler was wishing he had never undertaken to mop up Philadelphia, *The Man Nobody Knows* was selling its ten thousands-- and the Florida boom was at its height. The quotation is not, as you might imagine, from the collected lyrics of an enraptured schoolgirl, but from the conclusion of an article written for the *Miamian* by the vice-president of a bank. It faintly suggests what happened to the mental processes of supposedly hard-headed men and women when they were exposed to the most delirious fever of real-estate speculation which had attacked the United States in ninety years.

There was nothing languorous about the atmosphere of tropical Miami during that memorable summer and autumn of 1925. The whole city had become one frenzied real-estate exchange. There were said to be 2,000 real-estate offices and 25,000 agents marketing house-lots or acreage. The shirt-sleeved crowds hurrying to and fro under the widely advertised Florida sun talked of binders and options and water-frontages and hundred-thousand-dollar profits; the city fathers had been forced to pass an ordinance forbidding the sale of property in the street, or even the showing of a map, to prevent inordinate traffic congestion. The warm air vibrated with the clatter of riveters, for the steel skeletons of skyscrapers were rising to give Miami a skyline appropriate to its metropolitan destiny. Motor-busses roared down Flagler Street, carrying "prospects" on free trips to watch dredges and steam-shovels converting the outlying mangrove swamps and the sandbars of the Bay of Biscayne into gorgeous Venetian cities for the American homemakers and pleasure-seekers of the future. The Dixie Highway was clogged with automobiles from every part of the country; a traveler caught in a traffic jam counted the license-plates of eighteen states among the sedans and flivvers waiting in line. Hotels were overcrowded. People were sleeping wherever they could lay their heads, in station waiting-rooms or in automobiles. The railroads had been forced to place an embargo on imperishable freight in order to avert the danger of famine; building materials were now being imported by water and the harbor bristled with shipping. Fresh vegetables were a rarity, the public utilities of the city were trying desperately to meet the suddenly multiplied demand for electricity and gas and telephone service, and there were recurrent shortages of ice.

How Miami grew! In 1920 its population had been only 30,000. According to the state census of 1925 it had jumped to 75,000- -and probably if one had counted the newcomers of the succeeding months and Miami's share of the visitors who swarmed down to Florida from the North in one of the mightiest popular migrations of all time, the figure would have been nearer 150,000. And this, one was told, was only a beginning. Had not S. Davies Warfield, president of the Seaboard Air Line Railway, been quoted as predicting for Miami a population of a million within the next ten years? Did not the Governor of Florida, the Honorable John W. Martin, assert that "marvelous as is the wonder-story of Florida's recent achievements, these are but heralds of the dawn"?

Everybody was making money on land, prices were climbing to incredible heights, and those who came to scoff remained to speculate.

Nor was Miami alone booming. The whole strip of coast line from Palm Beach southward was being developed into an American Riviera; for sixty-odd miles it was being rapidly staked out into fifty-foot lots. The fever had spread to Tampa, Sarasota, St. Petersburg, and other cities and towns on the West Coast. People were scrambling for lots along Lake Okeechobee, about Sanford, all through the state; even in Jacksonville, near its northern limit, the "Believers in Jacksonville" were planning a campaign which would bring their city its due in growth and riches.

§ 2

For this amazing boom, which had gradually been gathering headway for several years but had not become sensational until 1924, there were a number of causes. Let us list them categorically.

1. First of all, of course, the climate--Florida's unanswerable argument.

2. The accessibility of the state to the populous cities of the Northeast--an advantage which Southern California could not well deny.

3. The automobile, which was rapidly making America into a nation of nomads; teaching all manner of men and women to explore their country, and enabling even the small farmer, the summer-boarding-house keeper, and the garage man to pack their families into flivvers and tour southward from auto-camp to auto-camp for a winter of sunny leisure.

4. The abounding confidence engendered by Coolidge Prosperity, which persuaded the four-thousand-dollar-a-year salesman that in some magical way he too might tomorrow be able to buy a fine house and all the good things of earth.

5. A paradoxical, widespread, but only half-acknowledged revolt against the very urbanization and industrialization of the country, the very concentration upon work, the very routine and smoke and congestion and twentieth-century standardization of living upon which Coolidge Prosperity was based. These things might bring the American businessman money, but to spend it he longed to escape from them--into the free sunshine of the remembered countryside, into the easy-going life and beauty of the European past, into some never-

never land which combined American sport and comfort with Latin glamour--a Venice equipped with bathtubs and electric iceboxes, a Seville provided with three eighteen-hole golf courses.

6. The example of Southern California, which had advertised its climate at the top of its lungs and had prospered by so doing: why, argued the Floridians, couldn't Florida do likewise?

7. And finally, another result of Coolidge Prosperity: not only did John Jones expect that presently he might be able to afford a house at Boca Raton and a vacation-time of tarpon-fishing or polo, but he also was fed on stories of bold business enterprise and sudden wealth until he was ready to believe that the craziest real-estate development might be the gold-mine which would work this miracle for him.

Crazy real-estate developments? But were they crazy? By 1925 few of them looked so any longer. The men whose fantastic projects had seemed in 1923 to be evidences of megalomania were now coining millions: by the pragmatic test they were not madmen but--as the advertisements put it--inspired dreamers. Coral Gables, Hollywood-by-the-Sea, Miami Beach, Davis Islands--there they stood: mere patterns on a blue-print no longer, but actual cities of brick and concrete and stucco; unfinished, to be sure, but growing with amazing speed, while prospects stood in line to buy and every square foot within their limits leaped in price.

Long years before, a retired Congregational minister named Merrick had bought cheap land outside Miami, built a many-gabled house out of coral rock, and called it "Coral Gables." Now his son, George Edgar Merrick, had added to this parcel of land and was building what the advertisements called "America's Most Beautiful Suburb." The plan was enticing, for Merrick had had sense enough to insist upon a uniform type of architecture--what he called a "modified Mediterranean" style. By 1926 his development, which had incorporated itself as the City of Coral Gables, contained more than two thousand houses built or building, with "a bustling business center, schools, banks, hotels, apartment houses and club houses"; with shady streets, lagoons, and anchorages. Merrick advertised boldly and in original ways: at one time he engaged William Jennings Bryan to sit under a sun-umbrella on a raft in a lagoon and lecture (at a handsome price) to the crowds on the shore--not upon the Prince of Peace or the Cross of Gold, but upon the Florida climate. (Bryan's tribute to sunshine was followed with dancing by Gilda Gray.) Merrick also knew how to make a romantic virtue of necessity: having low-lying land to drain and build on, he dug canals and imported real gondolas and gondoliers from Venice. The Miami-Biltmore Hotel at Coral Gables rose to a height of twenty-six stories; the country club had two eighteen-hole golf courses, and Merrick was making further audacious plans for a great casino, a yacht club, and a University of Miami. "Ten years of hard work, a hundred millions of hard money, is what George Merrick plans to spend before he rests," wrote Rex Beach in a brochure on Coral Gables. "Who can envisage what ten years will bring to that wonderland of Ponce de Leon's? Not you nor I. Nor Mr. Merrick, with all his soaring vision." (Alas for soaring vision! Among the things which ten years were to bring was an advertisement in the *New York Times* reminding the holders of nine series of bonds of the City of Coral Gables that the city had been "in default of the payment of principal and interest of a greater part of the above bonds since July 1, 1930.")

There were other miracle-workers besides Merrick. Miami Beach had been a mangrove swamp until Carl G. Fisher cut down the trees, buried their stumps under five feet of sand, fashioned lagoons and islands, built villas and hotels, and--so it was said--made nearly forty million dollars selling lots. Joseph W. Young built Hollywood-by-the-Sea on the same grand scale, and when the freight embargo cut off his supply of building materials, bought his own seagoing fleet to fetch them to his growing "city." Over on the West Coast, D. P. Davis bought two small islets in the bay at Tampa--"two small marshy clumps of mangrove, almost submerged at high tide"--and by dredging and piling sand, raised up an island on which he built paved streets, hotels, houses. On the first day when Davis offered his lots to the public he sold three million dollars' worth--though at that time it is said that not a single dredge had begun to scoop up sand!

Yes, the public bought. By 1925 they were buying anything, anywhere, so long as it was in Florida. One had only to announce a new development, be it honest or fraudulent, be it on the Atlantic Ocean or deep in the wasteland of the interior, to set people scrambling for house lots. "Manhattan Estates" was advertised as being "not more than three-fourths of a mile from the prosperous and fast-growing city of Nettie"; there was no such city as Nettie, the name being that of an abandoned turpentine camp, yet people bought. Investigators of the claims made for "Melbourne Gardens" tried to find the place, found themselves driving along a trail "through prairie muck land, with a few trees and small clumps of palmetto," and were hopelessly mired in the mud three miles short of their destination. But still the public bought, here and elsewhere, blindly, trustingly--natives of Florida, visitors to Florida, and good citizens of Ohio and Massachusetts and Wisconsin who had never been near Florida but made out their checks for lots in what they were told was to be "another Coral Gables" or was "next to the right of way of the new railroad" or was to be a "twenty-million-dollar city." The stories of prodigious profits made in Florida land were sufficient bait. A lot in the business center of Miami Beach had sold for $800 in the early days of the development and had resold for $150,000 in 1924. For a strip of land in Palm Beach a New York lawyer had been offered $240,000 some eight or ten years before the boom; in 1923 he finally accepted $800,000 for it; the next year the strip of land was broken up into building lots and disposed of at an aggregate price of $1,500,000; and in 1925 there were those who claimed that its value had risen to $4,000,000. A poor woman who had bought a piece of land near Miami in 1896 for $25 was able to sell it in 1925 for $150,000. Such tales were legion; every visitor to the Gold Coast could pick them up by the dozen; and many if not most of them were quite true--though the profits were largely on paper. No wonder the rush for Florida land justified the current anecdote of a native saying to a visitor, "Want to buy a lot?" and the visitor at once replying, "Sold."

Speculation was easy--and quick. No long delays while titles were being investigated and deeds recorded; such tiresome formalities were postponed. The prevalent method of sale was thus described by Walter C. Hill of the Retail Credit Company of Atlanta in the Inspection Report issued by his concern: "Lots are bought from blueprints. They look better that way. . . . Around Miami, subdivisions, except the very large ones, are often sold out the first day of sale. Advertisements appear describing the location, extent, special features, and approximate price of the lots. Reservations are accepted. This requires a check for 10 per cent of the price of the lot the buyer expects to select. On the first day of sale, at the promoter's office in town, the reservations are called out in order, and the buyer steps up and, from a beautifully drawn blueprint, with lots and dimensions and prices clearly shown, selects a lot or lots, gets a receipt in the form of a 'binder' describing it, and has the thrill of seeing 'Sold' stamped in the blue-lined square which represents his lot, a space usually fifty by a hundred feet of Florida soil or swamp. There are instances where these first-day sales have gone into several millions of dollars. And the prices! . . . Inside lots from $8,000 to $20,000. Water-front lots from $15,000 to $25,000. Seashore lots from $20,000 to $75,000. And these are not in Miami. They are miles out--ten miles out, fifteen miles out, and thirty miles out."

The binder, of course, did not complete the transaction. But few people worried much about the further payments which were to come. Nine buyers out of ten bought their lots with only one idea, to resell, and hoped to pass along their binders to other people at a neat profit before even the first payment fell due at the end of thirty days. There was an immense traffic in binders--immense and profitable.

Steadily, during that feverish summer and autumn of 1925, the hatching of new plans for vast developments continued. A great many of them, apparently, were intended to be occupied by what the advertisers of Miami Beach called "America's wealthiest sportsmen, devotees of yachting and the other expensive sports," and the advertisers of Boca Raton called "the world of international wealth that dominates finance and industry . . . that sets fashions . . . the world of large affairs, smart society and leisured ease." Few of those in the land-rush seemed to question whether there would be enough devotees of yachting and men and women of leisured ease to go round.

Everywhere vast new hotels, apartment houses, casinos were being projected. At the height of the fury of building a visitor to West Palm Beach noticed a large vacant lot almost completely covered with bathtubs. The tubs had apparently been there some time; the crates which surrounded them were well weathered. The lot, he was informed, was to be the site of "One of the most magnificent apartment buildings in the South"--but the freight embargo had held up the contractor's building material and only the bathtubs had arrived! Throughout Florida resounded the slogans and hyperboles of boundless confidence. The advertising columns shrieked with them, those swollen advertising columns which enabled the *Miami Daily News,* one day in the summer of 1925, to print an issue of 504 pages, the largest in newspaper history, and enabled the *Miami Herald* to carry a larger volume of advertising in 1925 than any paper anywhere had ever before carried in a year. Miami was not only "The Wonder City," it was also "The Fair White Goddess of Cities," "The World's Playground," and "The City Invincible," Fort Lauderdale became "The Tropical Wonderland," Orlando "The City Beautiful," and Sanford "The City Substantial."

Daily the turgid stream of rhetoric poured forth to the glory of Florida. It reached its climax, perhaps, in the joint Proclamation issued by the mayors of Miami, Miami Beach, Hialeah, and Coral Gables (who modestly referred to their county as "the most Richly Blessed

Community of the most Bountifully Endowed State of the most Highly Enterprising People of the Universe"), setting forth the last day of 1925 and the first two days of 1926 as "The Fiesta of the American Tropics"--"our Season of Fiesta when Love, Good Fellowship, Merrymaking, and Wholesome Sport shall prevail throughout Our Domains." The mayors promised that there would be dancing: "that our Broad Boulevards, our Beautiful Plazas and Ballroom Floors, our Patios, Clubs and Hostelries shall be the scenes where Radiant Terpsichore and her Sparkling Devotees shall follow with Graceful Tread the Measure of the Dance." They promised much more, to the extent of a page of flatulent text sprinkled with capitals; but especially they promised "that through our Streets and Avenues shall wind a glorious Pageantry of Sublime Beauty Depicting in Floral Loveliness the Blessing Bestowed upon us by Friendly Sun, Gracious Rain, and Soothing Tropic Wind."

Presumably the fiesta was successful, with its full quota of Sparkling Devotees and Sublime Beauty. But by New Year's Day of 1926 the suspicion was beginning to insinuate itself into the minds of the merrymakers that new buyers of land were no longer so plentiful as they had been in September and October, that a good many of those who held binders were exceedingly anxious to dispose of their stake in the most Richly Blessed Community, and that Friendly Sun and Gracious Rain were not going to be able, unassisted, to complete the payments on lots. The influx of winter visitors had not been quite up to expectations. Perhaps the boom was due for a "healthy breathing-time."

§ 3

As a matter of fact, it was due for a good deal more than that. It began obviously to collapse in the spring and summer of 1926. People who held binders and had failed to get rid of them were defaulting right and left on their payments. One man who had sold acreage early in 1925 for twelve dollars an acre, and had cursed himself for his stupidity when it was resold later in the year for seventeen dollars, and then thirty dollars, and finally sixty dollars an acre, was surprised a year or two afterward to find that the entire series of subsequent purchases was in default, that he could not recover the money still due him, and that his only redress was to take his land back again. There were cases in which the land not only came back to the original owner, but came back burdened with taxes and assessments which amounted to more than the cash he had received for it; and furthermore he found his land blighted with a half-completed development.

Just as it began to be clear that a wholesale deflation was inevitable, two hurricanes showed what a Soothing Tropic Wind could do when it got a running start from the West Indies.

No malevolent Providence bent upon the teaching of humility could have struck with a more precise aim than the second and worst of these Florida hurricanes. It concentrated upon the exact region where the boom had been noisiest and most hysterical--the region about Miami. Hitting the Gold Coast early in the morning of September 18, 1926, it piled the waters of Biscayne Bay into the lovely Venetian developments, deposited a five-masted steel schooner high in the street at Coral Gables, tossed big steam yachts upon the avenues of Miami, picked up trees, lumber, pipes, tiles, débris, and even small automobiles and sent them crashing into the houses, ripped the roofs off thousands of jerry-built cottages and villas, almost wiped out the town of Moore Haven on Lake Okeechobee, and left behind it some four hundred dead, sixty-three hundred injured, and fifty thousand homeless. Valiantly the Floridians insisted that the damage was not irreparable; so valiantly, in fact, that the head of the American Red Cross, John Barton Payne, was quoted as charging that the officials of the state had "practically destroyed" the national Red Cross campaign for relief of the homeless. Mayor Romfh of Miami declared that he saw no reason "why this city should not entertain her winter visitors the coming season as comfortably as in past seasons." But the Soothing Tropic Wind had had its revenge; it had destroyed the remnants of the Florida boom.

By 1927, according to Homer B. Vanderblue, most of the elaborate real-estate offices on Flagler Street in Miami were either closed or practically empty; the Davis Islands project, "bankrupt and unfinished," had been taken over by a syndicate organized by Stone & Webster; and many Florida cities, including Miami, were having difficulty collecting their taxes. By 1928 Henry S. Villard, writing in *The Nation,* thus described the approach to Miami by road: "Dead subdivisions line the highway, their pompous names half-obliterated on crumbling stucco gates. Lonely white-way lights stand guard over miles of cement sidewalks, where grass and palmetto take the place of homes that were to be. . . . Whole sections of outlying subdivisions are composed of unoccupied houses, past which one speeds on broad thoroughfares as if traversing a city in the grip of death." In 1928 there were thirty-one bank failures in Florida; in 1929 there were fifty-seven; in both of these years the liabilities of the failed banks reached greater totals than were recorded for any other state in the Union. The Mediterranean fruitfly added to the gravity of the local economic situation in 1929 by ravaging the citrus crop. Bank clearings for Miami, which had climbed sensationally to over a billion dollars in 1925, marched sadly downhill again:

1925 .... $1,066,528,000
1926 632,867,000
1927 260,039,000
1928 143,364,000
1929 142,316,000

And those were the very years when elsewhere in the country prosperity was triumphant! By the middle of 1930, after the general business depression had set in, no less than twenty-six Florida cities had gone into default of principal or interest on their bonds, the heaviest defaults being those of West Palm Beach, Miami, Sanford, and Lake Worth; and even Miami, which had a minor issue of bonds maturing in August, 1930, confessed its inability to redeem them and asked the bondholders for an extension.

The cheerful custom of incorporating real-estate developments as "cities" and financing the construction of all manner of improvements with "tax-free municipal bonds," as well as the custom on the part of development corporations of issuing real-estate bonds secured by new structures located in the boom territory, were showing weaknesses unimagined by the inspired dreamers of 1925. Most of the millions piled up in paper profits had melted away, many of the millions sunk in developments had been sunk for good and all, the vast inverted pyramid of credit had toppled to earth, and the lesson of the economic falsity of a scheme of land values based upon grandiose plans, preposterous expectations, and hot air had been taught in a long agony of deflation. For comfort there were only a few saving facts to cling to. Florida still had her climate, her natural resources. The people of Florida still had energy and determination, and having recovered from their debauch of hope, were learning from the relentless discipline of events. Not all Northerners who had moved to Florida in the days of plenty had departed in the days of adversity. Far from it: the census of 1930, in fact, gave Florida an increase in population of over 50 per cent since 1920--a larger increase than that of any other state except California--and showed that in the same interval Miami had grown by nearly 400 per cent. Florida still had a future; there was no doubt of that, sharp as the pains of enforced postponement were. Nor, for that matter, were the people of Florida alone blameworthy for the insanity of 1925. They, perhaps, had done most of the shouting, but the hysteria which had centered in their state had been a national hysteria, enormously increased by the influx of outlanders intent upon making easy money.

§ 4

The Florida boom, in fact, was only one--and by all odds the most spectacular--of a series of land and building booms during the Postwar Decade, each of which had its marked effect upon the national economy and the national life.

At the very outset of the decade there had been a sensational market in farm lands, caused by the phenomenal prices brought by wheat and other crops during and immediately after the war. Prices of farm property leaped, thousands of mortgages and loans were based upon these exaggerated values, and when the bottom dropped out of the agricultural markets in 1920-21, the distress of the farmers was intensified by the fact that in innumerable cases they could not get money enough from their crops to cover the interest due at the bank or to pay the taxes which were now levied on the increased valuation. Thousands of country banks, saddled with mortgages and loans in default, ultimately went to the wall. In one of the great agricultural states, the average earnings of *all* the national and state banks during the years 1924-29, a time of great prosperity for the country at large, were less than 1 $^{1}/_{2}$ per cent; and in seven states of the country, between 40 and 50 per cent of the banks which had been in business prior to 1920 had failed before 1929. Just how many of these failures were directly attributable to the undisciplined rise and subsequent fall in real-estate prices it is, of course, impossible to say; but undoubtedly many of the little country banks which suffered so acutely would never have gone down to ruin if there had been no boom in farm lands.

All through the decade, but especially during and immediately after the Florida fever, there was an epidemic of ambitious schemes hatched by promoters and boosters to bring prosperity to various American cities, towns, and resorts, by presenting each of them, in sumptuous advertisements, circulars, and press copy put out by hustling chambers of commerce, as the "center of a rising industrial empire" or as the "new playground of America's rich." Some of these ventures prospered; in California, for example, where the technique of boosting had been brought to poetic perfection long years previously, concerted campaigns brought industries, winter visitors, summer visitors, and good fortune for the businessman and the hotel-keeper alike. It was estimated that a million people a year went to California "just to look and play"--and, of course, to spend money. But not all such ventures could prosper, the number of factories and of wealthy vacationists being unhappily limited. City after city, hoping to attract industries within its limits, eloquently pointed out its "advantages" and tried to "make its personality felt" and to "carry its constructive message to the American people"; but at length it began to dawn upon the boosters that attracting industries bore some resemblance to robbing Peter to pay Paul, and that if all of them were converted to boosting, each of them was as likely to find itself in the role of Peter as in that of Paul. And exactly as the developers of the tropical wonderlands of Florida had learned that there were more land-speculators able and willing to gamble in houses intended for the polo-playing class than there were members of this class, so also those who carved out playgrounds for the rich in North Carolina or elsewhere learned to their ultimate sorrow that the rich could not play everywhere at once. And once more the downfall of their bright hopes had financial repercussions, as bankrupt developments led to the closing of bank after bank.

Again, all through the decade, but especially during its middle years, there was a boom in suburban lands outside virtually every American city. As four million discouraged Americans left the farms, and the percentage of city-dwellers in the United States increased from 51.4 to 57.6, and the cities grew in size and in stridency, and urban traffic became more noisy and congested, and new high buildings cut off the city-dweller's light and air, the drift of families from the cities to the urban-rural compromise of the neighboring countryside became more rapid. Here again the automobile played its part in changing the conditions of American life, by bringing within easy range of the suburban railroad station, and thus of the big city, great stretches of woodland and field which a few years before had seemed remote and inaccessible. Attractive suburbs grew with amazing speed, blossoming out with brand-new Colonial farmhouses (with attached garage), Tudor cottages (with age-old sagging roofs constructed by inserting wedge-shaped blocks of wood at the ends of the roof-trees), and Spanish stucco haciendas (with built-in radios). Once more the real-estate developer had his golden opportunity. The old Jackson farm with its orchards and daisy-fields was staked out in lots and attacked by the steam-shovel and became Jacobean Heights or Colonial Terrace or Alhambra Gardens, with paved roads, twentieth-century comforts, Old World charm, and land for sale on easy payments.

On the immediate outskirts of great cities such as New York, Chicago, Los Angeles, and Detroit huge tracts were less luxuriously developed. The Borough of Queens, just across the East River from New York, grew vastly and hideously: its population more than doubled during the decade, reaching a total of over a million. Outside Detroit immense districts were subdivided and numerous lots in them were bought by people so poor that they secured permits to build "garage dwellings"--temporary one-room shacks--and lived in them for years without ever building real houses. So furious was the competition among developers that it was estimated that in a single year there were subdivided in the Chicago region enough lots to accommodate the growth of the city for twenty years to come (at the rate at which it had previously grown), and that by the end of the decade enough lots had been staked out between Patchogue, Long Island, and the New York City limits to house the entire metropolitan population of six million.

For a time the Florida boom had a picturesque influence on suburban developments. Many of them went Venetian. There was, for example, American Venice, thirty-four miles from New York on Long Island, where the first bridge to be built was "a replica of the famous Della Paglia Bridge at Venice," and the whole scene, according to the promoters, "recalls the famous city of the Doges, only more charming--and more homelike." "To live at American Venice," chanted one of the advertisements of this proposed retreat for stockbrokers and insurance salesmen, "is to quaff the very Wine of Life. . . . A turquoise lagoon under an aquamarine sky! Lazy gondolas! Beautiful Italian gardens! . . . And, ever present, the waters of the Great South Bay lapping lazily all day upon a beach as white and fine as the soul of a little child." And there was Biltmore Shores, also developed on Long Island (by William Fox of the movies and Jacob Frankel of the clothing business) where, in 1926, "an artistic system of canals and waterways" was advertised as being "in progress of completion."

The Venetian phase of the suburban boom was of short duration: after 1926 the mention of lagoons introduced painful thoughts into the minds of prospective purchasers. But the suburban boom itself did not begin to languish in most localities until 1928 or 1929. By that time many suburbs were plainly overbuilt: as one drove out along the highways, one began to notice houses that must have stood long untenanted, shops with staring vacant windows, districts blighted with half-finished and abandoned "improvements"; one heard of suburban apartment houses which had changed hands again and again as mortgages were foreclosed, or of householders in uncompleted subdivisions who were groaning under a naïvely unexpected burden of taxes and assessments. Yet even then it was clear that, like Florida, the suburb had a future. The need of men and women for space and freedom, as well as for access to the centers of population, had not come to an end.

The final phase of the real-estate boom of the nineteen-twenties centered in the cities themselves. To picture what happened to the American skyline during those years, compare a 1920 airplane view of almost any large city with one taken in 1930. There is scarcely a city which does not show a bright new cluster of skyscrapers at its center. The tower-building mania reached its climax in New York--since towers in the metropolis are a potent advertisement--and particularly in the Grand Central district of New York. Here the building boom attained immense proportions, coming to its peak of intensity in 1928. New pinnacles shot into the air forty stories, fifty stories, and more; between 1918 and 1930 the amount of space available for office use in large modern buildings in that district was multiplied approximately by ten. In a photograph of uptown New York taken from the neighborhood of the East River early in 1931, the twenty most conspicuous structures were all products of the Post-war Decade. The tallest two of all, to be sure, were not completed until after the panic of 1929; by the time the splendid shining tower of the Empire State Building stood clear of scaffolding there were apple salesmen shivering on the curbstone below. Yet it was none the less a monument to the abounding confidence of the days in which it was conceived.

The confidence had been excessive. Skyscrapers had been over-produced. In the spring of 1931 it was reliably stated that some 17 per cent of the space in the big office buildings of the Grand Central district, and some 40 per cent of that in the big office buildings of the Plaza district farther uptown, were not bringing in a return; owners of new skyscrapers were inveigling business concerns into occupying vacant floors by offering them space rent-free for a period or by assuming their leases in other buildings; and financiers were shaking their heads over the precarious condition of many realty investments in New York. The metropolis, too, had a future, but speculative enthusiasm had carried it upward a little too fast.

§ 5

After the Florida hurricane, real-estate speculation lost most of its interest for the ordinary man and woman. Few of them were much concerned, except as householders or as spectators, with the building of suburban developments or of forty-story experiments in modernist architecture. Yet the national speculative fever which had turned their eyes and their cash to the Florida Gold Coast in 1925 was not chilled; it was merely checked. Florida house-lots were a bad bet? Very well, then, said a public still enthralled by the radiant possibilities of Coolidge Prosperity: what else was there to bet on? Before long a new wave of popular speculation was accumulating momentum. Not in real-estate this time; in something quite different. The focus of speculative infection shifted from Flagler Street, Miami, to Broad and Wall Streets, New York. The Big Bull Market was getting under way.

♦ XII ♦
THE BIG BULL MARKET

§ 1

One day in February, 1928, an investor asked an astute banker about the wisdom of buying common stocks. The banker shook his head. "Stocks look dangerously high to me," he said. "This bull market has been going on for a long time, and although prices have slipped a bit recently, they might easily slip a good deal more. Business is none too good. Of course if you buy the right stock you'll probably be all right in the long run and you may even make a profit. But if I were you I'd wait awhile and see what happens."

By all the canons of conservative finance the banker was right. That enormous confidence in Coolidge Prosperity which had lifted the businessman to a new preëminence in American life and had persuaded innumerable men and women to gamble their savings away in Florida real estate had also carried the prices of common stocks far upward since 1924, until they had reached what many hard-headed financiers considered alarming levels. Throughout 1927 speculation had been increasing. The amount of money loaned to brokers to carry margin accounts for traders had risen during the year from $2,818,561,000 to $3,558,355,000--a huge increase. During the week of December 3, 1927, more shares of stock had changed hands than in any previous week in the whole history of the New York Stock Exchange. One did not have to listen long to an after-dinner conversation, whether in New York or San Francisco or the lowliest village of the plain, to realize that all sorts of people to whom the stock ticker had been a hitherto alien mystery were carrying a hundred shares of Studebaker or Houston Oil, learning the significance of such recondite symbols as GL and X and ITT, and whipping open the early editions of afternoon papers to catch the 1:30 quotations from Wall Street.

The speculative fever had been intensified by the action of the Federal Reserve System in lowering the rediscount rate from 4 per cent to 3 $\frac{1}{2}$ per cent in August, 1927, and purchasing Government securities in the open market. This action had been taken from the most laudable motives: several of the European nations were having difficulty in stabilizing their currencies, European exchanges were weak, and it seemed to the Reserve authorities that the easing of American money rates might prevent the further accumulation of gold in the United States and thus aid in the recovery of Europe and benefit foreign trade. Furthermore, American business was beginning to lose headway; the lowering of money rates might stimulate it. But the lowering of money rates also stimulated the stock market. The bull party in Wall Street had been still further encouraged by the remarkable solicitude of President Coolidge and Secretary Mellon, who whenever confidence showed signs of waning came out with opportunely reassuring statements which at once sent prices upward again. In January 1928, the President had actually taken the altogether unprecedented step of publicly stating that he did not consider brokers' loans too high, thus apparently giving White House sponsorship to the very inflation which was worrying the sober minds of the financial community.

While stock prices had been climbing, business activity had been undeniably subsiding. There had been such a marked recession during the latter part of 1927 that by February, 1928, the director of the Charity Organization Society in New York reported that unemployment was more serious than at any time since immediately after the war. During January and February the stock market turned ragged and unsettled, and no wonder--for with prices still near record levels and the future trend of business highly dubious, it was altogether too easy to foresee a time of reckoning ahead.

The tone of the business analysts and forecasters--a fraternity whose numbers had hugely increased in recent years and whose lightest words carried weight--was anything but exuberant. On January 5, 1928, Moody's Investors Service said that stock prices had "over-discounted anticipated progress" and wondered "how much of a readjustment may be required to place the stock market in a sound position." On March 1st this agency was still uneasy: "The public," it declared, "is not likely to change its bearish state of mind until about the time when money becomes so plethoric as to lead the banks to encourage credit expansion." Two days later the Harvard Economic Society drew from its statistical graphs the chilly conclusion that "the developments of February suggest that business is entering upon a period of temporary readjustment"; the best cheer which the Harvard prognosticators could offer was a prophecy that "intermediate declines in the stock market will not develop into such *major* movements as forecast business depression." The National City Bank looked for gradual improvement in business and the Standard Statistics Company suggested that a turn for the better had already arrived; but the latter agency also sagely predicted that the course of stocks during the coming months would depend "almost entirely upon the money situation." The financial editor of the *New York Times* described the picture of current conditions presented by the mercantile agencies as one of "hesitation." The newspaper advertisements of investment services testified to the uncomfortable temper of Wall Street with headlines like "Will You 'Overstay' This Bull Market?" and "Is the Process of Deflation Under Way?" The air was fogged with uncertainty.

Anybody who had chosen this moment to predict that the bull market was on the verge of a wild advance which would make all that had gone before seem trifling would have been quite mad--or else inspired with a genius for mass psychology. The banker who advised caution was quite right about financial conditions, and so were the forecasters. But they had not taken account of the boundless commercial romanticism of the American people, inflamed by year after plentiful year of Coolidge Prosperity. For on March 3, 1928--the very day when the Harvard prophets were talking about intermediate declines and the *Times* was talking about hesitation--the stock market entered upon its sensational phase.

§ 2

Let us glance for a moment at the next morning's paper, that arm-breaking load of reading-matter which bore the date of Sunday, March 4, 1928. It was now many months since Calvin Coolidge had stated, with that characteristic simplicity which led people to suspect him of devious meanings, that he did not "choose to run for President in 1928"; and already his Secretary of Commerce, who eight years before had been annoyed at being called an amateur in politics, was corralling delegates with distinctly professional efficiency against the impending Republican convention. It was three months since Henry Ford had unveiled Model A, but eyes still turned to stare when a new Ford went by, and those who had blithely ordered a sedan in Arabian Sand were beginning to wonder if they would have to wait until September and then have to take Dawn Gray or leave it. Colonel

Lindbergh had been a hero these nine months but was still a bachelor: on page 21 of that Sunday paper of March 4, 1928, he was quoted in disapproval of a bill introduced in Congress to convert the Lindbergh homestead at Little Falls, Minnesota, into a museum. Commander Byrd was about to announce his plans for a flight to the South Pole. Women's skirts, as pictured in the department store advertisements, were at their briefest; they barely covered the kneecap. The sporting pages contained the tidings that C. C. Pyle's lamentable Bunion Derby was about to start from Los Angeles with 274 contestants. On another page Mrs. William Jay, Mrs. Robert Low Bacon, and Mrs. Charles Cary Rumsey exemplified the principle of *noblesse oblige* by endorsing Simmons beds. *The Bridge of San Luis Rey* was advertised as having sold 100,000 copies in ninety days. The book section of the newspaper also advertised *The Greene Murder Case* by S. S. Van Dine (not yet identified as Willard Huntington Wright), Willa Cather's *Death Comes for the Archbishop,* and Ludwig Lewisohn's *The Island Within.* The theatrical pages disclosed that "The Trial of Mary Dugan" had been running in New York for seven months, Galsworthy's "Escape" for five; New York theater-goers might also take their choice between "Strange Interlude," "Show Boat," "Paris Bound," "Porgy," and "Funny Face." The talking pictures were just beginning to rival the silent films: Al Jolson was announced in "The Jazz Singer" on the Vitaphone, and two Fox successes "with symphonic movietone accompaniment" were advertised. The stock market--but one did not need to turn to the financial pages for that. For on page 1 appeared what was to prove a portentous piece of news.

General Motors stock, opening at 139 $^3/_4$ on the previous morning, had skyrocketed in two short hours to 144 $^1/_4$, with a gain of more than five points since the Friday closing. The trading for the day had amounted to not much more than 1,200,000 shares, but nearly a third of it had been in Motors. The speculative spring fever of 1928 had set in.

It may interest some readers to be reminded of the prices brought at the opening on March 3rd by some of the leading stocks of that day or of subsequent days. Here they are, with the common dividend rate for each stock in parentheses:

American Can (2), 77
American Telephone & Telegraph (9), 179 $^1/_2$
Anaconda (3), 54 $^1/_2$
Electric Bond & Share (1), 89 $^3/_4$

General Electric (5 including extras), 128 $^3/_4$
General Motors (5), 139 $^3/_4$
Montgomery Ward (5 including extras), 132 $^3/_4$
New York Central (8), 160 $^1/_2$
Radio (no dividend), 94 $^1/_2$
Union Carbide & Carbon (6), 145
United States Steel (7), 138 $^1/_8$
Westinghouse (4), 91 $^5/_8$
Woolworth (5), 180 $^3/_4$

On Monday General Motors gained 2 $^1/_4$ points more, on Tuesday 3 $^1/_2$; there was great excitement as the stock "crossed 150." Other stocks were beginning to be affected by the contagion as day after day the market "made the front page": Steel and Radio and Montgomery Ward were climbing, too. After a pause on Wednesday and Thursday, General Motors astounded everybody on Friday by pushing ahead a cool 9 $^1/_4$ points as the announcement was made that its Managers Securities Company had bought 200,000 shares in the open market for its executives at around 150. And then on Saturday the common stock of the Radio Corporation of America threw General Motors completely into the shade by leaping upward for a net gain of 12 $^3/_4$ points, closing at 120 $^1/_2$.

What on earth was happening? Wasn't business bad, and credit inflated, and the stock-price level dangerously high? Was the market going crazy? Suppose all these madmen who insisted on buying stocks at advancing prices tried to sell at the same moment! Canny investors, reading of the wild advance in Radio, felt much as did the forecasters of Moody's Investors Service a few days later: the practical question, they said, was "how long the opportunity to sell at the top will remain."

What was actually happening was that a group of powerful speculators with fortunes made in the automobile business and in the grain markets and in the earlier days of the bull market in stocks--men like W. C. Durant and Arthur Cutten and the Fisher Brothers and John J. Raskob--were buying in unparalleled volume. They thought that business was due to come out of its doldrums. They knew that with Ford production delayed, the General Motors Corporation was likely to have a big year. They knew that the Radio Corporation had been consolidating its position and was now ready to make more money than it had ever made before, and that as scientific discovery followed discovery, the future possibilities of the biggest radio company were exciting. Automobiles and radios--these were the two most characteristic products of the decade of confident mass production, the brightest flowers of Coolidge Prosperity: they held a ready-made appeal to the speculative imagination. The big bull operators knew, too, that thousands of speculators had been selling stocks short in the expectation of a collapse in the market, would continue to sell short, and could be forced to repurchase if prices were driven relentlessly up. And finally, they knew their American public. It could not resist the appeal of a surging market. It had an altogether normal desire to get rich quick, and it was ready to believe anything about the golden future of American business. If stocks started upward the public would buy, no matter what the forecasters said, no matter how obscure was the business prospect.

They were right. The public bought.

Monday the 12th of March put the stock market on the front page once more. Radio opened at 120 $^1/_2$--and closed at 138 $^1/_2$. Other stocks made imposing gains, the volume of trading broke every known record by totaling 3,875,910 shares, the ticker fell six minutes behind the market, and visitors to the gallery of the Stock Exchange reported that red-haired Michael Meehan, the specialist in Radio, was the center of what appeared to be a five-hour scrimmage on the floor. "It looked like a street fight," said one observer.

Tuesday the 13th was enough to give anybody chills and fever. Radio opened at 160, a full 21 $^1/_2$ points above the closing price the night before--a staggering advance. Then came an announcement that the Stock Exchange officials were beginning an investigation to find out whether a technical corner in the stock existed, and the price cascaded to 140. It jumped again that same day to 155 and closed at 146, 7 $^1/_2$ points above Monday's closing, to the accompaniment of rumors that one big short trader had been wiped out. This time the ticker was twelve minutes late.

And so it went on, day after day and week after week. On March 16th the ticker was thirty-three minutes late and one began to hear people saying that some day there might occur a five-million-share day--which seemed almost incredible. On the 20th, Radio jumped 18 points and General Motors 5. On March 26th the record for total volume of trading was smashed again. The new mark lasted just twenty-four hours, for on the 27th--a terrifying day when a storm of unexplained selling struck the market and General Motors dropped abruptly, only to recover on enormous buying--there were 4,790,000 shares traded. The speculative fever was infecting the whole country.

Stories of fortunes made overnight were on everybody's lips. One financial commentator reported that his doctor found patients talking about the market to the exclusion of everything else and that his barber was punctuating with the hot towel more than one account of the prospects of Montgomery Ward. Wives were asking their husbands why they were so slow, why they weren't getting in on all this, only to hear that their husbands had bought a hundred shares of American Linseed that very morning. Brokers' branch offices were jammed with crowds of men and women watching the shining transparency on which the moving message of the ticker tape was written; whether or not one held so much as a share of stock, there was a thrill in seeing the news of that abrupt break and recovery in General Motors on March 27th run across the field of vision in a long string of quotations:

GM 50.85 (meaning 5,000 shares at 185) 20.80. 50.82. 14.83. 30.85. 20.86. 25.87. 40.88. 30.87. . . .

New favorites took the limelight as the weeks went by. Montgomery Ward was climbing. The aviation stocks leaped upward; in a single week in May, Wright Aeronautical gained 34 $^3/_4$ points to reach 190, and Curtiss gained 35 $^1/_2$ to reach 142. Several times during the spring of 1928 the New York Stock Exchange had to remain closed on Saturday to give brokers' clerks a chance to dig themselves out from under the mass of paper work in which this unprecedented trading involved them. And of course brokers' loans were increasing; the inflation of American credit was becoming steadily intensified.

The Reserve authorities were disturbed. They had raised the rediscount rate in February from 3 $^1/_2$ to 4 per cent, hoping that if a lowering of the rate in 1927 had encouraged speculation, a corresponding increase would discourage it--and instead they had witnessed a common-stock mania which ran counter to all logic and all economic theory. They raised the rate again in May to 4 $^1/_2$ per cent, but after a brief shudder the market went boiling on. They sold the Government bonds they had accumulated during 1927, and the principal result of their efforts was that the Government-bond market became demoralized. Who would ever have thought the situation would thus get out of hand?

In the latter part of May, 1928, the pace of the bull market slackened. Prices fell off, gained, fell off again. The reckoning, so long expected, appeared at last to be at hand. It came in June, after several days of declining prices. The Giannini stocks, the speculative favorites of the Pacific coast, suddenly toppled for gigantic losses. On the San Francisco Stock Exchange the shares of the Bank of Italy fell 100 points in a single day (June 11th), Bancitaly fell 86 points, Bank of America 120, and United Security 80. That same day, on the New York Curb Exchange, Bancitaly dove perpendicularly from 200 to 110, dragging with it to ruin a horde of small speculators who, despite urgent warnings from A. P. Giannini himself that the stock was overvalued, had naïvely believed that it was "going to a thousand."

The next day, June 12th, this Western tornado struck Wall Street in full force. As selling orders poured in, the prophecy that the Exchange would some day see a five-million-share day was quickly fulfilled. The ticker slipped almost two hours behind in recording prices on the floor. Radio, which had marched well beyond the 200 mark in May, lost 23 $\frac{1}{2}$ points. The day's losses for the general run of securities were not, to be sure, very large by subsequent standards; the *New York Times* averages for fifty leading stocks dropped only a little over three points. But after the losses of the preceding days, it seemed to many observers as if the end had come at last, and one of the most conservative New York papers began its front-page account of the break with the unqualified sentence, "Wall Street's bull market collapsed yesterday with a detonation heard round the world."

(If the Secretary of Commerce had been superstitious, he might have considered that day of near-panic an omen of troubles to come; for on that same front page, streamer headlines bore the words, "HOOVER CERTAIN ON 1ST BALLOT AS CONVENTION OPENS.")

But had the bull market collapsed? On June 13th it appeared to have regained its balance. On June 14th, the day of Hoover's nomination, it extended its recovery. The promised reckoning had been only partial. Prices still stood well above their February levels. A few thousand traders had been shaken out, a few big fortunes had been lost, a great many pretty paper profits had vanished; but the Big Bull Market was still young.

§ 3

A few weeks after the somewhat unenthusiastic nomination of Herbert Hoover by the Republicans, that coalition of incompatibles known as the Democratic party nominated Governor Alfred E. Smith of New York, a genial son of the East Side with a genius for governmental administration and a taste for brown derbies. Al Smith was a remarkable choice. His Tammany affiliations, his wetness, and above all the fact that he was a Roman Catholic made him repugnant to the South and to most of the West. Although the Ku Klux Klan had recently announced the abandonment of its masks and the change of its name to "Knights of the Great Forest," anti-Catholic feeling could still take ugly forms. That the Democrats took the plunge and nominated Smith on the first ballot was eloquent testimony to the vitality of his personality, to the wide-spread respect for his ability, to the strength of the belief that any Democrat could carry the Solid South and that a wet candidate of immigrant stock would pull votes from the Republicans in the industrial North and the cities generally--and to the lack of other available candidates.

The campaign of 1928 began.

It was a curious campaign. One great issue divided the candidates. As already recorded in Chapter Ten, Al Smith made no secret of his distaste for prohibition; Hoover, on the other hand, called it "a great social and economic experiment, noble in motive and far-reaching in purpose," which "must be worked out constructively." Although Republican spellbinders in the damply urban East seemed to be under the impression that what Hoover really meant was "worked out of constructively," and Democratic spellbinders in the South and rural West explained that Smith's wetness was just an odd personal notion which he would be powerless to impose upon his party, the division between the two candidates remained: prohibition had forced its way at last into a presidential campaign. There was also the ostensible issue of farm-relief, but on this point there was little real disagreement; instead there was a competition to see which candidate could most eloquently offer largesse to the unhappy Northwest. There was Smith's cherished water-power issue, but this aroused no flaming enthusiasm in the electorate, possibly because too many influential citizens had rosy hopes for the future of Electric Bond & Share or Cities Service. There were also, of course, many less freely advertised issues: millions of men and women turned to Hoover because they thought Smith would make the White House a branch office of the Vatican, or turned to Smith because they wished to strike at religious intolerance, or opposed Hoover because they thought he would prove to be a stubborn doctrinaire, or were activated chiefly by dislike of Smith's hats or Mrs. Smith's jewelry. But no aspect of the campaign was more interesting than the extent to which it reflected the obsession of the American people with bull-market prosperity.

To begin with, there was no formidable third party in the field in 1928 as there had been in 1924. The whispering radicals had been lulled to sleep by the prophets of the new economic era. The Socialists nominated Norman Thomas, but were out of the race from the start. So closely had the ticker tape bound the American people to Wall Street, in fact, that even the Democrats found themselves in a difficult position. In other years they had shown a certain coolness toward the rulers of the banking and industrial world; but this would never do now. To criticize the gentlemen who occupied front seats on the prosperity band-wagon, or to suggest that the ultimate destination of the band-wagon might not be the promised land, would be suicidal. Nor could they deny that good times had arrived under a Republican administration. The best they could do was to argue by word and deed that they, too, could make America safe for dividends and rising stock prices.

This they now did with painful earnestness. For the chairmanship of the Democratic National Committee, Al Smith chose no wild-eyed Congressman from the great open spaces; he chose John J. Raskob, vice-president and chairman of the finance committee of the General Motors Corporation, vice-president of the General Motors Acceptance Corporation, vice-president and member of the finance committee of the E. I. duPont de Nemours & Company, director of the Bankers Trust Company, the American Surety Company, and the County Trust Company of New York--and reputed inspirer of the bull forces behind General Motors. Mr. Raskob was new to politics; in *Who's Who* he not only gave his occupation as "capitalist," but was listed as a Republican; but what matter? All the more credit to Al Smith, thought many Democrats, for having brought him at the eleventh hour to labor in the vineyard. With John J. Raskob on the Democratic side, who could claim that a Democratic victory would prevent common stocks from selling at twenty times earnings?

Mr. Raskob moved the Democratic headquarters to the General Motors Building in New York--than which there was no more bullish address. He proudly announced the fact that Mr. Harkness, "a Standard Oil financier," and Mr. Spreckels, "a banker and sugar refiner," and Mr. James, "a New York financier whose interests embrace railroads, securities companies, real estate, and merchandising," did not consider that their interests were "in the slightest degree imperiled by the prospect of Smith's election." (Shades of a thousand Democratic orators who had once extolled the New Freedom and spoken harsh words about Standard Oil magnates and

New York financiers!) And Mr. Raskob and Governor Smith both applied a careful soft pedal to the ancient Democratic low-tariff doctrine--being quite unaware that within two years many of their opponents would be wishing that the Republican high-tariff plank had fallen entirely out of the platform and been carted away.

As for the Republicans, they naturally proclaimed prosperity as a peculiarly Republican product, not yet quite perfected but ready for the finishing touches. Herbert Hoover himself struck the keynote for them in his acceptance speech.

"One of the oldest and perhaps the noblest of human aspirations," said the Republican candidate, "has been the abolition of poverty. . . . We in America today are nearer to the final triumph over poverty than ever before in the history of any land. The poorhouse is vanishing from among us. We have not yet reached the goal, but, given a chance to go forward with the policies of the last eight years, we shall soon, with the help of God, be in sight of the day when poverty will be banished from this nation. There is no guarantee against poverty equal to a job for every man. That is the primary purpose of the policies we advocate."

The time was to come when Mr. Hoover would perhaps regret the cheerful confidence of that acceptance speech. It left only one loophole for subsequent escape: it stipulated that God must assist the Republican administration.

Mr. Hoover was hardly to be blamed, however, for his optimism. Was not business doing far better in the summer of 1928 than it had done during the preceding winter? Was not the Big Bull Market getting under way again after its fainting fit in June? One drank in optimism from the very air about one. And, after all, the first duty of a candidate is to get himself elected. However dubious the abolition of poverty might appear to Hoover the engineer and economist seated before a series of graphs of the business cycle, it appeared quite differently to Hoover the politician standing before the microphone. Prosperity was a sure-fire issue for a Republican in 1928.

Al Smith put up a valiant fight, swinging strenuously from city to city, autographing brown derbies, denouncing prohibition, denouncing bigotry, and promising new salves for the farmer's wounds; but it was no use. The odds against him were too heavy. Election Day came and Hoover swept the country. His popular vote was nearly 21,500,000 Smith's 15,000,000; his electoral vote was 444 to Smith's 87; and he not only carried Smith's own state of New York and the doubtful border states of Oklahoma, Tennessee, and Kentucky, but broke the Solid South itself, winning Florida, Texas, North Carolina, and even Virginia.

It was a famous victory, and in celebration of it the stock market--which all through the campaign had been pushing into new high ground--went into a new frenzy. Now the bulls had a new slogan. It was "four more years of prosperity."

§ 4

During that "Hoover bull market" of November, 1928, the records made earlier in the year were smashed to flinders. Had brokers once spoken with awe of the possibility of five-million-share days? Five-million-share days were now occurring with monotonous regularity; on November 23rd the volume of trading almost reached seven million. Had they been amazed at the rising prices of seats on the Stock Exchange? In November a new mark of $580,000 was set. Had they been disturbed that Radio should sell at such an exorbitant price as 150? Late in November it was bringing 400. Ten-point gains and new highs for all time were commonplace now. Montgomery Ward, which the previous spring had been climbing toward 200, touched 439 $7/8$ on November 30. The copper stocks were skyrocketing; Packard climbed to 145; Wright Aeronautical flew as high as 263. Brokers' loans? Of course they were higher than ever; but this, one was confidently told, was merely a sign of prosperity--a sign that the American people were buying on the part-payment plan a partnership in the future progress of the country. Call money rates? They ranged around 8 and 9 per cent; a little high, perhaps, admitted the bulls, but what was the harm if people chose to pay them? Business was not suffering from high money rates; business was doing better than ever. The new era had arrived, and the abolition of poverty was just around the corner.

In December the market broke again, and more sharply than in June. There was one fearful day--Saturday, December 7th--when the weary ticker, dragging far behind the trading on the floor, hammered out the story of a 72-point decline in Radio. Horrified tape-watchers in the brokers' offices saw the stock open at 361, struggle weakly up to 363, and then take the bumps, point by point, all the way down to 296--which at that moment seemed like a fire-sale figure. (The earnings of the Radio Corporation during the first nine months of 1928 had been $7.54 per share, which on the time-honored basis of "ten times earnings" would have suggested the appropriateness of a price of not much over 100; but the ten-times-earnings basis for prices had long since been discarded. The market, as Max Winkler said, was discounting not only the future but the hereafter.) Montgomery Ward lost 29 points that same nerve-racking Saturday morning, and International Harvester slipped from 368 $\frac{1}{2}$ to 307. But just as in June, the market righted itself at the moment when demoralization seemed to be setting in. A few uneasy weeks of ragged prices went by, and then the advance began once more.

The Federal Reserve authorities found themselves in an unhappy predicament. Speculation was clearly absorbing more and more of the surplus funds of the country. The inflation of credit was becoming more and more dangerous. The normal course for the Reserve banks at such a juncture would have been to raise the rediscount rate, thus forcing up the price of money for speculative purposes, rendering speculation less attractive, liquidating speculative loans, and reducing the volume of credit outstanding. But the Reserve banks had already raised the rate (in July) to 5 per cent, and speculation had been affected only momentarily. Apparently speculators were ready to pay any amount for money if only prices kept on climbing. The Reserve authorities had waited patiently for the speculative fever to cure itself and it had only become more violent. Things had now come to such a pass that if they raised the rate still further, they not only ran the risk of bringing about a terrific smash in the market--and of appearing to do so deliberately and wantonly--but also of seriously handicapping business by forcing it to pay a high rate for funds. Furthermore, they feared the further accumulation of gold in the United States and the effect which this might have upon world trade. And the Treasury had a final special concern about interest rates--it had its own financing to do, and Secretary Mellon was naturally not enthusiastic about forcing the Government to pay a fancy rate for money for its own current use. It almost seemed as if there were no way to deflation except through disaster.

The Reserve Board finally met the dilemma by thinking up a new and ingenious scheme. They tried to prevent the reloaning of Reserve funds to brokers without raising the rediscount rate.

On February 2, 1929, they issued a statement in which they said: "The Federal Reserve Act does not, in the opinion of the Federal Reserve Board, contemplate the use of the resources of the Federal Reserve Banks for the creation or extension of speculative credit. A member bank is not within its reasonable claims for rediscount facilities at its Federal Reserve Bank when it borrows either for the purpose of making speculative loans or for the purpose of maintaining speculative loans." A little less than a fortnight later the Board wrote to the various Reserve Banks asking them to "prevent as far as possible the diversion of Federal Reserve funds for the purpose of carrying loans based on securities." Meanwhile the Reserve Banks drastically reduced their holdings of securities purchased in the open market. But no increases in rediscount rates were permitted. Again and again, from February on, the directors of the New York Reserve Bank asked Washington for permission to lift the New York rate, and each time the permission was denied. The Board preferred to rely on their new policy.

The immediate result of the statement of February 2, 1929, was a brief overnight collapse in stock prices. The subsequent result, as the Reserve Banks proceeded to bring pressure on their member banks to borrow only for what were termed legitimate business purposes, was naturally a further increase in call-money rates. Late in March--after Herbert Hoover had entered the White House and the previous patron saint of prosperity had retired to Northampton to explore the delights of autobiography--the pinch in money came to a sudden and alarming climax. Stock prices had been falling for several days when on March 26th the rate for call money jumped from 12 per cent to 15, and then to 17, and finally to 20 per cent--the highest rate since the dismal days of 1921. Another dizzy drop in prices took place. The turnover in stocks on the Exchange broke the November record, reaching 8,246,740 shares. Once again thousands of requests for more margin found their way into speculators' mail-boxes, and thousands of participators in the future prosperity of the country were sold out with the loss of everything they owned. Once again the Big Bull Market appeared to be on its last legs.

That afternoon several of the New York banks decided to come to the rescue. Whatever they thought of the new policy of the Federal Reserve Board, they saw a possible panic brewing--and anything, they decided, was better than a panic. The next day Charles E. Mitchell, president of the National City Bank, announced that his bank was prepared to lend twenty million dollars on call, of which five million would be available at 15 per cent, five million more at 16 per cent, and so on up to 20 per cent. Mr. Mitchell's action--which was described by Senator Carter Glass as a slap in the face of the Reserve Board--served to peg the call money rate at 15 per cent and the threatened panic was averted.

Whereupon stocks not only ceased their precipitous fall, but cheerfully recovered!

The lesson was plain: the public simply would not be shaken out of the market by anything short of a major disaster.

During the next month or two stocks rose and fell uncertainly, sinking dismally for a time in May, and the level of brokers' loans dipped a little, but no general liquidation took place. Gradually money began to find its way more plentifully into speculative use despite the barriers raised by the Federal Reserve Board. A corporation could easily find plenty of ways to put its surplus cash out on call at 8 or 9 per cent without doing it through a member bank of the Federal Reserve System; corporations were eager to put their funds to such remunerative use, as the increase in loans "for others" showed; and the member banks themselves, realizing this, were showing signs of restiveness. When June came, the advance in prices began once more, almost as if nothing had happened. The Reserve authorities were beaten.

§ 5

By the summer of 1929, prices had soared far above the stormy levels of the preceding winter into the blue and cloudless empyrean. All the old markers by which the price of a promising common stock could be measured had long since been passed; if a stock once valued at 100 went to 300, what on earth was to prevent it from sailing on to 400? And why not ride with it for 50 or 100 points, with Easy Street at the end of the journey?

By every rule of logic the situation had now become more perilous than ever. If inflation had been serious in 1927, it was far more serious in 1929, as the total of brokers' loans climbed toward six billion (it had been only three and a half billion at the end of 1927). If the price level had been extravagant in 1927 it was preposterous now; and in economics, as in physics, there is no gainsaying the ancient principle that the higher they go, the harder they fall. But the speculative memory is short. As people in the summer of 1929 looked back for precedents, they were comforted by the recollection that every crash of the past few years had been followed by a recovery, and that every recovery had ultimately brought prices to a new high point. Two steps up, one step down, two steps up again--that was how the market went. If you sold, you had only to wait for the next crash (they came every few months) and buy in again. And there was really no reason to sell at all: you were bound to win in the end if your stock was sound. The really wise man, it appeared, was he who "bought and held on."

Time and again the economists and forecasters had cried, "Wolf, wolf," and the wolf had made only the most fleeting of visits. Time and again the Reserve Board had expressed fear of inflation, and inflation had failed to bring hard times. Business in danger? Why, nonsense! Factories were running at full blast and the statistical indices registered first-class industrial health. Was there a threat of overproduction? Nonsense again! Were not business concerns committed to hand-to-mouth buying, were not commodity prices holding to reasonable levels? Where were the overloaded shelves of goods, the heavy inventories, which business analysts universally accepted as storm signals? And look at the character of the stocks which were now leading the advance! At a moment when many of the high-flyers of earlier months were losing ground, the really sensational advances were being made by the shares of such solid and conservatively managed companies as United States Steel, General Electric, and American Telephone--which were precisely those which the most cautious investor would select with an eye to the long future. Their advance, it appeared, was simply a sign that they were beginning to have a scarcity value. As General George R. Dyer of Dyer, Hudson & Company was quoted as saying in the *Boston News Bureau,* "Anyone who buys our highest-class rails and industrials, including the steels, coppers, and utilities, and holds them, will make a great deal of money, *as these securities will gradually be taken out of the market.*" What the bull operators had long been saying must be true, after all. This was a new era. Prosperity was coming into full and perfect flower.

Still there remained doubters. Yet so cogent were the arguments against them that at last the great majority of even the sober financial leaders of the country were won over in some degree. They recognized that inflation might ultimately be a menace, but the fears of immediate and serious trouble which had gripped them during the preceding winter were being dissipated. This bull market had survived some terrific shocks; perhaps it was destined for a long life, after all.

On every side one heard the new wisdom sagely expressed: "Prosperity due for a decline? Why, man, we've scarcely started!" "Be a bull on America." "Never sell the United States short." "I tell you, some of these prices will look ridiculously low in another year or two." "Just watch that stock--it's going to five hundred." "The possibilities of that company are *unlimited."* "Never give up your position in a good stock." Everybody heard how many millions a man would have made if he had bought a hundred shares of General Motors in 1919 and held on. Everybody was reminded at some time or another that George F. Baker never sold anything. As for the menace of speculation, one was glibly assured that--as Ex-Governor Stokes of New Jersey had proclaimed in an eloquent speech--Columbus, Washington, Franklin, and Edison had all been speculators. "The way to wealth," wrote John J. Raskob in an article in the *Ladies' Home Journal* alluringly entitled "Everybody Ought to Be Rich," "is to get into the profit end of wealth production in this country," and he pointed out that if one saved but fifteen dollars a month and invested it in good common stocks, allowing the dividends and rights to accumulate, at the end of twenty years one would have at least eighty thousand dollars and an income from investments of at least four hundred dollars a month. It was all so easy. The gateway to fortune stood wide open.

Meanwhile, one heard, the future of American industry was to be assured by the application of a distinctly modern principle. Increased consumption, as Waddill Catchings and William T. Foster had pointed out, was the road to plenty. If we all would only spend more and more freely, the smoke would belch from every factory chimney, and dividends would mount. Already the old economic order was giving way to the new. As Dr. Charles Amos Dice, professor of the somewhat unacademic subject of business organization at Ohio State University, wrote in a book called *New Levels in the Stock Market,* there was taking place "a mighty revolution in industry, in trade, and in finance." The stock market was but "registering the tremendous changes that were in progress."

When Professor Dice spoke of changes in finance, he certainly was right. The public no longer wanted anything so stale and profitless as bonds, it wanted securities which would return profits. Company after company was taking shrewd advantage of this new appetite to retire its bonds and issue new common stock in their place. If new bonds were issued, it became fashionable to give them a palatably speculative flavor by making them convertible into stock or by attaching to them warrants for the purchase of stock at some time in the rosy future. The public also seemed to prefer holding a hundred shares of stock priced at $50 to holding twenty shares priced at $250-- it made one feel so much richer to be able to buy and sell in quantity!-- and an increasing number of corporations therefore split up their common shares to make them attractive to a wide circle of buyers, whether or not any increase in the dividend was in immediate prospect. Many concerns had long made a practice of securing new capital by issuing to their shareholders the rights to buy new stock at a concession in price; this practice now became widely epidemic. Mergers of industrial corporations and of banks were taking place with greater frequency than ever before, prompted not merely by the desire to reduce overhead expenses and avoid the rigors of cut-throat competition, but often by sheer corporate megalomania. And every rumor of a merger or a split-up or an issue of rights was the automatic signal for a leap in the prices of the stocks affected--until it became altogether too tempting to the managers of many a concern to arrange a split-up or a merger or an issue of rights not without a canny eye to their own speculative fortunes.

For many years rival capitalistic interests, imitating the brilliant methods of Sidney Z. Mitchell, had sought to secure control of local electric light and power and gas companies and water companies and weld them into chains; and as the future possibilities of the utilities seized upon the speculative imagination, the battle between these groups led to an amazing proliferation of utility holding companies. By the summer of 1929 the competing systems had become so elaborate, and their interrelations had become so complicated, that it was difficult to arrive at even the vaguest idea of the actual worth of their soaring stocks. Even the professional analyst of financial properties was sometimes bewildered when he found Company A holding a 20-per-cent interest in Company B, and B an interest in C, while C in turn invested in A, and D held shares in each of the others. But few investors seemed to care about actual worth. Utilities had a future and prices were going up--that was enough.

Meanwhile investment trusts multiplied like locusts. There were now said to be nearly five hundred of them, with a total paid-in capital of some three billion and with holdings of stocks--many of them purchased at the current high prices--amounting to something like two billion. These trusts ranged all the way from honestly and intelligently managed companies to wildly speculative concerns launched by ignorant or venal promoters. Some of them, it has been said, were so capitalized that they could not even pay their preferred dividends out of the income from the securities which they held, but must rely almost completely upon the hope of profits. Other investment trusts, it must be admitted, served from time to time the convenient purpose of absorbing securities which the bankers who controlled them might have difficulty in selling in the open market. Reprehensible, you say? Of course; but it was so easy! One could indulge in all manner of dubious financial practices with an unruffled conscience so long as prices rose. The Big Bull Market covered a multitude of sins. It was a golden day for the promoter, and his name was legion.

Gradually the huge pyramid of capital rose. While supersalesmen of automobiles and radios and a hundred other gadgets were loading the ultimate consumer with new and shining wares, supersalesmen of securities were selling him shares of investment trusts which held stock in holding companies owned the stock of banks which had affiliates which in turn controlled holding companies--and so on *ad infinitum*. Though the shelves of manufacturing companies and jobbers and retailers were not overloaded, the shelves of the ultimate consumer and the shelves of the distributors of securities were groaning. Trouble was brewing--not the same sort of trouble which had visited the country in 1921, but trouble none the less. Still, however, the cloud in the summer sky looked no bigger than a man's hand.

How many Americans actually held stock on margin during the fabulous summer of 1929 there seems to be no way of computing, but it is probably safe to put the figure at more than a million. (George Buchan Robinson estimated that three hundred million shares of stock were being carried on margin.) The additional number of those who held common stock outright and followed the daily quotations with an interest nearly as absorbed as that of the margin trader was, of course, considerably larger. As one walked up the aisle of the 5:27 local, or found one's seat in the trolley car, two out of three newspapers that one saw were open to the page of stock market quotations. Branch offices of the big Wall Street houses blossomed in every city and in numerous suburban villages. In 1919 there had been 500 such offices; by October, 1928, there were 1,192; and throughout most of 1929 they appeared in increasing numbers. The broker found himself regarded with a new wonder and esteem. Ordinary people, less intimate with the mysteries of Wall Street than he was supposed to be, hung upon his every word. Let him but drop a hint of a possible split-up in General Industries Associates and his neighbor was off hot-foot the next morning to place a buying order.

The rich man's chauffeur drove with his ear laid back to catch the news of an impending move in Bethlehem Steel; he held fifty shares himself on a twenty-point margin. The window-cleaner at the broker's office paused to watch the ticker, for he was thinking of converting his laboriously accumulated savings into a few shares of Simmons. Edwin Lefèvre told of a broker's valet who had made nearly a quarter of a million in the market, of a trained nurse who cleaned up thirty thousand following the tips given her by grateful patients; and of a Wyoming cattleman, thirty miles from the nearest railroad, who bought or sold a thousand shares a day--getting his market returns by radio and telephoning his orders to the nearest large town to be transmitted to New York by telegram. An ex-actress in New York fitted up her Park Avenue apartment as an office and surrounded herself with charts, graphs, and financial reports, playing the market by telephone on an increasing scale and with increasing abandon. Across the dinner table one heard fantastic stories of sudden fortunes: a young banker had put every dollar of his small capital into Niles-Bement-Pond and now was fixed for life; a widow had been able to buy a large country house with her winnings in Kennecott. Thousands speculated--and won, too--without the slightest knowledge of the nature of the company upon whose fortunes they were relying, like the people who bought Seaboard Air Line under the impression that it was an aviation stock. Grocers, motormen, plumbers, seamstresses, and speakeasy waiters were in the market. Even the revolting intellectuals were there: loudly as they might lament the depressing effects of standardization and mass production upon American life, they found themselves quite ready to reap the fruits thereof. Literary editors whose hopes were wrapped about American Cyanamid B lunched with poets who swore by Cities Service, and as they left the table, stopped for a moment in the crowd at the broker's branch office to catch the latest quotations; and the artist who had once been eloquent only about Gauguin laid aside his brushes to proclaim the merits of National Bellas Hess. The Big Bull Market had become a national mania.

§ 6

In September the market reached its ultimate glittering peak.

It was six months, now, since Herbert Hoover had driven down Pennsylvania Avenue in the rain to take the oath of office as President of the United States. He had appointed the Wickersham Commission to investigate law enforcement in general and prohibition in particular. At the President's instance Congress had passed the Agricultural Marketing Act; and Alexander Legge had assumed, among his duties as chairman of the new Federal Farm Board, the task of "preventing and controlling surpluses in any agricultural commodity." The Kellogg-Briand Treaty had been proclaimed in effect, and Ramsay MacDonald was preparing to sail for the United States to discuss a new treaty for the reduction of naval armaments. The long wrangle over the Harding oil scandals was at last producing definite results: Colonel Stewart, buried under a mountain of Rockefeller proxies, had left the chairmanship of the Standard Oil Company of Indiana, and Harry F. Sinclair was sitting in jail. Colonel Lindbergh, true to his rôle as the national super-hero, had married Miss Anne Morrow. Commander Byrd, the man who put heroism into quantity production, was waiting in the Antarctic darkness of "Little America" for his chance to fly to the South Pole. Nonstop flyers were zooming about over the American countryside, and emulation of the heroes of the air had reached its climax of absurdity in the exploit of a twenty-two-year-old boy who had climbed into the cabin of the *Yellow Bird* and had been carried as a stowaway by Assolant and Lefèvre from Old Orchard, Maine, to the Spanish coast. And on the sands of a thousand American beaches, girls pulled down the shoulder-straps of their bathing suits to acquire fashionably tanned backs, and wondered whether it would be all right to leave their stockings off when they drove to town, and whether it was true, as the journals of fashion declared, that every evening dress must soon reach all the way to the ground.

This was the season when Tilden won his seventh and last American amateur tennis championship. It was Bobby Jones's penultimate year as monarch of amateur golfers--his seventh successive year as winner of either the amateur or the open championship of the United States. Babe Ruth was still hammering out home runs as successfully as in 1920, but he too was getting older: a sporting cycle was drawing to its close. Dempsey had lost his crown to Tunney, Tunney had hung it on the wall to go and foregather with the *literati,* and there was no one to follow them as a magnet for two-million-dollar crowds.

Everybody was reading *All Quiet on the Western Front* and singing the songs which Rudy Vallee crooned over the radio. The literary journals were making a great fuss over humanism. But even sun-tan and Ramsay MacDonald's proposed good-will voyage and humanism and *All Quiet* were dull subjects for talk compared with the Big Bull Market. Had not Goldman, Sachs & Company just expressed its confidence in the present level of prices by sponsoring the Blue Ridge Corporation, an investment trust which offered to exchange its stock for those of the leading "blue chips" at the current figures--324 for Allied Chemical and Dye, 293 for American Telephone, 179 for Consolidated Gas, 395 for General Electric, and so on down the list?

Stop for a moment to glance at a few of the prices recorded on the overworked ticker on September 3, 1929, the day when the Dow-Jones averages reached their high point for the year; and compare them with the opening prices of March 3, 1928, when, as you may recall, it had seemed as if the bull market had already climbed to a perilous altitude. Here they are, side by side--first the figures for March, 1928; then the figures for September, 1929; and finally the latter figures translated into 1928 terms--or in other words revised to make allowance for intervening split-ups and issues of rights. (Only thus can you properly judge the extent of the advance during those eighteen confident months.)

	Opening price March 3, 1928	High price Sept. 3, 1929	Adjusted high price Sept. 3, 1929
American Can	77	181 $^7/_8$	181 $^7/_8$
American Telephone & Telegraph	179 $^1/_2$	304	335 $^5/_8$
Anaconda Copper	54 $^1/_2$	131 $^1/_2$	162
Electric Bond & Share	89 $^3/_4$	186 $^3/_4$	203 $^5/_8$
General Electric	128 $^3/_4$	396 $^1/_4$	396 $^1/_4$
General Motors	139 $^3/_4$	72 $^3/_4$	181 $^7/_8$
Montgomery Ward	132 $^3/_4$	137 $^7/_8$	466 $^1/_2$
New York Central	160 $^1/_2$	256 $^3/_8$	256 $^3/_8$
Radio	94 $^1/_2$	101	505
Union Carbide & Carbon	145	137 $^7/_8$	413 $^5/_8$
United States Steel	138 $^1/_8$	261 $^3/_4$	279 $^1/_8$
Westinghouse E. & M.	91 $^5/_8$	289 $^7/_8$	313
Woolworth	180 $^3/_4$	100 $^3/_8$	251

Note: The prices of General Electric, Radio, Union Carbide, and Woolworth are here adjusted to take account of split-ups occurring subsequent to March 3, 1928. The prices of American Telephone, Anaconda, Montgomery Ward, United States Steel, Westinghouse, and Electric Bond & Share are adjusted to take account of intervening issues of rights; they represent the value per share on September 3, 1929, of a holding acquired on March 3, 1928, the adjustment being based on the assumption that rights offered in the interval were exercised.

One thing more: as you look at the high prices recorded on September 3, 1929, remember that on that day few people imagined that the peak had actually been reached. The enormous majority fully expected the Big Bull Market to go on and on.

For the blood of the pioneers still ran in American veins; and if there was no longer something lost behind the ranges, still the habit of seeing visions persisted. What if bright hopes had been wrecked by the sordid disappointments of 1919, the collapse of Wilsonian idealism, the spread of political cynicism, the slow decay of religious certainty, and the debunking of love? In the Big Bull Market there was compensation.

Still the American could spin wonderful dreams--of a romantic day when he would sell his Westinghouse common at a fabulous price and live in a great house and have a fleet of shining cars and loll at ease on the sands of Palm Beach. And when he looked toward the future of his country, he could envision an America set free--not from graft, nor from crime, nor from war, nor from control by Wall Street, nor from irreligion, nor from lust, for the Utopias of an earlier day left him for the most part skeptical or indifferent; he envisioned an America set free from poverty and toil. He saw a magical order built on the new science and the new prosperity: roads swarming with millions upon millions of automobiles, airplanes darkening the skies, lines of high-tension wire carrying from hilltop to hilltop the power to give life to a thousand labor-saving machines, skyscrapers thrusting above one-time villages, vast cities rising in great geometrical masses of stone and concrete and roaring with perfectly mechanized traffic--and smartly dressed men and women spending, spending, spending with the money they had won by being far-sighted enough to foresee, way back in 1929, what was going to happen.

♦ XIII ♦
CRASH!

§ 1

Early in September the stock market broke. It quickly recovered, however; indeed, on September 19th the averages as compiled by the *New York Times* reached an even higher level than that of September 3rd. Once more it slipped, farther and faster, until by October 4th the prices of a good many stocks had coasted to what seemed first-class bargain levels. Steel, for example, after having touched 261 $^3/_4$ a few weeks earlier, had dropped as low as 204; American Can, at the closing on October 4th, was nearly twenty points below its high for the year; General Electric was over fifty points below its high; Radio had gone down from 114 $^3/_4$ to 82 $^1/_2$.

A bad break, to be sure, but there had been other bad breaks, and the speculators who escaped unscathed proceeded to take advantage of the lessons they had learned in June and December of 1928 and March and May of 1929: when there was a break it was a good time to buy. In the face of all this tremendous liquidation, brokers' loans as compiled by the Federal Reserve Bank of New York mounted to a new high record on October 2nd, reaching $6,804,000,000--a sure sign that margin buyers were not deserting the market but coming into it in numbers at least undiminished. (Part of the increase in the loan figure was probably due to the piling up of unsold securities in dealers' hands, as the spawning of investment trusts and the issue of new common stock by every manner of business concern continued unabated.) History, it seemed, was about to repeat itself, and those who picked up Anaconda at 109 $^3/_4$ or American Telephone at 281 would count themselves wise investors. And sure enough, prices once more began to climb. They had already turned upward before that Sunday in early October when Ramsay MacDonald sat on a log with Herbert Hoover at the Rapidan camp and talked over the prospects for naval limitation and peace.

Something was wrong, however. The decline began once more. The wiseacres of Wall Street, looking about for causes, fixed upon the collapse of the Hatry financial group in England (which had led to much forced selling among foreign investors and speculators), and upon the bold refusal of the Massachusetts Department of Public Utilities to allow the Edison Company of Boston to split up its stock. They pointed, too, to the fact that the steel industry was undoubtedly slipping, and to the accumulation of "undigested" securities. But there was little real alarm until the week of October 21st. The consensus of opinion, in the meantime, was merely that the equinoctial storm of September had not quite blown over. The market was readjusting itself into a "more secure technical position."

§ 2

In view of what was about to happen, it is enlightening to recall how things looked at this juncture to the financial prophets, those gentlemen whose wizardly reputations were based upon their supposed ability to examine a set of graphs brought to them by a statistician and discover, from the relation of curve to curve and index to index, whether things were going to get better or worse. Their opinions differed, of course; there never has been a moment when the best financial opinion was unanimous. In examining these opinions, and the outgivings of eminent bankers, it must furthermore be acknowledged that a bullish statement cannot always be taken at its face value: few men like to assume the responsibility of spreading alarm by making dire predictions, nor is a banker with unsold securities on his hands likely to say anything which will make it more difficult to dispose of them, unquiet as his private mind may be. Finally, one must admit that prophecy is at best the most hazardous of occupations. Nevertheless, the general state of financial opinion in October, 1929, makes an instructive contrast with that in February and March, 1928, when, as we have seen, the skies had not appeared any too bright.

Some forecasters, to be sure, were so unconventional as to counsel caution. Roger W. Babson, an investment adviser who had not always been highly regarded in the inner circles of Wall Street, especially since he had for a long time been warning his clients of future trouble, predicted early in September a decline of sixty or eighty points in the averages. On October 7th the Standard Trade and Securities Service of the Standard Statistics Company advised its clients to pursue an "ultra-conservative policy," and ventured this prediction: "We remain of the opinion that, over the next few months, the trend of common-stock prices will be toward lower levels." Poor's *Weekly Business and Investment Letter* spoke its mind on the "great common-stock delusion" and predicted "further liquidation in stocks." Among the big bankers, Paul M. Warburg had shown months before this that he was alive to the dangers of the situation. These commentators--along with others such as the editor of the *Commercial and Financial Chronicle* and the financial editor of the *New York Times*--would appear to deserve the 1929 gold medals for foresight.

But if ever such medals were actually awarded, a goodly number of leather ones would have to be distributed at the same time. Not necessarily to the Harvard Economic Society, although on October 19th, after having explained that business was "facing another period of readjustment," it predicted that "if recession should threaten serious consequences for business (as is not indicated at present) there is little doubt that the Reserve System would take steps to ease the money market and so check the movement." The Harvard soothsayers proved themselves quite fallible: as late as October 26th, after the first wide-open crack in the stock market, they delivered the cheerful judgment that "despite its severity, we believe that the slump in stock prices will prove an intermediate movement and not the precursor of a business depression such as would entail prolonged further liquidation." This judgment turned out, of course, to be ludicrously wrong; but on the other hand the Harvard Economic Society was far from being really bullish. Nor would Colonel Leonard P. Ayres of the Cleveland Trust Company get one of the leather medals. He almost qualified when, on October 15th, he delivered himself of the judgment that "there does not seem to be as yet much real evidence that the decline in stock prices is likely to forecast a serious recession in general business. Despite the slowing down in iron and steel production, in automobile output, and in building, the conditions which result in serious business depressions are not present." But the skies, as Colonel Ayres saw them, were at least partly cloudy. "It seems probable," he said, "that stocks have been passing not so much from the strong to the weak as from the smart to the dumb."

Professor Irving Fisher, however, was more optimistic. In the newspapers of October 17th he was reported as telling the Purchasing Agents Association that stock prices had reached "what looks like a permanently high plateau." He expected to see the stock market, within a few months, "a good deal higher than it is today." On the very eve of the panic of October 24th he was further quoted as expecting a recovery in prices. Only two days before the panic, the *Boston News Bureau* quoted R. W. McNeel, director of McNeel's Financial Service, as suspecting "that some pretty intelligent people are now buying stocks." "Unless we are to have a panic--which no one seriously believes--stocks have hit bottom," said Mr. McNeel. And as for Charles E. Mitchell, chairman of the great National City Bank of New York, he continuously and enthusiastically radiated sunshine. Early in October Mr. Mitchell was positive that, despite the stock-market break, "The industrial situation of the United States is absolutely sound and our credit situation is in no way critical. . . . The interest given by the public to brokers' loans is always exaggerated," he added. "Altogether too much attention is paid to it." A few days later Mr. Mitchell spoke again: "Although in some cases speculation has gone too far in the United States, the markets generally are now in a healthy condition. The last six weeks have done an immense amount of good by shaking down prices. . . . The market values have a sound basis in the general prosperity of our country." Finally, on October 22nd, two days before the panic, he arrived in the United States from a short trip to Europe with these reassuring words: "I know of nothing fundamentally wrong with the stock market or with the underlying business and credit structure. . . . The public is suffering from 'brokers' loanitis.'"

Nor was Mr. Mitchell by any means alone in his opinions. To tell the truth, the chief difference between him and the rest of the financial community was that he made more noise. One of the most distinguished bankers in the United States, in closing a deal in the early autumn of 1929, said privately that he saw not a cloud in the sky. Habitual bulls like Arthur Cutten were, of course, insisting that they were "still bullish." And the general run of traders presumably endorsed the view attributed to "one large house" in mid-October in the *Boston News Bureau's* "Broad Street Gossip," that "the recent break makes a firm foundation for a big bull market in the last quarter of the year." There is no doubt that a great many speculators who had looked upon the midsummer prices as too high were now deciding that deflation had been effected and were buying again. Presumably most financial opinion agreed also with the further statement which appeared in the "Broad Street Gossip" column on October 16th, that "business is now too big and diversified, and the country too rich, to be influenced by stock market fluctuations"; and with the editorial opinion of the *News Bureau,* on October 19th, that "whatever recessions (in business) are noted, are those of the runner catching his breath. . . . The general condition is satisfactory and fundamentally sound."

The disaster which was impending was destined to be as bewildering and frightening to the rich and the powerful and the customarily sagacious as to the foolish and unwary holder of fifty shares of margin stock.

§ 3

The expected recovery in the stock market did not come. It seemed to be beginning on Tuesday, October 22nd, but the gains made during the day were largely lost during the last hour. And on Wednesday, the 23rd, there was a perfect Niagara of liquidation. The volume of trading was over 6,000,000 shares, the tape was 104 minutes late when the three-o'clock gong ended trading for the day, and the *New York Times* averages for fifty leading railroad and industrial stocks lost 18.24 points--a loss which made the most abrupt declines in previous breaks look small. Everybody realized that an unprecedented number of margin calls must be on their way to insecurely margined traders, and that the situation at last was getting serious. But perhaps the turn would come tomorrow. Already the break had carried prices down a good deal farther than the previous breaks of the past two years. Surely it could not go on much longer.

The next day was Thursday, October 24th.

On that momentous day stocks opened moderately steady in price, but in enormous volume. Kennecott appeared on the tape in a block of 20,000 shares, General Motors in another of the same amount. Almost at once the ticker tape began to lag behind the trading on the floor. The pressure of selling orders was disconcertingly heavy. Prices were going down. . . . Presently they were going down with some rapidity. . . . Before the first hour of trading was over, it was already apparent that they were going down with an altogether unprecedented and amazing violence. In brokers' offices all over the country, tape-watchers looked at one another in astonishment and perplexity. Where on earth was this torrent of selling orders coming from?

The exact answer to this question will probably never be known. But it seems probable that the principal cause of the break in prices during that first hour on October 24th was not fear. Nor was it short selling. It was forced selling. It was the dumping on the market of hundreds of thousands of shares of stock held in the name of miserable traders whose margins were exhausted or about to be exhausted. The gigantic edifice of prices was honeycombed with speculative credit and was now breaking under its own weight.

Fear, however, did not long delay its coming. As the price structure crumbled there was a sudden stampede to get out from under. By eleven o'clock traders on the floor of the Stock Exchange were in a wild scramble to "sell at the market." Long before the lagging ticker could tell what was happening, word had gone out by telephone and telegraph that the bottom was dropping out of things, and the selling orders redoubled in volume. The leading stocks were going down two, three, and even five points between sales. Down, down, down. . . . Where were the bargain-hunters who were supposed to come to the rescue at times like this? Where were the investment trusts, which were expected to provide a cushion for the market by making new purchases at low prices? Where were the big operators who had declared that they were still bullish? Where were the powerful bankers who were supposed to be able at any moment to support prices? There seemed to be no support whatever. Down, down, down. The roar of voices which rose from the floor of the Exchange had become a roar of panic.

United States Steel had opened at 205 $^1/_2$. It crashed through 200 and presently was at 193 $^1/_2$. General Electric, which only a few weeks before had been selling above 400, had opened this morning at 315--now it had slid to 283. Things were even worse with Radio: opening at 68 $^3/_4$, it had gone dismally down through the sixties and the fifties and the forties to the abysmal price of 44 $^1/_2$. And as for Montgomery Ward, vehicle of the hopes of thousands who saw the chain store as the harbinger of the new economic era, it had dropped headlong from 83 to 50. In the space of two short hours, dozens of stocks lost ground which it had required many months of the bull market to gain.

Even this sudden decline in values might not have been utterly terrifying if people could have known precisely what was happening at any moment. It is the unknown which causes real panic.

Suppose a man walked into a broker's branch office between twelve and one o'clock on October 24th to see how things were faring. First he glanced at the big board, covering one wall of the room, on which the day's prices for the leading stocks were supposed to be recorded. The LOW and LAST figures written there took his breath away, but soon he was aware that they were unreliable: even with the wildest scrambling, the boys who slapped into place the cards which recorded the last prices shown on the ticker could not keep up with the changes--they were too numerous and abrupt. He turned to the shining screen across which ran an uninterrupted procession of figures from the ticker. Ordinarily the practiced tape-watcher could tell from a moment's glance at the screen how things were faring, even though the Exchange now omitted all but the final digit of each quotation. A glance at the board, if not his own memory, supplied the missing digits. But today, when he saw a run of symbols and figures like

R   WX

$6.5\ ^1/_2.5.4$ $9.8\ ^7/_8\ ^3/_4\ ^1/_2\ ^1/_4.8.7\ ^1/_2.7.$

he could not be sure whether the price of "6" shown for Radio meant 66 or 56 or 46; whether Westinghouse was sliding from 189 to 187 or from 179 to 177. And presently he heard that the ticker was an hour and a half late; at one o'clock it was recording the prices of half-past eleven! All this that he saw was ancient history. What was happening on the floor now?

At ten-minute intervals the bond ticker over in the corner would hammer off a list of selected prices direct from the floor, and a broker's clerk would grab the uncoiling sheet of paper and shear it off with a pair of scissors and read the figures aloud in a mumbling expressionless monotone to the white-faced men who occupied every seat on the floor and stood packed at the rear of the room. The prices which he read out were *ten or a dozen or more points below those recorded on the ticker.* What about the stocks not included in that select list? There was no way of finding out. The telephone lines were clogged as inquiries and orders from all over the country converged upon the Stock Exchange. Once in a while a voice would come barking out of the broker's rear office where a frantic clerk was struggling for a telephone connection: "Steel at ninety-six!" Small comfort, however, to know what Steel was doing; the men outside were desperately involved in many another stock than Steel; they were almost completely in the dark, and their imaginations had free play. If they put in an order to buy or to sell, it was impossible to find out what became of it. The Exchange's whole system for the recording of current prices and for communicating orders was hopelessly unable to cope with the emergency, and the sequel was an epidemic of fright.

In that broker's office, as in hundreds of other offices from one end of the land to the other, one saw men looking defeat in the face. One of them was slowly walking up and down, mechanically tearing a piece of paper into tiny and still tinier fragments. Another was grinning shamefacedly, as a small boy giggles at a funeral. Another was abjectly beseeching a clerk for the latest news of American & Foreign Power. And still another was sitting motionless, as if stunned, his eyes fixed blindly upon the moving figures on the screen, those innocent-looking figures that meant the smash-up of the hopes of years. . . .

GL.   AWW.   JMP.
8.7.5.2.1.90.89.7.6.   3.2 1/2.2.   6.5.3.2 1/2.

A few minutes after noon, some of the more alert members of a crowd which had collected on the street outside the Stock Exchange, expecting they knew not what, recognized Charles E. Mitchell, erstwhile defender of the bull market, slipping quietly into the offices of J. P. Morgan & Company on the opposite corner. It was scarcely more than nine years since the House of Morgan had been pitted with the shrapnel-fire of the Wall Street explosion; now its occupants faced a different sort of calamity equally near at hand. Mr. Mitchell was followed shortly by Albert H. Wiggin, head of the Chase National Bank; William Potter, head of the Guaranty Trust Company; and Seward Prosser, head of the Bankers Trust Company. They had come to confer with Thomas W. Lamont of the Morgan firm. In the space of a few minutes these five men, with George F. Baker, Jr., of the First National Bank, agreed in behalf of their respective institutions to put up forty million apiece to shore up the stock market. The object of the two-hundred-and-forty-million-dollar pool thus formed, as explained subsequently by Mr. Lamont, was not to hold prices at any given level, but simply to make such purchases as were necessary to keep trading on an orderly basis. Their first action, they decided, would be to try to steady the prices of the leading securities which served as bellwethers for the list as a whole. It was a dangerous plan, for with hysteria spreading there was no telling what sort of *débâcle* might be impending. But this was no time for any action but the boldest.

The bankers separated. Mr. Lamont faced a gathering of reporters in the Morgan offices. His face was grave, but his words were soothing. His first sentence alone was one of the most remarkable understatements of all time. "There has been a little distress selling on the Stock Exchange," said he, "and we have held a meeting of the heads of several financial institutions to discuss the situation. We have found that there are no houses in difficulty and reports from brokers indicate that margins are being maintained satisfactorily." He went on to explain that what had happened was due to a "technical condition of the market" rather than to any fundamental cause.

As the news that the bankers were meeting circulated on the floor of the Exchange, prices began to steady. Soon a brisk rally set in. Steel jumped back to the level at which it had opened that morning. But the bankers had more to offer the dying bull market than a Morgan partner's best bedside manner.

At about half-past one o'clock Richard Whitney, vice-president of the Exchange, who usually acted as floor broker for the Morgan interests, went into the "steel crowd" and put in a bid of 205--the price of the last previous sale--for 10,000 shares of Steel. He bought only 200 shares and left the remainder of the order with the specialist. Mr. Whitney then went to various other points on the floor, and offered the price of the last previous sale for 10,000 shares of each of fifteen or twenty other stocks, reporting what was sold to him at that price and leaving the remainder of the order with the specialist. In short, within the space of a few minutes Mr. Whitney offered to purchase something in the neighborhood of twenty or thirty million dollars' worth of stock. Purchases of this magnitude are not undertaken by Tom, Dick, and Harry; it was clear that Mr. Whitney represented the bankers' pool.

The desperate remedy worked. The semblance of confidence returned. Prices held steady for a while; and though many of them slid off once more in the final hour, the net results for the day might well have been worse. Steel actually closed two points higher than on Wednesday, and the net losses of most of the other leading securities amounted to less than ten points apiece for the whole day's trading.

All the same, it had been a frightful day. At seven o'clock that night the tickers in a thousand brokers' offices were still chattering; not till after 7:08 did they finally record the last sale made on the floor at three o'clock. The volume of trading had set a new record--12,894,650 shares. ("The time may come when we shall see a five-million-share day," the wise men of the Street had been saying twenty months before!) Incredible rumors had spread wildly during the early afternoon--that eleven speculators had committed suicide, that the

Buffalo and Chicago exchanges had been closed, that troops were guarding the New York Stock Exchange against an angry mob. The country had known the bitter taste of panic. And although the bankers' pool had prevented for the moment an utter collapse, there was no gainsaying the fact that the economic structure had cracked wide open.

§ 4

Things looked somewhat better on Friday and Saturday. Trading was still on an enormous scale, but prices for the most part held. At the very moment when the bankers' pool was cautiously disposing of as much as possible of the stock which it had accumulated on Thursday and was thus preparing for future emergencies, traders who had sold out higher up were coming back into the market again with new purchases, in the hope that the bottom had been reached. (Hadn't they often been told that "the time to buy is when things look blackest"?) The newspapers carried a very pretty series of reassuring statements from the occupants of the seats of the mighty; Herbert Hoover himself, in a White House statement, pointed out that "the fundamental business of the country, that is, production and distribution of commodities, is on a sound and prosperous basis." But toward the close of Saturday's session prices began to slip again. And on Monday the rout was under way once more.

The losses registered on Monday were terrific--17 $^1/_2$ points for Steel, 47 $^1/_2$ for General Electric, 36 for Allied Chemical, 34 $^1/_2$ for Westinghouse, and so on down a long and dismal list. All Saturday afternoon and Saturday night and Sunday the brokers had been struggling to post their records and go over their customers' accounts and sent out calls for further margin, and another avalanche of forced selling resulted. The prices at which Mr. Whitney's purchases had steadied the leading stocks on Thursday were so readily broken through that it was immediately clear that the bankers' pool had made a strategic retreat. As a matter of fact, the brokers who represented the pool were having their hands full plugging up the "air-holes" in the list--in other words, buying stocks which were offered for sale without any bids at all in sight. Nothing more than this could have been accomplished, even if it could have been wisely attempted. Even six great banks could hardly stem the flow of liquidation from the entire United States. They could only guide it a little, check it momentarily here and there.

Once more the ticker dropped ridiculously far behind, the lights in the brokers' offices and the banks burned till dawn, and the telegraph companies distributed thousands of margin calls and requests for more collateral to back up loans at the banks. Bankers, brokers, clerks, messengers were almost at the end of their strength; for days and nights they had been driving themselves to keep pace with the most terrific volume of business that had ever descended upon them. It did not seem as if they could stand it much longer. But the worst was still ahead. It came the next day, Tuesday, October 29th.

The big gong had hardly sounded in the great hall of the Exchange at ten o'clock Tuesday morning before the storm broke in full force. Huge blocks of stock were thrown upon the market for what they would bring. Five thousand shares, ten thousand shares appeared at a time on the laboring ticker at fearful recessions in price. Not only were innumerable small traders being sold out, but big ones, too, protagonists of the new economic era who a few weeks before had counted themselves millionaires. Again and again the specialist in a stock would find himself surrounded by brokers fighting to sell--and nobody at all even thinking of buying. To give one single example: during the bull market the common stock of the White Sewing Machine Company had gone as high as 48; on Monday, October 28th, it had closed at 11 $^1/_8$. On that black Tuesday, somebody--a clever messenger boy for the Exchange, it was rumored--had the bright idea of putting in an order to buy at 1--and in the temporarily complete absence of other bids he actually got his stock for a dollar a share! The scene on the floor was chaotic. Despite the jamming of the communication system, orders to buy and sell--mostly to sell--came in faster than human beings could possibly handle them; it was on that day that an exhausted broker, at the close of the session, found a large waste-basket which he had stuffed with orders to be executed and had carefully set aside for safekeeping--and then had completely forgotten. Within half an hour of the opening the volume of trading had passed 3,000,000 shares, by twelve o'clock it had passed 8,000,000, by half-past one it had passed twelve 12,000,000, and when the closing gong brought the day's madness to an end the gigantic record of 16,410,030 shares had been set. Toward the close there was a rally, but by that time the average prices of fifty leading stocks, as compiled by the *New York Times,* had fallen nearly forty points. Meanwhile there was a near-panic in other markets--the foreign stock exchanges, the lesser American exchanges, the grain market.

So complete was the demoralization of the stock market and so exhausted were the brokers and their staffs and the Stock Exchange employees, that at noon that day, when the panic was at its worst, the Governing Committee met quietly to decide whether or not to close the Exchange. To quote from an address made some months later by Richard Whitney: "In order not to give occasion for alarming rumors, this meeting was not held in the Governing Committee Room, but in the office of the president of the Stock Clearing Corporation directly beneath the Stock Exchange floor. . . . The forty governors came to the meeting in groups of two and three as unobtrusively as possible. The office they met in was never designed for large meetings of this sort, with the result that most of the governors were compelled to stand, or to sit on tables. As the meeting progressed, panic was raging overhead on the floor. . . . The feeling of those present was revealed by their habit of continually lighting cigarettes, taking a puff or two, putting them out and lighting new ones--a practice which soon made the narrow room blue with smoke. . . ." Two of the Morgan partners were invited to the meeting and, attempting to slip into the building unnoticed so as not to start a new flock of rumors, were refused admittance by one of the guards and had to remain outside until rescued by a member of the Governing Committee. After some deliberation, the governors finally decided not to close the Exchange.

It was a critical day for the banks, that Tuesday the 29th. Many of the corporations which had so cheerfully loaned money to brokers through the banks in order to obtain interest at 8 or 9 per cent were now clamoring to have these loans called--and the banks were faced with a choice between taking over the loans themselves and running the risk of precipitating further ruin. It was no laughing matter to assume the responsibility of millions of dollars' worth of loans secured by collateral which by the end of the day might prove to have dropped to a fraction of its former value. That the call money rate never rose above 6 per cent that day, that a money panic was not added to the stock panic, and that several Wall Street institutions did not go down into immediate bankruptcy, was due largely to the nerve shown by a few bankers in stepping into the breach. The story is told of one banker who went grimly on authorizing the taking over of loan after loan until one of his subordinate officers came in with a white face and told him that the bank was insolvent. "I dare say," said the banker, and went ahead unmoved. He knew that if he did not, more than one concern would face insolvency.

The next day--Wednesday, October 30th--the outlook suddenly and providentially brightened. The directors of the Steel Corporation had declared an extra dividend; the directors of the American Can Company had not only declared an extra dividend, but had raised the regular dividend. There was another flood of reassuring statements--though by this time a cheerful statement from a financier fell upon somewhat skeptical ears. Julius Klein, Mr. Hoover's Assistant Secretary of Commerce, composed a rhapsody on continued prosperity. John J. Raskob declared that stocks were at bargain prices and that he and his friends were buying. John D. Rockefeller poured Standard Oil upon the waters: "Believing that fundamental conditions of the country are sound and that there is nothing in the business situation to warrant the destruction of values that has taken place on the exchanges during the past week, my son and I have for some days been purchasing sound common stocks." Better still, prices rose-- steadily and buoyantly. Now at last the time had come when the strain on the Exchange could be relieved without causing undue alarm. At 1:40 o'clock Vice-President Whitney announced from the rostrum that the Exchange would not open until noon the following day and would remain closed all day Friday and Saturday--and to his immense relief the announcement was greeted, not with renewed panic, but with a cheer.

Throughout Thursday's short session the recovery continued. Prices gyrated wildly--for who could arrive at a reasonable idea of what a given stock was worth, now that all settled standards of value had been upset?--but the worst of the storm seemed to have blown over. The financial community breathed more easily; now they could have a chance to set their houses in order.

It was true that the worst of the panic was past. But not the worst prices. There was too much forced liquidation still to come as brokers' accounts were gradually straightened out, as banks called for more collateral, and terror was renewed. The next week, in a series of short sessions, the tide of prices receded once more--until at last on November 13th the bottom prices for the year 1929 were reached. Beside the figures hung up in the sunny days of September they made a tragic showing:

	High price Sept. 3, 1929	Low price Nov. 13, 1929
American Can	181 $\frac{7}{8}$	86
American Telephone & Telegraph	304	197 $\frac{1}{4}$
Anaconda Copper	131 $\frac{1}{2}$	70
Electric Bond & Share	186 $\frac{3}{4}$	50 $\frac{1}{4}$
General Electric	396 $\frac{1}{4}$	168 $\frac{1}{8}$
General Motors	72 $\frac{3}{4}$	36
Montgomery Ward	137 $\frac{7}{8}$	49 $\frac{1}{4}$
New York Central	256 $\frac{3}{8}$	160
Radio	101	28
Union Carbide & Carbon	137 $\frac{7}{8}$	59
United States Steel	261 $\frac{3}{4}$	150
Westinghouse E. & M.	289 $\frac{7}{8}$	102 $\frac{5}{8}$
Woolworth	100 $\frac{3}{8}$	52 $\frac{1}{4}$

The *New York Times* averages for fifty leading stocks had been almost cut in half, falling from a high of 311.90 in September to a low of 164.43 on November 13th; and the *Times* averages for twenty-five leading industrials had fared still worse, diving from 469.49 to 220.95.

The Big Bull Market was dead. Billions of dollars' worth of profits--and paper profits--had disappeared. The grocer, the window-cleaner, and the seamstress had lost their capital. In every town there were families which had suddenly dropped from showy affluence into debt. Investors who had dreamed of retiring to live on their fortunes now found themselves back once more at the very beginning of the long road to riches. Day by day the newspapers printed the grim reports of suicides.

Coolidge-Hoover Prosperity was not yet dead, but it was dying. Under the impact of the shock of panic, a multitude of ills which hitherto had passed unnoticed or had been offset by stock-market optimism began to beset the body economic, as poisons seep through the human system when a vital organ has ceased to function normally. Although the liquidation of nearly three billion dollars of brokers' loans contracted credit, and the Reserve Banks lowered the rediscount rate, and the way in which the larger banks and corporations of the country had survived the emergency without a single failure of large proportions offered real encouragement, nevertheless the poisons were there: overproduction of capital; overambitious expansion of business concerns; overproduction of commodities under the stimulus of installment buying and buying with stock-market profits; the maintenance of an artificial price level for many commodities; the depressed condition of European trade. No matter how many soothsayers of high finance proclaimed that all was well, no matter how earnestly the President set to work to repair the damage with soft words and White House conferences, a major depression was inevitably under way.

Nor was that all. Prosperity is more than an economic condition; it is a state of mind. The Big Bull Market had been more than the climax of a business cycle; it had been the climax of a cycle in American mass thinking and mass emotion. There was hardly a man or woman in the country whose attitude toward life had not been affected by it in some degree and was not now affected by the sudden and brutal shattering of hope. With the Big Bull Market gone and prosperity going, Americans were soon to find themselves living in an altered world which called for new adjustments, new ideas, new habits of thought, and a new order of values. The psychological climate was changing; the ever-shifting currents of American life were turning into new channels.

The Post-war Decade had come to its close. An era had ended.

◆ XIV ◆
AFTERMATH: 1930-31

§ 1

Not without long and unhappy protest did the country accept as an inevitable fact the breakdown of Coolidge-Hoover Prosperity. It was a bitter draught to swallow; especially bitter for the Republican party, which had so far forgotten the business cycle's independence of political policies as to persuade itself that prosperity was a Republican invention; and bitterest of all for Herbert Hoover, who had uttered such confident words about the abolition of poverty.

When the stock market went over the edge of Niagara in October and November, 1929, and the decline in business became alarming, the country turned to the President for action. Something must be done immediately to restore public confidence and prevent the damage from spreading too far. Mr. Hoover was a student of business, a superlative organizer, and no novice in the art of directing public opinion; whatever his deficiencies might be in dealing with politicians and meeting purely political issues, the country felt that in a public emergency of this sort he would know what to do and how to do it if anybody on earth did.

The President acted promptly. He promised a reduction in taxes. He called a series of conferences of business leaders who expressed public disapproval of the idea of lowering wages. He recommended the building of public works to take up the impending slack in employment. And he and his associates resolutely set themselves to build up the shaken morale of business by proclaiming that everything was all right and presently would be still better; that "conditions"--as the everlasting reiterated phrase of the day went-- were "fundamentally sound." "I am convinced that through these measures we have reëstablished confidence," said the President in his annual message in December. When the year 1930 opened, Secretary Mellon predicted "a revival of activity in the spring." "There is nothing in the situation to be disturbed about," said Secretary of Commerce

Lamont in February. . . . "There are grounds for assuming that this is about a normal year." In March Mr. Lamont was more specific: he predicted that business would be normal in two months. A few days later the President himself set a definite date for the promised recovery: unemployment would be ended in sixty days. On March 16th the indefatigable cheer-leader of the Presidential optimists, Julius H. Barnes, the head of Mr. Hoover's new National Business Survey Conference, spoke as if trouble were already a thing of the past. "The spring of 1930," said he, "marks the end of a period of grave concern. . . . American business is steadily coming back to a normal level of prosperity."

At first it seemed as if the Administration would succeed not only in preventing drastic and immediate wage cuts, but in restoring economic health by applying the formula of Doctor Coué. After sinking to a low level at the end of 1929 and throwing something like three million men upon the streets, the industrial indices showed measurable signs of improvement. The stock market collected itself and began a new advance. Common stocks had not lost their lure; every speculator who had not been utterly cleaned out in the panic sought eagerly for the hair of the dog that bit him. During the first three months of 1930 a Little Bull Market gave a very plausible imitation of the Big Bull Market. Trading became as heavy as in the golden summer of 1929, and the prices of the leading stocks actually regained more than half the ground they had lost during the *débâcle*. For a time it seemed as if perhaps the hopeful prophets at Washington were right and prosperity was coming once more and it would be well to get in on the ground floor and make up those dismal losses of 1929.

But in April this brief illusion began to sicken and die. Business reaction had set in again. By the end of the sixty-day period set for recovery by the President and his Secretary of Commerce, commodity prices were going down, production indices were going down, the stock market was taking a series of painful tumbles, and hope deferred was making the American heartsick. The Coué formula was failing; for the economic disease was more than a temporary case of nervous prostration, it was organic and deep-seated.

Grimly but with a set smile on their faces, the physicians at Washington continued to recite their lesson from *Self-Mastery Through Conscious Auto-Suggestion.* They had begun their course of treatment with plentiful publicity and could not well change the prescription now without embarrassment. Early in May Mr. Hoover said he was convinced that "we have now passed the worst and with continued unity of effort we shall rapidly recover." On May 8th the governor of the Federal Reserve Board admitted that the country was in "what appears to be a business depression" *("appears to be"*--with factories shutting down, stocks skidding, and bread-lines stretching down the streets!), but that was as far as anybody at Washington seemed willing to go in facing the grim reality. On May 28th Mr. Hoover was reported as predicting that business would be normal by fall. The grim farce went on, the physicians uttering soothing words to the patient and the patient daily sinking lower and lower--until for a time it seemed as if every cheerful pronouncement was followed by a fresh collapse. Only when the failure of the treatment became obvious to the point of humiliation did the Administration lapse into temporary silence.

What were the economic diseases from which business was suffering? A few of them may be listed categorically.

1. Overproduction of capital and goods. During the nineteen-twenties, industry had become more mechanized, and thus more capable of producing on a huge scale than ever before. In the bullish days of 1928 and 1929, when installment buying and stock profits were temporarily increasing the buying power of the American people, innumerable concerns had cheerfully overexpanded; the capitalization of the nation's industry had become inflated, along with bank credit. When stock profits vanished and new installment buyers became harder to find and men and women were wondering how they could meet the next payment on the car or the radio or the furniture, manufacturers were forced to operate their enlarged and all-too-productive factories on a reduced and unprofitable basis as they waited for buying power to recover.

2. Artificial commodity prices. During 1929, as David Friday has pointed out, the prices of many products had been stabilized at high levels by pools. There were pools, for example, in copper and cotton; there was a wheat pool in Canada, a coffee pool in Brazil, a sugar pool in Cuba, a wool pool in Australia. The prices artificially maintained by these pools had led to overproduction, which became the more dangerous the longer it remained concealed. Stocks of these commodities accumulated at a rate out of all proportion to consumption; eventually the pools could no longer support the markets, and when the inevitable day of reckoning came, prices fell disastrously.

3. A collapse in the price of silver, due partly to the efforts of several governments to put themselves on a gold basis--with a resulting paralysis to the purchasing power of the Orient.

4. The international financial derangement caused by the shifting of gold in huge quantities to France and particularly to the United States.

5. Unrest in foreign countries. As the international depression deepened, the political and economic dislocation caused by the war became newly apparent; the chickens of 1914-18 were coming home to roost. Revolutions and the threat of revolutions in various parts of the world added to the general uncertainty and fear, and incidentally jeopardized American investments abroad.

6. The self-generating effect of the depression itself. Each bankruptcy, each suspension of payments, and each reduction of operating schedules affected other concerns, until it seemed almost as if the business world were a set of tenpins ready to knock one another over as they fell; each employee thrown out of work decreased the potential buying power of the country.

And finally--

7. The profound psychological reaction from the exuberance of 1929. Fundamentally, perhaps, the business cycle is a psychological phenomenon. Only when the memory of hard times has dimmed can confidence fully establish itself; only when confidence has led to outrageous excesses can it be checked. It was as difficult for Mr. Hoover to stop the psychological pendulum on its down-swing as it had been for the Reserve Board to stop it on its up-swing.

What happened after the failure of the Hoover campaign of optimism makes sad reading. Commodity prices plunged to shocking depths. Wheat, for instance: during the last few days of 1929, December wheat had brought $1.35 at Chicago; a year later it brought only 76 cents. July wheat fell during the same interval from $1.37 to 61 cents. Mr. Legge's Federal Farm Board was not unmindful of the distress throughout the wheat belt caused by this frightful decline; having been empowered by law to undertake the task of "preventing and controlling surpluses in any agricultural commodity," it tried to stabilize prices by buying wheat during the most discouraging stages of the collapse. But it succeeded chiefly in accumulating surpluses; for it came into conflict with a law older than the Agricultural Marketing Act--the law of supply and demand. When the dust cleared away the Farm Board had upward of two hundred million bushels of wheat on its hands, yet prices had nevertheless fallen all the way to the cellar;

and although Mr. Legge's successor claimed that the Board's purchases had saved from failure hundreds of banks which had loaned money on the wheat crop, that was scant comfort to the agonized farmers. A terrific drought during the summer of 1930 intensified the prostration of many communities. Once more the farm population seemed pursued by a malignant fate. They had benefited little from Coolidge Prosperity, and now they were the worst sufferers of all from the nightmare of 1930-31.

Meanwhile industrial production was declining steadily. By the end of 1930 business had sunk to 28 per cent below normal. Stock prices, after rallying slightly during the summer of 1930, turned downward once more in September, and by December a long series of shudders of liquidation had brought the price-level well below the post-panic level of the year before. Alas! the poor Bull Market! Radio common, which had climbed to such dizzy heights in 1928 and 1929, retraced its steps down to--yes, and past--the point at which it had begun its sensational advance less than three years before; and in many another stock the retreat was even longer and less orderly. The drastic shrinkage in brokers' loans testified to the number of trading accounts closed out unhappily. The broker had ceased to be a man of wonderful mystery in the eyes of his acquaintances; he was approached nowadays with friendly tact, as one who must not be upset by unfortunate references to the market. Several brokerage houses tumbled; blue-sky investment companies formed during the happy bull-market days went to smash, disclosing miserable tales of rascality; over a thousand banks caved in during 1930, as a result of the marking down both of real estate and of securities; and in December occurred the largest bank failure in American financial history, the fall of the ill-named Bank of the United States in New York. Unemployment grew steadily, until by the end of 1930 the number of jobless was figured at somewhere in the neighborhood of six million; apple salesmen stood on the street corner, executives and clerks and factory hands lay awake wondering when they, too, would be thrown off, and contributed anxiously to funds for the workless; and a stroller on Broadway, seeing a queue forming outside a theater where Charlie Chaplin was opening in "City Lights," asked in some concern, "What's that--a bread-line or a bank?"

Early in 1931 there were faint signs of improvement and the deflated stock market took cheer, but by March the uncertain dawn was seen to have been false, and throughout the spring months the decline was renewed. Production ebbed once more; commodity prices fell; stock prices faded until the panic levels of November, 1929, looked lofty by comparison; and discouragement deepened as dividends were reduced or omitted and failures multiplied. Would the bottom never be reached?

The rosy visions of 1929 had not been utterly effaced: it was significant that the numbers of holders of common stock in most of the large corporations increased during 1930. Investors stubbornly expected the tide to turn some day, and they wanted to be there when it happened. Yet the shock of the drop into the apparently bottomless pit of depression was telling on their nerves. "There are far too many people, from businessmen to laborers," declared an advertisement inserted in the New York papers by the *Evening World* in December, 1930, "who are giving a too eager ear to wild rumors and spiteful gossip tending to destroy confidence and create an atmosphere of general distrust. The victims of vague fear, on the street and in the market place, are a menace to the community. . . . They are the feeders of that mob psychology which creates the spirit of panic."

"Mob psychology"! There had been mob psychology in the days of the Big Bull Market, too. Action and reaction--the picture was now complete.

Two years earlier, when Mr. Hoover had discussed the abolition of poverty, he had prudently added the words "with God's help." It must have seemed to him now that God had prepared for him a cruelly ironic jest. Mr. Hoover was hardly more responsible for the downfall of the business hopes of the nineteen-twenties than for the invasion of Belgium; yet he who had won renown by administering relief to the Belgians had now been called upon to administer relief to the Americans, lest the poverty of which he had once spoken so lightly make tragic inroads among them. He was an able economist and an able leader of men in public crises; yet his attempts to lead business out of depression had come to conspicuous failure. Other businessmen of wide experience had been as unconvinced as he that the deflation would have to be prolonged and painful; yet when business was on the road to ruin, these men forgot their own former optimism and blamed the President for lack of foresight, lack of leadership, lack of even elementary common sense. They had not been forced to put themselves unforgettably on record; he had. They were not expected to reintroduce prosperity; he was. By the spring of 1931 the President's reputation had declined along with prices and profits to a new low level, and the Democrats, cheered by striking gains in the November elections, were casting a hopeful eye toward 1932. Observing the plight of Mr. Hoover, Calvin Coolidge, syndicating two hundred daily words of mingled hard sense and soft soap from his secure haven at Northampton, must have thanked Heaven that he had not chosen to run for President in 1928; and Governor Smith must have felt like the man who just missed the train which went off the end of the open drawbridge. Doubtless the Administration's campaign of optimism had been overzealous, but Mr. Hoover's greatest mistake had been in getting himself elected for the 1928-32 term.

The truth was that what had taken place since the Big Bull Market was more than a cyclical drop in prices and production; it was a major change in the national economy. There were encouraging signs even when things were at their worst: the absence of serious conflict between capital and labor, for instance, and the ability of the Federal Reserve System to prevent a money panic even when banks were toppling. Doubtless prosperity was due ultimately to return in full flood. But it could not be the same sort of prosperity as in the nineteen-twenties: inevitably it would rest on different bases, favor different industries, and arouse different forms of enthusiasm and hysteria. The panic had written *finis* to a chapter of American economic history.

§ 2

There were other signs of change, too, as the nineteen-thirties began. Some of them had begun long before the panic; others developed some time after it; but taken together they revealed striking alterations in the national temper and the ways of American life.

One could hardly walk a block in any American city or town without noticing some of them. The women's clothes, for instance. The skirt length had come down with stock prices. Dresses for daytime wear were longer, if only by a few inches; evening dresses swept the ground. Defenders of the knee-length skirt had split the air with their protests, but the new styles had won out. Bobbed hair was progressively losing favor. Frills, ruffles, and flounces were coming in again, and the corset manufacturers were once more learning to smile. A measure of formality was gradually returning: witness the long white gloves, the masculine silk hats and swallow-tail coats. Nor did these changes follow any mere whim of manufacturers and stylists. Manufacturers and stylists may issue decrees, but not unless the public is willing to follow does the fashion actually change. Did not the clothing business try to bring back the long skirt early in the nineteen-twenties, but without success? The long skirts and draperies and white gloves of 1930 and 1931 were the outward signs of a subtle change in the relations between the sexes. No longer was it the American woman's dearest ambition to simulate a flat-breasted, spindle-legged, carefree, knowing adolescent in a long-waisted child's frock. The red-hot baby had gone out of style. Fashion advertisements in 1930 and 1931 depicted a different type, more graceful, more piquant, more subtly alluring; decorum and romance began to come once more within the range of possibilities.

What the fashions suggested was borne out by a variety of other evidence. The Revolution in Manners and Morals had at least reached an armistice.

Not that there was any general return to the old conventions which had been overthrown in the nineteen-twenties. The freedom so desperately won by the flappers of the now graying "younger generation" had not been lost, and it was difficult to detect much real change in the uses to which this freedom was put. What had departed was the excited sense that taboos were going to smash, that morals were being made over or annihilated, and that the whole code of behavior was in flux. The wages of sin had become stabilized at a lower level. Gone, too, at least in some degree, was that hysterical preoccupation with sex which had characterized the Post-war Decade. Books about sex and conversation about sex were among the commodities suffering from overproduction. Robert Benchley expressed a widely prevalent opinion when he wrote in his dramatic page in the *New Yorker,* late in 1930, "I am now definitely ready to announce that Sex, as a theatrical property, is as tiresome as the Old Mortgage, and that I don't want to hear it mentioned ever again--I am sick of rebellious youth and I am sick of Victorian parents and I don't care if all the little girls in all sections of the United States get ruined or want to get ruined or keep from getting ruined. All I ask is: don't write plays about it and ask me to sit through them."

Apparently a great many playgoers and readers were beginning to feel as Mr. Benchley did. George Jean Nathan noted the arrival on Broadway of a new crop of romantic and poetic playwrights, and reported that "the hard-boiled school of drama and literature . . . is all too evidently on the wane." Henry Seidel Canby, writing in the *Saturday Review of Literature,* came to the same conclusion. Reticence had returned from exile; indeed, even before the Post-war Decade closed, "Journey's End," which managed to make war real without the wholesale introduction of profanity or prostitutes, had been applauded with something like relief. The contrast between "Journey's End" and "What Price Glory?" was suggestive of the change in the popular temper. The success of such novels as *The Good Companions, Angel Pavement,* and *The Water-Gypsies* was perhaps a further indication of the change. There were enough exceptions to the rule to remind one that easy generalizations are dangerous, but two conclusions seemed almost inescapable: sex was no longer front-page news, and glamour was coming into its own again.

Nor, for that matter, were people quite so positive now that every manifestation of Victorianism and of the eighteen-nineties was to be laughed at uproariously by "moderns." Collectors were beginning to look with less scornful eyes upon Victorian furniture, and people who had read *The Mauve Decade* and the debunking biographies with an air of condescension toward pre-war conventions found themselves looking with wistful eyes, only a few years later, at William Gillette's revival of "Sherlock Holmes" and at the sentimentalization of the 'nineties in "Sweet Adeline."

The young people of the early nineteen-thirties presumably knew just as much about life as those of the early and middle twenties, but they were less conspicuously and self-consciously intent upon showing the world what advanced young devils they were. LaMar Warrick, who taught at a large Middle Western university, reported in *Harper's* in the autumn of 1930 that the biological novels of Aldous Huxley, the biological psychology of John B. Watson, and the biological philosophies of Bertrand Russell were "fast becoming . . . out of date" among the students in her classes. She found the new younger generation tiring of what one of these students called "a modernism which leaves you washed out and cynical at thirty." A staff reporter for the *Des Moines Sunday Register* queried professors and undergraduates at three colleges in Iowa as to the validity of Mrs. Warrick's contentions, and an impressive majority of those with whom he talked told him that what she had said held true in Iowa as well as in Illinois. One young Iowan remarked that at his college there was not now a single "Flaming Mamie" who could be compared with "the girls who five years ago were wearing leopard-skin coats, driving expensive roadsters, and generally raising hell." That hell-raising was actually on the decline seemed almost too much to expect of inflammable human nature; but at least the burden of testimony suggested that ostentatious hell-raising was not quite so certain a way to social renown as in the heyday of flapperism.

The Revolt of the Highbrows had spent its force. The voice of H. L. Mencken no longer shook the country from Provincetown to Hollywood, and people who were always denouncing George F. Babbitt and the dangers of standardization were beginning to seem a little tiresome. Many of the once distraught intellectuals were now wondering if life was such a ghastly farce as they had supposed. The philosophical and literary theme of futility had been almost played out. Even Hemingway, whom the young *émigrés* to Montparnasse in 1926 or thereabouts had hailed as a major prophet of the emptiness of everything, struck a new note, almost a romantic note, in his *Farewell to Arms,* published late in 1929; this novel told the story not of a series of shallow and fleeting passions, but of a great love which possessed the very values of whose future Joseph Wood Krutch had despaired. Lewis Mumford declared in 1931 that Mr. Krutch should have realized that civilization had merely been molting a dead skin, not going into dissolution; speaking for the young intellectuals of the nineteen-thirties, Mr. Mumford announced that "the mood of defeat is dead. We have not yet hauled down our flag, because, like Whitman's Little Captain, we can still say collectively, *We have not yet begun to fight."* Here again, easy generalizations are dangerous; yet one doubts if any representative of the intelligentsia could have spoken of fighting in 1925 and felt that he was representing the opinion of his up-to-date contemporaries. The fashionable posture in 1925 had not been belligerent; it had been the posture of graceful acquiescence in defeat. Now the mood of intellectual disillusionment was passing; the garment of hopeless resignation began to look a little worn at the elbows.

Whether religion was regaining any of its lost prestige was doubtful. The net gain in membership of all the churches in the United States was only a trifle over one-tenth of one per cent in 1930--the smallest gain since Dr. H. K. Carroll began his annual compilation in 1890. But at least the religious scene had changed. The Fundamentalists and Modernists were tiring of their battle. Dayton had become ancient history. The voice of science no longer seemed to deny so loudly and authoritatively the existence of spiritual values in the universe; and when readers of Eddington and Jeans concluded that there was a crack in the airtight system of scientific materialism after all, and the modernist clergy hastened to report that the crack was wide enough to admit God, their assertion attracted less excited rebuttal than formerly, if only because the new scientific philosophies were too hard to understand and the argument had been going on for so many weary years. The voice of psychology, once so deafening and bewildering, had especially lost authority; it was evident that neither Freud nor Watson had infallible answers for all the problems of humanity, and that the psychologists were no more united than the Democrats. Those who watched the religious life of the colleges as the nineteen-twenties gave way to the nineteen-thirties doubted if the ranks of the agnostics were decreasing, but found, nevertheless, a change in the general attitude: fewer young men and women bristled with hostility toward any and all religion, and there was a more widespread desire, even among the doubters, to find some ground for a positive and fruitful interpretation of life. What was true of the colleges was presumably true of the country as a whole: although the churches were hardly gaining ground, neither perhaps, was religion losing it. Like manners and morals, religion showed signs of stabilization on a different basis. Whether the change was more than temporary remained to be seen.

The great American public was just as susceptible to fads as ever. Since the panicky autumn of 1929, millions of radios had resounded every evening at seven o'clock with the voices of Freeman F. Gosden and Charles J. Correll, better known as Amos 'n' Andy; "I'se regusted" and "Check and double check" had made their way into the common speech, and Andy's troubles with the lunchroom and Madam Queen had become only less real to the national mind than the vicissitudes of business and the stock market. In September, 1930, the Department of Commerce had found at least one thoroughly prosperous business statistic to announce: there were almost 30,000 miniature golf courses in operation, representing an investment of $125,000,000, and many of them were earning 300 per cent a month. If the American people were buying nothing else in the summer of 1930, they were at least buying the right to putt a golf ball over a surface of crushed cottonseed and through a tin pipe.

Yet the noble art of ballyhoo, which had flourished so successfully in the nineteen-twenties, had lost something of its vigor. Admiral Byrd's flight to the South Pole made him a hero second only to Lindbergh in the eyes of the country at large, but in the larger centers of population there was manifest a slight tendency to yawn: his exploit had been over-publicized, and heroism, however gallant, lost something of its spontaneous charm when it was subjected to scientific management and syndicated in daily dispatches. A few months after Byrd reached the South Pole, Coste and Bellonte made the first completely successful non-stop westward flight across the Atlantic; yet at the end of 1930 it was probable that fewer Americans could have identified the names of Coste and Bellonte than the name of Ruth

Elder. Heroism in the air was commonplace by this time. Endurance flyers still circled about day after day in quest of new records, but they were finding the crowds more sparse and the profits in headlines and in cash less impressive. As for Shipwreck Kelly, premier flagpole sitter of the nineteen-twenties, he was reported to have descended from the summit of the Paramount Building in 1930 because no one seemed to be watching. Bathing-beauty contests? Something had happened to them, too. Atlantic City had given up its annual beauty pageant in 1927. And in all 1930 there was not one first-class murder trial of nation-wide interest, not one first-class prize-fight, not one great new sporting hero crowned.

Indeed, a sporting era was passing. Rickard, who had known how to surround two heavyweight fighters with a two-and-a-half-million-dollar crowd, was dead; pugilism had fallen again into shady repute. Dempsey was in retirement. Tunney was reading Shakespeare. Ruth still hammered out home runs, but Jones and Tilden had both turned professional, and Knute Rockne, the greatest football coach of the nineteen-twenties, had been killed in an airplane accident, to the official regret of the President of the United States. With the passing of Grover Whalen to the aisles of Wanamaker's, New York City, the fountain-head of ballyhoo, had lost some of its lavish taste for welcoming heroes to the Western Hemisphere; the precipitation of ticker tape and torn-up telephone books in lower Broadway in 1930 was the smallest in years. Perhaps hard times were responsible for the decline of the hero racket. But perhaps there was more to it than that. The ballyhoo technique possessed no longer the freshness of youth. Times had changed.

The post-war apathy toward politics and everything political continued apparently undiminished. In the autumn of 1929, when Ramsay MacDonald came to America with a message of peace and good will strikingly reminiscent of the preachments of Woodrow Wilson, he was received with astonishing enthusiasm, and for a time it seemed as if idealism were about to manifest itself once more as in the days before the coming of complacent normalcy. The mood persisted long enough for the London Treaty for renewed limitation of naval armaments to pass the Senate with flying colors, much to the credit of President Hoover and Secretary Stimson; otherwise, however, cynicism and hopelessness still prevailed. Chicago threw out the notorious Thompson and the Tammany scandals in New York City aroused some resentment; but the general attitude as the summer of 1931 approached still seemed to be "What's the use of trying to do anything about it?" and the racketeer still flourished like a hardy weed, as did the bootlegger, the rumrunner, and the prohibition issue.

But if the country still expected as little as ever of politics and politicians, and still submitted to the rule of the gangster, at least it was somewhat less satisfied with *laissez-faire* for business than in the days of Calvin Coolidge. The public attitude during the depression of 1930-31 presented an instructive contrast with that during previous depressions. The radical on the soap-box was far less terrifying than in the days of the Big Red Scare. Communist propaganda made amazingly little headway, all things considered, and attracted amazingly little attention; for one reason, perhaps, because many of the largest employers met the crisis with far-sighted intelligence, maintaining the wage-rate wherever possible and reducing hours rather than throwing off employees; for another reason, because during the Big Bull Market innumerable potential radicals had received from the stock-market page a conservative financial education. Naturally, however, there was a general sense that something had gone wrong with individualistic capitalism and must be set right--how could it be otherwise, with the existing system dragging millions of families down toward hunger and want?

There was a new interest in the Russian experiment, not unmixed with sober fear. Maurice Hindus's *Humanity Uprooted,* which had come out during the month of the panic and had sold very slowly at first, became a best seller during the gloomy autumn of 1930. In the summer of 1929 Russia had seemed as remote as China; in 1931, with breadlines on the streets, the Russian Five-Year Plan became a topic of anxious American interest. The longer the paralysis of industry lasted--and how it lasted!--the more urgent became the demand for some measure of American economic planning which might prevent such disasters from recurring, without handing over undue power to an incompetent or venal bureaucracy.

With the return of full prosperity this demand would doubtless weaken; nevertheless the inevitable slow drift toward collectivism, interrupted during the bumptiously successful nineteen-twenties, promised to be haltingly resumed once more. Despite the obvious distaste of the country for state socialism or anything suggesting it, there was no denying that the economic system had proved itself too complex, and machine production too powerful, to continue unbridled. The chief difficulty, perhaps, was to find any persons or groups wise enough to know how to apply the bridle and persuasive enough to be allowed to keep their grip upon it. The experience of the past few years had given no very convincing evidence of the ability of financiers or economists to diagnose the condition of the country's business, or of the emotional public to respond to treatment. Yet there stood the problem, a problem hardly dreamed of by most Americans when Coolidge Prosperity was blooming; and as 1931 dragged along, month after month, without any immediate promise of business revival, no other problem seemed to the country half so vital or so pressing.

§ 3

Many of these specific signs of change were of uncertain significance; possibly some of them were illusory. Yet the United States of 1931 was a different place from the United States of the Post-war Decade; there was no denying that. An old order was giving place to new.

Soon the mists of distance would soften the outlines of the nineteen-twenties, and men and women, looking over the pages of a book such as this, would smile at the memory of those charming, crazy days when the radio was a thrilling novelty, and girls wore bobbed hair and knee-length skirts, and a trans-Atlantic flyer became a god overnight, and common stocks were about to bring us all to a lavish Utopia. They would forget, perhaps, the frustrated hopes that followed the war, the aching disillusionment of the hard-boiled era, its oily scandals, its spiritual paralysis, the harshness of its gaiety; they would talk about the good old days. . . .

What was to come in the nineteen-thirties?

Only one thing could one be sure of. It would not be repetition. The stream of time often doubles on its course, but always it makes for itself a new channel.

APPENDIX

SOURCES AND OBLIGATIONS

I am under an immense debt to certain writers upon whose books I have drawn extensively in this chronicle. Naturally I have made frequent use, not only in Chapter Five, but elsewhere, of the extraordinarily varied and precise information collected in *Middletown,* that remarkable sociological study of an American city by Robert S. Lynd and Helen Merrell Lynd; I do not see how any conscientious historian of the Postwar Decade could afford to neglect this mine of material. The concluding chapters of *The Rise of American Civilization,* by Charles A. Beard and Mary R. Beard, have been helpful at many points, particularly in the preparation of my short account of the Washington Conference and the situation which led up to it. William Allen White's biography of Woodrow Wilson and his extended portraits of Warren G. Harding and Calvin Coolidge in *Masks in a Pageant* have been especially useful not only for the specific information which they contain, but also for their suggestive interpretations of these three Presidents. To Charles Merz I am indebted for many facts and conclusions about the prohibition experiment, which I have drawn from *The Dry Decade,* his admirably impartial account of the first ten years of prohibition; and also for other facts assembled by him in his other books, *And Then Came Ford* and *The Great American Bandwagon.* Finally, I have made constant use of the *World Almanac,* which is responsible for many of the statistics embodied in this volume; of the *New York Times Index;* and above all of the files of the *New York Times* itself in the New York Public Library. A book of this sort must inevitably rely very largely on contemporary newspaper and magazine sources; the newspapers are invaluable not only for their news accounts of important events, but also for the light which their advertising columns and picture sections throw upon the fashions, ideas, and general atmosphere of the period.

The account of the beginnings of radio broadcasting in Chapters One and Four is based partly upon an address given on April

21, 1928, by H. P. Davis, vice-president of the Westinghouse Electric and Manufacturing Company, before the Harvard Business School.

In the preparation of Chapter Two ("Back to Normalcy"), I found Ray Stannard Baker's *Woodrow Wilson and World Settlement* especially valuable for its exhaustive account of Wilson's part in the Peace Conference. Mr. Baker's findings have of course been compared with those of Colonel House, Secretary Lansing, and others. Lodge's secret memorandum to Henry White was disclosed in Allan Nevins's biography of White. The description of Woodrow Wilson in the last days of his life is based on a personal visit to him in November, 1923.

In Chapter Three ("The Big Red Scare"), I owe many of the facts about the Palmer raids to the account in Zechariah Chafee's *Freedom of Speech.* Senator Husting's pledge was quoted on the cover of the *New Republic* at the time of the coal strike of 1919. Much of the material about the super-patriots is derived from a series of articles contributed to the *New Republic* in 1924 by Sidney Howard. The account of the Chicago race-riot is based on the careful study embodied in Charles S. Johnson's *The Negro in Chicago;* and the account of the Wall Street explosion contains many facts from an article by Sidney Sutherland in *Liberty* for April 26, 1930.

In Chapter Four ("America Convalescent") the facts cited about the Sacco-Vanzetti propaganda came largely from a series of contemporary news stories in the *New York World.*

Chapter Five ("The Revolution in Manners and Morals") draws freely upon *Middletown,* as previously stated; upon Professor Paul H. Nystrom's *Economics of Fashion;* and upon Walter Lippmann's *A Preface to Morals* and Joseph Wood Krutch's *The Modern Temper.*

In writing Chapter Six ("Harding and the Scandals") I have made much use of White's *Masks in a Pageant* and Beard's *The Rise of American Civilization,* as stated above; of M. E. Ravage's *The Story of Teapot Dome,* a lively account of the progress of the oil cases up to 1924; and of Bruce Bliven's series of articles on the Ohio Gang in the *New Republic.* The quotation from Harry M. Daugherty which appears at the beginning of the chapter is printed as arranged and repunctuated by Mr. Bliven in one of his *New Republic* articles. George G. Chandler of the Philadelphia law firm of Montgomery & MacCracken gave me valuable help in connection with the account of the oil scandals.

Chapter Seven ("Coolidge Prosperity") is based in considerable degree upon the facts and generalizations in Stuart Chase's concise book, *Prosperity, Fact or Myth,* and also cites numerous figures drawn from *Recent Economic Changes.* The sections on the supersalesmen and on religion and business embody a quantity of material set forth by that able student of the ways of businessmen, Jesse Rainsford Sprague, in various articles in *Harper's Magazine.* Some of the data about the service clubs I owe to Charles W. Ferguson, who gathered them in the preparation of his forthcoming book, *The Joiners;* some of the facts about business courses and business methods in the universities come from Abraham Flexner's *Universities: American, English, German.*

The basic idea of Chapter Eight ("The Ballyhoo Years") is Silas Bent's, as any reader of his book, *Ballyhoo,* will be aware. I have taken many facts from that book. The statistical data on the status of religion during the decade are drawn from the "Preliminary Report on Organized Religion for the President's Study of Social Trends," by C. Luther Fry, to which Robert S. Lynd was good enough to give me access. The account of the Dayton trial makes considerable use of Arthur Garfield Hays's narrative in *Let Freedom Ring.* Richard F. Simon, of Simon & Schuster, provided me with much material about the cross-word-puzzle craze, and W. B. Miller, formerly of the *Louisville Courier-Journal,* told me at first hand the story of the Floyd Collins episode.

I am under special obligation both to Walter Lippmann's *A Preface to Morals* and to Joseph Wood Krutch's *The Modern Temper* for their remarkable analyses of disillusionment in the nineteen-twenties; the discussion of disillusionment in Chapter Nine ("The Revolt of the Highbrows") could never have been written without the aid of Mr. Krutch's penetrating book.

Chapter Ten ("Alcohol and Al Capone") makes especially lavish use of four sources: Charles Merz's *The Dry Decade,* the Wickersham Report, Fred D. Pasley's fascinating *Al Capone,* and *It's a Racket,* by Gordon L. Hostetter and Thomas Quinn Beesley.

Many figures and incidents and the quotation from Walter C. Hill in Chapter Eleven ("Home, Sweet Florida") are from two articles by Homer B. Vanderblue in the *Journal of Land and Public Utility Economics,* Volume 3. Among other sources, Gertrude Mathews Shelby's "Florida Frenzy" in *Harper's Magazine* for January, 1926, was especially valuable. The data about rentals of New York City office space were given me by the real-estate officer of a large local financial institution.

In Chapter Thirteen ("Crash!") I have cited a number of facts set forth by Richard Whitney in an address on "The Work of the New

York Stock Exchange in the Panic of 1929," given before the Boston Association of Stock Exchange Firms on June 10, 1930.

The optimistic statements by leaders of the Hoover Administration, cited in the last chapter ("Aftermath"), were collected in an article by James Truslow Adams ("Presidential Prosperity") in *Harper's Magazine* for August, 1930.

These are only a few of the innumerable sources drawn upon in the book; I single them out for mention only because they are not cited in the text or because my debt to them is especially large.

I am exceedingly grateful to numerous friends who have been kind enough either to hunt up material for me or to take the time to read and criticize parts of the manuscript; particularly to Rollin Alger Sawyer of the New York Public Library, Arthur Besse, John G. MacKenty, Earle Bailie, C. Alison Scully, Myra Richardson, Gordon Aymar, Agnes Rogers Hyde, Stuart Chase, Robert K. Haas, Arthur C. Holden, and Emily Linnard Cobb. I must especially thank Charles Merz for encouraging me, at the outset, to undertake what has proved an endlessly fascinating task. And finally I must record the fact that up to the time of her death, my wife, Dorothy Penrose Allen, helped me more than I can ever acknowledge.

FREDERICK LEWIS ALLEN
Scarsdale,
New York June, 1931

THE END

SINCE YESTERDAY

THE 1930s IN AMERICA

September 3, 1929--September 3, 1939

Frederick Lewis Allen

.

To

LETITIA CUNNINGHAM ROGERS

who has a wise head and a warm heart

PREFACE

Ever since, in *Only Yesterday,* I tried to tell the story of life in the United States during the nineteen-twenties I have had it in the back of my mind that some day I might make a similar attempt for the nineteen-thirties. I definitely began work on the project late in 1938 and had it three-quarters done by the latter part of the summer of 1939, though I did not yet know how the story would end. The outbreak of war in Europe provided an obvious conclusion, since it promised to end an era perhaps as definitely as the Panic of 1929 had ended one. By an odd chance, the declaration of war upon Germany by the British and French governments took place ten years to a day after that September 3, 1929, which I had already made the subject of my first chapter. It gave me a turn to realize how precisely the course of events had provided me with a decade to chronicle.

The span of time covered in *Only Yesterday* was from the Armistice of November 11, 1918, to the Panic of October-November, 1929, with a concluding chapter which recited the course of events between the Panic and the spring of 1931 and tried to suggest how the temper of the country had altered during that post-Panic interval. (The book was published in December, 1931.) When I came to plan the present volume it was clear that some overlapping would be necessary, for obviously the story of the nineteen-thirties should start before the Panic and give some idea of the high place from which the country fell during the economic collapse of 1929-32. Hence my decision to begin with a study of things as they were on September 3, 1929 (which I had written in somewhat different form as an article in *Harper's Magazine* in 1937), and in a second chapter to cover the Panic and the course of events up to the spring of 1931. The story of the Panic itself, however,

I have abbreviated in this book, since I told it in considerable detail in *Only Yesterday.*

The problem of selection and emphasis, always difficult, is of course doubly difficult when one is writing so close to the event. In *Only Yesterday* I brought into sharp relief manners and customs, fads and follies, and everyday circumstances of life. In the present volume I have done the same thing to some degree, but not quite as much; for the heart of the story of America in the nineteen-thirties was obviously the enormous economic and political transformation which took place, and such trivialities as had been of the essence of life in the United States in the nineteen-twenties were now, it seemed to me, less significant. Future events may make my selection and appraisal of material look very dated; in that case I can only hope my very miscalculations may have a certain paradoxical value as indicating the sort of pitfall into which one readily fell in 1939, even if one were conscientiously intent upon presenting a fair appraisal.

F. L. A.

Contents

Chapter One

PRELUDE: SEPTEMBER 3, 1929

§ 1

Do you remember what you were doing on September 3, 1929?

Probably not--unless you have an altogether exceptional memory.

Let me refresh your recollection. For if we are to understand the changes in American life during the nineteen-thirties, we must first recall what things were like before this period began--before the Panic which introduced the Depression. Perhaps the most convenient way of doing this is to imagine ourselves re-living a single day in 1929: seeing what things look like, listening to the talk, glancing at the newspapers and magazines and books, noticing what are the preoccupations and assumptions and expectations in people's minds--and doing all this with the eyes and ears and intellectual perspective of to-day.

I have chosen September 3, 1929, as the day to re-visit, for it was then that the Big Bull Market reached its peak: that the Dow-Jones average of stock-market prices, which had been rising so long and so furiously, made its high record for all time. If there was any single day when the wave of prosperity--and of speculation--which characterized the nineteen-twenties may be said to have attained its utmost height before it curled over and crashed, September 3, 1929, was that day.

So let us go back and look about us.

§ 2

It is a very hot day, this first Tuesday in September, 1929. Not everywhere, to be sure: in the Far West and South the temperatures are moderate. But from the coast of Maine to the wheatfields of Nebraska the sun beats down implacably.

Yesterday was Labor Day; and last night, as the long holiday week end came to its close, the suburban highways approaching the larger American cities were nightmares of congestion as endless lines of cars full of sunburned, sweltering vacationists and week-enders crept cityward through the night, inch by angry inch. On the New Jersey highways leading to New York the tie-up was so complete that people by the thousands, hopeless of reaching the Holland Tunnel for hours, parked their cars in Newark or Hoboken and finished the journey to New York by tube. The railroad stations, too, were jammed with people--not only vacationists and week-enders but boy and girl campers returning to town en masse; never had Labor Day traffic been so overwhelming, or the collective discomfort of Labor Day travel been greater. (There were, of course, no air-conditioned cars.)

As you get up on Tuesday morning, September 3, after an airless night, the weather prediction in the morning paper offers you no relief. "Fair and continued warm today and tomorrow," it says. You are in for it: for a temperature of 94.2° in New York; 90° in Chicago, Detroit, and Kansas City; 92° in St. Louis; 94° in Minneapolis; 97° in Boston.

After breakfast you go out on the street. The men you see there do not look so very different from those of a decade later, though more of them are wearing starched collars and waistcoats than in subsequent years, and not nearly so many of them are going hatless. But the women are different indeed. The fashionable figure is straight up and down--no breasts, no waist, no hips; and if few of the women you see can even approximate this ideal, at least they are visibly making the effort. Not yet have Mae West's curves become a national influence. The waistline--if it can be called one--is round the hips. The skirts are short, reaching only two or three inches below the knee: shorter than they will be again until 1939. (The new evening dresses--backless and sleeveless--have panels, godets, or drapery hanging about the ankles, but the dresses themselves are still short.) Every dress has a v-neck, almost every sweater even. If this were a wintry day, instead of one of the hottest days of summer, you would see every woman hugging herself energetically to hold in place her straight wraparound coat. The women's hats are small helmets that fit tightly right down to the nape of the neck and so closely surround the face that a profile view of a woman shows hardly more than an eye, the nose, mouth, and chin, a lock or two of hair to decorate the cheek--and the helmet. Not all women wear their hair short, but the approved style is to shingle it in the back and draw it forward over the ears.

Even in a large city you may see one or two backless dresses among the shoppers and a few pairs of stockingless legs, for the sun-tan craze is in the full flush of novelty. As the advertisements in the *Ladies Home Journal* declare, "This is a sun-worshipping year . . . all the world has gone in for sun-tan." You will have to look long and hard to detect any tinted nails, however; that style is still in the future.

The automobiles surging by you are angular; there isn't a streamline among them. Horizontal and perpendicular lines; square tops, with the upper rear angle hardly rounded at all; perpendicular or almost perpendicular windshields; perpendicular, flat radiator fronts. No pointed or rounded prows, no sloping rears, no draft ventilators.

You will not be able to go far, in the central part of any of the big cities, without hearing the deafening clatter of riveters, for although the Florida boom went to pieces in 1926, and the boom in suburban developments--which has been filling up the open spaces in the outskirts of the cities with Cotswold Terraces and Rosemont Groves and Woodmere Drives--has been lagging a bit since 1937, the boom in apartment-house construction and particularly in office-building construction is still going full tilt. Not in the poorer districts are the riveters noisiest, but at the centers of big business and of residential wealth, for it is the holders and manipulators of securities who are the chief beneficiaries of this last speculative phase of Coolidge-Hoover prosperity. That network of steel girders which you see rising so high above the street is going to be a luxurious cooperative apartment house; that place where the sidewalk is roofed over and the steam shovels are gobbling up an immense excavation is the site for a new skyscraper for brokers' offices and investment-trust offices and mortgage-bond salesmen.

In New York they are tearing down the old Waldorf-Astoria to make room for a skyscraper to end skyscrapers, the Empire State Building. John D. Rockefeller, Jr., has architects quietly at work making preliminary plans for a big mid-town development which he hopes will have a new Opera House as its central feature (he doesn't know yet that the Opera will decline to come in and that his colossal investment will have to take new shape in a Radio City). The Chrysler Building and several other major skyscrapers are still shooting upward. Most of the other cities of America are doing their best to emulate New York's frenzy for monuments of steel and stone ever loftier, more ambitious, and more expressive of the era of confident speculative finance.

As you walk on, a man passes you whistling "Singin' in the Rain," which at the moment rivals "The Pagan Love Song" and "Vagabond Lover" in popularity.

Here is a movie theatre advertising Al Jolson in "Say It with Songs"; across the street another one advertises "Our Modern Maidens," with Joan Crawford (still in her harum-scarum phase) and Rod La Rocque. A little further Ronald Colman may be seen in "Bulldog Drummond." The fact that this is advertised as Mr. Colman's "first all-talking picture" bears witness that the invasion of the movies by sound is not yet complete. Even in the big cities there are still silent pictures competing with the talking ones. The migration of Broadway stage celebrities to Hollywood has been under way for some time, as movie producers search for actors who can speak their parts acceptably, but still the studios are fumbling uncertainly with the new medium, and still the critics regard the "talkie" as something of an awkward parvenu. When your local theatre, succumbing to the trend of the times, gets itself wired for sound, the noises which blare forth are sometimes wonderful indeed. The actors lisp absurdly; the outbursts of song, coming after "silent sequences," are often cacophonous; and as Gilbert Seldes remarks in an article in the current *Harper's,* "The tinkle of a glass, the shot of a revolver, a footfall on a hardwood floor, and the noise of a pack of cards being shuffled, are all about alike."

Steadily, however, the medium is being improved; and indeed there are many people in this era of rapid engineering advance and bold business enterprise who are wondering whether the talking picture will not soon be superseded in its turn by television. "Within twelve months--eighteen months at the latest--the talkies will have to meet the competition of the talkie-projector in the home," writes Mr. Seldes. ". . . And within another year we shall probably have the simple and comparatively inexpensive mechanisms, now being perfected, which will throw on a small screen set up beside the home radio set a moving picture projected from a central broadcasting station."

If you are to be in New York this evening, perhaps the stage will be more to your taste than the movies. "Street Scene" is having a long run there, and so is that grim reminiscence of war, "Journey's End," which you may prefer if you have liked the current best-selling novel, *All Quiet on the Western Front.* Eddie Cantor is on the stage in "Whoopee," you can see Bert Lahr in "Hold Everything!" If you enjoy opening nights, you can go to the first performance of a new musical show called "Sweet Adeline," which exemplifies a budding tendency to turn back in nostalgic mood to the sentiments of the gay nineties. If you had rather sit quietly at home on such a hot night and listen to the radio, you can hear the Fada Symphony Orchestra, the Pure Oil Band, Whiteman's Old Gold Orchestra, or the Freed Orchestradians. Not yet has the technique of the radio variety show been perfected, nor can you listen in on a world-wide broadcast, but the crooners--led by Rudy Vallee--are on the air in full force. The average price of a radio set is still as high as $135, for the low-priced small sets have not yet come on the market. In these prosperous times, however, radios are being bought in quantity despite their size and price, and already some twelve million American families own them.

§ 3

Let us look at the newspapers. They may help us to orient ourselves. What will tomorrow morning's headlines say about today's events?

They will agree that the most exciting and important events of September 3, 1929, aside from the heat wave and purely local happenings, are a speech by the Prime Minister of England, a golf tournament, and two incidents in aviation.

The Prime Minister is Ramsay MacDonald; his speech is delivered at Geneva before the Assembly of the League of Nations. (Yes, the League, in 1929, is an important--though hardly determining--factor in international relations.) MacDonald announces in his speech that negotiations between Great Britain and the United States for the limitation of naval armaments are progressing favorably, and that full agreement seems near. He hopes shortly to visit the United States to further that agreement. (He will come, a little later, and he and President Hoover will sit and talk on a log by the Rapidan River near Hoover's rural camp.)

These armament negotiations of 1929 are incidents in the long post-war struggle for agreement--and for national advantage--in a Hitlerless world. Germany is a republic and a member of the League of Nations; the Dawes Plan of collecting reparations from Germany is about to be succeeded by the less oppressive Young Plan; France, the most powerful nation on the Continent, still occupies the Rhineland. Japan has not yet gone into Manchuria, let alone into China, nor Italy into Ethiopia; Spain is not yet torn by civil war; and Adolf Hitler is the little-regarded leader of a noisy minority of German Brown Shirts, his name quite unknown to most Americans.

There is plenty of tension, to be sure. National feelings run high, and for years past the attentive students of international affairs have been intermittently predicting a major war. At this very moment there is a grave threat of war between Russia and China. Mussolini is cherishing dreams of empire; there are Arab riots in Palestine; and Gandhi is giving trouble to the British in India. But still in the main the lines drawn at Versailles in 1919 are holding, and the democratically governed nations are on top.

Much more exciting than Ramsay MacDonald's address, to most Americans, is another front-page event of September 3: the National Amateur Golf Championship at Pebble Beach, California. The incomparable Bobby Jones is there, tying for first place with Gene Homans in the qualifying round. Will Jones go on victoriously to win his fifth American amateur title? (He will not; he will be beaten tomorrow by young Johnny Goodman, who in turn will be beaten by nineteen-year-old Lawson Little. Not till next year will Jones be able to perform the feat of taking the British amateur and open titles, and the American amateur and open, all in one season.) Meanwhile the question whether Jones will win is in millions of people's minds all over the country; for golf is in its heyday as the business man's game. For years past, aspiring executives have been drilled in the idea that afternoons spent in plus-fours provide not only enjoyment but useful business contacts, and country clubs have been becoming more palatial, more expensive, and more heavily mortgaged with membership bonds.

Of the two headlined incidents in aviation, one is a triumph, the other a disaster. The triumph belongs to the great German dirigible, the Graf Zeppelin. Having successfully circled the world, it is now on its way home across the Atlantic from Lakehurst to Friedrichshafen; by the evening of the third of September it has completed the ocean crossing, and observers in little Spanish towns see it floating overhead, its cabins brilliantly lighted against the sky. So impressive has been the Graf Zeppelin's demonstration of the possibilities of lighter-than-air flying that the designers of the Empire State Building are about to build a mooring mast on top of the skyscraper; they will announce their decision on December 11 with this somewhat premature prophecy: "The directors of Empire State, Inc., believe that in a comparatively short time the Zeppelin airships will establish transatlantic, transcontinental, and transpacific lines, and possibly a route to South America from the port of New York. Building with an eye to the future, it has been determined to erect this mooring tower."

In striking contrast to the Graf Zeppelin's triumph is the air disaster of September third: the crash of a Transcontinental Air Transport plane in New Mexico during a thunderstorm, with the loss of eight lives: a severe setback to heavier-than-air flying.

One might be misled by the word "Transcontinental." There is no coast-to-coast passenger service by air in 1929. During the summer the T.A.T., with Colonel Lindbergh as its adviser, has begun a pioneer service in conjunction with the Pennsylvania and Santa Fe railroads: passengers take an overnight train from New York to Columbus, Ohio; fly by day from Columbus to Waynoke, Oklahoma; take another overnight train to Clovis, New Mexico; and then continue by air to the Coast. In newspaper advertisements you may see Lionel Barrymore as he alights from the "Airway Limited," which has reduced the journey from New York to Los Angeles to the record-breaking time of forty-eight hours. No night flying is permitted. Yet now, before the first summer is over, one of the big Ford trimotor planes has gone smashing into Mount Taylor in New Mexico. The disaster is an ugly blow to the fledgling air-transport industry. Since Lindbergh's flight to Paris in 1927 the adventurers of the air have been crossing oceans boldly, airplane stocks have been soaring, and the Post Office Department has been successfully flying the mail across the country; but passenger flying in the United States is still in its hazardous and uncertain infancy.

The newspapers which record the events of September 3, 1929, contain other items of interest. You will learn in them that in Gastonia, North Carolina, a jury has been chosen for the trial of sixteen strikers and alleged Communists for the killing of the Chief of Police. (Yes, there is occasionally a bitter industrial conflict in the nineteen-twenties, even though unionism is weak, the membership of the American Federation of Labor has dwindled, and radicalism is almost negligible. There is, of course, no CIO.) You will learn that Commander Byrd--not yet an Admiral--is waiting in the snows of Little America for his flight over the South Pole. Babe Ruth, you will discover, is still top man in baseball: though he has made no home run on

8

September 3, his record for the season, so far, stands at 40 home runs as against 31 for Jimmy Foxx and 29 for Lou Gehrig. Bill Tilden is expected to win the amateur tennis championship at Forest Hills (and will do so--for the seventh time), but his era of supremacy, like Bobby Jones's and Babe Ruth's, has not long to run. (His seventh championship will be his last.) From the social columns of the newspaper you may learn that Alfred E. Smith has wandered far enough from the torrid sidewalks of New York to be the guest of honor at a luncheon at fashionable Southampton. Having been defeated by Herbert Hoover in the national election of 1928, Smith is now preparing himself for a loftier if narrower Presidency--that of the Empire State Building.

§ 4

But the event for which September 3, 1929, will probably be longest remembered in the United States, you will not find recorded in the newspapers at all. No headlines will announce tonight that the Big Bull Market has reached its climax; for no headline writers--nor anybody else for that matter--can see into the future. The financial reporters will remark, to be sure, that bullish enthusiasm has resulted in "another in the long series of consecutive new high records established by the share market," but the comment will be casual. Men do not whip themselves into frenzies over the usual. None of us is aware, on September 3, 1929, that the people of the United States are crossing one of the great divides of national history. The way ahead is hidden, as always, by fog. Surely, we imagine, there is higher ground just ahead. Yet at this very moment the path under our feet is about to turn downward.

Suppose we go into a broker's office this morning. It is crowded with men and women; every seat is taken, men are standing against the walls, and during the lunch hour there will be a dense cluster at the door as business men on their way to lunch stop by to see how their fortunes are faring. All eyes are riveted on the trans-lux screen, across which runs an endless procession of letters and figures--the record of sales taking place on the New York Stock Exchange. The tickers are having a hard time to keep up with the trading today, for the volume of transactions, though not phenomenal for 1929, is large: the day's total will run to nearly four and a half million shares. Probably half the people in this room have bought stocks on margin; in the whole United States, probably well over a million people are thus speculating with borrowed money, while several millions more are keeping a hopeful eye upon the daily fluctuations in market prices. The financing of all these speculative borrowings has sucked into the stock market a huge amount of credit; at this very moment the total of loans to brokers--loans by the banks, and by business corporations acting through the banks--comes to over eight billion dollars; yet still the demand so far exceeds the supply that the interest rate for loans to brokers stands today at nine per cent.

If you can interpret the symbols as they hurry across the lighted screen, notice the prices they record. United States Steel is edging up to 261 $^3/_4$; Anaconda Copper is at 130 $^7/_8$; American Telephone, at 302; General Electric, at 395; General Motors, at 71 $^7/_8$; and Radio Corporation, which recently split its shares five for one, is quoted on the new basis at 99 (which would be 495 on the old basis). Absurdly high, these prices? Not in the opinion of most of the men in this room. Wherever men of property gather these days--in business offices, in the suburban club cars, at the downtown lunch tables, in the country-club locker rooms--you will hear that this is a new era, that the future of the blue-ribbon stocks is dazzling, that George F. Baker never sells anything, that you can't go far wrong if you are a Bull on America. "These new investment trusts are taking the best stocks out of the market; better buy them now, while they're still within reach." "Prices too high? But look at the figures that the Blue Ridge Corporation has just announced that it'll pay! Those fellows know what they're doing." "One of the biggest men in the Street told me yesterday that he expects to see General Electric go to a thousand." "I tell you, Electric Bond and Share at 183 is dirt cheap when you consider what's ahead for the public utilities."

It is not only in the places where the wealthy congregate that one hears discussion of the market. In these days when janitors have put their savings into Montgomery Ward, when cowboys have margin accounts in American Can, and when nursemaids have just bought 300 shares of Cities' Service, stock-market talk is recurrent at dinner par-

ties, in streetcars, on commuting trains, among filling-station employees, among bookkeepers lunching at the automat. The stories
about big winnings, the conjectures about foolproof methods of stock-
market forecasting, the gossip about Packard's current earnings, form
the leitmotif of the times.

In every era young intellectuals tend to be rebellious. Do they,
in 1929, rebel against the speculative frenzy of finance capitalism?
Very few of them do. If most of them look askance at American business and American business men, it is only because they regard them
as vulgar and commercial-minded. The heaven of the young intellectuals of 1929 is not Moscow but Montparnasse; their gods are not
radical economists or novelists of proletarian revolt, but Proust, Ce-
zanne, Jung, Mencken, Hemingway (as a Left Bank author of terse
disillusionment), and T. S. Eliot.

In Chicago, Samuel Insull is now at the summit of his career;
he is watching the stock of Insull Utilities Investments--that stock
which was delivered to him only a few months ago at less than $8 a
share--reach a high price for the day of $115 a share; and he is prepar-
ing to launch yet another super-super-corporation, and to witness the
Civic Opera's first season in the mammoth building which he has provided for it. In Cleveland, men of vision are betting their shirts on
those wonder-boys of railroading, the brothers Van Sweringen, who
have so piled holding company upon holding company that they now
control six railroads and are acquiring control of a seventh. In Detroit
the big bankers and automobile executives, succumbing to the prevalent fever for financial concentration, are discussing a movement to
combine dozens of Michigan banks into huge groups. On the Pacific
Coast, the current financial sensation is Amadeo Giannini's Bank of
America, which seems well on its way to swallow up all California
business, if not to dominate a large part of American banking. Charlie
Mitchell's salesmen from the National City Company in New York are
selling South American bonds to the little crossroads bank, and Anaconda Copper stock to the bank's president. The optimism of
prosperity is everywhere.

Well, not quite everywhere. The farmers of America are not
prospering: hard times have been almost incessant on the farms since
the post-war collapse of agricultural prices in 1921. The textile towns

11

of New England are in a bad way. In the deep South and the uplands of the Alleghenies, and in the cut-over regions of northern Michigan, there is much privation. Nor can it be denied that there is unemployment. To paraphrase the words of F. C. Mills in his *Economic Tendencies in the United States,* the displacement of men by machines, the turnover of men within industries, and the shifting of men from industry to industry, are making men less secure in their jobs, and especially are making it harder for men past the prime of life to get back into new jobs once they are displaced. The rewards for employed men are often high, but mechanical improvements and a faster pace of work are making it harder to hold on. And it must be admitted, too, that when one uses the word prosperity one is using a relative term. According to the Brookings estimates, even in this banner year of 1929 no less than seventy-eight per cent of the American population have family incomes of less than $3,000 or individual incomes of less than $1,500, and something like forty per cent have family incomes of less than $1,500 or individual incomes of less than $750. Certainly such a state of affairs is far from Utopian. Yet by all current standards elsewhere in the world, and by all remembered standards in America, the average of well-being is high; and among the well-to-do it is glittering.

President Hoover has just returned to the blinding heat of Washington from a week end at his Rapidan camp, and this morning he meets with his Cabinet from 10:30 till 12. No record will be kept of what goes on at that meeting, but one may hazard a reasonable guess as to some of the topics under discussion. The talk may turn to the armament negotiations with Great Britain, or to some thorny questions of tariff adjustment, or to the danger of a Russo-Chinese war over the Chinese Eastern Railroad. Mr. Hoover may consult his Cabinet as to whether he should denounce the shipbuilding companies which retained William B. Shearer as an "observer" at the Geneva arms conference, presumably to hinder naval reduction. (He will denounce them, three days hence.) There are also awkward questions relating to Prohibition, farm relief, and Mexican policy which may come before the meeting. Are those men gathered about the long table in the White House offices turning their attention today to the question whether prosperity can be maintained? It is possible, but unlikely.

Not that Herbert Hoover shares the widespread belief that the speculative debauch in the stock market is a happy and healthy phenomenon. On the contrary, he has been supporting the Federal Reserve Board in its unavailing efforts to check the flow of credit into speculation, and he has done his share of worrying over the possible consequences of a collapse of prices. But by this time the boom is well beyond control, except by some drastic measure which might bring on the very crash it was intended to avert. Otherwise the economic skies seem clear. Business is undeniably booming. Perhaps the speculative storm will manage to blow itself out and all will be well. Prosperity, these days, has come to be taken for granted; and busy men whose desks are piled with problems pressing for solution do not borrow trouble by debating just when and how it might come to an unimaginable end.

Besides, the maintenance of general prosperity is not, in 1929, generally regarded as a presidential responsibility. The New York *Herald Tribune* is going to press tonight with a laudatory review of Hoover's first six months in office, and nowhere in that review will there be a word about the stock market or so much as a hint that the maintenance of general economic stability is the government's affair. In every political election, of course, the party in power, as a matter of routine, takes all credit for whatever good times have been enjoyed, and the party out of power excoriates it for whatever hard times have been suffered; but the most that is really expected of the government from month to month, in relation to the progress of the national economy, is that its policies of taxation, regulation, subsidy, and the like, shall if possible be helpful to business rather than hurtful, and particularly shall be helpful to those business interests which are able to write their wishes into legislation. Otherwise the government is expected to keep its hands off. Insofar as the economic machinery does not run of its own accord, automatically, the citizens look less to the political chiefs in Washington for economic leadership than to the financial chiefs in Wall Street. Not Herbert Hoover and his Cabinet but the bankers and industrialists and holding-company promotors are the architects and custodians of this prosperity.

§ 5

13

But if the maintenance of prosperity is not considered a current problem, Prohibition emphatically is. The Eighteenth Amendment is in full force, and so are the bootleggers and rumrunners. Al Capone, as it happens, is serving a year's sentence in Philadelphia for carrying a pistol, but he will be out soon; meanwhile his Chicago gang and similar gangster groups in other cities are taking an enormous toll from the illicit liquor business. Very few people believe that repeal of the Eighteenth Amendment is a reasonable possibility; any well-informed student of politics will tell you that a few dry states could block it indefinitely. Moralists are attributing the prevalence of crime to the dire influences of the speakeasy.

If your rambles this afternoon should take you through midtown New York, you may notice well-dressed men and women descending the steps to the basement entrances of certain brownstone houses. They are not calling on the cook, but making a routine entrance to a speakeasy: standing patiently at the door till Tony or Mino, within, has appraised them through a little barred window and decided to unbolt the door. The man-about-town carries in his wallet a collection of autographed speakeasy cards, certifying to membership in this or that "club," in case he should wish to go for a drink to some place where he is not already well known by sight as a patron or can identify himself as a "friend of Mr. Jones's."

President Hoover has appointed a commission to study the whole question of law enforcement and crime; and this very day its chairman, George W. Wickersham, is on a train from New York to Washington, going over the agenda for tomorrow's meeting. Prohibition is only one of the topics which this commission will investigate; indeed, though the minutes of tomorrow's meeting will cover five pages, only two lines will deal with liquor legislation. But to the general public nothing in the commission's program really matters except Prohibition. For the wet-or-dry issue is the hottest one in American politics.

§ 6

At any moment some currents in the great stream of history are diminishing, and other currents are gaining in volume and strength. At any moment there are things ending, waves of popular excitement subsiding, men moving into the twilight of their careers; and there are also things beginning, future events being quietly prepared for, men and women walking about unknown whose names will soon be on everybody's lips.

On this September day of 1929, the last surviving veteran of the Mexican War is dying. . . . Ex-President William Howard Taft, now the Chief Justice of the Supreme Court, is in declining health, and has but a few months more to live. . . . Thomas A. Edison's achievements as an inventor are behind him, for he is in his eighty-third year. On this hot day he is convalescing from an attack of pneumonia, but is sitting up in a chair and declaring that he expects to go to Dearborn in a few weeks to celebrate the fiftieth anniversary of his incandescent light. (The expectation is justified, for he still has two full years to live.) . . . Calvin Coolidge's life-work is behind him, too. Last March he left the White House for his simple duplex apartment on Massasoit Street, Northampton, where the rent is $36 a month; and although he is said to have made a hundred thousand dollars writing magazine articles since March 4, he still uses a little second-story office with a desk, two chairs, and a bookcase filled with old law books. Life is quiet for him, these days, too quiet; he longs for the days that are done. . . . In the day's news there is an echo of the oil scandal of the Administration which preceded Coolidge's: Harry F. Sinclair, serving a term in the District of Columbia jail for contempt of the Senate during the oil investigations, has been denied permission to leave the jail on errands as the jail physician's "pharmaceutical assistant."

It has been said that coming events cast their shadows before. But if this is true, the shadows are not recognized as such. On September 3, 1929, Governor Franklin D. Roosevelt of New York State, who ran for the Governorship last year at the urgent invitation of his old friend Al Smith, is awaiting replies to a questionnaire which he has just sent out to mayors and village presidents throughout the State. The questionnaire asks them on what basis their communities buy electric power--from private utilities or from municipal plants? and at what cost? This inquiry might seem prophetic, but to mortals denied the gift of prophecy it does not seem especially significant. The men who are pushing up the prices of public-utility stocks to Himalayan levels are not greatly disturbed. For anybody in Albany will tell you that Roosevelt is just collecting information which he thinks he needs in order to carry out Al Smith's power policy.

If you follow the liberal weeklies carefully, you will see occasional caustic references to that autocratic reactionary, that stubborn member of the A F of L bureaucracy, the leader of the United Mine Workers, John L. Lewis. . . . Father Coughlin of Royal Oak, outside Detroit, is well known within the range of the single broadcasting station which transmits his sermons but almost unknown beyond them. . . . In Long Beach, California, there is an elderly practicing physician named Francis E. Townsend, quite unknown save to his patients and personal friends: the time for the Townsend Pension Plan is still far away. . . . Huey Long is in the midst of a stormy term as Governor of Louisiana, but Northerners have heard little of him yet. . . . The people who are accustomed to sitting in a Greenwich Village speakeasy and occasionally hearing young Howard Scott--a none-too-successful engineer--expound his curious economic theories, would be amazed if they were told that within four years Technocracy will be the talk of the United States.

Broadcasters take a day off every week, and so on this September 3 Freeman F. Gosden and Charles J. Correll are getting a rest after their first fortnight on the NBC network as "Amos 'n' Andy." In two months their program will be changed from a late evening hour to 7 p.m., Eastern Standard Time, and within a year their popularity will be so immense that one will hardly be able to walk a block in an American town at that hour without hearing "I'se regusted" and "Dat's de propolition" issuing from open window after window. Have they any inkling of what is ahead for them? Does Garnet Carter of Lookout Mountain, Tennessee, who is today boarding a train for Miami to install the first miniature golf course in Florida, dream that by next summer miniature golf courses will be springing up by every highway all over the land? Does Walt Disney, who, after years of adversity, is at last finding a public for his Mickey Mouse pictures and has just brought out his first Silly Symphony, foresee his fame and fortune as the creator of "Three Little Pigs" and "Snow White"?

16

As the heat of the day begins to wane in Cazenovia, New York, a young writer named Hervey Allen sits down to work at the second chapter of a huge novel which will not be published for nearly four years: *Anthony Adverse. . . .* In the John Day publishing house in New York, the editors are making up their minds to publish a novel called *East Wind, West Wind,* which has been declined already by so many publishers that its author has not even bothered to tell her agents that she has left China for a visit to the United States. In her mind is taking shape another novel; who guesses that this yet unwritten book, *The Good Earth,* will win for Pearl Buck the Nobel Prize? . . . Who, for that matter, would ever pick a freckle-faced, fourteen-year-old boy in Oakland, California, named Donald Budge, as the future world's tennis champion? The boy hasn't even touched a racket since he was eleven. . . . Recent graduates of Cushing Academy at Ashburnham, Massachusetts, remember well their schoolmate Ruth Elizabeth Davis, but not in connection with Hollywood; for not until 1930 will she begin her screen career. (Later they will see her often as Bette Davis.) . . . In one of the Middle Western cities, if you drop into a theatre on the Orpheum vaudeville circuit tonight, you may be amused by a young ventriloquist named Edgar Bergen talking to a dummy that he calls Charlie McCarthy. . . . If you are in New York and the heat drives you to a roof garden for the evening, and you happen to choose the Park Central Hotel, you may appreciate the nimbleness of a twenty-year-old clarinetist in the band; but his name will be as unfamiliar to you as those of Bergen and McCarthy: it is Benny Goodman. Does anybody think of him--does he think of himself--as the future King of Swing?

Everybody who follows the newspapers at all closely in 1929 can identify for you instantly Bishop Cannon, Texas Guinan, Senator Heflin, Jimmy Walker, Hugo Eckener, Legs Diamond, Mabel Walker Willebrandt, Dolly Gann, or "Doug and Mary." But even your local newspaper editor, who prides himself on knowing the names of public characters, will probably have to go to books of reference to identify General Hugh S. Johnson, Alf M. Landon, Harry Hopkins, Thomas E. Dewey, or Eleanor Roosevelt. And not in any book of reference will he find Joe Louis, Bruno Richard Hauptmann, Robert Taylor, the WPA, or the New Deal.

In all the country there is no such thing as a streamlined train, a bar operating openly and legally, or a man living on Federal relief.

Shirley Temple is a baby less than five months old, and the Dionne quintuplets are unborn.

And so, for that matter, is the Depression. In fact, if you wished to be set down as the craziest of prophets by any of the men and women whom you have watched going about their affairs in the glaring sunlight of September 3, 1929, you would only have to tell them that within two months they are to witness the greatest financial panic in American history, and that it will usher in a prolonged and desperate economic crisis.

Chapter Two

EXIT PROSPERITY

§ 1

After September 3, 1929, the stock market dropped sharply, surged up again, dropped again--and did not surge back. Instead, as September came to an end, it sagged lower and lower.

Even so, there was not at first much uneasiness. Again and again, during the Big Bull Market of the two preceding years, there had been sharp breaks lasting several days, thousands of injudicious and unfortunate speculators had been shaken out, and yet prices had recovered and climbed on to new heights. Why worry now? Why not take advantage of these bargain prices? And so margin traders, large and small, who had previously sold out at big profits came floating in again, staking their previous winnings on the chance that Steel would climb back from 230 to 260, or General Electric from 370 to 395, and beyond; and accordingly the volume of brokers' loans rose to a new-- and final--peak of over eight and a half billion dollars. Meanwhile the chorus of financial prognosticators assuring all and sundry that nothing was amiss, and that prices were suffering only a temporary setback, rose louder than ever.

Yet still the market sagged. Foreign funds were being withdrawn from it, partly as a result of the collapse of Hatry's speculative bubble in England, partly, perhaps, because speculation in New York had seemed from the first a hazardous business to European investors and many of them were now having qualms. Some American investors, too, were prudently withdrawing as they noticed that the volume of industrial production was declining a little. All the time, as prices ebbed, insecurely margined traders were being forced to sell. As October continued and there was no smart recovery, a note of uncertainty, of urgency, of stridency even, came into the clamor that all was well. Perhaps, after all, it was not. . . . The decline became more rapid. Surely this must be the bottom, the last chance to buy cheap. Or was it the beginning of the end?

The short session of Saturday, October 19, was a bad one, such volatile stocks as Auburn and Case losing 25 points and 40 points respectively in two hours of trading, and even General Electric losing 9 $\frac{1}{4}$. Monday, October 21, was worse, for by this time more and more traders were reaching the end of their resources and being sold out; the volume of trading reached six million shares. Tuesday was better: did not the great Charles E. Mitchell of the National City Bank, returning from Europe, radiate assurance? But on Wednesday the storm broke anew and the losses were unprecedented: Adams Express lost 96 points during the day, Auburn lost 77, Westinghouse lost 25, and the stock-market page of the late afternoon papers showed a startling procession of minus figures down the column of "net change": -6 $\frac{1}{2}$, -3, -14 $\frac{3}{8}$, -7, -2 $\frac{1}{2}$, -16 $\frac{1}{4}$, -12 and so on. By this time the volume of selling was so great that the supposedly almost instantaneous ticker service was left far behind; at three o'clock, when the Exchange was closing for the day, the figures running across the trans-lux screens in brokers' offices all over the country were reporting transactions which had taken place at sixteen minutes past one--an hour and forty-four minutes before!

And on Thursday, October 24. . . .

That Thursday morning the selling came in a roaring and presently incredible deluge. How much of it was short selling will never be known, for no statistical record of the total was kept, but apparently the amount was not very great. Some of it, of course, was frightened selling, even at the outset: already men and women had discovered, to their great alarm, that the slow gains of weeks and months could be swept away in a few precipitous hours. But even in the first hour on Thursday the greater part of the selling was surely forced selling. In a market so honeycombed with credit, the beautifully contrived system whereby the stock gambler whose margin was exhausted by a fall in market prices was automatically sold out, became a beautifully contrived system for wrecking the price structure. In poured the selling orders by hundreds and thousands; it seemed as if nobody wanted to buy; and as prices melted away, presently the brokers in the howling melee of the Stock Exchange were fighting to sell before it was too late. The great Panic was on.

By noon that day, dismayed crowds of men and women in brokers' branch offices everywhere saw the ticker recording unbelievable prices, and realized furthermore that it was so hopelessly behind the market as to be well-nigh useless as a clue to what was actually taking place in the maelstrom of Wall Street, where Montgomery Ward was falling headlong from 83 to 50, Radio from 68 $^3/_4$ to 44 $^1/_2$, even United States Steel from 205 $^1/_2$ to 193 $^1/_2$.

To the rescue came the big bankers. A few minutes after noon, five of them--Messrs. Lamont of J. P. Morgan & Co., Mitchell of the National City Bank, Potter of the Guaranty Trust, Wiggin of the Chase National, and Prosser of the Bankers Trust--met at the House of Morgan and formed a pool to support prices. So high was the confidence of the financial world in their sagacity and power that even before they had decided upon anything, when simply the news went about that they were meeting, prices steadied, rallied; and by the time Richard Whitney, as the representative of the bankers' pool, went on the floor of the Stock Exchange at half past one to bid for stocks, he hardly had to do more than go through the motions: when he offered to buy 10,000 shares of Steel at 205, he found only 200 shares for sale at that price. The gods of Wall Street still could make the storm to cease.

Not till eight minutes past seven that evening, when night had darkened the windows of the brokers' offices, did the tickers stop chattering out prices from the Exchange floor. Nearly thirteen million shares had changed hands. Wild rumors had been going about all day-- that exchanges had been closed, that troops had been called out in New York, that eleven speculators had committed suicide. Panic this was, and no doubt about it. But the bankers, it was hoped, had saved the day.

For two more days the market, struggling, nearly held its own, while the lights burned all night in Wall Street as the brokers' clerks struggled to get their records straight, and the telegrams calling for more margin went out by hundreds and thousands. Then the avalanche began again; and this time the bankers could not conceivably have stopped it if they had tried. All they tried to do was to provide bids for stock where there were no bids at all: to give to the rout a semblance of order.

On Tuesday, October 29, came the climax. The official statistics of the day gave the volume of trading as 16,410,030 shares, but no one knows how many sales went unrecorded in the yelling scramble to sell: there are those who believe that the true volume may have been twenty or even twenty-five million. Big and small, insiders and outsiders, the high-riders of the Big Bull Market were being cleaned out: the erstwhile millionaire and his chauffeur, the all-powerful pool operator and his suckers, the chairman of the board with his two-thousand-share holding and the assistant bookkeeper with his ten-share holding, the bank president and his stenographer. Here are a few of the losses for that single day in individual stocks--and remember that they came on top of a long succession of previous losses: American Telephone and General Electric, 28 points apiece; Westinghouse, 19 points; Allied Chemical, 35 points; North American, 271 $1/2$ points; Auburn, 60 points; Columbian Carbon, 38 $3/4$ points--and these despite a sharp rally at the close!

Said the sober *Commercial & Financial Chronicle* in its issue of November 2, "The present week has witnessed the greatest stock-market catastrophe of all the ages."

Now at last there came a turn in the tide, as old John D. Rockefeller announced that his son and he were buying common stocks, and two big corporations declared extra dividends as a gesture of stubborn confidence. The Exchange declared a holiday and shortened the hours of trading to give the haggard brokers and sleepless clerks a chance to begin to dig themselves out from under the mass of accumulated work. Then prices went down once more, and again down. Day after day the retreat continued. Not until November 13 did prices reach their bottom for 1929.

The disaster which had taken place may be summed up in a single statistic. In a few short weeks it had blown into thin air *thirty billion dollars*--a sum almost as great as the entire cost to the United States of its participation in the World War, and nearly twice as great as the entire national debt.

§ 2

President Hoover went into action. He persuaded Secretary Mellon to announce that he would propose to the coming Congress a reduction in individual and corporate income taxes. He called to Washington groups of big bankers and industrialists, railroad and pub-lic-utility executives, labor leaders, and farm leaders, and obtained assurances that capital expenditures would go on, that wage-rates would not be cut, that no claims for increased wages other than those in negotiation would be pressed. He urged the governors and mayors of the country to expand public works in every practicable direction, and showed the way by arranging to increase the Federal public-buildings expenditure by nearly half a billion dollars (which at that time seemed like pretty heavy government spending). Hoover and his associates began at every opportunity to declare that conditions were "fundamentally sound," to predict a revival of business in the spring, to insist that there was nothing to be disturbed about.

Thereupon the bankers and brokers and investors and business men, and citizens generally, caught their breath and looked about them to take stock of the new situation. Outwardly they became aggressive-ly confident, however they might be gnawed inwardly by worry. Why, *of course* everything was all right. The newspapers and magazines car-ried advertisements radiating cheer: "Wall Street may sell stocks, but Main Street is still buying goods." "All right, Mister--now that the headache is over, LET'S GO TO WORK." It was in those days soon after the Panic that a new song rose to quick popularity--a song copyrighted on November 7, 1929, when the stock market was still reeling: "Happy Days Are Here Again!"

But it was useless to declare, as many men did, that nothing more had happened than that a lot of gamblers had lost money and a preposterous price-structure had been salutarily deflated. For in the first place the individual losses, whether sustained by millionaires or clerks, had immediate repercussions. People began to economize; indeed, during the worst days of the Panic some businesses had come almost to a standstill as buyers waited for the hurricane to blow itself out. And if the rich, not the poor, had been the chief immediate victims of the crash (it was not iron-workers and sharecroppers who were throwing themselves out of windows that autumn, but brokers and promoters), nevertheless trouble spread fast as servants were discharged, as jewelry shops and high-priced dress shops and other luxury businesses found their trade ebbing and threw off now idle employees, as worried executives decided to postpone building the extension to the factory, or to abandon this or that unprofitable department, or to cut down on production till the sales prospects were clearer. Quickly the ripples of uncertainty and retrenchment widened and unemployment spread.

Moreover, the collapse in investment values had undermined the credit system of the country at innumerable points, endangering loans and mortgages and corporate structures which only a few weeks previously had seemed as safe as bedrock. The Federal Reserve officials reported to Hoover, "It will take perhaps months before readjustment is accomplished." Still more serious was the fact--not so apparent then as later--that the smash-up of the Big Bull Market had put out of business the powerful bellows of inflation which had kept industry roaring when all manner of things were awry with the national economy. The speculative boom, by continually pouring new funds into the economic bloodstream, had enabled Coolidge-Hoover prosperity to continue long after its natural time.

Finally, the Panic had come as a shock--a first shock--to the illusion that American capitalism led a charmed life. Like a man of rugged health suffering his first acute illness, the American business man suddenly realized that he too was a possible prey for forces of destruction. Nor was the shock confined to the United States. All over

24

the world, America's apparently unbeatable prosperity had served as an advertisement of the advantages of political democracy and economic finance capitalism. Throughout Europe, where the nations were loaded down with war debts and struggling with adverse budgets and snarling at one another over their respective shares of a trade that would not expand, men looked at the news from the United States and thought, "And now, perhaps, the jig is up even there." . . .

But if business was so shaken by the Panic that during the winter of 1929-30 it responded only languidly to the faith-healing treatment being prescribed for it by the Administration, the stock market found its feet more readily. Presently the old game was going on again. Those pool operators whose resources were at least half intact were pushing stocks up again. Speculators, big and little, convinced that what had caught them was no more than a downturn in the business cycle, that the bottom had been passed, and that the prosperity band wagon was getting under way again, leaped in to recoup their losses. Prices leaped, the volume of trading became as heavy as in 1929, and a Little Bull Market was under way. That zeal for mergers and combinations and holding-company empires which had inflamed the rugged individualists of the nineteen-twenties reasserted itself: the Van Sweringers completed their purchase of the Missouri Pacific; the process of amalgamation in the aviation industry and in numerous others was resumed; the Chase National Bank in New York absorbed two of its competitors and became the biggest bank in all the world; and the investment salesmen reaped a new harvest selling to the suckers five hundred million dollars' worth of the very latest thing in investments--shares in fixed investment trusts, which would buy the very best stocks (as of 1930) and hold on to them till hell froze.

Who noticed that there was more zeal for consolidating businesses than for expanding them or initiating them? In the favorite phrase of the day, Prosperity was just around the corner.

But a new day was not dawning. This light in the economic skies was only the afterglow of the old one. What if the stock ticker-- recording Steel at 198 $^3/_4$, Telephone at 274 $^1/_4$, General Motors at 103 $^5/_8$, General Electric at 95 $^3/_8$, Standard Oil of New Jersey at 84 $^7/_8$-- promised fair weather? Even at the height of the Little Bull Market there were breadlines in the streets. In March Miss Frances Perkins,

Industrial Commissioner for New York State, was declaring that unemployment was worse than it had been since that state had begun
collecting figures in 1914. In several cities, jobless men by the hundreds or thousands were forming pathetic processions to dramatize
their plight--only to be savagely smashed by the police. In April the
business index turned down again, and the stock market likewise. In
May and June the market broke severely. While Hoover, grimly fas-
tening a smile on his face, was announcing, "We have now passed the
worst and with continued unity of effort we shall rapidly recover," and
predicting that business would be normal by fall--in this very season
the long, grinding, heart-breaking decline of American business was
beginning once more.

§ 3

Not yet, however, had the Depression sunk very deeply into
the general public consciousness. Of the well-to-do, in particular, few
were gravely disturbed in 1930. Many of them had been grievously
hurt in the Panic, but they had tried to laugh off their losses, to grin at
the jokes about brokers and speculators which were going the rounds.
("Did you hear about the fellow who engaged a hotel room and the
clerk asked him whether he wanted it for sleeping or jumping?" "No--
but I heard there were two men who jumped hand-in-hand because
they'd held a joint account!") As 1930 wore on, they were aware of the
Depression chiefly as something that made business slow and uncertain and did terrible things to the prices of securities. To business men
in "Middletown," a representative small mid-Western city, until 1932
"the Depression was mainly something they read about in the newspapers"--despite the fact that by 1930 every fourth factory worker in the
city had lost his job. In the country at large, nearly all executive jobs
still held intact; dividends were virtually as large as in 1929; few
people guessed that the economic storm would be of long duration.
Many men and women in the upper income brackets had never seen a
visible sign of this unemployment that they kept reading about until, in
the fall of 1930, the International Apple Shippers' Association, faced
with an oversupply of apples, had the bright idea of selling them on

credit to unemployed men, at wholesale prices, for resale at 5 cents apiece--and suddenly there were apple-salesmen shivering on every corner.

When the substantial and well-informed citizens who belonged to the National Economic League (an organization whose executive council included such notables as John Hays Hammond, James Rowland Angell, Frank O. Lowden, David Starr Jordan, Edward A. Filene, George W. Wickersham, and Nicholas Murray Butler) were polled in January, 1930, as to what they considered the "paramount problems of the United States for 1930," their vote put the following problems at the head of the list: 1. Administration of Justice; 2. Prohibition; 3. Lawlessness, Disrespect for Law; 4. Crime; 5. Law Enforcement; 6. World Peace--and they put Unemployment down in *eighteenth* place! Even a year later, in January, 1931, "Unemployment, Economic Stabilization" had moved up only to fourth place, following Prohibition, Administration of Justice, and Lawlessness.

These polls suggest not only how well insulated were the "best citizens" of the United States against the economic troubles of 1930, and how prone--as Thurman Arnold later remarked--to respond to public affairs with "a set of moral reactions," but also how deep and widespread had become the public concern over the egregious failure of Prohibition to prohibit, and over the manifest connection between the illicit liquor traffic and the gangsters and racketeers.

Certainly the Prohibition laws were being flouted more generally and more openly than ever before, even in what had formerly been comparatively sober and puritanical communities. As a "Middletown" business man told the Lynds, "Drinking increased markedly here in '27 and '28, and in '30 was heavy and open. With the Depression, there seemed to be a collapse of public morals. I don't know whether it was the Depression, but in the winter of '29-'30 and in '30-'31 things were roaring here. There was much drunkenness--people holding bathtub gin parties. There was a great increase in women's drinking and drunkenness." In Washington, in the fall of 1930, a bootlegger was discovered to have been plying his wares even in the austere precincts of the Senate Office Building. In New York, by 1931, enforcement had become such a mockery that the choice of those who wanted a drink was no longer simply between going to a speakeasy and calling up a bootlegger; there were "cordial and beverage shoppes" doing an open retail business, their only concession to appearances being that bottles were not ordinarily on display, and the show windows revealed nothing more embarrassing to the policeman on the beat than rows of little plaster figurines. By the winter of 1930-31, steamship lines operating out of New York were introducing a new attraction for the wholeheartedly bibulous--week-end cruises outside the twelve-mile limit, some of them with no destination at all except "the freedom of the seas."

With every item of gangster news--the killing of "Jake" Lengle of the Chicago *Tribune;* the repeated shootings of Legs Diamond in a New York gang war; the bloody rivalry between Dutch Schultz and Vincent Coll in the New York liquor racket; the capture of "Two-gun" Crowley (a youth who had been emulating gangster ways) after an exciting siege, by the police, of the house in which he was hiding out in New York's upper West Side; the ability of Al Capone, paroled from prison in Pennsylvania, to remain at large despite the universal knowledge that he had long been the dictator of organized crime in Chicago--with every such item of news the public was freshly reminded that the gangsters were on the rise and that it was beer-running and "alky-cooking" which provided them with their most reliable revenue. Preachers and commencement orators and after-dinner speakers inveighed against the "crime wave." District Attorney Crain of New York said the racketeers "have their hands in everything from the cradle to the grave--from babies' milk to funeral coaches"; and President Hoover said that what was needed to combat racketeering was not new laws, but enforcement of the existing ones.

Meanwhile sentiment against Prohibition was apparently rising: when the *Literary Digest,* early in 1930, took a straw vote of almost five million people, only 30 $\frac{1}{2}$ per cent favored continuance and strict enforcement of the Eighteenth Amendment and Volstead Act; 29 per cent were for modification, and 40 $\frac{1}{2}$ per cent for repeal. Nor was the cause of righteous enforcement aided when Bishop James Cannon, Jr., of the Methodist Episcopal Church, South, who had been one of the most active of dry leaders, was discovered--to the glee of the wets--to have been speculating in the stock market under the auspices of a New York bucket shop.

Perhaps the Wickersham Commission, when it came out of its long huddle over the law-enforcement problem, would throw a clear beam of light into this confusion? On the 19th of January, 1931, it reported upon Prohibition--and the confusion was thereby worse confounded. For, in the first place, the body of the Wickersham report contained explicit and convincing evidence that Prohibition was not working; in the second place, the eleven members of the Commission came to eleven separate conclusions, two of which were in general for repeal, four for modification, and five--less than a majority, it will be noted--for further trial of the Prohibition experiment. And in the third place, the commission *as a whole* came out, paradoxically, for further trial.

Confronted by this welter of disagreement and contradiction, the puzzled citizen could be sure of only one thing: that the supposedly enlightened device of collecting innumerable facts and trying to reason from them to an inevitable conclusion had been turned into a farce. The headache of the Prohibition problem remained to vex him.

§ 4

There were other diversions aplenty to take people's minds off the Depression. There was, for instance, the $125,000,000 boom in miniature golf. People had been saying that what the country needed was a new industry; well, here it was--in travesty. Garnet Carter's campaign to establish miniature golf in Florida during the winter of 1929-30 had been so sensationally successful that by the summer hundreds of thousands of Americans were parking their sedans by half-acre roadside courses and earnestly knocking golf balls along cotton-seed greenswards, through little mouse holes in wooden barricades, over little bridges, and through drainpipes, while the proprietors of these new playgrounds listened happily to the tinkle of the cash register and decided to go in for even bigger business in 1931--to lease the field across the way and establish a driving range, with buckets of balls and a squad of local boys as retrievers (armed with beach umbrellas against the white hail of slices and hooks).

There was the incredible popularity of Amos 'n' Andy on the radio, which made the voices of Freeman F. Gosden and Charles J. Correll the most familiar accents in America, set millions of people to following, evening by evening, the fortunes of the Fresh Air Taxicab Company and the progress of Madam Queen's breach-of-promise suit against Andy--and gave the rambunctious Huey Long, running for the Senate in Louisiana, the notion of styling himself the "Kingfish" as he careened about the State with two sound-trucks to advertise him to the unterrified Democracy. (Long won the election, incidentally, though he had to kidnap and hold incommunicado on Grand Isle, till primary day was past, two men who had been threatening him with embarrassing lawsuits.)

There was Bobby Jones's quadruple triumph in golf--the British and American amateur and open championships--which inspired more words of cabled news than any other individual's exploits during 1930, and quite outshone Max Schmeling's defeat of Jack Sharkey, the World's Series victory of the Philadelphia Athletics, the success of Enterprise in defending the America's Cup at Newport against the last of Sir Thomas Lipton's Shamrocks, and the winnings of Gallant Fox, Whichone, and Equipoise on the turf. Always the fliers could command excitement: Lindbergh, the prince charming of American aviators, inaugurated the air-mail route to the Canal Zone (and soon afterward became the father of a son destined for a tragic end); in September, 1930, Costes and Bellonte made the first successful westward point-to-point flight across the Atlantic, taking off at Paris in the "Question Mark" and landing at Long Island.

There was the utterly fantastic epidemic of tree-sitting, which impelled thousands of publicity-crazy boys to roost in trees by day and night in the hope of capturing a "record," with occasional misadventures: a boy in Fort Worth fell asleep, hit the ground, and broke two ribs; the owner of a tree at Niagara Falls sued to have a boy removed from its branches, whereupon the boy's friends cut a branch from another tree, carried him to a new perch, and enabled him to continue his vigil; a boy in Manchester, New Hampshire, stayed aloft till a bolt of lightning knocked him down. To this impressive conclusion had come the mania for flagpole-sitting and Marathon-dancing which had characterized the latter nineteen-twenties.

TICKER TAPE FOR BOBBY JONES
He disentangles himself from a streamer as he returns to New York on July 2, 1930, after winning two British golf championships. (Note Mrs. Jones's helmet-like hat and the almost perpendicular windshield of the car.)

As the winter of 1930-31 drew on, there were other things to talk about than the mounting unemployment relief problem and the collapse of the speculatively managed Bank of United States in New York. Some of the new automobiles were equipped for "free wheeling." (If you pulled out a button on the dashboard, the car would coast the moment you took your foot off the throttle. When you stepped on it again there was a small whirring sound and the engine took up its labor once more without a jolt.) The device was good for endless discussions: was it a help? did it save gas? was it safe? A lively backgammon craze was bringing comfort to department-store managers: however badly things might be going otherwise in the Christmas season, at least backgammon boards were moving. While the head of the house sat at his desk miserably contemplating the state of his finances, his eighteen-year-old son was humming "Body and Soul" and trying to screw up his courage to fill his hip flask with the old man's gin for the evening's dance, where he dreamed of meeting a girl with platinum-blonde hair like Jean Harlow's in "Hell's Angels."

Not everybody was worrying about the Depression--yet.

§ 5

But Herbert Hoover worried, and worked doggedly at the Presidency, and saw his prestige steadily declining as the downward turn in the business index mocked his cheerful predictions, and thereupon worried and worked the harder. Things were not going well for the great economic engineer.

The London Arms Conference, despite the most careful preparation--during which Ramsay MacDonald had come to Washington to confer--had produced a none-too-impressive agreement: it set "limitations" which the United States could not have attained without spending a billion dollars on new construction.

Congress, applying itself to tariff revision, had got out of hand and had produced, not the limited changes which Hoover had half-heartedly advocated, but a new sky-high tariff bill which (in the words of Denna Frank Fleming) was virtually "a declaration of economic war against the whole of the civilized world," giving "notice to other nations that retaliatory tariffs, quotas, and embargoes against American goods were in order . . . notice to our war debtors that the dollar exchange with which they might make their payments to us would not be available." It had been obvious to anybody beyond the infant class in economics that the United States could neither have a flourishing export trade nor collect the huge sums owing it from abroad unless it either lent foreign countries the money with which to pay (which it had been doing in the nineteen-twenties--and had now stopped doing) or else permitted imports in quantity. Over a thousand American economists, finding themselves in agreement for once (and for the last time during the nineteen-thirties) had protested against any general tariff increase. Hoover was no economic illiterate. But he was by nature and training an administrator rather than a politician, and he had been so outmaneuvered politically during the long tariff wrangle that when the Hawley-Smoot Tariff Bill was finally laid on his desk in June, 1930, he signed it--presumably with an inward groan.

His Farm Board had been trying to sustain the prices of wheat and cotton by buying them on the market, and had succeeded by the end of the 1930 season in accumulating sixty million bushels of wheat and a million and a third bales of cotton, without doing any more than slow up the price decline. As if the farm situation were not bad enough already, a terrific drought had developed during the summer in the belt of land running from Virginia and Maryland on the Eastern seaboard out to Missouri and Arkansas (a precursor of other and more dreadful droughts to come); and when wells failed and crops withered in the fields, new lamentations arose to plague the man in the White House. Nor had these lamentations ceased when it became apparent that the continuing contraction of business threatened an ugly winter for the unemployed, whose numbers, by the end of 1930, had increased from the three or four millions of the spring to some five or six millions.

Since Hoover's first fever of activity after the Panic, he had been leery of any direct governmental offensive against the Depression. He had preferred to let economic nature take its course. "Economic depression," he insisted, "cannot be cured by legislative action or executive pronouncement. Economic wounds must be healed by the action of the cells of the economic body--the producers and consumers themselves." So he stood aside and waited for the healing process to assert itself, as according to the hallowed principles of laissez-faire economics it should.

But he was not idle meanwhile. For already there was a fierce outcry for Federal aid, Federal benefits of one sort or another; and in this outcry he saw a grave threat to the Federal budget, the self-reliance of the American people, and the tradition of local self-rule and local responsibility for charitable relief. He resolved to defeat this threat. Although he set up a national committee to look after the unemployment relief situation, this committee was not to hand out Federal funds; it was simply to co-ordinate and encourage the state and local attempts to provide for the jobless out of state appropriations and local charitable drives. (Hoover was quite right, said those well-to-do people who told one another that a "dole" like the one in England would be "soul-destroying.") He hotly opposed the war veterans' claim for a Bonus--only to see the "Adjusted Compensation" bill passed over his veto. He vetoed pension bills. To meet the privation and distress caused by the drought he urged a Red Cross campaign and recommended an appropriation to enable the Department of Agriculture to loan money "for the purpose of seed and feed for animals," but fought against any handouts by the Federal government to feed human beings.

In all this Hoover was desperately sincere. He saw himself as the watchdog not only of the Treasury, but of America's "rugged individualism." "This is not an issue," he said in a statement to the press, "as to whether people shall go hungry or cold in the United States. It is solely a question of the best method by which hunger and cold shall be prevented. It is a question as to whether the American people, on one hand, will maintain the spirit of charity and mutual self-help through voluntary giving and the responsibility of local government as distinguished, on the other hand, from appropriations out of the Federal Treasury for such purposes. . . . I have . . . spent much of my life in fighting hardship and starvation both abroad and in the Southern States. I do not feel that I should be charged with lack of human sympathy for those who suffer, but I recall that in all the organizations with which I have been connected over these many years, the foundation has been to summon the maximum of self-help. . . . I am willing to pledge myself that if the time should ever come that the voluntary agencies of the country, together with the local and State governments, are unable to find resources with which to prevent hunger and suffering in my country, I will ask the aid of every resource of the Federal Government because I would no more see starvation amongst our countrymen than would any Senator or Congressman. I have faith in the American people that such a day will not come."

Such were Hoover's convictions. But to hungry farmers in Arkansas the President who would lend them Federal money to feed their animals, but not to feed their children, seemed callous. Jobless men and women in hard-hit industrial towns were unimpressed by Hoover's tributes to self-reliance.

Even the prosperous conservatives failed him as wholehearted allies. Business was bad, the President seemed to be doing nothing constructive to help them, and though they did not know themselves what ought to be done or were hopelessly divided in their counsels, they craved a leader and felt they were not being given one. They groused; some of them called Hoover a spineless jellyfish. Meanwhile Charles Michelson, the Democratic party's publicity director, was laying down a diabolically well-aimed barrage of press releases and speeches for Congressional use, taking advantage of every Hoover weakness to strengthen the Democratic opposition; and the President, suffering from his inability to charm and cajole the Washington correspondents, was getting a bad press. The Congressional and State elections of November, 1930, brought Democratic victories, confronting Hoover with the prospect, ere long, of a definitely hostile Congress.

Those elections brought, incidentally, a smashing victory in New York State to Governor Franklin D. Roosevelt, who was re-elected by the unexpectedly large plurality of 725,000. The afternoon following the election, Roosevelt's State chairman, an ex-boxing commissioner named James A. Farley, produced with the aid of Roosevelt's political mentor, Louis McHenry Howe, a statement which he was afraid the Governor might not like. It said: "I do not see how Mr. Roosevelt can escape being the next presidential nominee of his party, even if no one should raise a finger to bring it about." Having issued the statement at the Hotel Biltmore in New York, Farley telephoned the Governor in Albany to confess what he had done. Roosevelt laughed and said, "Whatever you said, Jim, is all right with me." Here too, had Hoover but known it, was another portent for him. But things were bad enough even without borrowing trouble from the future. In midwinter there was an encouraging upturn in business, but as the spring of 1931 drew on, the retreat began once more. Hoover's convictions were being outrun by events.

§ 6

During all this time, many men were earnestly citing the hardships suffered in the depressions of 1857 and 1875 and 1893 as proofs that nothing ailed America but a downswing in the business cycle. The argument looked very reasonable--but these men were wrong. Something far more profound than that was taking place, and not in America alone.

The nineteenth century and the first few years of the twentieth century had witnessed a remarkable combination of changes which could not continue indefinitely. Among these were:--

1. The rapid progress of the industrial revolution--which brought with it steam power, and then gasoline and electric power and all manner of scientific and inventive miracles; brought factory production on a bigger and bigger scale; drew the population off the farms into bigger and bigger cities; transformed large numbers of people from independent economic agents into jobholders; and made them increasingly dependent upon the successful working of an increasingly complex economy.

2. A huge increase in population. According to Henry Pratt Fairchild, if the population of the world had continued to grow at the rate at which it was growing during the first decade of the present century, at the end of 10,000 years it would have reached a figure beginning with 221,848 and followed by *no less than 45 zeros.*

3. An expansion of the peoples of the Western world into vacant and less civilized parts of the earth, with the British Empire setting the pattern of imperialism, and the United States setting the pattern of domestic pioneering.

4. The opening up and using up of the natural resources of the world--coal, oil, metals, etc.--at an unprecedented rate, not indefinitely continuable.

5. A rapid improvement in communication--which in effect made the world a much smaller place, the various parts of which were far more dependent on one another than before.

6. The rapid development and refinement of capitalism on a bigger and bigger scale, as new corporate and financial devices were invented and put into practice. These new devices (such as, for example, the holding company), coupled with the devices added to mitigate the cruelties of untrammeled capitalism (such as, for example, labor unionism and labor legislation), profoundly altered the working of the national economies, making them more rigid at numerous points and less likely to behave according to the laws of laissez-faire economics.

Which of these phenomena were causes, and which were effects, of the changes in the economic world during the century which preceded 1914, is a matter of opinion. Let us not concern ourselves with which came first, the hen or the egg. The point is that an immense expansion and complication of the world economy had taken place, that it could not have continued indefinitely at such a pace, and that as it reached the point of diminishing returns, all manner of stresses developed. These stresses included both international rivalries over colonies (now that the best ones had been exploited--and were incidentally no longer paying their mother countries so well) and internal social conflicts over the division of the fruits of industry and commerce. The World War of 1914-18, brought about by the international rivalries, had left Europe weakened and embittered, with hitherto strong nations internally divided and staggering under colossal debts.

Presently there were ominous signs that the great age of inevitable expansion was over. The population increase was slowing up. The vacant places of the world were largely preempted. The natural resources were limited and could hardly be exploited much longer so quickly and cheaply. As the economic horizons narrowed, the struggle for monopoly of what was visibly profitable became more intense. Nations sought for national monopoly of world resources; corporate and financial groups sought for private monopoly of national resources and national industries. Meanwhile each national economy became more complex, less flexible, and more subject to the hazards of bankruptcy by reason of unbearable debts.

One way of expansion still remained open. Invention did not stop; the possibilities of increased comfort and security through increasingly efficient mechanical production (and through improvement in the means of communication) remained almost limitless. But the economic apparatus which was at hand, and men's mental habits and outlook, were adjusted to the age of pioneering expansion rather than to reliance on increasing efficiency alone; and what sort of economic apparatus the new age might require no one knew.

During the nineteen-twenties the United States, comparatively unhurt by the war and adept at invention and mechanization, had continued to rush ahead as if the age of pioneering expansion were not over. Still, however, it was a victim of the vices of its pioneering youth--an optimistic readiness to pile up debts and credit obligations against an expanding future, a zest for speculation in real estate and in stocks, a tendency toward financial and corporate monopoly or quasi-monopoly which tended to stiffen a none-too-flexible economy. These vices combined to undo it. As Roy Helton remarks in this connection, when one is grown up one can no longer indulge with impunity in the follies of youth. While the bellows of speculation and credit inflation blew, the fires of prosperity burned brightly; but once the bellows stopped blowing, the fires dimmed. And when they dimmed in the United States, they dimmed all the more rapidly in Europe, where since the war they had burned only feebly.

As the contraction of one national economy after another set in, men became frantic. The traditional economic laws and customs no longer seemed to work; the men of learning were as baffled as anybody else; nobody seemed to know the answer to the economic riddle. Russia offered an alternative set of laws and customs, but enthusiasm for the Marxian way as exemplified in Russia was limited. What else was there for men to fasten their hopes upon? Nobody knew, for this emergency was unprecedented. So it happened that the world entered upon a period of bewilderment, mutual suspicion, and readiness for desperate measures.

Nor was the United States, falling from such a pinnacle of apparent economic success, to escape the confusion and dismay of readjustment.

Chapter Three

DOWN, DOWN, DOWN

§ 1

June, 1931: twenty months after the Panic.

The department-store advertisements were beginning to display Eugenie hats, heralding a fashion enthusiastic but brief; Wiley Post and Harold Gatty were preparing for their flight round the world in the monoplane "Winnie Mae"; and newspaper readers were agog over the finding, on Long Beach near New York, of the dead body of a pretty girl with the singularly lyrical name of Starr Faithfull.

On the New York stage, in June, 1931, Katharine Cornell was languishing on a sofa in "The Barretts of Wimpole Street," de Lawd was walking the earth in "The Green Pastures," and the other reigning successes included "Grand Hotel" and "Once in a Lifetime." At the movie theatres one might see African lions and hear native tom-toms in "Trader Horn," or watch Edward G. Robinson in "Smart Money" or Gloria Swanson in "Indiscreet." As vacationists packed their bags for the holidays, the novel that was most likely to be taken along was Pearl S. Buck's *The Good Earth,* which led the best-seller lists. The sporting heroes of the nineteen-twenties had nearly all passed from the scenes of their triumphs: Bobby Jones had turned professional the preceding fall; Tilden had lost the tennis championship the preceding summer; Dempsey and Tunney had long since relinquished their crowns, and boxing was falling into uncertain repute; Knute Rockne, the Notre Dame football coach, had recently been killed in an airplane crash; and even Babe Ruth was no longer the undisputed Sultan of Swat: Lou Gehrig was now matching him home run for home run.

During that month of June, 1931, there was a foretaste--and a sour one--of many a financial scandal to come, when three officers of the Bank of United States were convicted by a jury in New York, after shocking disclosures of the mismanagement of the bank's funds during the speculative saturnalia of 1928 and 1929. There was the inception of a romance that was to shake an empire to its foundations: on June 10 a young American woman living in London, a Mrs. Ernest Simpson, was presented at Court and met for the first time the Prince of Wales. At Hopewell, New Jersey, the scene was being unwittingly set for the most tragic crime of the decade: Colonel Lindbergh's new house--described in newspaper captions as "A Nest for the Lone Eagle"--was under construction, the scaffolding up, the first floor partly completed.

During that month a young man from St. Louis came on to New York, with arrangements all made, as he supposed, for the transfer to him of a seat on the New York Stock Exchange. But one detail had been neglected: the Exchange was virtually a club, and a candidate for membership must have a proposer and seconder. There was some delay before the young man from St. Louis, whose name was William McC. Martin, Jr., could be proposed and seconded, for he did not know anybody on the Exchange. The gentlemen of Wall Street, having no inkling of the changes in store for them during the next few years, would have been thunderstruck if they had been told that before the decade was out, this unknown youth would be President of an Exchange operating under close governmental supervision. The President in 1931 was Richard Whitney, hero of the bankers' foray against the Panic; on April 24, 1931, Mr. Whitney had made an impressive address before the Philadelphia Chamber of Commerce on "Business Honesty." Prices on the Exchange had been going down badly and brokers were pulling long faces, but there was still a little gravy left for those who knew what the next move would be in Case Threshing or Auburn Auto.

On a Sunday morning in June, 1931, two men spent some busy hours in a small room in a very big house in Hyde Park, New

York, poring over maps of the United States and railroad timetables and lists of names. They were the Governor of New York, Franklin D. Roosevelt, who had been so impressively re-elected the preceding November, and the Chairman of his Democratic State Committee, James A. Farley. Mr. Farley had conceived the idea of attending the forthcoming Elks' Convention at Seattle, and he and Governor Roosevelt were planning how he might make the most of the expedition, covering eighteen states in nineteen days and talking with innumerable Democratic leaders, with most of whom he had already been corresponding profusely and cordially. The object of this prophetic journey, needless to say, was to sound out Democratic sentiment in the West and to suggest as disarmingly as possible that the leaders might do well to unite behind Governor Roosevelt in 1932.

And it was during that month of June, 1931, that President Hoover gave up waiting for economic conditions to improve of their own accord and began his real offensive against the Depression--began it with a statesmanlike stroke in international finance which seemed briefly to be victorious, and which failed in the end only because the processes of economic destruction were too powerful and too far developed to be overcome by any weapon in the Hoover armory. On the hot afternoon of Saturday, June 20, Hoover proposed an international moratorium in war reparations and war debts.

§ 2

For a long time past, as business slowed up in Europe, a sort of creeping paralysis had been afflicting European finance. Debts--national and private--which had once seemed bearable burdens had now become intolerably heavy; new financial credits were hardly being extended except to shore up the old ones; prices fell, anxiety spread, and the whole system slowed almost to a standstill. During the spring of 1931 the paralysis had become acute.

It is ironical, in retrospect, to note that what made it acute was an attempt on the part of Germany and Austria to combine for limited economic purposes--to achieve a customs union--and the fierce opposition of the French to any such scheme. Anything which might bring Germany and Austria together and strengthen them was anathema to the French, who little realized then the possible consequences of Central European bankruptcy.

Already the biggest bank in Austria, the Credit Anstalt, had been in a tight fix. When the altercation over the customs union still further increased the general uncertainty, the Credit Anstalt had been obliged to appeal to the none-too-solvent Austrian government for aid. Immediately panic was under way. Quickly it spread to Germany. In May and June, 1931, capital was fleeing both countries, foreign loans were being withdrawn, and a general collapse seemed imminent--a collapse which might cause the downfall of Germany's democratic government. For that cloud on the German horizon which in 1929 had seemed no bigger than a man's hand was now growing fast: Hitler's Brown Shirts were becoming more and more powerful.

On the sixth of May, 1931, when few Americans had the faintest idea of how critical the European financial situation was becoming, the American Ambassador to Germany had dined with President Hoover at the White House; and since then the President, fearing that a collapse in Europe might have grave consequences to the United States, had been turning over in his mind the idea of an international moratorium--of postponing for a year all payments on intergovernmental debts, including the reparations which Germany was then obliged to pay and the war debts owed to the United States by her former European allies. Mr. Hoover had then begun a long period of consultation--with members of his Cabinet, with Federal Reserve officials, with ambassadors, with bankers. Always a terrific worker--at his desk before eight-thirty, taking only fifteen minutes for lunch unless he had White House guests, and often burning the lights in the Lincoln study late into the night--he now concentrated all the more fiercely. Before long he had drafted tentatively a moratorium statement, laboring over it so grimly that he broke pencil point after pencil point in the writing.

Yet he had delayed issuing it. The dangers of the scheme were apparent. Congress might object, and this would be fatal. Other nations, particularly proud and jealous France, might object. The budget-balancing on which he had set his heart might be imperiled by cutting off the debt payments to America. Furthermore such a proposal, by calling attention to the international panic, might accentuate rather than ease it. Meanwhile the storm in Europe spread. Hoover's advisers were pleading with him to act, but still he would not. He waited. In mid-June he was scheduled to go on a speaking trip through the Middle West (which included the somewhat dubious pleasure of speaking at the dedication of a memorial to President Harding); he went off with the proposal yet unmade, while almost hourly the inside news was relayed to him from Washington: the European collapse was accelerating.

By the time he got back to Washington it was clear that he must act at once or it would be much too late. He began telephoning senators and representatives to get their advance approval. Congress was not sitting, and the telephone operators had to catch for him men widely dispersed all over the country, on speaking trips, on motor trips, on golf courses, on fishing trips deep in the woods; one lawmaker, hearing that the White House wanted him, called it from a Canadian drugstore; another was reached just as he was about to rise for an after-dinner speech. Hour after hour the indefatigable Hoover sat at the telephone explaining to man after man what he wanted to do--and fearing that the news would leak before he could act. At last, on that broiling Saturday, June 20, the news was already leaking and he had to give out the announcement--with France still unconsulted.

He called the newspaper men to the White House and read them a long statement which contained both his proposal for an international moratorium and the names of 21 senators and 18 representatives who had already approved it. The newspaper men grabbed their copies and rushed for the telephones.

When the news was flashed over the world a chorus of wild enthusiasm arose. The stock market in New York leaped, stock markets in Europe rallied, bankers praised Hoover, editorial writers cheered; the sedate London *Economist* came out with a panegyric entitled "The Break in the Clouds" which called the proposal "the gesture of a great man"; and millions of Americans who had felt, however vaguely, that the government ought to "do something" and who had blamed Hoover for his inactivity, joined in the applause. Little as they might know about the international financial situation (which had been getting nowhere near as much space in the press as the Starr Faithfull mystery), this was action at last and they liked it. To the worried President's surprise, he had made what seemed to be a ten-strike. It was the high moment of his Presidency.

Only the French demurred. Hoover sent his seventy-seven-year-old Secretary of the Treasury, Andrew Mellon, to reason with them, and exhausted the old man with constant consultations by transatlantic telephone. After a long delay--over two weeks--the French agreed to the plan with modifications, and the day appeared to have been saved.

§ 3

But it was not saved at all.

Presently panic in Germany became intensified; the big Danat Bank was closed. The panic spread to England. The pound sterling was now in danger. A new National Government, headed by the Laborite MacDonald but composed mostly of Tories, took office to save the pound--and presently abandoned it. When England went off the gold standard, every nation still on gold felt the shock, and most of them followed England into the new adventure of a managed currency.

In the United States this new shock of September, 1931, was sharp. The archaic American banking system, which had never been too strong even in more prosperous days, was gravely affected; all over the United States banks were collapsing--banks which had invested heavily in bonds and mortgages and now found the prices of their foreign bonds cascading, the prices of their domestic bonds sliding down in the general rush of liquidation, and their mortgages frozen solid. In the month of September, 1931, a total of 305 American banks closed; in October, a total of 522. Frightened capitalists were hoarding gold now, lest the United States too should go off the gold standard;

safe-deposit boxes were being crammed full of coins, and many a mattress was stuffed with gold certificates.

American business was weakening faster than ever. In September the United States Steel Corporation--whose President, James A. Farrell, had hitherto steadfastly refused to cut the wage-rate--announced a ten-per-cent cut; other corporations followed; during that autumn, all over the United States, men were coming home from the office or the factory to tell their wives that the next pay check would be a little smaller, and that they must think up new economies. The ranks of the unemployed received new recruits; by the end of the year their numbers were in the neighborhood of ten millions.

So far, in a few months, had the ripples of panic and renewed depression spread from Vienna.

Again Hoover acted, and again his action was financial. Something must be done to save the American banking system, and the bankers were not doing it; the spirit of the day was *sauve qui peut.* Hoover called fifteen of the overlords of the banking world to a secret evening meeting with him and his financial aides at Secretary Mellon's apartment in Washington, and proposed to them that the strong banks of the country form a credit pool to help the weak ones. When it became clear that this would not suffice--for the strong banks were taking no chances and this pool, the National Credit Corporation, lent almost no money at all--Hoover recommended the formation of a big governmental credit agency, the Reconstruction Finance Corporation, with two billion dollars to lend to banks, railroads, insurance companies.

As the winter of 1931-32 arrived and the run on the country's gold continued, and it seemed as if the United States might presently be forced off the gold standard, Hoover issued a public appeal against hoarding and then proposed an alteration in Federal Reserve requirements which--embodied in the Glass-Steagall Act--eased this situation. Again with the idea of improving credit conditions, he urged, and secured, the creation of a chain of home-loan discount banks, and the provision of additional capital for the Federal Land Banks. Steadily he fought against those measures which seemed to him iniquitous: he appeared before the American Legion and appealed to the members not to ask for the immediate cash payment of the rest of their Bonus money; he vetoed a bill for the distribution of direct Federal relief; and again and again he made clear his opposition to any proposals for inflation or for (in his own words) "squandering ourselves into prosperity."

Still the Depression deepened.

Already the pressure of events had pushed the apostle of rugged individualism much further toward state socialism than any previous president had gone in time of peace. Hoover's Reconstruction Finance Corporation had put the government deeply into business. But it was state socialism of a very limited and special sort. What was happening may perhaps be summed up in this way:--

Hoover had tried to keep hands off the economic machinery of the country, to permit a supposedly flexible system to make its own adjustments of supply and demand. At two points he had intervened, to be sure: he had tried to hold up the prices of wheat and cotton, unsuccessfully, and he had tried to hold up wage-rates, with partial and temporary success; but otherwise he had mainly stood aside to let prices and profits and wages follow their natural course. But no natural adjustment could be reached unless the burdens of debt could also be naturally reduced through bankruptcies. And in America, as in other parts of the world, the economic system had now become so complex and interdependent that the possible consequences of widespread bankruptcy--to the banks, the insurance companies, the great holding-company systems, and the multitudes of people dependent upon them--had become too appalling to contemplate. The theoretically necessary adjustment became a practically unbearable adjustment. Therefore Hoover was driven to the point of intervening to protect the debt structure--first by easing temporarily the pressure of international debts without canceling them, and second by buttressing the banks and big corporations with Federal funds.

Thus a theoretically flexible economic structure became rigid at a vital point. The debt burden remained almost undiminished. Bowing under the weight of debt--and other rigid costs--business thereupon slowed still further. As it slowed, it discharged workers or put them on reduced hours, thereby reducing purchasing power and intensifying the crisis.

It is almost useless to ask whether Hoover was right or wrong. Probably the method he was driven by circumstances to adopt would have brought recovery very slowly, if at all, unless devaluation of the currency had given a fillip to recovery--and devaluation to Hoover was unthinkable. It is also almost useless to ask whether Hoover was acting with a tory heartlessness in permitting financial executives to come to Washington for a corporate dole when men and women on the edge of starvation were denied a personal dole. What is certain is that at a time of such widespread suffering no democratic government could *seem* to be aiding the financiers and *seem* to be simultaneously disregarding the plight of its humbler citizens without losing the confidence of the public. For the days had passed when men who lost their jobs could take their working tools elsewhere and contrive an independent living, or cultivate a garden patch and thus keep body and soul together, or go West and begin again on the frontier. When they lost their jobs they were helpless. Desperately they turned for aid to the only agency responsible to them for righting the wrongs done them by a blindly operating economic society: they turned to the government. How could they endorse a government which gave them--for all they could see--not bread, but a stone?

The capitalist system had become so altered that it could not function in its accustomed ways, and the consequences of its failure to function had become too cruel to be borne by free men. Events were marching, and Herbert Hoover was to be among their victims, along with the traditional economic theories of which he was the obstinate and tragic spokesman.

§ 4

As the second year of the Depression drew to an end and the third one began, a change was taking place in the mood of the American people.

"Depression," as Peter F. Drucker has said, "shows man as a senseless cog in a senselessly whirling machine which is beyond human understanding and has ceased to serve any purpose but its own." The worse the machine behaved, the more were men and women driven to try to understand it. As one by one the supposedly fixed principles of business and economics and government went down in ruins, people who had taken these fixed principles for granted, and had shown little interest in politics except at election time, began to try to educate themselves. For not even the comparatively prosperous could any longer deny that something momentous was happening.

The circulation departments of the public libraries were reporting an increased business, not only in the anodyne of fiction, but also in books of solid fact and discussion. As a business man of "Middletown" later told the Lynds, "Big things were happening that were upsetting us, our businesses, and some of our ideas, and we wanted to try to understand them. I took a lot of books out of the library and sat up nights reading them." Ideas were in flux. There was a sharp upsurge of interest in the Russian experiment. Lecturers on Russia were in demand; Maurice Hindus's *Humanity Uprooted* and *New Russia's Primer* were thumbed and puzzled over; Ray Long, editor of Hearst's usually frivolous *Cosmopolitan* magazine, had gone to Moscow to sign up Soviet writers and gave a big dinner to a Russian novelist at the massively capitalistic Metropolitan Club in New York; gentle liberals who prided themselves on their open-mindedness were assuring one another that "after all we had something to learn from Russia," especially about "planning"; many of the more forthright liberals were tumbling head over heels into communism.

For more orthodox men and women, the consumption of Walter Lippmann's daily analysis of events--written for the New York *Herald Tribune* and syndicated all over the country--was becoming a matutinal rite as inevitable as coffee and orange juice. When the New York *World*--famous for its liberalism and the wit of its columnists-- had ceased publication in February, 1931, Lippmann, its editor, had gone over to the *Herald Tribune* and to sudden national fame. Clear, cool, and orderly in his thinking, he seemed to be able to reduce a senseless sequence of events to sense; he brought first aid to men and women groping in the dark for opinions--and also to men and women who foresaw themselves else tongue-tied and helpless when the conversation at the dinner party should turn from the great Lenz-Culbertson bridge match to the Reconstruction Finance Corporation and the gold standard.

The autumn of 1931 brought also an outburst of laughter. When old certainties topple, when old prophets are discredited, one can at least enjoy their downfall. By this time people had reached the point of laughing at *Oh, Yeah,* a small book in which were collected the glib prophecies made by bankers and statesmen at the onset of the Depression; of relishing the gossipy irreverence of *Washington Merry-Go-Round,* which deflated the reputations of the dignified statesmen of Washington; of getting belly-laughs from a new magazine, *Ballyhoo,* whose circulation rocketed to more than a million as it ridiculed everything in business and politics, even the sacred cow of advertising; and of applauding wildly the new musical comedy, "Of Thee I Sing," which made a farce of the political scene, represented a vice-president of the United States, Alexander Throttlebottom, as getting lost in a sight-seeing party in the White House, represented a presidential candidate as campaigning with Love as his platform, and garbled the favorite business slogan of 1930 into a slogan for newly-weds: "Posterity is just around the corner."

As Gilbert Seldes has noted, when Rudy Vallee, at the opening of George White's "Scandals" on September 13, 1931, sang softly

"Life is just a bowl of cherries.
Don't make it serious.
Life's too mysterious. . . ."

he summed up both the disillusionment and bewilderment of Depression, and the desire to take them, if possible, lightly.

49

§ 5

Statistics are bloodless things.

To say that during the year 1932, the cruelest year of the Depression, the average number of unemployed people in the country was 12 $^1/_2$ million by the estimates of the National Industrial Conference Board, a little over 13 million by the estimates of the American Federation of Labor, and by other estimates (differently arrived at, and defining unemployment in various ways) anywhere from 8 $^1/_2$ to 17 million--to say this is to give no living impression of the jobless men going from office to office or from factory gate to factory gate; of the disheartening inevitability of the phrase, "We'll let you know if anything shows up"; of men thumbing the want ads in cold tenements, spending fruitless hours, day after day and week after week, in the sidewalk crowds before the employment offices; using up the money in the savings bank, borrowing on their life insurance, selling whatever possessions could be sold, borrowing from relatives less and less able to lend, tasting the bitterness of inadequacy, and at last swallowing their pride and going to apply for relief--if there was any to be got. (Relief money was scarce, for charitable organizations were hard beset and cities and towns had either used up their available funds or were on the point of doing so.)

A few statistical facts and estimates are necessary, however, to an understanding of the scope and impact of the Depression. For example:--

Although the amount of money paid out in interest during the year 1932 was only 3.5 per cent less than in 1929, according to the computations of Dr. Simon Kuznets for the National Bureau of Economic Research, on the other hand the amount of money paid out in salaries had dropped 40 per cent, dividends had dropped 56.6 per cent, and wages had dropped 60 per cent. (Thus had the debt structure remained comparatively rigid while other elements in the economy were subjected to fierce deflation.)

Do not imagine, however, that the continuation of interest payments and the partial continuation of dividend payments meant that business as a whole was making money. Business as a whole lost between five and six billion dollars in 1932. (The government figure for all the corporations in the country--451,800 of them--was a net deficit of $5,640,000,000.) To be sure, most of the larger and better-managed companies did much better than that. E. D. Kennedy's figures for the 960 concerns whose earnings were tabulated by Standard Statistics-- mostly big ones whose stock was active on the Stock Exchange--show that these 960 leaders had a collective profit of over a third of a billion. Yet one must add that "better managed" is here used in a special sense. Not only had labor-saving devices and speed-ups increased the output per man-hour in manufacturing industries by an estimated 18 per cent since 1929, but employees had been laid off in quantity. Every time one of the giants of industry, to keep its financial head above water, threw off a new group of workers, many little corporations roundabout sank further into the red.

While existing businesses shrank, new ones were not being undertaken. The total of domestic corporate issues--issues of securities floated to provide capital for American corporations--had dropped in 1932 to just about *one twenty-fourth* of the 1929 figure.

But these cold statistics give us little sense of the human reali- ties of the economic paralysis of 1932. Let us try another approach.

Walking through an American city, you might find few signs of the Depression visible--or at least conspicuous--to the casual eye. You might notice that a great many shops were untenanted, with dusty plate-glass windows and signs indicating that they were ready to lease; that few factory chimneys were smoking; that the streets were not so crowded with trucks as in earlier years, that there was no uproar of riveters to assail the ear, that beggars and panhandlers were on the si- dewalks in unprecedented numbers (in the Park Avenue district of New York a man might be asked for money four or five times in a ten- block walk). Traveling by railroad, you might notice that the trains were shorter, the Pullman cars fewer--and that fewer freight trains were on the line. Traveling overnight, you might find only two or three other passengers in your sleeping car. (By contrast, there were more filling stations by the motor highways than ever before, and of all the retail businesses in "Middletown" only the filling stations showed no large drop in business during the black years; for although few new automobiles were being bought, those which would still stand up were being used more than ever--to the dismay of the railroads.)

Otherwise things might seem to you to be going on much as usual. The major phenomena of the Depression were mostly negative and did not assail the eye.

But if you knew where to look, some of them would begin to appear. First, the breadlines in the poorer districts. Second, those bleak settlements ironically known as "Hoovervilles" in the outskirts of the cities and on vacant lots--groups of makeshift shacks constructed out of packing boxes, scrap iron, anything that could be picked up free in a diligent combing of the city dumps: shacks in which men and some-times whole families of evicted people were sleeping on automobile seats carried from auto-graveyards, warming themselves before fires of rubbish in grease drums. Third, the homeless people sleeping in doorways or on park benches, and going the rounds of the restaurants for leftover half-eaten biscuits, piecrusts, anything to keep the fires of life burning. Fourth, the vastly increased number of thumbers on the highways, and particularly of freight-car transients on the railroads: a huge army of drifters ever on the move, searching half-aimlessly for a place where there might be a job. According to Jonathan Norton Leo-nard, the Missouri Pacific Railroad in 1929 had "taken official cognizance" of 13,745 migrants; by 1931 the figure had already jumped to 186,028. It was estimated that by the beginning of 1933, the country over, there were a million of these transients on the move. Forty-five thousand had passed through El Paso in the space of six months; 1,500 were passing through Kansas City every day. Among them were large numbers of young boys, and girls disguised as boys. According to the Children's Bureau, there were 200,000 children thus drifting about the United States. So huge was the number of freight-car hoppers in the Southwest that in a number of places the railroad police simply had to give up trying to remove them from the trains: there were far too many of them.

Among the comparatively well-to-do people of the country (those, let us say, whose pre-Depression incomes had been over $5,000 a year) the great majority were living on a reduced scale, for salary cuts had been extensive, especially since 1931, and dividends were dwindling. These people were discharging servants, or cutting servants' wages to a minimum, or in some cases "letting" a servant stay on without other compensation than board and lodging. In many pretty houses, wives who had never before--in the revealing current phrase--"done their own work" were cooking and scrubbing. Husbands were wearing the old suit longer, resigning from the golf club, deciding, perhaps, that this year the family couldn't afford to go to the beach for the summer, paying seventy-five cents for lunch instead of a dollar at the restaurant or thirty-five instead of fifty at the lunch counter. When those who had flown high with the stock market in 1929 looked at the stock-market page of the newspapers nowadays their only consoling thought (if they still had any stock left) was that a judicious sale or two would result in such a capital loss that they need pay no income tax at all this year.

Alongside these men and women of the well-to-do classes whose fortunes had been merely reduced by the Depression were others whose fortunes had been shattered. The crowd of men waiting for the 8:14 train at the prosperous suburb included many who had lost their jobs, and were going to town as usual not merely to look stubbornly and almost hopelessly for other work but also to keep up a bold front of activity. (In this latter effort they usually succeeded: one would never have guessed, seeing them chatting with their friends as train-time approached, how close to desperation some of them had come.) There were architects and engineers bound for offices to which no clients had come in weeks. There were doctors who thought themselves lucky when a patient paid a bill. Mrs. Jones, who went daily to her stenographic job, was now the economic mainstay of her family, for Mr. Jones was jobless and was doing the cooking and looking after the children (with singular distaste and inefficiency). Next door to the Joneses lived Mrs. Smith, the widow of a successful lawyer: she had always had a comfortable income, she prided herself on her "nice things," she was pathetically unfitted to earn a dollar even if jobs were to be had; her capital had been invested in South American bonds and United Founders stock and other similarly misnamed "securities," and now she was completely dependent upon hand-outs from her relatives, and didn't even have carfare in her imported pocketbook.

The Browns had retreated to their "farmhouse" in the country and were trying to raise crops on its stony acres; they talked warmly about primal simplicities but couldn't help longing sometimes for elec-

53

tric light and running hot water, and couldn't cope with the potato bugs. (Large numbers of city dwellers thus moved to the country, but not enough of them engaged in real farming to do more than partially check the long-term movement from the farms of America to the cities and towns.) It was being whispered about the community that the Robinson family, though they lived in a $40,000 house and had always spent money freely, were in desperate straights: Mr. Robinson had lost his job, the house could not be sold, they had realized on every asset at their command, and now they were actually going hungry--though their house still looked like the abode of affluence.

Further down in the economic scale, particularly in those industrial communities in which the factories were running at twenty per cent of capacity or had closed down altogether, conditions were infinitely worse. Frederick E. Croxton's figures, taken in Buffalo, show what was happening in such communities: out of 14,909 persons of both sexes willing and able to work, his house-to-house canvassers found in November, 1932, that 46.3 per cent were fully employed, 22.5 per cent were working part time, and as many as 31.2 per cent were unable to find jobs. In every American city, quantities of families were being evicted from their inadequate apartments; moving in with other families till ten or twelve people would be sharing three or four rooms; or shivering through the winter in heatless houses because they could afford no coal, eating meat once a week or not at all. If employers sometimes found that former employees who had been discharged did not seem eager for re-employment ("They won't take a job if you offer them one!"), often the reason was panic: a dreadful fear of inadequacy which was one of the Depression's commonest psychopathological results. A woman clerk, offered piecework after being jobless for a year, confessed that she almost had not dared to come to the office, she had been in such terror lest she wouldn't know where to hang her coat, wouldn't know how to find the washroom, wouldn't understand the boss's directions for her job.

For perhaps the worst thing about this Depression was its inexorable continuance year after year. Men who have been sturdy and self-respecting workers can take unemployment without flinching for a few weeks, a few months, even if they have to see their families suffer; but it is different after a year . . . two years . . . three years. . . . Among the miserable creatures curled up on park benches or standing in

54

dreary lines before the soup kitchens in 1932 were men who had been jobless since the end of 1929.

At the very bottom of the economic scale the conditions may perhaps best be suggested by two brief quotations. The first, from Jonathan Norton Leonard's *Three Years Down,* describes the plight of Pennsylvania miners who had been put out of company villages after a blind and hopeless strike in 1931: "Reporters from the more liberal metropolitan papers found thousands of them huddled on the mountainsides, crowded three or four families together in one-room shacks, living on dandelions and wild weed-roots. Half of them were sick, but no local doctor would care for the evicted strikers. All of them were hungry and many were dying of those providential diseases which enable welfare authorities to claim that no one has starved." The other quotation is from Louise V. Armstrong's *We Too Are the People,* and the scene is Chicago in the late spring of 1932:--

"One vivid, gruesome moment of those dark days we shall never forget. We saw a crowd of some fifty men fighting over a barrel of garbage which had been set outside the back door of a restaurant. American citizens fighting for scraps of food like animals!"

Human behavior under unaccustomed conditions is always various. One thinks of the corporation executive to whom was delegated the job of discharging several hundred men: he insisted on seeing every one of them personally and taking an interest in each man's predicament, and at the end of a few months his hair had turned prematurely gray. . . . The Junior League girl who reported with pride a Depression economy: she had cut a piece out of an old fur coat in the attic and bound it to serve as a bathmat. . . . The banker who had been plunged deeply into debt by the collapse of his bank: he got a $30,000 job with another bank, lived on $3,000 a year, and honorably paid $27,000 a year to his creditors. . . . The wealthy family who lost most of their money but announced bravely that they had "solved their Depression problem" by discharging fifteen of their twenty servants, and showed no signs of curiosity as to what would happen to these fifteen. . . . The little knot of corporation officials in a magnificent skyscraper office doctoring the books of the company to dodge bankruptcy. . . . The crowd of Chicago Negroes standing tight-packed before a tenement-house door to prevent the landlord's agents from evicting a neighbor family: as they stood there, hour by hour, they sang hymns. . . . The onetime clerk carefully cutting out pieces of cardboard to put inside his shoes before setting out on his endless job-hunting round, and telling his wife the shoes were now better than ever. . . . The man in the little apartment next door who had given up hunting for jobs, given up all interest, all activity, and sat hour by hour in staring apathy. . . .

It was a strange time in which to graduate from school or college. High schools had a larger attendance than ever before, especially in the upper grades, because there were few jobs to tempt any one away. Likewise college graduates who could afford to go on to graduate school were continuing their studies--after a hopeless hunt for jobs--rather than be idle. Look, for example, at a sample page of the first report of the Harvard College Class of 1932, made up in the spring of 1933. At first glance it would seem to testify to a remarkable thirst for further knowledge (I quote it verbatim, omitting only the names):

--does not give his occupation

--is studying abroad

--is a student at the Harvard Law School, 1st year

--is at the University of North Carolina, Chapel Hill, N. C.

--is a student in the Harvard Medical School, 1st year

--has not been heard from

--is a student in the Harvard Engineering School, 4th year

--is interested in the Communist movement

--is a student in the Harvard Law School, 1st year

--is a student in Harvard College

--is a student in the Harvard School of Architecture, 1st year

--is with the Cleveland Twist Drill Co.

--is a student in the Harvard School of Business Administration, 1st year

--is manufacturing neckwear

--is a student in the Harvard Graduate School of Arts and Sciences, 1st year

--is a student in the Harvard Law School, 1st year

--is a student in the Harvard Graduate School of Business Administration, 1st year

--is a student in Manhattan College

The effects of the economic dislocation were ubiquitous. Not business alone was disturbed, but churches, museums, theatres, schools, colleges, charitable organizations, clubs, lodges, sports organizations, and so on clear through the list of human enterprises; one and all they felt the effects of dwindling gifts, declining memberships, decreasing box-office returns, uncollectible bills, revenue insufficient to pay the interest on the mortgage.

Furthermore, as the tide of business receded, it laid bare the evidence of many an unsavory incident of the past. The political scandals which were being investigated in New York City by Samuel Seabury, for instance, came to light only partly as a result of a new crusading spirit among the citizenry, a wave of disgust for machine graft; it was the Depression, bringing failures and defaults and then the examination of corporate records, which had begun the revelations. The same sort of thing was happening in almost every city and town. As banks went under, as corporations got into difficulties, the accountants learned what otherwise might never have been discovered: that the respected family in the big house on the hill had been hand-in-hand with gangsters; that the benevolent company president had been living in such style only because he placed company orders at fat prices with an associated company which he personally controlled; that the corporation lawyer who passed the plate at the Presbyterian church had been falsifying his income-tax returns. And with every such disclosure came a new disillusionment.

§ 6

On the evening of the first of March, 1932, an event took place which instantly thrust everything else, even the grim processes of Depression, into the background of American thought--and which seemed to many observers to epitomize cruelly the demoralization into which the country had fallen. The baby son of Colonel and Mrs. Charles A. Lindbergh was kidnapped--taken out of his bed in a second-story room of the new house at Hopewell, New Jersey, never to be seen again alive.

Since Lindbergh's flight to Paris nearly five years before, he had occupied a unique and unprecedented position in American life. Admired almost to the point of worship by millions of people, he was like a sort of uncrowned prince; and although he fiercely shunned publicity, everything he did was so inevitably news that the harder he tried to dodge the limelight, the more surely it pursued him. Word that he had been seen anywhere was enough to bring a crowd running; he was said to have been driven at times to disguise himself in order to be free of mobbing admirers. He now occupied himself as a consultant in aviation; late the preceding summer he and his wife, the former Anne Morrow, had made a "flight to the Orient" which Mrs. Lindbergh later described in lovely prose; and since his meeting with Dr. Alexis Carrel late in 1930 he had begun experiments in the construction of perfusion pumps which were to bring him a high reputation as a biological technician. His new house at Hopewell, remote and surrounded by woods, had been built largely as a retreat in which the Lindberghs could be at peace from an intrusive world.

LINDBERGH KIDNAPPING POSTER
Sent to police chiefs in 1400 American communities in March, 1932

And now, suddenly, this peace was shattered. Within a few hours of the discovery that the Lindbergh baby's bed was empty--the blankets still held in place by their safety pins--a swarm of police and newspaper men had reached the house and were trampling about the muddy grounds, obliterating clues. And when the news broke in the next morning's newspapers, the American people went into a long paroxysm of excitement.

More police and reporters arrived; the nearest railroad station was transformed into a newspaper headquarters; news from Hopewell crowded everything else to the back pages of the papers; President Hoover issued a statement, the Governor of New Jersey held police conferences, anti-kidnapping bills were prepared by legislators in several states, the *New York Times* reported the receipt on a single day of 3,331 telephone calls asking for the latest news. Bishop Manning of New York sent his clergy a special prayer for immediate use, declaring, "In a case like this we cannot wait till Sunday." William Green asked members of the American Federation of Labor to aid in the hunt for the criminal. Commander Evangeline Booth urged all commanding officers of the Salvation Army to help, and referred to "the miraculous accomplishments with which God has honored our movement along these very lines through our lost and found bureau." Clergymen of three denominations prayed over the radio for the baby's deliverance. Wild rumors went about. Babies resembling the Lindbergh child were reported seen in automobiles all over the country. The proprietor of a cigar store in Jersey City brought the police on the run by reporting that he had heard a man in a telephone booth say something that sounded like a kidnapper's message. And the Lindberghs received endless letters of advice and suggestion--the total running, in a few weeks, to one hundred thousand.

From day to day the drama of the search went on--the Lindberghs offering immunity to the kidnapper in a signed statement, giving out the pathetic details of the baby's accustomed diet, asking two racketeering bootleggers named Spitale and Bitz to serve as intermediaries with the underworld; and soon the chief actors in the Hopewell drama became as familiar to the American newspaper-reading public as if the whole country had been engaged in reading the same detective story. Mr. and Mrs. Oliver Whateley, the butler and his wife; Betty Gow, the nurse; Arthur Johnson, her sailor friend; Colonel

Schwarzkopf of the New Jersey State Police; Violet Sharpe, the maid at the Morrows' house, who committed suicide; and Dr. John F. Condon ("Jafsie"), the old gentleman in the Bronx who made the first personal contact with the kidnapper--these men and women became the subjects of endless conjectures and theorizings. When a stranger asked one, "Have they found the baby?" there was never an instant's doubt as to what baby was meant, whether the question was asked in New Jersey or in Oregon. One would hear a hotel elevator man saying out of the blue, to an ascending guest, "Well, I believe it was an inside job"--to which the guest would reply heatedly, "Nonsense, it was that gang in Detroit." If the American people had needed to have their minds taken off the Depression, the kidnapping had briefly done it.

On March 8, a week after the crime, old Dr. Condon--college lecturer and welfare worker in "the most beautiful borough in the world," as he called the Bronx--conceived the odd idea of putting an advertisement in the Bronx *Home News,* to the effect that he would be glad to serve as an intermediary for the return of the Lindbergh child. The next day he received a letter, misspelled in an odd Germanic way, containing an enclosure addressed to Colonel Lindbergh. He called up the house at Hopewell, was asked to open the enclosure, described some curious markings on it, and at once was asked to come and see Colonel Lindbergh--for those markings were identical with the code symbols on a ransom note which had been left on the window sill of the baby's room! On March 12, Dr. Condon received a note which told him to go to a hot-dog stand at the end of the Jerome Avenue elevated railroad. He found there a note directing him to the entrance of Wood-lawn Cemetery. He presently saw a man in the shrubbery of the cemetery, and he went with this man to a bench near by, where they sat and talked. The kidnapper had a German or Scandinavian accent, called himself "John," and said he was only one of a gang.

Further negotiations--which left no doubt that "John" was indeed the kidnapper, or one of the kidnappers--led to the payment of $50,000 in bills to "John" by Dr. Condon (accompanied by Colonel Lindbergh) in St. Raymond's Cemetery in the Bronx on April 2--whereupon "John" handed Dr. Condon a note which said that the baby would be found safe on a "boad" (meaning *boat)* near Gay Head on Martha's Vineyard. The Colonel made two flights there by plane and found no "boad"; clearly the information given was false.

Then on the evening of May 12, 1932, about six weeks after the kidnapping, the newsboys chanted extras in the streets once more: the child's body had been found by chance in a thicket near a road five and a half miles from the Lindbergh place. Whether he had been killed deliberately or accidentally would never be known; in any event, the kidnapper had chosen that spot to half-bury the little body.

"BABY DEAD" announced the tabloid headlines: those two words sufficed.

A great many Americans whose memories of other events of the decade are vague can recall just where and under what circumstances they first heard that piece of news.

The story seemed to have reached its end, but still the reverberations of horror continued. Soon it was clear, not only that the kidnapper had added the cruelty of Lindbergh's hopeless search by plane to the barbarity of the original crime; not only that Gaston B. Means had wangled $100,000 out of Mrs. McLean of Washington on the criminally false pretense that he could get the child back; but also that John Hughes Curtis of Norfolk, Virginia, who had induced Colonel Lindbergh to go out on a boat in Chesapeake Bay to make contact with the kidnappers, had concocted--for whatever reason--one of the most contemptible hoaxes ever conceived. These revelations, coming on top of the shock of seeing the Lindberghs forced to deal with representatives of the underworld (as if the underworld were quite beyond the law), brought thunders of dismay from preachers, orators, editorial-writers, columnists: there was something very rotten indeed in the State of Denmark. And the tragic sense that things were awry was deepened.

There the Lindbergh case rested in 1932. But we must go ahead of our history to recount the sequel. It came over twenty-eight months later, on September 19, 1934, when the kidnapper was arrested. Ironically, one of the things which facilitated his capture was that in the meantime the New Deal had come in, the United States had gone off the gold standard, and the gold certificates which had been handed over to the kidnapper had become noticeable rarities.

The kidnapper proved to be not a member of the organized underworld but a lone criminal--a fugitive felon from Germany, illegally in the United States--one Bruno Richard Hauptmann. He was arrested in the Bronx, was tried at the beginning of 1935 at the Hunterdon County Court House at Flemington, New Jersey, was convicted, and--after an unsuccessful appeal and a delay brought about by the inexplicable unwillingness of Governor Harold Hoffman of New Jersey to believe in his guilt--was electrocuted on April 3, 1936.

The evidence against Hauptmann was overwhelming. Leaving aside the possibly debatable identifications of him and other dubious bits of evidence, consider these items alone: 1. Hauptmann lived in the Bronx, where Dr. Condon's advertisement had appeared, where Dr. Condon had met "John" and where "John" had received the ransom money. 2. The numbers of the ransom bills had been recorded: many of these bills had been passed in parts of New York City accessible to a resident of the Bronx; it was the passing of one by Hauptmann in a Bronx garage which led to his arrest. 3. When arrested, Hauptmann had a $20 ransom bill on his person. 4. No less than $14,600 in ransom bills was found secreted in his garage. 5. He was a German, his tricks of speech corresponded roughly to those in the ransom letters, he had once used in an account book the spelling "boad," and he used other misspellings and foreign locutions like those in the ransom notes. 6. His handwriting was similar to those in the notes. 7. He had had no regular means of support after March 1, 1932, but had nevertheless spent money freely and had had a brokerage account of some dimensions (with which he was quite unsuccessful). 8. His story of how he got his money, through an alleged partnership in a fur business with one Frisch, and how he kept it in a shoe box on a shelf, was vague and unconvincing. 9. Furthermore, the kidnapper had left behind, at Hopewell, a ladder of odd construction. An expert from the Department of Agriculture, Arthur Koehler, not only found, from the sort of wood used in the making of this ladder and from peculiarities in its cutting, that it had been a part of a shipment to a Bronx firm, but also that irregularities in the planing of it corresponded to irregularities in a plane in Hauptmann's possession. 10. Finally, one piece of the wood used in the ladder fitted precisely a piece missing from a floor board in Hauptmann's attic, even the old nail holes in it matching to a fraction of an inch!

§ 7

Down, down, down went business.

Calvin Coolidge, who had been the chief patron saint of the prosperity of the nineteen-twenties, paced in unhappy bewilderment about the lawn at "The Beeches," his Northampton estate. One day he dropped in at his barber's for his monthly haircut. "Mr. Coolidge," said the barber deferentially, "how about this depression? When is it going to end?" "Well, George," said the ex-President, "the big men of the country have got to get together and do something about it. It isn't going to end itself. We all hope it will end, but we don't see it yet."

Andrew Mellon, who had been shunted into the Ambassadorship to the Court of St. James's to give Ogden Mills, a younger and livelier man, a chance to run the Treasury, no longer wore the halo in Wall Street which had once been his; when he left the Treasury the stock market--which in other years would have expressed itself sharply--never wavered; yet Mellon had been one of those "big men" of the country to whom Coolidge presumably referred, a man of vast wealth, financial acumen, financial prestige. What did he have to say? In the spring of 1932 he spoke in London. "None of us has any means of knowing," said he, "when and how we shall emerge from the valley of depression in which the world is traveling. But I do know that, as in the past, the day will come when we shall find ourselves on a more solid economic foundation and the onward march of progress will be resumed." And again, before the International Chamber of Commerce: "I do not believe in any quick or spectacular remedies for the ills from which the world is suffering, nor do I share the belief that there is anything fundamentally wrong with the social system under which we have achieved, in this and other industrialized countries, a degree of economic well-being unprecedented in the history of the world. . . ."

Not much satisfaction there for men and women in trouble!

A few months later another great man of finance spoke in London--Montagu Norman, governor of the Bank of England. Even making allowance for the hopeful passages in his address, and for British self-deprecation, those who read his cabled remarks got a shock from them. Speaking of the world-wide economic crisis, he said: "The difficulties are so vast, the forces so unlimited, so novel, and precedents are so lacking, that I approach this whole subject not only in ignorance but in humility. It is too great for me."

Didn't *he* know either?

Nor did Wall Street seem to have any answer. The men of Wall Street were complaining that the trouble lay in a "lack of confidence" (how often had we all heard, how often were we all to hear those hoary words parroted!); and that this lack of confidence arose from fear of inflation and from the unpredictable and dangerous behavior of Congress, which was all-too-lukewarm about balancing the Federal budget and was full of unsound notions. The defenders of the old order seemed as bewildered as any one else; they didn't know what had hit them. Said a banker noted for his astuteness, in a newsreel talk, "As for the cause of the Depression, or the way out, you know as much as I do." And Charles M. Schwab of Bethlehem Steel, who had once been unfailingly optimistic, was quoted as saying at a luncheon in New York, ". . . . I'm afraid, every man is afraid. I don't know, we don't know, whether the values we have are going to be real next month or not."

The astrologers and fortunetellers were in clover; Evangeline Adams and Dolores were getting letters by the basketful--and from financiers as well as from those of humbler station. When all other prophets failed, why not try the stars?

The spring of 1932 was a bad season for financial reputations. On that very March 12 when "Jafsie" met Hauptmann and talked with him beside Woodlawn Cemetery, a strange thing happened in Paris: one of the supposed miracle workers of international industry and finance, the Swedish match king, Ivar Kreuger, carefully drew the blinds of the bedroom in his apartment in the Avenue Victor Emmanuel III, smoothed the covers of the unmade bed, lay down, and shot himself an inch below the heart. During the following weeks, out trickled the story behind the suicide: that Kreuger's operations had been fraudulent, and that he had readily deceived with false figures and airy lies the honorable members of one of the most esteemed

American financial houses. On April 8 Samuel Insull, builder of a lofty pyramid of public-utility holding companies--that same Insull of whom it had been said, only a few years before, that it was worth a million dollars to anybody to be seen talking with him in front of the Continental Bank--went to Owen D. Young's office in New York, confronted there Mr. Young and a group of New York bankers, was told that the jig was up for him, and said sadly, "I wish my time on earth had already come"; Insull's house of cards, too, had gone down. A Senate investigation was beginning to show up the cold-blooded manipulations by which stocks had been pushed up and down in the stock market by corporate insiders of wealth and prominence and supposed responsibility. The president of Hoover's Reconstruction Finance Corporation, Charles G. Dawes, had to resign and hurry to Chicago in order that the Corporation might authorize the lending of ninety million dollars to save his bank, caught in a Chicago banking panic. Rumors of all sorts of imminent collapses were going about. Of whom and of what could one be sure?

By the middle of 1932 industry was operating at less than half its maximum 1929 volume, according to the Federal Reserve Board's Adjusted Index of Industrial Production: the figure had fallen all the way from 125 to 58. Cotton was selling below 5 cents, wheat below 50 cents, corn at 31 cents; bond prices had taken a headlong tumble; and as for the stock market, once the harbinger of so many economic blessings, it had plumbed such depths as to make the prices reached at the end of the Panic of 1929 look lofty by comparison. Here are a few comparisons in tabular form:--

	High Price on Sept. 3, 1929	Low Price on Nov. 13, 1929 after the Panic	Low Price for 1932
American Telephone	304	197 $^1/_4$	70 $^1/_4$
General Electric	396 $^1/_4$	168 $^1/_2$	34*
General Motors	72 $^3/_4$	36	7 $^5/_8$
New York Central	256 $^3/_8$	160	8 $^3/_4$
Radio	101	26	2 $^1/_2$
U. S. Steel	261 $^3/_4$	150	21 $^1/_4$

*Adjusted to take account of a split-up in the meantime. The actual price was 8 $^1/_2$.

Thus spoke the stock market, that "sensitive barometer" of the country's economic prospects. Thus had departed the hopes of yesteryear. Was there no savior anywhere in sight?

Chapter Four

A CHANGE OF GOVERNMENT

§ 1

It began to look as if the job of saving the United States would fall into the willing hands of Franklin D. Roosevelt.

Early in June, 1932, the Republicans held a dull convention with their Old Guard in full control, wrote a dull and verbose platform, and nominated Herbert Hoover for re-election because they had to. Considering what was going on in the world, the general aspect of the Republican deliberations was ichthyosaurian.

When the Democrats went to Chicago for their convention--to a Chicago still reeling from a local panic in which nearly forty banks had gone under and the Dawes bank had been hard hit--Roosevelt had a long lead for the Democratic nomination. For his aides had been doing hard and effective work. Jim Farley--large, amiable, energetic, shrewd in the politics of friendships and favors--had been rushing about the country with glad hand outstretched and had been using to the utmost his incredible capacity for mass production of personal correspondence. He sometimes called in six stenographers at a time, spent eight consecutive hours signing letters in green ink; at night, when safe from interruption, he could sign at the rate of nearly two thousand letters an hour. While Farley commanded the Roosevelt forces in the field, the Roosevelt chief-of-staff was Louis McHenry Howe, a little wizened invalid with protruding eyes and unkempt clothes who worshipped Roosevelt and lived to further his career. Remaining in a shabby office in Madison Avenue, New York, sitting at a desk littered with newspapers and pamphlets, or lying on an old day bed when his chronic asthma exhausted him, Howe studied the political map and gave Farley sage advice. "Louis would sit in front of me in his favorite pose," writes Farley, "his elbows resting on his knees, and his face cupped in his hands so that practically nothing was visible of his features except his eyes." A masterly strategist of politics, Howe thought out the plan of campaign.

While these men gathered delegates for Roosevelt, others gathered ideas for him. In March, 1932--the month of the Lindbergh kidnapping and the Kreuger suicide--Roosevelt's friend and adviser Samuel I. Rosenman had suggested to him that it might be a good idea to get a group of university professors to help him formulate his program; and, when Roosevelt smilingly agreed that it might, Rosenman had invited Professor Raymond Moley of Columbia to dinner and had thrashed the matter out with him over coffee and cigars. Moley had been working with Roosevelt for months on various New York problems and thus naturally became the recruiting officer and unofficial chairman of a group of advisers which included (in addition to Moley and Rosenman) Rexford Guy Tugwell and Adolph A. Berle, Jr., both of Columbia, and Basil O'Connor, Roosevelt's law partner. Roosevelt at first dubbed the group his "privy council"; in July, James Kieran of the *New York Times* christened it the "brains trust"; the general public took over this name but inevitably changed the awkward plural into a singular and spoke of the "brain trust." Members of the group would go to Albany, dine with Governor Roosevelt, talk with vast excitement for hours, and return to New York to study and report on national problems for the candidate and to draft memoranda and rough out speeches for him.

But at first Roosevelt was very cautious in his use of such material or in taking a definite position upon anything. He was handsome, friendly, attractive; he had the smiling magnetism, the agreeable voice which Hoover so dismally lacked; he had not only had political and administrative experience as Governor of New York, but knew Washington as a former Assistant Secretary of the Navy. With Farley and Howe to help him, and with delegates flocking to him because of his political "availability," all he apparently needed in order to win the nomination--and the election, for that matter--was to exercise his charm, look just conservative enough to fall heir to the votes of Republicans who were sick of Hoover, look just radical enough to keep the rebellious from turning socialist or communist, and not make enemies. So he spoke kindly of "the forgotten man at the bottom of the economic pyramid" but failed to specify exactly how this man should be remembered; he said that "the country demands bold, persistent experimentation" but engaged, in his speeches, chiefly in the sort of experimentation practiced by the chameleon. So gentle was he with the Tammany graft being disclosed by Samuel Seabury, and so tentative was he in expressing economic ideas, that Walter Lippmann warned those Western Democrats who regarded Roosevelt as a courageous progressive and an "enemy of evil influences" that they did not know their man.

"Franklin D. Roosevelt," wrote Lippmann, "is an amiable man with many philanthropic impulses, but he is not the dangerous enemy of anything. He is too eager to please. . . . Franklin D. Roosevelt is no crusader. He is no tribune of the people. He is no enemy of entrenched privilege. He is a pleasant man who, without any important qualifications for the office, would very much like to be President."

On the first ballot for the nomination, taken in the Chicago Stadium in a sweltering all-night session after interminable nominating speeches, Roosevelt already had a majority of the delegates. The only obstacles now remaining were the ancient rule which required a two-thirds vote for the nomination, and the possibility that the opposition forces of John Nance Garner of Texas or of Roosevelt's former friend and mentor, Al Smith, might be unbreakable. Two more ballots followed without important change as night gave way to day, and at 9:15 on the morning of July 1st the delegates--"stupefied by oratory, brass bands, bad air, perspiration, sleeplessness, and soft drinks," as Walter Lippmann said--stumbled out of the Stadium into the sunshine with no decision taken.

Only Huey Long, the Louisiana Kingfish, had seemed unwilted during that exhausting night: Heywood Broun saw him dash down to the aisles to soothe a swaying delegation, pause to greet a blonde stenographer with "How are you, baby?" and continue energetically on his political errand. When Farley got back to Louis Howe's room to report, he found Howe lying on the floor in his shirt sleeves, his head on a pillow, two electric fans blowing on him; Farley sprawled on the carpet beside him to confer on the strategy of the hour. The two men decided that Farley should look for Sam Rayburn of Texas and see if the Texas delegation could be persuaded to forsake Garner for Roosevelt, in return for aid in getting Garner the vice-presidential nomination. Farley then dragged himself to Pat Harrison's rooms in search of Rayburn; and when he found that Rayburn had not yet arrived, Farley sat down to wait and presently was snoring in his chair. Under such conditions do our statesmen make their vital choices.

But soon it was all over. Rayburn arrived at the Harrison suite. He did not commit himself definitely but said, "We'll see what can be done"; and Farley felt that victory was on the way. That afternoon Garner telephoned from Washington to recommend that his leaders should release their delegations. (What part Hearst, who had been backing Garner, had in this surrender is uncertain.) When that night, the delegates assembled once more, the opposition lines had broken. On the first ballot that night--the fourth for the nomination--Roosevelt was chosen. Garner thereupon got the vice-presidential nomination.

Dramatically, Roosevelt refused to wait weeks for a notification ceremony. Throwing aside tradition, he chartered a plane, flew to Chicago, and made an immediate speech of acceptance promising a "new deal." (This was the first public appearance of the phrase. Moley, perhaps thinking of Stuart Chase's book, *A New Deal,* had used it in a memorandum to Roosevelt six weeks before, and Roosevelt had seized upon it.)

The origin of this acceptance speech was a little drama in itself. For weeks Roosevelt and the Brain Trust had been working on a draft of the address. During the plane trip Roosevelt had made a few last-minute revisions. But at the airport at Chicago he was met by Louis Howe, who thrust another manuscript into his hand. Howe, in Chicago, had been shown a copy of the Brain Trust draft by Moley, had disliked it, and had written a revised version: it was this new version which he was now handing to the nominee. As Roosevelt rode to the Stadium through roaring crowds he had no chance to compare the two documents; not until he was on the platform, facing the Convention, could he lay them side by side. During the cheering he glanced them over. Then he began to speak. The beginning of his address was his faithful Howe's first page; the rest was the original Brain Trust draft!

Nothing in the speech was as bold as Roosevelt's flight to make it. "Taking note, apparently, of the charges of straddling that had been flung at him," wrote Elmer Davis, "he promised to make his position clear; and he did--upon the Prohibition plank [demanding Repeal] which the party had adopted by a vote of five to one. For the rest, you could not quarrel with a single one of his generalities; you seldom can. But what they mean (if anything) is known only to Franklin D. Roosevelt and his God."

In the speech there were many passages which foreshadowed the subsequent vigorous measures of his Presidency, but they were vague in phrasing. In only one place, where he suggested that a force of unemployed men be put at conservation work, did he seem to have a really novel plan (this was the germ of the CCC). He endorsed some ideas which he was later to forsake, as when he said that government "costs too much" and that the Federal government should set an example of solvency. And he accepted "one hundred per cent" the new Democratic platform: a short specific document which, though it called for financial reforms such as Roosevelt was later to push through Congress, and called also for "control of crop surpluses," represented in the main an old-fashioned liberalism--a return to the days of small and simple business units and modest and frugal governmental units--and certainly gave no hint of any intention to expand enormously the Federal power.

Events were moving fast in that summer of 1932, ideas were boiling, and counsels were divided. The Democratic candidate was astute: he had less to lose by facing two ways than by standing fast; by talking about candor than by exercising it.

§ 2

Not only were ideas boiling; the country was losing patience with adversity. That instinct of desperate men to rebel which was swelling the radical parties in a dozen Depression-hit countries and was gathering stormily behind Hitler in Germany was working in the United States also. It was anything but unified, it was as yet little organized, and only in scattered places did it assume the customary European shape of communism. It had been slow to develop--partly because Americans had been used to prosperity and had expected it to return automatically, partly because when jobs were vanishing those men who were still employed were too scared to be rebellious, and simply hung on to what they had and waited and hoped. (It is not usually during a collapse that men rebel, but after it.) There had been riots and hunger-marches here and there but on the whole the orderliness of the country had been striking, all things considered. Yet men could not be expected to sit still forever in the expectation that an economic system which they did not understand would right itself. The ferment of dissatisfaction was working in many places and taking many forms, and here and there it was beginning to break sharply through the orderly surface of society.

In the summer of 1932 the city of Washington was to see an exciting example of this ferment--and a spectacular demonstration of how not to deal with it.

All through June thousands of war veterans had been streaming into Washington, coming from all over the country by boxcar and by truck. These veterans wanted the government to pay them now the "adjusted compensation" which Congress had already voted to pay them in 1945. They set up a camp--a shanty-town, a sort of big-scale "Hooverville"--on the Anacostia flats near the city, and they occupied some vacant land with disused buildings on it on Pennsylvania Avenue just below the Capitol. More and more of them straggled to Washington until their number had reached fifteen or twenty thousand.

Among such a great crowd there were inevitably men of many sorts. The Hoover Administration later charged that many had had

73

criminal records, or were communists. But unquestionably the great majority of them were genuine veterans; though there was one small communist group, it was regarded with hostility by the rest; in the main this "Bonus Expeditionary Force" consisted of ordinary Americans out of luck. They were under at least a semblance of military discipline and were on the whole well-behaved. Many brought their wives and children along, and as time went on the Anacostia camp took on an air half military and half domestic, with the family wash hanging on the line outside the miserable shacks, and entertainers getting up impromptu vaudeville shows.

General Pelham D. Glassford, the Washington superintendent of police, sensibly regarded these invaders as citizens who had every right to petition the government for a redress of grievances. He helped them to get equipment for their camp and treated them with unfailing consideration. But to some Washingtonians their presence was ominous. A group of the veterans--under a leader who wore a steel neckbrace and a helmet with straps under the chin, to support a broken back--picketed the Capitol for days while the Bonus bill was being considered; and on the evening when the bill was to come to a vote, the great plaza before the Capitol was packed with veterans. The Senate voted No. What would the men do? There were people looking out the windows of the brightly lighted Senate wing who wondered breathlessly if those thousands of ragged men would try to rush the building. But when their leader announced the news, a band struck up "America" and the men dispersed quietly. So far, so good.

Some of them left Washington during the next few days, but several thousand stayed on, hopelessly, obstinately. (Where had they to go?) Officialdom became more and more uneasy. The White House was put under guard, its gates closed and chained, the streets about it cleared, as if the man there did not dare face the unrest among the least fortunate of the citizenry. It was decided to clear the veterans out of the disused buildings below the Capitol (to make way for the government's building program); and on the morning of July 28, 1932, General Glassford was told that the evacuation must be immediate. He set about his task.

It began peacefully, but at noon somebody threw a brick and there was a scuffle between the veterans and the police, which quickly

subsided. Two hours later there was more serious trouble as a policeman at whom the veterans had thrown stones pulled his gun; two
veterans were killed before Glassford could get the police to stop
shooting. Even this battle subsided. All Glassford wanted was time to
complete the evacuation peacefully and without needless affront. But
he was not to get it.

Pictures, Inc.
BONUS MARCHERS ON THE CAPITOL STEPS
The siege of the Senate at Washington, July, 1932

Earlier in the day he had told the District Commissioners that if the evacuation was to be carried out speedily, troops would be required. This statement had been needlessly interpreted as a request for military aid, which Glassford did not want at all. President Hoover had ordered the United States Army to the rescue.

Down Pennsylvania Avenue, late that hot afternoon, came an impressive parade--four troops of cavalry, four companies of infantry, a machine-gun squadron, and several tanks. As they approached the disputed area they were met with cheers from the veterans sitting on the curb and from the large crowd which had assembled. Then suddenly there was chaos: cavalrymen were riding into the crowd, infantrymen were throwing tear-gas bombs, women and children were being trampled and were choking from the gas; a crowd of three thousand or more spectators who had gathered in a vacant lot across the way were being pursued by the cavalry and were running wildly, pell-mell, across the uneven ground, screaming as they stumbled and fell.

The troops moved slowly on, scattering before them veterans and homegoing government clerks alike. When they reached the other end of the Anacostia bridge and met a crowd of spectators who booed them and were slow to "move on," they threw more gas bombs. They began burning the shacks of the Anacostia camp--a task which the veterans themselves helped them accomplish. That evening the Washington sky glowed with fire. Even after midnight the troops were still on their way with bayonets and tear-gas bombs, driving people ahead of them into the streets of Anacostia.

The Bonus Expeditionary Force had been dispersed, to merge itself with that greater army of homeless people who were drifting about the country in search of an ever-retreating fortune. The United States Army had completed its operation "successfully" without killing anybody--though the list of injured was long. The incident was over. But it had left a bitter taste in the mouth. Bayonets drawn in Washington to rout the dispossessed--was this the best that American statesmanship could offer hungry citizens?

§ 3

The farmers were rebellious--and no wonder. For the gross income of American agriculture had declined from nearly 12 billion dollars in 1929--when it had already for years been suffering from a decline in export sales--to only 5 $\frac{1}{4}$ billions in 1932. While most manufacturing businesses dropped their prices only a little and met slackened demand with slackened production, the farmer could not do this, and the prices he got went right down to the cellar. Men who found themselves utterly unable to meet their costs of production could not all be expected to be philosophical about it.

Angry Iowans, organized by Milo Reno into a Farmers' Holiday Association, were refusing to bring food into Sioux City for thirty days or "until the cost of production had been obtained"; they blockaded the highways with spiked telegraph poles and logs, stopped milk trucks and emptied the milk into roadside ditches. Said an elderly Iowa farmer with a white mustache to Mary Heaton Vorse, "They say blockading the highway's illegal. I says, 'Seems to me there was a Tea Party in Boston that was illegal too.'"

Elsewhere farmers were taking the obvious direct means to stop the tidal wave of mortgage foreclosure sales. All through the prairie country there were quantities of farmers who not only had heavy mortgages on their property but had gone deeply into debt for the purchase of farm machinery or to meet the emergencies of years of falling prices; when their corn and wheat brought to even the most industrious of them not enough money to meet their obligations, they lost patience with the laws of bankruptcy. If a man sees a neighbor of his, a formerly successful farmer, a substantial, hard-working citizen with a family, coming out of the office of the referee in bankruptcy stripped of everything but an old team of horses, a wagon, a few dogs and hogs, and a few sticks of furniture, he is likely to see red. Marching to the scene of the next foreclosure sale, these farmers would drive off prospective bidders, gather densely about the auctioneer, bid in horses at 25 cents apiece, cows at 10 cents, fat hogs at a nickel--and the next morning would return their purchases to the former owner.

In a quiet county seat, handbills would appear: "Farmers and workers! Help protect your neighbors from being driven off their property. Now is the time to act. For the past three and a half years we have waited for our masters, who are responsible for the situation, to find a way out. . . . On Friday the property of ------ is to be sold at a forced auction at the courthouse. . . . The Farmers Committee has called a mass protest meeting to stop the above-mentioned sale." And on Friday the trucks would drive up to the courthouse and men by the hundreds, quiet, grim-faced, would fill the corridors outside the sheriff's office while their leaders demanded that the sale be not held.

They threatened judges in bankruptcy cases; in one case a mob dragged a judge from his courtroom, beat him, hanged him by the neck till he fainted--and all because he was carrying out the law.

These farmers were not revolutionists. On the contrary, most of them were by habit conservative men. They were simply striking back in rage at the impersonal forces which had brought them to their present pass.

All through the summer and autumn of 1932--when the Olympic Games were being held with high pageantry at Los Angeles, when people were gathering in the open fields of Maine and New Hampshire to witness as much of a total eclipse of the sun as drifting clouds would permit, when Mayor Jimmy Walker of New York was being tried before Governor Roosevelt for misconduct in office and was resigning to seek a temporary exile in the south of France, when the report that a nudist camp had been established anywhere was enough to bring the reporters on the dead run, and when Roosevelt was campaigning against Hoover--all through that summer and autumn the ferment of ideas, plans, notions for defeating the Depression increased.

In July and August, barter schemes were going into effect in Dayton and Yellow Springs, Ohio, and soon they were being set up in numerous communities: men and women were organizing the dispossessed to pool their various abilities and make goods for one another-- only to discover, after months or even years of heroic effort, that "mutual exchanges" and attempts to set up little systems of production within the existing system could be only makeshifts at best. Towns from which money had almost disappeared were adopting scrip currency--issuing local money good in the local shops. Huey Long, who had arrived in Washington as a Senator in January and had electrified the gentlemen of the press by receiving them in lavender pajamas, had proposed a Share-our-Wealth scheme in March; and although Huey now occupied an ostentatious position on the Roosevelt band wagon, he had not forgotten his slogan: the time was ripe for it. Father Cough-lin's big radio audience heard him excoriating both the New York financiers and the Hoover Administration and calling Morgan, Mellon, Meyer, and Mills the "Four Horsemen"; the radio priest was getting ready to come out for revaluation of the currency.

Magazine editors were being inundated with manuscripts ex-plaining how the Depression could be ended--manuscripts proposing huge bond issues for public works, recommending inflation, recom-mending all sorts of other expedients, rational or ridiculous: "hot money" which would decline in value if unspent; the Douglas credit plan; other complex improvements in the banking and credit system; schemes for the general reduction of debts; "work-sharing" schemes for shorter hours of labor to soak up unemployment; proposals for the seizure and operation of industries by the government. Communism was notably gaining strength, both among the unemployed workers and--more rapidly--among the urban intellectuals: Edmund Wilson, John Dos Passos, Malcolm Cowley, V. F. Calverton, Theodore Dreis-er, and other able writers were fighting the good fight for Marx, and young novelists by the dozens were sitting down to write proletarian fiction.

The yeast was slowly working, and with the advent of winter it suddenly produced an astonishing and significant phenomenon: the frenzy of interest in Technocracy.

§ 4

To nobody was this frenzy more bewildering than to Howard Scott, the father of the Technocratic idea. He was an eccentric, boast-ful, haphazard young man who claimed to have had an important career in engineering and certainly had conducted a small paint and floor-wax business. For years he had been buttonholing people at The Meeting Place or Van's Place or other Greenwich Village speakeasies and restaurants to expound his strange economic theories--and had been finding it difficult to get people to listen. But when the Depression routed economic orthodoxy, heterodox notions began to look less crazy; Scott got enough backing to put a squad of unemployed architects to work at Columbia University on an "Energy Survey of North America." Then the *Living Age* came out with an article about Technocracy; and then, abruptly--in December, 1932--the thing was everywhere: in the newspapers, in the magazines, in sermons, in radio-actors' gags, in street-corner conversation. The amazed Scott, who a little while before had been jubilant when a newspaper gave a few lines to Technocracy, was now pursued by interviewers ready to hang upon his lightest word.

Scott's theory--developed partly from the writings of Veblen and Soddy--had a basis of good hard sense. He argued that it was not necessary for our economic system to falter and slow down; our enormous scientific and technical progress and the vast potentialities of machine power offered a basis for unparalleled prosperity--if only our money and credit arrangements could be prevented from jamming the works. The trouble with the system, argued Scott, was that discoveries and improvements which should cause us to be able to enjoy the affluence of plenty did not do so, but added to the debt burden and stalled the economic machinery.

At this point the argument became more difficult. What was wrong, insisted Scott, was the price system. What we needed was a price system based on energy--in units like ergs and joules. And the people who could put such a system into effect and operate it were the technologists--the scientists and engineers.

To try to put into effect a new price system seemed a sufficiently hazardous proceeding--considering the vast number of changes it would necessitate in everyday transactions--even if Scott and his disciples had been able to explain how this very difficult change was to be brought about. (No adequate explanation was forthcoming.) Practical men boggled at such a proposal. Practical men also smiled at putting the vital decisions in a society into the hands of scientific specialists. They remembered that politicians are always needed in the making of social decisions, because they know how to take account of human nature. Other critics of Technocracy pointed out that Scott's statements about the great potentialities of new engineering devices like the electric eye were optimistic at best. Still others were irritated by the abstruse language and the complicated mathematical formulae in which the Technocrats expressed themselves: when Scott himself wrote for publication he said of Technocracy that "its methods are the result of a synthetic integration of the physical sciences that pertain to the determination of all functional sequences of social phenomena," and he defined science as "the methodology of the determination of the most probable."

But the Technocratic idea fitted precisely the American mood of the moment. It offered an answer to the pervasive riddle of the times. This answer was new; it did not--as did communism--run head on into ingrained prejudices and emotional conflicts. It seemed to be scientific, and thus commended itself to a people who venerated science as the source of progress. As a new fad, it was as much fun as a round-the-world flight or Amos 'n' Andy. The very fact that it was abstruse, that it broke clean away from the world of practical problems and intelligible statements, gave it a mystical irresistibility to a nation searching for a magic key to recovery, for something which would both bring prosperity and serve as a religion. Technocracy was hopeful, too, looking forward as it did to an era of possible plenty; this fact helped to make it palatable to a public of habitual optimists. And its vogue came at the moment when millions of Americans had decided that they were sick of the old order and were ready for a new one--they didn't know what.

During the last month of 1932 and the first month of 1933 America took up the idea with a whoop. The columns of newspapers and magazines were full of it; bankers and taxi drivers alike argued its merits and fallacies; *The ABC of Technocracy* leaped into the best-seller lists, half-forgotten volumes by Soddy and Veblen suddenly met a lively demand, and several new books on Technocracy were hurriedly announced. When ship-news reporters boarded an incoming liner, the first question they asked a returning banker or movie star was "What do you think of Technocracy?" Howard Scott was invited by the largest apartment house in New York to act as Santa Claus at its

Christmas tree celebration, quite as if he were a Channel swimmer or a nonstop flyer. A rift between Scott and his Columbia associates became a front-page news sensation.

Then the interest almost as quickly waned. Technocracy was too far removed from the practical issues of the day to remain in the forefront of attention. By the time the New Deal arrived, it was already *vieux jeu* to most Americans--like a memory of a half-forgotten folly.

Yet in the meantime it had offered an object-lesson in the readiness of the American people for a new messiah and a new credo. In a lesser degree they were exhibiting the same emotional willingness to get up and go, they knew not where, that was being exhibited in Germany by multitudes of men and women who were not convinced by Hitler but followed him because he was marching and seemed sure of his destination, and because they could face a hopeless future no longer.

§ 5

Poor Hoover!

In June he had made a bold disarmament proposal in the hope of ending a long European deadlock over arms limitations, a deadlock which was deepening the bitterness in Germany--but French and British opposition brought it to nought, and the move had come too late anyhow. He labored with a recalcitrant Congress in the fervent hope of balancing the budget--and won only a partial victory. Anxiety sat heavy upon him. As he hurried from his desk to a quick luncheon and back again, he hardly spoke to members of the White House staff in the corridors, but passed them half-unseeing, a frown upon his face. Democrats like Garner who gave him scant co-operation he regarded with wrath; the White House correspondents found him suspicious, unwilling to hold press conferences, resentful of attacks upon him in the press. No man in the White House had ever struggled harder and seen his efforts so scantily rewarded.

In August things seemed to be looking better. The Bonus Army--that hateful reminder of a bitterness and distress of which he was already painfully conscious--had been driven from the city. Better still, the business index had turned upward. A conference in Lausanne, which had ended German reparations, appeared to have eased the financial tension in Europe. Gold was no longer leaving the United States; indeed, by the end of August over a third of the gold that had been frightened away in the latter months of 1931 and the early months of 1932 had returned. The RFC had slowed up the rate of bank failures. And once again the stock market was showing healthy plus signs. Perhaps at last the corner to prosperity had been turned, and even if Hoover lost the election he might go down in history as the man who had seen the United States through the crisis.

Already, however, the campaign was upon him, and to the terrific burdens of the Presidential office he had to add the burden of drafting long speeches in self-defense--dictating them in the Lincoln study to relays of stenographers, correcting the typewritten copy, rushing it to the printer, and then laboriously going over the proofs sentence by sentence with his advisers. Every statistical evidence of improvement in the economic situation must be used to the utmost; every Hoover move against the Depression must be dramatized as a battle in a winning war; he must defend even the Smoot-Hawley tariff and warn his audience that if a Democratic tariff were put into effect "the grass will grow in the streets of a hundred cities" and "weeds will overrun the fields of millions of farms."

Sometimes, on his speech-making tours, he was heartened by roars of vigorous applause--but again there would be evidences of hostility, as when a group of jeering demonstrators gathered opposite a station when his train stopped and threw into a group of his aides a 150-watt electric-light bulb which exploded with a startlingly bomb-like sound. So near was Hoover to complete exhaustion that on one of the last nights of the campaign, when he was on his way across the country to vote at Palo Alto, he lost his place repeatedly in his address at St. Paul, and throughout the address a man sat behind him gripping the arms of a chair and ready to push it under the President if he should collapse.

More debonair was Roosevelt as he went about the country preaching his New Deal. The Democratic candidate was less vague, now, than he had been. For his Brain Trust, now much enlarged and established in a suite in the Roosevelt Hotel in New York, was strenuously rounding out a program for him--or rather, a series of programs which sometimes conflicted with the plans of his more conservative advisers, if not with one another.

Roosevelt was explicit in his promise of financial reforms such as the regulation of securities and commodity exchanges, the regulation of holding companies, the separation of commercial and investment banking, the protection of investors through demands for full publicity about issues of securities. He was explicit about the need for a "competitive tariff" and for reciprocal tariff negotiations. He demanded that the Federal government develop power projects on the Columbia and Tennessee Rivers, and elsewhere, and use them as "yardsticks" with which to measure the service given by private utilities. Calling for control of crop surpluses, he defined the objectives of what was later to be the AAA, and he promised that the Federal government would lighten the load of farm mortgages. He insisted that it owed its citizens the positive duty of stepping into the breach when the states were unable to meet the burdens of relief. He came out for old-age insurance and unemployment insurance. At the Commonwealth Club in San Francisco he gave a real indication of the attitude he was to take during his Presidency when he insisted that "private economic power is . . . a public trust," and that "continued enjoyment of that power by any individual or group must depend upon the fulfillment of that trust." Yet at the instance of his more conservative advisers he came out also for a "definite balancing of the budget," berated the Hoover Administration for its extravagance, and promised drastic Federal economies. Furthermore, he said definitely, when questioned, that he was for "sound money"--which was generally taken to mean the gold standard; he said that "no responsible government would have sold to the country securities payable in gold if it knew that the promise--yes, the covenant-embodied in these securities was . . . dubious. . . ." Needless to say, he was explicit about repeal of the Prohibition

Amendment; on this point opinion had so clearly swung his way that there was next to no danger in being positive.

Those critics who had earlier been uneasy at Roosevelt's light-footedness were still uneasy. There were still ambiguities and contradictions in the program: how, for example, could a Federal government assume so many duties and obligations and simultaneously reduce expenses? And just what did "sound money" mean? It was difficult to judge the real significance of a program which contained so many potential contradictions. But Roosevelt's confidence was infectious, his smile was winning, and the times were on his side. The business upturn which had so encouraged Hoover in the late summer was flattening out, the stock market was definitely turning down after its sally, and with every month of continued hard times the general desire for change became more intense.

Election Day came--and that night the rejoicing was not in Palo Alto but at the Democratic headquarters at the Biltmore Hotel in New York, where Roosevelt and Farley and one or two others heard the good news in a secluded room while happy crowds of Democrats milled about outside. For Roosevelt had won 472 electoral votes to Hoover's 59--had carried every state but Connecticut, Delaware, Maine, New Hampshire, Pennsylvania, and Vermont.

So Franklin D. Roosevelt was to be President. But what sort of President? That depended upon events to come as well as upon himself--upon circumstances which neither he nor anybody else could foresee.

§ 6

There followed a strange interregnum. Business recovery was stalled again (from fears of what Roosevelt might do, claimed the Republicans). Congress, meeting in December, was more definitely insurgent than ever, and turned a deaf ear to the defeated President.

Nor was the President-elect co-operative. Hoover wished to make preparations for a world economic conference, and also to set up a debt-funding commission to deal with European requests for revision of the war debts, and he felt that he could not fairly do either of these things without the approval of Governor Roosevelt as the incoming President. He invited Roosevelt to a conference; Roosevelt politely came to the White House, where he and Hoover sparred conversationally, each man being attended by a second as if for a verbal battle. But nothing came of the conference, nor of a second one, nor of other Hoover suggestions for joint action in "restoring confidence." Hoover suggested that Roosevelt issue a statement assuring the country that "there will be no tampering or inflation of the currency," and Roosevelt--after a long delay--replied that he doubted if a mere statement would do much good. The President-elect wouldn't play ball.

To Hoover it seemed perfectly clear that a recovery which he had helped to start was being dissipated through Roosevelt's refusal to co-operate. And his anger was all the more vehement because he believed that the bank panic which was developing was due to Roosevelt's silence (now that the campaign was over) about inflation of the currency, and to a general fear of what the wild men of the Democracy might do after March 4. There were explicit stories going about to the effect that Roosevelt had said he favored inflation. Hoover was told that Professor Tugwell had spoken jauntily of the danger of a general bank closing and had said, "We should worry about anything except rehabilitating the country after March 4," adding that one of the first Roosevelt moves might be "reflation if necessary." ("Reflation" was a current euphemism for inflation.) This was too much: Hoover wrote furiously to his informant that Tugwell "breathes with infamous politics devoid of every atom of patriotism." The unhappy President believed that Roosevelt was irresponsibly ready to see the country go to pot in order to get the credit for rescuing it.

On the other hand, Roosevelt felt that as a private citizen until March 4, he himself must not join in Presidential action; and also that it was unreasonable to expect him to tie himself to the policies of an unsympathetic and already discredited administration--especially when the situation was changing fast and his own plans, different from Hoover's at many points, were still in flux. Both positions were natural under the circumstances; one need only add that the real villain of the

86

piece was the antiquated political arrangement by which an administration had to remain in nominal power for nearly four months after it
had been rejected at the polls.

Slowly and uncertainly the drama of Presidential frustration
proceeded--and then suddenly, about the middle of February, 1933,
when Hoover's term of office had less than three weeks to run, it went
into double-quick time. The banking system gave way.

Again and again during the preceding year or two there had
been local bank panics; the Federal Reserve had come to the rescue,
RFC money had been poured in, and a total collapse had been averted.
Now a new panic was beginning, and it was beyond the power of these
agencies to stop. Perhaps the newspaper publication of the facts about
RFC loans was a factor in bringing about this panic--though to say this
is to beg the question whether a banking system dependent upon secret
loans from a democratic government is not already in an indefensible
position. Probably the banks would have collapsed anyhow, so widely
had their funds been invested in questionable bonds and mortgages, so
widely had they been mismanaged through holding companies and
through affiliation with investment companies, so lax were the standards imposed upon them in many states, and so great was the strain
upon the national economy of sustaining the weight of obligations
which rested in their hands. At any rate, here at the heart of the national debt-and-credit structure a great rift appeared--and quickly widened.

On the 14th of February the condition of some of the banks in
and about Detroit had become so critical that Governor Comstock of
Michigan ordered an eight-day bank holiday for the State. All over the
country there began a whispering, barely audible at first, then louder
and louder: "Trouble's coming. They say there's a run on the trust
company down the street. Better get your money out of the bank." The
murmur ran among the bankers: "Trouble's coming. Better sell some
bonds and get cash before it's too late. Better withdraw your balances
on deposit in New York." It ran among the men of wealth: "Better put
everything into cash. Get gold if you can." It spread to Europe: "Better
get gold out of the United States. Better sell the dollar." The financial
machinery of the country began to freeze into rigidity, the industrial
and commercial machinery to slow down. Nor was there anything that
Hoover could do to stop the panic. Laboring ceaselessly, sleeping no

more than five hours a night, he saw all the ground he had gained since June being lost.

§ 7

Faster moved the clock of history.

On the 15th of February--the day after the Michigan bank closing--the whole course of events in America was nearly altered by an assassin. In Miami a man named Zangara fired several shots at Roosevelt in a crowd, missed him, fatally wounded Mayor Cermak of Chicago.

The next day--the 16th--the Senate voted to repeal the Prohibition Amendment. Four days later--on the 20th--the House followed, and the issue of repeal went to the States for their action, which by the following December was to make the country legally wet again. (This change in the Constitution required not only a two-thirds vote in both Senate and House--which had been secured--but the approval of conventions in three-quarters of the states.) The supposedly impossible was happening, with consequences to be felt in every American community; another landmark was being quickly swept away by the tide of change.

During all these days there were continuous and feverish attempts to set the Michigan banking situation straight. In Detroit the bankers and motor manufacturers labored over rescue plans; the wires between Detroit and New York and Washington hummed with anxious talk between the President, the RFC officials, the Federal Reserve officials, Ford and Chrysler and Sloan, Senator Couzens, and the Michigan bankers and officials--and no solution was found. Meanwhile armored trucks were running by night from city to city, carrying cash for beleaguered banks. The Federal Reserve figures were showing sharp increases in hoarding, sharp losses of gold by the United States, as the panic became intensified.

On Tuesday, February 21, Roosevelt announced that his Secretary of State would be Cordell Hull of Tennessee and his Secretary of the Treasury would be the smiling little manufacturer, William H. Woodin of New York. (Roosevelt had wanted Carter Glass for the Treasury, but Glass had realized that Roosevelt was ready if necessary to leave the gold standard and inflate the currency, and would not accept; Woodin, a comparatively unknown man, was a second choice.)

On the same day began the disclosure, by witnesses before a Senate committee, of some of the most disturbing facts yet revealed about the behavior of the lords of American finance during the preceding years. Charles E. Mitchell, chairman of the big National City Bank in New York, admitted under the questioning of Ferdinand Pecora that he had received bonuses totaling over three million dollars from his bank and its affiliates during 1927, 1928, and 1929--and yet, by selling some bank stock to a member of his family at a loss, he had avoided paying any income tax in 1929, even though he later repurchased the stock. The next day it was learned that after the Panic of 1929 the bank had protected its high officials who had been trading in its own stock, but that underlings in the bank's employ had had to pay in full, in installments, for stock which had meanwhile lost most of its value. Though there was nothing criminal about these operations--there were worse things brought out by Pecora later--they were peculiarly infuriating to the sense of democratic fair play. The effect of such disclosures as these, at such a time, upon the attitude of the country toward the big bankers was profound; it was as if a smouldering fire of distrust and disapproval had burst suddenly into flame.

On Friday, the 24th, there were runs on Baltimore banks and Governor Ritchie declared a Maryland bank holiday. On Saturday and Sunday the panic became serious in three Ohio cities. On Monday, the 27th, Mitchell resigned from the chairmanship of the National City Bank; the champion of bull market banking had abdicated before a rising public opinion. The panic was now spreading through Ohio and Indiana into Kentucky and Pennsylvania.

Nor were the only dramatic changes in America. On the evening of the 27th the Nazis burned the German Reichstag, attributing the fire to the Communists; in that conflagration German democracy was effectively destroyed. The new Chancellor, Adolf Hitler, was now swiftly on his way to supreme dictatorship. At the other side of the world, the Japanese government, which had invaded Manchuria in 1931 when the Western world was distracted with financial panic, was marching on into Jehol in complete defiance of the disapproval of the League of Nations. Internationally as well as within the United States, an old order was giving place to new.

Faster, faster.

On Wednesday, the first of March, two more states declared state bank holidays; that evening another four were added to the list. On March 2, ten more fell in line. In numerous cities outside the bank-holiday states, banks were by this time remaining open only on a restricted basis. That same day Roosevelt went by special train from New York to Washington--and spent most of the journey talking with Farley about men's need of religion in the crises of their lives. Jaunty and carefree as he seemed, he knew that he was riding into a hurricane which would presently confront him with the responsibility, not only for making instant and unprecedented decisions, but also for directing in America that insurgency which, the world over, was following upon economic collapse. The unrest which was spreading among the farmers and the unemployed; the anger which was rising against the financial overlords; the longing for a magic formula, manifested in the excitement over Technocracy--these resentments and hopes were his to satisfy. If he could not satisfy them . . .

By March 3--the eve of inauguration--the financial storm was battering at Chicago and New York, the financial strongholds of the country. The tie-up was almost complete. Hoover was making desperate last-minute efforts to work out a solution, but they were unavailing. And at 4:30 in the morning of March 4, the strongholds surrendered: Governor Lehman of New York proclaimed a state bank holiday, and almost simultaneously Governor Horner proclaimed one in Illinois. At 6 o'clock a worn and haggard Hoover got up to perform the last routine tasks of his Presidency. He was told that on his last morning of office the banking system of the United States had stopped functioning.

"We are at the end of our string," said he. "There is nothing more we can do."

90

The stage manager of history had been too cruelly precise. For all Hoover's asperities, his awkwardness, his political ineptitudes, he had been a resourceful and resolute soldier of a doomed order, and deserved no such personal humiliation. But now the curtain was coming down and he could do no more.

Chapter Five

NEW DEAL HONEYMOON

§ 1

Saturday, March 4, 1933.

Turn on the radio. It's time for the inauguration.

There is a tension in the air today--a sense of momentousness and of expectation. When you went downtown this morning you found the banks shut; if you lived in New York State or in Illinois this may have been your first inkling of the general bank closing, since the closing orders in those states had come too late for the early editions of the morning papers of March 4. On the door of each bank was pasted a little typewritten notice that it had been closed at the Governor's order; people by twos and threes went up and read the sign and walked away. Your first thought, perhaps, was that you had only a little money in the house--five dollars, was it? ten dollars?--and you wondered how you would manage when this was used up, and what would happen next. Then you began to realize the significance of this financial stoppage.

Well, it's come at last, you thought. Here is that day of doom that people have been dreading. Just now it isn't so bad; there is a tingle of excitement, the sort of thrill you get from a three-alarm fire. But what next? This may be only the beginning of the crack-up. The one thing you want to hear, that everybody wants to hear, is the inaugural address. All over the country people are huddled round their radios, wondering what Roosevelt's answer to disaster will be.

Here's the voice of a radio reporter describing the preparations for the inauguration ceremony at the east front of the Capitol in Washington--the notables coming to their places on the platform, the dense crowds flooding the Capitol square below under a chill, cloudy sky. The reporter is talking with all the synthetic good cheer of his kind-- bearing down hard on the note of optimism, in fact, for he knows that worried and frightened people are listening to him. He describes Hoover coming alone, gravely, to his place on the platform; then Roosevelt coming up a ramp on the arm of his son James. The ceremony begins. You hear Chief Justice Hughes administer the oath of office; you hear Roosevelt's reply, phrase by phrase, uttered clearly and firmly. Then comes the inaugural.

The new President's voice is resolute. It comes into your living room sharply.

"President Hoover, Mr. Chief Justice, my friends," the voice begins. "This is a day of national consecration, and I am certain that my fellow Americans expect that on my induction into the Presidency I will address them with a candor and a decision which the present situation of the nation impels. This is pre-eminently the time to speak the truth, frankly and boldly. Nor need we shrink from honestly facing conditions in our country today. This great nation will endure as it has endured, will revive and will prosper. So, first of all, let me assert my firm belief that the only thing we have to fear is fear itself--nameless, unreasoning, unjustified terror which paralyzes needed efforts to convert retreat into advance."

This doesn't sound like "prosperity is just around the corner" talk. It sounds like real confidence.

The voice goes on to blame "the rulers of the exchange of mankind's goods" for the troubles of the country. "True, they have tried, but their efforts have been cast in the pattern of an outworn tradition. . . . The money changers have fled from their high seats in the temple of our civilization." Through the radio comes a burst of applause: after the bank smash-ups and scandals, this condemnation of the big financiers expresses the mood of millions of Americans.

The voice speaks of the primary need of putting people to work; of the need for "making income balance outgo"; of the need for an "adequate but sound currency" (sharp applause for that!); promises a "good neighbor" policy in foreign affairs, but says domestic affairs must come first. Most striking of all, however, is the constant emphasis upon the need for action. Again and again comes the word "action." And after the new President has said he believes that the sort of action which is needed may be taken under the Constitution, the loudest applause of all comes for his declaration that if the occasion warrants he will not hesitate to ask for "broad executive power to wage a war against the emergency, as great as the power that would be given to me if we were in fact invaded by a foreign foe."

A ten-strike, this declaration. For the people have been sick of watching an Executive devote his strongest energies to opposing action, however questionable: they want a positive policy.

"We do not distrust the future of essential democracy," the President continues. "The people of the United States have not failed. In their need they have registered a mandate that they want direct, vigorous action. They have asked for discipline and direction under leadership. They have made me the present instrument of their wishes. In the spirit of the gift I take it."

You can turn off the radio now. You have heard what you wanted to hear. This man sounds no longer cautious, evasive. For he has seen that a tortured and bewildered people want to throw overboard the old and welcome something new; that they are sick of waiting, they want somebody who will *fight* this Depression for them and with them; they want leadership, the thrill of bold decision. And not only in his words but in the challenge of the very accents of his voice he has promised them what they want.

If only the performance measures up to the promise!

Pictures, Inc.

THE OLD ORDER CHANGETH
President Hoover and President-elect Roosevelt ride together to
the Inauguration, March 4, 1933

§ 2

Action there was, in abundance; and it came fast.

On Sunday, March 5, the day after the inauguration, the new President not only called Congress to meet in special session on Thursday, but also issued a proclamation putting the bank holiday on a national basis and prohibiting the export of gold and all dealings in foreign exchange. (Thus the country went at least part way off the gold standard--on a temporary basis.)

On Thursday Congress met and passed with a whoop a law validating everything that the executive had done to date and tightening still further its control over banking operations, gold, silver, currency, and foreign exchange.

On Friday the President asked Congress for immediate action to cut Federal expenses to the bone--and Congress rushed at the task, despite the political distastefulness of slashing the veterans' allowances.

On Saturday--after a week of furious activity at the Treasury, during which regulations were devised and altered, plans for the issue of clearing-house certificates were made and abandoned, plans for the issue of new currency were promulgated, and a rough classification of banks into more and less sound was made with the aid of advice from Federal Reserve Banks and chief national bank examiners--the President announced that most of the banks of the country would open the following Monday, Tuesday, and Wednesday.

On Sunday night the President, in his first "fireside chat," explained to the people of the country with admirable simplicity, clarity, and persuasiveness just how the re-opening of the banks would be managed and how his hearers could help to make the process orderly.

On Monday, the 13th of March, the banks began to open. And on the same day the President asked Congress to legalize beer--thus closing his tremendous first ten days of office on a note of festivity.

Such were the bare facts of those ten days. But the mere catalogue of them gives little idea of their overtones of significance, or of what those ten days were like to the American people.

The predicament of the incoming Administration was staggering. A new President and new Cabinet, unaccustomed even to the ordinary routine of their positions, largely unacquainted with their staffs, and forced to rely heavily upon the services of Hoover officials who stayed on to help them, had to deal with an unprecedented emergency which confronted them with unforeseen problems. Everything had to be done at top speed. Nobody could tell what might be the future cost of mistakes made under such pressure. Nobody could be sure, for that matter, that this was not just the first of a progressive series of emergencies which would bring conditions infinitely worse. Never did a green Administration seem to be walking into such a potential hornet's nest of difficulties.

But other circumstances aided them. In the first place, the accident of fate which had been so cruel to Hoover gave the country an Administration which could start from scratch in its race against panic, unhandicapped by memories of previous failures. It is traditional for the American people to feel kindly toward a new administration and support its first moves; in this case the friendly feeling was not only ready-made but intense. An enormous majority of the population desperately wanted the New Deal to succeed. Even the Wall Street bankers were ready to give Roosevelt full powers and wish him well, wince though they might at being called money changers who had "fled from their high seats in the temple." They were badly frightened, their institutions were demoralized, their collective reputation was besmirched anyhow, their only hope lay in Roosevelt's success. The newspapers, too, were loud now with enthusiasm. For weeks they had been burying bank-panic news in the back pages; now they could let go--and out gushed, on the news pages and in the editorials, all that zest for whooping it up, for boosting, for delivering optimistic fight talks, that was innate and habitual in the American temperament. Congress, usually divided in opinion and intractable, became almost as unanimous and enthusiastic as a cheering section--because public opinion told them to. The Congressmen's mail was heavy, and the burden of it was "Support the President." It was as if a people rent by discords suddenly found themselves marching in step.

There was another favorable circumstance. In *The Folklore of Capitalism,* Thurman W. Arnold tells of a conversation he had, before the bank panic, with a group of bankers, lawyers, and economists. They were one and all aghast at the possibility of a general bank closing. "My mind," said one of them, "fails to function when I think of the extent of the catastrophe that will follow when the Chase National Bank closes its doors." Mr. Arnold told his friend Professor Edward S. Robinson about this conversation, and found him unaccountably cheerful. "Do you think," asked Professor Robinson, "that when the banks all close people will climb trees and throw coconuts at each other?" Mr. Arnold replied that this seemed to him a little unlikely but that a bank crash of such magnitude suggested to him rioting and perhaps revolution. Whereupon Professor Robinson said, "I will venture a prediction. . . . When the banks close, everyone will feel relieved. It will be a sort of national holiday. There will be general excitement and a feeling of great interest. Travel will not stop; hotels will not close; everyone will have a lot of fun, though they will not admit that it's fun at the time."

Despite the fact that indirectly the bank holiday brought new distress, through new curtailments of business and new layoffs, and intensified the suffering of many people who were already hard hit, Professor Robinson was essentially right. The majority of Americans felt a sense of relief at having the lid of secrecy blown off. Now everything was out in the open. They felt that this trouble was temporary. They felt no shame now in being short of money--everybody seemed to be. They were all in the same boat. And they responded to one another's difficulties good-naturedly.

The grocer lent credit (what else could he do?), most hotels were glad to honor checks, shops were cordial about charge accounts. The diminished advertising columns of the newspapers contained such cheerful announcements as "IN PAYMENT FOR PASSAGE WE WILL ACCEPT CHECKS OR PROPERLY AUTHORIZED SCRIP" (this was in the early days of the bank holiday, when the issue of clearing-house scrip appeared likely); "RADIO CITY HAS CONFIDENCE IN AMERICA AND ITS PEOPLE--until scrip becomes available our box offices will accept checks"; "WE WILL TAKE YOUR CHECK DATED THREE MONTHS AHEAD for a three months' supply of Pepsodent for yourself and your family."

True, the shopping districts were half deserted; on the upper floors of department stores, clerks were standing about with no customers at all; there was a Saturday air about the business offices, trains were sparsely filled, stock exchanges and commodity exchanges were closed. But in the talk that buzzed everywhere there was less of foreboding than of eager and friendly excitement. "Are they going to put out scrip?--and how do we use it?" "What's a 'conservator'--is that a new word?" "You say you had thirty dollars on you when the banks closed? Well, you're in luck. I had only three-fifty--I'd planned to go to the bank that morning." "They say the Smiths stocked their cellar with canned goods last week--three months' supply; they thought there was going to be a revolution!" "Did you see those pictures of the gold hoarders bringing bags full of gold back to the Federal Reserve Bank? Those birds are getting off easy, if you ask me." "Mrs. Dodge beat the bank holiday all right--overdrew her account last Friday. No, not intentionally. Just a mistake, she says. Shot with luck, I call it." "Stop me if you've heard this banker story: it seems that a banker died and when he got to the gates, St. Peter said. . . ."

To this public mood President Roosevelt's first fireside chat was perfectly attuned. Quiet, uncondescending, clear, and confident, it was an incredibly skillful performance. (According to Raymond Moley's *After Seven Years,* the first draft of this chat was written by Charles Michelson of the Democratic publicity staff; Arthur Ballantine, Under Secretary of the Treasury for Hoover, completely rewrote it; Roosevelt revised it.) The banks opened without any such renewed panic as had been feared. They might not have done so had people realized that it was impossible, in a few days, to separate the sound banks from the unsound with any certainty, and that errors were bound to be made. The story goes that one bank had been in such bad shape that its directors decided not even to put in an application to reopen; through a clerical slip this bank was put on the wrong list, received a clean bill of health, and opened with flying colors! In some places, to be sure, there were bank runs even after the opening--runs which had to be met unquestioningly with Federal funds, lest the whole trouble begin over again. And so many banks had to be kept shut anyhow that ten per cent or more of the deposits of the country were still tied up after March 15, and the national economic machinery thus remained partially crippled. On the whole, however, the opening was an immense success. Confidence had come back with a rush; for the people had been captivated and persuaded by a President who seemed to believe in them and was giving them action, action, action.

The New Deal had made a brilliant beginning.

§ 3

The next few months in Washington provided a spectacle unprecedented in American history. The pace at which the New Deal had started its career slackened hardly at all. The administrative hopper produced bill after bill, the President passed the bills on to Congress with terse recommendations for passage, and Congress--almost as if mesmerized--passed them, often with scant debate, sometimes without an opportunity for all the members to read them, much less comprehend their full significance. Never before except in wartime had the Executive been so dominant over Congress. Never before, even in wartime, had a legislative program been pushed through with such terrific speed and daring.

The very air of Washington crackled. Suddenly this city had become unquestionably the economic as well as the political capital of the country, the focus of public attention. The press associations had to double their staffs to fill the demand for explanatory dispatches about the New Deal bills. And into Washington descended a multitude of men and women from all over the country.

First there were bankers by the thousands, thronging the corridors of the Treasury, buttonholing their Senators to explain just why their banks should be permitted to re-open, and converging upon an emergency office set up in the Washington Building by the Acting Comptroller of the Currency--an office in which four men found themselves the bottleneck of communication between the banking system and the government. Amid the hammering of workmen putting up partitions, these men were trying simultaneously to hire stenographers and clerks, to draft regulations and letters, to interview importunate bankers, and to deal with incoming telephone calls which were backed up two and three days by the congestion of appeals from all over the country. Every banker had his own story to tell--his own account of how his mortgages had been undervalued by the bank examiners, or an entire community was dependent upon his institution. Some of them brought their directors along. Who could deal with these men? So terrific was the strain of those first days that on at least two nights the Acting Comptroller of the Currency went home only to take a shower, change his clothes, and go back to work; when he did snatch a few hours' sleep, his wife had to sit by a constantly ringing telephone and explain that he might not be disturbed. Another high official would lie down on a couch in the office of the Secretary of the Treasury, go to sleep, be awakened by a question, answer it, and drop off to sleep again.

In that GHQ at the Treasury during the bank holiday there was an almost continuous executive conference, day and night. Woodin and Moley, Democrats; Mills, Ballantine, and Awalt, Republicans, were the nucleus of a group which labored without thought of party. Even in their brief intervals of rest the problems remained with them; at breakfast on the Tuesday morning after the Inauguration little Woodin reported to Moley how he had solved the knotty question of whether and how to issue scrip: "I played my guitar a little while and then read a while and then slept a little while and then awakened and then thought about this scrip thing and then played some more and read some more and slept some more and thought some more. And, by gum, if I didn't hit on the answer that way! . . . We don't have to issue scrip!" The ordeal of twenty-hour days was too much for Secretary Woodin; his health had not been good, and there are those who think that it was the labor and responsibility of those weeks in March which killed him; he died the following year.

Droves of Democratic office-seekers, too, were descending upon Washington: so many of them that Postmaster-General Farley, whom they knew to be the chief patronage dispenser of the Administration, found them haunting the corridors of his hotel; he "virtually had to slip back and forth to his office like a man dodging a sheriff's writ," and he found that the only way to get rid of the hordes that packed his reception room at the Old Post Office Building was to make the rounds of the room five or six times a day with his secretary, taking down the name of each individual and a brief description of the sort of job he sought.

Experts and specialists of all sorts were coming into town to help in the framing of new laws and regulations and in the setting up of new government agencies. Financiers and their lawyers and brief-case-toting assistants were coming to take the witness stand in Ferdinand Pecora's intermittently sensational investigation of the scandals of the banking world. Special emissaries from Great Britain, Canada, France, Italy, Argentina, Germany, Mexico, China, Brazil, Japan, and Chile arrived in quick succession, each with his entourage, to consult with the President and his advisers on economic and diplomatic problems; from Great Britain came Ramsay MacDonald, the Prime Minister; from France came Edouard Herriot, the Premier; there were receptions, conferences, dinners, long discussions between groups of experts, in endless and fatiguing succession.

To Washington as by a magnet were drawn, too, innumerable idealists, enthusiasts, radical national-planners, world-savers of all degrees of hard- and soft-headedness, each with his infallible prescription for ending the Depression.

Meanwhile into the White House poured thousands of plans for recovery, for the great American public wanted to help. They ranged, these plans, from semi-literate scrawls on ruled paper to 175-page mimeographed booklets with graphs and statistical tables, and they displayed a touching confidence that the President himself would carefully consider their suggestions. (All these plans were read, considered, and politely acknowledged--but not by him.) "In the present national emergency," began a characteristic letter, "surely I will be pardoned if it is presumptuous to bring views to your attention. If the ideas are in the least beneficial then the end will justify the beginning." And another: "Being one of those Americans who love their country and having a sort of an idea which may have some merit, I am taking

ALLEN

the presumptuous liberty of passing it along to you in this letter."
Business men, bankers, students, housewives, unemployed laborers,
they had ideas and threw them into the hopper.

Furious work was being done in Washington in that spring of
1933. The lights burned late in government offices as the architects of
the New Deal, official and unofficial, drafted bills and regulations and
memoranda, tore their drafts to pieces and began all over again, and
then rushed off to consult other groups and revise and revise again. In
the vast new office buildings along the Mall there was sublime confusion as new jobholders arrived and began searching for their offices,
for desks, for people who could tell them what they were supposed to
do. Government departments were overflowing into office buildings
everywhere; and the streets were full of apartment-hunters, while the
real-estate men of Washington rubbed their hands at the sudden boom
in the housing market.

§ 4

Out of all this pandemonium emerged in short order an extraordinary array of new legislative measures. To summarize the chief
ones very briefly:--

1. Devaluation.

After the banks opened there was a prompt improvement in
business, but during the first few weeks it was only moderate. The
President became impatient; and Congress, likewise impatient, became
so enamoured of the idea of inflating the currency that a bill sponsored
by Senator Wheeler of Montana, providing for the free coinage of silver on the old Bryan basis of 16 to 1, almost passed the Senate despite
Roosevelt's opposition. Under these circumstances Roosevelt took the
plunge off the gold standard. Half convinced that some sort of inflation was necessary anyhow as a shot in the arm for the American
economy; unwilling to let Congress take the initiative away from him

and force the country into some ill-devised inflation scheme; and convinced that if it were done when 'tis done, then 'twere well it were done quickly, Roosevelt on April 19th placed an embargo on gold--thus serving notice that the gold standard had been definitely abandoned. Then he laid before Congress a bill--which was passed--giving him permissive authority to inflate in any one of five ways if he saw the need to do so.

Shortly afterward there followed a law which forbade the issue of bonds, governmental or corporate, payable in gold, and which abrogated all existing contractual obligations to pay bonds in gold. Still later, when the World Economic Conference, assembling in London, turned to the international stabilization of currencies as its first important task, Roosevelt heaved a bombshell into it--with distressing damage to the prestige of his own delegation--by refusing to let the United States be a party to even a vague and general stabilization agreement at that juncture. And from time to time, while these moves were going on, he declared his intention to raise American prices "to such an extent that those who have borrowed money will, on the average, be able to repay that money in the same kind of dollar which they borrowed." (It was not until later in 1933 that he devalued the American dollar progressively to 59.06 cents, in terms of its former gold value, through the amazing--and none too successful--scheme of progressively raising the price which the United States would bid for gold.)

The result of these various orders, laws, and statements in the spring of 1933 was to bring about a quick jump in prices, a burst of upward activity on the stock exchanges and commodity exchanges, a hurried buying of supplies by business men for their inventories in expectation of further rises in prices, and a much sharper recovery of business than had previously seemed likely. It is difficult to disentangle causes and effects when a government is doing everything at once, but the evidence would seem to show that the shot in the arm administered in the spring of 1933 had a definitely stimulating effect. (In fact, there would seem to be room for the somewhat cynical comment that of all the economic medicines applied to the United States as a whole during the nineteen-thirties, only two have been of proved general effectiveness, and both of these have a habit-forming tendency and may be lethal if too often repeated: these two medicines are devaluation and spending.)

2. Crop Control.

The New Deal came to the rescue of the farm population with a bill which aimed to raise the prices of the major American farm crops by offering payments to farmers to leave part of their acreage unplanted. The money for the payments was to be raised by a processing tax, which in effect was a light sales tax on the consumption of these crops--penalizing everybody a little in order to help the hard-hit farm population. (With cotton the method was different: the crop having already been planted, rewards were offered for plowing up part of it.) The complicated business of administering this Act was entrusted to an Agricultural Adjustment Administration--AAA for short.

The promise of the AAA program, along with the promise of inflation, lifted farm prices sharply in the spring of 1933, and thus brought early and substantial relief to the farmers; the effect of the AAA after it went into full operation in 1934 was more debatable, and was obscured anyhow by subsequent droughts.

3. Stimulating Employment.

Roosevelt's pet scheme for putting a quarter of a million young men into the woods for conservation work was quickly approved by Congress, and presently the young men of the CCC were off to army camps and then to the forests. There was also passed a bill providing $3,300,000,000 for public works--a staggering sum by Hoover standards. (Roosevelt's heart was not in the public-works program, it was difficult to spend any large amount of money quickly and yet wisely on dams, bridges, and other major works, and therefore slow progress was made; a good deal of the $3,300,000,000 was diverted into relief and national defense.)

4. Federal Relief.

To aid the unemployed--whose condition was desperate--the Federal government went for the first time on a large scale into the distribution of relief funds. These, in the early months of the New Deal, were mostly dispensed through state and local machinery; but the new assumption of responsibility was nevertheless significant.

5. The Tennessee Valley Experiment.

Not only did a bill passed in May, 1933, provide for the Federal operation of that subject of long previous argument, the dam at Muscle Shoals; it provided also for an ambitious development of the whole Tennessee Valley through the building of other Federal dams, through the sale of power from them at low prices, and through Federal subsidizing of conservation measures in the Valley. This bill--which went considerably beyond Roosevelt's campaign proposals--was perhaps the most revolutionary measure of the early New Deal in its long-term significance, for it put the government directly into industry and into a dominating position in developing a whole section of the country.

6. Lightening the Debt Burden.

Federal agencies were set up to refinance farm and home mortgages, lowering the interest rate on them and putting a Federal guarantee behind them, thus easing the back-breaking pressure of debt on farmers and other householders--and, incidentally, further freezing the debt-structure of the country.

7. Financial Reforms.

A Securities Act was passed which provided that those who issued securities must provide the government with full--in fact voluminous--information about the enterprises to be financed. And a banking act was passed which, though it did not grapple with the knotty problem of unifying the banking system of the country, struck at certain conspicuous abuses: it provided that no banking house might both accept deposits and issue securities, and it forbade commercial banks to have securities affiliates. (These reforms were the forerunners of others to come.)

Last in our list, but far from least, there was set up

106

8. The NRA.

The genesis and motivation of the NRA provide a beautiful example of the wild confusion of those honeymoon days of the New Deal, and deserve special mention. The NRA's paternity was multiple, to say the least.

Soon after the bank holiday Senator Hugo Black (of subsequent Supreme Court fame) pushed through the Senate a bill decreeing a thirty-hour week in all businesses engaged in interstate commerce; and although the measure was held up by a motion to reconsider, the size of the Senate vote and the fact that the House was giving a favorable reception to a similar measure (the Connery Bill), showed that Congress meant business. (Here was NRA idea No. 1: spread employment by shortening hours of labor.) Thereupon Secretary of Labor Frances Perkins insisted any such bill must contain a minimum-wage provision. (Here was idea No. 2: "put a floor under wages.") By this time the President and various members of his Administration had become worried over the possibility that wholesale and inflexible legislation on hours and wages might prove a Pandora's box of troubles, and had begun to wrestle with ideas for a more flexible and comprehensive Administration measure, which could be substituted somewhat as the discretionary inflation bill had been substituted for the Wheeler Bill.

A number of business men also swung into action. For a long time the Chamber of Commerce of the United States had been opposing what it called "cut-throat competition" and had wanted the Sherman Anti-Trust Act modified so that trade associations might set wages and adopt "codes of practice" with governmental permission. Hoover had flatly opposed any such scheme as monopolistic--as allowing established companies to combine to prevent, not only "cutthroat competition," but all real competition of any sort. Roosevelt seemed to have no such fears--and the business men saw their opportunity. (Thus arose idea No. 3: "self-government for business," with the trade associations doing the governing under government auspices.)

Meanwhile there was also much enthusiasm among the young liberals in Washington for the idea of "national planning" for industry.

Impressed by the Russian Five-Year Plan, they wanted the government to regulate the functioning of the helter-skelter American business system. (Here was idea No. 4.) There was a widespread hope, too, chiefly among these same liberals, that purchasing power might be expanded by a concerted raising of wages--on the theory that if the raising were general no business would suffer and all would benefit. (Idea No. 5.)

Each of these ideas was represented in the framing of the National Industrial Recovery Act.

After numerous conferences of various groups of men of diverse economic philosophies, there emerged as the principal artificer of the project a man whose own central interest was in the Chamber of Commerce idea: a former Army officer, former plow manufacturer, and protégé of Bernard Baruch named General Hugh S. Johnson, who had worked in the Brain Trust group during the campaign and now had a desk in the office of Raymond Moley, the new Assistant Secretary of State. And there emerged a bill which provided that each industry, through its trade association, would write for itself a "code" prescribing maximum hours and minimum wages and rules of fair competition for that industry, subject to the approval of the government. What was thus prescribed and approved might be done regardless of the Sherman Act, and in fact might not be transgressed under penalty of the law. Since the men who were thus to be allowed to organize and write their own codes were the employers, the Department of Labor insisted that their employees should also be permitted to organize; and so was written into the National Industrial Recovery Act the famous Section 7a, which stated that "employees shall have the right to organize and bargain collectively through representatives of their own choosing, and shall be free from the interference, coercion, or restraint of employers of labor or their agents." For further protection for labor and for consumers there were elaborate provisions for setting up Labor Advisory Boards and Consumers' Advisory Boards, to make sure that every interest was consulted.

On June 16, 1933, the National Industrial Recovery Act was signed amid much fanfare. Said President Roosevelt, "History probably will record the National Industrial Recovery Act as the most important and far-reaching legislation ever enacted by the American Congress." On that same day General Johnson was named Administrator of the NRA. And it became obvious that this unprecedented organization was to be the focal point of the whole New Deal program of 1933.

Having produced the NRA, Congress adjourned, bringing to an end what was indeed an extraordinary session.

§ 5

The contrasts between this 1933 New Deal program and the Hoover program were sharp. It was not a program of defense but of multiple and headlong attack. In most of the laws and certainly in the intent behind them there was a new emphasis on the welfare of the common man; a new attempt, as was often said, to build prosperity from the bottom up rather than from the top down. There was a new willingness to expand the scope of government operations; for a long time past these had been expanding out of sheer political and economic necessity, as the inevitable long-term tendency toward centralization took effect upon government as well as upon business, but now the brakes were removed and the expansion was abrupt. Also in contrast was the visible distrust by Roosevelt of the bankers and corporate insiders of Wall Street; Hoover had leaned upon them for advice and assistance (which was not always forthcoming), Roosevelt disregarded them. He preferred the assistance of supposedly impartial (if impractical) professors to that of supposedly practical (if partial) business men. There was a new encouragement of labor unions, a new hospitality to liberal and radical ideas which would reduce the power of the owning class. The governmental center of gravity had moved to the left.

At the same time the program represented a strange jumble of theories. For example, the Economy Act--and to a certain extent the financial reform measures--had a deflationary effect; whereas devaluation--and to a certain extent the public-works plan and the Federal relief plan--had an inflationary effect. The AAA bill tried to bring recovery by inducing scarcity--as did much of the NRA as it later developed; whereas the public-works and TVA plans operated on the abundance theory. The conferences with foreign emissaries and the plans for international economic cooperation ran head on into the devaluation policy--with a resounding explosion in London. The financial reform measures sought to discourage concentrations of economic power; the NRA--in practice--tended to encourage them.

In addition to these conflicts of theory, there were numerous collisions between governmental organizations trying to do the same thing, between organizations trying to do opposite things, between old policies being pursued as a matter of habit and new ones being introduced.

Some of these conflicts were due, of course, to the sheer impossibility of achieving legislative and administrative perfection at a hand gallop. Some were due to the fact that Washington was full of able and eager men with contrasting ideas: in a multitude of counselors there is confusion. Some were due to the political necessity of devising measures which could win the support of diverse interests. And some were due to the fact that the New Deal program of those first few months was like a geological formation built up in several layers. At the bottom were the old-fashioned liberal measures, the economy and reform measures, of the 1932 platform. On top of these were the more ambitious programs adumbrated by the Brain Trust during the campaign and after, and other measures hustled into action when the bank panic produced a much graver crisis than had been foreseen in early 1932. Then there were the measures which grew, perforce, out of the bank panic itself--including, if you wish, devaluation. On top were the bright ideas that bloomed in the fertile spring of 1933; chief among these was the NRA, which was a whole plum pudding of contrasting elements in itself. Yet even if one took account of all these reasons for inconsistency, there remained something in Roosevelt's try-everything attitude which reminded one of the man who, feeling unwell, took in quick succession all the tonics on the shelf.

But if the President preferred bold action to careful deliberation, so too did the country. The sickness of the economic system was infinitely complicated and little understood. Now a physician had come along who had a lot of medicines in his bag, who had an air of authority and an agreeable bedside manner; and the American people hailed him with delight. His medicines were better than most which were currently suggested, and certainly the patient's morale was improved by having a friendly physician who was willing to do something and not just wait for nature to effect a cure. In the spring and summer of 1933 the American economic system took its new medicines cheerfully, sat up in bed, and said, "I feel better already."

§ 6

What a flood tide of returning hope was running in those first six months of the New Deal!

That was the season when the Chicago Fair opened--that Fair whose intention to chronicle "A Century of Progress" had seemed only a few months before so unmitigatedly ironical. What did Chicagoans care if Sally Rand stole the show with her fan dance? She too had been a victim of the Depression, earning a precarious living dancing in smalltime cabarets in Western cities, and her fortunes had sunk low in 1932; in her own reported words, she had "never made any money until she took off her pants"; but now the crowds surged to see her come down the velvet-covered steps with her waving fans (and apparently nothing else) before her, and Chicago profited. General Balbo's armada of Italian airplanes flew to the fair; and in that same summer of 1933 Charles and Anne Lindbergh, leaving behind them for a time the scenes of their tragedy, flew to Greenland, to proceed thence to Europe and Africa and--*Listen! The Wind*--toSouth America.

That was the season when the Senate Banking Committee drew from the Morgan partners the story of the "preferred lists" of subscribers to the stock of their corporations; and when the orderly processes of financial exemplification were interrupted, to everybody's dismay, by a circus promoter who placed a midget in J. P. Morgan's lap. It was the season when the country first became wonderingly aware of the extent to which the amiable First Lady of the land embodied the law of perpetual motion; and when her husband, after putting his name to the National Industrial Recovery Act, climbed aboard the

111

little *Amberjack II,* put on his oilskins, and went sailing up the New England coast to Campobello.

That was the season when Max Baer knocked out Schmeling in the tenth, and the massive Primo Camera knocked out champion Jack Sharkey in the sixth, and an unidentified man almost knocked out Huey Long in the Sands Point washroom, and Glenn Cunningham began breaking the running records for the mile, and *Anthony Adverse* began breaking records for fiction sales as it enthralled lovers of vicarious adventure on thousands of summer porches.

Once more the business men of the country began to know hope. The Federal Reserve Board's adjusted index figure for Industrial Production in the bank-holiday month of March, 1933, had been 59 (as against 58 for the preceding July, the month of the Bonus March). In April it jumped from 59 to 66; in May it jumped to 78; in June, to 91; in July, to 100 (as against a 1929 high of 125). There was no such proportionate gain in employment, to be sure; for as the pace of business increased, there was much slack to be taken up simply by working factories full time that had been working part time, by working office clerks overtime, by keeping shopgirls on the run. Still there remained millions of unemployed men, whose poverty was as yet unrelieved by any Federal expenditures for their aid. So greatly had the Depression stimulated working efficiency and the installation of labor-saving devices that a far sharper increase in production than this would be needed to give jobs to those men. Nor were the men who went back to work any too tractable. They had suffered, they had become embittered, and as hope returned, anger rose with it: strikes began to increase in number. The mood of the farm population was still rebellious, for until their crops were harvested the rise in farm prices would do them little good; the speculators would get the money. There were still riots and disorders in the farm belt. But the prospects were promising. "Give us just a few months more of this improvement . . ." men said to themselves.

The speculators leaped into action. As the stock market spurted, out of the highways and byways came the little stock gamblers. For three and a half years they had been telling themselves--if they had any money left--that speculation was no more for them. During the past few months they had been in the grip, most of them, of a mounting distrust of Wall Street bankers in particular and all bankers in general, and had been telling and re-telling derisive anecdotes in which bankers figured. But when they began to see the plus signs among the stock quotations, back to the brokers' offices they thronged, ready to stake their last savings on Commercial Solvents and Standard Brands and the alcohol stocks; and meanwhile as cold-blooded a lot of pool operators as had ever been seen in the unregenerate days of 1929 manipulated and unloaded, manipulated and unloaded. The Securities Act had been signed, reform was the order of the New Deal day, one might have expected these gentry to be newly cautious; but all such considerations apparently meant nothing to them. So violently did the stock market boil, so frequently were there five- and six-million-share days, that the total volume of trading in the month of June, 1933, and again in the month of July, 1933, was greater than it had been in any single month in the Big Bull Market of 1929--with the sole exception of the Panic month of October. Meanwhile the grain market and the other commodity markets boiled too. Who could lose? argued the little speculators. "If we don't have prosperity we'll at least have inflation." (In 1932 the thought of inflation had prompted selling, now it prompted buying: the mood had changed.)

Late in July the stock and commodity markets broke badly, and day after day the speculators' favorites tumbled; one of these favorites, American Commercial Alcohol, actually collapsed from 89 $^7/_8$ to 29 $^1/_8$ in four days. But at that very moment the President was having distributed to business men all over the country the blanket NRA code that would "start the wheels turning." It was difficult to find a daily paper which did not contain somebody's glowing tribute to the NRA. It had "abolished child labor," it was introducing "a new era of co-operation between industry and government," it was "an attempt to substitute constructive co-operation for destructive competition," it would cause "management and labor to join hands," it would "end the flat-wallet era," and it held out "the promise of a new day." The break in the markets checked confidence a bit; but was it not predicted that millions of men would go back to work "before the snow flies"?

In Washington the excitement was still feverish. Congress had adjourned, but now the business men were there by the bewildered thousands to draw up NRA codes. Up and down the interminable corridors of the Commerce Building they tramped, buttonholing any hatless man to ask their way, under the impression that he must be a high official. They wanted their own codes, industry by industry, and each of them had his own idea of what ought to go into his code to stop the particular kind of "cut-throat competition" that his company hated. But first these men had to find out what industry they belonged to. Was candlewick-bedspread-making a part of the cotton-textile industry, or should it have a code of its own? Shouldn't the dog-food industry insist on special treatment? And where should the academic costume men go to solve their code problems? And the fly-swatter manufacturers? Where was General Johnson's office? And who was this "Robbie" whose ear it was considered so valuable to get? And might it not be better to go back to the Mayflower and confer there, even though the hotel telephone service was so jammed that you couldn't get a connection?

In the center of this wild confusion--as Jonathan Mitchell wrote--General Johnson "sat at ease, coat off, blue shirt open at the neck, red-faced, and looking uncannily like Captain Stagg in Stallings and Anderson's 'What Price Glory.' Like captured peasants, squads of sweating business men . . . were led in before him." Part cavalry officer, part veteran business man, part economic seer, part government administrator (he could assume any of these roles at will, said Mitchell), the General coaxed or prophesied or wisecracked or thundered as the occasion seemed to warrant, and the business men would go forth obediently--or so they felt at the moment--to do his bidding. So completely did the General captivate the Washington newspaper men that they began to regard the NRA as the center of the government exhibit and the White House as a side show. His vehement oratory, his references to "cracking down on the chiselers" and to the "dead cats" of criticism, his torrential enthusiasm, held the country spellbound. General Johnson had become the personification of Recovery.

HE CAPTURED THE HEADLINES

Pictures, Inc.

General Hugh S. Johnson, head of the NRA, who during the latter part of 1933 was (with the possible exception of the President) the most publicized citizen of America

When you went to the movies to see "Cavalcade" (that life-preserver with TITANIC on it!), or "Mädchen in Uniform," or "Reunion in Vienna," you would see also a short picture, accompanied by a voice thrilling with patriotism, telling how America was marching on to prosperity under the slogan "We do our part." The Blue Eagle appeared in shop windows, in advertisements. There were splendid NRA parades, with thousands marching and airplanes droning overhead. Grover Whalen organized a New York compliance campaign enlivened by the appearance of Miss Nira (short for National Industrial Recovery Act) and Miss Liberty; 150 women from the Bronx marched to NRA headquarters bearing 250,000 pledges and accompanied by a brass band; it was estimated that a quarter of a million people marched in New York and a million and a half looked on, and it cost $4,980.70 to clean up the streets afterwards.

Yes, America was on its way. Though the stock market looked ragged as the summer came to an end, and the business indices had slipped back from the pinnacle of July, and doubts and disagreements were beginning to cloud the brightness of the economic and political skies, still the prevailing mood of the general public was aptly reflected in the song of the three little pigs in Disney's new picture, then going the rounds of the movie houses: America had learned to sing "Who's Afraid of the Big Bad Wolf?"

Chapter Six

A CHANGE OF CLIMATE

§ 1

The processes of social change are continuous and endlessly complex. To contrast the manners and morals and customs of one historical "period" with those of another is surely to over-simplify and almost surely to exaggerate. Yet the social climate does alter, just as the seasons do change--even though the shifts in temperature from day to day may be highly spasmodic and Detroit may be enjoying its "first day of spring" while Philadelphia is being swept by a blizzard. Looking back, one notices various contrasts between the social climate of the nineteen-twenties and that of the nineteen-thirties; and one notices, too, that most of these changes did not become clearly marked until about the year 1933, when the New Deal came in and the Eighteenth Amendment was repealed. It is almost as if the people of the United States had walked backward into the Depression, holding for dear life to the customs and ideals and assumptions of the time that was gone, even while these were one by one slipping out of reach; and then, in 1933, had given up their vain effort, turned about, and walked face-forward into the new world of the nineteen-thirties.

The post-war decade had brought to America a sharp revolution in manners and morals--a revolution the shock troops of which were a younger generation addicted to knee-length skirts, hip flasks, mixed drinking in the speakeasy, petting in the parked car, uninhibited language, a secondhand knowledge of Freudian complexes, and a disposition to defy their more puritanical parents and ridicule the whole Puritan tradition. Already by the end of the nineteen-twenties the revolution was playing itself out, at least in the centers of population where Puritanism had been most readily undermined. The older generation were gradually becoming accustomed to the outlandish ways of their progeny and relaxing somewhat their own codes of conduct, and the younger generation were getting older and learning the practical advantages of moderation. By the time of the Panic, the "Flaming Mamie" of the coeducational campus, though she still won admirers, was a little less likely to be regarded as a portent of the future than as a relic of the past. As the nineteen-thirties got under way, the change in the climate became clearly discernible.

Not that there was any measurable increase in abstinence, continence, or modesty; indeed there were some areas--some Middle-Western towns, many country villages--where the proprieties of an earlier day had been only slowly broken down and the sound of breakage was still loud; where the behavior of the "young married set" at the Saturday night rout at the local country club was more abandoned than ever, and where parents were comparing horrified notes about that appalling "new" phenomenon, the tendency of girls of fifteen and sixteen to come back from high-school parties smelling of gin and disturbingly rumpled. Said the Lynds of their findings in "Middletown," ". . . one got in 1935 a sense of sharp, free behavior between the sexes (patterned on the movies), and of less disguise among the young. A high-school graduate of eight years ago, now in close touch professionally with the young people of the city, was emphatic as regards the change: 'They've been getting more and more knowing and bold. The fellows regard necking as a taken-for-granted part of a date. We fellows used occasionally to get slapped for doing things, but the girls don't do that much any more.'"

Yet in the country at large there was a change of mood, a change of emphasis. The revolution was being consolidated. The shock troops were digging in in the positions they had won.

Otto F. Hess

THE BIG APPLE
Taken at Glen Island Casino, New Rochelle, N. Y., 1938

A neat measure of this change was offered in Hornell Hart's study of social attitudes in *Recent Social Trends,* which appeared at the beginning of 1933. Mr. Hart set forth the results of a careful statistical study of the beliefs and points of view reflected in the magazines of the country at various times. This study showed that the rebellion against the traditional code of sex morals--or, to put it another way, the rush of sentiment in favor of sex freedom--had reached its peak in the years 1923-1927; and although the magazines contained more discussions of family and sex problems during 1930 and 1931 than at any time during the preceding years, the tone was on the whole more conservative. In the year 1930 the magazines expressed more approval of marriage and family life, more approval of "comradeship, understanding, affection, sympathy, facilitation, accommodation, integration, cooperation" than in 1920.

If the change of mood became more striking as the years rolled by and the Depression deepened, one may ascribe this to a number of causes: the fact that any idea palls after a time, any bright new revolution begets doubts and questionings; the fact that young Mr. X, whose alcoholic and amorous verve had seemed so brilliantly daring in 1925, was now beginning to show not altogether attractive signs of wear and tear; the fact that Mrs. Y, who had so stoutly believed in her right to sleep where she pleased and had been sure that she didn't care with whom Mr. Y slept, had found she couldn't take it after all and had marched off to Reno; the fact that the Z children were having nightmares which the school psychiatrist attributed to the broken home from which they came; and the fact that the younger brothers and sisters of the X's and Y's and Z's were tired of seeing their elders carom against the furniture and make passes at one another, and concluded that these old people were a messy lot. But the most important reason for the change was probably the Depression.

Hundreds of thousands of young people who wanted to get married could not afford to. The song "I Can't Give You Anything But Love, Baby" dated from 1928, but it might well have been the theme-song of the nineteen-thirties. The marriage rate per thousand population fell from 10.14 in 1929 to 7.87 in 1932. (Likewise the birth rate per thousand population also fell, from 18.9 in 1929 to 17.4 in 1932 and 16.5 in 1933--the 1933 figure reflecting, of course, largely the economic conditions of 1932.) When it was so difficult to marry, an increase in pre-marital sex relations was almost inevitable. "A confidential check-up of one group of more than two dozen young business-class persons in their twenties," reported the Lynds, "showed seven out of every ten of them, evenly balanced as to sex, to have had sexual relations prior to marriage." The huge sales of contraceptives--totaling, annually, according to various authorities, from an eighth to a quarter of a billion dollars, and transacted not only in drugstores but in filling stations, tobacco stores, and all sorts of other establishments--were certainly not made only to the married.

Yet the new state of affairs was hardly conducive to a frivolous or cynical attitude toward marriage and the family; and it pushed into the forefront of attention a relatively new problem: what was to be the future of the jobless young man and his girl, who loved each other deeply and really wanted to marry? Were they to postpone marriage and live resolutely apart? Or prevail upon their families to support them, perhaps letting them live in the spare room or the attic or some other corner of a parental home?

Often the elders could ill afford to feed another mouth; and many a father who had slaved and scrimped for years, dreaming of retirement, and who now wondered how long his own job would last, blazed with anger to hear that young Harry had brought home a bride to consume the family savings. There were other elders who could well afford to shelter a young couple but who had been brought up to believe that no self-respecting young man married until he could support a wife, and who would cling to this idea, talk about a spoiled generation, tell how *they* hadn't *thought* of marrying till they were making forty dollars a week, and refuse to countenance any such nonsense. As a result, many young couples accepted as an alternative to immediate marriage an occasional night in a cheap hotel room or an auto-tourist cabin (many of these tourist cabins accepted, knowingly or innocently, a large proportion of local traffic). Hating the furtiveness of such meetings, hating the conventions which made them furtive, these young couples nevertheless felt their behavior was right--a response to necessity.

To many others, even less fortunate, the jobless children of jobless parents, the wandering nomads of the Depression, hitch-hiking through the country, riding the freight cars, sex became something that you took when you could; marriage was too remote to think about. Yet even here there was something new about the mood. There was little sense of a change in the moral code being willfully made, little sense

121

that stolen love was "modern" adventure. The dilemma was practical. One managed as best one could, was continent or incontinent according to one's individual need and one's individual code, whether of morals or aesthetics or prudence or convenience. If the conventions were in abeyance, it was simply because the times were out of joint and no longer made sense; but that did not mean that one might not long for wedded security.

Among the hatless and waistcoatless young men of the college campuses, with their tweed coats and flannel slacks, and among the college girls in their sweaters and tweed skirts and ankle socks, there was little of the rebellious talk about sex and marriage that had characterized the nineteen-twenties, little of the buzz of excitement that had accompanied the discussion of Freud and Havelock Ellis and Dora Russell. Whether there was less actual promiscuity is doubtful: a study of 1364 juniors and seniors in 46 colleges and universities of all types from coast to coast--made by Dorothy Dunbar Bromley and Florence Haxton Britten--showed that half the young men and a quarter of the girls had had pre-marital sex intercourse. The striking thing was that there was less to-do about sex. One's personal affairs were one's personal affair. As the editors of *Fortune* said in their account of the college youth of 1936: "As for sex, it is, of course, still with us. But the campus takes it more casually than it did ten years ago. Sex is no longer news. And the fact that it is no longer news is news."

The Depression also cut the divorce rate sharply: it dropped from 1.66 per thousand population in 1929 to only 1.28 per thousand population in 1932. Divorces cost money; and besides, in times of stress the fancy is likely to be less free. There was a good deal of pious talk about the way in which couples were re-united in love by hardship, but it is likely that in most cases what the hardship did was to subordinate everything to the stark necessity for getting along, love or no love. After the worst years the divorce rate rose again; no great reform had been effected; people who couldn't get on still separated when they must and could. Yet here again there was a change in emphasis: a more widespread sense of the damage inevitably done by a wrecked marriage to the children and to the separated partners themselves. It was perhaps significant that a public-opinion poll taken by *Fortune* in 1937 showed a majority against easy divorce. A similar poll in 1936 showed 63 per cent in favor of the teaching and practice of birth control, and in 1937 as many as 22.3 per cent approved of pre-marital experience *for both men and women:* there was no return to the old Puritan code. Yet there was a strong disposition to protect going marriages.

In short, although there was considerable public acceptance of pre-marital sex relations as inevitable and not sinful, and a tendency to approve of what one observer had called "a single standard, and that a low one," nevertheless marriage seemed to have become more highly prized as an institution than in the nineteen-twenties. The family seemed to have become more highly prized as an institution. "Sixty per cent of the college girls and fifty per cent of the men would like to get married within a year or two of graduation, and fifty per cent of each sex would like to have children soon after marriage," reported the editors of *Fortune* in their 1936 survey. The fact that the college girls of the nineteen-thirties were more eager for early marriage than those of the nineteen-twenties was noted by many college administrators. These same undergraduates and their contemporaries were on the whole less scornful of their parents and of parental ideas, less likely to feel that family life was a mockery, than the young people of ten years before.

Not only had the Depression made them more respectful of a meal ticket and of security; they had become preoccupied with other things besides intimate personal relationships, as we shall presently see.

§ 2

The vagaries of fashion are so haphazard and are influenced by so many business expediencies that one cannot ascribe them wholly to changes in the social climate. Yet in their main outlines they at least provide suggestions worth correlating with other evidences of the social trend.

123

If, for example, the women's fashions of the nineteen- twenties called for short skirts, a great reduction in the weight and cumbersomeness of clothes, a long-waisted, flat-fronted figure, and short hair cut in a Dutch bob or shingled almost like a boy's, surely here was a hint that women had become tired of the restrictions and responsibilities of conventional maturity and wanted a freedom and gaiety that they associated with immaturity: not the freedom of an old-fashioned little girl, sheltered and innocently pretty, but of an aggressively "modern" one--hard-boiled, "sophisticated" (to use a favorite complimentary term of that day), and ready to carry on with the boys. If the mannikins in the shop-windows and the sketches in the department-store advertisements gave the well-dressed woman a hard, blank, world-weary expression, here again was a hint as to the feminine ideal of the nineteen-twenties: she was a girl who, even before her figure had ripened, had become old in experience, had passed beyond the possibility of shock or enduring enthusiasm. And if, during the early years of that decade, the tail coat was a rarity among men and the dinner jacket was the standard wear even for the most formal occasions, here was a hint that the men, as well as the women, were in revolt against dignity and formality. In the nineteen-twenties, Americans wanted to be boys and girls together, equipped for a wild party but refusing to let it be thought that even the wildest party would arouse in them more than a fleeting excitement.

Now notice what happened later. Already before the end of the nineteen-twenties the tail coat was coming in again, with all the dignity that it conveyed. By 1929 the women's evening dresses were tentatively reaching for the floor--and for an effect of graciousness impossible to achieve with a knee-length gown. By 1930 they definitely were long--to remain thus, actually or virtually sweeping the floor, for the rest of the decade. And the women's daytime dresses gradually lengthened too until by 1933 they reached to within a foot or even nine inches of the ground. The severe helmet hat of 1929, pulled down on the back of the head, gave way to a variety of styles all of which sought at prettiness, pertness, a gentler or more whimsical effect than had been aimed at in the 'twenties. Women's hair, too, became less severe, was curled at the back of the head more gaily. Ruffles came in, bows, furbelows, with nostalgic hints of the prettiments of long-dead days. Gone was the little-girl long-waisted effect; the waist returned where it belonged.

124

As for the flat figure, that was abandoned too. Said *Vogue* in April, 1932, "Spring styles say 'CURVES'!" By 1933, when the amply contoured Mae West was packing the motion-picture theatres in "She Done Him Wrong," Lily of France was advertising "the new boneless Duo-Sette," saying, "It beautifully emphasizes the uplift bust," and Formfit, illustrating a new creation with pictures of young women whose breasts were separately and sharply conspicuous, was calling attention to "the youthful, pointed, uplifted lines it will give you." The flat-breasted little girl of the nineteen-twenties had attained maturity and was proud of it; indeed so striking was the change between the ideal figure of 1929 and that of 1933 that one might almost have thought a new anatomical species had come into being.

There was a subtle change, too, in the approved type of femininity as represented in the department-store advertisements and the shop-window mannikins. The new type of the early nineteen-thirties was alert-looking rather than bored-looking. She had a pert, uptilted nose and an agreeably intelligent expression; she appeared alive to what was going on about her, ready to make an effort to give the company a good time. She conveyed a sense of competence. This was the sort of girl who might be able to go out and get a job, help shoulder the family responsibilities when her father's or husband's income stopped; who would remind them, in her hours of ease, of the good old days before there were all-determining booms and depressions, the sentimental old days which Repeal itself reminded them of; and who would look, not hard, demanding, difficult to move deeply, but piquantly pretty, gentle, amenable, thus restoring their shaken masculine pride.

Nothing stands still, and as the years went on new changes took place. So many more women of the upper and middle classes were working now than had worked in the pre-Depression years that in their daytime costumes simplicity and practicality were in demand. The prevailing style of hairdress for younger women (a shoulder-length or almost shoulder-length page-boy or curled bob) was likewise simple--and incidentally very lovely: in years to come it may be that one of the most charming recollections of the nineteen-thirties will be of hatless girls striding along like young blond goddesses, their hair tossing behind them. (One recalls the complaint of a young man that almost every girl appeared good-looking from behind: it was only when he overtook her that disillusionment came.) When in the fall of

1938 an attempt was made to get women to put their short hair up, it only half-succeeded: it was too hard to manage.

Yet the impulse toward old-fashioned decoration, frivolity, and impractical eccentricity was all the time at work. There were attempts to re-introduce, in evening dresses, such ancient encumbrances as the bustle and the hoop skirt. Ruffled and pleated shirtwaists--with jabots--reappeared. The sandal idea, winning a rational approval for evening wear, was carried over irrationally into daytime wear, so that during the latter years of the decade half the younger women in the country were equipped with shoes with a small hole in front, which presented a stockinged toe to the eye and offered easy entrance to dust, gravel, and snow. As for the hats of those same latter years, here the modern principle of standardized functional utility surrendered utterly to the modern principle of surrealist oddity.

There were huge hats, tiny hats, hats with vast brims and microscopic crowns, hats which were not hats at all but wreaths about the hair; high fezzes perched atop the head; flat hats, dinner-plate size, which apparently had been thrown at the wearer from somewhere out in front and had been lashed where they landed with a sort of halter about the back of the head; straw birds' nests full of spring flowers, hats with a single long feather pointing anywhere--but why continue the interminable catalogue of variations? It was characteristic of the times that a woman lunching at a New York tearoom in 1938 took the bread-basket off the table, inverted it on her head, and attracted no attention whatever.

Maturity, too, began to pall. Gradually the skirts became shorter and shorter (except in the evening); by 1939 they had retreated almost to the knees. "Little-girl" costumes, "girlish ginghams," "swing" outfits "adapted from skating skirts" were bidding for attention, and the massive president of the woman's club was wondering whether she should try to insert herself into a bolero suit and put one of those bows in her hair. Apparently the old-fashioned little girl was becoming the standard type of the new day--unless the fashion makers should succeed in their attempt, late in 1939, to make her a grown-up old-fashioned woman (at least after nightfall), with a bustle, a wasp waist, and a boned corset startlingly like that in which her grandmother had suffered. Whether the new fashions would last or not, and just what they signified, it was still too early to predict.

§ 3

At thirty-two and a half minutes past three (Mountain Time) in the afternoon of the 5th of December, 1933, the roll call in the ratification convention in Utah was completed, and Utah became the 36th State to ratify the Twenty-first Amendment to the Constitution, repealing the Prohibition Amendment. A telegram went off to Washington, and presently the Acting Secretary of State and the President declared that Prohibition was at an end, after a reign of nearly fourteen years.

Crowds of men and women thronged the hotels and restaurants waiting for the word to come through that the lid was off, and when at last it did, drank happily to the new era of legal liquor. They thronged, too, to those urban speakeasies which had succeeded in getting licenses, and remarked how readily the front door swung open wide at the touch of the doorbell. But the celebration of the coming of Repeal was no riot, if only because in most places the supply of liquor was speedily exhausted: it took time for the processes of distribution to get into motion. And as for the processes of legal manufacture--which for distilled liquors are supposed to include a long period of aging-- these were so unready that an anomalous situation developed. The available liquor was mostly in the hands of bootleggers; even the legal liquor was mostly immature. Among the people who, during the first days and months of repeal, rejoiced in at last being able to take a respectable drink of "good liquor" instead of depending upon "this bootleg stuff," thousands were consuming whisky which consisted simply of alcohol acceptably tinted and flavored. To a public whose taste had been conditioned for years by bootleg liquor, good bush needed no wine.

Drinking, to be sure, did not become legal everywhere. Eight States remained dry--all of them Southern except North Dakota, Kansas, and Oklahoma. (These states received--at least in the years immediately following repeal--very little assistance from the Federal government in protecting their aridity.) Fifteen States made the selling of liquor a State monopoly--though seven of these permitted private sale under varying regulations, most of which, in a determined effort to prevent "the return of the saloon," forbade perpendicular drinking and insisted--at least for a time--that drinkers be seated at restaurant tables.

Despite these qualifications, the change in the American *mores* which began in 1933 was tremendous.

Hotels and restaurants blossomed with cocktail lounges and taprooms and bars, replete with chromium fittings, mirrors, bright-colored modern furniture, Venetian blinds, bartenders taken over from the speakeasies, and bartenders who for years had been serving at the oyster bar or waiting on table, and now, restored to their youthful occupation, persuaded the management to put on the wine list such half-forgotten triumphs of their ancient skill as Bronx and Jack Rose cocktails. So little building had been going on during the Depression that the architects and decorators had had almost no chance for years to try out the new principles of functional design and bright color and simplified furniture; now at last they had it, in the designing of cocktail lounges--with the odd result that throughout the nineteen-thirties most Americans instinctively associated modernist decoration with eating and drinking.

Hotels in cities which in days gone by would have frowned upon the very notion of a night club now somewhat hesitantly opened night clubs with floor shows--and found they were a howling success. Neat new liquor stores opened--in some States operated by government authority, in others under private ownership. It took some time for customers to realize that it was no longer necessary for a man carrying home a package of rum to act the part of a man carrying home a shoe box; and in some towns where the dry sentiment was still strong, there were men who continued to patronize bootleggers rather than subject themselves to the embarrassment of walking into the State liquor shop.

Restaurants which in pre-prohibition days would never have dreamed of selling liquor installed bars and made prodigious sales; the

128

tearoom proprietor wrestled with her conscience and applied for a license; and even the Childs' restaurants, unmindful of their traditional consecration to dairy products, pancakes, and calories, opened up slick circular bars and sold Manhattans and old-fashioneds. And if most of the metropolitan speakeasies withered and died, if the speakeasy tickets grew dog-eared in the pocketbook of the man-about-town and at last were thrown away, if the hip flask became a rarity, if the making of bathtub gin became a lost art in metropolitan apartment houses, and the business executive no longer sallied forth to the trade convention with two bottles of Scotch in his golf bag, so many bright new bars appeared along the city streets that drinking seemed to have become not only respectable but ubiquitous.

For a time there was a wishful thought among those of gentle tastes that when good wines became more accessible a good many Americans would acquire fastidious palates. G. Selmer Fougner, Julian Street, Frank Schoonmaker, and other experts in the detection and savoring of rare vintages preached their gospel of deference to the right wine of the right year, and for a time ladies and gentlemen felt themselves to be nothing better than boors if they did not warm inwardly to the story of how somebody found a little French inn where the Chateau Latour 1929 was incomparable. But the crass American nature triumphed; pretty soon it was clear that even in the politest circles whisky was going to be the drink in greatest demand.

Whether there was more drinking after repeal than before cannot be determined statistically, owing to the obvious fact that the illicit sale of liquor was not measured. The consensus of opinion would seem to be that drinking pretty surely increased during the first year or two, and probably increased in quantity thereafter, but that on the whole it decreased in stridency.

"Less flamboyant drinking is the present-day rule," said the *Fortune* survey of youth in college in 1936; "there is no prohibition law to defy, hence one can drink in peace." There were signs here and there of a reaction against drinking among the boys and girls of college age; observers reported some of them, at least, to be less interested in alcohol than their elders, and were amazed at the volume of their consumption of Coca-Cola and milk (Coca-Cola, long the standard soft drink of the South, had followed its invasion of the campuses of the Middle West by extending its popularity among the young people in the Northeast as well). The American Institute of Public Opinion, taking a poll in 1936 as to whether conditions were "better" or "worse" since repeal, or showed no significant change, arrived at a singularly inconclusive result: 36 per cent of the voters thought things were better, 33 per cent thought they were worse, 31 per cent saw no significant change: not only was the division almost even, but there was no way of knowing what each voter may have meant in his heart by "conditions" being "better."

One change was manifest: there was now more mixed drinking than ever, just as there was more smoking by both sexes. (In the six years from 1930 to 1936 the production of cigarettes went up from 123 billion to 158 billion, while the production of cigars decreased a little and that of smoking tobacco increased a little.) In fact, a phenomenon which had been conspicuous during the nineteen-twenties, when women smokers invaded the club cars of trains and women drinkers invaded the speakeasies, appeared to be continuing: there were fewer and fewer bars, restaurants, smoking cars, and other haunts set apart for men only: on the whole men and women were spending more of their time in one another's company and less of their time segregated from one another. Perhaps it was not an altogether unrelated fact that most men's clubs were still somewhat anxiously seeking members throughout the nineteen-thirties and that many of the lodges were in dire straits. Was it not possible to infer that the male sex, for one, was enjoying mixed company too well to want very urgently to get away from it? Possibly the cause of feminism was triumphing in a way which the earnest suffragists of a generation before would never have expected--and at which they might have been dismayed.

And what became of the bootleggers? Some of them went into the legitimate liquor business or other legitimate occupations, some of them went into business rackets and gambling rackets, some joined the ranks of the unemployed--and a large number of them went right on bootlegging. For one of the most curious facts about the post-Repeal situation was that the manufacture and smuggling and wholesaling of illicit liquor continued in great volume. The Federal government and the States, in their zeal to acquire revenue from the sale of liquor, had clapped upon it such high taxes that the inducement to dodge them was great. Year after year the Internal Revenue agents continued to seize and destroy stills at the rate of something like 15,000 a year, and straightway new ones sprang up. In his report for the fiscal year ending June 30, 1938, the Commissioner of Internal Revenue, reporting that only 11,407 stills had been seized, noted, "This is the first year since the enactment of the Twenty-first Amendment that there has been a decline in illicit distillery seizures." Likewise rumrunning--or, to be more accurate, the smuggling of alcohol--continued to provide a headache for the customs officers and the Coast Guard; in February, 1935, more than a year after Repeal, the Coast Guard found twenty-two foreign vessels lying at sea *at one time* beyond our customs waters, waiting for a chance to sneak in.

So easy was it to operate illicit stills, to store bottles and counterfeit labels and counterfeit revenue stamps and alcohol cans in separate places, bottle the illicit liquor, transport it in trucks or automobiles equipped with traps, and offer a liquor store or saloonkeeper a consignment of spurious liquor at a bargain, that a year or two after repeal the best expert opinion was that anywhere from fifteen to sixty per cent of the liquor consumed in the United States was bootleg.

Were the American people glad that they had ended Prohibition? Apparently they were. A *Fortune* Quarterly Survey made late in 1937 showed that only 15.1 per cent of the men of the country and 29.7 per cent of the women wanted complete Prohibition back again. Even combining with this dry group those who were in favor of prohibition of hard liquors but would permit the sale of wine and beer, there was still approximately a two-thirds majority in favor of a wet regime. Americans might or might not think "conditions" were "better," but they did not--most of them--want to reopen the question.

Here and there a new wave of dry sentiment appeared to be forming. In Virginia, for instance, a scholarly book on the effects of alcohol, which was to have been distributed to the schools as a public document, came to the shocked attention of the WCTU at the end of 1937. Because the book contained such statements as, "It has been proved that we cannot abolish drinking by legislation nor frighten a person into sobriety" and "small quantities [of alcohol] may favor digestive activities," the WCTU exerted pressure on the legislature and the whole edition was solemnly burned in the Capitol furnace. In most communities, however, what had been a lively issue till 1933 had dropped almost completely out of the focus of general public attention, as if settled once and for all.

Could it really have been true, the men and women of 1939 asked themselves, that in 1929 Prohibition had been the topic of hottest debate in American public life?

§ 4

We come now to a series of changes in everyday American life during the nineteen-thirties which might seem at first glance to have been unrelated, but which combine, perhaps, into a sort of pattern--a pattern of relaxation.

1. *The five-day week.* During 1931 and 1932, when factories and business offices were short of work, there were very general reductions in hours--intended partly to "spread the work" and partly to appease workers whose pay must be reduced. When the NRA codes came into being in 1933 and 1934 these reductions were continued or extended. After the NRA was abolished most of them--though not all--were continued. The result was that millions of people, rich and poor, found themselves with Saturdays free during part of the year if not all of it. A study made by the National Industrial Conference Board in 1937 showed the extent of the five-day week: out of 2,452 companies (mostly manufacturing companies) reporting, 57.3 per cent had a five-day week for their wage earners, 45.3 per cent had a five-day week for their clerical workers, and 7.5 per cent reported a five-day week but did not specify what types of workers were included. "While five years ago the five-day week was exceptional," summarized the report, "it has now become quite general." Business offices followed a similar pattern in the larger cities (especially New York); and although few shops were closed on Saturdays, there was an increasing tendency among them to stagger the hours of their employees.

Perhaps no change that took place during the decade more sharply altered the weekly routine of millions of men and women. It altered the pattern of automobile and train traffic too, increasing the Friday rush out of the cities, decreasing the Saturday rush. I recall a certain train which until the Depression used to leave New York for Westchester County in two crowded sections every Saturday noon; by 1933 it was running in one modest section, so thin was the Saturday traffic--and presently a second section was added to one of the Friday evening trains. The two-day week end was supplanting the day-and-a-half week end. On Saturday mornings, especially in summer, the business districts of the larger cities were coming to wear a Sunday aspect. Quantities of people had gained new leisure--quite apart from those millions upon whom an unwelcome idleness had been thrust. The long slow trend toward shorter work periods and longer play periods, a trend which had been under way in America for as long as any living man could remember, had been sharply accelerated.

2. *A democratization of sport.* To the aid of men and women who had more leisure and less money came the relief and public-works agencies, putting millions of unemployed men to work building motor parkways, public bathing beaches, playgrounds, and other conveniences for people who were looking for sport. According to the 1935 *Year Book of National Recreation* the number of public bathing beaches, public golf courses, ice-skating areas, and swimming pools in 2,204 communities had already *doubled* since 1925. Some of these new facilities were built on a modest scale, but others were huge: Jones Beach on Long Island, for example, as magnificent an example of enlightened public planning as the decade produced, could and did comfortably accommodate one hundred thousand people or more on a sunny Sunday in midsummer.

Consider what happened to the game of golf. The Depression hit the private golf clubs hard. As many as 1,155 clubs had belonged to the United States Golf Association in 1930; by 1936 the number had been reduced to 763--and this despite frantic drives for new members, special summer-membership schemes, and other rescue devices. The golf clubs of the country were said to have lost something like a million members since 1929. But the number of municipal golf courses grew from 184 in 1925 to 576 in 1935, and there were over a thousand courses--most of them probably private-club courses which had gone

133

bankrupt--now operating on a daily-fee basis. In short, expensive golf had lost ground; inexpensive golf had gained.

In general the simpler and less pretentious sports made the best headway. Although school and college basketball, professional baseball, and college football were still preeminent as sports to watch, nevertheless in the older colleges and schools they attracted a somewhat less devout interest than in earlier years. Let the editors of *Fortune* (writing in 1936) summarize one element in the change: "The football star, the crew captain, the 'muscular Christian' from the college Y.M.C.A., the smoothie from the big prep school who becomes track manager, the socially graceful prom leader--these still have honor and respect. But the intellectually curious person, who used to be considered queer or 'wet' unless he had extra-intellectual characteristics to recommend him, is climbing past the conventional big man. Englishmen, long accustomed to spotting future undersecretaries of the Foreign Office . . . on visits to Cambridge and Oxford, have remarked on this mutation in American campus leadership, and are inclined to set 1932 as the date at which the mutation became apparent." Meanwhile there was a significant increase, in many colleges and schools, in the interest taken in *playing* games such as soccer, lacrosse, rugby, squash racquets, and tennis, which existed without benefit of massive stadia.

In the country at large, the game which made the biggest gain in popularity was softball--that small-scale version of baseball which had once been known chiefly as "indoor baseball." Coming into its own at about the beginning of the decade, it grew so fast that by 1939 there were said to be half a million teams and more than five million players of all ages; there were numerous semi-professional teams, there were world's series matches, and among the semi-professionals were girls' teams, the members of which delighted the crowds by wearing very abbreviated shorts but occasionally sliding to bases nonetheless. The Depression also brought minor booms in such sports as bicycling and roller skating. The bicycling boom began as a fad in the Hollywood area in the winter of 1932-33 (when it gave California girls a fine excuse for putting on "trousers like Dietrich's") and spread widely during the next two or three years, chiefly, perhaps, because it was inexpensive.

The simultaneous skiing craze was a more complex phenomenon. For country dwellers who lived where the terrain and winter temperature were suitable it was inexpensive; for city dwellers who had to carry their equipment long distances, it was not. Perhaps one secret of its rise was the increasing vogue of winter holidaying, which itself had a complex ancestry (the discovery of the delights of winter holidaying in the warmth of Florida or California, the rising popularity of winter-cruising and of motoring outside the country to escape from Prohibition, the shortening of the work week, the secularization of Sunday and the rise of the week-end habit, etc.). At any rate the skiing craze grew rapidly during the Depression, stimulated in 1932 by the holding at Lake Placid, New York, of the winter Olympics. The Boston & Maine Railroad had made such a success of the experiment of running Sunday "snow trains" into the comparatively wide open spaces north of Boston that by 1937 snow trains or snow busses were running out of New York, Pittsburgh, Chicago, Portland, San Francisco, and Los Angeles; department stores were importing Norwegian specialists and building ski-slides; the Grand Central Station in New York was posting prominently in its concourse the daily temperature and snow data for a dozen skiing centers in New England and New York, and rural hotelkeepers in icy latitudes were advertising their unequaled skiing facilities and praying nightly throughout the winter for the snowfall upon which their fortunes depended.

The skiing craze was beyond the means of the urban poor and was geographically limited; nevertheless it confirmed in one respect the general trend. More Americans were getting out into the sun and air; learning to play themselves instead of simply paying to see others play.

Women were purchasing strange new play garments, ranging from shorts to beach pajamas, overalls, slacks, and "play suits." More and more men were going hatless in summer, to the anguish of the hatters. For that matter, more and more men were going waistcoatless and soft-collared and garterless and undershirtless; it is said that when Clark Gable, in the undressing scene in "It Happened One Night" (1935), disclosed that he wore no undershirt, the knitwear manufacturers reeled from the shock to their sales. The bathing suit top had been generally discarded. Men at play were even beginning to break out into bright-colored play-shirts, slacks, and shorts. By 1939 one saw

135

men of conservative taste strolling unabashed through summer-resort villages in costumes whose greens and blues and reds would have drawn stares of amazement in 1929.

In short, so far as the tension of the times would permit, Americans were apparently learning to relax.

3. *An increase in bridge playing.* If one superimposes upon a graph of business conditions during the decade a graph showing the taxes collected on playing cards, one notices an odd variation. While the business index was plunging into the depths from 1929 to 1932, the index of playing cards manufactured, after dropping between 1929 and 1930, actually *rose* between 1930 and 1931, only to sag thereafter and never recover to its 1931 point. The year 1931, it will be recalled, was the year when Mr. and Mrs. Ely Culbertson played contract against Sidney S. Lenz and Oswald Jacoby in a green-and-rose drawing-room at the Hotel Chatham in New York, with favored spectators peeking at them through a screen, star reporters clustering in a neighboring room to study the play-by-play bulletins, and direct news wires flashing to an eager public the narrative of some rather indifferent play. Throughout the following year Culbertson's books on bridge ranked high among the best sellers.

For a long time bridge had been a standard after-dinner sport among the adult prosperous; but now its vogue was spreading. The Lynds reported that in "Middletown" there was much more bridge played in 1935 than in 1925; there was more playing for money; the game had reached down through the high school to children in the sixth grade; and it was invading the working class, "spreading there first through the women's groups and then more slowly to a more resistant group of men, who prefer their pinochle and poker."

4. *An increase in gambling.* Allied, perhaps, to the increase in bridge playing was a notable increase in the number of gambling devices made accessible to the American people. Most of these were devices for wagering a small amount of money in the hope of a big return, and their rise may have been due largely to Depression desperation--the wild hope of winning in a gamble what the ordinary processes of the economic system stubbornly withheld. But they bore

witness also to that weakening of the Puritan traditions which helped bring Repeal, the week end of motoring or sport, and the bridge vogue.

According to Samuel Lubell, the business of manufacturing and operating slot machines, punchboards, pinball games, jar deals, and other similar contrivances for separating the public from its nickels grew during the Depression to giant proportions, and in 1939 "its annual take was somewhere between one half and three quarters of a billion dollars--between ten and fifteen billion nickels"--as much money as was spent annually in the shoe stores. There was nothing new in principle about the slot machine, the improved model of which looked like a cash register and was known as a "one-armed bandit": the founder of the leading company engaged in manufacturing them had begun business in 1889 and had died in 1929, a millionaire. Slot machines had had a bad reputation, having been widely in the control of gangs and dependent for operation upon political "fix," yet they continued to flourish widely, sometimes one jump ahead of the police, sometimes with police connivance. And in 1932 a new game, pinball, was introduced which could be played simply for fun, at a nickel a turn, as well as with gambling intent, and it swept the country: pinball boards were to be found in unmolested operation in drugstores, tobacco stores, hotel corridors, cafés, and all sorts of other places. It was based upon the old game of bagatelle: the player shot marbles out of a chute and watched them run down a slope into holes partially protected by pins. The punchboard and jar games--the latter invented in 1933--also prospered; between 1933 and 1939 some two million jar games were sold.

A quite different kind of gamble was represented in the tremendous American participation in the Irish Sweepstakes, a lottery inaugurated in 1930 on behalf of a group of Irish hospitals, and conducted with such honesty and efficiency that within five years it had become the most successful lottery in the world. Although a Federal statute made lottery information unmailable in the United States and this at first prevented newspapers from printing accounts of the Sweeps in their mail editions, the ban on news publication was later relaxed, every Sweeps drawing became a front-page story, and Americans grew used to reading of janitors and unemployed chefs into whose astonished hands a hundred and fifty thousand dollars had dropped. Many of the tickets sold in the United States never reached

Ireland; but if, in the drawing for the 1933 Derby, over six and a half million tickets were in the drum (as was estimated) and 214 of the 2,404 winners (or more than one in fifteen) were American, one may reasonably guess that there may have been over four hundred thousand Americans whose tickets actually got into that particular draw.

Nor should we forget, in any survey of the trend, the relaxation in many States of the laws against race-track betting; the "Bank Night" device of drawing for cash prizes in the movie theatres--a device introduced by Charles Urban Yeager in the Egyptian Theatre at Delta, Colorado, and the Oriental Theatre at Montrose, Colorado, in the winter of 1932-33, and subsequently copyrighted by him as it spread to thousands of other theatres, which by 1937 were paying Yeager's firm a total of $30,000 to $65,000 a week; the game of bingo (or beano, or keno), which became immensely popular as a money-making entertainment for churches, and in various forms was widely played in movie theatres and elsewhere, till in 1938 some people were referring to it as the most popular money game in the country; and possibly the pathetic epidemic of chain-letter writing which spread from Denver all over the United States in 1934-35 ("Scratch out the top name and send a dime"). Nor has this brief survey taken account of various older gambling devices which persisted, sometimes in new guises and under new sponsorship--as did the numbers racket when Dutch Schultz, the liquor racketeer, took over its management in the Harlem section of New York and systematized it during the last days of Prohibition.

In 1938 a Gallup poll revealed that during the preceding year an estimated 29 per cent of the American people--meaning, one supposes, adults--had taken part in church lotteries (presumably including bingo parties), 26 per cent had played punch boards, 23 per cent had played slot machines, 21 per cent had played cards for money, 19 per cent had bet on elections, 13 per cent had taken sweepstakes tickets, 10 per cent had bet on horse races, and 9 per cent had indulged in numbers games. There were no Gallup polls in the preceding decade, but one wonders if any score even approaching that would have been made in the nineteen-twenties--unless, perhaps, playing the stock market and buying Florida real estate had been included in the gambles.

§ 5

Yet despite all these manifestations of gaiety, relaxation, and sport there was a new tension, a disquiet. For the Depression had wrecked so many of the assumptions upon which the American people had depended that millions of them were inwardly shaken.

Let us look for a moment at the pile of wreckage. In it we find the assumption that well-favored young men and women, coming out of school or college, could presently get jobs as a matter of course; the assumption that ambition, hard work, loyalty to the firm, and the knack of salesmanship would bring personal success; the assumption that poverty (outside of the farm belt and a few distressed communities) was pretty surely the result of incompetence, ignorance, or very special misfortune, and should be attended to chiefly by local charities; the assumption that one could invest one's savings in "good bonds" and be assured of a stable income thereafter, or invest them in the "blue-chip" stocks of "our leading American corporations" with a dizzying chance of appreciation; the assumption that the big men of Wall Street were economic seers, business forecasters could forecast, and business cycles followed nice orderly rhythms; and the assumption that the American economic system was sure of a great and inspiring growth.

Not everybody, of course, had believed all of these things. Yet so many people had based upon one or more of them their personal conceptions of their status and function in society that the shock of seeing them go to smash was terrific. Consider what happened to the pride of the business executive who had instinctively valued himself, as a person, by his salary and position--only to see both of them go; to the banker who found that the advice he had been giving for years was made ridiculous by the turn of events, and that the code of conduct he had lived by was now under attack as crooked; to the clerk or laborer who had given his deepest loyalty to "the company"--only to be thrown out on the street; to the family who had saved their pennies, decade after decade, against a "rainy day"--only to see a torrent of rain sweep every penny away; to the housewife whose ideal picture of herself had been of a person who "had nice things" and was giving her

139

children "advantages," economic and social--and who now saw this picture smashed beyond recognition; and to the men and women of all stations in life who had believed that if you were virtuous and industrious you would of course be rewarded with plenty--and who now were driven to the wall. On what could they now rely? In what could they now believe?

One might have expected that in such a crisis great numbers of these people would have turned to the consolations and inspirations of religion. Yet this did not happen--at least in the sense in which the clergy, in innumerable sermons, had predicted it. The long slow retreat of the churches into less and less significance in the life of the country, and even in the lives of the majority of their members, continued almost unabated.

The membership rolls of most of the larger denominations, to be sure, showed increases. Between 1929 and 1937-38, for example, the Roman Catholic population increased from 20,203,702 to 21,322,608--a modest gain. The Methodist, Baptist, and Lutheran churches also grew in numbers. Yet membership figures are a notoriously uncertain measure of religious vitality. As regards the large Protestant--or nominally Protestant--population of the country, the observations of the Lynds, returning to "Middletown" in 1935 and contrasting the religious life of the city then with what it had been in 1925, offer probably a fairer measure.

The Lynds found some imposing new churches in "Middletown"--products of the hopeful days of the Big Bull Market--but inside the churches they saw little visible change. "Here, scattered through the pews," they reported, "is the same serious and numerically sparse Gideon's band--two-thirds or more of them women, and few of them under thirty--with the same stark ring of empty pews 'down front.'" The congregations seemed to the Lynds to be older than in 1925, the sermon topics interchangeable. Consulting the ministers, they gathered such comments as these:--

"The Depression has brought a resurgence of earnest religious fundamentalism among the weak working-class sects . . . but the uptown churches have seen little similar revival of interest."

140

"There has been some turning to religion during the Depression, but it has been very slight and not permanent."

From a local editor they gleaned the possibly revealing comment that "All the churches in town, save a few denominations like the Seventh Day Adventists, are more liberal today than in 1925. Any of them will take you no matter what you believe doctrinally." They quoted as typical of the attitude of the "Middletown" young people toward formal religion the comment of a college boy on Christianity: "I believe these things but they don't take a large place in my life." Their analysis concluded with the judgment that religion, in "Middletown," appeared to be "an emotionally stabilizing agent, relinquishing to other agencies leadership in the defining of values."

The preponderance of evidence from other parts of the country would seem to sustain this judgment. Put on one side of the balance such phenomena as the upsurge of intense interest, here and there, in the refined evangelism of the Oxford Groups led by Dr. Frank Buchman, and their "Moral Rearmament" campaign in 1938-39; put on the other side the intensified hostility of radicals who regarded the churches as institutions run for the comfort of the rich and the appeasement of the poor; recall how briefly the stream of Sunday-pleasuring automobiles was halted by the men and women straggling at noontime out of the church on Main Street; compare the number of people to whom Sunday evening was the hour of vespers with the number of people to whom it was the evening when Charlie McCarthy was on the air--and one can hardly deny that the shock of the Depression did not find the churches, by and large, able to give what people thought they needed.

§ 6

Yet in the broader sense of the word religion--meaning the values by which people live, the loyalties which stir them most deeply, the aspirations which seem to them central to their beings--no such shock could have failed to have a religious effect. One thinks of the remark of a young man during the dark days of 1932: "If someone came along with a line of stuff in which I could really believe, I'd follow him pretty nearly anywhere." That remark was made, as it happens, in a speakeasy, and the young man was not thinking in terms of puritan morality or even of Christian piety, but in terms of economic and political and social policy. For such as he the times produced new creeds, new devotions.

But these were secular.

Their common denominator was social-mindedness; by which I mean that they were movements toward economic or social salvation--whether conceived in terms of prosperity or of justice or of mercy--not so much for individuals as such but for groups of people or for the whole nation, and also that they sought this salvation through organized action.

In political complexion these secular religionists ranged all the way from the communists at one end of the spectrum to the more fervent members of the Liberty League at the other. They included the ardent devotees of technocracy, Upton Sinclair's "Epic," Huey Long's "Share-Our-Wealth," Father Coughlin's economic program, the Townsend Plan, the CIO, and, of course, the New Deal. Of the way in which the battles between them raged--and the whole battlefield gradually moved to the left, so to speak--we shall hear more in chapters to come. At this point it need only be remarked that most of the new religions of social salvation did not gather their maximum momentum until after the New Deal Honeymoon was over; or perhaps it is more accurate to say that the New Deal, during its Honeymoon, gathered up or overshadowed nearly all of them. It was during the next two or three years that the fires of zeal burned most intensely: that one man in three at a literary party in New York would be a communist sympathizer, passionately ready to join hands, in proletarian comradeship, with the factory hand or sharecropper whom a few years before he had scorned as a member of Mencken's "booboisie"; that daughters of patrician families were defiantly marching to the aid of striking garment workers, or raising money for the defense of Haywood Patterson in the long-drawn-out Scottsboro case; that college intellectuals were nibbling at Marx, picketing Hearst newsreels, and--with a flash of humor--forming the "Veterans of Future Wars."

142

How completely the focus of public attention had become political, economic, and social, and how fully the rebelliousness of the
rebellious had turned into these channels, may be suggested by the fact
that H. L. Mencken, whose *American Mercury* magazine had been the
darling of the young intellectuals of the 'twenties, lost ground as it became evident that Mr. Mencken, though liberal in matters of literature
and morals, was a tory in matters of politics and economics--until by
1933, when he resigned his editorship, the new highbrows were dis-
missing him airily as a back number. Nor did the intellectuals rise in
furious defense of freedom of expression when the Catholic Legion of
Decency imposed a censorship upon the movies in 1934-35. They
were tired of all that, and their protests were faint. They had turned to
fresh woods and pastures new.

§ 7

Underneath the tumult and the shouting of argument, underneath the ardor for this cause or that, there remained, however,
gnawing doubts. The problems were so bewildering, so huge. The un-
settlement of ideas had been so shaking. Things changed so frightfully
fast. This plan, this social creed, looked all right today--but would it
hold tomorrow? To many Americans, if not most, the complexity of
the problems, the hopelessness of arriving at sure solutions, were so
great that no social ardor could really move them. While the social
Salvationists marched in earnest procession toward their various goals
of revolution or reforms, these others stood silent and bewildered by
the roadside. Something had gone wrong with the country but they
didn't know what, couldn't figure it out, wondered if anybody could
figure it out.

Toward the end of the decade, when Archibald MacLeish published his *Land of the Free,* through the poem he introduced the
recurring words, "We don't know--we can't say--we're wondering. . . ."
and observers who had talked with numbers of the drought refugees
said that these very words were constantly on the refugees' lips. So it
was with innumerable others whose lives had been overturned by the

Depression, and with still others who had suffered no bitter hurt them-selves but realized that something queer and incomprehensible was happening to the community. They didn't know; and they were likely to fall back into apathy or fatalism, into a longing for a safe refuge from the storm of events.

To quote the editors of *Fortune* once more (speaking of the majority of college students, not the intellectual minority): "The present-day college generation is fatalistic . . . the investigator is struck by the dominant and pervasive color of a generation that will not stick its neck out. It keeps its shirt on, its pants buttoned, its chin up, and its mouth shut. If we take the mean average to be the truth, it is a cau-tious, subdued, unadventurous generation, unwilling to storm heaven, afraid to make a fool of itself, unable to dramatize its predicament. . . . Security is the summum bonum of the present college generation." This sort of caution was not confined to the campuses. One saw it in business men: "We used to feel pretty sure about what would happen. Now we don't know what will happen." One felt it in the constant ite-ration, in economic discussions, of the word "confidence"--which enters the vocabulary only when confidence is lacking. One detected it in the strength of the movements for old people's pensions, in the push for social security. The sons and daughters of the pioneers might ha-zard their small change on bingo or the one-armed bandit, but they did not want life to be a gamble.

Except during the hopeful interval of the New Deal Honey-moon, when hope suddenly and briefly rode high, through the shifting moods of the American people ran an undercurrent of fear. They wanted to feel certainty and security firm as a rock under their feet--and they did not, and were afraid.

144

Chapter Seven

REFORM--AND RECOVERY?

§ 1

The New Deal Honeymoon ended in the latter months of 1933--not abruptly but (like many a marital infatuation) in a series of annoyances and disappointments and discords.

The upsurge of business, which in the spring of 1933 had carried the Federal Reserve Board's Adjusted Index of Industrial Production all the way from 59 in March up to 100 in July, was followed by a bad setback--the result of over-speculation and over-purchasing for inventories. In August the index receded from 100 to 91; in September it slipped to 84, in October to 76; by November it had reached 72. Two-thirds of the ground which had been gained during that wonderful springtime rise had now been lost--and during the very months when the NRA, vehicle of so many high hopes, was accumulating momentum! No wonder people began to ask themselves whether this New Deal recovery had been just a flash in the pan; to note how the hurriedly devised New Deal machinery was creaking; to turn a more skeptical ear to the President's optimistic assurances and to General Johnson's mighty tub-thumping.

Already the NRA was producing friction and evasion. Henry Ford was refusing to sign the automobile code. William Randolph Hearst, in full-page newspaper advertisements, was attacking the Recovery Act as "a measure of absolute state socialism" and "a menace to political rights and constitutional liberties," and was proclaiming that the letters NRA stood for "No Recovery Allowed." As the various industrial codes were at last worked out and approved, after endless arguments and confusions, some employers were planning to comply with their provisions fairly and honorably; others were welcoming the chance given them to gather round a table and quietly fix prices, but were resolving to evade the wage and hour clauses and to make a dead letter of Section 7a of the Recovery Act, which guaranteed collective bargaining. These companies were piously introducing company unions which looked like the real thing but weren't, or were deciding to have no truck with unions at all and to trust to the courts to uphold them in their defense of their "liberties." Simultaneously the large-waisted officials of the American Federation of Labor were being stirred to unwonted activity, chartering new unions by the hundreds, and workmen who took Section 7a at its face value were striking fiercely for their government-guaranteed rights. From industrial centers came reports of bloody fighting along the picket lines, of tear gas drenching angry crowds, of National Guardsmen marching to action.

Late in the autumn of 1933, George R. Leighton, investigating for *Harper's Magazine* the facts behind the Blue Eagle ballyhoo in four Eastern states, came back with the report that "the spirit and intent of the National Industrial Recovery Act and the codes are being frustrated, openly or in secret." He found that the government's aim to raise wages was being defeated, either by the sheer refusal of employers to obey the minimum-wage provisions of the blanket code, or by their raising some wages up to the minimum and lowering others down to it. He found employees too scared to peep about what was happening. "For God's sake," cried one workman, "don't tell anybody that you've been here. . . . There are men in cement plants near here who have complained and now they're out in the cold." Compliance boards--which were supposed to enforce the codes--were sometimes, Mr. Leighton found, packed with men who saw eye to eye with hard-boiled employers and had no notion of protecting labor or the consumers. He found local NRA officials timid in dealing with powerful industrialists; one official spoke of a big factory owner in his town in revealing words: "It is so hard to get an audience with him."

The evidence was fast accumulating: the Administration's great experiment in "business self-rule" had come into full collision

146

with the ingrained determination of business executives to hold down their costs of doing business, to push up prices if they could, and in general to run their companies as they pleased, come hell, high water, or General Johnson. Where they could turn the machinery of the NRA to their own ends, they did so--and it was they, not labor or the consumers, who held the initiative in framing the codes. Where they could not turn this machinery to their own ends, some of them complied, others fought the law or nullified it. Certain benefits accrued from the NRA experiment: a virtual ending of child labor; some increases in wages, reductions of over-long hours, and elimination of demoralizing practices, especially in the more enlightened industries; some stabilizing of business. But there seemed to be no increase in employment beyond what sprang directly from the shortening of hours, and prices to the ultimate consumer tended to rise along with wages--in some cases faster than wages. Meanwhile as business lagged and strike threats multiplied, the business community in general was becoming more and more antagonistic toward the new dispensation.

Roosevelt himself was deeply concerned by the loss of business momentum and by the downward drift of farm prices. He who had once referred to himself as the quarterback of the offensive against the Depression now saw the game going against him and decided to try a forward pass. He had been listening to the advice of Professor George F. Warren of Cornell, who had persuaded Farm Credit Administrator Henry Morgenthau that if the government deliberately raised the price at which it could buy gold, the dollar might be cheapened not only in terms of gold, but in terms of other goods as well: in short, that prices should rise. William H. Woodin, the Secretary of the Treasury, was gravely ill, and Dean G. Acheson, who as Under Secretary was in active charge of the Treasury Department, had no use for the Warren gold-buying scheme; but the President, full of his new idea, went ahead regardless, and on October 22, 1933, announced that the Reconstruction Finance Corporation was going to buy gold for the government.

So it happened that at nine o'clock each morning during the late autumn of 1933, two or three men gathered in the President's bedroom at the White House: usually Professor Warren, Henry Morgenthau, and Jesse Jones of the Reconstruction Finance Corporation. While the President breakfasted in bed, they decided what the

147

day's price for gold would be. The President would scribble a couple of "chits"--one for Jones, authorizing the day's gold price; the other for Acheson, breaking the news to the Treasury Department. Presently Acheson left his untenable position at the Treasury and Morgenthau took his place (to succeed to the Secretaryship upon Woodin's resignation); Professor O. M. W. Sprague, financial adviser to the government, also left the Treasury in indignation at such monetary high-jinks; Al Smith was heaping ridicule upon the President's "baloney dollar"; and Wall Street resounded with angry cries: the United States was on its way to the sort of uncontrolled inflation which had run wild in Germany in 1923; over-spending and "rubber-dollar" experimentation would soon result in ruining the government's credit.

Not until the end of January, 1934, did the gold-buying episode come to an end. By that time the dollar had been devalued (in terms of gold) to 59.06 cents. Prices had risen somewhat, but nowhere near proportionately. The great experiment was a failure. Moreover the financial community--which had long since quite recovered from its sheer panic of the preceding spring, and now felt, with rising indignation, that it was being made the scapegoat of the Depression--had become an almost solid anti-Roosevelt phalanx.

(Footnote upon the prophecies of the wise men of Wall Street: Within the following five and a half years there took place no uncontrolled inflation, no collapse of the credit of the government. What did take place was an embarrassingly huge accumulation of gold in the underground vaults of Fort Knox in Kentucky: over fourteen billion dollars' worth of it, at the $35-an-ounce price which the United States was willing to pay and others did not care to pay because most of the nations of the world had gone off the gold standard.)

As the winter of 1933-34 set in, the New Deal's once-solid support was falling into fragments. Most of the radicals had become impatient with Roosevelt: he was moving too slowly, they charged, he was proposing mere palliatives instead of revolutionary remedies. Thousands of farmers were angry at the failure of the AAA thus far to bring them high prices for their crops, and disorder still flared along the highways of the corn belt and the wheat belt. Laboring men, though they credited the government with an intention to let them organize and to be generous with unemployment relief, resented its inability to enforce Section 7a and the capture of the NRA machinery by the employers. Business men who had imagined that Roosevelt, after putting through his rapid-fire program of reforms and recovery measures in the spring of 1933, would rest on his oars, were discovering to their dismay that he had no such intention; what wild scheme, they asked one another, would this man hatch next?

Already he had set up the Civil Works Administration, a vast and unwieldy--and expensive--system of Federal work relief for the unemployed. In his budget message to Congress at the beginning of 1934, he calmly stated that during the fiscal year 1933-34 the excess of government expenditures over government receipts would be over seven billion dollars and that during the fiscal year 1934-35 it would probably be two billion dollars. "This excess of expenditures over revenues, amounting to over nine billion dollars during two fiscal years," announced the President, "'has been rendered necessary to bring the country back to a sound condition after the unexampled crisis which we encountered last spring. It is a large amount, but the immeasurable benefits justify the cost." The words were confident, but what economy-minded business man struggling with his year-end accounts could fail to ask himself just how "immeasurable" the benefits *to him* had turned out to be, or whether this man who contemplated so coolly a nine-billion-dollar increase in the Federal deficit could be the same Franklin Roosevelt who in 1932 had berated the Republicans for gross extravagance and in March, 1933, had introduced the Economy Bill?

The truth was that a major deflation, if it should occur, would be even more damaging to Franklin Roosevelt than it would have been to Herbert Hoover. Under the existing debt structure Roosevelt had now placed, at many new points, the credit of the government itself. He had committed himself to recovery through rising prices and large-scale business expansion, rather than through falling prices and the writing-off of debts. He must keep his foot pressed down on the accelerator, not on the brake. Dark though the road might look ahead, he must drive on. A costly course to take? Perhaps. But it was too late to turn back now.

§ 2

Intermittently throughout the year 1933 the Senate Committee on Banking and Currency, with the aid of its inexorable counsel, Ferdinand Pecora, had been putting on one of the most extraordinary shows ever produced in a Washington committee room: a sort of protracted coroner's inquest upon American finance. One by one, a long line of financial overlords--commercial bankers, investment bankers, railroad and public-utility holding-company promoters, stockbrokers, and big speculators--had filed up to the witness table; and from these unwilling gentlemen, and from their office files, had been extracted a sorry story of public irresponsibility and private greed. Day by day this story had been spread upon the front pages of the newspapers.

The investigation showed how pool operators in Wall Street had manipulated the prices of stocks on the Exchange, with the assistance of men inside the companies with whose securities they toyed. It showed how they had made huge profits (which represented the exercise of no socially useful function) at the expense of the little speculators and of investors generally, and had fostered a speculative mania which had racked the whole economic system of the country-- and this not only in 1928 and 1929, but as recently as the spring of 1933, when Roosevelt was in the White House and Wall Street had supposedly been wearing the sackcloth and ashes of repentance. The investigation showed, too, how powerful bankers had unloaded stocks and bonds upon the unwary through high-pressure salesmanship and had made millions trading in the securities of their own banks, at the expense of stockholders whose interests they claimed to be serving. It showed how the issuing of new securities had been so organized as to yield rich fruits to those on the inside, and how opportunities to taste these fruits had been offered to gentlemen of political influence. It showed how that modern engine of financial power, the holding company, had been misused by promoters: how some of these promoters had piled company upon company till their structures of corporate influence were seven or eight stories high; how these structures had become so complex that they were readily looted by unscrupulous men, and so unstable that many of them came crashing down during the Depression. It showed how grave could be the results when the holding-company technic was applied to banking. It showed how men of wealth had used devices like the personal holding company and tricks like the sale of stock (at a loss) to members of their families to dodge the tax collector--at the very moment when men of humbler station had been paying the taxes which supported the government. Again and again it showed how men occupying fiduciary positions in the financial world had been false to their trust.

Naturally the composite picture blocked out by these revelations was not fair to the financiers generally. The worst scandals got the biggest headlines. Yet the amount of black in the picture was shocking even to the most judicial observer, and the way in which the severity of the Depression had been intensified by greedy and short-sighted financial practices seemed blindingly plain. So high did the public anger mount that the New Deal was sure of strong support as it drove on to new measures of reform.

The first move was into Wall Street. The Securities Act of 1933 was followed by the Securities and Exchange Act of 1934, which put the stock exchanges of the country under Federal regulation, lest the next boom (if it ever came) end in another speculative crash. This Act gave the Federal Reserve Board the authority to limit speculative margins; required all directors, officers, and principal stockholders of big corporations to report all their transactions in the securities of their companies; and created a Securities and Exchange Commission--to be known familiarly as the SEC--which was intended to act as chaperon and policeman of the stock exchanges and the investment market generally, and by slow degrees subdue them to the useful and the good.

The next year the New Deal moved against the misuse of the holding company in the area where its performances had been most egregious--in the public utilities. The Public Utility Holding Company Act provided that holding-company structures must not be more than two stories high, that they must be simplified, and that they must limit themselves to the management of economically integrated groups of operating companies.

Turning to the banking system of the country, the New Deal made no attempt to unify it (bringing the national banks and the forty-eight groups of state banks into one system) but in 1935 increased the supervisory power of the Federal Reserve Board over the various Federal Reserve Banks, centering a more effective authority in

Washington, and incidentally made permanent the insurance by the government of small bank deposits, as temporarily arranged in 1933.

Other new powers of regulation and compulsion were assumed by the Federal government. For example, the power of the Interstate Commerce Commission was extended to cover not only railroads, as of yore, but interstate bus and truck traffic as well; and for the old Radio Commission was substituted a new Communications Commission which was not only to police the air waves but also to supervise the telegraph and telephone systems. Not until September 2, 1935, did the President announce--in a letter to Roy W. Howard of the Scripps-Howard newspapers--that the New Deal's legislative program had "reached substantial completion" and that business might expect a "breathing spell."

Throughout a large part of the years 1934 and 1935 the hue and cry over these reform measures of the New Deal reverberated across the country.

No longer, to be sure, did the news from Washington still make the front pages of the newspapers as automatically as it had in the first wild days of the new Administration. Other events, important and unimportant, now claimed a fresher attention. During the winter of 1933-34--a piercingly cold winter in the North, when the Atlantic Ocean was blocked with ice all the way from Nantucket Island to the mainland, and Army fliers, hastily ordered to carry the air mails after Roosevelt's mistakenly sudden termination of the air-mail contracts, were flying to their deaths in ice and fog--there was foreign news to contest for front-page space with General Johnson's latest admonitions and expletives and with Roosevelt's monetary experiments and reform proposals. There were riots in Paris which seemed for a time to presage civil war in France. Foreign excitements continued during the summer of 1934: there came Hitler's blood purge and the assassination of little Chancellor Dollfuss of Austria, which threatened a general European war (with Italy opposed to Germany!). That spring there took place in a humble Canadian home an event which for sheer human interest was the feature-editor's answer to prayer: on May 28, Mrs. Oliva Dionne gave birth to five little girls--and incidentally to a major Canadian industry, the exploitation of the Quintuplets as five modern wonders of the world.

As the summer of 1934 drew to its close the country supped on horror: the Ward Liner *Morro Castle* was burned, with a loss of 137 lives, off the coast of New Jersey. Men and women who were hardly aware what the letters SEC stood for could have told you in detail how the *Morro Castle* fire was first discovered in a locker off the port-side writing room; how Chief Officer William F. Warms had found himself in precarious command of the vessel owing to the death of the captain from indigestion a few hours previously; how the fire could not be stopped and the passengers took to the boats--or to the open Atlantic; and how the red-hot hulk of the ship was later beached right beside the convention hall at Asbury Park, where it boomed briefly a grim sight-seeing trade.

While the visitors to Asbury Park were still staring at the *Morro Castle,* the most exciting detective-and-trial-scene story of the decade began to unfold itself, as Bruno Richard Hauptmann was captured in the Bronx and was put on trial for the kidnapping of the Lindbergh baby. The furiously ballyhooed trial at Flemington brought once again to everybody's lips the names of Dr. Condon and the Whateleys and Betty Gow, and lifted into brief public prominence new names such as those of Attorney General Wilentz of New Jersey, Justice Trenchard, counsel Reilly for the defense, and the mysterious German of Hauptmann's incredible testimony, Isidor Fisch.

It was during the following summer--the summer of 1935--that public attention was diverted from the debate over the Holding-Company Bill and other Administrative measures by Jim Braddock's capture of the heavyweight boxing championship from Max Baer; by the deaths of Will Rogers and Wiley Post in an airplane crash in Alaska; and by the slow gathering of war clouds over unhappy Ethiopia. All through 1934 and 1935, furthermore, an event of major importance to America--of which we shall hear more in the next chapter of this book--was taking place on the Great Plains: the farms of the Dust Bowl were blowing away.

Yet never quite inaudible, during all the time when these events were taking place, was the rumble of battle over the New Deal financial reforms. The outcry of protest from Wall Street--which was echoed generally in the conservative press--was terrific. The Securities and Exchange Bill, if passed, would end the liquidity of the investment markets and bring general economic ruin! Roosevelt was taking the high road to communism! Had not Dr. William A. Wirt of Gary, Indiana, told of being at a "brain trust" dinner party where, he insisted, government employees had spoken of Roosevelt as merely the Kerensky of a new American revolution? Did not Rexford Tugwell, the Assistant Secretary of Agriculture, appear to be practically a communist--especially to those newspaper proprietors who feared that his proposed bill to regulate food and drug advertising might cut into their revenues? The government was out to ruin all investors in public utilities: it was enlarging the TVA's sphere of competition with Southern private utilities, it was subsidizing municipalities which wanted to have municipal power and light systems and take their power from the TVA, it was building new dams at Grand Coulee and Bonneville in the West, which would enlarge the area served by public power--and now it was proposing, through the Holding-Company Bill, to apply a "death-sentence" to a lot of helpless holding companies! The issue was clear, shouted the conservatives: it was economic dictatorship versus democracy.

Back from the New Dealers came the reply: Wall Street's record of mismanagement had been spread upon the books of the Senate Committee. "The people of the United States will not restore that ancient order." The New Deal intended to protect the average man against "the selfish interests of Wall Street."

Thus the thunder of battle rolled--while Franklin Roosevelt, still overwhelmingly in command of Congress, pushed the reforms through to enactment.

§ 3

Not only did the New Deal try to restore prosperity through the NRA, the AAA, currency changes, and other measures, and to prevent the recurrence of economic disaster through its reform measures; it also tried to protect individual citizens against the hardships of economic adversity, past, present, and future. It set up so many agencies to lend money to organizations and individuals that the mere listing of them would be wearisome. Through an enactment of major importance in 1935, the Social Security Act, it set up a vast system of unemployment insurance and of old-age assistance for the greater part of the working population of the country--taxing pay rolls to set up a colossal fund out of which might be paid old-age benefits in the long future. Year after year it struggled, too, with the problem of unemployment relief.

The attack upon this desperate problem threw into sharp outline the essential strength of the New Deal, its essential weakness, and the dilemma of the national economy as a whole.

When in the spring of 1933 the Federal government had assumed the responsibility for seeing that men and women and children did not go hungry or shelterless in the United States, it had set aside half a billion dollars out of the public-works fund to aid the states in carrying the burden of unemployment relief; and President Roosevelt had appointed as Federal Emergency Relief Administrator a thin, narrow-faced, alert-looking young Iowan named Harry Hopkins, who had been a zealous and idealistic social worker and had served as relief administrator in New York during Roosevelt's governorship. The distribution of this fund appeared to be simply a temporary expedient, for in those hopeful days recovery was seemingly on its way at the double-quick. Then came the downturn of the fall of 1933, and the prospect of another dreadful winter. Most of the cities and states of the country were on the verge of bankruptcy and quite unable to bear the relief burden unaided--and unemployment during the winter of 1933-34 was pretty surely going to be almost as severe as during that of 1932-33! Another "temporary" plan was needed, and on no niggardly scale.

So the Civil Works Administration was set up and Harry Hopkins found himself in command of a huge and hasty organization of mercy; and Roosevelt, as we have seen, asked Congress for billions to meet this new need. Surely things would be better next year. In the spring of 1934 the Civil Works Administration--which was proving terrifically expensive--was abandoned, and the organization of relief was altered again.

But things did not prove much better the next year. And so once more the President called for billions of dollars and once more the organization was overhauled: early in 1935 the Works Progress Administration--the WPA--came into being.

Although the WPA was destined to remain throughout the rest of the decade, it was destined also to be subject to constant reorganization and revision. In essence, the history of those first years was to be repeated again and again. Year after year the Administration found the number of unemployed men unexpectedly large, found its funds running out, confronted the new crisis with a new appeal to Congress for more billions, and hastily improvised new and glowing plans. The prevailing pattern was one of administrative makeshift.

The principle upon which Federal relief operated was magnificent. The government said in effect: "These millions of men who are out of work are not to be considered paupers. They are not to be subjected to any humiliation which we can spare them. They are to be regarded as citizens and friends who are the temporary victims of an unfortunate economic situation for which the nation as a whole is responsible. Not only is it far too late in the day, now, to follow the Hoover principle that the acceptance of Federal money undermines men's self-respect; it is even too late in the day to be content with giving handouts. These men want to *work* for the money they receive. Very well, we shall put them to work--as many of them as we possibly can. We shall put them at useful work which will not compete with private business. They shall become government employees, able to hold up their heads again. If putting them to work costs more than a cash dole, the benefits in morale restored will outweigh the expense."

But these things were easier said than done, on the scale on which the government had to operate. Stop for a minute to feel the impact of these figures: The CWA at its peak employed *over four million workers*--enough to man some twenty General Motors Corporations. The WPA began operations with the aim of employing *three and a half million.* (The total number of people dependent upon Federal, state, or local relief--including the families of those to whom payments were made--was variously estimated at various times at from *twenty to twenty-five million.*) How to put this vast horde to work?

First of all, there was the difficulty of finding work that had value, and would not compete with private business, and was fitted to the endlessly varied abilities and experience of millions of individuals. It was decided that the reliefers were not to work on private property, engage in manufacturing, or set up rival merchandising systems. The money went at first mostly into such projects as the repair and building of roads (especially farm-to-market roads), repairs on public buildings and schools, the construction of parks and playgrounds; and--for the professional and clerical workers, the white-collar class--into research projects for the government and for universities, and into engaging reliefers who had some special skill or knowledge to teach it to others who did not have it. Some of the jobs were trivial, or too many men were assigned to them, or these men were conspicuously inexpert; hence the criticisms one constantly heard of "leaf-raking" and of men idling on the job.

During an aldermanic inquiry into New York City relief early in 1935--in which it was discovered that money was being spent for the teaching of tap dancing and the manipulation of shadow puppets, and for such academic enterprises as "a study of the predominating non-professional interests of teachers in nursery schools, kindergarten, and first grade" and "a study of the relative effectiveness of a supervised correspondence course in elementary Latin"--one Robert Marshall testified that he was a "training specialist" who taught the reliefers "boon doggies," explaining that this was an old pioneer term for useful everyday tricks of handicraft such as making belts by weaving ropes. The strange term entranced newspaper-readers, and presently the conservative press everywhere was referring to relief projects of questionable value as "boondoggling."

Another great difficulty was that of enrolling and investigating and assigning workers. Should a job go to the person who could do it best, or to the person in the direst need? If need was to be the criterion, how could any standards of work be maintained? The determination of wage scales offered another series of headaches. Presumably the wages should be lower than those for private business--but what if local wages were on the starvation level? These were only a few of the practical questions for which there seemed to be no possible answer which did not produce either injustice or inefficiency.

Again, there was the grave difficulty of setting up a proper organization, of keeping the control of relief out of the hands of grafters
and political hacks, of resolving the endless conflicts between Federal
and local agencies. Though the division of authority between Federal
and state and local governments varied bewilderingly in different places and at different times, the whip hand was held in the main by the
Hopkins organization in Washington, which was vigilant against graft
and--at least in the early years--pretty independent of politics. As time
went on, the taint of politics became somewhat more noticeable: the
relief system was all too valuable to the Democratic party, relief expenditures had a way of rising to a maximum as Election Day
approached, and there was ugly evidence here and there of the gross
misuse of funds, as in Pennsylvania; but on the whole the record was
astonishingly clean considering the vastness of the funds disbursed and
the generally low level of political ethics in American local government.

Beyond all these difficulties was the final, inescapable one.
Try as Hopkins and his aides might to make the work vital and pride-
worthy, the fact remained that it was made work, ill-paid, uncertain,
undemanding of real quality of workmanship; and that the reliefers
became perforce, by degrees, a sort of pariah class, unwelcomed by
private industry, dwelling in an economic twilight.

That is a generalization. Against it should be set some high
triumphs, including notably those of the Federal Theatre, Music, and
Arts projects. Who would have believed, during the Hoover period,
that within a few years, under the WPA, orchestras would be getting
relief aid for playing to enthusiastic audiences, government-subsidized
theatre groups would be packing the playhouses with excellent shows,
and able painters who had not sold a picture for months or even years
would be getting government assignments to paint post-office murals?

Of all the forms which Federal relief took there is not space
here to speak. Yet a word at least should be said of the Transient
Camps which offered shelter to those hundreds of thousands of Americans who were traveling about in search of work and could not
qualify for regular relief after they left their home towns (who wants to
support a non-resident?); of the National Youth Administration, which
helped to pay for the education and training of young people who

158

would otherwise have gone without; and of the WPA's purchase of surplus commodities--especially farm products--and their distribution to the needy. (Nor should it be forgotten that the great enterprises-- bridges, dams, public buildings, etc.--constructed by the Public Works Administration, and the forest-conservation work of the Civilian Conservation Corps, while not administratively a part of Federal relief, supplemented the relief system.)

Two more generalizations must be made, however, before we leave this twilight zone. The first is that, despite all the inefficiencies of the relief system, its frequent upheavals of organization, its confusion, and its occasional political subversion, it commended itself to the bulk of the American people because of its essential friendliness, of the human decency of its prevailing attitude toward those whom the Depression had thrust into want. Possibly those privileged people who denounced the system as a coddling and spoiling of the unfit may have owed their security from civil revolution during the nineteen-thirties to the fact that the government in power treated the reliefers as citizens worthy of respect.

The second generalization is that the terrific cost of such a relief system bore down upon the working and income-receiving past of the population, even while the expenditures were helping to keep trade going; and that that part of the cost which was not met by current taxes remained, in the form of Federal debt, to bear down upon the jobholding and income-receiving Americans for long years to come. Human decency came very high.

Here was the essential dilemma of the New Deal. Just as it wanted, reasonably enough, to apply the lessons of the 1929-33 débâcle and reform the financial system, but apparently could not do this without setting up a Federal supervisory bureaucracy, without inflicting upon the financial world endless rules and regulations, endless tasks of questionnaire-answering, report-writing, and prospectuswriting, and filling Wall Street with paralyzing fears, rational and irrational, thus delaying recovery; so also it apparently could not deal humanely with the unemployed men and women of the country without imposing heavy taxes, incurring heavy deficits, raising very natural qualms as to its ability to carry on indefinitely with a mounting debt, and thus once again delaying recovery. It had to march toward its goal under a veritable Christian's pack--the burden of the very inadequacies which it was trying to resolve.

Pictures, Inc.

J. P. MORGAN AT THE WITNESS TABLE
This picture was taken at the Senate Munitions Committee hearing in
1936. Left, Frank Vanderlip. Right (behind Morgan), George Whitney
of J. P. Morgan & Co.

§ 4

Early in the evening of July 22, 1934, a group of agents of the Department of Justice, armed with pistols, gathered unobtrusively about a movie theatre on Lincoln Avenue, Chicago. The leader of the group, Melvin H. Purvis, parked his car near the theatre door and care-fully scanned the faces of the men and women who entered. At length Purvis recognized the man he wanted--though this man had dyed his hair, had had his face lifted, had grown a mustache, and had put on gold-rimmed glasses.

For two hours Purvis waited in his car, until the man came out of the theatre. Then Purvis signaled to his aides by thrusting an arm out of the car, dropping his hand, and closing it. The aides closed in on the movie-goer, and when he started to draw an automatic they shot him down. The next morning the headlines shouted that John Dillin-ger, Public Enemy No. 1, had been destroyed.

Another offensive of the reform spirit against things-as-they-had-been was well under way.

During the early years of the decade, as we have seen, there had been immense indignation at the prevalence of crime in America and the inability of the police to cope with it. This indignation had been sharpened by the Lindbergh kidnapping early in 1932. From that time on, every kidnapping case leaped into such prominence in the newspaper dispatches that most Americans imagined that a wave of kidnapping was sweeping the country. The public indignation took an ugly form at San Jose, California, late in 1933, when two men who had kidnapped young Brooke Hart, and had shot him, weighted his body, and thrown it into San Francisco Bay, were taken out of the San Jose jail by an angry mob and hanged on trees near by--whereupon the Governor of California, who had a curious notion of law and order, commented that the lynchers had done "a good job."

Proceeding upon the theory that the states could not be sure of catching criminals (any more than they could be sure of stopping undesirable business practices) without Federal aid, Congress had passed laws giving the Federal authorities a limited jurisdiction over crimes which had hitherto been wholly under state jurisdiction. J. Edgar Hoover, the resourceful head of the Bureau of Investigation of the Department of Justice, saw his chance. When John Dillinger, a bank robber and hold-up man of the Middle West, proved to have a remarkable ability to shoot his way out of difficulty, Hoover sent his Federal men on the trail--though Dillinger's only Federal offense up to that time was said to have been the interstate transportation of a stolen car. Dillinger was labeled "Public Enemy No. 1" (now that Al Capone was in prison), and the public began to take notice.

The Federal agents caught up to Dillinger at St. Paul but he escaped, wounded. A few days later he appeared in a surgeon's office, leveled a gun, compelled the surgeon to give him treatment for his wound, and got away safely. Again he was found, at a summer resort in Northern Wisconsin; but although agents surrounded the building where he was staying, he escaped after a battle in which two men were killed and two were wounded. At last Purvis caught him in Chicago, as we have seen, and the story of John Dillinger came to an end.

But not the story of J. Edgar Hoover and his Federal agents. For these Federal sleuths now proceeded to capture, dead or alive, "Pretty Boy" Floyd, "Baby Face" Nelson, and so many other public enemies, one after another, that after Alvin Karpis was taken alive in 1936 the public quite lost track of the promotions in the Public Enemy class.

Hoover and his men became heroes of the day. The movies took them up, taught people to call them G-men, and presented James Cagney in the role of a bounding young G-man, trained in the law, in scientific detection, in target practice, and incidentally in wrestling. Presently mothers who had been noting with alarm that their small sons liked to play gangster on the street corner were relieved to observe that the favored part in these juvenile dramas was now that of the intrepid G-man, whose machine gun mowed down kidnappers and bank robbers by the score. The real G-men--with the not-quite-so-heavily-advertised aid of state and local police--continued to follow up their triumphs until by the end of 1936 they could claim that every kidnapping case in the country since the passage of the Lindbergh law in 1932 had been closed.

But kidnapping and bank robbery, sensational as they were, were hardly the most menacing of crimes. The depredations of professional gangster-racketeers were more far-reaching and infinitely more difficult to combat. During the nineteen-twenties various gangster mobs, the most notorious of which was Al Capone's in Chicago, had built up larger, better organized, and more profitable systems of business-by-intimidation than the country had ever seen before. The foundation of these rackets was usually beer-running, but a successful beer-runner could readily handle most of the bootlegging trade in whisky and gin as a sideline, branch out to take over the gambling and prostitution rackets, and also develop systems of terrorization in otherwise legitimate businesses, by using what purported to be an employer's association or a labor union but was really a scheme for extortion backed by threats to destroy the members' business--or kill them--if they did not pay. The pattern was different in every city and usually there were many rival gangs at work, muscling in on one another's territory from time to time to the accompaniment of machine-gun battles.

During the early nineteen-thirties the racketeers--like legitimate business men--found business bad. The coming of Repeal, by breaking the back of the illicit liquor business, deprived these gentry of a vital source of revenue. But the technique of politically protected intimidation had been so well learned that racketeering went right on in many cities. Even in New York--a city which had never been so racket-ridden as Chicago and had elected in 1933 an honest and effective mayor, Fiorello LaGuardia--dozens of businesses were in the grip of rackets and their victims were too terrified to testify to what was going on.

But New York was to provide a classic demonstration of what the new reform spirit, properly directed, could do.

The story of the demonstration really began on November 21, 1933--when Roosevelt was engaged in his breakfast-in-bed gold-buying plan, and General Johnson was approving NRA codes, and Mae West was appearing on the screen in "I'm No Angel," and Katha-

163

rine Hepburn in "Little Women," and copies of *Anthony Adverse* were everywhere, and the first bad dust storm had just raged in the Dust Bowl, and the Century of Progress Fair at Chicago had just ended its first year, and the CWA had just been organized, and the United States had just recognized Soviet Russia. On that day the New York papers had carried on their inside pages an item of local news: the appointment as local Federal Attorney of one Thomas E. Dewey, who was only thirty-one years old. During the next year and a half young Dewey did well at this job. In the spring of 1935 a grand jury in New York, investigating racketeering, became so dissatisfied with the way in which the evidence was presented to it by the Tammany District Attorney that it rose up in wrath and asked Governor Lehman to appoint a special prosecutor. Governor Lehman appointed the valiant Dewey and on July 29, 1935, he set to work.

There followed one of the most extraordinary performances in the history of criminal detection and prosecution. Dewey mobilized an able staff of young lawyers and accountants in a highly protected office in the Woolworth Building, sent them out to get the evidence about racketeering, and to everybody's amazement got it, despite the terrified insistence of the very people whom he was trying to protect that they knew nothing at all. This evidence Dewey marshaled so brilliantly that presently he began a series of monotonously successful prosecutions. He put out of business the restaurant racket, to which at least 240 restaurants had paid tribute. He sent to prison Toots Herbert, who in the guise of a labor leader, head of Local 167, had collected large sums from the poultry business. He convicted Lucky Luciano, who had levied toll upon the prostitutes and madams of New York (with such smooth-running political protection that although during 1935 no less than 147 girls who worked for this combination had been arrested, not one of them had got a jail sentence). Within two years Dewey had indicted 73 racketeers and convicted 71 of them: and all this despite the unwillingness of witnesses to talk, the constant need of protecting against violence those who agreed to talk, and constant attempts at bribery and intimidation. Elected District Attorney in 1937, Dewey continued his onslaught, and in 1939 he secured the conviction of an important Tammany leader, James J. Hines. (Hines appealed, and at the end of the decade his case was still pending.)

The intimidation industry was not destroyed, of course, any more than kidnapping and bank robbery had been ended; but Dewey, like the G-men, had shown that crime could be successfully combated, and the lesson was widely noted. When the worthy members of the National Economic League, who in 1930 and 1931, as we have previously seen, voted that "Administration of Justice" and "Crime" and "Lawlessness" were--along with Prohibition--the important issues before the country, voted again in 1937, they decided that "Crime" offered a less important problem than "Labor," "Efficiency and Economy in Government," "Taxation," or "The Federal Constitution."

The drive against crime had won at least a temporary victory.

§ 5

Through the years 1934 and 1935, President Roosevelt was sore beset.

Economic recovery was lagging badly. For a measure of what was happening, let us return once more to the Federal Reserve Board's Adjusted Index of Industrial Production, which gives perhaps the best general indication of economic health. We have seen that the index figure had dropped from its prosperity peak of 125 in 1929 all the way to 58 in the summer of 1932, and again to 59 in the bank-panic month of March, 1933; that it had then bounded to 100 during the New Deal Honeymoon, and slid down to 72 in November, 1933, as the Honeymoon came to an end. Slowly it crept up again, but only to 86 in the spring of 1934. Back it slipped to a discouraging 71 in the fall of 1934. Once more it gained, till at the beginning of 1935 it had reached 90. Then during the spring of 1935 it receded to 85. Not until the last month of 1935 had it fought its way up again to the hundred mark it had attained during those first frenzied months of the New Deal--and this despite the pouring of billions of dollars of relief money into the bloodstream of trade.

The President's confident proposals for new legislation could not altogether distract public attention from the administrative difficulties which tangled the agencies he had already set up. The NRA appeared to be stimulating dissension rather than production. On the one hand it had virtually invited labor to organize; on the other hand it had turned over the formulation and administration of its hundreds of codes mainly to employers, and was unable to require these employers to recognize the rapidly mushrooming unions, dominated in many cases by inexperienced and over-combative leaders; hence it could not make good on its promise. Disillusioned auto workers were saying that NRA stood for "National Run Around." A fierce dock strike on the Pacific Coast grew into an attempt to tie up the whole city of San Francisco by a general strike in July, 1934. When the textile code authority called for a cut in production that same summer--a cut which meant grievous reductions in hard-driven textile workers' wages--another great strike began, with flying squadrons of strikers driving from mill town to mill town in the South, with National guardsmen called out in seven states, and with a list of dead and wounded growing ominously day by day. That fall General Johnson left the NRA under a storm of criticism--or, as he delicately put it himself, a "hail of dead cats."

The AAA was a storm center too, and its effect upon the farmers' income was a matter of dispute, since the rise in farm prices in 1934 might be partly attributed to the deadly drought which was blighting the prairies and the Great Plains. Unemployment and the resulting drain upon the national budget continued almost unabated.

Politically, the President came through the Congressional elections of 1934 with flying colors; the Democrats gained nine seats in the Senate and even enlarged slightly their big majority in the House. But how long would this supremacy last? Cannon were being unlimbered not only to the right of Roosevelt, but to the left of him too. That the forces of capital and management--bankers, investors, big business men, and their sympathizers--should have closed ranks against him was natural in view of his reform legislation, his monetary unorthodoxy, his huge spendings for relief, his intermittent hostility to big business, and his expansion of the area of government authority. But what if he could not hold the support of the have-nots, and found himself the leader of a centrist minority, raked by a cross fire from both sides?

On the left Roosevelt must reckon with Huey Long, the Kingfish of Louisiana, who had always been a maverick in national politics and had definitely quit the New Deal since that day in June, 1933, when he had called at the White House, had kept his jaunty straw hat on throughout most of his interview with the President, had been told that the Administration could not appoint some of his nominees for office, and had remarked to Jim Farley as he left, "What the hell is the use of coming down to see this fellow? I can't win any decision over him." Long was one of the most extraordinary figures in all American political history. He was of the stuff of which dictators are made, and he ruled Louisiana with an iron hand, smashing opposition as ruthlessly as a racketeer. Blatant, profane, witty, unscrupulous, violent; possessed of the demagogue's habit of promising the impossible, together with the statesman's ability to provide good roads, better schools, free schoolbooks, and a generally better standard of living among the poor, both black and white, and at the same time to keep the state government solvent--Huey had blustered and bludgeoned his way into a stormy national prominence.

No use for Senators to try to silence him in Washington by leaving the Senate Chamber when he began to speak; his invective was the one thing the crowds in the galleries wanted most to hear.

When Huey toured the South in the spring of 1935, ten thousand people gathered in Atlanta to hear him denounce the Administration. "Pour it on 'em, Kingfish!" they yelled in delight. He was getting the headlines that spring by calling for an investigation of Postmaster General Jim Farley, of whom he said later, by way of explanation, "Jim was the biggest rooster in the yard, and I thought that if I could break his legs the rest would be easy." Radio audiences chuckled with delight at Huey's barnyard wit, as when he said, commenting on Herbert Hoover's call for a militant Republicanism, "Hoover is a hoot owl. Roosevelt is a scrootch owl. A hoot owl bangs into the roost and knocks the hen clean off and catches her while she's falling. But a scrootch owl slips into the roost and scrootches up to the hen and talks softly to her. And the hen just falls in love with him, and the next thing you know, there ain't no hen." Had there ever been be-

167

fore, in American political life, a man who could rule a state with machine guns, subdue a legislature completely to his will, and yet produce the sort of hilarity represented by a remark in the course of his comment on the Mardi Gras: "Once I got invited to one of their balls. I went down to a pawn shop and bought a silk shirt for six dollars with a collar so high I had to climb up on a stump to spit"?

Huey Long had a fantastic, Utopian "Share Our Wealth" program for the country, very explicit as to objectives but very vague as to methods. It began with "Every family to be furnished by the government a homestead allowance, free of debt, of not less than one-third the average family wealth of the country, which means, at the lowest, that every family shall have the reasonable comforts of life up to a value of from $5,000 to $6,000." It ended with a clause proclaiming, "The raising of revenue for the support of this program to come from the reduction of swollen fortunes from the top." No wonder the New Deal, champion of the "forgotten man," feared Huey's rising power! When during 1935 the Democratic National Committee conducted a secret poll on a national scale, it found that on a third-party ticket Long would be able to command between three and four million votes for the Presidency. And nobody could tell how much further he might go.

Roosevelt must reckon also with another one-time ally who, like Long, had left the New Deal reservation: Father Coughlin of the Shrine of the Little Flower, whose eloquence over the radio had gained for his National Union for Social Justice an immense following, somewhat similar to Huey Long's. Father Coughlin's voice was raised in behalf not only of "a living annual wage" but of "nationalization of banking and currency and of national resources." How much strength might this prophet of the air waves command by 1936, if recovery continued to lag, and how would he dispose it?

Even more portentous, for a time, seemed the incredible organization headed by Dr. Francis E. Townsend of Long Beach, California. Not until the first of January, 1934, had this elderly physician announced his plan for a government allowance of $200 a month to every citizen 60 years of age or older, the pension to be financed by a sales tax--and to be spent by each recipient within 30 days, thus assuring (so the argument ran) such a wave of spending that business

168

would boom and the sales tax would easily be borne. Yet so glowing was the appeal of the Townsend Old Age Revolving Pensions plan, and so clever was Townsend's aide Robert L. Clements in organizing Townsend Clubs, welding them into a hierarchic national system, and providing the faithful with a *Townsend National Weekly* and with speakers' manuals, Townsend buttons, stickers, tire covers, and automobile plates, that within a year the Townsend planners were said to possess the balance of political power in eleven states west of the Mississippi and were entrenched even in Ohio, Indiana, Illinois, and Massachusetts.

Smile as one might at the naïve devotion of these embattled old folks, in their annual convention, as they heard Townsend and Clements likened to George Washington and Alexander Hamilton, and rose to sing

Onward, Townsend soldiers,
Marching as to war,
With the Townsend banner
Going on before.
Our devoted soldiers
Bid depression go;
Join them in the battle,
Help them fight the foe!

it was no smiling matter for the Democratic general staff that the number of Townsend Club members was conservatively estimated at three million, and that the movement, by the end of 1935, had gained at least ten million supporters. Old age, it appeared, must be served.

And what of the communists? They were few in number compared with these other groups, but the influence of their scattered agents in provoking labor disputes and offering aggressive labor leadership was disproportionately great, the intellectual offensive waged by their journalists and writers was powerful, and they formed the spearhead for a wide-ranging attack upon the New Deal from the left--an attack epitomized in such books as *The Economic Consequences of the New Deal,* by Benjamin Stolberg and Warren Jay Vinton, which denounced Roosevelt for trying to "organize scarcity" instead of "organizing abundance" and for trying merely to shore up the vicious and doomed system of capitalism, instead of wholeheartedly siding with the proletariat in the coming "irreconcilable conflict between capital and labor." To the communists and their allies, in 1934 and early 1935, a liberal who did not stand for unrelenting war in this conflict was a fascist in sheep's clothing. Alien to the American temper and American habits of thought as the communist credo was, it had a boldness, a last-resort ferocity, that might commend itself to millions of desperate men.

What of the future possibilities of some such movement as Upton Sinclair's EPIC (End Poverty in California) campaign? Sinclair had recommended that the unemployed be set to work producing for one another, setting up--by an extension of the barter plans which had been so hopefully tried at the bottom of the Depression--a sort of economy-within-the-going-economy. Sinclair had scared prosperous Californians half to death in the elections of 1934, and had been defeated only with the aid of motion pictures faked by the Hollywood studios, showing dreadful-looking bums arriving in California by the carload to enjoy the new Eden that Sinclair promised.

And what of the farmer-labor movement in the Northwest, and of the aggressive Governor Floyd Olson of Minnesota as a possible leader?

In dealing with these various political menaces on the left the quarterback showed himself to be a brilliant broken-field runner. Roosevelt smiled upon Sinclair--without embracing him. Pushing forward the Social Security Bill, he gave implicit assurance to the Townsendites that he intended to secure for them at least half a loaf. Not without a side glance at Huey Long and Father Coughlin, he suddenly produced in the summer of 1935 a proposal to increase the taxes upon the rich--to levy a big toll upon inheritances and large incomes and a graduated tax upon corporation incomes. The tax did not produce much revenue and its effect upon the wealthy was apoplectic; but

170

Huey was so delighted that he moved back on the New Deal reservation--for how long, nobody could predict.

Yet all the broken-field dodging in the world could hardly have got Roosevelt past all these captains of dissent had not luck, too, intervened on his side. The luck assumed strange guises. Who would have guessed that Stalin, fearing the rise to power of Hitler and Mussolini, would have called upon good communists everywhere to join forces with liberal democrats in Popular Fronts--as he did in the summer of 1935--and that the advice from Moscow would soon spike the guns which the communists had been leveling at Roosevelt? Or that the powerful Olson of Minnesota would fall fatally ill and be unable to head a third party? Or that Huey Long, walking down the corridor of his own State Capitol in Baton Rouge in the evening of September 8, 1935, would be shot by a young physician, Carl Austin Weiss, Jr., and fatally wounded--while Huey's bodyguards, leaping too late to his defense, drilled the assassin with sixty-one bullets?

§ 6

While these assorted threats were still menacing the New Deal from the left, there fell from the right such a body blow that almost its whole program seemed in danger of annihilation. In a unanimous decision on May 27, 1935, the United States Supreme Court invalidated the NRA.

By implication, furthermore, the Court did much more than that. Had it struck down the NRA alone, the blow would not have been staggering; for the NRA, as we have seen, had long since been recognized as the problem child of the New Deal. Had the Court's objection simply been to the drafting of the statute, the blow would not have been staggering; for Congress and the Executive were accustomed to being reminded that he who legislates in haste must expect to be invalidated at leisure. Had the Court even been content with objecting--as it did object--to the way in which the National Industrial Recovery Act had delegated lawmaking powers to trade associations, the blow would

171

not have been staggering. What was lethal about the decision was that--as Charles and Mary Beard have put it--"In the opinion that supported the decision, the Chief Justice seemed to block every loophole for the regulation of procedures, hours, and wages in industries by Federal law."

The decision implied that it would be unconstitutional for the Federal government to deal with a national industrial or social or agricultural problem by dictating to individual factories, stores, or farmers what they should do. For the operation of a factory, according to the Court's reasoning, was an intrastate operation--even if the raw materials which it manufactured came from another state, and the factory competed with factories in other states. The operation of a store was intrastate, even if this store was operated by a national chain incorporated in another state, sold goods made in other states, and was at a hundred other points affected by the economic conditions in other states. The growing of crops was an intrastate process, even if when grown they moved into interstate commerce and the price which the farmer received was dependent upon a national market. No, said the Court: under the Constitution the Federal government may regulate only interstate commerce, and none of these things are interstate commerce as we interpret it. Not even in a national emergency may the Federal government deal with them. "Extraordinary conditions do not create or enlarge constitutional power."

If the decision of May 27, 1935, was remarkable, so was the President's manner of replying to it. Four days later, more than two hundred newspaper men crowded into the Executive Offices at the White House to hear what he had to say. Jammed shoulder to shoulder in the hot room--for it was a warm day outside--and too cramped for ready note-taking, they listened to a discussion of the decision which lasted for an hour and twenty-five minutes. While Mrs. Roosevelt, sitting beside the President, knitted steadily on a blue sock, Roosevelt began by reading a few of the telegrams that had reached him since the decision--telegrams asking whether there wasn't something he could do to "save the people"--and then, placing a fresh cigarette in his holder, began a measured and carefully thought-out, if informal, analysis of the meaning of the decision, which he said was "more important than any decision probably since the Dred Scott case." Only two or three times did his voice rise in anger, but it thrilled with intensity throughout, and the reporters could have no doubt that he was profoundly moved.

"The big issue," said the President, "is this: Does this decision mean that the United States Government has no control over any economic problem?" And again--after a long analysis of the changes in the nature of the national economy since the Interstate Commerce Clause was written, and of the increase in economic interdependence since the days of the early Court decisions interpreting that clause strictly--"We have been relegated to the horse-and-buggy definition of interstate commerce." A great question, he said, had been raised for national decision--"The biggest question that has come before this country outside of time of war, and it has to be decided. And, as I say, it may take five years or ten years."

Before the correspondents filed out, there came a question from one of them: "You made a reference to the necessity of the people deciding within the next five or ten years. Is there any way of deciding that question without voting on a constitutional amendment or the passing of one?"

"Oh, yes, I think so," said the President. "But it has got to come, in the final analysis."

"Any suggestion as to how it might be made, except by a constitutional amendment?"

"No; we haven't got to that yet."

Nor was he to get to it for nearly two years.

Chapter Eight

WHEN THE FARMS BLEW AWAY

§ 1

It was on Armistice Day of 1933 that the first of the great dust storms swept across South Dakota.

"By mid-morning a gale was blowing, cold and black. By noon it was blacker than night, because one can see through night and this was an opaque black. It was a wall of dirt one's eyes could not penetrate, but it could penetrate the eyes and ears and nose. It could penetrate to the lungs until one coughed up black. If a person was outside, he tied his handkerchief around his face, but he still coughed up black; and inside the house the Karnstrums soaked sheets and towels and stuffed them around the window ledges, but these didn't help much.

"They were afraid, because they had never seen anything like this before. . . .

"When the wind died and the sun shone forth again, it was on a different world. There were no fields, only sand drifting into mounds and eddies that swirled in what was now but an autumn breeze. There was no longer a section-line road fifty feet from the front door. It was obliterated. In the farmyard, fences, machinery, and trees were gone, buried. The roofs of sheds stuck out through drifts deeper than a man is tall."

I quote from an account by R. D. Lusk, in the *Saturday Evening Post,* of the way in which that first great storm of blowing dust hit the 470-acre Karnstrum farm in Beadle County, South Dakota. But the description might apply equally well to thousands of other farms on the Great Plains all the way from the Texas Panhandle up to the Canadian border, and to any one of numberless storms that swept the Plains during the next two years. For the "great black blizzard" of November 11, 1933--which darkened the sky in Chicago the following day and as far east as Albany, New York, the day after that--was only a prelude to disaster. During 1934 and 1935 thousands of square miles were to be laid waste and their inhabitants set adrift upon desperate migrations across the land.

Long afterward, an elderly farm woman from the Dust Bowl-- one of that straggling army of refugees whose predicament has been made vivid to hundreds of thousands of readers in Steinbeck's *The Grapes of Wrath*--told her story to Paul Taylor and Dorothea Lange in California. She described how her family had done pretty well on their Arkansas farm until the Depression, when prices had fallen and they had found themselves in hard straits. "And then," said she, "the Lord taken a hand."

To many others it must have seemed as if the Lord had taken a hand in bringing the dust storms: as if, not content with visiting upon the country a man-made crisis--a Depression caused by men's inability to manage their economic affairs farsightedly--an omnipotent power had followed it with a visitation of nature: the very land itself had risen in revolt. (To other people, omnipotence may have seemed to be enjoying a sardonic joke at the expense of the New Deal's Agricultural Adjustment program: "So it's crop-reduction you want, is it? Well, I'll show you.") Yet this was no blind stroke of nature such as that of the hurricane which, wandering far from the paths usually followed by hurricanes, tore across New England in the fall of 1938, swamping towns, ripping up forests, and taking nearly seven hundred lives. There was a long story of human error behind it.

Pictures, Inc.

BLACK BLIZZARD COMING!
Looking along a western Oklahoma highway in December, 1935,
as a cloud black with powdered topsoil rolls up

During the latter part of the nineteenth century the Great Plains--a region of light rainfall, of sun and high winds, of waving grasses, "where seldom is heard a discouraging word, and the skies are not cloudy all day"--had been the great cattle country of the nation: a vast open area, unfenced at first, where the cowboys tended the cattle-kings' herds. Before the end of the century this range had been badly damaged by over-grazing, according to contemporary Federal reports, and the land was being heavily invaded by homesteaders, who tried manfully to wring a living from the semi-arid soil. But it was not until the Great War brought a huge demand for wheat, and tractors for large-scale machine farming became available, that the Plains began to come into their own as a crop-producing country, and the sod-covering which had protected them was plowed up on the grand scale.

Throughout the nineteen-twenties the area devoted to big wheat farms expanded. A new power era had come, it was said, to revolutionize American agriculture; factory methods were being triumphantly applied to the land.

To be sure, there wasn't much rain. The mean annual rainfall was only between 10 and 20 inches on the Plains (as compared with, for example, 20 to 40 in the Mississippi Valley region, 40 to 50 in the North Atlantic region, 40 to 60 in the Ohio and Tennessee basins, and 75 and more in the Pacific Northwest). But there was a pretty favorable series of years during the nineteen-twenties and the farmers were not much disturbed.

In a recent report of the National Resources Committee there is a revealing map. It shows--by means of black dots scattered over the United States--the regions where there was an increase, between 1919 and 1929, in the acreage of land in harvested crops: in short, it shows the regions newly invaded by the crop farmer. Easily the most conspicuous feature of the map is an irregular blur of those black dots running from north to south just a little east of the Rocky Mountains-- running from the Canadian border at the northern edge of Montana and North Dakota, down through the Dakotas, western Kansas and Nebraska and eastern Colorado, and then into Oklahoma and northern Texas. This, very roughly, was the next region of promise--and the region of future tragedy.

Nineteen-thirty was a bad year in parts of this territory--and worse elsewhere; it was then, you may recall, that President Hoover was agitated over the question whether Federal money should be granted to drought-distressed farmers. Nineteen-thirty-one was worse in the Dakotas; 1932 was better. Then came 1933: it was a swinger, hot and dry. During that first summer of the New Deal, farmers in South Dakota were finding that they couldn't raise even enough corn to feed the livestock. In western Kansas not a drop of rain fell for months. Already the topsoil was blowing; there were places in Kansas where it was said that farmers had to excavate their tractors before they could begin to plow. That fall came the Armistice Day black blizzard.

But it was during 1934 and 1935--the years when Roosevelt was pushing through his financial reforms, and Huey Long was a national portent, and the languishing NRA was put out of its misery by the Supreme Court--that the thermometer in Kansas stayed week after week at 108 or above and the black storms raged again and again. The drought continued acute during much of 1936. Oklahoma farms became great dunes of shifting sand (so like seashore dunes, said one observer, that one almost expected to smell the salt). Housewives in the drought belt kept oiled cloths on the window sills and between the upper and lower sashes of the windows, and some of them tried to seal up every aperture in their houses with the gummed paper strips used in wrapping parcels, yet still the choking dust filtered in and lay in ripples on the kitchen floor, while outside it blew blindingly across a No Man's Land; roads and farm buildings and once green thickets half-buried in the sand. It was in those days that a farmer, sitting at his window during a dust storm, remarked that he was counting the Kansas farms as they came by.

Retribution for the very human error of breaking the sod of the Plains had come in full measure. And, as often happens, it was visited upon the innocent as well as upon the guilty--if indeed one could single out any individuals as guilty of so pervasive an error as social shortsightedness.

§ 2

Westward fled the refugees from this new Sahara, as if obedient to the old American tradition that westward lies the land of promise. In 1934 and 1935 Californians became aware of an increasing influx into their state of families and groups of families of "Okies," traveling in ancient family jalopies; but for years the streams of humanity continued to run. They came along U. S. Highway 30 through the Idaho hills, along Highway 66 across New Mexico and Arizona, along the Old Spanish Trail through El Paso, along all the other westward trails. They came in decrepit, square-shouldered 1925 Dodges and 1927 La Salles; in battered 1923 Model-T Fords that looked like

178

relics of some antique culture; in trucks piled high with mattresses and cooking utensils and children, with suitcases, jugs, and sacks strapped to the running boards. "They roll westward like a parade," wrote Richard L. Neuberger. "In a single hour from a grassy meadow near an Idaho road I counted 34 automobiles with the license plates of states between Chicago and the mountains."

They left behind them a half-depopulated countryside. A survey of the farmhouses in seven counties of southeastern Colorado, made in 1936, showed 2878 houses still occupied, 2811 abandoned; and there were also, in that area, 1522 abandoned homesites. The total number of drought refugees who took the westward trek over the mountains was variously estimated in 1939 at from 200,000 upwards-- with more coming all the time.

As these wanderers moved along the highways they became a part of a vast and confused migratory movement. When they camped by the wayside they might find themselves next to a family of evicted white Alabama sharecroppers who had been on the move for four years, snatching seasonal farm-labor jobs wherever they could through the Southwest; or next to tenant families from the Arkansas Delta who had been "tractored off" their land--expelled in order that the owner might consolidate two or three farms and operate them with tractors and day labor; or next to lone wanderers who had once held industrial jobs and had now for years been on relief or on the road--jumping freights, hitchhiking, panhandling, shunting back and forth across the countryside in the faint hope of a durable job. And when these varied streams of migrants reached the Coast they found themselves in desperate competition for jobs with individuals or families who for years had been "fruit tramps," moving northward each year with the harvests from the Imperial Valley in southern California to the Sacramento Valley or even to the apple-picking in the Yakima Valley in Washington.

Here in the land of promise, agriculture had long been partly industrialized. Huge farms were in the control of absentee owners or banks or corporations, and were accustomed to depend upon the labor of migratory "fruit tramps," who had formerly been mostly Mexicans, Japanese, and other foreigners, but now were increasingly Americans. Those laborers who were lucky enough to get jobs picking cotton or

179

peas or fruit would be sheltered temporarily in camps consisting typically of frame cabins in rows, with a water line between every two rows; they were very likely to find in their cabin no stove, no cots, no water pail. Even the best of the camps offered a way of life strikingly different from that of the ruggedly individualist farmer of the American tradition, who owned his farm or else was preparing, by working as a resident "hired man," or by renting a farm, for the chance of ultimate ownership. These pickers were homeless, voteless nomads, unwanted anywhere save at the harvest season.

When wave after wave of the new migrants reached California, the labor market became glutted, earnings were low, and jobs became so scarce that groups of poverty-stricken families would be found squatting in makeshift Hoovervilles or bunking miserably in their awkward old Fords by the roadside. Being Americans of native stock and accustomed to independence, they took the meager wages and the humiliation bitterly, sought to organize, talked of striking, sometimes struck. At every such threat, something like panic seized the growers. If this new proletariat were permitted to organize, and were to strike at picking time, they might ruin the whole season's output of a perishable crop. There followed anti-picketing ordinances; the spectacle of armed deputies dislodging the migrants from their pitiful camps; violence by bands of vigilantes, to whom these ragged families were not fellow-citizens who had suffered in a great American disaster but dirty, ignorant, superstitious outlanders, failures at life, easy dupes for "red" agitators. This engulfing tide of discontent must be kept moving.

Farther north the refugees were likely to be received with more sympathy, especially in regions where the farms were small and not industrialized; here and there one heard of instances of real hospitality, such as that of the Oregon town which held a canning festival for the benefit of the drought victims in the neighborhood. The well-managed camps set up by the Farm Security Administration were havens of human decency. But to the vast majority of the refugees the promised land proved to be a place of new and cruel tragedy.

§ 3

These unhappy wanderers of the West were only a small minority of the farmers of the United States. What was happening to the rest of them?

We have already seen the AAA beginning the colossal task of making acreage-reduction agreements with millions of farmers in the hope of jacking up the prices of crops and thus restoring American agriculture to economic health. We have seen it making credit available to farmers and trying, through the Farm Mortgage Moratorium Act and other legislation, to free them of the immediate hazards of debt. Just how successful the AAA program could be considered was still, at the end of the decade, a subject of ferocious controversy, if only because one could not separate its effect upon prices from the effects wrought by the drought and by the general improvement in economic conditions after 1933. But certainly farm prices rose. For example, the farmer who had received, on the average, only 33 cents a bushel for wheat in 1933 received 69 cents in 1934, 89 cents in 1935, 92 cents in 1936, $1.24 in 1937, and 88 cents in 1938. The cotton farmer who had received an average price of 5.6 cents a pound for his cotton in 1933 received between 10 and 13 cents during the next four years, and 7.9 cents in 1938. And certainly there was a general improvement in the condition of those farmers who owned their own farms--and lived outside the worst drought areas. A survey of 3,000 farms in various parts of the country--mostly better-than-average farms--made by the Department of Agriculture in 1938 showed a distinct gain in equipment and in comfort; more of these farms had electricity than in 1930, more had tractors and trucks, more had bathrooms, automobiles, and radios. But this was not a complete picture of what had happened.

To begin with, quantities of farmers had lost their farms during the hideous early years of the Depression--lost them by reason of debt. These farms had mostly fallen into the hands of banks or insurance companies, or of small-town investors who had held the mortgages on them, or were being held by government bodies for non-payment of taxes, or had been bought in at tax sales. As early as 1934, the National Resources Board stated that nearly thirty per cent of the total value of farm land in the West North Central States was owned by "creditor or government agencies which have been compelled to take over the property." At the small prairie city, the local representative of a big New York insurance company was a very busy man, supervising the management of tracts of property far and wide. The tentacles of the octopus of metropolitan financial control reached more deeply than ever before into the prairie country--though one must add that this octopus was a most unwilling one, and would have been only too glad to let go if it could only get its money back. (As time went on, the Metropolitan and other insurance companies made determined efforts to find buyers for their farm properties, financing these buyers on easy terms.) In the callous old Wall Street phrase, the farms of the United States had been "passing into stronger hands"; and that meant that more and more of them, owned by people who did not live on them, were being operated by tenants.

For over half a century at least, farm tenancy had been on the increase in the United States. Back in 1880, only 25 per cent of American farms had been run by tenants. Slowly the percentage had increased; now, during the Depression, it reached 42. The growth of tenantry caused many misgivings, for not only did it shame the fine old Jeffersonian ideal of individual landholding--an ideal in which most Americans firmly believed--but it had other disadvantages. Tenants were not likely to put down roots, did not feel a full sense of responsibility for the land and equipment they used, were likely to let it deteriorate, and in general were less substantial citizens than those farmers who had a permanent share in the community. In 1935, less than two-thirds of the tenant farmers in the United States had occupied their present land for more than one year! In the words of Charles and Mary Beard, "Tenants wandered from farm to farm, from landlord to landlord, from region to region, on foot, in battered wagons, or in dilapidated automobiles, commonly dragging families with them, usually to conditions lower in the scale of living than those from which they had fled."

The passing of farms into "stronger hands" was accompanied by another change. More and more the farm owner, whether or not he operated his own farm, was coming to think of himself as a business man, to think of farming as a business. He was less likely to use his farm as a means of subsistence, more likely to use as much of it as possible for the growing of crops for sale. He was more interested in bookkeeping, more alert to the advantages of farm machinery, and especially of operating with tractors on the largest possible scale. A striking example of this trend was the appearance of the "suitcase farmer"--a small-town business man who bought a farm or two, cleared them of houses and barns, spent a few weeks of each year planting and harvesting them (using his own tractor or a hired one), and otherwise devoted himself to his business, not living on the land at all. A Kansas banker told Ladd Haystead, toward the end of the decade, that he estimated that between twenty and thirty per cent of the land in western Kansas was owned by suitcase farmers. This was what was happening to the territory whence the victims of drought had fled!

In certain parts of the South and Southwest this trend toward making a mechanized business of farming took a form even more sinister in the eyes of those who believed in the Jeffersonian tradition. In these districts farm tenancy was becoming merely a way station on the road to farm industrialism. The tenants themselves were being eliminated. Furthermore, the AAA, strangely enough, was unwittingly assisting the process.

How easy for an owner of farm property, when the government offered him a check for reducing his acreage in production, to throw out some of his tenants or sharecroppers, buy a tractor with the check, and run his farm mechanically with the aid of hired labor--not the sort of year-round hired labor which the old-time "hired man" had represented, but labor engaged only by the day when there happened to be work to be done! During the nineteen-thirties large numbers of renters and sharecroppers, both black and white, were being displaced in the South--to the tune of angry protests by the Southern Tenant Farmers' Union, equally angry retaliation by the landlords and their allies, and a deal of the sort of barbarous cruelty which we have noted in California. In the areas where large-scale cotton farming with the aid of machinery was practicable, tenants were expelled right and left. *Fortune* told of a big Mississippi planter who bought 22 tractors and 13 4-row cultivators, evicted no less than 130 of his 160 sharecropper families, and kept only 30 for day laborers. During the years 1930-37, the sales of farm tractors in ten cotton states increased no less than ninety per cent--and the indications were that at the end of that period the increase was accelerating. While the number of farms operated by tenants was growing elsewhere in the country between 1930 and 1935, it actually declined a little in the West South Central States. In two cotton counties of the Texas Panhandle, studied by Paul S. Taylor in 1937, it declined sharply. And here was the reason: "Commonly, the landlord who purchases a tractor throws two 160-acre farms operated by tenants into an operating unit, and lets both tenants go. Sometimes the rate of displacement is greater, rising to 8, 10, and even 15 families of tenants."

Where did the displaced tenants go? Into the towns, some of them. In many rural areas, census figures showed an increased town population and simultaneously a depopulated countryside. Said the man at a gas station in a Texas town, "This relief is ruining the town. They come in from the country to get on relief." Some of them got jobs running tractors on other farms at $1.25 a day. Some went on to California: out of farming as a settled way of life into farming as big business dependent on a large, mobile supply of labor.

So far this new pattern was only fragmentary and was confined mostly to the South and West, though the number of migratory farm workers was growing fast even along the Atlantic seaboard. Perhaps the onrushing agricultural industrialism would prove as short-lived as the earlier epidemic of tractor farming which had promised so much for the Great Plains during the nineteen-twenties--would lead once more to depletion of the soil and thus to its own undoing as well as the land's. Perhaps those agrobiologists were right who believed that the trend of the future would be toward smaller farms and more intensive yields. The relatively new science of farm chemurgy was revealing all sorts of new industrial uses for farm products; du Pont, for example, was using farm products in the making of cellophane, Duco, motion-picture film, rayon, pyralin, plastecele, fabrikoid, sponges, window shades, hair ornaments, handbags, alcohols, and a lot of other things which one would hardly associate with the old-fashioned farm. Yet even if the farmer of the future who applied new methods to the growing of specialized crops for specialized uses would be able to operate best with a small tract of land, as some people expected, would he be able to operate without more capital than most farmers possessed? That question was still unanswered.

Meanwhile large-scale tractor farming was spreading fast, and was repeating the harshnesses of mid-nineteenth century industrialism--as if America had learned nothing in the interim.

How far would the new trend go? Would great mechanized farm corporations, perhaps controlled from the metropolitan cities, gradually put out of business the smaller farms of those rolling areas, such as abounded in the Old Cotton South, where tractors could not readily be used? Would the cotton picker invented by the Rust brothers of Memphis accelerate this change? What would become, then, of the already miserable sharecroppers? Were other parts of the country destined sooner or later to go through the same sort of transition that was taking place in the South and West, producing a huge, roving, landless proletariat of the land, helpless if unorganized, menacing if organized because it had no stake in the land and its settled institutions? These questions, too, waited for answers.

§ 4

For a generation or more the conservationists had been warning the country that it was squandering its heritage of land and forests and fields and minerals and animal life: that in effect it was living riotously on its capital of national resources. But to most citizens the subject had seemed dull, academic. Now, in the Dust Bowl, the Lord had "taken a hand" in instruction. And hardly had the black blizzards blown themselves out when--as if distrustful whether the country properly realized that droughts and floods were not incompatible phenomena, but were associated results of human misuse of the land--the Lord drove the lesson home. The rivers went on a rampage.

"In 1936"--I quote from Stuart Chase's summary--"the Merrimac, Connecticut, Hudson, Delaware, Susquehanna, Potomac, Allegheny, and Ohio all went wild. The Potomac was up twenty-six feet at Washington and long barriers of sandbags protected government buildings. . . . Pittsburgh was under ten to twenty feet of water and was without lights, transport, or power. The life of 700,000 people was paralyzed. The food supply was ruined, the steel industry at a standstill." The following January, the unseasonably warm and rainy January of 1937, the Ohio River produced what was perhaps, all things considered, the worst flood in American history.

The bare facts of that flood are impressive. The Ohio rose 7.9 feet higher than it had ever risen before at Cincinnati, 6.8 feet higher than it had ever risen before at Louisville. Nine hundred people were estimated to have lost their lives by drowning or by other casualties resulting from the flood. The number of families driven from their homes was set at 500,000; the number still homeless a month after the worst of the crisis was set by the Red Cross at 299,000.

But these figures give no impression whatever of what men and women experienced in each town during the latter days of January as the swirling waters rose till the Ohio seemed a great rushing muddy lake full of floating wreckage, and the cold rain drizzled inexorably down, and every stream added its swollen contribution to the torrent. Railroad tracks and roads washed away. Towns darkened as the electric-light plants were submerged. Business halted, food supplies stopped, fires raging out of control, disease threatening. The city of Portsmouth, Ohio, opening six great sewer valves and letting seven feet of water rush into its business district, lest its famous concrete flood wall be destroyed. Cincinnati giving City Manager Dykstra dictatorial powers. The radio being used to direct rescue work and issue warnings and instructions to the population as other means of communication failed: a calm voice at the microphone telling rescuers to row to such-and-such an address and take a family off the roof, to row somewhere else and help an old woman out of a second-story window. Breadlines. The Red Cross, the Coast Guard, the WPA aiding in the work of rescue and reorganization. Martial law. Churches above the water line being used as refuges. Dead bodies of horses and cattle-- yes, and of men and women--floating through the streets, along with tree branches, gasoline tanks, beams from collapsed houses. Mud everywhere, as the waters receded--mud and stench. Most dramatic of all, perhaps, the triumphant fight to save Cairo, Illinois: men piling more and more sandbags atop the levee, standing guard day and night, rushing to strengthen the wall of defense wherever it weakened, as the waters rose and rose--and did not quite break over.

186

By this time everybody with any capacity for analysis was ready to begin to understand what the government technicians had long been saying in their monographs; what Stuart Chase and Paul B. Sears and David Cushman Coyle, the Mississippi Valley Committee and the National Resources Committee, and Pare Lorenz's very fine films, "The River" and "The Plough that Broke the Plains," were repeating in more popular terms: that floods as well as dust storms were largely the result of reckless misuse of the land. Indeed, as early as the beginning of 1936, when the Supreme Court threw out the Agricultural Adjustment Act, Congress took account of the new understanding in revamping its farm program. The new law was labeled a Soil Conservation and Domestic Allotment Act, and the new crop adjustments were called "soil-erosion adjustments."

Already at many points the government was at work restoring a deforested and degrassed and eroded countryside. In the CCC camps, young men were not only getting healthy employment, but were renewing and protecting the forest cover by planting trees, building firebreaks, removing inflammable underbrush, and building check dams in gullies. The experts of the Soil Conservation Service were showing farmers how to fight erosion by terracing, contour plowing, rotation of crops, strip cropping, and gully planting. After the dust storms, for example, they demonstrated how the shifting dunes of Dalhart, Texas, could be held in place by planting them with milo, Sudan grass, and black amber cane. Under the supervision of the Forest Service, the government between 1935 and 1939 planted 127,000,000 trees to serve as windbreaks on the Great Plains. The Taylor Grazing Act of 1934 stopped homesteading on the great range and gave the Department of the Interior power to prevent over-grazing on eighty million acres.

PWA funds were going into the construction of dams which would aid in flood control (and also extend navigation), such as that at Fort Peck in eastern Montana, which was to create a lake 175 miles long. The TVA--that most combative and most remarkable of New Deal agencies--was not simply creating a new electric-light and power system in competition with privately owned utilities (though this part of its work stirred up ten times as much excitement as all the rest put together); its dams were also controlling floods, and it was showing farmers how to deal with erosion, how to use phosphates. (In 1937, during the Ohio River flood, the Tennessee River did not misbehave.) Other PWA funds were providing a better irrigation system for parts of Utah where water was running short. The colossal dam at Grand Coulee, Washington--the biggest thing ever built by man--was getting ready to pump water for the irrigation of 1,200,000 acres of desert land, as well as to provide hydroelectric power in quantity (like its sister dam at Bonneville) for the future development of the Northwest. These were only a few of the numerous enterprises going ahead simultaneously.

Nor was the government undertaking these enterprises in a wholly piecemeal manner: through its National Resources Committee and other agencies it was making comprehensive studies of the country's resources and equipment, so that the movement of restoration and regeneration could proceed with a maximum of wisdom.

§ 5

With the aid of these studies--and of the lessons taught by drought and flood--more and more Americans, during the latter nineteen-thirties, were beginning to see the problem of their country's future in a new light. They were beginning to realize that it had reached maturity. No longer was it growing hand-over-fist.

Immigration was no longer adding appreciably to its numbers: indeed, during the years between 1931 and 1936, the number of aliens *emigrating* from the United States had been larger each year than the number *immigrating:* the tide had actually been trickling in reverse. If, beginning in 1936, the incoming tide had increased again as Europeans sought to escape from the shadow of Hitlerism, even so the total remained tiny in comparison with those of pre-war years. Ellis Island was no longer a place of furious activity. The time was at hand when the number of foreign-born people in the United States would be sharply diminished by death, and the sound of foreign languages would be heard less and less in the streets of American cities. Already the schools, the manufacturers of children's clothing, and the toy manufacturers were beginning to notice the effects of the diminished birth rate (accentuated by the sharp drop during the early Depression years). Writing in the spring of 1938, Henry Pratt Fairchild reported that there were over 1,600,000 fewer children under 10 in the United States than there had been five years earlier. School principals, confronting smaller entering classes of children, could well understand what the population experts were talking about when they predicted a slower and slower population growth for the country, with an increasing proportion of old people and a decreasing proportion of young ones. They could see the change taking place before their own eyes.

That the frontier was closed was not yet quite true, a generation of historians to the contrary notwithstanding; for the Northwest was still a land of essentially frontier possibilities. Yet for a long time past, young men and women bent on fortune had mostly been going, not west, but to the cities. If the victims of the Dust Bowl and the tractor had pushed west, their fate had been ironic. The brief return to the country of great numbers of jobless city dwellers during the early Depression years had only temporarily slowed down the movement from farm to city and town. For a long time past, the fastest-growing communities had been, by and large, not Western boom towns but the suburbs which ringed the big cities--and during the nineteen-thirties these suburbs were still adding to their numbers. Industry, by and large, was no longer moving westward; the great bulk of the country's manufacturing was still done along the north Atlantic seaboard and in the strip of territory running thence out through Pennsylvania and Ohio to Chicago and St. Louis--and some observers, even believed they detected during the nineteen-thirties a slight shift back toward the East.

American individuals and families were becoming more nomadic. This was partly due to the omnipresence of the automobile; there were three million more cars on the road in 1937 than in 1929, for though fewer cars were sold, more old ones were still in use. Partly, as we have seen, it was due to the Depression search for jobs and to the eviction of farm tenants. But American *institutions* appeared, geographically, to be settling down.

Still there was a chance for a far richer development of the country, and the chance was most visible west of the Great Plains. Yet if this development was to be durable, the new pioneering must be more disciplined than the old. The hard fact that the days were over when Americans could plunder and move on, stripping off forests, ripping out minerals, and plowing up grasslands without regard to the long consequences, was now penetrating the public consciousness-- even while the men and women whose farms had blown away were still wandering homeless through the land.

Chapter Nine

THE VOICE WITH THE SMILE WINS

§ 1

Dance orchestras were blaring forth "The Music Goes 'Round and 'Round" and one could hardly turn a radio dial without hearing the ubiquitous refrain. Major Bowes was the current radio sensation, so warmly did he inquire into the life histories of the yodelers and jews-harp-players on his Amateur Hour, and so spontaneous and unexpected seemed the well-rehearsed programs. At the movie houses Fred Astaire and Ginger Rogers were dancing nimbly in "Follow the Fleet." Gary Cooper was about to introduce his audiences to the word "pixillated" in the hilarious courtroom scene of "Mr. Deeds Goes to Town." Seven-year-old Shirley Temple was becoming the rising star of Hollywood. She had no such income-tax troubles as had Mae West, whose salary of $480,833 for the preceding year had been second only, in all the United States, to that of William Randolph Hearst; nor could any Shirley Temple picture attract at its opening such crowds as greeted Charlie Chaplin's "Modern Times"; but her curls and her childish smile made the great American heart throb with sentiment. (She was about to appear in "Captain January.")

To scores of thousands of readers, *Life with Father* was still offering an acquaintance with the rambunctious Clarence Day, senior; *North to the Orient,* an air ride with the Lindberghs. Among best-selling novels, *Vein of Iron* and *It Can't Happen Here* were yielding their leadership to *The Last Puritan,* and people who believed in the finer things of life were expressing pleasure that a genuine hundred-percent philosopher like George Santayana should have been able to hit commercial success on the nose. In the fastnesses of the publishing house of Macmillan the editors were wondering whether a forthcoming novel of theirs, Margaret Mitchell's *Gone with the Wind,* might possibly sell as well as *Anthony Adverse.* (It would not only do that but within its first six months would sell over a million copies--a prodigious record--and would set ladies' luncheon tables from coast to coast buzzing with the question whether Scarlett O'Hara really got Rhett Butler back--and who ought to play Scarlett on the screen.)

It was a cold winter in the North, with heavy drifts of snow. Sales of skiing equipment were noteworthy, and the snow trains bore away to the uplands innumerable incipient experts in the slalom--or in the lesser art of teetering safely down a very small hill. Over in Germany the Olympic winter sports were being held, as a prelude to that monstrous summer carnival of athletics in which it was to be revealed to the eyes even of Adolf Hitler that Nordics, whatever their transcendent virtues, could not run as fast as black Jesse Owens. (The Germans, however, would have their reply ready: had not their Max Schmeling confounded the sports writers by defeating Joe Louis at the Yankee Stadium by a technical knockout in the twelfth round?)

If the zest of ladies and gentlemen for corporate finance was being circumscribed by the SEC, they at least could undertake imaginary feats of financial daring in the parlor game of "Monopoly." The time was approaching when a popular if short-lived diversion among otherwise reasonable Americans would be the exchange of such curious pleasantries as these: "Knock, knock." "Who's there?" "Eskimo, Christian, and Italian." "Eskimo, Christian, and Italian who?" "Eskimo, Christian, and Italian no lies."

In short, the year 1936 was getting under way--the year when President Roosevelt's New Deal would have to face the voters.

How much water had gone under the bridge since 1932, when Roosevelt had first been a candidate for the White House! Gone was the prospect of imminent financial catastrophe. Gone was popular distrust of the solvency of the banks: bank failures now were few and far between. Gone was any real hope of collecting the war debts (except from Finland); was it possible that only five years previously, Herbert Hoover had tried to halt the Depression by proposing a year's delay in payments? Gone was any hope of early return to the traditional international gold standard: managed currencies had become the order of the day. Waning at least, if not gone, was the fear of immediate headlong inflation of the currency. (Although the huge Federal deficits--larger than any in Hoover's time--caused grave headshakings, nevertheless people went right on buying government bonds.) Yet waning also was any real expectation of an abrupt economic upsurge which would eliminate speedily the unemployment problem. Although people still talked of "the emergency" or "the crisis," clearly they were no longer thinking of any "sudden juncture," any "moment of danger," such as dictionary definitions of those terms would imply; this "emergency" had become semi-permanent. The economic system had pulled out of its sinking spell of 1929-33 only to become a chronic invalid, whose temperature was lower now in the mornings but showed no signs of returning quickly to normal. Americans were getting used to the fact that nine or ten million of their fellow-countrymen were out of work.

No longer was there any question, in the minds of most Americans capable of realistic thought, that the government must carry a heavy responsibility for the successful or unsuccessful working of the economic system. Having once intervened, it could not extricate itself even if it would. The debate was only about the extent to which the intervention should go. The economic headquarters of the country had not only moved from Wall Street to Washington, but apparently had settled down there for an indefinite stay. If, as we have seen, economic authority still tended to gravitate from the countryside to the cities and from the lesser cities to New York, until great tracts of land in the Mississippi Valley were subject to the dictates of New York executives, no longer did those executives issue their dictates as they pleased; when Washington spoke, they knew they heard their master's voice. Even the great House of Morgan--head, front, and symbol of the one-time sovereignty of Wall Street--had been forced to divide itself into two concerns, one for commercial banking, the other for investment banking. No major decision could any longer be made in Wall Street without the question being asked, "What will Washington say to this?"

The government was growing in size and complexity as well as in power. Whenever a new fever attacked the body politic, new Federal agencies multiplied--like white corpuscles in the blood--to fight it. The custom of the time decreed that each agency must be known by the initials of its title, but soon there were so many that only an expert could identify them by these alphabetical designations. RFC, NRA, and WPA might be easy even for the elementary class in governmental nomenclature; AAA, CCC, SEC, and TVA for the intermediate class; but what did HOLC stand for, and FHA, and FCA and NYA--to mention only a few?

Because the riddles which the New Deal faced were beyond its ability (or, probably, anybody's ability) to solve with real success, and because anyhow it was easier to hand out subsidies to the victims of a maladjustment than to bring the maladjustment to an end, this swelling government establishment had become a huge subsidizing machine--handing out Federal relief payments, farm allotment payments, and other "emergency" benefits innumerable, to say nothing of war bonuses and such venerable subsidies as kept the color in the wan cheeks of the merchant marine; until by 1936 an appropriation of a hundred million dollars looked like small change, and even a billion seemed no bigger than a light-year seems to an astronomer.

All this development of the Federal power the Republicans viewed with loud alarm; yet with such an air of inevitability did the growth take place that one wondered whether the Republicans, should they come to power, would be able to reverse the trend. It seemed likely that the difference between the two parties would be that one of them, in moving toward the concentration of power in Washington, would move with the throttle open; the other, with the brakes on.

In the world outside the United States the changes between 1932 and 1936 were even more striking. No longer could France be thought of as the pre-eminent power on the Continent. British diplomacy was beginning that series of surrenders and evasions which was presently to reduce sharply the prestige of the Empire. The League of Nations, which had failed to make Japan regret its invasion of Manchuria in 1931, and was now failing to make Mussolini regret his invasion of Ethiopia in 1935, was in its death throes. The Nazi government of Germany, though only three years old, was already

194

alarming the Continent; and was about to begin, with its march into the Rhineland, that series of bold territorial moves which were to keep all Europe in fear of immediate general war. Mussolini, the father of fascism, was shifting from opposition to Hitler to alliance with this younger and more furious disciple of the totalitarian idea. The European center of gravity was moving definitely toward Berlin.

No longer were vital economic decisions made at international conferences of bankers; now they were made only by the political leaders of states. That trend toward concentration of national authority in the government which was noticeable in Washington was noticeable almost everywhere else--even in Britain and France. Russia was becoming less and less the exponent of a revolutionary form of economic and social organization and more and more a nation whose dictatorial government pursued nationalist ends in a world of national rivalries. In Germany, the central power was now absolute. National Socialism had become the most dynamic religion of the day, and the head of the state was rapidly becoming an object of worship. Watching the German spectacle, American observers were wondering whether the world was irresistibly due for an era of political, racial, religious, and intellectual intolerance.

It had been expected that the economic barriers between nations would gradually be lifted after the worst of the Depression was over. But now these barriers were stronger than ever. In Germany the objective of the Nazi government was no longer primarily to solve the insoluble economic problems which confronted every government in the nineteen-thirties, but to give its people the thrill and pride of conquest; and to achieve prosperity incidentally by putting the unemployed to work (as in a vast public-works campaign) at armament-making, and by controlling its inflated currency and well-nigh every other economic activity through the exercise of central authority. The Nazis were defying half the economic axioms of the days of free business enterprise and--at least temporarily--getting away with it. They were in fact abolishing economics entirely, in the sense that the word implies an organization of the decisions of free men, and were substituting for it an organization of compulsions and conquests.

As Germany re-armed, so did the other governments. By 1936 an international armaments boom was in full swing. Indeed, so depen-

dent were the various national economies becoming upon arms manufacturing that some observers were beginning to wonder which would
be worse, the general war which so many people dreaded, or the true
peace which so many people longed for and which would put out the
fires in hundreds of factories and might light the fires of rebellion in
millions of hungry men.

Whenever people thought of "the danger of war," they thought
of such a general headlong conflict as had broken out in 1914. Experts
on foreign affairs had been predicting at intervals ever since the early
nineteen-twenties that such a conflict would surely break out next
month or next year or within two or three years at the most; and now
their predictions were more urgent than ever. Yet the pattern of international relations which was being established in Europe was a pattern
neither of general war nor of true peace. It was a pattern of continuous
half-war: of nations remaining partially mobilized, partially on a war
footing; making quick sallies to grab this territory or that, knowing
that the dread of another 1914 would prevent anybody from stopping
them until it was too late; of nations gaining new spheres of influence
by subsidizing revolts in other countries (or even aiding these revolts
by force of arms) as the Italians and Germans were shortly to aid Franco's revolt in Spain. In short, it was a pattern of shifting, localized,
undeclared, unceasing conflict. War? Peace? This was neither, by the
vocabulary even of 1932: it was something in between, to which the
words of an earlier day no longer applied.

Truly it was a new world upon which Americans were looking
in 1936: a world full of the wreckage of the verities not merely of
1929 but even of 1932.

§ 2

At last business conditions in the United States were definitely
improving. The Federal Reserve Board's Adjusted Index of Industrial
Production (which as you may recall had sunk as low as 58 and 59 in
the crises of 1932 and early 1933, had leaped to 100 during the New

Deal Honeymoon, had then slipped back to 72 by November, 1933, and had obstinately hung in the seventies and eighties throughout 1934) had now begun to show a pretty definite upward trend. By the beginning of 1935 it had risen as far as 90. By the end of 1935 it had reached 101. And after a brief relapse into the nineties, it swept on during 1936 to 104 in June, 108 in July and August, 109 in September, 110 in October, 114 in November, and 121 in December--within striking distance of the record figure of 125 which had been set in 1929.

A very pretty picture indeed--yet one could not appraise it rightly without noting several disquieting facts. One was that the production figure would have to rise much higher than 125 to absorb the bulk of the unemployed. Labor saving machinery, speed-up methods of work, and executive efficiency had now made it possible to produce more goods with less workers. Perhaps there was significance also in the fact that as a result of the drop in the birth rate and the closing down of immigration, a larger proportion of the people of the country than ever before were of working age. Another disquieting fact was that the improvement was being secured at a price--the price of a rising Federal debt. The net deficits of the United States government had been running as follows:--

Fiscal year ending June 30, 1933 (which straddled the Hoover and Roosevelt Administrations): $2,602,000,000

Fiscal year ending June 30, 1934: $3,630,000,000

Fiscal year ending June 30, 1935: $3,002,000,000

To which was now being added the 1936 figure of $4,361,000,000

This latter enormous figure for 1936 was by no means attributable solely to New Deal policies; for it was not only affected by the destruction by the Supreme Court of the processing taxes levied by the AAA, but was also very gravely enlarged by Congress's voting of the Bonus over Roosevelt's veto. On June 15, 1936, the postmen sallied forth to distribute over a billion and a half dollars in bonds and checks. Most of these were cashed within the next three months. What wonder that the deficit was larger than ever before--and that, with these new funds being spent all over the country, the business index was rising?

Throughout these early years of the New Deal the levels of prices and wages and the structure of corporate and private debt were being artificially supported by government spending--or, to put it another way, by the failure of the government to levy high enough taxes to take care of the spending. If it had been possible for the law of supply and demand to work unhindered, prices and wages--and the volume of corporate and private debt--would theoretically have fallen to a "natural" level and activity could have been resumed again. But it was not possible for the law of supply and demand to work unhindered. In a complex twentieth-century economy, deflation was too painful to be endured. Hoover had set up the RFC because the banks couldn't take it; Roosevelt had set up the Federal relief system because human beings couldn't take it. Some of Roosevelt's advisers, embracing the theory of John Maynard Keynes (and also making a virtue of necessity), had been arguing for some time that when the government, by over-spending, poured new money into the economic bloodstream, business would be stimulated and a new adjustment would be reached at a higher level, thus rendering the anguish of deflation unnecessary. The new money would "prime the pump" of business; presently all sorts of new businesses would be undertaken, there would be a boom, the unemployed would be absorbed in industry, and all would be well. Roosevelt hoped that this would happen, and so far the process seemed to be beginning. Business was picking up. But where, oh, where, were the new enterprises?

During the preceding year there had been a considerable volume of capital flotations, but chiefly these flotations had been undertaken merely to refund old issues of securities at lower interest rates: interest rates having gone down, corporations had been seizing the happy opportunity to substitute $3 \frac{3}{4}$ per cent bonds for 5 per cent bonds. Few of the flotations had represented the investment of money in the expansion of old businesses or in the inauguration of new ones. Uninvested money was piling up in the banks instead of being spent in building and equipping new factories. In short, the pump was not working right.

Of course it was not working right, argued most business men. The trouble was that investors were frightened. Naturally they were distrustful of the New Deal's reformist zeal and of the very spending policy which was supposed to entice their money into the capital markets. Surely the pump would work really well before long, replied the New Dealers; and how could they cut expenses without destroying buying power and perhaps starving their fellow-citizens? Eagerly they continued to prime the pump. Year after year, in his Budget messages, the President who had berated Hoover in 1932 for failing to balance the Budget expressed the hope that next year, or the year after, the balance would at last be achieved; but like the man who swears that this little drink is positively his last one, presently he began to sound as if he did not convince even himself.

There were other somewhat unsettling facts about this recovery, too. The Lynds noticed, for example, that in "Middletown" it was harder now for a man to start a small business than it had been even a decade before. "The Middletown tradition is all in favor of an enterprising man with an idea and a shoestring of capital," they noted. "But it is this type of small enterprise that has gone under in Middletown in the Depression." Personal savings had been eaten up, bankers were cautious, the trend in manufacturing was toward such large and expensively equipped shops that the small manufacturer was at a disadvantage, and the going concerns in many lines of business were inclined, with or without the aid of their trade associations, to make things hot for a newcomer. It was the big corporations, by and large, which were making the profits; small ones were lucky indeed to break even. Here was a barrier to new investment (which will be noted more fully in the last chapter of this book): the odds were against making money in fledgling enterprises.

Even inside going businesses, as the Lynds also pointed out, the ladder of opportunity was not so readily climbed as it once had been. The skilled laborer was finding that the higher-paid and more important positions were going to a different class of specially trained men. "In other words," said the Lynds, "Andrew Carnegie's advice to enterprising young men to begin at the bottom no longer appears to be sound advice. Men of his type are advising young men today to get a toehold in one of the managerial or technical departments halfway up the ladder."

Was this a sign of a gradual crystallization of class structure in American society? Certainly it was hard for reliefers to get themselves out of the relief class. It was hard for dispossessed farmers to get back on the land. If it was also harder than it had been for the man without a higher education or influential friends to get a job in the upper ranks of business, how would fare the American dream of a classless democracy in which anyone could go to the top?

§ 3

But how welcome was even this modest and dubiously founded recovery of 1936! The railroads, to be sure, were not getting much of it; but the automobile companies were selling more cars than in any previous season save 1928 and 1929, the steel industry was operating close to capacity at last, the consumers' goods industries and chain stores were mostly going strong, and even the building industry--which had come to a prolonged and almost complete halt during the worst of the Depression--was climbing briskly (with government aid) up the lower foothills of recovery. (No longer was it inevitably embarrassing to ask an architect what he was doing these days.) There seemed to be plenty of free-and-easy spending among the prosperous: Miami was having its best season since the collapse of the Florida boom in the distant days of Calvin Coolidge, there were lavish débutante parties in the big cities, the race tracks were crowded, the cash registers were tinkling in the night clubs. Apparently the men of means, looking ruefully back on what had happened to their investments under Hoover and meditating fearfully on what might happen to them under Roosevelt, were putting their money where they could enjoy it right away.

There were visible promises, too, if one looked about one, of what might prove to be a new industrial age. A few of the more progressively managed railroads, shaking themselves out of their long technological nap, were running slick new streamlined trains made of duralumin, stainless steel, or corten. The Union Pacific had started the new movement by completing a dural train early in 1934, the Burling-

200

ton had followed with a stainless steel Zephyr, and by the end of 1936 there were 358 cars made of these new materials in operation or under construction for the Class I railroads of the country. Whenever one of the fancy new trains was put on exhibition, crowds surged through it, entranced: here was a symbol of the new America they wanted. Air-conditioning was coming in fast, too, not only in the movie theatres and railroad trains but in restaurants and shops and offices as well. As for streamlining, it had become a briefly overworked fad. In 1934 and 1935 some of the automobile companies had produced cars so bulb-ous, so obesely curved as to defy the natural preference of the eye for horizontal lines; the city streets were being invaded by new busses streamlined against the terrific air resistance built up while edging through urban traffic at ten miles an hour; and the streamline idea was being applied by designers even to quite stationary buildings and to objects of furniture which would never have to confront a stronger draft than that of an electric fan.

New ocean liners were breaking records for size and speed. In June, 1935, the New York waterfront had been lined with crowds and the harbor had resounded with tootings of welcome as the *Normandie* arrived; a year later the reception was to be repeated as the *Queen Mary* swept in from England. As for airplanes, one had only to com-pare the great silvery Douglas DC3 of June, 1936, which had a cruising speed of 200 miles an hour, with the 110-mile-an-hour trans-port planes of 1932. Coast-to-coast travel in overnight air sleepers had become a matter of routine. In October, 1936, the China Clipper fi-nished its first scheduled round-trip passenger flight across the Pacific to Manila and back. Not yet was there any passenger service across the Atlantic by plane, but there was service by air nonetheless: Germany's newest dirigible, the *Hindenburg,* began in 1936 a regular series of flights--nor did any one then guess what would happen to that graceful ship of the air on May 6, 1937.

The motorist too could get, here and there, a glimpse of the promise of a new world when he found himself cruising at 60 miles an hour on a huge well-banked highway, with underpasses and majestic clover-leaf intersections--a highway which smoothly skirted the towns in which, a few years before, his car would have been clogged in local traffic. It was all new and exciting, this world of beautiful speed, as exciting as it was to follow a guide about Rockefeller Center, New

York, the one and only skyscraper group to rise in the United States during the nineteen-thirties, and to see how a combination of cool design and gay planting and shining new materials could brighten the metropolitan scene.

New materials? Why, it was beginning to seem as if the chemists and metallurgists could produce any sort of substance that was needed. Lighter, tougher steels, made with nickel, chromium, tungsten, vanadium, molybdenum. Plastics suited to the making of anything from automobile steering wheels to tableware, from radio cabinets to dice. New artificial fibers made from cellulose, and new processes for extracting cellulose from Southern pines. Plywood with absurdly unwoodlike qualities. Certainly the technical men were making ready the materials for the world of tomorrow, however discouragingly the production of these marvels lagged. What boundless possibilities might be locked in the development of tray agriculture? What marvels of efficiency might not the photo-electric cell make possible? What would television do to entertainment and news distribution in the future? Would the two-cycle Diesel engine revolutionize the production and transmission of power? And how would people live when the prefabricated house moved out of the phase of experiment into the phase of mass production? Questions like these were running through people's minds; the American imagination was beginning to break loose again.

Was there, perhaps, some new machine, some new gadget the furious demand for which would set in motion a new boom--something like the automobile or the radio? In the spring and summer of 1936 a great many people thought they had found one. Way back in the summer of 1929, just before the Panic, a bacteriologist named Arthur G. Sherman had built for his family a little house on wheels which could be towed behind his car on vacations. It attracted so much favorable attention wherever he went that he built a few more, and exhibited one of them at the Detroit Automobile Show in 1930. Presently he was manufacturing them on an expanding scale, other manufacturers were leaping in, householders with a knack for tools were building their own trailers in their backyards. By 1936 the number of house trailers on the road was estimated by *Automotive Daily News* at 160,000. On New Year's Day, 1937, Florida observers reported that these contrivances were crossing the state line at the rate of 25 an hour. Roger

Babson declared that within twenty years half the population of the United States would be living in them. What more lovely vision could there be--provided one did not focus one's attention on real-estate values, taxes, steady jobs, schooling for the children, sanitation problems, and other such prosy details--than the vision of the coming of a care-free era when the restless American could sell his house, climb into his trailer, and go forth to live the life of the open road?

§ 4

The amount of money which was going into new things like the trailer industry, however, was but a fraction of what was needed. What was holding back the rest?

However economists might disagree upon this point, there was very little disagreement among the potential investors themselves, the possessors of capital, the well-to-do, and especially the very rich. What was wrong, they were sure, was "lack of confidence"--and this lack of confidence was caused by the arbitrary rule of an Administration which spent money recklessly, followed unsound and inflationary principles of public finance, yielded to the advice of semi-communist brain-trusters, burdened business with grievous taxes, wasted the tax money on crazy boondoggling schemes for the pampering and political bribing of the unenterprising poor, harassed business men with hasty and unpredictable and paralyzing reforms and with government competition, slaughtered little pigs to win votes from the farmers, encouraged labor agitators to tie up industry, generally opposed the "profit system," and threatened American freedom by dictating to Congress, discrediting the Supreme Court, and undermining the Constitution.

On these and other charges against the Administration endless changes were rung in the conservative press, in the speeches of conservative business men and political leaders, in the circulars of such varied organizations as the Liberty League, the Crusaders, the Defenders, and the American Nationalists, Inc., and above all in the private conversation of the well-to-do.

That the large property owners and the managers of large businesses should have become indignant was not at all surprising. Buffeted and frightened by the Depression, they had at first hailed Roosevelt as a deliverer. Presently they had discovered that he did not intend the "recovery" for which he was working to be a recovery of things as they had been in 1929; he wanted things changed. He not only continued to press for reforms, he tore to bits the fiscal promises of the 1932 Democratic platform and of his own campaign speeches. He set out to champion the less fortunate, to denounce such financiers and big business men as stood in his way; and as their opposition to him hardened, so also did his opposition to them. Raymond Moley has told how Roosevelt, sitting with a group of men discussing the tenor of an impending Presidential speech, would listen to their accounts of the derogatory Roosevelt stories that were going the rounds of Wall Street and State Street and Chestnut Street and La Salle Street, and how his face would stiffen, till it became clear that the speech would be--as Moley said--"more like a thistle than an olive branch."

It was natural, then, that men and women of means should feel that the President had changed his course and singled them out as objects of the enmity of the government. It was natural that they should have become confirmed in this feeling when, with half an eye to undermining Huey Long's "Share Our Wealth" offensive, he backed in the summer of 1935 a revenue bill which stepped up taxes on the rich. It was even natural that they should have felt so strongly about what had happened since 1933 as to seem to forget that there had been anything wrong with the country before 1933.

Yet the lengths to which some of them went in their opposition, and the extent to which this opposition became concentrated, among a great many of them, into a direct and flaming hatred of Roosevelt himself, constituted one of the memorable curiosities of the nineteen-thirties.

All the fumblings of a government seeking to extricate the country from the world-wide Depression which had followed the slackening of nineteenth-century expansion; all the maneuvers of an

Administration trying to set right what seemed to have gone wrong in the financial world during the previous decade, to redress the disadvantages under which the common man labored, and simultaneously to maintain its political appeal to this common man--all these things were reduced, in the minds of thousands of America's "best people," to the simple proposition that Franklin D. Roosevelt was intent upon becoming a dictator at their expense. Much that Roosevelt did lent a color of justification to this version of history; yet in reducing so much to so little these people performed one of the most majestic feats of simplification in all American history.

This hatred of Roosevelt was strong, though far from unanimous, among the well-to-do in all sections of the country. It was strongest and most nearly unanimous among the very rich and in those favored suburbs and resorts where people of means were best insulated against uncomfortable facts and unorthodox opinions. (To live in Locust Valley or Greenwich, let us say, to work in Wall Street, and to read only the New York *Herald Tribune* in the morning and the New York *Sun* at night, offered excellent insulation, especially if one concentrated devotedly upon the daily lamentations of Mark Sullivan and the uniformly sour interpretations of Administration policies in the financial columns of the *Sun*.) In general, the hatred was most intense in the cities along the Atlantic seaboard, with the exception of Washington, where there were moderating opportunities to see New Dealers in the flesh and to discover that they were human after all. It flared higher and higher during 1934 and 1935 and continued at a high temperature until about 1938, when it appeared to weaken somewhat, if only through exhaustion.

Sometimes the anti-Roosevelt mood was humorous. On the commuting trains and at the downtown lunch clubs there was an epidemic of Roosevelt stories, like that of the psychiatrist who died and arrived in Heaven to be whisked off to attend God Himself: "You see, He has delusions of grandeur--He thinks He's Franklin D. Roosevelt." But there was nothing humorous in the attitude of the gentlemen sitting in the big easy chairs at their wide-windowed clubs when they agreed vehemently that Roosevelt was not only a demagogue but a communist. "Just another Stalin--only worse." "We might as well be living in Russia right now." At the well-butlered dinner party the company agreed, with rising indignation, that Roosevelt was "a traitor to

his class." In the smoking compartment of the Pullman car the traveling executives compared contemptuous notes on the President's utter
ignorance of business. "He's never earned a nickel in his life--what has
he ever done but live off his mother's income?" In the cabañas at Miami Beach the sun-tanned winter visitors said their business would be
doing pretty well if it weren't for THAT MAN. In the country-club
locker room the golfers talked about the slow pace of the stock market
as they took off their golf shoes; and when, out of a clear sky, one man
said, "Well, let's hope somebody shoots him," the burst of agreement
made it clear that everybody knew who was meant.

There was an epidemic, too, of scurrilous Roosevelt gossip.
Educated and ordinarily responsible people not only insisted, but sincerely believed, that "everybody in Washington knew" the whole
Roosevelt family was drunk most of the time; that the reason why Mrs.
Roosevelt was "so all over the place" was that she was planning to
succeed her husband in the Presidency "until it's time for the sons to
take over"; and that Roosevelt was insane. Hadn't a caller recently sat
with him and tried to talk public affairs, only to be greeted with prolonged and maniacal laughter? From this point the gossip ran well over
the line into the unprintable.

A good deal of the bitter anti-Roosevelt talk could not, of
course, be taken at its face value. Often it was a form of conscious
self-indulgence in the emotional satisfaction of blaming a personal
scapegoat for everything that went wrong. When, as in a *New Yorker*
cartoon, a group of ladies and gentlemen sallied forth to the trans-lux
theatre "to hiss Roosevelt," they enjoyed the sort of release that many
liberals had enjoyed when they blamed all the ills of the economic system on the personal wickedness of bankers, or that Nazis enjoyed
when they blamed all the ills of Germany on the Jews. To find a scapegoat is to be spared, for the moment, any necessity for further
examination of the facts or for further thought.

Yet to the extent that it stopped factual inquiry and thought,
the Roosevelt-hating was costly, not only to recovery, but to the haters
themselves. Because as a group (there were many exceptions) the
well-to-do regarded the presence of Roosevelt in the White House as a
sufficient explanation for all that was amiss and as a sufficient excuse
for not taking a more active part in new investment, they inevitably

lost prestige among the less fortunate. For the rich and powerful could maintain their prestige only by giving the general public what it wanted. It wanted prosperity, economic expansion. It had always been ready to forgive all manner of deficiencies in the Henry Fords who actually produced the goods, whether or not they made millions in the process. But it was not disposed to sympathize unduly with people who failed to produce the goods, no matter how heart-rending their explanations for their failure. Roosevelt-hating thrust the owners and managers of business into inaction--into trying to resist the tide of affairs, to set back the clock. It made them conservatives in the sense that they were trying to hold on to old things, whereas before 1929 they had been, in their own way, innovators, bringers of new things. It made them, as a group, sterile. And they were soon to learn that sterility does not stir public applause.

§ 5

The Presidential campaign of 1936 was approaching. Whom would the Republicans nominate to embody and galvanize the widespread indignation against the New Deal, not only among the rich but also among the majority of business men, and a host of others who regarded Roosevelt as dangerously radical, extravagant, or untrustworthy?

Hoover? No, his name recalled too many bitter memories of economic and political defeat. Borah? He had strong popular backing, especially in the West, but he was fiscally unorthodox and too old and too much of a maverick. Frank Knox of Chicago? Senator Vandenberg of Michigan? All were passed over. As the time for the Cleveland convention drew near, the Republican choice settled upon a candidate who had been virtually unknown to the country before 1936 but who seemed supremely "available"--Governor Alfred Mossman Landon of Kansas.

A successful independent oil producer, Landon should appeal, the Republican leaders felt, to business men. A Governor who had balanced his State budget in trying times, he should be a fitting standard-bearer in a fight against Federal spending (though his opponents pointed out that he had had to balance the budget anyhow because the Kansas Constitution decreed it; and also that Kansas had leaned heavily on the Federal government for relief funds). A former Bull Mooser, a man of generally liberal views, Landon should invite the support of men and women in the middle of the political road. (The conservative die-hards were his anyhow: they would vote for the Devil himself to beat Roosevelt.) An adroit political adjuster, Landon should be amenable to the suggestions of men on the Hill who thought Roosevelt too dictatorial toward Congress. A friendly, likable person, with an attractive family, he should personally be a good vote-getter. If his record contained little evidence of brilliance, he could be presented as an unassuming average man, a regular fellow who didn't set himself up to be a superman but possessed plain common sense and would stick to "the American way." As the delegates assembled in Cleveland, Landon was clearly so far in the lead that no other name was even placed in nomination. Landon was nominated with a whoop. The "Kansas Coolidge," "the Careful Kansan," with a Kansas sunflower as his emblem, was sent forth to do battle with Roosevelt.

Landon was provided with a platform likewise intended to appeal to those in the middle of the road. Though it bristled with denunciations of the New Deal, in certain respects it wore a surprisingly liberal aspect. It did not utterly decry Federal participation in relief, though it advocated the "return of responsibility for relief administration to non-political local agencies." It did not utterly decry Federal participation in agricultural regulation, but proposed a national land-use plan not wholly different from the Democratic scheme--with, however, a greater reliance upon the state governments. It did not call for the repeal of the Securities Act, the Stock Exchange Act, or the Public Utility Holding Company Act, upon which the men of Wall Street had poured such vitriol, but called for "Federal regulation, within the Constitution, of the marketing of securities to protect investors," and added, "We favor also Federal regulation of the interstate activities of public utilities." Indeed, if a visitor from Mars had compared the two party platforms of 1936, concentrating his attention not on the denunciations and pointings-with-pride but merely upon the positive recommendations which they contained, he might have wondered why feeling ran so high in this campaign.

If the Republicans demanded a balanced budget and "a sound currency to be preserved at all hazards," the Democrats also spoke of their "determination to achieve a balanced budget" and "approved the objective of a permanently sound currency." Both platforms inveighed against monopolies, approved collective bargaining, promised to protect civil liberties, approved the merit system in the civil service, and spoke friendly words about old-age security (though the Republicans proposed an altered Social Security system). And if the Republicans hammered at the Democrats for "flaunting" the "integrity and authority of the Supreme Court" and for "insisting on passage of laws contrary to the Constitution," if they pledged themselves to "resist all attempts to impair the authority of the Supreme Court of the United States," the Democrats also proposed "to maintain the letter and spirit of the Constitution," explaining that if national problems could not be "effectively solved by legislation within the Constitution, we shall seek such clarifying amendment as will assure to the Legislatures of the several states and the Congress of the United States, each within its proper jurisdiction, the power to enact those laws which the State and Federal Legislatures, within their respective spheres, shall find necessary. . . ." Surely, the visitor from Mars would have said, these parties which so denounce each other are virtually as Tweedledum and Tweedledee.

The reference in the Democratic platform to the possible need of a "clarifying" amendment to the Constitution was a master-stroke of rhetorical precision. For during the preceding year the Supreme Court had emerged as the one conservative force able and ready to withstand the New Deal offensive. Not only had it thrown out the NRA, unanimously; in January, 1936, it had thrown out the AAA too, by a vote of 6 to 3; it had also vetoed the Farm Mortgage Moratorium Act, the Guffey Coal Act, and several other measures; and in these decisions it had interpreted so narrowly the interstate commerce clause of the Constitution that almost every important New Deal law seemed likely in due course to fall before its scythe. Only two of the Court's decisions thus far had favored the Administration--a 5 to 4 Gold Clause verdict and an 8 to 1 verdict on certain limited phases of the TVA. Under the circumstances the New Dealers' opinion of the "nine old men" of the Court--or, more particularly, of the right-wing justices--was blistering; and by contrast the Court had become to conservatives an object of unprecedented veneration. (Above the rear number plate of the conservative's Cadillac was now affixed a plate reading SAVE THE CONSTITUTION, in the very place where, four years before, had been affixed a plate reading REPEAL THE EIGHTEENTH AMENDMENT.)

Roosevelt was deeply indignant at the Court and longed to checkmate it, but had not yet decided how to attempt to do this. He did not want to propose during the campaign to amend the Constitution, for it would have been difficult to frame any amendment of the inter-state-commerce clause which might not be represented by the Republicans as a wide-open door to complete government regimentation of business. He wanted to dodge the issue of the Court for the time being. That word "clarifying"--so innocent-looking, so suggestive of a mere attempt to prevent misinterpretation--helped in the dodging.

Luck helped Roosevelt, too, and in ironical fashion. For just as the elder Republicans were packing their bags to go to Cleveland for the convention, the Supreme Court did a strange thing. Previously it had thrown out Federal wages-and-hours legislation. Now, taking the bit in its teeth, it threw out *State* wages-and-hours legislation by ruling against a New York State minimum wage law for women. The result was staggering: *nobody* could legislate on wages and hours! Not even the Republican leaders could swallow that and remain smiling. As a result, after the Republicans had declared in their platform that they would "protect women and children with respect to maximum hours, minimum wages, and working conditions" by state laws, adding somewhat lamely, "We believe that this can be done within the Constitution as it now stands," Governor Landon felt it necessary to inform the convention that if necessary he would seek an amendment to make this possible. Somehow this took the edge off the Republican championship of the Court. Unwittingly the nine gentlemen in black had scored a point for the embarrassed President.

In other ways fortune favored Roosevelt. One of Landon's earliest discoverers had been William Randolph Hearst, and by 1936 the support of Hearst was less than an asset. At the beginning of 1936 Al Smith, once Roosevelt's good friend and mentor, had threatened to "take a walk" and had urged other Democrats to join him in leaving the New Dealers; but the threat had been made at a dinner of the Liberty League, an organization so studded with millionaire industrialists as to become a political liability for the Republicans. (Even in Republican politics, millionaires are customarily kept in the background, behind a convincing front of small business men and "plain people.") Adroitly seizing the opportunity thus offered, the Democratic strategists conducted their campaign as though they were opposed merely by the millionaire Liberty League, not the Republican party. When at the close of the Democratic convention in Philadelphia--a rubber-stamp, Roosevelt-controlled convention which was dragged out for five days to make the merchants and hotel-keepers of Philadelphia happy and to fill the ears of radio listeners with triumphant if vacuous New Deal oratory--Roosevelt went to Franklin Field to accept renomination, he made a ringing speech in which the Republicans were not even once mentioned. The enemy, according to this speech, was the "economic royalists," who "complain that we seek to overthrow the institutions of America" when "what they really complain of is that we seek to take away their power." Whether one calls such a phrase good demagoguery or good politics, it scored with the voters. The phrase became as popular as an earlier Roosevelt's reference to "malefactors of great wealth."

Even the elements favored the President. During the summer of the campaign he made an ostensibly non-political tour of inspection of the drought-stricken Great Plains--and as he went he was preceded by such torrents of rain that one of the reporters on the Presidential special, waking one morning to look out a streaming train window at a soaking countryside, remarked, "What's this? A flood-control trip?"

But the President's greatest advantage lay in his superior personal appeal to the voters. Whether or not the Republicans, succumbing to old habit, had selected an available candidate when they needed a crusader, the fact was that Landon did not throw out sparks. He spoke sensibly, thoughtfully, moderately, including among his campaign speeches a fine defense of freedom; but his voice was harsh compared to Roosevelt's, especially over the radio, where Roosevelt could swing thrillingly from apparently confidential persuasion to sharp-edged exhortation; and though Landon had an amiable smile, it lacked the contagious expansiveness of Roosevelt's. Whatever may have been Landon's potential abilities, as a campaigner--in opposition to one of the master politicians of American history--he was hardly a man to encourage the van or to harass the foe from the rear.

211

§ 6

Roosevelt, by contrast, was in his element as the battle cries began to resound.

The group of aides which surrounded him during this campaign was different from the Brain Trust which had surrounded him in 1932. Sam Rosenman, to be sure, was still unobtrusively at his side in policy-making discussions. Raymond Moley, although supposedly he had left the New Deal as well as his office in the State Department in the fall of 1933, had remained a confidential Presidential adviser, though with waning influence and growing exasperation at the President's offensive against big business. Throughout 1934 and 1935 Moley had been a constant back-door visitor to the White House, and he remained in close touch with Roosevelt until the time of the Democratic convention of 1936. But the divergence between their views had become so patent that after the "economic royalists" speech Moley was definitely through. Tugwell was no longer so close to the throne as he had been; nor was Berle. And although Jim Farley was still on hand to direct the political management of the campaign, the devoted and astute Louis Howe was not. After a lingering illness in the White House, Howe had died in April, 1936.

The leading newcomer to the ranks of Presidential aides and intimate advisers was a young man named Tom Corcoran, an Irishman from Pawtucket, Rhode Island, who had been a protégé of Felix Frankfurter's since his Harvard Law School days, had been recommended by Frankfurter to Moley to draft the Securities Act of 1933, along with James M. Landis and Benjamin Cohen, and had subsequently, with Cohen, drafted both the Stock Exchange Act and the Public Utility Holding Company Act. Corcoran's skill in bill-drafting, his indefatigable energy, his devotion to the New Deal and to a high ideal of public service, his gay brilliance, and his knack for playing the accordion had all endeared him to Roosevelt, and now within a year he had become one of the innermost circle. His acquaintance among the liberals in the Administration was large; he became a natural leader of the young liberal lawyers and a sort of unofficial employment officer for them inside the government; and already he and his close ally, the shy, rumpled, unobtrusive, clear-headed Ben Cohen, who lived with Corcoran and other young New Dealers at a little red house on R Street, were men of mark in the new Washington.

They were by no means the extreme radicals which current conservative opinion made them out to be (their draft of the Public Utility Holding Company Act, for example, was the mildest of three submitted to the President). They wanted the government to hold big business in check, to discipline it, and if necessary to take over some of its functions, but largely in order to clear the way for small business, which, they believed, was being crowded out of the economic race by big business. Corcoran and Cohen were closer to the elder La Follette in their economic philosophy, or to Woodrow Wilson, than to Moscow. This philosophy, however, involved them in hostility to the great corporations and great financial interests; and they readily stimulated a similar hostility in Roosevelt, who--though he had never formulated a consistent economic policy--was angry at the rich men's hatred for him and also believed that only by inveighing against "economic royalists" could he hold in his own ranks the disaffected millions who had followed leaders like Huey Long. Moley, on the contrary, wanted no continuing onslaught upon the power of concentrated wealth, wanted collaboration between it and the government. There was real significance in the fact that during the campaign of 1936 Corcoran succeeded Moley as one of the chief Presidential speech-drafters (along with Stanley High, Ben Cohen, William C. Bullitt, and others) and as an intimate (along with Relief Administrator Harry Hopkins, Secretaries Morgenthau and Ickes, Judge Rosenman, and others). The apostles of ever-strict business regulation (and also of spending for recovery) had definitely gained the Presidential ear.

During the campaign, one or more of the inner group would prepare drafts of a speech for Roosevelt. At a White House conference a number of them would argue out with him questions of policy and epigram. Then the President would dictate his own draft from the others, utilizing an idea here, a telling phrase there. The copy would be revised, perhaps again and again, and then Roosevelt would sally forth to deliver it. The main themes of his speeches were that the whole country was bound together and what benefited one interest, one locality, benefited all; that only a beginning had been made in the work of national conservation, not only of physical but of human resources;

that if the public debt was rising, so also was the national income; that things were demonstrably better in 1936 than in 1932. On awkward points such as budget-balancing Roosevelt was agile if not actually slippery in his logic. On past government measures he was explicit; on future ones, vague--for the truth was that his legislative program, so far as it had been thought out, had been completed. He had no future program but only a sense of direction. His demeanor was generally friendly; only in the Madison Square Garden speech at the end of the campaign--when he had been enraged by some misguided Republican propaganda about Social Security--did he turn to bitterness (with no Moley or Louis Howe at hand to tone down his wrath). It was in that philippic that he cried, "I should like to have it said of my first Administration that in it the forces of selfishness and of lust for power met their match. I should like to have it said of my second Administration that in it these forces met their master." During the rest of the campaign he appeared a happy man reporting encouraging progress and almost completely neglecting to take notice of Landon or the Republican party.

Nor did the long, exhausting journeys of the campaign--the sleeping-car nights, the goldfish-bowl publicity, the incessant speech-making, the hand-shaking, the hurried conferences, the incessant uproar of cheering--seem to tire Roosevelt in the least, cripple though he was, unable to walk alone. On the contrary, he wore out his companions and emerged from every day of his ordeal fresher than ever, like an Antaeus renewed in strength by every contact with the political element. Smiling, always smiling, the silver voice ringing, he swung through the country in a triumph.

Where were the rivals on the left who a year or two before had looked so menacing? Huey Long was dead. Father Coughlin and the Townsendites, together with a remnant of the Huey Long following, had joined in backing for the Presidency Representative Lemke of North Dakota; but it was early apparent that the Lemke opposition would be weak. Governor Olson of Minnesota was dead. The socialists, nominating Norman Thomas as was their habit, were weak. And as for the communists, though they nominated Earl Browder for the Presidency, so anxious were they to be true to the Popular Front principle dictated by Moscow, and so anxious to defeat Landon, whom they called the "fascist" candidate, that one could hardly be sure

214

whether they were really revolutionary Marxians or just another group of New Dealers. The contest had become Roosevelt against Landon, with no important third-party opposition.

Bitterly the campaign progressed. Not since 1896, certainly, had public feeling run so high over an election. To hear angry Republicans and angry Democrats talking, one would have supposed the contest was between a tyrant determined to destroy private property, ambition, the Constitution, democracy, and civilization itself, and a dupe of Wall Street who would introduce a fascist dictatorship.

Who would win? The *Literary Digest,* which for years had been conducting election straw votes on a huge scale, predicted a Landon victory, with Roosevelt getting only 161 electoral votes as against Landon's 320. Dr. George Gallup, whose American Institute of Public Opinion had been reporting the results of its more scientific polls since October go, 1935--thereby inaugurating a new kind of political measurement, with unguessable possibilities for the future--showed Roosevelt in the lead throughout the campaign, and gaining through most of it: Gallup predicted that Roosevelt would get 477 electoral votes, that Landon would get 42 (with two states left in the doubtful column). Jim Farley predicted that Roosevelt would get 523 electoral votes, carrying every state but Maine and Vermont--but who ever believes a campaign manager's prophecies? Doggedly, the Republicans held to their hope that Landon would carry the country.

Then came Election Day, and as they gathered by their radios that evening to hear the returns, they were thunderstruck. For Jim Farley had been right. The Roosevelt landslide was overwhelming. The old political adage had to be altered to "As Maine goes, so goes Vermont." The Democrats won every state but those two. Roosevelt's popular vote was 27 $^3/_4$ millions to Landon's 16 $^2/_3$ millions. Congress was now to be more than three-quarters Democratic in both Houses--a terrific majority. The New Deal had been upheld by the great electorate, and in no uncertain terms.

Why did this happen? Some reasons have already been suggested. But there were two which have not hitherto been mentioned in this account. One was that the New Deal was a vast dispenser of pecuniary aid to individuals, chiefly in the form of relief. In some areas these payments were crassly used for political advantage. In most, they were not. To argue that the billions spent for relief were in essence a vast Democratic campaign fund, paid for by the taxpayers, was to exaggerate cynically. Nevertheless the argument for the New Deal was implicit in every payment, whether spoken or not: "We are looking after you. Maybe these other people won't. Better vote for us." The momentum of governmental subsidies is tremendous; anybody who suggests reducing them does so at his political peril.

Pictures, Inc.

ROOSEVELT RIDES IN TRIUMPH
Returning with Mrs. Roosevelt from the rainy Inauguration of
January 20, 1937

The other reason was that although Roosevelt was bitterly hated by most of the well-to-do, he was genuinely admired and trusted by most of the poorer people of the country. Between the lines of his speeches as well as of the legislation which he sponsored they read a genuine friendliness toward them, a genuine desire to help them. Part of the failure of the press (which, in the cities, was overwhelmingly pro-Landon) either to sway the small voters or to predict their vote undoubtedly lay in the failure of editors to understand the impress on these people's minds of the New Deal relief policy and of Roosevelt's own personality. Newspaper articles about the scandalous waste of relief funds or about nonsensical boondoggling were discounted by these small voters, not simply because some of them were getting money themselves and wanted the flow of cash to continue, but because they saw in the New Deal a badly needed angel of mercy which stood sincerely ready to help them. Above all, they saw in Roosevelt himself a friend who did not talk down to them, did not patronize them, but respected them as American citizens and wanted his Administration to serve them. What did they care what the papers said? They knew what the McGarritys in the next block, what the Nelsons on the next farm, had been up against, and what the Federal government had done for them; they had heard Roosevelt's friendly voice themselves, over the radio, again and again. They felt that they *knew,* and they voted accordingly.

§ 7

Gradually Europe was drawing nearer.

During 1936 Hitler's armies had marched unopposed into the Rhineland. Mussolini's armies, completing their Ethiopian campaign, had marched into Addis Ababa. Civil war had broken out in Spain, and by the time of Roosevelt's re-election the forces of Francisco Franco, backed by German and Italian support, were drawing close to Madrid. With more and more disquiet the American people were taking note of an outside world whose orderly foundations were crumbling as the aggressors of the new German-Italian Axis moved step by threatening step toward domination.

But the event which was presently to bring the average American man and woman closer to the European theatre than they had been since Versailles, and which for days on end was to overshadow in interest anything that was happening on the American continent, leaping into the American headlines and becoming the predominant topic of American conversation, was no affair of armies or conquests. Though this event might be regarded as a sign of the weakness of the British Empire--or, conversely, of the ability of that Empire to adjust its weaknesses, close ranks, and carry on--to most observers it was simply a personal drama on an imperial stage: the drama of a king forced to choose between his kingdom and a woman. That the king should be Edward VIII of Great Britain and Ireland and of the British Dominions Beyond the Seas, King, Defender of the Faith, Emperor of India, and that the woman should be a Baltimore girl, Wallis Warfield Simpson, heightened the drama into what H. L. Mencken called "the greatest news story since the Resurrection."

All through the summer and fall of 1936, while Roosevelt and Landon had been stumping the United States, the American press had been conspicuously aware of the royal romance. Americans had seen photographs of Edward and Wallis together on a Mediterranean cruise, he (in swimming trunks) paddling in a rubber boat, she (in a bathing suit) sitting on a pier-end above him. When on October 27 she was granted a divorce from Ernest Simpson, the news from the Ipswich Assizes made the front pages in the United States. Not for weeks thereafter were the great mass of the English people even to learn of the existence of Mrs. Simpson, so strict was the unofficial censorship on news uncomfortable to royalty; not, in fact, until after the Bishop of Bradford, on December 1, spoke (at a diocesan convention) of the King's need of God's grace, said he hoped the King was aware of this need, and added sadly, "some of us wish he gave more positive signs of such awareness." This sentence, indirect and discreet as it was, opened the way to the revelation in England. But in America the way did not need to be opened. Americans had been asking one another for weeks whether the King and Mrs. Simpson were really to be married; and as the drama unfolded to its climax, the dispatches from Downing

Street and Westminster and Fort Belvedere let loose a tumult of argument from one end of the United States to the other.

"Good for him. Best thing he's ever done. Let him marry her. Can't a king be a human being?" "No, no, no. He accepted a responsibility and now he's chucking it. If he was going to welsh on his job, why did he ever take it in the first place?" "Well, he never was good for much but nightclub work anyhow. Did you see the bawling-out Westbrook Pegler gave him in his column?" "Kind of a sock for Wallis, I guess. She was all set to be Queen--and now where is she?" "I'll bet it was the Archbishop of Canterbury that spoiled the thing. Those divorces of hers, you know." "Nonsense--they'd have swallowed the divorces all right if she hadn't been an American. Now if she'd been a duchess . . ." "You have to hand it to her at that--a Baltimore girl who can bring about an imperial crisis single-handed."

Endlessly the talk buzzed, till Wallis Warfield Simpson had fled England for the seclusion of the Rogers' villa at Cannes, and Stanley Baldwin had told the House of Commons the long story of his activities as a match-breaker, and the headlines had shrieked, THE KING QUITS, and millions of Americans had gathered at their radios on the afternoon of December 11, 1936, to hear, above the crackle of static, the slow, measured words of Edward himself:

"At long last I am able to say a few words of my own. I never wanted to withhold anything, but until now it has not been constitutionally possible for me to speak. . . . *(Try another station--I can't hear. What was that he said?)* . . . I have found it impossible to carry the heavy burden of responsibility and to discharge my duties as King as I should wish to do, without the help and support of the woman I love. . . . *(There, that's better. No, try the other one again.)* . . . And now we all have a new King. I wish him and you, his people, happiness and prosperity with all my heart. God bless you all! God save the King!"

With this last speech of Edward's, so perfect in its eloquent simplicity, the curtain fell upon the drama of British royalty. Now Americans could turn their minds again to what was happening at home. Their own chief of state, re-elected, had been given virtually a blank check. What would he write upon it?

219

Chapter Ten

WITH PEN AND CAMERA THROUGH DARKEST AMERICA

§ 1

If in the year 1925 (or thereabouts) you had gone to a cocktail party in New York attended by writers, critics, artists, musicians, and professional men and women interested in the newest ideas and the newest tendencies in the arts, you would probably have heard some of the following beliefs expressed or implied in the conversation screamed over the Martinis:--

That there ought to be more personal freedom, particularly sex freedom.

That reformers were an abomination and there were too many laws.

That Babbitts, Rotarians, and boosters, and indeed American business men in general, were hopelessly crass.

That the masses of the citizenry were dolts with thirteen-year-old minds.

ALLEN

That most of the heroes of historical tradition, and especially of Victorian and Puritan tradition, were vastly overrated and needed "debunking."

That America was such a standardized, machine-ridden, and convention-ridden place that people with brains and taste naturally preferred the free atmosphere of Europe.

If after a lapse of ten years you had strayed into a similar gathering in 1935 (or thereabouts) you would hardly have been able to believe your ears, so sharp would have been the contrast. It is unlikely that you would have found anybody showing any conversational excitement over sex freedom, or the crudeness of Babbitts, or the need for debunking Henry Wadsworth Longfellow. (It was characteristic of the nineteen-thirties that the Queen Victoria with whom Strachey had dealt sharply in the previous decade became a popular heroine as portrayed on the stage by Helen Hayes, and that Longfellow himself and other worthies of Victorian Boston were largely restored to favor in Van Wyck Brooks's *The Flowering of New England* in 1936.) In the conversation screamed over the somewhat more palatable Martinis of 1935 you would probably have heard some of the following beliefs expressed or implied:--

That reform--economic reform, to be sure, but nevertheless reform by law--was badly needed, and there ought to be more stringent laws. (Some members of the company might even scout reform as useless pending the clean sweep of capitalist institutions which must be made by the inevitable Communist Revolution.)

That the masses of the citizenry were the people who really mattered, the most fitting subjects for writer and artist, the people on whose behalf reform must be overtaken. (Indeed, if you had listened carefully you might have heard a literary critic who had been gently nurtured in the politest of environments referring to *himself* as a proletarian, so belligerently did he identify himself with the masses.)

221

That America was the most fascinating place of all and the chief hope for freedom; that it was worth studying and depicting in all its phases but particularly in those uglier phases that cried most loudly for correction; and that it was worth working loyally to save, though perhaps it was beyond saving and was going to collapse along with the rest of civilization.

"What has happened in these ten years?" you might have asked. "Have these people got religion?"

They had. The religion, of course, was not the religion of the churches; one of the few points of resemblance between the prevailing attitude of such a group in 1925 and its prevailing attitude in 1935 was that at both times its members were mostly agnostic if not atheist. What animated these men and women was the secular religion of social consciousness to which a reference was made in Chapter VI of this book. Deeply moved by the Depression and the suffering it had caused; convinced that the economic and social system of the country had been broken beyond repair, that those who had held the chief economic power before 1929 had been proved derelict and unworthy, and that action was desperately needed to set things right; wrung by compassion for the victims of economic unbalance, these men and women no longer set such store as formerly upon art as art. They wanted it to have a social function, to illuminate the social scene, to bring its darkest places clearly into view. "What's the use of being a connoisseur of the arts when people are starving?" cried a New York woman of means who had prided herself on her judicious purchases of modern paintings; "I feel as if I'd been wasting my money." "What's the use of writing pretty novels about ladies and gentlemen?" thought the young fiction-writers of 1935. "If we write about the sharecroppers we're getting at the sort of thing that matters--and we may accomplish something."

To understand the thrust of American literature during the nineteen-thirties one must realize how strong was this mood of social evangelism among writers and critics and the intellectual élite generally.

§ 2

At this point careful qualification is necessary. The new mood was most widespread in New York, which had long been the center of intellectual ferment in the United States and an extremely sensitive barometer of the pressure of new and radical ideas. It was more widespread among the young and rising--and frequently jobless--intellectuals than among the older and better-established. Many successful practitioners of the craft of writing to sell were quite untouched by it. It was not strikingly prevalent among well-to-do "nice people" of culture who had always been surrounded with books and had always subscribed to the more decorous magazines, or among academic gentry remote from the fever of new creative effort in the arts. It was likely to bewilder and perhaps frighten the clubwoman who enjoyed literary lectures and wanted to beautify her town and subscribed to all the best concerts and belonged to the Book-of-the-Month Club. As for the banker who was a college trustee and helped to make up the annual deficit of the symphony concerts and had every right to be considered a sustainer of the arts, he was likely to be angered by it--if indeed he was aware of it at all.

Now and again some expression of the mood leaped into wide popularity. There was, for example, the play "Tobacco Road," written by Jack Kirkland from a novel by Erskine Caldwell. Produced in New York on December 4, 1935 (just as Prohibition gave way to Repeal), this study of a poverty-stricken and depraved Southern tenant family seemed at first about to fail but gradually found its public and, to the amazement of Broadway, ran on and on, year after year, until by the autumn of 1939 it had easily broken the phenomenal record for successive New York performances set by "Abie's Irish Rose" in the nineteen-twenties. Undoubtedly the success of "Tobacco Road" was due in part to its frank and profane dialogue, its exhibitions of uninhibited love-making, and James Barton's fine gift for both comic and tragic effects as Jeeter Lester; but at least the success was not prevented by the fact that the play showed relentlessly and compassionately the interworking of poverty and degeneracy--showed it without blinking the fact that the Lesters had become a dirty, irresponsible, mentally defective, disreputable family.

Another quite different embodiment of the mood was the musical revue "Pins and Needles," produced on November 27, 1937, by Labor Stage, Inc., a company of garment workers (of which no actor was paid more than $55 a week). This revue likewise went on and on until late in 1939 it had broken all previous musical-show endurance records. Playfully pleading the cause of the labor unions and satirizing their enemies, "Pins and Needles" was different from anything previously seen on the musical stage. Who would have imagined, in the nineteen-twenties, that a revue would run for years whose catchiest air was called "Sing Me a Song of Social Significance"?

Only one or two books which could fairly be said to reflect the mood of social consciousness reached the top of the bestseller list during the nineteen-thirties. One was Sinclair Lewis's *It Can't Happen Here,* published late in 1935, which showed how fascism might come to the United States. A still better example was John Steinbeck's *The Grapes of Wrath,* a very vivid and finely wrought account of the plight of a family of migrant "Okies" in California, which not only met with thunders of critical applause when it appeared early in 1939 but jumped at one bound to the top of the list. Here, even more than in "Tobacco Road," the components of the young intellectuals' credo were brought together: a sense of the way in which economic and social forces worked together to bring tragedy to innocent people; a deep sympathy for those people, combined with a willingness to reveal all their ignorance, their casual carnality, their inability to understand their own plight; a sense of the splendor of America, its exciting challenge to artist and to social engineer alike; and a resolve to arouse an indifferent public by showing the worst in poverty and cruelty that America could offer.

Otherwise an examination of the annual best-seller lists would seem to suggest how limited in size was the public which wanted social documents. To command the attention of two or three hundred thousand readers in its original full-price edition, a book succeeded best by addressing itself to other impulses.

There was, for example, the desire to escape from the here and now of Depression and anxiety. May not *The Good Earth,* by Pearl S. Buck, which led the fiction list in 1931 and 1932, have had an additional appeal because it took its readers away to China? May not the appearance of *The Fountain,* by Charles Morgan, on the best-seller list for 1932 have been partly due to the fact that it told of a man who escaped from the outward world of ugly circumstance into a world of inward reflection? Surely the success of *Shadows on the Rock,* by Willa Cather (1931), the even greater success of *Anthony Adverse,* by Hervey Allen (which led all comers in 1933 and 1934), and the superlative success of *Gone with the Wind,* by Margaret Mitchell (which was the overwhelming favorite in 1936 and 1937)--to say nothing of Stark Young's *So Red the Rose* (1934), Kenneth Roberts's *Northwest Passage* (1937), and a number of other books, was the greater because they offered an escape into history. For a time the likeliest recipe for publishing profits was to produce an 800-page romance in old-time costume.

Indeed, it is possible that *The Grapes of Wrath,* if it had appeared a few years earlier, would not have been the big popular hit that it was in 1939. It would have seemed to many readers too painful, too disturbing. By 1939 they had become accustomed to unemployment--even complacent about it--and had acquired new worries to be diverted from (Hitler and the threat of war). They could now take the Steinbeck medicine with less flinching.

There were suggestions of other moods, too, in the bestseller lists. The fact that *The Strange Death of President Harding* in 1930 and *Washington Merry-Go-Round* in 1931 both stood high may be regarded as an indication of the growing public disillusionment with the government as the Hoover Administration battled vainly with the Depression. *The Epic of America,* best-selling non-fiction book of 1932, may have appealed to a mood of inquiry into the background and traditions of a nation which could get itself into such a fix. When the economic tide turned in 1933, what more natural than that men and women whose dreams of a career had been thwarted by the Depression and who now began to hope that they could make a second start should have rushed to buy *Life Begins at Forty* by Walter B. Pitkin (first on the non-fiction list in 1933, second in 1934)?

Americans have always wanted guideposts to personal success and the more rewarding life, and it might be pushing inference too far to suggest that the big sales of *Live Alone and Like It* by Marjorie Hillis in 1936, *Wake Up and Live* by Dorothea Brande in 1936, and *How*

225

to Win Friends and Influence People by Dale Carnegie in 1937 had
any close relation to the state of business, or that the rise of *The Importance of Living,* by Lin Yutang, to the top of the list in 1938 was a sign
that during the business Recession there was once more a wish to learn
how to be happy by denying the need for worldly advancement. But
the popularity of Vincent Sheean's *Personal History* (1935), Negley
Farson's *Way of a Transgressor* (1936), John Gunther's *Inside Europe*
and *Inside Asia* (1936 and 1939), and other books on foreign affairs
(not to mention *It Can't Happen Here),* surely reflected the rising excitement over the news from Europe as the Nazis and fascists
advanced through crisis after crisis to ever greater power.

Some books during the decade rode high with the aid of very
special circumstances. The best-selling non-fiction book of 1934 was
Alexander Woollcott's *While Rome Burns,* a collection of anecdotes
and whimsies which would hardly have fared so well had its author
not invented a new sort of radio program well adapted to the intelligence of bookish people, and had he not been delighting huge
audiences on the air by collecting old poems and old eyeglasses, telling stories about Katharine Cornell, and extolling Kipling, Harpo
Marx, Laura E. Richards, and the wonderful dogs of the Seeing Eye.
(To Mr. Woollcott's audible enthusiasm was also due in no small
measure the success of *Goodbye Mr. Chips.*) *North to the Orient*
(1935) and *Listen, the Wind* (1938) sold in great volume not simply
because they were exquisitely written but also, perhaps, because Anne
Morrow Lindbergh was the wife of an idolized hero and was admired
in her own right. No correlation between the successful books of any
given period and the general trend of opinion and taste during that period can be pushed far: there is always a vast diversity of talent among
the writers, a vast diversity of taste among the readers, and an element
of chance in the whole process. For example, throughout most of the
decade there was an undeniable public interest in economic problems
and a considerable sale of economic treatises. Yet no book on the economic condition of America got to the top of the best-seller list,
although there were big sales for *100,000,000 Guinea Pigs* (a diatribe
for consumers on the difference between what they thought they were
buying and what the manufacturers were actually selling them) and
fairly big sales for several of Stuart Chase's lively simplifications of
the economic dilemma. Perhaps economics was, after all, the dismal

science--or, let us say, the dismal area of disagreement, assumption, and conjecture.

§ 3

Limited in size as were their audiences, the writers who were engaged in the search for social significance produced perhaps the most vital and certainly the most characteristic work of the decade. John Dos Passos with his *U.S.A.* trilogy, in which he suggested the hollowness and wastefulness of pre-Depression American life, interlarding his passages of fiction with impressionistic portraits of famous Americans (in which, of course, J. P. Morgan was roundly condemned, Woodrow Wilson sharply satirized, and Thorstein Veblen extolled), and closing the trilogy with a word-picture of an unemployed man trying hopelessly to thumb his way down a fine American highway; Erskine Caldwell packing his pages with the cruelty and misery of the lower ranges of Southern life; Ernest Hemingway trying (not very successfully) to make a proletarian lesson out of the story of Harry Morgan, a disreputable Key West rumrunner; James T. Farrell showing how environment got the best of Studs Lonigan, a lower-middle-class Irish Catholic boy of Chicago; Albert Halper presenting the factory workers of *The Foundry;* Robert Cantwell dealing with striking fruit pickers; and John Steinbeck later following the Joads from drought-ridden Oklahoma to vigilante-ridden California--these and others like Fielding Burke and Grace Lumpkin were the pace-setters for the period in fiction (though of course there were very able novels produced by writers of different intent, such as Thomas Wolfe, Pearl Buck, Ellen Glasgow, Margaret Mitchell, and William Faulkner). Even Sinclair Lewis engaged in the politico-social battle, though not on the side of rebellion; in *The Prodigal Parents* his effort was to show that the Babbitt whom he had once satirized was a kindlier and better man than the youngsters of the radical left.

Among the poets, Archibald MacLeish and Edna St. Vincent Millay were turning likewise to political and social themes; Carl Sandburg was writing

Stocks are property, yes.
Bonds are property, yes.
Machines, land, buildings are property, yes.
A job is property,
no, nix, nah, nah.

and numerous younger men and women were struggling with the almost impossible task of writing sagas and songs of the masses in idioms intelligible only to those who had learned to follow the abstruse indirections of T. S. Eliot and Ezra Pound.

In the theatre, Clifford Odets made energetic use of proletarian themes; Maxwell Anderson, in "Winterset," turned social injustice to the uses of poetic tragedy; as the decade grew older and fascism became more menacing, Robert E. Sherwood epitomized the democratic faith in his moving tableaux from the life of "Abe Lincoln in Illinois"; the Federal players dramatized current politics in "Triple A Plowed Under" and "One Third of a Nation."

At the same time ardent historians and literary sociologists were bringing out harsh biographies of the robber barons and Mellons and Morgans of the American past; delving into aspects of the history of American cities and regions which had been carefully neglected by chambers of commerce; taking to pieces the life of American communities and assembling their findings in statistical and graphic profusion. With more amiable intent, the Writers' Project of the WPA was going over the country inch by inch for a series of guidebooks. Surveys supported by the Federal government or by foundations were analyzing every public problem in exhaustive detail. The nineteen-thirties were a golden age of literary sociology. America had discovered itself to be a fascinating subject for exploration, dissection, and horrified but hopeful contemplation.

§ 4

At the heart of the literary revolt against the America that had been stood the communist intellectuals. Numerically they were hardly important, but from them the revolt caught the fire of burning conviction, and from the curious nature of the communist position it derived most of its weaknesses. Many an author was handicapped by his conviction that, as a Marxian, he must take for his hero a kind of American he did not really know, or that he must make his characters conform to a Marxian pattern and argue the Marxian case, or that he must depict his proletarians both as men rendered cruel and vicious by their lot and as the heroic standard-bearers of a glorious revolution, or that he must present anybody with more than $3,000 a year only in caricature, or that he must preach a collective uniformity which ran counter to his own natural instinctive preference for individual dissent. Especially in the early years of the decade, the Marxian pattern was a strait jacket into which American literature could not readily be fitted. As Malcolm Cowley has remarked, in those early years at least six novels and two plays were based on a single actual strike (at Gastonia in 1929), and "strike novels began to follow a pattern almost as rigid and conventional as that of a Petrarchan sonnet. The hero was usually a young worker, honest, naïve and politically undeveloped. Through intolerable mistreatment, he was driven to take part in a strike. Always the strike was ruthlessly suppressed, and usually its leader was killed. But the young worker, conscious now of the mission that united him to the whole working class, marched on toward new battles." (Later, especially after the communists accepted the idea of the Popular Front, the bonds of doctrine became progressively less constricting.)

The truth was that many of the young rebels had embraced--or at least dallied with--communism chiefly because they saw it as the end-station of the road of disillusionment. First one saw that the going order was not working right; then one progressed to the consideration of reforms, one read *The Autobiography of Lincoln Steffens,* and decided that half-measures would not suffice to redeem America; one went on to the idea that nothing short of revolution would serve; and there at the terminus of one's journey sat Karl Marx waiting to ask one's unquestioning devotion, there was the Communist Party promising to make a clean sweep of all that was hateful in American life. How welcome to find the end of the road, how easy to be able to ascribe everything one disliked to capitalism! (Did not Robert Forsythe, in *Redder Than the Rose,* a book of left-wing comment which succeeded in being both vehement and humorous, argue that Dillinger was a product of capitalism, that the vulgarities of the Hauptmann trial were American capitalism's "own narcotic to deaden its death pains," that Mae West showed "in her frank cynical way the depths to which capitalistic morality has come"?) Yet how hard, nevertheless, to swallow the belief that any deceit was justified by the cause--even if the cause appealed to one's most generous instincts--and to follow unquestioningly the twists and turns of the Moscow party line, now damning Roosevelt as the best friend of the rich, now embracing him as a partner in the Popular Front!

During the latter nineteen-thirties there appeared a crop of autobiographies full of nostalgic memories of the Bohemian Greenwich Village of the early nineteen-hundreds, when young intellectuals were manning the silk strikers' picket lines, seeing Big Bill Haywood plain, cheering for the Armory Show of independent art, and experimenting with free verse and free love. Perhaps the day would come when a new crop of autobiographies would recall the dear dead days of the nineteen-thirties when the young rebels saw themselves as soldiers in the class war, regarded Union Square as their G.H.Q., debated endlessly about "ideology," were lashed into their wildest furies of controversy over the "trial" of Trotsky in Mexico City, and were heartened every day by the knowledge that as capitalism withered, communism was inevitably rising to take its place.

§ 5

Through the ranks of the painters, too, swept the contagion of social concern and of enthusiasm for putting American life on record. Thomas H. Benton's muscular and turbulent groups, Grant Wood's formalized Midwestern landscapes and satirical portraits, John Stuart Curry's scenes of farm life on the plains, Charles Burchfield's gaunt mansions of the Rutherford B. Hayes era, Edward Hopper's grim streets and cool New England lighthouses, Reginald Marsh's pageants of New York slum life attracted many disciples. The Federal government, wisely including artists among its relief beneficiaries, put scores of them to work painting murals on post-office walls; and presently the young painter's model found that she was no longer simply to lie on a couch while he experimented with the treatment of planes of color and bulges of significant form, but was to strike a pose as a pioneer mother or embody the spirit of America insisting upon slum clearance. The value of the new trend was debatable, but at least it promised to decrease the wide gap between the artist and the general public, which at last began to feel that it knew what was going on. Simultaneously there was a sharp increase in the number of young people who, at places like the School of Fine Arts of the University of Iowa, were actually learning to paint; and there, too, was hope for the future of American art.

Not altogether unrelated to this change in emphasis in American painting, perhaps, was the rise to sudden popularity of an art hitherto seldom regarded with serious attention--the art of photography. It rose on the crest of a camera craze of remarkable dimensions--a craze which otherwise served chiefly as a new and amusing hobby, with aesthetic values and satisfactions thrown in for good measure.

During the early years of the Depression one began to notice, here and there, young men with what appeared to be leather-cased opera glasses slung about their necks. They were the pioneers of the camera craze who had discovered that the Leicas and other tiny German cameras, which took postage-stamp-size pictures capable of enlargement, combined a speed, a depth of focus, and an ability to do their work in dim light which opened all sorts of new opportunities to the photographer. The number of "candid camera" addicts grew rapidly as the experts showed how easily an executive committee or a tablefull of night-club patrons might be shot sitting. During the eight years from 1928 to 1936 the importation into America of cameras and parts thereof--chiefly from Germany--increased over five-fold despite the Depression.

By 1935 and 1936 the American camera manufacturers and the photographic supply shops found their business booming. Candid cameras were everywhere, until before long prominent citizens became accustomed to having young men and women suddenly rise up before them at public events, lift little cameras to one eye, and snap them--of course without permission. At intermissions during theatrical openings and gala concerts the aisles would sometimes be full of camera sharpshooters. Schoolboys were pleading with their parents for enlargers and exposure-meters. Camera exhibitions were attracting unprecedented crowds.

During the two years 1935-37 the production of cameras in the United States jumped 157 per cent--from less than five million dollars' worth in 1935 to nearly twelve and a half million dollars' worth in 1937. An annual collection of distinguished photographic work, *U. S. Camera,* became a bestseller. A flock of new picture magazines appeared and a few of these jumped to wide popularity, led by the more dignified *Life* and the less dignified *Look.* One had only to lay *U. S. Camera* beside the camera magazines of a few years before, with their fancy studies of young women in Greek draperies holding urns, their deliberately blurred views of sailboats with rippled reflections, and their sentimental depictions of cute babies, to realize how this art had grown in range, imagination, and brilliance.

Some of the new photographers centered their interest upon snapping friends and relatives (including, of course, their children) and immortalizing their travels; some of them tried to capture the sentimental loveliness of scenes that they had enjoyed; and some went on to experiment in the making of abstract patterns of light and shade. But a great many others found themselves becoming unsentimental reporters--of events, of the social scene, even of the uglier parts of the social scene. Able professionals like Margaret Bourke-White, like Dorothea Lange of the Farm Security Administration, like Walker Evans, often worked with the same sort of sociological enthusiasm that had caught the young novelists and was here and there catching the young painters. When S. T. Williamson, reviewing for the *New York Times* a book of Walker Evans's uncompromising pictures (brought out by the Museum of Modern Art in 1938), denied that Mr. Evans had revealed the physiognomy of America and insisted that it would be "nearer the mark to say that bumps, warts, boils, and blackheads are here," he was saying the sort of thing that might be said about half the novels written by the devotees of social significance. What was significant about this

232

aspect of the camera craze was that photographers like Mr. Evans with their grim portrayals of dismal streets, tattered billboards, and gaunt, sad-eyed farm women, were teaching the amateur--whose name was legion--that the camera need not necessarily be shut up in its case until a beauty spot was reached, that there was excitement in catching characteristic glimpses even of the superficially ugly manifestations of life, that these too could be made beautiful in their way, and that when one began to see the everyday things about one with the eye of an artist who was simultaneously a reporter or a sociologist, one began to understand them.

§ 6

One morning in the winter of 1937-38 a crowd began to gather outside the Paramount Theatre in Times Square, New York, as soon as it was light. By 6 A. M. there were three thousand people assembled in the otherwise empty streets--mostly high-school boys and girls in windbreakers and leather jackets. By 7:30 the crowd had so swelled that ten mounted policemen were sent from the West 47th Street station to keep it under control. At 8 o'clock the doors of the theatre were carefully opened to admit 3,634 boys and girls; then the fire department ordered the doors closed, leaving two or three thousand youngsters out in the cold.

Benny Goodman and his orchestra were opening an engagement at the Paramount. Benny Goodman was the King of Swing, and these boys and girls were devotees of swing, ready to dance in the aisles of the theatre amid shouts of "Get off, Benny! Swing it!" and "Feed it to me, Gene! Send me down!" They were jitterbugs, otherwise "alligators," equipped with the new vocabulary of swing ("in the groove," "spank the skin," "schmaltz," "boogie-woogie," "jam session," "killer-diller," and so on endlessly); members of that army of young swing enthusiasts all over the country who during the next year or two knew the names and reputations of the chief band leaders and instrumentalists of swingdom--Goodman, Tommy Dorsey, Artie Shaw, Gene Krupa, "Count" Basie, Teddy Wilson, Louis Armstrong,

Jack Teagarden, Larry Clinton, and others without number--as a seasoned baseball fan knows his professional ball players.

To trace fully the origins of this craze one would have to go back very far. Suffice it to say here that during the nineteen-twenties, the jazz craze--which had begun long before in the honky-tonks of New Orleans and had burst into general popularity with the success of "Alexander's Ragtime Band" and the rising vogue of the one-step and foxtrot as dances between 1911 and 1916--had become tamed into decorum and formality; but that even during this time there were obscure jazz bands, mostly of Negro players, which indulged in a mad improvisation, superimposing upon the main theme of the dance music they were playing their own instrumental patterns made up on the spur of the moment (and sometimes later committed to writing). During the early years of the Depression there was little popular interest in this "hot jazz" in the United States; what a worried public wanted was "sweet" music, slow in rhythm and soothingly melodious, like "Some Day I'll Find You" (1931) and "Star Dust" (very popular in 1932), or poignantly haunting, like "Night and Day" (1932) and "Stormy Weather" (1933). But Europe had acquired a belated enthusiasm for jazz rhythms and in France there grew up something of a cult of "le jazz hot." Phonograph records of the playing of such experts as Louis Armstrong and his band sold well abroad. In the fall of 1933--at about the time of the NRA parades and the coming of Repeal--an English company arranged with a young New Yorker who was crazy about hot jazz to try to get some good records made by a band of American whites; and young John Henry Hammond, Jr., persuaded the scholarly-looking clarinetist, Benny Goodman, who was playing in a radio orchestra, to gather a group of players for this purpose.

Otto F. Hess

BENNY GOODMAN IN ACTION
At a "Battle of Swing" at the Savoy Ballroom, Harlem, New York City

The resulting records not only sold well in England but made an unexpected hit in the United States; and thus began a public enthusiasm for "swing"--as the hot jazz full of improvisation came to be called--which welled to its climax in the winter of 1937-38, when the bespectacled Mr. Goodman, playing at the Paramount and later in Boston and elsewhere, found that the boys and girls so yelled and screamed and cavorted when his band began to "send" that a concert became a bedlam. When in the spring of 1938 a Carnival of Swing was held at Randall's Island in New York, with twenty-five bands present, over 23,000 jitterbugs listened for five hours and forty-five minutes with such uncontrollable enthusiasm that, as a reporter put it in the next morning's *Times,* the police and park officers had all they could do to protect the players from "destruction by admiration."

Among many of the jitterbugs--particularly among many of the boys and girls--the appreciation of the new music was largely vertebral. A good swing band smashing away at full speed, with the trumpeters and clarinetists rising in turn under the spotlight to embroider the theme with their several furious improvisations and the drummers going into long-drawnout rhythmical frenzies, could reduce its less inhibited auditors to sheer emotional vibration, punctuated by howls of rapture. Yet to dismiss the swing craze as a pure orgy of sensation would be to miss more than half of its significance. For what the good bands produced--though it might sound to the unpracticed ear like a mere blare of discordant noise--was an extremely complex and subtle pattern, a full appreciation of which demanded far more musical sophistication than the simpler popular airs of a preceding period. The true swing enthusiasts, who collected records to the limit of their means and not only liked Artie Shaw's rendering of "Begin the Beguine" but knew precisely why they liked it, were receiving no mean musical education; and if Benny Goodman could turn readily from the playing of "Don't Be That Way" to the playing of Mozart, so could many of his hearers turn to the hearing of Mozart. It may not have been quite accidental that the craze for swing accompanied the sharpest gain in musical knowledge and musical taste that the American people had ever achieved.

This great gain in the appreciation of good music was one of the most remarkable phenomena of the nineteen-thirties. Some credit for it belongs to the WPA, which, doing valiant work in music as in literature and the theatre and the plastic arts, not only offered music classes and other aids to the potentially musical, but maintained no less than 36 symphony orchestras. But the chief credit probably must go to the radio, which had been demonstrating the ancient truth that if you throw at people enough of the products of any art, good, bad, and indifferent, some of these people will in time learn to prefer the good.

For a long time the radio had been spilling into the ears of millions of Americans an almost continuous stream of music of all sorts, mostly trite. At the beginning of the nineteen-thirties it was still accepted as axiomatic by most radio people--and particularly by those business executives whose task it was to approve the programs devised by advertising agencies to promote the sale of their goods--that good music was not widely wanted. Long before this, however, the broadcasting companies had been experimenting with putting music of high quality on the air, partly for the sake of prestige, partly to convince the people who wanted the radio to be more educational that the radio companies themselves were hot for culture. The National Broadcasting Company had put on the New York Symphony Orchestra as early as 1926, the Boston Symphony in 1927, the Philadelphia in 1929. By 1929 the Philadelphia Orchestra program had actually secured an advertising sponsor: Philco took the plunge. In 1930 the Columbia Broadcasting System began a series of concerts of the New York Philharmonic on Sunday afternoons, and the next year the NBC began putting the Metropolitan Opera on the air on Saturday afternoons. Before long the opera broadcast, too, acquired sponsors: a cigarette company and a mouth-wash company signified their willingness to pay for it if only a few well chosen words about the advantages of the right sort of smoke or gargle might accompany the works of Wagner and Puccini. What was happening was that these classical programs were obviously attracting listeners and more listeners.

So the movement swept on until on the first day of February, 1937--just a little while before President Roosevelt brought out his plan for the enlargement of the Supreme Court--an emissary of David Sarnoff of the National Broadcasting Company, calling upon Arturo Toscanini in his native Milan, told him that the NBC wanted him to conduct a radio orchestra the following winter.

"Did you ever hear of the NBC?" the emissary, Samuel Chotzinoff, is said to have begun.

"No," replied Toscanini.

Some explanation was required; and then Chotzinoff handed over a memorandum which suggested several alternative plans for Toscanini concerts on the air. The great conductor peered at it near-sightedly, ran his finger down the list, and presently stopped.

"I'll do this," said he. He was pointing at a suggestion of a concert a week for ten weeks.

He did it--with an orchestra especially recruited to do him justice. When, at Christmas time of 1937, he stepped upon the podium in the biggest broadcasting studio in the NBC Building in New York, facing a visible audience of a thousand or so men and women (equipped with satin programs guaranteed not to make crackling noises) and an invisible audience of millions more at their radios all over the country, it was clear that a milestone had been reached. Things had come to the point where the huge radio public was ready to be given the best that could be got, and given it direct--not simply granted a chance to overhear what was intended in the first place for the musically elect.

The remarkable rise in American musical appreciation may best be measured, perhaps, by citing a few figures collected by Dickson Skinner in *Harper's Magazine* in the spring of 1939. Here they are:--

In 1915 or thereabouts there had been 17 symphony orchestras in the United States. By 1939 there were over 270.

It was estimated that in 1938-39 the combined audiences on the air for the Metropolitan Opera on Saturday afternoon, the NBC symphony on Saturday evening, and the New York Philharmonic and Ford hour on Sunday, numbered 10,230,000 families *each week.* (Figure for yourself how many families had been able--and willing--to hear music of such calibre before 1930.)

As evidence that these audiences were increasing, it was estimated by the Coöperative Analysis of Broadcasting that the audience
for the Ford Sunday evening hour, offering the Detroit Symphony, was
118 per cent larger in 1937 than in 1935; and that by 1938 it was fifth
among all radio programs in national popularity, being exceeded only
by the news broadcast and by three other commercial programs.

The NBC Music Appreciation Hour, conducted by Walter
Damrosch, was being heard each week in 1938 by more than seven
million children in some 70,000 schools--and probably by three or four
million adults also.

And finally, during 1938, broadcasts of symphony orchestras
and of grand opera were being carried by the two NBC networks at a
rate which averaged more than an hour a day.

After reciting these statistics, it would seem hardly necessary
to add that the biggest phonograph company reported that its sales of
records increased 600 per cent in the five years 1933-38. The phonograph, once threatened with virtual extinction by the radio, had come
into its own again, not only because of the swing craze but even more
importantly because of the widespread desire to hear "classical" music
of one's own choice without having to wait till a radio orchestra got
round to playing it.

Thus far very little benefit from the growth of this huge audience had come to American composers. But that time would
presumably arrive before long. For the testimony of concert perfor-
mers who found that their audiences now wanted not simply the old
sure-fire favorites, but the less familiar symphonies and concertos; the
number of school and college glee clubs that now preferred to sing
valid music; the growing number of listeners to Station WQXR in
New York, which specialized in good music; the demeanor of the
crowds who came to such music festivals as that held each summer in
the Berkshires: these were among the accumulating fragments of evidence that a great American musical public of real discrimination was
being built up.

§ 7

One does not expect a piece of music to carry a political or economic message, but one might well expect newspapers, magazines, the radio, and the movies to do so. These were the chief agencies of day-to-day adult instruction and entertainment, reaching audiences vastly bigger than even the most popular book or play could command. What was their function in the struggle over the future of America?

Inevitably the influence of the newspapers tended to be conservative. Newspaper publishing had become a branch of big business, obedient to the economic law which concentrated power into fewer and fewer hands. Although the tendency of newspapers to be combined into chains under a single ownership seemed to have been halted during the nineteen-thirties (during the latter years the Hearst chain actually showed signs of weakening), the tendency toward monopoly or duopoly of newspaper control in each city but the very largest continued. By 1938 a number of good-sized American cities--such as Denver, Des Moines, Grand Rapids, Hartford, Louisville, Memphis, Nashville, Omaha, Toledo, and St. Paul--had each only one morning and one afternoon paper; several of the biggest cities--Baltimore, Buffalo, Cleveland, Detroit, Kansas City, Pittsburgh, St. Louis, and Seattle--had only one morning and two afternoon papers; and in three of these latter cities the one morning paper was under the same ownership as one of the two afternoon papers. So complex and expensive an enterprise did a city newspaper have to be to survive that its controlling owners were perforce capitalists on a considerable scale, and their influence was likely to be exerted on behalf of property rights, of big business, and of the interests of important advertisers.

Not that the newspaper editors and reporters were conservative by preference. Many if not most of these, in fact, were aggressive supporters of the underdog. Indeed, the decrease in the number of newspapers, the increasing use of syndicated material, and the drastic economies required by the Depression had thrown so many newspaper men out on the street that what had once been hopefully spoken of as the "profession of journalism" had become one of the most crowded and ill-paid of all white-collar occupations, and the reporter might well regard *himself* as an underdog. Out of these circumstances emerged such anomalies as newspapers whose editors and reporters were mostly New Dealers (or even communists) and members of the Newspaper Guild affiliated with the CIO, yet whose editorial pages warred fiercely against Roosevelt and whose news columns were "slanted" against labor. Where the tradition of factual, objective reporting was strong, as on the *New York Times,* the slanting was only minor and occasional; where this tradition was weaker, as on the Chicago *Tribune,* it was sharp.

But if the newspapers tended toward conservatism, at least they did not tend toward evasion of political and economic issues. One of the most striking phenomena of the decade was the rising importance of the political columnist whose writings were syndicated all over the country and whose audiences were numbered by the millions. The readers of a small-city newspaper might find on their breakfast tables not only the advice of Dorothy Dix on affairs of the heart, the gossip of Walter Winchell, the Broadway talk of O. O. McIntyre, but also the opinions on national affairs of people like Walter Lippmann, David Lawrence, Frank Kent, Dorothy Thompson, Drew Pearson and Robert S. Allen, and Westbrook Pegler (and also Eleanor Roosevelt, whose "My Day" seldom touched national issues directly but had an indirectly persuasive effect). Being permitted usually more latitude of expression than a local editor, these syndicated columnists--who incidentally were mostly conservative--became national oracles. When Walter Lippmann turned against the New Deal he carried thousands of readers with him; when Westbrook Pegler took issue with a political adversary, people from coast to coast watched the fur fly. Lippmann in 1932, Dorothy Thompson in 1937, were among the most influential of all Americans. Strange that the old tradition of personal journalism, so nearly killed by the transformation of the American newspaper into a standardized corporated entity, should thus reassert itself on the grand scale!

In the magazine world--if one excepts such liberal weeklies of small circulation as the *New Republic* and the *Nation* and such organs of the solid intellectuals as *Harper's*--the tendency was toward a very timid discretion in the treatment of public affairs. This discretion was relaxed somewhat in 1932 and 1933, when readers clamored to know

241

what was wrong with the management of American business and the upholders of the status quo were too bewildered to offer confident resistance, but reasserted itself after the New Deal Honeymoon. Among the big popular magazines with circulations of two or three million the only sort of militancy likely to be manifest thereafter was a militancy such as that of George Horace Lorimer of the *Saturday Evening Post,* who risked considerable losses in circulation (but, of course, few losses in advertising) by his incessant hammering at the Roosevelt Administration. Otherwise these magazines--particularly the women's magazines--touched controversial issues timidly if at all and confined themselves mostly to highly expert fictional entertainment and to the discussion of matters to which neither their owners, their advertisers, nor their more tender-minded readers could conceivably take exception. When an attempt was made to provide, in *Ken,* a liberal-radical periodical of large circulation, advertisers held off and thus condemned it to an early death. But on the whole it would be inexact to say that direct pressure from advertisers affected very largely the policy of the successful big-circulation magazines. What chiefly affected them was the desire of their owners to see their own opinions echoed, to make money by pleasing and flattering their advertisers, and at the same time to provide agreeable and innocuous entertainment.

That there was money to be made nevertheless by the sharp presentation of facts, and particularly of facts about America, was shown by the growing success of *Time*--an expertly edited, newsy, and withal irreverent (though not at all radical) weekly--and its younger sister *Fortune* (founded in 1930), which although edited by liberals for the benefit chiefly of the rich, developed such a brilliant technic of team-research and team-authorship and trimmed its sails so skillfully to the winds of conservatism that it not only became a mine of factual material for future historians but subtly broadened reactionary minds. None of the other periodical successes of the decade promised to have so acute an effect upon the status of the writer as this adventure in writing a magazine inside the office; there were those who saw in it a threat of extinction to the free-lance journalist, a threat of the coming of the day when the magazine writer would have to look for an office job or be shut out from publication. (The rise of the *Reader's Digest* to huge popularity appeared to prove chiefly that readers liked to save time, if their reading could be ably condensed and reassuringly simplified; the rise of the picture magazines, led by *Life* and *Look,* proved chiefly that the camera craze had produced enough good photographers to satisfy a public that always liked pictures.) Yet even such new successes as these hardly affected the basic generalization that the way of the popular magazines was the way of evasion and sheer entertainment.

Of radio's coming-of-age during the nineteen-thirties something has already been said. We have noted its contribution to the cause of music. But it developed in other ways also. As a news agency it invaded more and more successfully a field in which the press had stood alone. During the early and middle years of the decade the "commentators" of the air waves became rivals in influence of the political columnists of the press: men like Edwin C. Hill, William Hard, Lowell Thomas, Boake Carter, and H. V. Kaltenborn interpreted national affairs to huge numbers of auditors. Summary, explanation, and interpretation were in demand, especially on the crises in Europe. But personal opinion was likely to be dampened unless safely conservative. The radio commentators added little to the fires of domestic revolt.

Otherwise perhaps the most significant development in radio was the improvement and standardization of the variety show of the air, an hour's or half-hour's program of alternating light music and humorous dialogue, featuring such national favorites as Jack Benny, Rudy Vallee, Fred Allen, George Burns and Gracie Allen, Bing Crosby, and Edgar Bergen and Charlie McCarthy. Throughout most of the decade, unless there was an election, a prize fight, a European crisis, or a Presidential "fireside chat" to demand brief attention, it was the variety shows which commanded the biggest audiences. Their chief rivals for popularity were the numerous serial stories of the air, ranging from Amos 'n' Andy (which reached its biggest number of listeners in 1930 but continued *ad infinitum)* to the Lone Ranger, a wild West thriller, which first was heard on January 30, 1933, and rose in favor until by 1939 it was a three-times-a-week treat to some twenty million people who received it from 140 stations.

Almost without exception both the variety shows and the serials were innocent of any political or economic or social import whatever, save for the announcer's occasional interposition with a suave tribute to the products and policies of the corporation which

243

footed the bill for the entertainment. Charlie McCarthy, for instance, took one into a safe little world of small boys' pranks, a world in which nothing more distressing happened than that Edgar Bergen grew bald, a world in which there were no unemployed men, no budget deficits, no marching dictators. How close were the heroic exploits of the Lone Ranger to observed reality may be suggested by the fact that-- according to J. Bryan, III, in the *Saturday Evening Post*--neither Fran Striker, who wrote the innumerable scripts, nor Earle W. Graser, whose voice made "Hi-Yo, Silver!" familiar the country over, had ever been west of Michigan.

§ 8

As for the movies, so completely did they dodge the dissensions and controversies of the day--with a few exceptions, such as the March of Time series, the brief newsreels, and an occasional picture like "I Am a Fugitive from a Chain Gang" or "They Won't Forget"-- that if a dozen or two feature pictures, selected at random, were to be shown to an audience of 1960, that audience would probably derive from them not the faintest idea of the ordeal through which the United States went in the nineteen-thirties.

Upon these movies were lavished huge sums of money. For them the stage was robbed of half its ablest actors and playwrights; the literary world, of many of its ablest writers--to say nothing of the engineering and photographic skill which brought to adequacy that cacophonous novelty of 1929, the talking picture, and which toward the end of the decade was bringing more and more pictures in reasonably convincing color. A large number of excellent pictures were produced, with capital acting--whether comedies like "It Happened One Night," or adventure stories like "Mutiny on the Bounty," or historical dramas like "The Life of Emile Zola," or picturizations of fictional classics like "A Tale of Two Cities"; and there was a far greater number of pictures which, whatever their unreality, served as rousing entertainment for an idle evening. But although the secular religion of social consciousness was rampant in Hollywood--especially in 1937 and 1938, when numerous script-writers and actors and technical men were ready to do or die for their guilds, for Tom Mooney, for the Spanish Loyalists, or even for the communist version of the Popular Front--nevertheless in the pictures upon which they worked there was hardly a glimpse of the real America. The movies took one to a never-never land of adventure and romance uncomplicated by thought.

The capital invested in the movies preferred to steer clear of awkward issues, not to run the risk of offending theatre-goers abroad or at home. The moralists must be placated; as a result of the campaign of the Legion of Decency in 1934, Joseph Breen had been installed in the office of the Motion Picture Producers and Distributors of America, ready to censor before production any picture which showed too prolonged a kiss, which showed small boys bathing naked, which permitted a character to say "damn" or "hell." (The immediate effect of the Legion of Decency campaign, oddly enough from the point of view of censorship-haters, appeared to be salutary; it frightened the producers into launching, during 1935 and 1936, some of the best pictures yet seen.) Foreign opinion must be placated lest foreign sales be lost: when "Idiot's Delight" was adapted from stage to screen, it must be set in an anonymous country whose inhabitants spoke not Italian but Esperanto; when "Beau Geste" was refilmed in 1939, the villains of the original silent version must be given Russian names rather than Italian and Belgian names because film trade with Russia was comparatively small. Neither capital nor labor, neither the Administration nor its enemies, must be given any opportunity to criticize. If one wanted to show a crusading reformer, better to make him a Frenchman of the past, like Emile Zola, than an American of the present: for how could an American engage in a crusade without implying that something was wrong?

It was significant that the pre-eminent artist of the motion picture during the nineteen-thirties, Walt Disney, was a maker of fantasies, and that the motion-picture event in January, 1938, which Westbrook Pegler called "the happiest thing that has happened in this world since the armistice" was the production of "Snow White," a fairy story of the screen. Only in unreality could genius have free rein.

The Disney film was a huge popular success; it set the whole country humming "Heigh-ho" and "Whistle While You Work" and incidentally was a godsend to the toy business: during the bleak first third of 1938, when the Recession was at its worst, over $3,000,000 worth of Disney toys were sold, and that summer, when the wheels of most factories were turning intermittently, the Sieberling-Latex plant near Akron was three weeks behind orders (after running 24 hours a day for months)--making rubber statuettes of Dopey and the other dwarfs!

Not merely did the movies avoid temptations to thought about the condition of the country; in effect their producers played, half unwittingly, a gigantic joke upon the social Salvationists, and particularly upon those men and women who would have liked to make the American masses class conscious. For the America which the movies portrayed--like the America of popular magazine fiction and especially of the magazine advertisements--was devoid of real poverty or discontent, of any real conflict of interests between owners and workers, of any real ferment of ideas. More than that, it was a country in which almost everybody was rich or about to be rich, and in which the possession of a huge house and a British-accented butler and a private swimming pool not merely raised no embarrassing questions about the distribution of wealth, but was accepted as the normal lot of mankind. So completely did the inveterate movie-goer come to take this America for granted--at least during his two hours in the theatre--that he was unlikely to be surprised to find a couple of stenographers pictured as occupying an apartment with the newest built-in kitchen equipment and a living-room 35 feet long and 20 feet wide; or to hear Bette Davis, in "Dark Victory," expressing satisfaction that she had given up the life in which she "had had everything" for a life in which she "had nothing"--"nothing," in this case, being a remodeled Vermont farmhouse which (according to the careful computations of E. B. White in *Harper's Magazine*) must have cost at least $11,000 or $12,000 a year to live in.

While the writers and artists in whom burned a fierce desire to reveal to their fellow-countrymen the inequalities and miseries of their lot were resolutely addressing a public numbered in the thousands, another public numbering *eighty-five millions each week* was at the movies watching Gary Cooper, Clark Gable, Myrna Loy, Katharine

246

Hepburn, Ronald Colman, Carole Lombard, and the other gods and goddesses of Hollywood disporting themselves in a dreamland of wide-sweeping stairways, marble floors, and magnificent drawing-room vistas. And these eighty-five millions were liking it.

Was not the lesson of all this that America was not--or not yet, if you prefer--proletarian-minded? True, its citizens were capable of organizing hotly to redress wrongs and secure themselves benefits, were quite ready to have these wrongs redressed and these benefits provided by the government if no other agency would do it; and some Americans might even fight, if need be, to get what they wanted. Yet still in the back of their minds there was room for an Horatio Alger paradise where young men of valour rose to the top and young women of glamour married the millionaire's son, and lived happily ever after.

Chapter Eleven

FRICTION AND RECESSION

§ 1

In a cold rain which slanted viciously down upon sodden throngs before the Capitol, Franklin D. Roosevelt, standing with head bared to the gusts, took the oath of office for his second term as President of the United States and began his Inaugural Address.

It was an eloquent address. Describing in glowing terms the improvement in national conditions which had taken place since 1933, he went on to ask, "Shall we pause now and turn our back upon the road that lies ahead?" His answer, of course, was No; and he proceeded in biting sentences to summarize the poverty and wretchedness that still remained to be defeated. "I see one-third of a nation ill-housed, ill-clad, ill-nourished," said he. "It is not in despair that I paint for you that picture. I paint it for you in hope, because the nation, seeing and understanding the injustice in it, proposes to paint it out. We are determined to make every American citizen the subject of his country's interest and concern, and we will never regard any faithful law-abiding group within our borders as superfluous. The test of our progress is not whether we add more to the abundance of those who have much, it is whether we provide enough for those who have too little."

Down in the crowd below, New Dealers tried to hold on to their streaming umbrellas and clap simultaneously--and cheered anyhow. This was the sort of fighting humanitarianism they liked. Yet everybody in the crowd, New Dealer or skeptic or opponent, was listening intently for something more specific. How did Roosevelt propose to proceed along the "road that lies ahead," and in particular how did he propose to deal with the Supreme Court, which stood right in the middle of that road as Roosevelt saw it? During the almost twenty months that had elapsed since the Court had smashed the NRA he had been biding his time. All through the 1936 campaign he had left the Court issue severely alone. Now, with the seal of majority approval upon him, would he speak?

Twice already today he had drawn the minds of the crowd to the overarching question. When he took the oath of office he had not been content to answer Chief Justice Hughes with a simple "I do," but with his left hand upon the Bible and his right hand upraised he had repeated the whole historic oath, with sharp emphasis upon the word "Constitution." Early in the Inaugural Address he had remarked, "The Constitution of 1787 did not make our democracy impotent." What more would there be? The crowd waited, the rain beating down upon them. There was no further reference to the Court, direct or indirect.

The deluge from the heavens on that twentieth of January, 1937, might have been taken as an unhappy omen. In a direct physical sense it was indeed to be one; for that rainstorm, following previous rains and being followed by others, was presently to set in motion the great Ohio River flood. Already down a thousand hillsides from Pennsylvania to Arkansas were coursing the muddy rivulets which would join to inundate Cincinnati, Louisville, and many another city and town. And in another, broader sense those who regarded the storm as an ill omen were to be justified. For the new year of 1937 was to be marked by discords and disappointments. At that very moment, in Flint, Michigan, thousands of sit-down strikers were occupying the factories of the General Motors Corporation in what was to prove the first major conflict of a widespread and ugly industrial war. By the time this war waned, the national economy was to slide down into a new crisis which would dash, for a long time to come, the high hopes set forth in the Inaugural Address. As for the President himself, even at that moment--though only his Attorney-General and perhaps three or four other men had an inkling of what was afoot--he had formulated and was having drafted in detail a plan of campaign against the Supreme Court, a plan which, although in the end it would bring him an indirect victory, would in the meantime lead him to a painful and damaging defeat.

§ 2

The General Motors Corporation was one of the mightiest of American economic principalities. It employed nearly a quarter of a million men and annually produced, in factories and assembly plants all over the country and abroad, some two million cars and trucks-- over two-fifths of all those made in the United States, and well over a third of all those made in the whole world. Its management was theoretically answerable to over a third of a million stockholders, but was actually free from any direction or restraint by any but a handful of the biggest of them. (This army of stockholders wanted dividends; when dividends are not forthcoming, the innumerable small stockholders of such a monster corporation do not revolt--they sell.) The Corporation's net earnings, though they had dwindled to the vanishing point in 1932, had swelled in 1936 to nearly a quarter of a billion dollars--just about a thousand dollars per employee. The Corporation was half immune to competition of the traditional sort, for now it shared with Ford and Chrysler well over 90 per cent of the American automobile business; only those two other monster organizations could combat it. It had become virtually independent of the banking houses of Wall Street, since it could finance out of earnings and depreciation allowances not only replacements and improvements and additions to its plants, but all manner of adventures in other economic fields; the building of ice boxes, airplane engines, Diesel locomotives, and so on; engineering research more effective than private inventors could manage. All in all, the General Motors inner management--a few men in New York and Detroit--exercised a power in American life probably greater than that of any state government.

Yet since the end of December, 1936, this principality had been paralyzed by groups of employees who had seized its key plants by simply sitting down at their jobs and defying all who would dislodge them. The stream of car production, dammed at these vital points, slowed to a halt; while the little city of Flint, Michigan, where most of the key plants were situated, became the scene of something close to civil war.

Behind the defiance of these workers lay a long story of business regimentation, labor insurgency, and government inefficacy.

When the New Deal, in 1933, had given to business managements the permission to organize, it had also, as we have seen, acknowledged the right of labor to organize. There was nothing revolutionary about this acknowledgement: previous laws such as the Clayton Act and Norris-La Guardia Act had included similar provisions--though the courts tended to whittle them down. But the express permission, written into Section 7a of the National Industrial Recovery Act and into the resulting NRA codes, had started a rush to join labor unions.

With this rush most of the leaders of the American Federation of Labor--slow-moving, inflexible, conservative-minded men, devoted to old-fashioned craft unionism and jealous of their jurisdictional rights--had been quite unable to cope. A few of them, however, had been galvanized into sudden activity, and one in particular, John L. Lewis, the beetle-browed boss of the United Mine Workers, had seemed to become a new man. In previous years Lewis had been noted chiefly for his dictatorial and obstructive ways and had become unpopular among the Mine Workers themselves, but now he staked every last penny in the union treasury upon a whirlwind organizing campaign, sent out bands of organizers to tell the miners that "The law is on our side," and signed them up by the hundreds of thousands.

Presently the transformed Lewis became the strong leader of an aggressive group inside the Federation, a group which stood for industrial unionism--for collecting in a single organization all the workers in a given industry, whatever special crafts they might be engaged in. Along with Lewis the group included such men as Sidney Hillman, the astute head of the International Garment Workers; Charles P. Howard of the International Typographers; and David Dubinsky of the International Ladies Garment Workers. Believing that the craft-unionists of the Federation were consistently muffing opportunities to mobilize the workers in the yet-unorganized mass-production industries--steel, automobiles, rubber, and so on--these men gathered on October 9, 1935, to form a special organization of their own, inside the A. F. of L. They called it the Committee for Industrial Organization: the CIO. The rift deepened and the next year, 1936, the CIO was read out of the A. F. of L. and became, under Lewis's leadership, a competing federation--more alert, more headlong, better able to undertake rapid, large-scale organization, and quite prepared to go into party politics: its fast-growing unions contributed nearly half a million dollars to help Roosevelt defeat Landon.

Meanwhile the NRA had been tossed into the wastebasket by the Supreme Court. Congress had quickly passed a new law, the Wagner Labor Relations Act, to supplant Section 7a and specifically authorize collective bargaining, and had set up a National Labor Relations Board to enforce the Act. From the outset this Board faced a well-nigh impossible task. Many employers were coolly proceeding as if there were no Wagner Act at all, driving away union organizers and firing union members in the confident hope that the Supreme Court would upset the new law and things would return to the *status quo ante.* Other employers were setting up "company unions"; and though some of these were really representative agencies for genuine conciliation and adjustment, others were essentially fake unions, under the management's thumb. There was an ugly temper in the industrial towns, where men who had suffered acutely during the Depression, and had lost all respect for the princes of industry who hired and fired them, were ready to make trouble just as soon as they had full stomachs and a glimmer of hope. With labor in a rebellious mood, many unions inexperienced and undisciplined, racketeers and adventurers making hay as union organizers, jurisdictional disputes frequent, the labor high command divided, the status and meaning of the law uncertain, the attitude of the government shifting and ambiguous, many employers openly heedless of the law, and conflicting propagandas misrepresenting the issues, there was confusion everywhere. Anger deepened and strikes multiplied.

Among the automobile workers the militancy became especially hot. They complained of their low wages, arguing that although the hourly rates were higher than in most other industries, employment was spasmodic and the annual wage uncertain and unsatisfactory.

252

They complained of the inexorable speed of the factory assembly lines. Especially they were angry at the way in which the corporations spied on union members and found pretexts to discharge them in order to break the union movement. According to the official summary of the report of the La Follette Committee of the Senate, during the period of a little over two and a half years between January 1, 1934, and July 31, 1936, the General Motors Corporation alone "paid $994,855.68 to detective agencies for spy services." Union leaders were shadowed, there were stool pigeons in the unions, and no man in the assembly line knew whether a casual reference to the union in a conversation with a fellow-workman might not be followed by his discharge on the ground of inefficiency.

An industrial union, the United Automobile Workers, had been formed among these men. In 1936 it was taken under the wing of the CIO and thereafter it grew with angry speed. In December, 1936, its new head, an energetic ex-minister, Homer Martin, tried to arrange a meeting with William S. Knudsen, the vice-president of General Motors, only to be told that labor matters should be taken up with the heads of the various plants; the vast General Motors principality, so well integrated in many respects, preferred not to act as if labor policy were a matter for integration. The plant managers were indisposed to negotiate. Thereupon the dispute boiled over.

John L. Lewis wanted no strike then in General Motors. He had his hands full organizing other industries, particularly steel. An automobile strike now might wreck the CIO in its infancy. Besides, the General Motors Corporation was far from unpopular with the general public, which liked its cars and thought of it as paying high wages. But the rebellion was irrepressible.

In plant after plant the men abruptly sat down--in the Cleveland Fisher Body plant, in Fisher Body No. 1 and Fisher Body No. 2 at Flint, in the Fleetwood and Cadillac plants at Detroit, and elsewhere. They kept enough men inside each factory to hold it as a fortress, and while these men idled, played cards, and stood guard at doors and windows, food was sent in to them from union kitchens outside. Thus began one of the most gigantic industrial conflicts in American history.

The sit-down strike was not a new phenomenon. It had been tried, briefly but successfully, by employees of the Hormel Packing Company in Austin, Minnesota, as far back as 1933. There had been several sit-downs in Europe in 1934, and subsequently the method had been utilized on an immense scale in France and to a limited extent in the United States, particularly at Akron. But the General Motors strike was the first to bring it forcibly to the attention of the great American public, and the country buzzed with indignation, enthusiasm, and bewilderment, according to its various predilections, as it read the news from Flint.

Pretty clearly the sit-down was illegal. Liberal observers might point out that the traditional concepts of ownership did not seem quite applicable to a colossal corporation the ownership of which rested, not with the management, but with a third of a million stockholders, very few of whom were anywhere near as close to it as the workmen whose daily lives were bound up with it; but no new legal concepts applicable to such a principality had been formulated. And anyhow the angry men at Flint were beyond bothering about the law. They had discovered that the sit-down gave them new strategic advantages. Not only did it enable them to capture and hold the corporation's productive machinery; it also removed from them the usual temptation to violence, or the appearance of violence, which would alienate the general public. From the moment they sat down they were on the defensive, and the temptation to attack rested with the management. Behind the walls of the great factories they had only to sit and wait while Governor Murphy of Michigan and Secretary of Labor Frances Perkins sought tirelessly to induce the General Motors management to sit down at a table with the United Automobile Workers.

On January 11 the management took the offensive. It turned the heat off in one of the besieged plants, Fisher Body No. 2, and the police gathered to prevent food from being sent in. The union leaders sent a sound truck to the scene, and with the magnified voice of an organizer to cheer them on, rushed food past the police to their friends inside. A few hours later the police stormed the plant, and were beaten off in a pitched battle in which the weapons included buckshot and tear gas (on the part of the police) and door hinges, metal pipes, and soda-pop bottles (on the part of the strikers). The sit-downers remained in possession. The National Guard was called out; but Governor Murphy--who was willing to let the law go unenforced if only he might prevent further violence--forbade the troops to attack. Still the sit-downers remained in possession.

The management turned to the courts for aid, securing an order that the factories must be evacuated--an order which failed of its moral effect when the judge who had issued it was revealed to be a large stockholder in General Motors. Again the management secured an evacuation order, from another judge, which threatened the strikers with imprisonment and a fine of no less than fifteen million dollars if they did not get out by three o'clock on the afternoon of February 3. The men, inflamed now by the sort of spirit which sends soldiers over the top, had no intention of getting out; and as three o'clock on that fiercely cold winter afternoon approached, and thousands of CIO members and sympathizers gathered from Detroit and Toledo and Akron and massed in the streets, armed with clubs, pokers, and crow-bars, while the soldiers of the National Guard waited grimly for the order to advance, one could see impending a tragic battle the scars of which might remain for generations.

But there was no battle. Instead, there was hilarious square dancing on the frozen lawns outside Fisher No. 1. For at the last moment Governor Murphy wired that he had induced Knudsen to confer, and told the sheriff to make no move. After an anxious week of conferences, the Governor was able to announce that a settlement had been reached. General Motors recognized the United Automobile Workers as the exclusive bargaining agency in seventeen of its plants, and would negotiate for a contract with it.

The strike was over--after lasting 44 days, involving 44,000 workers directly and 110,000 indirectly, and paralyzing 60 factories in 14 states. Governor Murphy had succeeded in settling it--at the expense of the prestige of the law--with a minimum of bloodshed. And the CIO had won a great victory: a chance to participate in the government of the General Motors principality.

What wonder that after this intoxicating triumph workers all over the country caught the sit-down fever and stopped work in factories, ten-cent stores, restaurants, all manner of workplaces, until the total of sit-down strikers in America from September 1936, through

May, 1937, was brought to almost half a million? Or that partisanship for and against the CIO reached the boiling point? Or that John L. Lewis became the man of the hour, sagely discussed as a looming presidential candidate for 1940--a portentous dictator-in-the-making in the eyes of the conservatives, a hero immaculate in those of the liberals?

§ 3

Where would the next struggle come? In United States Steel?

That was what men were asking one another. But they were due for a surprise. For already the drama of the CIO and United States Steel was far advanced--in complete secrecy.

On Saturday, January 9, 1937--when the General Motors strike was still young--John L. Lewis had been lunching with Senator Guffey of Pennsylvania at the Mayflower Hotel in Washington when Myron C. Taylor, the dignified chairman of the board of United States Steel, entered the dining-room with Mrs. Taylor. Taylor bowed to the Senator and the big labor leader as he threaded his way past their table; a moment later he came back to chat with them briefly; and after Lewis and Senator Guffey had finished lunch and the Senator had left, Lewis went over to the Taylors' table and remained with them for twenty minutes or so, in what appeared to be the most affable conversation. Other luncheon guests throughout the room were agog at the spectacle of the leader of the CIO and the leader of the most famous corporation in the country hobnobbing agreeably. They would have been much more surprised had they guessed that during the conversation the labor leader had said he would like to have a leisurely talk with Taylor, and Taylor had suggested that they confer the next day--Sunday--at his suite at the Mayflower. When Lewis arrived at the Mayflower the next day and took the elevator, nobody in that hotel lobby in news-hungry Washington had an inkling of where he was bound.

There followed a series of conferences, most of them at Taylor's house in New York--still without anybody's being the wiser. The result of these conferences was an agreement upon a formula by which the Steel Corporation would recognize and sign contracts with the Steel Workers Organizing Committee, a unit of the CIO. Taylor submitted this agreement to his astonished directors and won their consent to it; and on Monday, March 1, the news broke that Steel and the CIO were signing up.

"One of the steel workers just came in and said he heard over the radio that U. S. Steel was meeting with the CIO," said an organizer over the telephone to Philip Murray of the SWOC; "I told him he was crazy and kicked him out of the office." "I can't believe you!" cried the president of one of the lesser steel companies when President Irwin of U. S. Steel called him on the telephone to tell him the news. No reconciliation during the nineteen-thirties until the reconciliation of Stalin and Hitler in 1939 caused more amazement. The steel industry as a whole had gone on record against the CIO unionization drive only the preceding summer. The Steel Corporation had been historically noted as an implacable foe of organized labor. The CIO's attitude toward corporation properties during the General Motors strike had brought most conservative industrialists almost to the point of apoplexy. Yet here was the Corporation making friends with the CIO--running up the white flag of surrender, cried the angry industrialists--without even a struggle! The news was too good to be true, cried the partisans of labor; surely there must be a catch in it somewhere! But there was no catch. The chairman of the Steel Corporation had simply recognized that the SWOC had already signed up enough workers--even out of the Corporation's own company unions--to cause a very ugly strike; that such a strike would cost the Corporation money, for foreign orders for steel for armaments were booming; that it would also cost the Corporation good will, for U. S. Steel had had a bad labor record in the past; and that the way of conciliation was the way of prudence.

Would there, then, be peace throughout the steel industry? There would not. "Little Steel"--the Bethlehem, Republic, National, Inland, and Youngstown Sheet and Tube companies--refused to sign contracts with the CIO. A strike was called that spring, for the insurgent workers could not be held back; and the companies fought it with all the weapons at their command. "Loyal workers" were protected with riot guns and gas grenades. These "loyal workers" were fed inside company plants with supplies sent them by airplane and by parcel post. "Back-to-work" movements were organized and well publicized. Local police and deputies broke up picket lines (a crowd of picketers in South Chicago were pursued and shot down as they ran, leaving behind them four killed, six fatally injured, and ninety wounded, some thirty of them by gunfire). And there was a barrage, throughout the strike, of persuasive publicity, which represented the steel companies as defending the "right to work," as protecting men who wanted to work from the "intimidation, coercion, and violence" of "outside agitators" sent into peaceable and contented communities by the CIO. "I won't have a contract, verbal or written," said Tom M. Girdler, head of the Republic company and leader of the managements' side in the conflict, "with an irresponsible, racketeering, violent, communistic body like the CIO, and until they pass a law making me do it, I am not going to do it."

The strike was broken. The CIO was defeated.

Already the sit-down epidemic and the strike epidemic generally were waning, somewhat to the relief of most of the general public, which had become sick and tired of reading about riots, plug-ugly strikebreakers, and new strikes started by new labor factions after settlements had been reached; sick and tired of picket lines, vigilantes, and all the discords of industrial friction. And presently the ubiquitous disputes were to be almost automatically subdued by the approach of the business Recession of 1937-38.

THE SOUTH CHICAGO "RIOT," MEMORIAL DAY, 1937
Police routing a picket-line outside the Republic Steel plant in the Little Steel
strike: 10 dead, 90 wounded

Pictures, Inc.

§ 4

During the very months in the spring and summer of 1937 when the country was most sharply divided by the disputes over the CIO, it was torn also by another major conflict. For on February 5-- when President Roosevelt's second term was hardly more than two weeks old, and the receding flood waters of the Ohio were leaving wreckage and slime in the streets of Louisville and Cincinnati, and Governor Murphy was beginning his conferences with Knudsen and Lewis for the settlement of the General Motors strike--the President almost nonchalantly tossed to Congress his plan for the liberalization of the Supreme Court. It was like tossing a cannon cracker into a munitions dump.

No President who was not buoyed up by a great confidence in the willingness of the majority of Congress and of the public to follow him wherever he might lead, and who was not by nature both daring and impulsive, would have gambled on such a plan without a preliminary sounding of opinion. For nearly two years Roosevelt had shown by his caution that he knew there was dynamite in the Supreme Court issue. But now he walked blithely up and set off the charge almost single-handed.

On the afternoon of February 4 the President asked the Speaker of the House, the Democratic leaders in the Senate and House, and the chairman of the two judiciary committees of Congress to meet with the Cabinet the following morning; and when, on the morning of the 5th, these gentlemen assembled in the Cabinet room at the White House, he explained to them briefly his new proposal and dismissed them with the word that he had a press conference to attend and would be sending his message to Congress, together with a draft of the proposed bill, at noon. Nobody in the room, according to the best evidence available at this writing, had had the least foreknowledge of the proposal except Attorney-General Homer Cummings, who had drafted it in consultation with the President. To all the rest of the Cabinet, and to the Congressional leaders, it came as a complete surprise. In the current vernacular, the President was not asking them, he was telling them.

It seems that some time in December, 1936, Cummings remembered that he had once found in the files of the Department of Justice a document drafted back in 1913 by Attorney-General McReynolds, who subsequently had become the most violently anti-New-Deal justice on the Supreme bench: this document was a suggestion that younger men be provided for the Federal judiciary by appointing a new judge for each judge who had reached the age of seventy (after serving at least ten years) and had failed to retire. Cummings had taken his discovery over to the White House, suggesting to Roosevelt that this principle might be applied now to the Federal judiciary--*including the Supreme Court.* Thus the Court would be enlarged to a maximum of fifteen members, Roosevelt would have a chance to nominate as the new members men who would not torpedo progressive legislation, and there would be no necessity for a Constitutional amendment. The whole thing would be done simply as a part of a mere plan for the provision of a larger and more alert judiciary.

Cummings had suggested other methods too of meeting the situation, but this one met with Roosevelt's immediate delight--a delight not decreased by the fact that there would be in it a well-concealed joke on Justice McReynolds. "That's the one, Homer!" cried the President, and straightway Cummings went to work upon it.

Not until January was well advanced, apparently, was anyone else except Solicitor-General Stanley Reed (and perhaps one or two subordinates in the Department of Justice) let in on the secret; then-- according to Joseph Alsop and Turner Catledge--the plan was shown to Judge Rosenman and Donald Richberg; a little later it was shown to Tom Corcoran and perhaps two or three other intimate Presidential advisers. (Corcoran, for one, disliked it because of the indirection with which a major matter of governmental policy was attacked; he had been working on a quite different plan.) The rest of the Cabinet and the Congressional leaders, as we have seen, were completely in the dark. Very much on his own responsibility, the Presidential quarterback gave the signal for the boldest of trick forward passes.

That not all the players on the team relished making interference for such a play was immediately apparent. As Hatton Sumner, chairman of the House judiciary committee, walked away from the meeting at the White House he remarked grimly to his colleagues, "Boys, here's where I cash in my chips." He was thereafter in opposition. And although the Presidential message made public at noon that day was innocent-looking to the last degree--it argued that "the personnel of the Federal judiciary is insufficient to meet the business before them," spoke of the tendency of judges to continue on the bench "in many instances far beyond their years of physical or mental capacity," and argued that "a constant and systematic addition of younger blood will vitalize the courts and better equip them to recognize and apply the essential concepts of justice in the light of the needs and the facts of an ever-changing world"--a previously amenable Congress began at once to show signs of scattered but rising insurgency. Nor did there come from the country at large that overwhelming shout of approval which would have swept the plan to victory.

The reason was that three minority groups of voters combined in disapproval of the plan. First there was the large anti-New-Deal group who were ready to leap savagely upon any Roosevelt measure. Second, there were people who, however adverse their opinion of the Supreme Court of 1937, had a sharp emotional bias against interfering with the Court as an institution. Third, there were those who did not mind seeing the Court interfered with but thought the Roosevelt scheme too breezily disingenuous, and were offended at the idea of treating a grave governmental issue as a mere matter of arterial hardening. Even at the outset these three groups added up to make a majority; and they were enlarged by subsequent events.

A group of wily Republican strategists in the Senate managed to persuade ex-President Hoover and other Republican leaders outside Congress to muffle their protests, knowing that if the Court plan were allowed to take on the color of a party issue the Democrats would rally round the flag. These Republican strategists were happy to let Senator Burton Wheeler, a Democrat, be the shining leader of the opposition. Then Chief Justice Hughes was persuaded to write a letter to Senator Wheeler explaining that the Supreme Court was keeping up with its calendar and thus undermining the implication that the "nine old men" could not get through their work. Most effective of all, the Court itself had a sharp attack of prudence.

If anybody had supposed that the black-robed gentlemen of the Court were not very human--that the processes of the Court were impersonal and unpolitical, an Olympian matching of the text of an Act with the text of the Constitution--he was due for a shock in March and April, 1937. Realizing that a series of rejections of liberal laws would strengthen the Roosevelt attack, the Court suddenly turned as mild as any sucking dove. It upheld the Railway Labor Act and the new version of the Frazier-Lemke Farm Mortgage Moratorium Act. It reversed itself upon minimum wages for women and children, upsetting the decision which had so embarrassed Governor Landon at the time of his nomination less than a year before. More remarkable still, it upheld the Wagner Labor Relations Act by a vote of 5 to 4, Justice Roberts moving quietly from the die-hard group into the liberal group, and thus confounding those industrialists who had cheerfully expected the National Labor Relations Board to be blown into oblivion. A little later the Court upheld the Social Security Act. The climax came when Justice Van Devanter resigned, thus giving Roosevelt the chance to make his first appointment to the Court--and presumably to convert what had been usually a narrow anti-New-Deal majority into a narrow liberal majority.

All these moves weakened the Roosevelt side in Congress. "Why run for a train after you've caught it?" remarked Senator Byrnes after he heard the news of the Van Devanter resignation. An eloquent fireside chat by the President over the radio early in the battle over the bill had not started the snowball of public opinion rolling; a *Fortune* poll made during the spring indicated that only about one-third of the voters were definitely in favor of the plan. But the President would consider no compromise. The battle in Congress became more bitter. Not until June 3 did the President give ground. On that day he saw Senator Joseph T. Robinson, the Democratic leader (who was in an agony of embarrassment because he had long since been promised a seat on the Supreme bench, and the Van Devanter seat was now vacant, and nothing had been done about filling it) and agreed to let Robinson work out whatever compromise seemed necessary. But by this time the factions in Congress had become so ugly-tempered that even a compromise would be difficult to obtain.

Furiously, belligerently, exhaustingly, Robinson labored week after week as June gave way to July and the Washington heat became more sullen and Senatorial tempers became more frayed--until at last he came to the end of his elderly strength. On the morning of July 14 the Senator's maid became uneasy when he did not appear for breakfast. She looked in his bedroom and in the bathroom, did not see him and rang for the elevator boy to ask whether the Senator had gone out. He had not. The frightened maid returned with the elevator boy to the apartment. They found the Senator sprawled dead upon the bedroom floor--out of sight of the door--with a copy of the Congressional

Record lying beside his outstretched hand. Roosevelt's strongest musterer of Senatorial votes had gone down in the battle.

Eight days later came the end of the inevitable Presidential retreat, when Senator Logan rose and moved to recommit the Supreme Court bill to the judiciary committee in order that this committee might substitute for it a bill providing for certain changes in the Federal judiciary but not touching the Supreme Court.

"Is the Supreme Court out of it?" asked Senator Johnson of California.

"The Supreme Court is out of it," replied Senator Logan.

"Glory be to God!" exclaimed Johnson.

Thereupon the motion to recommit was passed, 70 to 21. The Supreme Court bill was definitely beaten.

Still the President had not moved to fill Justice Van Devanter's seat. On August 12 he did so--and sprung another surprise. For on the nomination form which he sent by messenger to the Senate he had filled in in his own hand the name of Hugo L. Black of Alabama--a liberal Senator whose enthusiasm for the New Deal had been constant. Black's legal experience had been so limited that leaders of the legal profession were outraged at his selection, but Roosevelt counted on the nomination going through because Black was a Senator and his colleagues would hesitate to oppose him. He was right: the Senate consented. Many Senators, already embittered by the Court plan fight, were further angered, however; and in a few weeks a new storm broke. The Pittsburgh *Post-Gazette* produced what looked like substantial documentary proof that many years before, when the Ku Klux Klan had been strong in Alabama, Black had joined it. A member of the Supreme Court, guardian of the civil liberties of America, was shown to have been a member of an organization whose business it had been to promote racial and religious intolerance!

The outcry was terrific. Justice Black had gone to England; virtually besieged there by newspaper men, he refused to say a word. Not until the first of October, when he had returned to the United

States, did he break his silence. On that evening he spoke over the radio from the living room of his friend, Claude E. Hamilton, Jr., in Chevy Chase; and millions of Americans heard him, in his soft Southern voice, confess that he had joined the Klan "about fifteen years ago," that he had "later resigned" and "never rejoined," and that he had "no sympathy whatever with any organization or group which, anywhere or at any time, arrogates to itself the un-American power to interfere in the slightest degree with complete religious freedom." The new Justice's concern for civil liberties was so apparent in his discourse that thereafter the storm of protest at his appointment died to a rumble.

Soon afterward Black took his seat on the bench, there to occupy a position considerably to the left, politically, of even the liberal justices already sitting. Now there was a definite liberal majority on the Court--which was later to be reinforced when the seats vacated by Justices Sutherland and Brandeis, who resigned, and Justice Cardozo, who died, were filled by the appointment of Solicitor-General Reed, Chairman William O. Douglas of the Securities and Exchange Commission, and Felix Frankfurter, long a behind-the-scenes adviser to the President. The Court's new inclination to look with a favorable eye upon the extension of Federal power became a settled trend.

Had Roosevelt, then, really lost his campaign? In one sense he had won: the Court no longer stood in his way. There was more than political ingenuity to his claim, in 1939, that he had attained his ultimate objective despite the defeat of his plan for reaching it. Yet in another sense he had lost. Many members of Congress hitherto glad to meet his wishes had been left sore and vindictive by the pressure put upon them to vote for a measure thrown at them as the Court plan had been; and there were also Senators who were piqued at the Black incident, feeling that they had somehow been tricked into endorsing an appointment which later brought them embarrassment at home. When, a year later, Roosevelt tried to bring about the defeat at the polls of various Senators who had voted against the Court plan, these wounds were further inflamed. There was nothing new about the attempt of a President to reward his loyal supporters and eliminate his disloyal ones--although the Roosevelt offensive of 1938, to which the opposition press attached the opprobrious term of "purge," was unusually bold and inclusive--but to make the vote upon the Supreme Court plan the test of loyalty was galling. The offensive failed. In friendships within Congress, in prestige within and without Congress, the President had suffered. In this sense the campaign over the Supreme Court had been for him a costly defeat.

§ 5

Sometimes the historian wishes that he were able to write several stories at once, presenting them perhaps in parallel columns, and that the human brain were so constructed that it could follow all these stories simultaneously without vertigo, thus gaining a livelier sense of the way in which numerous streams of events run side by side down the channel of time. The chronicle of American life during the spring and summer of 1937 offers a case in point. The drama of insurgent labor and the drama of Roosevelt against the Court were being played simultaneously, and all the while other disturbances and excitements were distracting our attention to other stages, other currents of tendency were flowing alongside these roaring torrents of change. How to give any sense of the multiplicity and heterogeneity of events without endless interruptions of what must, if anybody is to be able to read it, be an orderly and consecutive narrative?

It was on the showery evening of May 6, 1937--while the CIO was getting ready for the strike in Little Steel and Administration emissaries were coaxing Congressmen to vote for the Roosevelt Court plan--that the great German airship Hindenburg, nosing toward the mooring mast at Lakehurst to complete its first transatlantic flight of 1937, suddenly became a torch flaming in the dusk, and the cheerful inconsequentialities that poured out of American radios were broken into by staccato reports of the horror on the New Jersey plain. Down went the hopes which had built a mooring mast on the Empire State Building and had risen high as the Hindenburg made crossing after crossing safely in 1936. Now the future of transatlantic lighter-than-air transport looked black indeed. Within a few weeks, as if to point the contrast, Pan-American clippers and Imperial Airways flying boats

266

were making survey flights between Britain and America in preparation for the inauguration of a regular passenger service.

Pictures, Inc.

THE HINDENBURG BURSTS INTO FLAME
This photograph was taken just as the fire broke out while the dirigible was
approaching her mooring-mast at Lakehurst, N. J., at dusk on May 6, 1937

During those same months of 1937 the armies of Francisco
Franco were besieging Madrid, the farce of "nonintervention" was
permitting Mussolini to help him, American liberals were "eating
lunch against Franco" (in Elmer Davis's phrase), and American Catholics were arguing that Franco's offensive was a holy crusade against
communist hordes which burned churches and slew priests.

In midsummer (just as the Supreme Court plan was coming to
defeat in the Senate) the Japanese began a systematic attack upon China, thus adding a new major invasion to the lengthening list of
international aggressions; soon Japanese bombs were falling in Shanghai and Americans were wondering whether the United States would

267

have to choose between the loss of all its traditional privileges in Chi-na--and perhaps the lives of oil salesmen and missionaries--and war with Japan. What would happen if a stray bomb should hit Admiral Yarnell's flagship on the Whangpoo? And ought American women to wear lisle stockings on behalf of suffering China?

No picture of the America of the spring and summer of 1937 would be fully revealing which was not a montage of innumerable and varied scenes. It would show Walter Reuther and Richard Frankens-teen, officials of the United Automobile Workers, being slugged and kicked and thrown bodily down on the concrete floor of a street over-pass beside the Ford factory at River Rouge by "loyal employees," who according to the testimony of observers were hired thugs of the Ford "Service" organization. (Thus was the "American system" de-fended.) It would show American living rooms littered with books of reference and public librarians distracted by the fury of contestants in the Old Gold Puzzle Contest. (That picture of two women saying "All London is now sporting the wide-awake hat!" and "Do you know that Palmerston quits today as Foreign Sec?"--could the answer to that be Jenny Lind? And those two people picking oxeye daisies--would that be Sitting Bull or Morgan Dix?)

It would show Leon Henderson, the burly economic adviser of the WPA, becoming worried by the rising trend of prices, concocting a memorandum entitled "Boom or Bust," and communicating his fears of a business collapse to Secretary Morgenthau, who in turn communi-cated them to the President; whereupon the President issued a warning to the effect that certain prices--notably that of copper--were too high. (Henderson was right: trouble was coming, nor could such a statement avert it.)

It would show Americans bent over their newspapers as they devoured another series of installments of the royal romance that had so entranced them the preceding December: Wallis Warfield Simp-son's divorce being declared absolute on May 3, 1937; the Duke of Windsor rushing from his Austrian retreat to join her in France; their wedding taking place at Monts, France, on June 3; while, during the month's interval, the Duke's brother George was crowned King at Westminster with pomp and circumstance. "Yes, I set my alarm clock for five in the morning and listened to the whole coronation on the air and I could hear the crowds cheering as the King and Queen went by in the golden coach." "Wallis may not have got to be Queen, but that trousseau was *something*."

The montage of American life in the spring and summer of 1937 would include endless other pictures: glimpses of Dust Bowl drought victims climbing into their jalopies to seek a newer world in the orchards of California; Joe Louis knocking out Jim Braddock at Chicago and becoming the titular heavyweight champion of the world (though not for another year would he bring down Max Schmeling); Edgar Bergen leaping into national popularity as he and his dummy Charlie McCarthy became features of the Chase and Sanborn radio hour in May, 1937, and shortly made it the most popular program of all. (Bergen had been almost unknown before he appeared at the Rainbow Room in New York on November 11, 1936. He made such a hit there that on December 17 he went on the air. Within a few months he was a national celebrity. Was there any area of American life, except the entertainment area, where success could come so swiftly?)

The montage would show Amelia Earhart Putnam flying from New Guinea toward Howland Island, never to be seen again, though the Navy searched the Pacific rollers long and hard; visitors to New York running through the theatre advertisements and trying to make up their minds whether to see "You Can't Take It With You" or "Brother Rat" or "Room Service," or Maurice Evans in "King Richard II"; a private car bearing northward from Ormond Beach the body of John D. Rockefeller, dead at the age of ninety-seven; men and women in darkened movie theatres visiting the peaceful gardens of Shangri La with Ronald Colman in Frank Capra's screen version of *Lost Horizon,* or listening to Jeanette MacDonald and Nelson Eddy in "Maytime"; bright billboards (donated by Outdoor Advertising, Inc., to the National Association of Manufacturers' campaign against labor-union influence) flaring with pictures of happy workmen over the title, "The American Way"; and Carolina students working out the steps of "The Big Apple," a modified square dance which would presently break the monotony of fox-trotting for hundreds of thousands of their agile contemporaries.

The montage would show American women putting on the oddest-looking peaked hats and openwork hats that had balanced on feminine heads for many a year. And, as the stock-market ticker stopped at noon on Saturday, August 14, 1937, it would show brokers debating whether Steel at 121 and Chrysler at 118 $^5/_8$ were still attractive purchases, or whether it might be a sensible idea to play a bit safe for a time.

It would have been a distinctly sensible idea to play safe. For the Recession of 1937-38 was at hand.

§ 6

When it came, it came fast--and apparently out of a clear sky.

Toward the end of August, 1937, the stock market sold off and business showed signs of slackening. After Labor Day the retreat became sharper. Stocks went down fast and far. On the morning of October 19 the market seemed near demoralization, with support for some stocks apparently quite lacking and selling orders pouring in from all over the country; the tape lagged twenty-five minutes behind the trading, and when at last the gong rang for the closing, the total of transactions had come to 7,290,000 shares--the biggest total since the collapse of the New Deal Honeymoon bull market in the summer of 1933. All through the autumn of 1937 the decline continued. Only the fact that speculation previous to August had been moderate and well-margined, with the SEC watching carefully to prevent manipulation, kept the annihilation of values from having disastrous consequences outside the exchanges. Meanwhile business operations contracted steadily and rapidly. Not until the end of March, 1938, did the stock market touch bottom; not until May did business do so. Never even during the collapse of 1929-32 had the industrial index shrunk at such a terrific rate.

Look first at what happened to the prices of some leading stocks in the space of only seven and a half months:

	Closing Price on August 14, 1937	Low Reached in March, 1938
American Telephone & Telegraph	went from 170 $^7/_8$	to 111
Chrysler	from 118 $^5/_8$	to 35 $^3/_8$
General Electric	from 58 $^3/_8$	to 27 $^1/_4$
General Motors	from 60 $^1/_8$	to 25 $^1/_2$
New York Central	from 41 $^1/_2$	to 10
U. S. Steel	from 121	to 38
Westinghouse E. & M.	from 159 $^1/_2$	to 61 $^3/_4$

Then see what happened to our familiar measure of the state of business in general, the Federal Reserve Board's adjusted Index of Industrial Production. (Do you recall its previous ups and downs? Its high of 125 in 1929, its low of 58 in 1932 and of 59 in the bank-panic month of 1933, its rush up to 100 during the New Deal Honeymoon, its decline to 72 as the Honeymoon ended, and its wobbling rise thereafter?) At the end of 1936 the index had touched 121, which looked distinctly promising. As late as August, 1937, it stood at 117. Then it ran downhill, month after month, until by May, 1938, it had sunk to 76. *In nine months it had lost just about two-thirds of the ground gained during all the New Deal years of painful ascent!*

What had happened? During the latter part of 1936 and the early part of 1937 there had taken place sharp increases in the prices of goods--some of them following increases in wages during the CIO's offensive, some of them affected by armament orders from Europe, many of them accentuated by a general impression, among business men, that "inflation" might be coming and that one had better buy before it was too late. The price of copper--which you will recall

271

especially disturbed the President--had jumped in five months from 10 cents a pound to 16. Business concerns had been accumulating big inventories. When the time came to sell these goods at retail to the public, the purchasing power to absorb them just was not there.

For new investment still lagged; and what was more, the government spending campaign, which had kept pumping new money into the economic system, had been virtually halted. During the summer of 1937, Henry Morgenthau, the Secretary of the Treasury, had persuaded the President to make a real attempt to balance the budget; and although it did not yet seem to be quite in balance, nevertheless when one took into account the Social Security taxes which were being levied (and were not counted on the credit side of the budget, being set apart in a separate account), the government was for a time actually taking in from the public more than it paid out.

Result: the goods which were piled up on the shelves moved slowly. Business men became alarmed and cut production. Two million men were thrown out of work in the space of a few months--and became all the less able to buy what was for sale. The alarm increased, for men well remembered what a depression was like and were resolved to cherish no false hopes this time. The vicious spiral of deflation moved with all the more rapidity. Thus out of that apparently clear sky--no great speculative boom in stocks or real estate, no tightness in credit, no overexpansion of capacity for making capital goods (in fact, not nearly enough expansion)--came the Recession of 1937-38.

It brought its ironies. Precisely a year after the beginning of the great sit-down strikes in General Motors, the president of the Corporation announced that about 30,000 production men were to be laid off immediately, and the remaining men would be reduced to a three-day week. What price CIO gains now? (If you had visited a General Motors dealer and seen the used cars accumulated on his hands, you would have realized why the Corporation had to stop glutting the market.)

Another irony was provided by the collapse of values on the New York Stock Exchange. Eight years before, when prices were tumbling, Richard Whitney had walked out on the floor and stemmed the panic by offering to buy Steel at 205; now Richard Whitney, deeply in debt, was misappropriating trust funds in the frantic attempt to save himself from bankruptcy. On Tuesday, March 8, 1938, just as trading for the day was beginning, President Gay of the Exchange mounted the rostrum and, as the gong rang to halt the brokers, read the amazing announcement that Richard Whitney & Company were suspended for "conduct inconsistent with just and equitable principles of trade." A few weeks later the hero of the 1929 panic, having confessed his all-too-obvious guilt, was on his way to Sing Sing.

Early the following winter--in December, 1938--the metropolis provided an even more extraordinary business scandal. F. Donald Coster, head of the reputable drug house of McKesson & Robbins, was discovered not only to have doctored the books of its crude drug department to the extent of many millions of dollars, but actually to be an ex-convict named Philip Musica who had changed his name and appearance and had successfully conducted a long masquerade as a respectable corporation official. When the police were closing in upon him, Coster-Musica gave this almost unbelievable episode its final touch of melodrama by committing suicide in his fine house at Fairfield, Connecticut. Again Wall Street was shaken, as men asked one another how bankers and accountants could have been so easily fooled. The Musica scandal, however, had no such overtones of significance as the collapse of Whitney. For Whitney had been the leader of the Old Guard of the Exchange. With his downfall during the Recession crumbled the last opposition to a reorganization of the Exchange in accordance with the wishes of Chairman William O. Douglas of the Securities and Exchange Commission. Soon the Exchange had a new paid President--a young man who had not even been acquainted with any member of it when he arrived in New York in 1931! Verily the old order had changed.

There was irony, too, in the earnest effort of Administration leaders to remain calm and hopeful-looking as they issued statements predicting an early upturn, while the economic landslide was roaring downhill. Hadn't there been another Administration, not so many years before, which they had ridiculed for doing much the same thing?

As the Recession deepened, there rose angry voices from the business community and the conservative press. The whole thing was the Administration's fault. This was a "Roosevelt Depression." With malicious glee they quoted a previous boast of the President's, made while the business indices were climbing: "We planned it that way." Well, this was what his planning came to. Especially they blamed the undistributed profits tax--a curious measure which was proving one of the less successful bright ideas of the Administration and which stirred the business world to particular wrath.

"Five years ago, with magnificent courage and resoluteness of purpose, President Roosevelt gave the financial and business communities of the nation an invigorating hope that banished fear," wrote David Lawrence on March 28, 1938. "Today, the same man has aroused in the financial and business communities a fear amounting almost to terror and a distrust which has broken down the morale of the whole economic machinery. . . . What Mr. Roosevelt has done-- and I believe he has not done it intentionally--is to break down the spirit and faith of the business and financial world in the actual safety of a citizen's property and his savings. To strike down this bulwark of the whole economic system is to breed panic and fear of indescribably dangerous proportions."

Strong words--yet they were not unrepresentative of business opinion generally. So obsessed had many business men become with their *idée fixe* that nothing the Administration could do would mollify them. On November 10, 1937, Secretary Morgenthau, in a speech before the New York Academy of Political Science, announced that the Administration would do everything possible to balance the budget. His audience appeared half-pleased, half-amused, and wholly unconvinced. (The Morgenthau speech, as it happened, had been carefully revised and approved by the President.) Addressing Congress at the beginning of 1938, Roosevelt spoke in cordial terms of the need for co-operation between government and business. There was no resulting uprush of "confidence." At that moment the President was making a deliberate effort to pursue a conservative and conciliatory course, conferring with big business men and calling a conference of little business men--which turned into a virtual riot. No friendly gesture seemed to have any real effect.

It is true that there was a contest of policy going on inside the Administration ranks. Certain men of the well-defined liberal group which Joseph Alsop and Robert Kintner called the "New Dealers"--including among others Tom Corcoran, Ben Cohen, Leon Henderson, Herman Oliphant of the Treasury, and Solicitor-General Robert H. Jackson--had composed speeches for delivery by Jackson in which the blame for the Recession was laid upon "monopolies" and "the sixty families" (meaning that they blamed the controllers and managers of the great corporations for pushing up prices by tacit agreement and then, when goods could no longer be sold at these prices, slowing production and throwing off workers lest their profits be unduly cut). They had encouraged Secretary Ickes to make a similar speech. But these speeches had been written without express Presidential authorization, and the young New Dealers had been risking their jobs and their influence in thus expressing their private opinions. What happened was that jittery business men read these New Deal speeches, listened to the calmer utterances of the President, and decided that no blandishments from Washington meant anything.

For this fact the impulsiveness of a President who seemed smilingly unaware of inconsistencies among New Deal pronouncements was partly to blame; indeed, the President commended Ickes for his "sixty families" speech on the eve of composing his own appeal for co-operation. Nevertheless it was true that as 1937 turned into 1938 Roosevelt was trying to balance the budget and to refrain from proposing measures which would frighten business men unduly; that the conservative business community, in its wrath, seemed oblivious of the attempts being made to appease it; and that slowly the Administration leaders were becoming convinced that no policy of retrenchment and appeasement would bear fruit.

All the while the New Dealers were urging a resumption of deficit spending, and on April 2--as things were getting worse and worse--the President threw up the sponge. At lunch on the train from Warm Springs to Washington he told Harry Hopkins and Aubrey Williams that he was ready to abandon the budget-balancing effort and go in for heavy spending again. On April 14 he went on the air to explain that he was asking Congress to appropriate three billion dollars for relief, public works, housing, flood control, and other recovery efforts.

That spring the legislation went through Congress, and simultaneously business began to show faint signs of improvement. In the latter half of June the stock market sprang to life. Recovery began again.

Economists might disagree as to whether the recovery was stimulated by the spending or was a mere coincidence, but among the young New Dealers there was no doubt at all. Look at the industrial index, they argued. It did no good to try to appease business; it did a lot of good to spend. Q.E.D.

The young New Dealers now rode high (so high, in fact, that in the autumn of 1938 they ventured into the comparatively unfamiliar field of politics and persuaded the President to make a dolefully unsuccessful attempt to defeat the Democrats in Congress who had voted against his Court plan). But the Administration as a whole had been struck a very heavy blow by the Recession. Meeting a new economic crisis, it had disclosed itself as neither able to generate "confidence" in business men nor to concoct any new and effective measures of recovery. The best it could do was to take down from the shelf a bottle of medicine to which it had been addicted for years--pump-priming.

§ 7

It had been a proud President who stood before the Capitol in the rain in January, 1937, and declared his intention to paint out the picture of "one-third of a nation ill-housed, ill-clad, ill-nourished." His pride had come before a fall. During a subsequent year and a half of friction and Recession his prestige in Congress had been sorely weakened; his economic policies had been tried in the balance and found wanting; the hateful picture of unemployment and poverty had been altered, if anything, for the worse.

Was the New Deal, then, played out?

Perhaps; but if so, the fact was becoming obscured by the approach of a new sort of crisis which would cause the citizens to look upon their country and its government with new eyes. For now the American skies were being slowly darkened by storm clouds rolling in from Europe.

Chapter Twelve

THE SHADOW OF WAR

§ 1

Studio Nine was a room "about the size of an average family living room." In it stood three desks and an old army cot with an army blanket. On each desk there was a microphone, and before one of these microphones sat a gray-haired man, wearing ear-phones. He was talking quietly in a crisp, precise voice. He looked tired and a bit disheveled, as if he had just risen from the rumpled cot. As he talked, he kept one eye on a plate-glass window, beyond which, in an adjoining room, sat a man watching him from behind a panel of instruments and occasionally signaling to him with a wave of the hand. From time to time other men would steal into the room, shove sheets of paper under his nose, and depart; he would glance at the sheets of paper and talk on, his crisp articulation unimpeded.

He was talking to millions of Americans--nobody knew how many. To hear what he had to say, girls in strapless evening dresses stilled their debate over whether to put their hair up for the winter season; lawyers turned from discussing Judge Pecora's declaration of a mistrial in the case of James J. Hines, whom District-Attorney Thomas E. Dewey of New York was attempting to convict as the "man higher up" in metropolitan racketeering; politicians laid aside the fascinating topic of the failure of President Roosevelt's attempt to "purge," in the Democratic primaries, the men who had failed to join his offensive against the Supreme Court in 1937; literary critics paused in their talk of what would become of Thomas Wolfe's mountains of manuscripts, now that he was dead; families in gray tenements stopped arguing about the chances for a reconciliation between the still hostile CIO and AF of L; actors and actresses interrupted their conjectures about the rising success of the hilarious Broadway production, "Hellzapoppin." For what the man in Studio Nine was telling these people seemed of more vital importance just then than anything else in the world.

The time was the latter part of September, 1938; the man was H. V. Kaltenborn, news commentator for the Columbia Broadcasting System; and Studio Nine was his headquarters at the center of the Columbia plexus in New York. He was interpreting the up-to-the-instant news of the Czechoslovak crisis in what he called "Yirrup," that crisis which was revealing to all the world what happens when an irresistible force meets a conciliatory body.

Ever since September 12 Kaltenborn had kept vigil day and night in Studio Nine, snatching sleep briefly on the army cot. Not until September 30--the day when Neville Chamberlain, just returned from Munich, came to the window of No. 10 Downing Street and said to the cheering crowd below, "I believe it is peace for our time"--would the Kaltenborn vigil end; not until he had delivered, in 18 days, a record total of 85 extempore broadcasts.

Kaltenborn was by no means the only interpreter of European affairs during those September weeks; every broadcasting system, every radio station was hurling news and interpretation into the ether. The names of Hitler, Henlein, Benes, Hodza, Chamberlain, and Daladier screamed persistently from front-page headlines, recurred in page after page of newsprint, sounded in the half-intelligible chanting of the men selling extras on the streets. In New England on the afternoon of September 21 a tropical hurricane struck without warning (the New York weather prediction that morning had been "Rain and cool today. Tomorrow cloudy, probably rain, little change in temperature"). The hurricane ripped seashore villages into kindling wood or swamped them under tons of roaring water, it laid fine groves of trees in lines on the ground, made rivers out of the streets of cities, derailed trains, blocked highways, broke off communication by telephone and telegraph, and took an estimated 682 lives. Yet even in New England, when householders repaired from their darkened houses to their automobiles to listen over their automobile radios (uncrippled by the storm) and find out how wide-ranging was this havoc that had separated them from the rest of the world, the twist of the dial brought them into the midst of the man-made hurricane that was raging in Europe.

Out of the night came the familiar refrains of "A Tisket, a Tasket" . . . then, as the dial turned, a bit of comedy on the Rudy Vallee hour . . . and then, as the dial was twisted again, a voice swelling forth in the midst of a sentence: . . . "town of Godesburg where Prime Minister Chamberlain held a second historic conference with Chancellor Hitler. The effects of that meeting already have brought reactions from world news centers. Now, tonight we'll attempt first to receive a broadcast direct from Prague, the capital of Czechoslovakia, where Maurice Hindus, well-known authority on Central European affairs, has been observing the day's happenings. We take you now to Prague." A pause, while the mind leaped the Atlantic in anticipation; then another voice: "Hello, America, this is Prague speaking. . . ."

How the world had shrunk! In July, 1914, when Karl von Wiegand of the United Press had cabled a mere 138 words from Berlin to New York on the Austro-Hungarian ultimatum to Serbia--one of the grave events which produced the World War of 1914-18--he had been admonished for wasting cable tolls. Now, in September, 1938, the news of another grave event in the same part of the world--the submission of Czechoslovakia to dismemberment--stood in the very center of American attention. Not until 1930 had there been such a thing as a world-wide news broadcast; now one could hear, in quick succession, voices from London, Paris, Berlin, and Prague, and millions of Americans were hanging on every word.

Far back in the distance, already, seemed those lively events of the earlier part of the summer of 1938 which had so captured the public mind: Joe Louis knocking out Max Schmeling at the Yankee Stadium in the first round--actually before some radio listeners had got tuned in on the fight; Howard Hughes flying round the world in the incredible time of 3 days, 19 hours, 8 minutes, 10 seconds; the "wrong-way" pilot, Douglas Corrigan, starting in an antiquated plane from Long Island "for California" and fetching up in Ireland, to return and be feted in America, still wearing his smile and his brown leather jacket; the demented John Warde tying New York traffic into knots as he stood for eleven hours on a narrow ledge on the seventeenth floor of the Hotel Gotham, contemplating his leap to suicide. Even American events and problems of real significance were being thrust into the background. The hesitant upward progress of the business indices, as a nation still beset by large-scale unemployment tried to come back from its Recession; the application of the new wages-and-hours act; the still-unsolved farm problem; the perennial headache of relief--all these things seemed to fall away into unimportance as Hitler demanded the Sudetenland, Chamberlain flew to Berchtesgaden and Godesburg with his furled black umbrella, and the heads of four nations met at Munich to sign and seal the destruction of Czechoslovakia. The war clouds from Europe were blotting out the American landmarks one by one.

§ 2

The chain of events which had dragged foreign problems into the forefront of American attention was a curious one, full of kinks.

At the beginning of the decade the United States had seemed to be drifting from a policy of national isolation toward a policy of acting in concert with other nations to maintain world peace. To be sure, there was no popular disposition to enter the League of Nations or to make foreign commitments, but there was a tendency in the State Department to come as close to doing this as public opinion would permit. In 1931, when Japan, seeing the European powers preoccupied by the Depression, seized its happy opportunity to invade Manchuria, it was Henry L. Stimson, Hoover's Secretary of State, who led the chorus of international condemnation. An American representative sat at Geneva as an "observer" while the League of Nations discussed Japan's offense; Secretary Stimson proclaimed that the United States would not recognize the Japanese conquest; he also sought to invoke the Nine-Power Pact against Japan, only to be rebuffed by Sir John Simon on behalf of Britain. Nothing that the League could or would do, none of the outcries of disapproval from Europe or America, stopped Japan; the first great breach in the post-war system of territorial arrangements was successfully completed--but not for lack of active interest on the part of the American government. America was in the thick of the diplomatic battle throughout. Its policy in 1931 was far from being isolationist.

The next great act of international aggression did not come for several years, and in the meantime the relations between the United States and the outside world went into a new crisis--this time economic. During the early Depression years, as nation after nation in its agony had lifted tariffs, devalued currencies, and otherwise dammed the international currents of trade and financial exchange in its attempts to save itself, the government at Washington had looked on in alarm. It was true that we had laid new bricks on top of our own tariff wall in 1930, but of course we considered our own tariff a purely domestic matter; we felt differently when other countries did such things. It was axiomatic in the minds of Hoover, the Treasury officials, the financial experts of Wall Street, and dominant American opinion generally that barriers to commerce must be removed, that the international gold standard was sacrosanct, that there could be no real American recovery without world recovery. But then came the New Deal--and the shoe was on the other foot. For now *we* wanted to do things which might upset international monetary and trade relations.

At first few people foresaw the impending clash of policies. President Roosevelt, to be sure, in his first inaugural in 1933, said explicitly that "our international trade relations, though vastly important, are in point of time and necessity secondary to the establishment of a sound national economy"--but had he not already appointed as his Secretary of State Cordell Hull, an inheritor of Woodrow Wilson's world-mindedness, and a passionate devotee of the stimulation of international trade by tariff reduction? Roosevelt, to be sure, took the United States off the gold standard, to the confusion of foreign currencies--but was he not simultaneously inviting foreign delegates to come and discuss measures of international economic co-ordination? Not even Roosevelt himself realized how sharp a collision he was headed for. He cheerfully entered into the preliminary plans for an economic conference to be held in London, in June, 1933, and sent to this conference, with inadequate instructions, a delegation headed by Secretary Hull which at once began arranging for the stabilization of currencies. A bit later, fearing that the United States might be tied into a hard-and-fast agreement for stabilization just as the inflation boom was lifting prices and delightfully stimulating business in America, Roosevelt sent to London his chief brain-truster, Assistant Secretary of State Raymond Moley, to restrain the delegates. But it was not until Moley had arrived in London that Roosevelt, becoming more and more entranced with the idea of prosperity through currency manipulation, decided abruptly that the conversations at London must not be allowed to endanger his domestic plans. When Moley agreed to a rather mild statement approving of stabilization in general principle, the President suddenly pulled the floor out from under everybody--Hull, the delegation, Moley, and for that matter the whole London conference--by refusing to have anything done about stabilization at all. An impulsive man had resolved the conflict between economic nationalism and economic internationalism by throwing his weight belatedly and without notice on the national side--to the utter discomfiture of his representatives.

After that--or rather after the experiment in gold-buying which followed it--the United States returned gradually to the ways of international economic facilitation. Secretary Hull doggedly carried on as if nothing had happened. He was permitted to get his reciprocal tariff bill enacted in 1934, and under it to ease the flow of goods between the United States and various other countries. In due course Secretary Morgenthau and the chiefs of British and French finance stabilized the currencies of Britain, France, and America. The adventure in economic isolation appeared to be over, though it had left its scars.

In the meantime, too, an olive branch had been held out to Latin America. In his first inaugural Roosevelt had proclaimed a "good neighbor" policy. To show the Latin Americans that this was no mere phrase, the United States took its troops out of Nicaragua, did away with those parts of the Platt Amendment that had permitted intervention in Cuba, and assured the nations south of the Rio Grande that it interpreted the Monroe Doctrine as a doctrine of co-operation and mutual aid, not as a doctrine of domination. Such was Secretary Hull's patent sincerity that the assurance was on the whole well taken. Toward the end of the decade the United States was better liked and better trusted in most of Latin America than ever before.

But long before that the smashing of international frontiers had begun again. In 1935 Mussolini invaded Ethiopia in extremely cold blood. Britain and France and the League could or would do nothing effective to discipline Italy, and Mussolini was not stopped. Early in 1936 Adolf Hitler, whose attempt to engineer a Nazi coup in Austria had failed in 1934, entered the Rhineland--and was not stopped. Later in the same year the Spanish Revolution broke out; Mussolini, and Hitler too, began using the Spanish Revolution for their own imperial ends--and were not stopped. In 1937, the Japanese attacked China--and were not stopped. In March, 1938, Hitler swept into Austria--and was not stopped. And as the summer and spring of 1938 wore on, he began confidently polishing his knife for Czechoslovakia.

At the time when this series of crises began, American public opinion was perhaps more isolationist than at any time since before the World War. By 1935 the "revisionist" view of the World War of 1914-18 had become the majority view. According to this version there had been guilt on both sides, not simply on the German side, and the United States had been unhappily sucked into participation in the war by British propaganda and by its economic stake in an Allied victory. As late as April, 1937, a Gallup poll on the question "Do you think it was a mistake for the United States to enter the World War?" drew a Yes from 71 per cent of those polled. In 1935 Walter Millis's *Road to War,* which presented the American decision of 1917 as a lamentable tragedy, became a best seller, influential among the highbrows. Several books and magazine articles drew sensational attention to the part played by munitions-makers in fomenting wars; and simultaneously the Nye committee of the Senate embroidered the same theme in a long investigation, showing up the unholy profits of American arms manufacturers from 1915 on, exposing the pretty little deals made by munitions salesmen abroad, and dragging Morgan partners to Washington to answer an implied charge that they had schemed to get the United States to fight Germany in 1917 in order to pull their chestnuts out of the fire. The picture of war as a horror into which the innocent common people were lured by the machinations of conscienceless bankers and big business men was the more readily accepted because the general public still had a very lively memory of the failure of such men to lead the country out of the valley of Depression, and of the shoddy conduct of many bankers and big business men as laid bare in the investigations of 1933.

It must be remembered, too, that in 1935 the American radicals were nearly all hotly anti-war. Nor was there, then, any widespread American fear that the dictators in Europe might actually harm the United States from the outside; when people spoke of "the fascist menace" in 1935, most of them meant the menace of an American fascist movement, which they variously imagined as being led by Roosevelt, or by somebody like Huey Long, or perhaps by an army officer supported by big business. So general was the belief that America must hoe its own row, and take preventive measures in advance so that it could not be seduced into hostilities, that in a Gallup poll taken in the fall of 1935 no less than 75 per cent of the voters thought Congress should get the approval of the people in a national vote before declaring war.

In this very isolationist state of mind, the country welcomed the passage by Congress in 1935 of a Neutrality Act which decreed that when war broke out anywhere, Americans must not sell munitions to either of the belligerents. The Neutrality Act was at once applied to the Italian-Ethiopian conflict.

But the Administration--and the permanent staff of the State Department--did not like compulsory neutrality. They wanted the United States to be free to use its diplomatic influence in international affairs and they felt that a blanket law might be embarrassing in some unforeseen circumstance. They liked to play along with the British in foreign policy, and the Neutrality Act might hobble them. When the Spanish Revolution broke out, they fell in with the British scheme for non-intervention (a scheme which notoriously failed to prevent Mussolini from intervening in behalf of Franco) and pushed through Congress a strange act which applied the neutrality principle to the Spanish dissension, despite the fact that this was not a war between nations but a rebellion against a government recognized by the United States. When, a little later, Japan went into China, the Administration wobbled this way and that, first telling all Americans to leave China or remain at their own risk, then proposing to defend Americans in China, and *never applying the Neutrality Act at all!* They were able to do this by taking advantage of a loophole. The Act as passed in revised form in 1937 provided that the mandatory ban on shipments of munitions should take effect either when war was declared or when the President "found" that a state of war existed. Neither Japan nor China

285

declared war--and the President failed to "find" that a state of war existed, though the Japanese were blasting at China with everything they had.

Presently the Administration departed still further from the isolationist idea and the idea of compulsory neutrality. In a speech at Chicago in October, 1937, Roosevelt said that "the moral consciousness of the world . . . must be aroused to the cardinal necessity . . . of putting an end to acts of aggression," added that an "epidemic of world lawlessness" was spreading, and that "when an epidemic of physical disease starts to spread, the community approves and joins in a quarantine of the patients in order to protect the health of the community against the spread of the disease." This looked like intervention against the aggressive nations with a vengeance. Later in 1937, in a letter to Governor Landon, Roosevelt insisted that "we owe some measure of co-operation and even leadership in maintaining standards of conduct helpful to the ultimate goal of general peace." When the American gunboat *Panay* was sunk by Japanese bombers early in 1938, the Administration made much of the incident, though it had occurred in the interior of a country at war and the *Panay* had been convoying Standard Oil tankers--in other words, had been engaged in just the sort of enterprise which the neutrality advocates of 1935 had sought to eliminate as a possible *casus belli*. At about the same time the Administration used its political influence with Congress to bury in committee the Ludlow Resolution which would have required a national referendum to get the United States into war; this measure, it said, would "cripple any President in the conduct of our foreign relations." Clearly the intention was to give full defense to American rights in China--even the right to convoy tankers with our own gunboats close to a battlefront; to impress the Japanese with the extent of American disgust at their behavior; and in general to use American influence wherever possible to keep aggressive nations within bounds.

Such a policy offered such a sharp contrast with what public opinion had wanted in 1935 that it might have been expected to lead to general public condemnation of President Roosevelt and Secretary Hull. It did not--though the "quarantine" speech required some quick and deft explaining. There was grumbling, but never enough to prevent the continued nullification of the Neutrality Act. The basic reason was that American public opinion, too, was shifting ground. With each new crisis, American dislike of Hitler, Mussolini, and the Japanese war lords was becoming sharper.

It is not, to be sure, clear that there was any great weakening of the underlying preference for "keeping out of foreign entanglements" on the part of the great mass of the American people, particularly in the interior of the country. A study of the Gallup polls from 1935 to 1938 gives no sure evidence of any such shift. But informed and audible opinion, especially on the Eastern seaboard, had undeniably altered. Influential Republicans like Governor Landon and ex-Secretary Stimson stood back of the President in his anti-aggressor moves. Specialists in foreign affairs like the members of the Council on Foreign Relations felt strongly that America must uphold the "democracies" against the "dictatorships." And radical opinion had changed almost unrecognizably.

The communists had shifted from an anti-war policy to an anti-fascist policy and had become almost as warlike as the Daughters of the American Revolution. Back in 1934, Earl Browder (who became the communist candidate for President in 1936) had declared, "The only way to fight war is to begin by fighting the war-makers in our own land. . . . The Roosevelt Administration is carrying on the greatest war program ever seen in peace time." When Roosevelt made his "quarantine" speech in 1937, on the other hand, Browder applauded it as a "declaration of a positive peace policy." The half-somersault executed by the American Student Union, a somewhat leftist youth organization, offered a perfect illustration of the general change in radical and liberal thought: at its meeting at the end of 1936 it had endorsed the Oxford pledge "not to support any war which the government may undertake"; at the end of 1937 it called for "immediate steps to restrain fascist aggression, . . . American leadership in naming aggressors, employing embargoes against aggressors, and organizing these efforts through international collaboration," and it urged "repeal or modification of the present Neutrality Act so as to discriminate between aggressor and attacked and to give aid to the latter." Young men and women who in 1934 and 1935 had spoken scornfully of war as a device for the enrichment of capitalists were by 1937 and 1938 making bonfires of silk stockings to express their detestation of Japan. Still they did not want war, but they were militantly taking sides in foreign quarrels.

Britain and Germany in Compact Never to Fight Each Other Again; Nazi Troops Cross Czech Border

Hitler's Vanguard Passes Austro-Czech Frontier at 1 A.M., an Hour After Deadline He Had Fixed

General Settlement Expected in Berlin

Deal on Spanish War, an Air Pact and Limit on Arms Due, Plus 4-Power Accord Sought by Italy

By The Associated Press

BERLIN, Oct. 1 (Saturday).—The contingent of German troops over the Czechoslovak frontier near Asov, Upper Austria, early today, starting the Nazi occupation of territory granted to Chancellor Hitler by the four-power accord.

The gray-clad German infantry-men marched over the border shortly after 1 a. m. (7 p. m. Eastern standard time, Friday), little more than an hour after the midnight deadline Hitler had set for his occupation.

An infantry battalion, numbering 600 men, advanced along several roads from Asov to take control of posts immediately before the Czechoslovak frontier in western Czechoslovakia. It was explained this movement was merely a vanguard operation, entering the terrain and preparing for the main army today, to march in later today, moving over the first of four districts granted to Hitler by the Munich pact.

The main body of troops, 30,000, assembled along the border of

Chamberlain Reveals New Pact of Friendship to Crowds Wildly Cheering Him on Return Home

Tells Them He Won 'Peace With Honor'

'I Believe It Is Peace for Our Time,' He Asserts; Later Parley Expected to Give Reich Colonies

By Joseph Driscoll

From the Herald Tribune Bureau
Copyright, 1938, New York Tribune Inc.

LONDON, Sept. 30.—Prime Minister Neville Chamberlain, returning tonight to receive a grateful welcome from hundreds of thousands of peace-loving Britons, brought from Munich not only the four-power agreement which authorizes Nazi Germany to take over Czechoslovakia's Sudetenland by gradual stages; but an Anglo-German pact of friendship, by which the two nations resolve never to go to war against each other and to settle all disputes by consultation and negotiation.

When his American Lockheed, airliner brought him back to English soil at Heston Airport, this afternoon Chamberlain received his first hearty welcome, which was followed by stirring street scenes the like of which had not been equaled in London since Armistice Day, 1918. The Prime Minister responded by reading, for the benefit of the newsreels and television apparatus, the text of the peace pact to which he and Hitler had affixed their signatures.

Prime Minister Chamberlain at Heston Airdrome yesterday
Herald Tribune radio photo—Acme

Czechs, Bowing to Munich Pact, Get an Ultimatum From Poland

Warsaw Demands Evacuation of Teschen Today; 'We Want to Fight,' Prague Crowds Reply to Plan; 50,000 Non-Nazis Flee Sudetenland

"PEACE" AFTER MUNICH, 1938
From the front page of the New York Herald Tribune, October 1, 1938

In some respects, too, general public opinion was changing. The Gallup polls showed a swelling majority in favor of a larger American navy, army, and air force. When in February, 1938--just before Hitler's conquest of Austria--the Gallup poll-takers propounded the question, "If Germany and Italy go to war against England and

288

France, do you think we should do everything possible to help England and France win, except go to war ourselves?" the vote came out Yes, 69 per cent. (If the issue had been differently phrased, there might not have been such a heavy affirmative vote; nevertheless the two-thirds majority was impressive.)

Still the great majority of Americans were earnestly anxious to keep out of war. But as the Hitler advance continued, crisis by crisis, more and more people began to feel that it menaced America too, that deliberate non-participation in foreign quarrels would be difficult and might be morally wrong. Then, almost on the heels of Hitler's Austrian coup, came his Czechoslovak coup of September, 1938, and shook America from end to end.

§ 3

A feeling of insecurity and apprehension, a feeling that the world was going to pieces, that supposedly solid principles, whether of economics or of politics or of international ethics, were giving way under foot, had never quite left thoughtful Americans since the collapse of Coolidge-Hoover prosperity in 1929 and 1930. It had been intense during the worst of the Depression, had been alleviated somewhat as business conditions improved, and had become more acute again as the international aggressors went on the rampage (and as, simultaneously, the United States slid into the Recession). The Munich crisis of September, 1938, produced a new attack of nerves.

Whether the strange incident of the Orson Welles broadcast should be considered a manifestation of this attack of nerves cannot be proved one way or the other--but at least it is significant that at the time a great many observers thought that it was one. On the evening of Sunday, October 30, 1938--a month after Munich--Orson Welles of the Mercury Theatre gave, over the Columbia Broadcasting System, a scheduled radio dramatization of an old fantasy by H. G. Wells, *The War of the Worlds*. To make it vivid, he arranged it to simulate a current news broadcast. After an announcer had clearly explained the nature of the program, a voice gave a prosaic weather forecast; then another voice said that the program would be continued from a hotel, with dance music; shortly this music was interrupted by a "flash" to the effect that a professor at "Mount Jennings Observatory," Chicago, reported seeing explosions at regular intervals on the planet Mars; then the listeners were "returned" in orthodox radio fashion "to the music of Ramon Raquello . . . a tune that never loses favor, the popular 'Star Dust'"; then came an interview with an imaginary Princeton professor, with more information about disturbances on Mars--whereupon a series of further "news bulletins" described the arrival of Martians in huge metal cylinders which landed in New Jersey. The broadcast gathered speed, bulletin following bulletin. More Martians landed--an army of them, which quickly defeated the New Jersey State Militia. Presently the Martian attack was vividly described as being general all over the United States, with the population of New York evacuating the city and Martian heat-rays and flame-throwers and other diabolical devices causing terrific destruction, till all was laid waste.

Despite the announcer's introduction, despite the fact that this was a scheduled program, that one needed only to twist a dial to hear the reassuring voice of Charlie McCarthy, that all names given were fictitious, that the program was once interrupted in the routine manner for an explanatory station identification, and that in numerous respects the "news" given out was preposterous on its face, the following remarkable reactions to the program took place:

All over the country, people called up newspapers or the police in wild panic to find out what to do. (The *New York Times* alone received 875 calls; the Associated Press had to send out an explanatory bulletin to its member papers.) In many communities terror-stricken people rushed out of their houses and milled about in the streets, not quite sure whether they were being attacked by Martians or by Germans, but sure that destruction was on the way and they must flee somewhere. In Newark, New Jersey, several families, convinced that a "gas attack" had begun, put wet cloths on their faces and tried to pack all their belongings in a car; the traffic was jammed for blocks around. A woman in Pittsburgh prepared to take poison, crying, "I'd rather die this way than that!" A woman in Indianapolis rushed into a church screaming, "New York destroyed; it's the end of the world. You might as well go home to die. I just heard it on the radio," and the church service came to a hurried end. When a church service in New Jersey was similarly interrupted, the congregation prayed for deliverance from catastrophe. A man in the Bronx section of New York rushed to the roof when he heard the news and thought he saw "the smoke from the bombs" drifting over the city. In a town in the State of Washington the electric-light service was interrupted during the broadcast, convincing listeners that the terror was close at hand, and women fainted.

So it went, with endless variations, all over the country. Even if only one person in twenty among those who heard the program took it at its face value, this credulous minority--together with the people whom they alarmed with their garbled stories of what they thought was happening--caused enough panic to serve as a remarkable case study in national hysteria.

But let us not argue whether the broadcast incident showed that people's nerves had been shaken by the September war scare. (Perhaps there was better proof of nerve strain in some of the observations made upon the incident. Dorothy Thompson, for example, in her syndicated column, called the episode "the news story of the century-- an event which made a greater contribution to an understanding of Hitlerism, Mussolinism, Stalinism, anti-Semitism, and all the other terrorisms of our times than all the words about them that have been written by reasonable men," and said that it "cast a brilliant and cruel light upon the failure of popular education." That was pretty tall talk.) There was other and more reliable evidence of mounting apprehension. Throughout the United States in the winter of 1938-39 there was a marked upsurge of anti-Semitism, noticeable even in Western towns where Jews were few, and even in the behavior of men and women who had no use for Hitler. Father Coughlin's anti-Semitic broadcasts did much to accelerate this sort of uneasy scapegoat-hunting. Among many liberals there was manifest a new and lively fear of Nazi influence within the United States; people who all their lives had laughed at red scares and had made light of the Russian connections of the Communist Party saw nothing to laugh at in Nazi propaganda in America and cried out that organizations with German connections must be investigated and broken up. Dinner-table conversations turned to the alarming increase in German trade with Latin America (which actually was no larger, relatively, than in 1913 and was less than half as great as United States trade with Latin America) and to the ominous question whether Nazi planes operating from South American bases could not quickly smash the Panama Canal and destroy American cities. Many lovers of peace had become obsessed with a sense that the United States, along with the rest of the world, was on its way to an inevitable doom. "When war breaks out in Europe, we'll be in it in six months--nothing on earth can stop it." The best that sanity seemed able to offer by way of reply was, "If in 1929 our best thinkers thought capitalism was triumphant, and in 1933 they thought communism was becoming triumphant, and in 1938 they think fascism is becoming triumphant, what will they think in 1943?"

All the while the Administration was quickening its efforts to make American influence felt by upholding the British and French, excoriating Hitler, and trying to impress him with the idea that if he went on he might have America against him. When in November, 1938, there were new and cruel German attacks on Jews, the American Ambassador at Berlin was called home "for report and consultation"; he did not return. Roosevelt said that the news from Germany had "deeply shocked public opinion in the United States." The American delegation at the Lima Conference in December sought strenuously to line up the Latin American nations against interference by European dictators--and met with a limited success. In his annual message to Congress in January, 1939, Roosevelt called for American unity in the face of foreign threats to free institutions, and for a heavy increase in American armaments--which was granted him. Pointedly he said (and he might have added "Berlin papers please copy") that there were "many ways short of war, but stronger and more effective than mere words, of bringing home to aggressor governments the aggregate sentiments of our own people." Later that month a Douglas attack plane crashed at Los Angeles, and soon it was discovered that the passenger in this plane built to United States Army specifications had been a Frenchman; obviously France was being permitted, with the Administration's blessing, to order good new American fighting planes. Then the President held a long secret session with the Senate Committee on Military Affairs, and after this meeting came senatorial rumors--which were sharply denied--that the President had said that if war came, America's frontier would be in France.

On Easter Sunday, as he left Warm Springs, Roosevelt called out to the crowd in the station, "I'll be back in the fall if we don't have a war"; he afterwards made it clear to the press that "we" had been meant to include, however vaguely, the United States. Secretary Ickes, long famed for the deadliness of his epithets, and other members of the Administration, were turning their rhetorical artillery upon the German government. When in due course Roosevelt issued a plea for peace to Hitler and Mussolini in mid-April of 1939--an eloquent document to which Hitler replied, not in a letter, but in a belated speech of great length, refusing guarantees--many observers felt that the plea had been weakened in advance by too much loose anti-Nazi talk by American officials.

Concurrently the pace of aggression in Europe was quickening. In January, 1939, Barcelona fell, and soon the Spanish Civil War was over: a fascist victory. In March Germany broke her promises at Munich, overran the rest of Czechoslovakia, and annexed Memel. In April Mussolini, not to be quite outdone, seized Albania. Then followed a pause; the news from Europe dropped for a time out of the American headlines. But already there had been a new intensification of the American dismay at these constant and frightening disturbances.

In March, 1939, a Gallup poll on the question "In case war breaks out, should we sell Britain and France food supplies?" had brought a Yes from 76 per cent of those polled; in April the question was repeated and the percentage jumped from 76 to 82. In March the further question "Should we sell them airplanes and other war materials?" brought a Yes from 52 per cent; in April the figure had gone way up to 66--a striking increase. True, only 16 per cent of those polled thought we should send the Army and Navy abroad to help England and France. But the great majority of Americans wanted to help somehow--and more than half of the Gallup voters expressed the ominous expectation (though not by any means the wish) that if war broke out America would be "drawn in."

Was the United States moving along that road to war which only a few years previously it had tried so hard to block off with red lights?

§ 4

On the morning of Sunday, April 30, 1939, the gates of the New York World's Fair were thrown open. The theme of the Fair was "The World of Tomorrow"; the opening ceremonies were held in a vast enclosure called the "Court of Peace." Could anybody in that throng of tens of thousands, gathered under a blue sky in which hung mountainous clouds, fail to reflect upon the question ironically posed by those two phrases?

Here, all about one, was the embodiment of the American dream, 1939 model. Bold modern architecture, sometimes severe, sometimes garish, but always devoid of the traditional classical or Gothic decoration, and glowing with color--offering the first chance most of the visitors had ever had to see what modern architects might do if the economic condition of the country let them go in for large-scale construction. Gardens, fountains, waterfalls leaping off buildings; music resounding everywhere; at night, the splendor of superb lighting. Miracles of invention and of industrial efficiency to goggle at. A sense of festival. Here every man could briefly feel himself, if not a king, at least the citizen of a gay and friendly country, the beneficiary of spotless industrial engineering, privileged to idle along the lagoons, to watch the fireworks flower in orange and blue and green, to see the trylon piercing the sky behind the young trees turned silver by the lights. Here General Motors and Remington Rand sat cheek by jowl with the WPA, Soviet Russia presented her delights to people who would presently compare them with Eastman Kodak's delights; in this fantastic paradise there were visible no social classes, no civil feuds, no international hates, no hints of grimy days in dreary slums, no depression worries. Here was a dream of wealth, luxury, and lively beauty, with coca-cola at every corner and the horns of the busses jauntily playing "The Sidewalks of New York."

Outside the gates was a nation one-third of whose citizens were still "ill-housed, ill-clad, ill-nourished," and a world from which the hope of true peace seemed to have passed forever. What would the real world of tomorrow hold for America?

Still the basic economic problem of America remained unsolved. An uncertain climb out of the pit of the Recession brought the Federal Reserve Board's adjusted index up to 102 in August, 1939. But that was only a shade higher than the point it had reached during the New Deal Honeymoon; and still there were nine and a half million people unemployed, according to the estimates of the National Industrial Conference Board. The colossal enterprise of work relief was becoming every day more clearly a tragic makeshift, demoralizing, as the years dragged on, to many if not to most of those unfortunate enough to be dependent upon it. Though it had been generously conceived, had produced some fine achievements in the arts and some welcome civic improvements, and had at least kept millions of men and women from the extremities of want and despair, nevertheless as a permanent institution the WPA offered an intolerable prospect--and it was getting to look all too permanent. The farm problem was still unsolved, despite Secretary Wallace's herculean efforts; instead of an ever-normal granary the United States seemed to be saddled with an ever-subsidized granary. A kindly government could alleviate the lot of families forced off the land, but could not yet catch up with the tractor as it drove new families, east and west, into homeless migration. Fine things as well as foolish things had been done in Washington, but still the prosperity which had vanished in 1929 looked as unattainable as a rainbow.

Must America at last be reconciled to the dictum that as its population growth slowed up its economic growth must slow up too? Must it accept either a continuance of this twilight-prosperity, with the burden of carrying the unemployed becoming progressively greater, or else a grim deflation of prices and wages and debts till the labor surplus could become absorbed--a deflation which might be even less endurable than that of 1929-33? No one could relish either of those prospects. Well then--a war boom? No gain thus made could be lasting. A speculative boom? That, too, would carry with it the seeds of its own destruction. No healthy expansion of the American economy could be achieved without a steady flow of money into new investment (along with a maintenance of popular purchasing power), and this flow was still dammed.

What dammed it? That question could not be answered adequately without taking into account one of the most significant economic developments of the nineteen-thirties: the increased importance of the great corporations which I have called economic principalities. Everybody was aware that the power of the Federal government had grown enormously during the decade, until its fingers reached into every nook and cranny of the country. Everybody was aware that all manner of activities and enterprises which had been managed on an individual or small-group basis were now becoming socialized--until even that company of rugged individualists, the medical profession, found itself fighting a rear-guard action against the gradual advance of group medicine, even of state medicine. Not everybody was aware of the extent to which the general trend toward centralization, toward bigger and bigger units of social and economic action, was affecting business as well.

Gone since 1929, it was true, were the dizzy days when promoters merged companies into super-companies and super-companies into super-super-companies, when holding-company pyramids were built four and six and eight stories high, and little groups of men in Wall Street, playing with paper stock certificates, thought they were well on their way to the control of all American enterprise. Some of the pyramids had fallen down in the Depression, others had been at least partly razed by a disapproving government; and as for the rest, their days of skyscraping growth were over--for the present at least. The public wanted no more Insulls or Van Sweringens to flourish. Yet most of the great corporate structures which had been put together in the generation before 1929, and especially in the decade before 1929, still stood intact after the storm.

Not only that: it was these great corporations, generally speaking, which during the nineteen-thirties had been making whatever money was made in business. Look at these revealing figures from E. D. Kennedy's *Dividends to Pay*. In the year 1935 there were nearly half a million corporations in the United States, and they made, between them, a tidy profit of over a billion and two-thirds dollars--but if one omitted from the reckoning 960 of the biggest (the 960 companies, with stocks active on the New York Exchange, for which the Standard Statistics Company tabulated earnings) that collective profit turned into a deficit. In short, in 1935 the 960 big companies were, collectively, making a profit; the 475,000 or so smaller companies were, collectively, losing money. Mr. Kennedy was not able to show what happened in 1937 to the great mass of corporations because the government figures had not yet appeared, but he was able to trace the further fortunes of the 960 at the top, and his findings provided more illumination. Of all the money made in 1937 by these 960 aristocrats of business, well over a half--60 per cent--was made by just 42 of them; and nearly a quarter--24 per cent--was made by a mere six of the very biggest. (You would like the names of these six? They were General Motors, American Telephone, Standard Oil of New Jersey, United States Steel, du Pont, and General Electric.)

Imagine yourself setting up a new company to compete against one of these giants or even a group of lesser giants, with their huge resources and their ability to maintain prices by mutual custom and business understanding if by no more devious means, and you will begin to understand one of the reasons why new investments did not flourish. Too many of the roads on which it might wish to proceed were already occupied by marchers able to keep the highway to themselves.

Parenthetically it should be added that the great principalities were now becoming less dependent upon the investment houses of Wall Street for capital; they could maintain and modernize and even expand their plants out of their own ample pockets. Perhaps the palmy days of the Wall Street bankers were over--not only because of government restrictions but also because the great principalities were becoming more powerful than the banks. Was it wholly irrelevant that during the last two or three years of the decade several big corporations, notably U. S. Steel and General Motors, moved in one way or another to reduce the authority of officers and directors who represented essentially Wall Street and the traditional power of capital, to increase the power of men who represented the active management, or to add directors who represented local business interests outside Wall Street? True, there was doubtless a political motive behind such moves. The managers of the principalities had waked up to the fact that they were in politics whether they wanted to be or not. "Public relations" were no longer a mere press-agent's job, but demanded the attention of at least a vice-president. The big corporations were spending millions to win popularity. Wall Street was not popular; why not go through the motions, at least, of casting it off? Nevertheless there may have been more to it than that. Perhaps the day was at hand when, figuratively speaking, Mr. Sloan would not call on Mr. Morgan; Mr. Morgan would call on Mr. Sloan.

The profits of these great principalities went into millions of American homes, for their cohorts of stockholders had never been so numerous. But to only a tiny minority of wealthy stockholders did enough money go to be potentially an important factor in new investment. This tiny minority, beset with taxes, were in no mood for gambles in the areas where the great principalities did not stifle competition. "Why take a chance?" they would say; "if we lose, we lose; if we win, the government will take most of it away." They preferred to keep their money invested in the principalities and in tax-exempt bonds, or even to hold it uninvested in cash. Give us a government that will free us from burdens and restrictions, they had been shouting, and you will see new investment burgeon. But the behavior of the business indices in 1938 and 1939, when the New Deal had certainly become less adventurous and more willing to conciliate capital, had given little indication that such would be the case. There was always some good reason why the burgeoning must be postponed: the man who in 1937 had sworn that the return of "confidence" waited only for the repeal of the undistributed profits tax lamented in 1938 and 1939 that new investment was being held back by the fear of war. The banks continued to be glutted with idle money.

There were other reasons, of course, why the money lay idle. Who, for example, would risk money in new building when costs were held so high--by crushing real-estate taxes, high prices for materials, high hourly wages for labor, antiquated and inefficient building methods, etc.--that no profit could be anticipated? Here the difficulty was not that a few great corporations monopolized the field, but that a multitude of suzerainties, large and small, and a multitude of frozen debts and unresolved Depression problems, prevented great corporations from entering the field at all with the economies of large-scale production. Yet on the whole the generalization appeared to stand. The highways of industry and trade were well filled with going concerns with which only big, well-heeled companies could compete, and the men who could afford to bring such companies to birth had no enthusiasm for the battle. They thought their troubles were mostly political; actually, the evidence suggested that they were mostly economic.

During 1938 and 1939 the government, through a Temporary National Economic Committee, set out to investigate the blocking of new investment, especially by the competition-stifling practices of the principalities (which for political reasons were referred to by the good old fighting term "monopolies"). Some of the New Dealers were studying the prospects for investments by the government itself to take up the slack. But the problem was thorny; and when in the spring of 1939 the President made a gesture in the direction of investment by the government--combining the idea with that of unemployment relief in what was called the Lending-Spending Bill--Congress threw the whole scheme out the window. (Not content with thus rebuffing Roosevelt, Congress cut the admirable Theatre Project out of the WPA and decreed that wage-rates for skilled workmen on the WPA should be cut, thus provoking a strike which the columnist Bugs Baer called the "mutiny on the bounty.") The 1940 elections were becoming visible to the naked political eye, ardent New Dealers were prophesying a third term for Roosevelt, Republicans and conservative Democrats were taking a rich delight in demolishing his domestic proposals, and the economic issues were becoming lost in the political shuffle.

Now at last it looked as if the New Deal was really through. It had played its cards and had no more new ones to offer--or, if it had them, it could no longer induce Congress to let it play them. The country was manifestly wearying of economic experiment; the Republican party had taken advantage of this weariness to make substantial gains in the 1938 elections. The social Salvationists were losing their zeal for legislating prosperity. Now, like Roosevelt himself, they had become tense with excitement about foreign affairs and had half forgotten the dismal unsolved problems on the domestic front; they were either forming committees for the defense of freedom and tolerance against dictatorship, or breaking up into new alignments over the question whether America should stay out of war at all costs or come to the rescue of Britain and France. Yet still the secret of prosperity remained undiscovered.

For three and a half of the ten years since the Panic of 1929 the Hoover Administration had fought valiantly but vainly against disaster. For six and a half years the Roosevelt Administration had experimented and palliated, and had merely kept disaster at bay--to the tune of an increase of not far from twenty billion dollars in the public debt of the United States.

But was that all that could be said?

On the credit side of the national ledger there were certain entries to be made. *Item 1.* No revolution, no dictatorship born of the Depression had done away with the essential civil liberties of Americans. *Item 2.* The government in power had never willfully denied the principle stated in Roosevelt's second inaugural, that "we are determined to make every American citizen the subject of his country's interest and concern, and we will never regard any faithful law-abiding group within our borders as superfluous." Whatever sins were to be charged against the New Deal, at least it had done its task humanely. (This item loomed large in the eyes of men who looked abroad in 1939 and thought of the hordes of refugees seeking footholds where they would not be "regarded as superfluous.") *Item 3.* Despite all the miseries of the Depression and the recurrent fears of new economic decline and of war, the bulk of the American people had not yet quite lost their basic asset of hopefulness.

It was still their instinct to transform a suburban swamp into a city of magic and call it "The World of Tomorrow." In that world of tomorrow the show which they liked best of all and stood in hour-long queues to enjoy was the General Motors Futurama, a picture of the possible delights of 1960. They still liked to build the biggest dam in all creation and toy with the idea of the happy farmsteads it would water, the enormous engines it would drive, the new and better business it would stimulate. They still liked to stand with elbows on the fence at the edge of the farm and say, "Sooner or later I aim to buy those forty acres over there and go into this thing on a bigger scale." They still scrimped to give their sons and daughters "a better education than we ever had," feeling obscurely that a better education would be valued in the years to come.

A nation tried in a long ordeal had not yet lost heart.

§ 5

So one meditated as the summer of 1939 slipped by. But always now the meditation was interrupted by the recurring question: What will happen in Europe, and what will it mean to us here?

That question could hardly fail to be in the back of one's mind when, early in June, the King and Queen of England visited the United States. The Roosevelts tactfully made the most of this opportunity to cement the bonds of Anglo-American amity and erase whatever unfavorable memories lingered from *l'affaire Simpson*--and from Munich. Their reception of their royal guests was carefully arranged to be both dignified and heartily American, with more than a touch of the military.

When the King and Queen arrived in Washington--on a day of terrific heat which must have made the King's epauletted admiral's uniform almost intolerable--ten "flying fortress" bombing planes roared over the route of the procession to the White House, and the cars in which rode the King and the President, and the Queen and Mrs. Roosevelt, were preceded by sixty businesslike-looking baby tanks. After the state dinner that evening, there was a White House concert the program for which included Negro spirituals, cowboy ballads, and square dances, with well-assorted solos: not only by Lawrence Tibbett but also by Marian Anderson, the great Negro singer--with Kate Smith contributing that perennial radio favorite, "When the Moon Comes Over the Mountain." Three days later, their Royal Highnesses picnicked with the Roosevelts at Hyde Park, and the King consumed hot dogs and beer. (He could have dodged the hot dogs, for the menu also included cold ham, smoked and plain turkey, and various salads, as well as baked beans and brown bread, doughnuts and ginger bread, cookies, coffee, and soft drinks--but he knew well that a hot dog eaten smilingly in America might be worth a dozen battleships.) When the guests boarded their train at Hyde Park that evening, the President clasped his hands together high over his head in democratic farewell and the crowd sang "Auld Lang Syne" and "For He's a Jolly Good Fellow."

Nor did Mrs. Roosevelt, in her amiable newspaper column "My Day," fail to take the American public into her confidence about her concern over the domestic arrangements for the visit--such as the care taken to provide the guests with early morning tea and with water chilled but not iced--and about those small mishaps which would cause every hostess who read of them to vibrate with sympathy--such as the fact that a butler entering the big library at Hyde Park with a tray of drinks slipped and dropped the tray with a crash.

Wide World

ENTENTE CORDIALE, JUNE, 1939
The King and Queen of England at Hyde Park with President and Mrs. Roosevelt
and Mrs. James Roosevelt (center)

The King and Queen in their turn were by universal consent cordial, unassuming, and engaging. The crowds both in Washington and New York were enormous and enthusiastic; in fact, Mrs. Roosevelt remarked in her column that during the procession in Washington she had been quite unable to explain to the Queen what buildings they were passing because the roars of applause drowned every word. No untoward incident marred the triumphal royal progress. Altogether, the visit was an almost incredible success.

A few weeks after this success, the President tried hard to get Congress to rewrite the Neutrality Act and do away with the mandatory ban on the export of arms and munitions to warring countries. Not yet, however, was Congress ready to take this leap. In a matter which might determine the issue of war or peace, a majority of the men on the Hill were still unwilling to yield to this volatile man who so firmly believed that Hitler must be stopped and that the United States must help stop him by making it plain that if he did not hold his hand he would have American planes and guns, if not American soldiers and sailors, to reckon with.

Wherever one turned, that summer, the thought of Europe followed.

The Transatlantic Clippers (41-ton planes with a wing-spread of 152 feet) began carrying passengers from Long Island Sound to France and England--a potential link between allies, one asked oneself, or between belligerency and neutrality? The American submarine *Squalus* sank off Portsmouth in 240 feet of water, and 33 of her 59 men were rescued by diving bell--was it just a coincidence that a British submarine and a French submarine were lost at about the same time? *The Grapes of Wrath* lay upon the summer-porch table--and beside it lay *Days of Our Years, Inside Asia,* and *Not Peace, But a Sword,* all three of which took the American reader overseas. The long quarrel between the TVA and the Commonwealth & Southern utility system was moderated with the government's purchase of the Tennessee Electric Power Company's properties--and one realized that the hatred of Roosevelt which had burned for years in the hearts of big business men was already dying to embers. A salesman could still get orders by sending in a card which said

If You Don't Give Me An Order

I'll Vote For Him Again

but some of the once-indignant business men were even beginning to like Roosevelt now--for his foreign policy.

Prospective débutantes were wondering, that summer, who would succeed Brenda Diana Duff Frazier as the "glamour girl" of the new season; the idea of glamour (or "oomph" if you preferred) was now so ubiquitous that *Life* was calling Thomas E. Dewey "Republican Glamour Boy No. 1," and Attorney-General Murphy "New Deal Glamour Boy No. 1." The fashion experts were returning from Europe with the news that Paris said corsets and hour-glass figures. Summer vacationists were bending over their Chinese checkers; trying to emulate the swimming mermaids and mermen of Billy Rose's Aquacade; comparing Grover Whalen's financial troubles, as he tried to prevent the "World of Tomorrow" from going bankrupt, with the troubles of the managers of the San Francisco Fair; discussing Johnstown's speed on the racetracks; driving to the movies to see Robert Donat in "Goodbye Mr. Chips," or Bette Davis in "Dark Victory." Would all these everyday trifles of the 1939 summer season come back to memory, some day, as incidents of the happy lull before the storm?

One thing was almost certain. If war broke out in Europe, we should look back upon the day of declaration as the day when a line was drawn across our national life. Whatever strange form the war might take, whatever might be America's relation to it, it would bring America new problems, new alignments, new hopes and fears.

But surely there wouldn't be war. Things were really rather quiet in Europe, on the surface, in July and early August. And if Hitler should make a new crisis over Danzig and the Polish corridor, surely somebody would back down before it was too late. Somebody always had.

§ 6

The storm moved up late in August.

First, like a rumble of premonitory thunder, came the report that von Ribbentrop was to fly to Moscow to sign a German-Russian agreement. Then came the agreement itself; it was proclaimed in streamer headlines in the papers of August 24:--

GERMANY AND RUSSIA SIGN 10-YEAR NON-AGGRESSION PACT; BIND EACH OTHER NOT TO AID OPPONENTS IN WAR ACTS; HITLER REBUFFS LONDON; BRITAIN AND FRANCE MOBILIZE

That announcement sent ideas, expectations, and assumptions reeling the world over. In America, the supposed experts on world affairs stumbled for a foothold in reality as their logical premises fell away from under them. The communists performed quick ideological contortions as they saw the party line coming to a hairpin turn. Business men decided not to put in that buying order yet awhile, to wait till the shape of things was clearer; steamship officials debated the canceling of sailing dates; the stock market hesitated, sold off a little, wobbled uneasily. Americans went again to their radios for last-minute European bulletins.

Days of negotiations, mobilizations, frantic efforts for settlement, threats and counter-threats--then, very early on the morning of September 1, Hitler's armies marched into Poland.

It had begun. But still there was a question hanging in the air--what about Britain and France?

All that day--it was a Friday--the question remained not quite answered, and all the next day too. It traveled along with Labor Day week-enders departing for their three-day holiday, burned in their minds even on the golf links and the bathing beaches.

The answer was delivered at last on Sunday morning, September 3--ten years to a day from that hot September 3 of 1929 with which this chronicle opened. Over the radio came from London the voice of Neville Chamberlain, an infinitely unmartial voice, speaking in tones low and tired and sad:--

"This morning the British Ambassador in Berlin handed to the German government a final note stating that unless we heard from them by eleven o'clock that they were preparing at once to withdraw their troops from Poland, a state of war would exist between us. I have to tell you that no such undertaking has been received and in consequence this country is at war with Germany."

With those sentences, spoken so quietly thousands of miles away, an era ended for America and another one began.

APPENDIX

SOURCES AND OBLIGATIONS

In the Appendix to *Only Yesterday* I spoke first of all of my debt to Robert S. Lynd and Helen Merrell Lynd for "the extraordinarily varied and precise information collected in *Middletown*," of which I had "made frequent use"; and I added, "I do not see how any conscientious historian of the Post-war Decade could afford to neglect this mine of material." *Mutatis mutandis,* I must now say the same thing of their *Middletown in Transition* (Harcourt, Brace, 1937). I have quoted from it more frequently in the present volume than from any other source, and have leaned more upon it than the number of quotations would suggest.

In writing my first four chapters, I have made much use of *The Hoover Administration, A Documented Narrative,* by William Starr Myers and Walter H. Newton (Charles Scribner's Sons, 1936), and *Hoover Off the Record,* by Theodore G. Joslin (Doubleday, Doran, 1934). These two books, one formal, the other informal, both have proved helpful for reference and quotation, partisan though they are. Similarly I have found the five volumes of *The Public Papers and Addresses of Franklin D. Roosevelt* (Random House, 1938) of great value for the New Deal period. Two other books which came out while mine was in preparation have been useful to me at many points and would be even more useful to writers who could take fuller advantage of them than I was able to: the splendid *America in Midpassage,* by Charles A. Beard and Mary R. Beard (Macmillan, 1939), and Raymond Moley's detailed and searching first-hand account of the New Deal, *After Seven Years* (Harper, 1939). Needless to say, I have made constant use of the successive volumes of the *World Almanac,* and especially the Chronology which appears in it annually and is invaluable to anyone engaged in a project of this sort; and also the files of the *New York Times* in the New York Public Library.

My other sources--books, newspapers, magazines, and ideas and anecdotes and observations picked up throughout the decade-- have been so voluminous that it would be wearisome to recite them all. But certain sources I should like to mention either by way of explanation or to express special obligation, and these I shall arrange chapter by chapter for convenience:

In Chapter I ("Prelude: September 3, 1929") the quotations from Gilbert Seldes are from "Talkies' Progress," in *Harper's Magazine,* September, 1929. The paraphrase of F. C. Mills is based on a quotation from him in *Middletown in Transition,* pp. 53-54. The late George W. Wickersham very kindly wrote me shortly before his death and showed me a copy of the Commission minutes for September 4, 1929. From newspaper data, Calvin Coolidge did not move to his larger house in Northampton until 1930, although William Allen White's biography of him would seem to imply an earlier move. The 1929 data about Dr. Francis E. Townsend are based on a letter from Old Age Revolving Pensions, Ltd.; about "Amos 'n' Andy" and Edgar Bergen, on information kindly supplied through Julian Street, Jr., when he was with the NBC; about Garnet Carter and Hervey Allen, on letters from them; about Pearl Buck, on a letter from Richard J. Walsh. For these letters I am grateful.

In Chapter II ("Exit Prosperity") the polls of the National Economic League are from reproductions of them in *The Folklore of Capitalism,* by Thurman W. Arnold (Yale University Press, 1937). The quotation of Denna Frank Fleming is from his book, *The United States and World Organization, 1920-1933* (Columbia University Press, 1938), p. 325. The item about Roosevelt and Farley at election time, 1930, is drawn from James A. Farley's book *Behind the Ballots* (Harcourt, Brace, 1938). Henry Pratt Fairchild's population estimate is from an article by him, "When the Population Levels Off," in *Harper's Magazine,* May, 1938. The concluding pages of this chapter repeat (with some revisions) passages in a talk I gave at Bennington College, Commencement, 1938, which was printed by the Catamount Press at North Bennington, Vt., with the title "In a Time of Apprehension."

In Chapter III ("Down, Down, Down") the item about William McC. Martin, Jr., he kindly gave me himself. The Roosevelt-Farley item is again from Farley's *Behind the Ballots* (see above). The details of my story of the Hoover moratorium are based chiefly on Myers and Newton, Joslin, and Mark Sullivan's article on "President Hoover and the World Depression" in the *Saturday Evening Post* for March 11, 1933. The Peter F. Drucker quotation was taken from the manuscript of his book *The End of Economic Man* (John Day, 1939). The National Credit Corporation item was drawn from *Three Years Down,* by Jonathan Norton Leonard (Carrick & Evans, 1939), a lively and useful, if bitter, account of the years 1929-33 to which I am also indebted for several items about the effects of the Depression on individuals. The Kuznets figures on interest payments are from "National Income, 1929-32," by Simon Kuznets, which is Bulletin 49 of the National Bureau of Economic Research. The E. D. Kennedy figures are from his valuable book *Dividends to Pay* (Reynal & Hitchcock, 1939), pp. 16-17. The figures on domestic corporate issues are from *The United States, a Graphic History,* by Hacker Modley, and Taylor (Modern Age Books, 1937). The Croxton figures for Buffalo were cited in *The Christian Century,* December 28, 1932. My account of the Lindbergh case is in large degree based upon Sidney B. Whipple's exceptionally interesting and careful account in *The Trial of Bruno Richard Hauptmann* (Doubleday, Doran, 1937), to which I am greatly indebted.

In Chapter IV ("A Change of Government") the account of the Chicago Convention draws much from Farley's *Behind the Ballots* (see above); the incident of the Acceptance Address manuscript is from Raymond Moley's *After Seven Years* (see above). The Elmer Davis quotation is from "The Collapse of Politics" in *Harper's Magazine* for September, 1932. My account of the Bonus Army episode is based on a comparison of many versions, including especially Paul Y. Anderson's personal observations in *The Nation* for August 17, 1932. The farmer's remark to Mary Heaton Vorse is from her article, "Rebellion in the Corn Belt," in *Harper's Magazine,* December, 1932. My description of a farmers' protest meeting follows the account of one in *We Too Are the People,* Louise V. Armstrong (Little, Brown, 1938), which is helpful also to an understanding of relief problems. For Hoover's unsmiling demeanor see *42 Years in the White House* by Irwin Hood Hoover (Houghton Mifflin, 1934). My account of Hoover and Roosevelt in the interregnum is based largely on a comparison of the versions Myers and Newton, Joslin, Moley, Farley, and others. In my account of the bank crisis I have used *28 Days: A History of the Banking Crisis,* by C. C. Colt and N. S. Keith (Greenberg, 1933).

In Chapter V ("New Deal Honeymoon") the beginning of Roosevelt's Inaugural is taken from the *New York Times* for March 5, 1933; the version given in *The Public Papers and Addresses of Franklin D. Roosevelt* omits the "national consecration" clause. The quotations from letters embodying plans for recovery are actual quotations from letters I was kindly shown in the NRA files at the Department of Commerce. The genesis of the NRA is based on many accounts, including chiefly "Whose Child is the NRA?" by John T. Flynn in *Harper's Magazine* for September, 1934. Jonathan Mitchell's article, "The Versatility of General Johnson," appeared in *Harper's Magazine* for October, 1934.

In Chapter VI ("A Change of Climate") I have made use of a study of *Youth and Sex* by Dorothy Dunbar Bromley and Florence Haxton Britten (Harper, 1938), and at several points have used an especially interesting article on "Youth in College," *Fortune,* June, 1936, which was reprinted in *American Points of View,* edited by William H. Cordell and Kathryn Coe Cordell (Doubleday, Doran, 1937). On bootlegging after Repeal, I have used *After Repeal,* by Leonard V. Harrison and Elizabeth Raine (Harper, 1936). The Virginia bookburning was described in *Ken,* August 28, 1938. My mention of slot machines, pinball, etc., draws heavily from Samuel Lubell's article, "Ten Billion Nickels," in the *Saturday Evening Post,* May 12, 1939; of the Irish Sweepstakes, from an article by John J. McCarthy in *Harper's Magazine,* June, 1934; of "Bank Night," from "Bank Night Tonight," by Forbes Parkhill, *Saturday Evening Post,* December 4, 1937; of softball, from "Baseball's Precocious Baby," by Ted Shane, *American Magazine,* June, 1939. The Gallup poll on gambling was cited in the *New York Times* for November 27, 1938.

In Chapter VII ("Reform--and Recovery?") I have quoted from George R. Leighton's article, "In Search of the NRA," which appeared in *Harper's Magazine,* January, 1934. On relief, *Spending to Save,* by Harry L. Hopkins (W. W. Norton, 1936) is the source of some facts. On Huey Long I have drawn plentifully from *Huey Long, A Candid Biography,* by Forrest Davis (Dodge, 1935); the White House incident is from Farley's reminiscences (see above). On the Townsend Plan, many facts are from "The Old People's Crusade," by Richard L. Neuberger and Kelley Loe, *Harper's Magazine,* March, 1936.

In Chapter VIII ("When the Farms Blew Away") the opening quotation is from "Life and Death of 470 Acres," by R. D. Lusk, *Saturday Evening Post,* August 13, 1938. The map which I mention is in *Problems of a Changing Population,* National Resources Committee (May, 1938), p. 65. The Neuberger quotation is from *Our Promised Land* (Macmillan, 1938). On the changes in American agriculture I am especially indebted to Paul S. Taylor, from whose "Power Farming and Labor Displacement in the Cotton Belt, 1937" (published by the U. S. Department of Labor and Bureau of Labor Statistics, serial No. R 737, Government Printing Office) I have quoted, and to Ladd Haystead's memorandum for Arthur Kudner, Inc., "The Farmer Looks at Himself." On farm tenancy, I am indebted to (and have quoted from) the chapter on "Labor in Evolving Economy" in the Beards' *America in Midpassage.* The Stuart Chase quotation on the flood of 1936 is from *Rich Land, Poor Land* (Whittlesey House, 1936), which was a helpful source also on government conservation measures.

In Chapter IX ("The Voice with the Smile Wins") the figures I have given on Federal deficits are net (after subtracting the amount paid out for statutory debt retirements); I have not attempted to go into the very intricate and debatable question of the extent to which the expenditures in these years represented in part money which should come back to the Federal government. In the discussion of Moley and Corcoran and Cohen I have used chiefly that illuminating little book, *Men Around the President,* by Joseph Alsop and Robert Kintner (Doubleday, Doran, 1939), and also Moley's *After Seven Years* (see above), checking the latter against the former. For many details in this chapter *In 1936,* by Alvin C. Eurich and Elmo C. Wilson (Henry Holt, 1937), came in handy.

In Chapter X ("With Pen and Camera Through Darkest America") the quotation from Malcolm Cowley is from an advance proof of the *New Republic* for November 8, 1939. My passage on Benny Goodman and swing leans heavily on "The Killer-Diller," by Frank Norris, *Saturday Evening Post,* May 7, 1938, and "No. 1 Swing Man," by Irving Kolodin, *Harper's Magazine,* September, 1939; the Toscanini-Chotzinoff item is from "Toscanini on the Air," *Fortune,* January, 1938; the figures on music appreciation are from an excellent summary, "Music Goes into Mass Production," by Dickson Skinner, *Harper's Magazine,* April, 1939. The data about centralized newspaper control are taken from John Cowles's chapter on "Journalism-- Newspapers," in *America Now,* by 36 Americans, edited by Harold E. Stearns (Scribner's, 1938). On the movies, I have taken a number of facts from advance proofs of Margaret Farrand Thorp's fine survey, *America at the Movies* (Yale University Press, 1939).

In Chapter XI ("Friction and Recession") I have made extensive use, in the labor section, of Edward Levinson's valuable *Labor on the March* (Harper, 1938), and am also indebted to Herbert Harris for his *American Labor* (Yale University Press, 1939), another useful source. The account of the meetings between Lewis and Taylor is drawn from "It Happened in Steel," in *Fortune,* May, 1937. My account of the Supreme Court battle follows pretty closely three fine articles by Joseph Alsop and Turner Catledge in the *Saturday Evening Post* for September 18, September 25, and October 16, 1937, entitled "The 168 Days" (later published in book form). The Leon Henderson item is from *Men Around the President* (see under Chapter IX); and I have also leaned somewhat on that book in my account of the Administration shifts of policy during the Recession.

In Chapter XII ("The Shadow of War") the quotation of the international broadcast is from bound volumes of the Columbia Broadcasting System's Broadcasts, at the New York Public Library. As to Studio Nine, I have drawn on H. V. Kaltenborn's *I Broadcast the Crisis* (Random House, 1938). My account of the London Economic Conference of 1933 naturally makes use of Moley's detailed narrative in *After Seven Years.* In this chapter I have made much use of the Gallup public-opinion polls on foreign affairs, as handily collected for reference in F. S. Wickware's "What the Polls Say," in *Harper's Magazine,* September, 1939; such polls sometimes seem to indicate more than they actually do (for much depends on the wording of the questions) but they at least help to show trends, especially when the same question is asked at intervals. E. D. Kennedy's book, from which I have drawn figures on corporate earnings, I have already cited above (under Chapter III).

I cannot list all the people who have been good enough to help me in one way or another, but I should like especially to thank the William Zuills of Orange Grove, Bermuda, for their thoughtful hospitality while I was at work on the opening chapters; and, for assistance of various sorts, Letitia C. Rogers, Oliver Ellsworth Allen, Margaret MacMullen, Charles W. MacMullen, Cathleen Schurr, the David Cushman Coyles, Charles C. Colt, John A. Kouwenhoven, Paul S. Taylor, George R. Leighton, Luther H. Gulick, Remley J. Glass, Daniel I. McNamara, Julian Street, Jr., Deems Taylor, Florence Alonso, and the staff of the New York Public Library (especially in the Newspaper Room and the Economics and Sociology Division). My wife, Agnes Rogers Allen, is to be thanked above all--for helpful ideas and criticism and for much hard work on behalf of this project.

F.L.A.

New York City

November 10, 1939